My Fellow Americans

My Fellow Americans

Presidents and Their Inaugural Addresses

Edited by
YUVRAJ SINGH

Introduction by
TED WIDMER

OXFORD
UNIVERSITY PRESS

OXFORD
UNIVERSITY PRESS

Oxford University Press is a department of the University of Oxford. It furthers
the University's objective of excellence in research, scholarship, and education
by publishing worldwide. Oxford is a registered trade mark of Oxford University
Press in the UK and certain other countries.

Published in the United States of America by Oxford University Press
198 Madison Avenue, New York, NY 10016, United States of America.

© Oxford University Press 2024

All rights reserved. No part of this publication may be reproduced, stored in
a retrieval system, or transmitted, in any form or by any means, without the
prior permission in writing of Oxford University Press, or as expressly permitted
by law, by license, or under terms agreed with the appropriate reproduction
rights organization. Inquiries concerning reproduction outside the scope of the
above should be sent to the Rights Department, Oxford University Press, at the
address above.

You must not circulate this work in any other form
and you must impose this same condition on any acquirer.

Library of Congress Cataloging-in-Publication Data
Names: Singh, Yuvraj, editor.
Title: My fellow Americans : presidents and their inaugural addresses /
Edited by Yuvraj Singh ; Introduction by Ted Widmer.
Other titles: My fellow Americans (Oxford University Press)
Description: New York : Oxford University Press, [2024] |
Includes bibliographical references.
Identifiers: LCCN 2024020051 (print) | LCCN 2024020052 (ebook) |
ISBN 9780197644997 (hardback) | ISBN 9780197645000 (epub) |
ISBN 9780197645345
Subjects: LCSH: Presidents—United States—Inaugural addresses—History. |
United States—Politics and government.
Classification: LCC J81.4 .M922 2024 (print) | LCC J81.4 (ebook) |
DDC 352.23/860973—dc23/eng/20240824
LC record available at https://lccn.loc.gov/2024020051
LC ebook record available at https://lccn.loc.gov/2024020052

DOI: 10.1093/oso/9780197644997.001.0001

Printed by Sheridan Books, Inc., United States of America

Dedicated to all of my fellow Americans

Contents

Acknowledgments	xv
Preface	xvii
Introduction TED WIDMER	1
George Washington's First Inaugural Address	21
Inaugurator: George Washington's First Inaugural Address STEPHEN H. BROWNE	25
George Washington's Second Inaugural Address	28
The American Cincinnatus: The Second Inaugural Address of George Washington KEVIN BUTTERFIELD	29
John Adams's Inaugural Address	33
The Colossus of Independence: The Inaugural Address of John Adams R. M. BARLOW	38
Thomas Jefferson's First Inaugural Address	41
The Sage of Monticello: The First Inaugural Address of Thomas Jefferson PETER S. ONUF	45
Thomas Jefferson's Second Inaugural Address	50
The Man of the People: The Second Inaugural Address of Thomas Jefferson ANNETTE GORDON-REED	55

James Madison's First Inaugural Address	60
The Father of the Constitution: The First Inaugural Address of James Madison STUART LEIBIGER	63
James Madison's Second Inaugural Address	66
The First Wartime President: The Second Inaugural Address of James Madison J. C. A. STAGG	69
James Monroe's First Inaugural Address	72
The Era of Good Feelings: The First Inaugural Address of James Monroe DANIEL F. PRESTON	79
James Monroe's Second Inaugural Address	83
The Last Cocked Hat: The Second Inaugural Address of James Monroe SANDRA MOATS	92
John Quincy Adams's Inaugural Address	96
The Corrupt Bargain: The Inaugural Address of John Quincy Adams C. JAMES TAYLOR	103
Andrew Jackson's First Inaugural Address	106
Calm before the Storm: The First Inaugural Address of Andrew Jackson HARRY L. WATSON	109
Andrew Jackson's Second Inaugural Address	113
Old Hickory: The Second Inaugural Address of Andrew Jackson THOMAS COENS	116
Martin Van Buren's Inaugural Address	120
The Little Magician: The Inaugural Address of Martin Van Buren MICHAEL J. GERHARDT	128
William Henry Harrison's Inaugural Address	132
Old Tippecanoe: The Inaugural Address of William Henry Harrison DANIEL WALKER HOWE	149

John Tyler's Address upon Assuming the Office of President of the United States	153
The President without a Party: John Tyler's Address upon Assuming the Office of President of the United States Christopher J. Leahy	157
James K. Polk's Inaugural Address	161
Dark Horse: The Inaugural Address of James K. Polk Walter R. Borneman	171
Zachary Taylor's Inaugural Address	175
Old Rough and Ready: The Inaugural Address of Zachary Taylor Michael F. Holt	178
Millard Fillmore's Announcement to Congress of the Death of President Taylor	182
Millard Fillmore's First Annual Message	183
A Strict Constitutionalist: Millard Fillmore's First Annual Message Claude Welch	201
Franklin Pierce's Inaugural Address	205
Handsome Frank: The Inaugural Address of Franklin Pierce Peter A. Wallner	212
James Buchanan's Inaugural Address	214
Doughface: The Inaugural Address of James Buchanan Jean H. Baker	220
Abraham Lincoln's First Inaugural Address	224
Trying to Stave off War: The First Inaugural Address of Abraham Lincoln David S. Reynolds	232
Abraham Lincoln's Second Inaugural Address	236
The Great Uniter: The Second Inaugural Address of Abraham Lincoln Richard John Carwardine	238

Andrew Johnson's Address upon Assuming the Office of President of the United States	242
On Opposite Ends: Andrew Johnson's Address upon Assuming the Office of President of the United States MICHAEL LES BENEDICT	244
Ulysses S. Grant's First Inaugural Address	248
The Hero as President: The First Inaugural Address of Ulysses S. Grant JOAN WAUGH	251
Ulysses S. Grant's Second Inaugural Address	255
"Errors of Judgement, Not of Intent": The Second Inaugural Address of Ulysses S. Grant JOHN F. MARSZALEK	258
Rutherford B. Hayes's Inaugural Address	261
The End of Reconstruction: The Inaugural Address of Rutherford B. Hayes DUSTIN MCLOCHLIN	267
James A. Garfield's Inaugural Address	271
The Preacher President: The Inaugural Address of James A. Garfield CHARLES W. CALHOUN	278
Chester A. Arthur's Address upon Assuming the Office of President of the United States	282
"Chet Arthur? President of the United States? Good God!": Chester A. Arthur's Address upon Assuming the Office of President of the United States WALTER NUGENT	284
Grover Cleveland's First Inaugural Address	288
"A Fine Man, a Grand Man": The First Inaugural Address of Grover Cleveland MARK W. SUMMERS	292
Benjamin Harrison's Inaugural Address	298

Little Ben: The Inaugural Address of Benjamin Harrison ALLAN B. SPETTER	307
Grover Cleveland's Second Inaugural Address	310
Grover the Good: The Second Inaugural Address of Grover Cleveland MATTHEW ALGEO	315
William McKinley's First Inaugural Address	318
The Front Porch Campaign: The First Inaugural Address of William McKinley CHRISTOPHER CAPOZZOLA	326
William McKinley's Second Inaugural Address	330
The Imperial Presidency: The Second Inaugural Address of William McKinley CHRISTOPHER MCKNIGHT NICHOLS	335
Theodore Roosevelt's Inaugural Address	342
The Bully Pulpit: The Inaugural Address of Theodore Roosevelt JEAN M. YARBROUGH	345
William Howard Taft's Inaugural Address	349
Between Giants: The Inaugural Address of William Howard Taft JONATHAN LURIE	360
Woodrow Wilson's First Inaugural Address	364
The Schoolmaster: The First Inaugural Address of Woodrow Wilson ROBERT A. ENHOLM	368
Woodrow Wilson's Second Inaugural Address	373
The Eve of War: The Second Inaugural Address of Woodrow Wilson JOHN MILTON COOPER, JR.	377
Warren G. Harding's Inaugural Address	380
Return to Normalcy: The Inaugural Address of Warren G. Harding JAMES D. ROBENALT	388
Calvin Coolidge's Inaugural Address	392

Cool Cal: The Inaugural Address of Calvin Coolidge AMITY SHLAES	401
Herbert Hoover's Inaugural Address	404
The Great Humanitarian: The Inaugural Address of Herbert Hoover KENDRICK A. CLEMENTS	413
Franklin D. Roosevelt's First Inaugural Address	416
Fear Itself: The First Inaugural Address of Franklin D. Roosevelt CYNTHIA M. KOCH	420
Franklin D. Roosevelt's Second Inaugural Address	425
"One-Third of a Nation...": The Second Inaugural Address of Franklin D. Roosevelt DAVID M. KENNEDY	430
Franklin D. Roosevelt's Third Inaugural Address	434
Pathbreaker: The Third Inaugural Address of Franklin D. Roosevelt MICHAEL KAZIN	438
Franklin D. Roosevelt's Fourth Inaugural Address	441
Unprecedented: The Fourth Inaugural Address of Franklin D. Roosevelt DAVID B. WOOLNER	443
Harry S. Truman's Inaugural Address	447
Cold Warrior: The Inaugural Address of Harry S. Truman ANDREW E. BUSCH	453
Dwight D. Eisenhower's First Inaugural Address	457
Ike: The First Inaugural Address of Dwight D. Eisenhower MICHAEL J. BIRKNER	463
Dwight D. Eisenhower's Second Inaugural Address	467
The Price of Peace: The Second Inaugural Address of Dwight D. Eisenhower LOUIS PAUL GALAMBOS	471
John F. Kennedy's Inaugural Address	474

Camelot: The Inaugural Address of John F. Kennedy BARBARA ANN PERRY	478
Lyndon B. Johnson's Inaugural Address	482
The Dawn of the Great Society: The Inaugural Address of Lyndon B. Johnson MARK K. UPDEGROVE	486
Richard M. Nixon's First Inaugural Address	490
"The Title of Peacemaker": The First Inaugural Address of Richard M. Nixon KEN HUGHES	495
Richard M. Nixon's Second Inaugural Address	498
A Moment of Triumph before Disaster: The Second Inaugural Address of Richard M. Nixon THOMAS ALAN SCHWARTZ	503
Gerald Ford's Remarks upon Taking the Oath of Office as President	506
"Just a Little Straight Talk": Gerald Ford's Remarks upon Taking the Oath of Office as President JOHN ROBERT GREENE	509
Jimmy Carter's Inaugural Address	512
The Peanut Farmer: The Inaugural Address of Jimmy Carter MARK ATWOOD LAWRENCE	515
Ronald Reagan's First Inaugural Address	519
The Great Communicator: The First Inaugural Address of Ronald Reagan GIL TROY	525
Ronald Reagan's Second Inaugural Address	529
The Teflon President: The Second Inaugural Address of Ronald Reagan IWAN MORGAN	535
George H. W. Bush's Inaugural Address	539

"A Thousand Points of Light": The Inaugural Address of George H. W. Bush MARY KATE CARY	544
Bill Clinton's First Inaugural Address	547
The Comeback Kid: The First Inaugural Address of Bill Clinton STEVEN M. GILLON	551
Bill Clinton's Second Inaugural Address	555
The Politician: The Second Inaugural Address of Bill Clinton RUSSELL L. RILEY	560
George W. Bush's First Inaugural Address	564
Common Ground: The First Inaugural Address of George W. Bush JAMES MANN	568
George W. Bush's Second Inaugural Address	572
A Vision of America: The Second Inaugural Address of George W. Bush MARK J. ROZELL	577
Barack Obama's First Inaugural Address	580
A New Birth of Freedom: The First Inaugural Address of Barack Obama TRACY DENEAN SHARPLEY-WHITING	586
Barack Obama's Second Inaugural Address	589
Faith in America's Future: The Second Inaugural Address of Barack Obama JAMES T. KLOPPENBERG	594
Donald Trump's Inaugural Address	597
Uniquely American: The Inaugural Address of Donald Trump NICHOLAS F. JACOBS	601
Joe Biden's Inaugural Address	606
"Democracy Is Precious, Democracy Is Fragile": The Inaugural Address of Joe Biden KATE MASUR	614
Contributors	621

Acknowledgments

TREMENDOUS THANKS GO to those that helped make this book possible through their recommendations: Sara Martin at the Massachusetts Historical Society, Elizabeth Chew at Montpelier, Jack Rakove at Stanford University, Robert Cherny at San Francisco State University, Jeffrey Rosen at the National Constitution Center, Ira Katznelson at Columbia University, and Sidney M. Milkis at the University of Virginia.

Special thanks go to Peter Onuf, who helped me get the ball rolling; Mark Atwood Lawrence, without whom this print edition wouldn't have been possible; and Susan Ferber at Oxford University Press for taking on this project in the first place.

I can draw an exact line through the events that led to this book. The first was a blog post from 2017 on daringfireball.net, a blog run by John Gruber. He had linked to a website, Standard Ebooks, that took ebooks on Project Gutenberg, a large repository of public domain works, and modernized them so they were enjoyable to read on any device. The creator, Alex Cabal, created a free toolset that anyone could use for their own project and which I used extensively. To export the manuscript in Word, I used Scrivener for macOS. Tools are important to get a job done, and usually go unmentioned.

Thanks also to my family, who have been supportive as I worked on this book throughout a pandemic. Special thanks to my late paternal grandparents, Parmjit Singh Sanghera and Ranjit Kaur Sanghera—both were teachers and instilled in me a love of reading in my youth; to my maternal grandparents, Amarjit Singh Khangura and Pritam Kaur Khangura; to my sister, Dilveen; and to my parents, Jasvir Kaur Sanghera and Jaswinder Singh Sanghera.

Finally, this book would have been impossible without the kindness, generosity, and grace of others. I will remain indebted to each scholar and historian who devoted the time necessary to contribute an essay.

Preface

Yuvraj Singh

IN JANUARY 2020, I came across a collection of presidential inaugural addresses on Project Gutenberg. My first thought was to clean up the edition I came across (since all the addresses were in the public domain, I didn't have to worry about copyright) and release an ebook version. The presidency has long fascinated me and 2020 was an election year, so my interest was at a quadrennial high. Even so, I didn't quite make the connection to the book you're reading now. Over several weeks, the idea of the final format—an essay written by a different historian to accompany each address—crystallized.

A number of factors led to that decision. One was my long-standing interest in American history. Part of the reason is best expressed in L. P. Hartley's *The Go-Between*: "The past is a foreign country: they do things differently there." As a first-generation American, that feeling of the past as a "foreign country" is all the more poignant (especially as it pertains to the presidency, an office barred to naturalized citizens). But knowing that it is *our* past means that, however hard or painful it is, we must try to understand it in order to make sense of our present and our future.

Inaugural addresses are fascinating snapshots of American history because they capture all three—past, present, and future. They're like an iceberg—what is said aloud on one day is only the tip of a presidential administration. One can say only so much with 135 words, as George Washington did in his second inaugural address, or even 8,445, as William Henry Harrison did with his only address. What lies below the surface—the social, political, economic, and military situation in the United States; the personal experiences, influences, learnings, philosophies, prejudices, and status of each president; events that occur during a presidency and how the president handles them; situations sown by predecessors—has a tremendous impact on what is said. Contemporary events that seem unimportant can have a profound impact that does not become visible or obvious until seen in retrospect. Time and distance are necessary to judge not just what happened, but also why it happened and in that particular way. Probing for answers to these questions can help trace a line—though not always a straight one—between then and now.

My process of assembling this book was simple: find a historian who specialized in or had published works on a particular president or his era to write about that president's inaugural address. This approach would allow for many—sixty-four, to be exact—voices and interpretive angles. Different historians tackling two separate inaugural addresses by the same president could arrive at different conclusions about that presidency, drawing on their unique contributions and research.

This approach differs from that of books on the inaugural addresses already available. Some volumes of the inaugural addresses only had the speeches, without commentary (such as the version on Project Gutenberg). A few—such as *Fellow Citizens*, edited by Robert V. Remini and Terry Golway, and *My Fellow Citizens*, edited by Arthur M. Schlesinger, Jr., and Fred L. Israel—featured interpretive essays by the main editors. As far as I could tell, though, there weren't any volumes in which each inaugural address was interpreted and contextualized by a different historian.

My personal reading habits also contributed to the conceptualization of this book. I tend to get engrossed in what I'm reading, which naturally leads me to learn more about a book, its author, and its context. Norton's Critical Editions and Oxford World's Classics were instrumental in helping me form this habit. The content surrounding the main text in these editions—the introductions, footnotes, endnotes, notes on different translations, glossaries, literary criticism—enable a learning experience greater than the sum of its parts. Norton Critical Editions in particular brought in criticism and interpretation by multiple authors, an approach adapted for this volume.

My original goal was a self-published ebook, as I didn't have the resources for a traditional print publication. January 20, 2021—Inauguration Day—would be the release date. (I missed my goal just shy of a week.) Each essay would immediately follow the text of the inaugural address; that way, the reader could read the address with fresh eyes.

The most significant challenge was finding all the authors and asking them to contribute, despite my not being a historian. All I knew about the subject at hand was what I had learned through extensive reading and some education. I had no network to speak of. None of the authors who agreed to write for this project knew me; all received an unsolicited email about the book and an invitation to contribute. Some contributors were recommended to me by historians who were unable to participate due to other commitments. Some were interested in a different inaugural address than the one I initially asked them to write about and suggested someone else for my original invitation.

Preface xix

To my immense gratification and relief, these factors did not prove to be impediments. Virtually every historian I contacted—even those who couldn't participate—was receptive and interested in the idea. Although my lack of professional status raised a couple of questions, no one refused to participate because of it. I was blown away by the kindness, generosity, and patience shown by every contributor—especially because I wasn't able to pay them anything.

I began searching for authors on February 4, 2020. I sent three emails regarding two early presidents who fascinated me: George Washington and Thomas Jefferson. One I didn't hear back from; one was supportive of the project but was unable to participate; and the third, Peter Onuf, professor emeritus at the University of Virginia and a leading Jeffersonian scholar, was happy to speak about the project. In a follow-up email, before we spoke, I added a couple more notes on what I was looking for: an essay of between 1,500 and 2,000 words that would help contextualize Jefferson's first inaugural. To my delight and surprise, at the end of the call, Dr. Onuf agreed to write the essay and suggested an author to write about George Washington's first inaugural—Stephen H. Browne at Penn State. He too agreed to participate.

Some writers were somewhat familiar to me. Peter Onuf, for example, has an online course, "Age of Jefferson," that I had watched years ago on Coursera. org. Others I knew from books they had written or citations in the footnotes or endnotes of biographies of presidents or history books. Still others were recommended by historians whom I knew I could trust. The search for contributors ran from February through October of 2020. This doesn't mean that the search was without its issues. A couple of contributors who had initially agreed were later unable to participate, so I had to find others to replace them. But such issues are part and parcel of an edited volume, I've learned. Of the roughly 150 historians I emailed, approximately 110 replied and 64 agreed to be part of this volume.

The essays that follow each address are neither panegyrics nor invectives in their analysis of the presidents in question. Nor are they meant to be in-depth looks at the president's term in office. Obviously, full books are written about single events that occur during a presidency, let alone the entire presidency. Rather, the essays here are intended to contextualize each inaugural address. Contributors were free to take different approaches. Some put more emphasis on the exact content of the address, while others explore what was going on at the time—a personal situation the president was dealing with, or a unique military, economic, or political situation that marked their presidency.

This volume contains sixty-four speeches and sixty-four accompanying essays from leading historians of the presidents or their eras. Some additional notes about the speeches are in order.

Fifty-nine of the pieces are proper inaugural addresses; that is, these speeches were given at an inaugural ceremony that signified re-election or a peaceful transfer of power (or, in George Washington's case, the instantiation of the office of the president). After being sworn in, the president took the oath of office and then delivered the inaugural address. The Joint Congressional Committee on Inaugural Ceremonies, a special committee formed every four years to manage the inauguration, was my source for this figure.

Three of speeches are not proper inaugural addresses but are speeches the president delivered upon assuming the presidency. In this volume, they are referred to as the president's "Address upon Assuming the Office of President of the United States." These were delivered by John Tyler, who succeeded William Henry Harrison after his monthlong tenure; Chester A. Arthur, who succeeded James A. Garfield after the latter died from a gunshot wound; and Gerald R. Ford, who succeeded Richard M. Nixon after the latter's resignation.

Two presidents—Millard Fillmore, who assumed office after the death of Zachary Taylor, and Andrew Johnson, after the assassination of Abraham Lincoln—have neither an inaugural address nor something that can be considered an address or speech upon becoming president. Instead, both communicated written messages to Congress that touched on the death of their predecessor and their assumption of the office. Their first major speeches would be their respective annual messages (or State of the Union Address). Johnson, however, indicated what his presidency would look like, whereas Fillmore had the barest of all messages, touching only on the circumstances surrounding Taylor's death. To compensate, this volume also includes the text of Millard Fillmore's annual message, which provides insight into how he intended to govern.

Four vice presidents became presidents after the death of their predecessor and then went on to be re-elected—Theodore Roosevelt, Calvin Coolidge, Harry Truman, and Lyndon B. Johnson. Only the inaugural delivered at the commencement of their full term in office is included.

For the five presidents who lack proper inaugural addresses, there seemed to be two options: skip them entirely, as other volumes of inaugural addresses do, or use the text that bears the closest proximity to a bona fide inaugural—short messages they delivered, often just to Congress, upon becoming president. It seemed more problematic to skip a president entirely—and the consequences of his ascent—than to justify his inclusion, though it will remain an imperfect choice.

The unabridged speeches and the historical contexts of the essays provide opportunities to draw lessons and make comparisons. No perfect parallels exist between then and now, but similarities abound. They highlight issues that the presidents thought were important—because they were important to the people. They show us how much progress has been made over more than 230 years—and how much progress still lies ahead for the nation to realize its ideals.

My Fellow Americans

Introduction

Ted Widmer

WHEN ASSEMBLED TOGETHER, the inaugural addresses of the presidents constitute an essential record of American history. Without a doubt, they offer important insights into the forty-six individuals who have held our highest elected office, and the circumstances that shaped each of their individual moments on America's grandest stage.

But they also tell a larger story, about a nation seeking to prove itself, against internal demons as well as foreign adversaries, and finding its way to extraordinary global preeminence. Like the Bayeux Tapestry, they present a continuous scroll of a great national epic—although this epic, unlike the tapestry, is still unscrolling.

At the outset of the story, it was unclear just how *epic* it would turn out to be. The founders entertained great hopes for the new nation, but they also quarreled among themselves and they did their best to paper over the internal contradictions that were already threatening to undermine the "last great experiment for promoting human happiness," as George Washington referred to the United States, in a letter of 1790.[1] Slavery was divisive from the outset, and the various ways in which the Constitution legitimized it did not inspire hope for a nation that had claimed, in the Declaration of Independence, to stand for the rights that inhere in all people. Other debates pitted small states against large states, urban interests against farmers, creditors against debtors, and the advocates of a strong government against those who preferred freedom from any central authority. The latter category was capacious indeed, with Americans already racing into the vast interior of North America, far from any governing councils, even before the American Revolution had ended. The last thing they wanted to see was a strong new government infringing on their liberties.

But surely some meaningful authority was necessary to give direction to this ambitious new nation, which claimed to be blazing a new path in human history, though it often failed to unite thirteen states that were not especially inclined to follow each other's lead. Accordingly, a new office had to be created, not present during the War for Independence, or the aimless years of weak government under the Articles of Confederation. It would have to be designed with great care, because the idea of a hierarchical structure touched upon every one of the debates that were already dividing Americans.

In the late spring of 1787, during the deliberations that led to the Constitution, the new office began to have a name. In response to a proposal from the Virginia delegation that a new federal government be considered, South Carolina delegate Charles Pinckney proposed that its executive power be vested in a "President of the United States of America."[2]

That was the beginning of an intense debate that awakened many of the fears that troubled the founders. Even with an official title, it was unclear what powers would reside in the presidency, or whether these immense powers should be parceled out among co-presidents from different regions. Several founders, including Edmund Randolph of Virginia, feared an excess of "one-man power" and proposed that the presidency be divided into a committee, with three executives from the North, the South, and the middle states. He thought a "unity," by which he meant one person, would concentrate too much authority in a single individual.[3]

Others agreed. George Mason of Virginia agreed that an executive "vested in three persons" would "contribute to quiet the minds of the people, and convince them that there will be proper attention paid to their respective concerns."[4] Other founders felt that a triumvirate would dilute the idea of a president. On June 1, James Wilson of Pennsylvania made a motion that the national executive should "consist of a single person."

At the outset of these debates, James Madison noted that "a considerable pause ensued," as if the founders realized just how dangerous it would be to the entire project if they got it wrong. Benjamin Franklin added to the solemnity of the moment by standing up and expressing his desire for a full debate on such an important question. That led to a searching conversation, and eventually to a vote, over whether the president should be a single person or not. It could be said that this was the first presidential election, even before a candidate was nominated. Should the powerful office exist at all?[5] In the end, the motion carried.

But many other questions remained, including the means of electing the president. Should it be a popular vote? Or should the state legislatures play a role? Many founders argued against the right of the people to vote directly for their leader, arguing, as George Mason did, that "it would be as unnatural to refer the choice of a proper character for Chief Magistrate to the people, as it would to refer a trial of colors to a blind man." Finally, on July 19, the proposal of Oliver Ellsworth was adopted that the president would be chosen by slates of "electors," appointed by the legislatures of each state.[6]

Throughout the summer, they deliberated some more, and the "considerable pause" led to a long list of checks and balances, ensnaring the presidency with responsibilities and boundaries that would prevent this one branch from dominating the others—or so they hoped. The length of a term was debated—some felt a longer term of six or seven years would be better, to give presidents a necessary independence. But in the end, a four-year term was decided upon—independent, but not *too* independent.

Balance was essential to preserve the fragile internal mechanisms of the carefully calibrated system they were building. Presidents could not become kings—that was the very office they had rebelled against during the American Revolution. It was imperative that America's leaders spring from the people and return to the people after their service to the republic.

As the founders were contemplating these weighty issues, it helped that they already knew who the first president would be. Throughout the summer of 1787, he was guiding the discussion with his moral authority, and his silences, which often spoke as loudly as his words. George Washington had lived his entire life according to an internal code of checks and balances, and he was already well-known for his carefully worded farewell speeches. That was encouraging to the founders, who worried that future presidents might grow so enchanted with the office that they would never leave.

To a degree, Washington was already occupying the role, even before he was elected. On May 25, 1787, he was elected to "preside" over the Constitutional Convention, and his prestige was crucial to the proceedings. As the founders debated the presidency-to-be, it was hard not to look at the presidential example, right there in the room. When the first election was held, in the winter of 1788–1789, Washington won unanimously.

Even with the choice made so clearly, much remained in doubt. How would a president travel to the place of inauguration, and what would the ceremony of investiture look like? How could Congress confer this high privilege without turning the event into a coronation? And how, exactly, should the president receive the tremendous power he was being given from the people? To be silent on such an important occasion seemed somehow less than presidential. But to speak for too long, or with too much self-regard, would bring different kinds of problems and invite the criticisms that were already coming in from Americans who were quick to pounce on any signs of privilege.

The new Constitution said nothing about these matters. But they were consequential and touched on deep anxieties. The founders understood that, if they provided too much pomp and circumstance, the office would begin to resemble the royal example that they were going to such lengths to avoid. But they needed an active president, to occupy a role that symbolized the stronger government coming into existence. To speak, or not to speak, was therefore a crucial question as the first inauguration neared.

Once again, Washington instinctively showed the way. His long journey from his home at Mount Vernon to his inauguration in New York was a triumph of moderation. It helped that he felt so little desire for the office. Even before the journey, Washington worried that his "movements to the chair of government will be accompanied with feelings not unlike those of a culprit who is going to the place of his execution."[7] Then, when the trip began, on April 16, 1789, Washington described "a mind oppressed with more anxious and painful sensations than I have words to express."[8]

Even if burdened with doubts, Washington understood that he needed to step into the role. The general struck just the right balance as he made his way through the country roads of Maryland, Delaware, Pennsylvania, and New Jersey, heading toward his inauguration in New York. He traveled like an ordinary citizen, stopping along the way in modest taverns and exchanging pleasantries with the well-wishers who crowded up close. Although a crown of laurels was placed on his head in Philadelphia, by a small child, the dangers of monarchy were largely avoided during the procession. There were other benefits as well, as Americans discovered that they liked the idea of a president traveling from one state to another, subtly drawing them together, into the federal idea.[9]

The crowning moment, as it were, came on April 30, when Washington took the oath of office before Federal Hall, just above Wall Street, in lower Manhattan. Again, he took care to avoid any royal trappings, wearing a suit of brown Connecticut homespun instead of his military uniform. Appearing before the crowd, he bowed to them, instead of the other way around, and "laid his hand on his heart," according to the account of a young girl watching from across the street.[10]

There was more to the ceremony than the oath. Although Washington was hardly known for his spontaneity, he added his own words to the event, in a most innovative way. For months, he had been contemplating a speech, to be delivered in these first moments, and he asked for drafts from his advisers, David Humphreys and James Madison. The latter figure was especially important in shaping the speech to come, another way in which he was busy applying mortar behind the scenes, so that each brick would fit into place.[11]

Even if the Constitution was silent on the topic of an inaugural address, Washington understood, intuitively, that something more was needed. The new office needed to be justified—certainly to the people, and perhaps to himself as well. The very idea was revolutionary for a people who had until recently lived under British rule. Kings don't persuade, they command. Monarchs have never been known for their eloquence and certainly do not speak at coronations. To the extent that they ever give famous speeches, they give them on the eve of battle or at their own executions (Louis XVI's moving address to the mob on the day he was guillotined took place four years after Washington became president).

Once again, Washington understood that he needed to survey a path into the wilderness. Accordingly, he gave an address inside Federal Hall that found the correct path between royal hauteur and a more egalitarian approach. It would have been difficult to begin with a humbler statement, expressing his "anxieties" about taking the position, and worrying that his "inferior endowments from nature" made him unfit for the job, along with other "deficiencies." So nervous did he seem while speaking that his hands were shaking, and his voice was "a little tremulous, and so low as to call for close attention."[12] An audience member expressed his amazement that the great general, so brave in the fact of "leveled cannon or pointed musket," seemed to tremble with stage fright.[13]

There was a grandeur in the moment, too. It came from the people listening reverentially to their new leader. It came from the Congress, seated respectfully (but not standing, as English protocols would have required for an oration by a king). And it came especially from the figure at the center of the ceremony, speaking haltingly, but always in command of himself. His sincerity of purpose carried the day. It would have been difficult to find a more apt way to launch this experiment in self-government. The speech set the precedent we still follow, more than fifty inaugurals later. It is the mold into which we pour our loftiest political language.

In short, Washington's inaugural address was not incidental to his presidency—it defined it. By declaring his intentions before his constituents, he showed an instinctive understanding of the new office and breathed life into it. His speech was respectful of Congress and the people, as it needed to be. But it was not entirely deferential, either. By seizing the initiative to speak, Washington revealed a considerable power in the new office—the freedom to lead.

Washington's inaugural address was consequential, not just for his own presidency, but for all of the others. It is a commonplace of American oratory to claim that "the eyes of the world are upon us," to borrow a phrase used by John Winthrop in 1630 and by hundreds of others since then.

Washington was genuinely in the spotlight, as the embodiment of democracy to his own and other peoples, wondering about the strange new form of government beginning. "I walk on untrodden ground," he wrote nervously, understanding that "there is scarcely any part of my conduct that may not hereafter be drawn into precedent." A huge range of questions presented themselves in the early days of the presidency. What sort of clothes should he wear? Should he wear a wig? Should he appear in public at all? Was it acceptable to attend a tea party? With a touching earnestness, Washington wrote his fellow Founders asking for their advice on these matters, which, no matter how quotidian, went to the heart of the presidency and democracy itself.[14]

With his usual instinct for the correct solution, Washington groped toward a satisfying compromise between the old ways and the new, beginning with the first day of his presidency. He validated democracy by going to Congress for the ceremony and then, immediately afterward, by walking seven blocks to a church service, through a large crowd in lower Manhattan. He validated monarchy with his natural aloofness and his tolerance of regal adoration: the giant transparencies of the new King George, and the thousands of new objects designed with his image—tankards, watch fobs, buttons, and other cheap souvenirs, presidential customs that continue to this day. Washington's personal gravitas would not allow for the relaxed, telegenic public behavior that we now expect from our presidents, nor was he comfortable with the deification that was already underway in his lifetime. Before settling on "Mr. President," the Senate debated a number of loftier honorifics, including "His Mightiness," "His Serene Highness," "His Elective Highness," and "His Highness, the President of the United States, and Protector of the Rights of the Same."

Four years after the first inaugural, Washington observed his own precedent and gave another inaugural address, this time in Philadelphia, where the government had relocated. Then, when approaching the end of his presidency, he again consulted Hamilton and Madison, for help preparing a valedictory. The famous Farewell Address was a printed essay, and not a speech, but it built upon the scaffolding Washington had already erected with his two inaugurals and deepened the important idea that the people needed to hear directly from their presidents.

His successors would continue to build on that scaffolding in the years to come. In 1797, John Adams was elected, and if that was not exactly a surprising result, still, it was the first time a new president took the stage. To do so with George Washington there added to the pressures he was facing at the first transitional moment. Once again, the inaugural address strengthened the presidency, as Adams acquitted himself with a detailed description of his plans for the future, a significantly more expansive speech than either of Washington's addresses.

Four years later, when Adams lost a bitter race to Thomas Jefferson, the transition was more difficult, for obvious reasons. Here was a genuine test for the new system, with a defeated incumbent turning over the reins of power to the man who defeated him. But once again, the inaugural address served as an advertisement for the larger project of democracy. Adams calmly left the new capital city of Washington. And Jefferson, too, rose to the occasion, delivering a speech of reconciliation and healing, and claiming, with some exaggeration, "we are all Republicans, we are all Federalists." That might have come as news to the bitter partisans in the audience, but it read beautifully and inspired Americans reading the proceedings in the newspapers.

As the job grew, so did the speech. With time, presidents began to understand that the inaugural address offered a rare opportunity to frame the nation's political agenda as a new quadrennial was beginning. Far from being a burden, as it always seemed to Washington, a major speech offered a chance to command the nation's attention and build political momentum. The tradition deepened as the government expanded, and Americans began to accept that all of these ideas—a president, and a federal capital along the Potomac—were becoming a permanent part of the landscape.

It helped that Americans were a people who loved oratory. They heard different kinds of public remarks in all of the places where they lived—in church, certainly, and in schools, and in the rude taverns where politics was constantly debated. As the Capitol grew in size and stature, the two chambers of the House and Senate were especially renowned for oratorical performances, with the Senate especially becoming a place for booming statements and rejoinders, like the debate between Daniel Webster of Massachusetts and Robert Hayne of South Carolina in 1830, which already seemed to foreshadow the great sectional divide to come.

Even with these tremendous performances inside the building, there was something special about the inaugural addresses that were delivered outside, on the East Portico, as a new president came into office. As this collection makes clear, with its superb commentary from so many distinguished scholars, and its organizing impulse from Yuvraj Singh, there were variants between the addresses, and they were not all delivered in the same place. But in general, a pattern was established, and every four years, the American people came out in large numbers to hear a new leader speak outside the building that stood as a shrine to their democracy.

The speeches were especially exciting when there was a new party coming into power, and Americans could feel the winds of change coming in with the new administration. However, those same winds proved to be the downfall of William Henry Harrison, the ninth president. After defeating Martin Van Buren and ending twelve years of Democratic rule, Harrison delivered a long speech, across an hour and forty minutes, in a snowstorm. Unwisely, Harrison added to his speech a tedious excursus into ancient history, despite the efforts of Daniel

Webster to edit out some of the more boring passages (Webster claimed that he "killed seventeen Roman proconsuls as dead as smelts").[15] That added substantially to a speech that was already growing wooly and meant that Harrison had to stand out in the cold even longer. He contracted an illness, probably pneumonia, as a result, and died a month into his tenure. Some felt it was divine retribution. He is the only president for whom the inaugural address proved terminal.

At other times, when democracy felt imperiled, the speech could bring it back to life. After the so-called Corrupt Bargain of 1824, when the House of Representatives handed the presidency to John Quincy Adams, he delivered an impressive address that reassured Americans of his formidable qualifications for the office.

Four years later, after Adams was defeated by Andrew Jackson (who had never surrendered his grievance over the loss of 1824), Jackson also won over detractors who worried about his lack of qualifications. Over and over again, the inaugural tended to heal the wounds of the campaigns and bring Americans back together. Standing symbolically by a door, at the top of the stairs to the Capitol, these presidents seemed to be welcoming Americans back into the laboratory, where they could work out their problems together.

Even when they could not, as the Civil War proved, the inaugural address offered a crucial moment of self-reflection, twice, as the nation plunged into the abyss in 1861 and re-emerged, stronger and better, in 1865. Lincoln's two inaugurals are already in the pantheon of great American speeches—his second one, in my opinion, is the greatest of them all. But they are even more moving to read in the context of all of the inaugural addresses, side by side—especially after a long train of addresses, before 1861, asserting that presidents had no right to criticize the "domestic institutions" of the South.

For all these reasons, it is important to have this modern edition of the inaugural addresses, telling the story of the nation as well as the speeches. It is all the more important to have in an era of flagging faith in democracy, as measured by the depressing annual reports on "Freedom in World" issued by Freedom House and the well-chronicled divisions between Americans over everything from Supreme Court decisions to the outcome of the 2020 election. We need to reread these inaugural addresses for the same reasons that Americans drifted to the steps of the Capitol in the past, eager to hear where the country was going. It grounds us to have these texts, reminding us how far we have already come.

As astonishing amount of history is available in these primary sources and the essays that explain them to us. We see, among other things, a kind of private conversation between the presidents, acknowledging each other even as they seek to build up presidencies of their own. Sometimes the sentences are even co-written by presidents—not only did James Madison contribute to Washington's inaugural, but John Quincy Adams also contributed to James Monroe's, and in a moving way the beautiful peroration of Lincoln's first inaugural was co-written by the man he defeated for the Republican nomination, William H. Seward.[16]

In other ways, too, they populate each other's speeches. For a long time, after George Washington, he reappeared in the speeches of presidents eager to retell the story of the country's founding. In 1861, as Lincoln was heading to Washington, D.C., in the worst crisis of our history, he found George Washington a comforting presence and talked often about his illustrious predecessor. In fact, he talked about him so well that he outmaneuvered Jefferson Davis, whose command of American history was nowhere near as strong as his own. It could be argued that Washington once again helped to keep his countrymen together.

Among other things, the presidents are bearers of historical witness at the time of giving the inaugural address. They assess the country's progress to that point and inevitably color their histories with their own judgments. After Lincoln's presidency, he rose up to a level nearly as heroic as Washington's, as the presidents of the late nineteenth century reckoned with the ongoing legacy of the Civil War. As late as 1905, Theodore Roosevelt brought some of Lincoln's DNA for good luck, by wearing a ring that enclosed a strand of Lincoln's hair.

The twentieth century brought upheavals of its own, including the two world wars and the Great Depression. The Second World War was as important a defining experience for presidents as the Civil War and Revolution had been, for earlier generations, and affected leaders as different as Dwight D. Eisenhower, John F. Kennedy, Richard Nixon, and George H. W. Bush in profound ways. That legacy was evident not just in their personal stories, but in their general belief that the United States must play a strong role defending freedom in the world—a belief that was largely missing during the first century of inaugural addresses.

Even in recent years, we have seen subtle alterations of the histories that presidents present to us. Bill Clinton, from a very different generation than his predecessor, succeeded in describing the Civil Rights Movement as a major turning point of American history, a stance that only deepened with the election of Barack Obama.[17]

Donald Trump, on the other hand, paid no heed to the Civil Rights Movement, or to the Second World War, instead urging Americans to heed their own interests. But if that stance seemed ahistorical when it was uttered, a deep reading of this volume reminds us that there were many precedents for American isolationism, including Warren Harding, Calvin Coolidge, and most of the nineteenth-century presidents. As Harding said in his inaugural, "a world supergovernment is contrary to everything we cherish."

We have also seen an extraordinary growth in the amount of attention paid to inaugural addresses over the past century. Despite the enormous import of

Lincoln's two inaugurals, they were relatively casual affairs in which crowds could arrive without tickets and get quite close to the Capitol. In the twentieth and twenty-first centuries, with the advent of radio, television, and social media, a global audience hangs on every syllable. The transition began with Theodore Roosevelt, who understood that the White House was becoming a "bully pulpit." It deepened with Woodrow Wilson, who said, "there is but one national voice in the country and that is the voice of the president," and governed from that premise.[18] It deepened still more with the addresses of Franklin Roosevelt and John F. Kennedy, who understood clearly that presidents were standing on a global stage, and not merely a national one.

It has also become, among other things, a major event in television and therefore an entertainment spectacle, with poetry and parades, in addition to all of the pomp and circumstance. The highest ratings ever achieved for an inaugural address were by Ronald Reagan, who spoke to 41.8 million people in 1981; the second-highest ratings were achieved by Barack Obama in 2009, when 37.93 million tuned in. Surprisingly, a former reality television star, Donald Trump, attracted only 30.64 million in 2017.[19]

Has the inaugural address peaked? I doubt it, although it now stands out as something quite different from what it was when George Washington delivered his first. Then it was a radical innovation, designed to explain the new office of the presidency and Washington's quite specific intentions. Now, it is an old-fashioned burst of oratory, longer than most speeches delivered by politicians, full of bombast and rodomontade. There are usually very few specifics; it is more of a celebratory pep talk for a nation that has (usually) tired of a predecessor president and is looking for a new storyline.

Well before this collection was assembled, I was thinking about the tradition of the inaugural address and went on a reader's pilgrimage through all of them. It began for professional reasons—I spent four years as a speechwriter in the Clinton White House, in the late 1990s. I enjoyed reading through older speeches, both to excavate felicitous turns of phrase and to deepen my sense of the rhetorical tradition I was working within. But as I kept reading in the old addresses, I felt the stirrings of a deeper historical interest, almost as if they offered a form of time travel.

There were three libraries within the White House compound, each fascinating for its architecture as well as its collections. One, in the Old Executive Office Building, groaned with collections of old government documents, held behind iron balustrades that seemed to stretch as far as the eye could see. The sheer amount of government verbiage encased in those old volumes was overwhelming—not just the major speeches of presidents, but the executive orders, and the debates in Congress, and the parliamentary maneuvers, and the publication of proclamations in the *Congressional Record*, recognizing 100th birthdays, and high school football championships, and all the ways in which Americans were living their lives, far from the ivory towers of Washington.

Reading all of the inaugural addresses is not a task for the fainthearted. No one can enter those endless paragraphs about tariffs and civil-service reform and emerge undamaged. But in that library, where America's treaties and founding documents were long kept under lock and key, I found the old speeches had new life breathed into them. Without too much difficulty, a reader can imagine the exhilaration with which America heard the earliest presidential thoughts of a Zachary Taylor, a Grover Cleveland, a Herbert Hoover. Taken all together, in sequence, the inaugural addresses comprise an advanced course in American history, a Book of the Republic.

Even after my White House career was finished, the speeches stayed with me. I edited an anthology of speeches for the Library of America and wrote an essay for *The American Scholar*, about the long history of the address.[20] In that essay, I researched many of the rituals connected to the speech, including the date itself. In the Catholic Church, January 20 is the feast day of Saint Fabian, a third-century pope who was appointed in a most unusual way. Before 236, he was a simple layperson, leading an utterly obscure life, even by third-century standards. That year, Fabian came to Rome and found himself unexpectedly in the middle of a crowd choosing the successor to Pope Anteros, recently deceased. At a dramatic point in the proceedings, according to the chronicler Eusebius, a dove flew down from the ceiling and landed on Fabian's head, in "clear imitation of the descent of the Holy Spirit in the form of a dove upon the Savior." The rest of the story can be divined without too much difficulty: within moments, Fabian found himself nominated, elected, and handed the keys to the papacy. Surprisingly, he made quite a good pope.

But January 20 has only been the inaugural date since 1937. In 1933, after a terrifyingly long transition during the darkest days of the Great Depression, Congress moved the date up from where it had been for most of our history, March 4. That date, too, had a certain resonance—it was perfect for announcing new plans ("March Forth!"), and it was enshrined in the Constitution. There are only twenty-five amendments to the Constitution, and two of them, the twelfth and twentieth, treat the date of the inaugural.

Despite the fact that inaugurals now take place in winter—hardly the best time to sing a song of renewal—the ceremony remains a very grand spectacle, much of it outdoors. Inaugurals happen rarely enough to be genuinely arresting spectacles. Once every four years, between the Olympics and the World Cup, we embrace the rituals that launch a new presidentiad—Walt Whitman's word. The parades, the seating charts, the jets streaking overhead, the swearing-in ceremony—and then, of course, the inaugural address, when the most powerful official in the world elucidates his vision for the next four years of history.

But it's an odd moment, really. Very few states, with the possible exception of the Vatican, place such a high premium on the rituals attending the transfer of power. These elaborate ceremonies tease out a tension that is as present in the twenty-first century as it was in the eighteenth, when the United States was still an iffy proposition. Simply put, it is difficult to conduct a democracy without resorting to monarchical role models. Despite George Washington's precautions, the inauguration remains a barely concealed coronation, drawing on ancient antecedents. There are traveling delegations from across the realm, elaborate hierarchies and protocols, balls, minstrels, horses, equerries—a veritable Renaissance Faire.

Yet it cannot be a coronation, so it is different. The new leader wears no crown (hats have been optional since 1960, when John F. Kennedy held a silk top hat but did not wear it). His tenure begins not with a religious ceremony symbolizing the church's approval, but with the swearing of a legal oath, thirty-five words written very specifically into the Constitution—along with the four words perhaps ad-libbed by George Washington in 1789, "so help me God." The ceremony that "makes a president" lasts only about six minutes, as the journalist Richard Harding Davis noted in 1897, while "six hours are required to fasten the crown upon the Czar of Russia and to place the sceptre in his hand."[21]

That tension continues throughout the day, when the new president is expected to walk some of the distance to the White House, waving jubilantly, but unable to walk free in any normal sense, surrounded by phalanxes of Secret Service agents, bulletproof glass, and other interpositions between the theory and reality of democracy. We have traveled a long way from Andrew Jackson's inaugural of 1829, when anyone could attend a White House reception, and did. Jackson was nearly crushed to death by the exuberant mob that showed up to congratulate him; he escaped by jumping out the nearest window.

The old spontaneity is impossible, given the prodigious pressures to organize a suitably telegenic entertainment spectacle. That means a small army of technicians must build a small city next to the Capitol, including a stage, where they will design a set and rope off the uninvited, while making sure that all of the incoming president's donors and supporters are reasonably nearby. At the same time, the uninvited are still relevant in their way, and great crowds on the Mall are desirable, especially to presidents who measure audience size as a kind of divine commentary on their right to govern.

The inaugural speech, the central spectacle of the day, remains sacrosanct, undiminished by the passage of centuries. Why has it endured? Surely part of the answer lies in the enormous expectations we freight the office with. We have very complicated, contradictory notions of who we expect our presidents to be. The leader of a political party . . . the symbol of the nation . . . the military commander-in-chief . . . the sparkplug for the economy . . . the boss of an organization, the executive branch, that employs two million people (not counting the military) . . . the oracle, therapist, and self-empowerment guru for 335 million people. With so many questions floating in the air about this father figure, we need the roots that a long speech, even a bad speech, can sink into the nation's topsoil.

At their best, these secular sermons tell us where we have been, where we are going, and who we will be when we get there. It is curious that we expect the most important speech to come at the beginning of a presidency rather than at its end. But undeniably, Lincoln's two inaugurals, Roosevelt's first, Jefferson's first, and Kennedy's rank among the most significant speeches in our history.

Of course, the inaugural tradition has grown since 1789, picking up piecemeal new rituals the way a shaggy dog accumulates burrs. The parade dates from 1829 when Andrew Jackson, trying to flee the huge crowds smothering him with affection, raced down Pennsylvania Avenue from the Capitol toward the White House and found that the crowd, to his horror, was following him. The White House reviewing stand dates from 1861, when a simple wooden platform with a canvas canopy was built for Abraham Lincoln to review the troops coming to defend Washington from the threat of invasion from the South.

The backdrop has changed as well. The first inaugural address given in Washington was Jefferson's, in 1801. When Jefferson spoke, so quietly that most of the room could not hear him, he was standing in the newly built Senate wing of the Capitol. In fact, that's all there was to the Capitol; it was little more than a hallway in search of an idea. Looking at prints of the successive inaugurals in the early nineteenth century is almost a cinematic experience. In each image, an indistinct president is in the foreground, giving an oration, while the Capitol gets a little bigger every time.

Real photographs begin in 1857, with the inauguration of James Buchanan. The daguerreotype shows the washy effects of what was still a very sketchy chemical process—one person's hat is far more distinct than the rest of his body, and focus is far better at the center of the image than at its margins, aptly symbolizing the nation's aimlessness as the United States drifted toward civil war.

Four years later, we have a more focused photograph of Lincoln's first inaugural, and four years after that, with the Capitol dome finally completed, we have a remarkable shot of Lincoln in the act of delivering his second. Historians argue about whether John Wilkes Booth is perceptible in the shot—nearly everyone looks like him—but the most fascinating figure is Lincoln himself, blurry and indistinct (did he move his head when he saw the photographer?), already growing spectral.

Then the photographs become better, as the technology improves, and the ceremony has been filmed from William McKinley's first inaugural (1897) on. Americans could hear Calvin Coolidge giving his speech on the radio (1925), and they could see Harry Truman on television (1949). In 1981, Ronald Reagan shifted the ceremony from the East Front of the Capitol to the West, having an actor's sense that this was the building's best profile. In 1997, Bill Clinton's speech went live on the Internet.[22]

Even with ever-more powerful means of communication, the inaugural remains recognizable as the descendant of the speech George Washington gave in 1789. Reading all of the inaugurals together reveals how much they have in common. It is remarkable how much history is covered by presidents—instead of simply announcing their plans for the future, many look backward, searching for clues to the country's greatness. That can be instructive; when John Adams reflects upon the Revolution and the Constitution, it's worth listening. It can also be pedestrian in a lesser figure (say, James Monroe). There is a thin line between a cliché and a genuinely moving statement about a personal belief or experience.

Needless to say, there are mountains of bad writing that need to be taken with a grain of salt. We should not forget that Americans enjoying long, stemwinding orations in the long night that preceded television, and there is no shortage of them here. Even the great figures stumbled. Why did John Adams, sailing along smoothly, suddenly embark on an interminable single sentence that took up approximately a quarter of his address and required 732 words to complete? Why did Martin Van Buren include an exclamation point—a rarity in inaugural address history—after a sentence that was neither funny nor shocking? What inner child in George H. W. Bush forced him to say "freedom is like a beautiful kite that can go higher and higher with the breeze"? Why did John F. Kennedy, usually so literate, wonder if "a beachhead of cooperation may push back the jungle of suspicion"? Was Ronald Reagan daydreaming of Mitch Miller and his television Sing Along with his odd paean to "the American Sound"?

Of course, we err in applying modern standards of literary quality to what was neither modern nor literary. A speech is not a poem or even an essay; it is a highly ritualistic kind of theater that combines words, gestures, and backdrops to create a stylized effect. As with Japanese kabuki, the audience derives much of its pleasure from its knowledge of the ritual. In our modern world of rapid sensations, we frown upon hearing any thought we have heard before, but such repetition was reassuring to earlier American audiences. It's clear that verbosity, far from being a sin, was a positive virtue for the people who assembled every four years to hear these elaborate performances. John Quincy Adams's first sentence, while unreadable today, must have thrilled a certain kind of listener: "In compliance with an usage coeval with the existence of our Federal Constitution, and sanctioned by the example of my predecessors in the career upon which I am about to enter, I appear, my fellow-citizens, in your presence and in that of Heaven to bind myself by the solemnities of religious obligation to the faithful performance of the duties allotted to me in the station to which I have been called." What writing class could ever teach that?

But there is a problem worse than swollen writing. The urge to write at great length is often tied to the need to conceal something, and there were unmentionable parts of the American story that never made it close to the inaugural stage. The silences are important.

In their haste to please, nearly every early American president went to great lengths to avoid the word slavery, preferring tortured euphemisms like "domestic institutions" or no mention at all. One cringes a bit when James Monroe asks, gloatingly, "On whom has oppression fallen in any quarter of our Union? Who has been deprived of any right of person or property?" In 1857, on the eve of the Civil War, James Buchanan wanted to end the argument over slavery so that he could move on to "more pressing" matters, like the spread of "liberty throughout the world"! But at the very moment of delivering his address, he was conniving with the chief justice of the Supreme Court, Roger Taney, about to issue the infamous Dred Scott decision. It's no wonder that their contemporary Herman Melville wrote in *Moby Dick*, "Woe to him who seeks to please rather than to appall!"

It is difficult to know which omissions will strike our descendants as glaring, but that, too, is important to consider when reading these addresses. In 1789, the year it all began, Jefferson wrote a letter to Madison that included a striking line: "the earth belongs in usufruct to the living." That was a healthy corrective for a new nation, seeking an untrammeled way forward, unimpeded by the ancient traditions of European precedent. But to place so high a value on the usufruct of the present is to deny something to our children, who will inhabit the future, and the Earth, that we bequeath to them. May our usufruct be as wise as possible, with them in mind.

The kabuki of the typical inaugural can be broken down into specific set pieces, the thoughts arranged in a comforting sequence that would have been instantly familiar one hundred, even two hundred, years ago.

1. I am not worthy of this great honor.
2. But I congratulate the people that they elected me.
3. Now we must all come together, even those of us who really hate each other.
4. I love the Constitution, the Union, and George Washington.
5. I will work against bad threats.
6. I will work for good things.
7. We must avoid entangling alliances.

8. America's strength = democracy.
9. Democracy's strength = America.
10. Thanks, God.

Not every speech follows that scheme. But quite a lot do. Still, a few inaugural addresses jump out from behind the damask curtain of nineteenth-century sensibilities. Who knew that James Garfield was a passionate champion of the rights of ex-slaves? Or that Rutherford B. Hayes daringly called for the creation of a single six-year term for the president? Or that Benjamin Harrison, another Republican beard, was a sensitive writer?

There is something about the generals that compels admiration. Military exigencies pruned their writing styles long before they entered politics. Washington's second inaugural is all of 135 words—about what it would take Taft to clear his throat. Jackson says more in fewer words than any of his contemporaries. Grant weeds out needless adjectives like so many Confederate sharpshooters: After discussing Reconstruction and problems with Black suffrage, he clenches his jaw and says, "This is wrong, and should be corrected." What else is there to say? Grant's no-nonsense style is even more appealing when one learns that halfway through his speech, his young daughter, lonely, came up to the podium to hold his hand while he was speaking.

These human moments are not written into the *Messages and Papers of the Presidents*, a ten-volume collection of presidential utterances between 1789 and 1897 that was the standard source for generations. But they too are an inexorable part of the story. Should we not know that James Garfield suffered from crippling writer's block and simply could not finish his speech until 2:30 on the morning of the inaugural? As the day approached, he had an anxiety dream in which he fell off a canal boat and was suddenly standing naked in the wilderness during a wild storm. After finding a few pieces of cloth to cover himself and embarking on "a long and tangled journey," he found his way to a house where "an old negro woman took me into her arms and nursed me as though I were a sick child." Comforted, he awoke to face his presidency.

If there is a single theme that unites all of the inaugurals, it is the need to explore the central mystery of God's relationship to the American experiment. This is hardly a simple topic, and some handle it better than others. John Quincy Adams preferred to place his hand on the Constitution rather than the Bible. Dwight D. Eisenhower, on the other hand, allowed a vehicle called "God's Float" to enter his parade. A religion writer compared it to "an oversized model of a deformed molar left over from some dental exhibit."

The tradition goes back to the oft-told story that Washington blurted out "So help me God" after taking the oath in 1789. That tradition may be invented (helpfully, Kevin Butterfield explains in this volume that he did not say those words in 1793). But it has entered our folklore, and presidents now routinely add those four words to the oath.[23] The mere mention of God's name signals the end of the speech, as if the manager of a vaudeville house had appeared onstage to thank the audience and urge its members to gather their belongings before leaving. God appears in forty-two of fifty-four perorations, and only one speech dares to leave Him out completely—Washington's second inaugural. The conformity ends, however, when it comes to naming Him. The founders avoided invoking God by name and instead resorted to a dizzying array of divine identifiers: "the benign Parent of the Human Race" (Washington), "that Being who is supreme over all" (Adams), "that Infinite Power which rules the destinies of the universe" (Jefferson), "that Power whose providence mercifully protected our national infancy" (Jackson), and "Him Who has not yet forsaken this favored land" (Lincoln). It is worth noting that Jesus has never been mentioned in an inaugural address.

Lincoln remains aloof from the rest, fascinating, slightly subversive. To read Lincoln in the context of his surrounding inaugurals is to see a gifted genius so ahead of his time that we are still in some ways catching up to him. For him, religion, like patriotism, was not a boast to be brayed in public, but an aspiration to be quietly, relentlessly sought in the dark chambers of the human heart.

Each of Lincoln's inaugural addresses struck the perfect tone for its moment. An eyewitness to the first (1861), Benjamin Brown French, wrote, "words could not have been selected & framed into sentences that could better express the ideas of those who have elected Abraham Lincoln to the Presidency." With a lawyer's precision and a friend's patience, Lincoln pleaded the cause of the Union with the South and reminded them, delicately but firmly, how much was at stake (he artfully delayed the words "civil war" until the penultimate paragraph).

The final paragraph is a miniature masterpiece and still teaches editors and aspiring speechwriters what a few line changes can do to strengthen an argument. William Seward, the incoming secretary of State, proposed these lines:

> I close. We are not we must not be aliens or enemies but fellow countrymen and brethren. Although passion has strained our bonds of affection too hardly they must not, I am sure they will not be broken. The mystic chords which proceeding from so many battle fields and so many patriot graves pass through all the hearts and all the hearths in this broad continent of ours will yet again harmonize in the ancient music when breathed upon by the guardian angel of the nation.

Lincoln's translation:

I am loath to close. We are not enemies, but friends. We must not be enemies. Though passion may have strained it must not break our bonds of affection. The mystic chords of memory, stretching from every battlefield and patriot grave to every living heart and hearthstone all over this broad land, will yet swell the chorus of the Union, when again touched, as surely they will be, by the better angels of our nature.

Lincoln's second inaugural (1865) is more majestic still. Though one of the shortest inaugurals, it remains the best. Everything about it is different—its lack of interest in the minutiae of politics, its stately retelling, in short, lapidary building blocks, of the war's story. The remarkable four-word sentence, "And the war came," surely preceded by a pause when he spoke it, seems almost to have sprung from the Old Testament. The brilliant disquisition on God's indecipherability ("The Almighty has his own purposes") flies in the face of all presidential oratory before and since. This least hermeneutic of all inaugurals is also in many ways the most religious, offering searing passages from the Bible along with Lincoln's mystical reflections on human responsibility to a God that is not always responsive, even to Americans. Finally, it is a literary gem, containing small surprises around every corner, including this prose poem near the end:

> Fondly do we hope,
> Fervently do we pray,
> That this mighty scourge of war
> May speedily pass away.

There are countless inaugural highlights in the more crowded twentieth century. Wilson's musings are cerebral and eloquent, befitting a parson. Franklin D. Roosevelt is interesting four times in a row—no mean feat—and breaks down the distance between speaker and listener with colloquialisms ("thank God"), sound bites ("fear itself"), and contagious optimism.

Eisenhower's second, while unknown to most, bears a close rereading today for its shrewd assessment of imperial overreach. Kennedy was our most exciting inaugural speaker, and no one should discount the importance of the way the words are performed—in his case, barked out on a day so cold that wisps of air visibly escaped from his mouth, like smoke from a dragon ready to slay the hoary Washington establishment seated behind him. His words were well chosen, too. Ted Sorensen, his speechwriter, studied Lincoln's Gettysburg Address and noticed something that had eluded almost all presidents in between: Lincoln communicated big ideas with very small words. Accordingly, he began lopping off adjectives and syllables to stunning effect (speechwriting can be a science as well as an art). The use of the second person ("ask not what your country can do for you..."), rare in presidential oratory, was another bright innovation. Eisenhower used *Thou* in 1953, but he was speaking to God at the time.

Still, none of the great speeches of the last century has quite the audacity of Lincoln's second, which becomes more revolutionary as modern politicians increasingly claim that God approves their actions. In the greatest essay on speechwriting ever written, "Politics and the English Language" (1946), George Orwell warns against the subtle and serial ways in which stately language can be placed in the service of violence. Obviously, Orwell deplored Nazism and Stalinism, but he was equally discouraged by ways in which Western politicians resorted to euphemism, stale imagery, and overreliance on safe words like *freedom* to obscure policies he disliked (including British rule in India and the dropping of the atomic bomb on Japan). "Political language," he wrote, "is designed to make lies sound truthful and murder respectable."[24]

It would be an exaggeration to claim that the inaugurals achieved a lasting literary impact. They were serviceable in their time, and, but for some iconic lines, virtually all soon forgotten after delivery.

Might we hope for more great inaugurals in the years to come? If Lincoln is any guide—and I believe that he is—the right words will come again to presidents when we need them most. It is in the darker moments, generally, that the most luminous speeches have been given. That is hardly an encouraging note to end on, but it does give some reassurance to read these addresses and realize how much we have already overcome.

In the current, vexed political climate, we will have all kinds of speeches—speeches that divide as well as unite Americans. But the ones that last will remind us how much we still have in common, despite our obvious differences. It goes without saying that we like soothing phrases about the remarkable nation we all inhabit. But we also need concrete, grounded ideas about America's place in the world. More than anything, we need to reconnect to each other as fellow Americans, to borrow a favorite presidential phrase, and the title of this volume. We have rarely needed that more.

Given how venerable the inaugural tradition is, it is becoming more difficult to claim, as so many presidents have, that we are a very young country. But age has its compensations, not the least of which is that our history just keeps getting richer. Future inaugural addresses will take place on a very crowded stage, as usual. But let us not forget all the other presidents who will be there in spirit, adding their voices to the sounds of the ceremony and straining to "harmonize in the ancient music," to use Seward's discarded phrase. Surely it does no harm to pause for a moment and listen to what they have to say, still speaking to us faintly over the din of the republic.

Notes

1. https://www.themorgan.org/exhibitions/the-great-experiment.
2. Stefan Lorant, *The Glorious Burden: The American Presidency* (New York: Harper & Row, 1968), 3.
3. Lorant, *The Glorious Burden*, 4.
4. Wayne Fields, *Union of Words: A History of Presidential Eloquence* (New York: Free Press, 1986), 6.
5. Lorant, *The Glorious Burden*, 6.
6. Lorant, *The Glorious Burden*, 11.
7. Ron Chernow, *George Washington: A Life* (New York: Penguin Press, 2010), 559.
8. https://www.mountvernon.org/george-washington/the-first-president/inauguration/.
9. https://www.mountvernon.org/george-washington/the-first-president/inauguration/; Lorant, *The Glorious Burden*, 18; Nathaniel Philbrick, *Travels with George: In Search of George Washington and His Legacy* (New York: Viking, 2021).
10. Philbrick, *Travels with George*, 48–49.
11. https://founders.archives.gov/documents/Madison/01-12-02-0078.
12. Chernow, *George Washington*, 568.
13. Philbrick, *Travels with George*, 50; Lorant, *The Glorious Burden*, 18–23.
14. Lorant, *The Glorious Burden*, 26–27.
15. Fields, *Union of Words*, 128.
16. Fields, *Union of Words*, 9.
17. Fields, *Union of Words*, 115.
18. Fields, *Union of Words*, 8.
19. https://www.statista.com/statistics/250929/us-presidential-inauguration-viewer-numbers/.
20. Ted Widmer, "So Help Me God," *The American Scholar* 74 (Winter 2005): 29–41.
21. Richard Harding Davis, "The Inauguration," *Harper's New Monthly Magazine* 95 (1897): 345.
22. https://en.wikipedia.org/wiki/United_States_presidential_inauguration.
23. https://www.mtsu.edu/first-amendment/article/1718/so-help-me-god#:~:text=Much%20of%20the%20debate%20has,oath%20that%20the%20Constitution%20prescribed.
24. George Orwell, "Politics and the English Language," The Orwell Foundation, 1946, retrieved from https://www.orwellfoundation.com/the-orwell-foundation/orwell/essays-and-other-works/politics-and-the-english-language/.

George Washington's First Inaugural Address

THURSDAY, APRIL 30, 1789

FELLOW-CITIZENS OF THE Senate and of the House of Representatives:
Among the vicissitudes incident to life no event could have filled me with greater anxieties than that of which the notification was transmitted by your order, and received on the 14th day of the present month. On the one hand, I was summoned by my country, whose voice I can never hear but with veneration and love, from a retreat which I had chosen with the fondest predilection, and, in my flattering hopes, with an immutable decision, as the asylum of my declining years—a retreat which was rendered every day more necessary as well as more dear to me by the addition of habit to inclination, and of frequent interruptions in my health to the gradual waste committed on it by time. On the other hand, the magnitude and difficulty of the trust to which the voice of my country called me, being sufficient to awaken in the wisest and most experienced of her citizens a distrustful scrutiny into his qualifications, could not but overwhelm with despondence one who (inheriting inferior endowments from nature and unpracticed in the duties of civil administration) ought to be peculiarly conscious of his own deficiencies. In this conflict of emotions all I dare aver is that it has been my faithful study to collect my duty from a just appreciation of every circumstance by which it might be affected. All I dare hope is that if, in executing this task, I have been too much swayed by a grateful remembrance of former instances, or by an affectionate sensibility to this transcendent proof of the confidence of my fellow-citizens, and have thence too little consulted my incapacity as well as disinclination for the weighty and untried cares before me, my error will be palliated by the motives which mislead me, and its consequences be judged by my country with some share of the partiality in which they originated.

Such being the impressions under which I have, in obedience to the public summons, repaired to the present station, it would be peculiarly improper to omit in this first official act my fervent supplications to that Almighty Being who rules over the universe, who presides in the councils of nations, and whose providential aids can supply every human defect, that His benediction may consecrate to the liberties and happiness of the people of the United States a Government instituted by themselves for these essential purposes, and may enable every instrument employed in its administration to execute with success the functions allotted to his charge. In tendering this homage to the Great Author of every public and private good, I assure myself that it expresses your sentiments not less than my own, nor those of my fellow-citizens at large less than either. No people can be bound to acknowledge and adore the Invisible Hand which conducts the affairs of men more than those of the United States. Every step by which they have advanced to the character of an independent nation seems to have been distinguished by some token of providential agency; and in the important revolution just accomplished in the system of their united government the tranquil deliberations and voluntary consent of so many distinct communities from which the event has resulted can not be compared with the means by which most governments have been established without some return of pious gratitude, along with an humble anticipation of the future blessings which the past seem to presage. These reflections, arising out of the present crisis, have forced themselves too strongly on my mind to be suppressed. You will join with me, I trust, in thinking that there are none under the influence of which the proceedings of a new and free government can more auspiciously commence.

By the article establishing the executive department it is made the duty of the President "to recommend to your consideration such measures as he shall judge necessary and expedient." The circumstances under which I now meet you will acquit me from entering into that subject further than to refer to the great constitutional charter under which you are assembled, and which, in defining your powers, designates the objects to which your attention is to be given. It will be more consistent with those circumstances, and far more congenial with the feelings which actuate me, to substitute, in place of a recommendation of particular measures, the tribute that is due to the talents, the rectitude, and the patriotism which adorn the characters selected to devise and adopt them. In these honorable qualifications I behold the surest pledges that as on one side no local prejudices or attachments, no separate views nor party animosities, will misdirect the comprehensive and equal eye which ought to watch over this great assemblage of communities and interests, so, on another, that the foundation of our national policy will be laid in the pure and immutable principles of private morality, and the preeminence of free government be exemplified by all the attributes which can win the affections of its citizens and command the respect of the world. I dwell on this prospect with every satisfaction which an ardent love for my country can inspire, since there is no truth more thoroughly established than that there exists in the economy and course of nature an indissoluble union between virtue and happiness; between duty and advantage; between the genuine maxims of an honest and magnanimous policy and the solid rewards of public prosperity and felicity; since we ought to be no less persuaded that the propitious smiles of Heaven can never be expected on a nation that disregards the eternal rules of order and right which Heaven itself has ordained; and since the preservation of the sacred fire of liberty and the destiny of the republican model of government are justly considered, perhaps, as *deeply*, as *finally*, staked on the experiment entrusted to the hands of the American people.

Besides the ordinary objects submitted to your care, it will remain with your judgment to decide how far an exercise of the occasional power delegated by the fifth article of the Constitution is rendered expedient at the present juncture by the nature of objections which have been urged against the system, or by the degree of inquietude which has given birth to them. Instead of undertaking particular recommendations on this subject, in which I could be guided by no lights derived from official opportunities, I shall again give way to my entire confidence in your discernment and pursuit of the public good; for I assure myself that whilst you carefully avoid every alteration which might endanger the benefits of an united and effective government, or which ought to await the future lessons of experience, a reverence for the characteristic rights of freemen and a regard for the public harmony will sufficiently influence your deliberations on the question how far the former can be impregnably fortified or the latter be safely and advantageously promoted.

To the foregoing observations I have one to add, which will be most properly addressed to the House of Representatives. It concerns myself, and will therefore be as brief as possible. When I was first honored with a call into the service of my country, then on the eve of an arduous struggle for its liberties, the light in which I contemplated my duty required that I should renounce every pecuniary compensation. From this resolution I have in no instance departed; and being still under the impressions which produced it, I must decline as inapplicable to myself any share in the personal emoluments which may be indispensably included in a permanent provision for the executive department, and must accordingly pray that the pecuniary estimates for the station in which I am placed may during my continuance in it be limited to such actual expenditures as the public good may be thought to require.

Having thus imparted to you my sentiments as they have been awakened by the occasion which brings us together, I shall take my present leave; but not without resorting once more to the benign Parent of the Human Race in humble supplication that, since He has been pleased to favor the American people with opportunities for deliberating in perfect tranquillity, and dispositions for deciding with unparalleled unanimity on a form of government for the security of their union and the advancement of their happiness, so His divine blessing may be equally *conspicuous* in the enlarged views, the temperate consultations, and the wise measures on which the success of this Government must depend.

Inaugurator

GEORGE WASHINGTON'S FIRST INAUGURAL ADDRESS

Stephen H. Browne

GEORGE WASHINGTON DID not invent the inaugural address, but he did establish it as an abiding ritual of American political life. The Constitution requires no such statement: an oath of office, yes, and an annual report to Congress on the nation's business. But of the inaugural address, nothing is said or even implied. Why then did Washington feel obliged to deliver a speech on the occasion of his assumption to office? Because the first president commanded a very keen grasp of power and how it ought to be managed on behalf of republican government. Citizens of the republic, in turn, expected power to show itself, to identify and explain the principles underwriting the officeholder's claim to the public trust. No one, of course, was more entrusted with power at the time than George Washington. That he, of all people, should nevertheless perform such a duty tells us much about the man, the moment, and the functions of the inaugural address.

On April 14, 1789, a thoroughly fatigued Charles Thomson, secretary of the Continental Congress, dismounted in front of Mount Vernon. He then informed Washington that he had been "elected to the office of President of the United States of America." No one, safe to say, would have been surprised at this news, least of all its illustrious recipient. Washington indeed had prepared a statement for just this occasion, and reading from it declared: "While I realize the arduous nature of the task, which is conferred on me and feel my inability to perform it, I wish there may not be reason for regretting the choice. All I can promise is only that which can be accomplished by an honest zeal." Two days later, the president-elect, Thomson, and Washington's secretary and future biographer David Humphreys set out on what can only be described as a republican variant on the royal procession. The journey would take them from Mount Vernon to nearby Alexandria for a brief round of toasts and speeches, and from there to Baltimore, through Delaware and into Philadelphia; thence up to Trenton, Elizabethtown, and on a barge into the Upper Harbor. On April 23, 1789, Washington debarked onto the streets of lower Manhattan amidst much noise, festivity, and collective pride. The house on Cherry Street was readied for the president's occupation; Congress had figured out most of the protocols; and in a week's time Federal Hall would host the new nation's first presidential inaugural address. On the appointed day, Washington was accompanied onto the balcony by New York Chancellor Robert Livingston, who administered the oath of office. Immediately upon its completion, Livingston let out, "Long live George Washington, President of the United States." Thirteen cannons roared their approval, and back into the chambers stepped the chief executive of the new nation.

What kind of speech might his fellow citizens expect? Washington was no orator, no Patrick Henry, and he never pretended otherwise. But whether on the fields of battle, at Mount Vernon, or in politics, he appreciated the power of language; and if Washington was not eloquent by nature, he knew how to get the best people around him to craft words for optimal effect. To this end he had enlisted Humphreys's aid in composing the inaugural message. James Madison, taking one look at the seventy-page jumble, nixed it and composed, with Washington's support, a rather more precise, coherent, and compelling draft. From this document he would deliver his address before the House and Senate gathered on the second floor of Federal Hall on April 30, 1789.

Just what executive power meant in the new order of things was as yet uncertain. But the new nation had fought a war in part to ensure that those who commanded such power were motivated by principles consistent with widely held ideals of republican virtue. This meant above all a regard for the public good over and above private desire. Americans wanted to be certain that the president was there for the right reasons. Washington accordingly devoted the first two of the address's five paragraphs to assuring the people that, though longing to remain at Mount Vernon, "the asylum of my declining years," he had accepted the "summon[s] by my Country, whose voice I can never hear but with veneration and love." In truth Washington had little to gain in any material way from assuming the office; he needed no boost to his reputation; and he certainly had no particular taste for the tumble of politics. Washington accepted the call because it was the right thing to do. For guidance he would look to Congress and the people, but ultimately "to that Almighty Being who rules over the universe, who presides in the councils of nations," confident that, in the end, "No people can be bound to acknowledge and adore the Invisible Hand which conducts the affairs of men more than those of the United States."

The assembled lawmakers that day would hear little in the way of specific recommendations or legislative priorities. Concerns about the military establishment, or commerce, or treaty relations with Indigenous peoples, or indeed foreign policy, are not even mentioned. Washington sought instead to underscore the essential tenets of republican government and the shared commitments upon which it must rest. Above all, he wished to stress the unprecedented obligations shouldered by those gathered before him that day because "the preservation of the sacred fire of liberty and the destiny of the republican model of government are justly considered, perhaps, as *deeply*, as *finally*, staked, on the experiment entrusted to the hands of the American people."

Ensuing presidents might and did on occasion insinuate into their inaugural address particular measures. Washington for the most part chose to emphasize just those principles with which the new nation could, without contest, give their unreserved assent: "reverence for the characteristic rights of freemen and a regard for the public harmony." He did make it a point to remind his listeners that Article Five of the Constitution provided a preferred method for amendment, and he attempted (unsuccessfully) to decline compensation. Beyond these brief comments, Washington hoped only to impart such sentiments as he thought proper to the occasion, praying, finally, that the blessings of "the benign Parent of the Human Race" may "be equally *conspicuous* in the enlarged views, the temperate consultations, and the wise measures on which the success of this Government must depend."

Everything Washington did as president was, as he acknowledged, a precedent of some kind. The first inaugural address was no exception; the very fact that he chose to deliver it remains a lasting contribution to American civic life. That afternoon and evening, New Yorkers spilled onto the streets to celebrate, vessels in the harbor festooned their masts, guns bellowed, and troops marched. Judging from the evidence, all America seemed to rejoice. At 1,431 words, the speech was not particularly long, nor was it especially colorful or provocative. The aim was rather to establish firmly and with utmost clarity the essential values necessary for making the republican experiment a success. In this the address might justly be said to have achieved its ends. On a personal level, the address served as a fair reflection of the man speaking: as the comte de Moustier recalled, the speech prompted "remembrances of that great man's past services, his actual elevation, his modesty."[1] As a statement of political principles it extends well beyond the circumstances of the moment. More than two centuries later, the ritual of the presidential inauguration continues to function as a crucial means to republican ends.

Note

1. Clarence Winthrop Bowen, *The History of the Centennial Celebration of the Inauguration of George Washington as First President of the United States* (New York: D. Appleton, 1892).

George Washington's Second Inaugural Address

MONDAY, MARCH 4, 1793

FELLOW CITIZENS:

I am again called upon by the voice of my country to execute the functions of its Chief Magistrate. When the occasion proper for it shall arrive, I shall endeavor to express the high sense I entertain of this distinguished honor, and of the confidence which has been reposed in me by the people of united America.

Previous to the execution of any official act of the President the Constitution requires an oath of office. This oath I am now about to take, and in your presence: That if it shall be found during my administration of the Government I have in any instance violated willingly or knowingly the injunctions thereof, I may (besides incurring constitutional punishment) be subject to the upbraidings of all who are now witnesses of the present solemn ceremony.

The American Cincinnatus

THE SECOND INAUGURAL ADDRESS OF GEORGE WASHINGTON

Kevin Butterfield

GEORGE WASHINGTON'S SECOND Inaugural Address is, by a good margin, the shortest inaugural address ever delivered. Using just 135 words, Washington focused directly on what is, of course, the key element of the inaugural ceremony—the oath of office, and the responsibilities that the oath imposes—and said little else. The speech seems to fit awkwardly in the company of inaugural addresses to come, ones that articulate policy visions and make grand statements of what the American nation should aspire to become. It has, on at least one occasion, simply been left out of a comprehensive account of presidential inaugural speeches.

Nonetheless, Washington's Second Inaugural—all four sentences of it—merits our close attention. That it happened at all is itself important, the result of a thoughtful assessment by Washington and his Cabinet, including Thomas Jefferson, Alexander Hamilton, and Henry Knox, of what was appropriate to the moment. And in the address's focus upon the oath of office, Washington underscored an element of the presidency that can be overlooked: that the occupant of the office, while vested with substantial power, is also bound to adhere to the specific terms of an oath found in the Constitution itself.

There was no model to follow for what precisely should happen when a sitting president was elected to another term of office. The rituals of the American presidency were his to shape. In the election of 1792, Washington again had been elected president, unanimously, and again had great reluctance to take on the burdens of the office. There was a performative element in his repeated denials that he desired anything other than a long-delayed retirement, to be sure. But it is also true that Washington primarily saw his continuation in the presidency as the performance of a duty owed to the nation, not as a personal accomplishment or, as so many subsequent presidents would see things, as a mandate to follow through on a specific political agenda. All of these things likely shaped his thinking about how, if at all, to talk publicly about his election to a second term in office.

On February 27, 1793, just days before the new term was to begin on March 4, Washington wrote to his Cabinet members and asked the four of them—Jefferson, Knox, Hamilton, and Edmund Randolph—to put their heads together and propose to him their "opinions as to the time, place & manner of qualification," or oath. When they gathered at the War Office at 9:00 the following morning, the Cabinet members discovered that they could not agree. Jefferson and Hamilton, interestingly enough, both believed that Washington should simply take the oath privately, at his Philadelphia home, administered with no ceremony at all by Justice William Cushing of the Supreme Court, whose circuit included the nation's capital. Knox and Randolph, on the other hand, advocated for a public event, in the presence of the members of Congress. In Jefferson's recollection, Knox was "stickling for parade" and "got into great warmth" about the personal indispensability of Washington in the government's survival: "it is the President's character," Jefferson remembered Knox arguing, "and not the written constitution which keeps it together."[1] Pomp and ceremony with Washington at the center, Knox believed, would serve a good purpose.

Ultimately, the four men recommended a public swearing-in, at noon, in the Senate Chamber with members of Congress and other dignitaries, such as foreign ministers, invited to observe. Hamilton acknowledged his initial concerns in a postscript he penned for President Washington, appended to the formal Cabinet recommendation that Washington take the oath in a ceremony before Congress, but he did "think it right in the abstract to give publicity to the Act in question." Washington agreed.

That Monday, Washington became the first man to be inaugurated president a second time. He also became the first president inaugurated on March 4, which would thereafter become one of the most important dates in the American political calendar—that is, until the ratification of the Twentieth Amendment in 1933, which moved the beginning of a presidential term to January 20. While the First Congress had been called to convene on March 4, 1789, Washington's inauguration that year had come in late April, unavoidably delayed by the process of organizing the government. Beginning in 1793 and for nearly a century and a half, March 4 would become the standard date when one presidential term ended and another began.

Washington entered the Senate chamber precisely at noon, before an audience that included members of both houses of Congress, his own Cabinet, justices of the Supreme Court, foreign ministers, and "a number of private citizens, ladies and gentlemen," according to the Philadelphia *National Gazette*. Vice President John Adams, who in many accounts is often mistakenly described as present, had left Philadelphia to attend to his wife, Abigail, during an illness. In his place, President Pro Tempore John Langdon called the proceedings to order by addressing Washington directly: "Sir, one of the Judges of the Supreme Court of the United States is now present, and ready to administer to you the oath required by the constitution, to be taken by the President of the United States."

Washington stood and, to put it simply, briefly explained to Congress why it was that he had chosen to take the oath "in your presence." He first noted that he would wait until "the occasion proper for it shall arrive" to go into more detail about "the high sense I entertain of this distinguished honor." That time would come nine months later, in early December 1793, when Washington delivered his annual message to Congress and described both his "gratitude" and his "earnest wish for . . . retirement." On this day, at his second inaugural ceremony, Washington chose to focus on the oath itself and the public accountability it demanded. Should it be found that he had "in any instance violated willingly or knowingly the injunction" of that constitutional oath, Washington asked to be held accountable, both to the strictures of "constitutional punishment" (he refers here, of course, to impeachment) and to "the upbraidings of all who are now witnesses of the present solemn ceremony." The man whom Americans most trusted to hold power spent the entirety of his Second Inaugural asking those around him to hold him accountable, both legally and morally, to the oath he was about to take.

Washington's focus on the oath should not be surprising. Oaths and affirmations were extraordinarily important to the founding of the new nation, one that despite its powerful racial hierarchies and exclusions was nonetheless held together primarily by shared belief, not by history or an ethnic nationalism more typical to European states. The War for Independence itself had driven this point home for Washington, who wrote to John Hancock in February 1777 to "strongly recommend every State to fix upon some Oath or Affirmation of Allegiance to be tendered to all the Inhabitants without exception, and to out law those that refuse it."[2] As a wartime leader in a chaotic environment in which allegiances were constantly up for grabs, Washington saw that "by our inattention" to oaths as a way to bind the people together "we lose a considerable Cement to our own Force, and give the Enemy an opportunity to make the first tender of the oath of allegiance to the King." Interestingly, it was in this same letter that Washington advocated to Congress that steps be taken to inoculate the Continental Army against smallpox. The goal, in some ways, was similar: to prevent the spread of danger by securing people against it in advance.

With independence won and, after the Constitutional Convention of 1787, a new federal government created, the oath remained a crucial component in holding things together. In fact, the very first bill signed into law under the new government, on June 1, 1789, was "An Act to Regulate the Time and Manner of Administering Oaths," which dictated the precise oath to be taken by all state and federal officials as called for in Article VI of the Constitution—everyone, that is, except the president, whose oath was found in the text of the Constitution itself. Nearly four years later when entering a second term in office, Washington took an opportunity to underscore just why those oaths were important. They bound the officers of the government to remain faithful and to fulfill their constitutional duties.

His short speech concluded, Washington stood opposite Justice William Cushing, who administered the oath. It is worth noting that the contemporary account in the Philadelphia *National Gazette* makes clear that Washington did not add the words "so help me God" at the end, further evidence that the myth that he had added those words four years earlier in New York is without any basis. After taking the oath, Washington left "as he had come," wrote the *National Gazette*, "without pomp or ceremony." Though brief, though distinctly different from the addresses that would come from all those who would later assume the office, Washington's Second Inaugural Address had one point to make, and it made it well: in a constitutional order full of checks, balances, and structural limitations on arbitrary power, the presidential oath was yet another safeguard to protect the American republic.

Notes

1. Thomas Jefferson, "Notes on Washington's Second Inauguration and Republicanism, 28 February 1793," Founders Online, National Archives and Records Administration, retrieved from https://founders.archives.gov/documents/Jefferson/01-25-02-0265.
2. George Washington, "From George Washington to John Hancock, 5 February 1777," Founders Online, National Archives and Records Administration, retrieved from https://founders.archives.gov/documents/Washington/03-08-02-0268.

John Adams's Inaugural Address

SATURDAY, MARCH 4, 1797

WHEN IT WAS first perceived, in early times, that no middle course for America remained between unlimited submission to a foreign legislature and a total independence of its claims, men of reflection were less apprehensive of danger from the formidable power of fleets and armies they must determine to resist than from those contests and dissensions which would certainly arise concerning the forms of government to be instituted over the whole and over the parts of this extensive country. Relying, however, on the purity of their intentions, the justice of their cause, and the integrity and intelligence of the people, under an overruling Providence which had so signally protected this country from the first, the representatives of this Nation, then consisting of little more than half its present number, not only broke to pieces the chains which were forging and the rod of iron that was lifted up, but frankly cut asunder the ties which had bound them, and launched into an ocean of uncertainty.

The zeal and ardor of the people during the Revolutionary war, supplying the place of government, commanded a degree of order sufficient at least for the temporary preservation of society. The Confederation which was early felt to be necessary was prepared from the models of the Batavian and Helvetic confederacies, the only examples which remain with any detail and precision in history, and certainly the only ones which the people at large had ever considered. But reflecting on the striking difference in so many particulars between this country and those where a courier may go from the seat of government to the frontier in a single day, it was then certainly foreseen by some who assisted in Congress at the formation of it that it could not be durable.

Negligence of its regulations, inattention to its recommendations, if not disobedience to its authority, not only in individuals but in States, soon appeared with their melancholy consequences—universal languor, jealousies and rivalries of States, decline of navigation and commerce, discouragement of necessary manufactures, universal fall in the value of lands and their produce, contempt of public and private faith, loss of consideration and credit with foreign nations, and at length in discontents, animosities, combinations, partial conventions, and insurrection, threatening some great national calamity.

In this dangerous crisis the people of America were not abandoned by their usual good sense, presence of mind, resolution, or integrity. Measures were pursued to concert a plan to form a more perfect union, establish justice, insure domestic tranquillity, provide for the common defense, promote the general welfare, and secure the blessings of liberty. The public disquisitions, discussions, and deliberations issued in the present happy Constitution of Government.

Employed in the service of my country abroad during the whole course of these transactions, I first saw the Constitution of the United States in a foreign country. Irritated by no literary altercation, animated by no public debate, heated by no party animosity, I read it with great satisfaction, as the result of good heads prompted by good hearts, as an experiment better adapted to the genius, character, situation, and relations of this Nation and country than any which had ever been proposed or suggested. In its general principles and great outlines it was conformable to such a system of government as I had ever most esteemed, and in some States, my own native State in particular, had contributed to establish. Claiming a right of suffrage, in common with my fellow-citizens, in the adoption or rejection of a constitution which was to rule me and my posterity, as well as them and theirs, I did not hesitate to express my approbation of it on all occasions, in public and in private. It was not then, nor has been since, any objection to it in my mind that the Executive and Senate were not more permanent. Nor have I ever entertained a thought of promoting any alteration in it but such as the people themselves, in the course of their experience, should see and feel to be necessary or expedient, and by their representatives in Congress and the State legislatures, according to the Constitution itself, adopt and ordain.

Returning to the bosom of my country after a painful separation from it for ten years, I had the honor to be elected to a station under the new order of things, and I have repeatedly laid myself under the most serious obligations to support the Constitution. The operation of it has equaled the most sanguine expectations of its friends, and from an habitual attention to it, satisfaction in its administration, and delight in its effects upon the peace, order, prosperity, and happiness of the nation I have acquired an habitual attachment to it and veneration for it.

What other form of government, indeed, can so well deserve our esteem and love?

There may be little solidity in an ancient idea that congregations of men into cities and nations are the most pleasing objects in the sight of superior intelligences, but this is very certain, that to a benevolent human mind there can be no spectacle presented by any nation more pleasing, more noble, majestic, or august, than an assembly like that which has so often been seen in this and the other Chamber of Congress, of a Government in which the Executive authority, as well as that of all the branches of the Legislature, are exercised by citizens selected at regular periods by their neighbors to make and execute laws for the general good. Can anything essential, anything more than mere ornament and decoration, be added to this by robes and diamonds? Can authority be more amiable and respectable when it descends from accidents or institutions established in remote antiquity than when it springs fresh from the hearts and judgments of an honest and enlightened people? For it is the people only that are represented. It is their power and majesty that is reflected, and only for their good, in every legitimate government, under whatever form it may appear. The existence of such a government as ours for any length of time is a full proof of a general dissemination of knowledge and virtue throughout the whole body of the people. And what object or consideration more pleasing than this can be presented to the human mind? If national pride is ever justifiable or excusable it is when it springs, not from power or riches, grandeur or glory, but from conviction of national innocence, information, and benevolence.

In the midst of these pleasing ideas we should be unfaithful to ourselves if we should ever lose sight of the danger to our liberties if anything partial or extraneous should infect the purity of our free, fair, virtuous, and independent elections. If an election is to be determined by a majority of a single vote, and that can be procured by a party through artifice or corruption, the Government may be the choice of a party for its own ends, not of the nation for the national good. If that solitary suffrage can be obtained by foreign nations by flattery or menaces, by fraud or violence, by terror, intrigue, or venality, the Government may not be the choice of the American people, but of foreign nations. It may be foreign nations who govern us, and not we, the people, who govern ourselves; and candid men will acknowledge that in such cases choice would have little advantage to boast of over lot or chance.

Such is the amiable and interesting system of government (and such are some of the abuses to which it may be exposed) which the people of America have exhibited to the admiration and anxiety of the wise and virtuous of all nations for eight years under the administration of a citizen who, by a long course of great actions, regulated by prudence, justice, temperance, and fortitude, conducting a people inspired with the same virtues and animated with the same ardent patriotism and love of liberty to independence and peace, to increasing wealth and unexampled prosperity, has merited the gratitude of his fellow-citizens, commanded the highest praises of foreign nations, and secured immortal glory with posterity.

In that retirement which is his voluntary choice may he long live to enjoy the delicious recollection of his services, the gratitude of mankind, the happy fruits of them to himself and the world, which are daily increasing, and that splendid prospect of the future fortunes of this country which is opening from year to year. His name may be still a rampart, and the knowledge that he lives a bulwark, against all open or secret enemies of his country's peace. This example has been recommended to the imitation of his successors by both Houses of Congress and by the voice of the legislatures and the people throughout the nation.

On this subject it might become me better to be silent or to speak with diffidence; but as something may be expected, the occasion, I hope, will be admitted as an apology if I venture to say that if a preference, upon principle, of a free republican government, formed upon long and serious reflection, after a diligent and impartial inquiry after truth; if an attachment to the Constitution of the United States, and a conscientious determination to support it until it shall be altered by the judgments and wishes of the people, expressed in the mode prescribed in it; if a respectful attention to the constitutions of the individual States and a constant caution and delicacy toward the State governments; if an equal and impartial regard to the rights, interest, honor, and happiness of all the States in the Union, without preference or regard to a northern or southern, an eastern or western, position, their various political opinions on unessential points or their personal attachments; if a love of virtuous men of all parties and denominations; if a love of science and letters and a wish to patronize every rational effort to encourage schools, colleges, universities, academies, and every institution for propagating knowledge, virtue, and religion among all classes of the people, not only for their benign influence on the happiness of life in all its stages and classes, and of society in all its forms, but as the only means of preserving our Constitution from its natural enemies, the spirit of sophistry, the spirit of party, the spirit of intrigue, the profligacy of corruption, and the pestilence of foreign influence, which is the angel of destruction to elective governments; if a love of equal laws, of justice, and humanity in the interior administration; if an inclination to improve agriculture, commerce, and manufacturers for necessity, convenience, and defense; if a spirit of equity and humanity toward the aboriginal nations of America, and a disposition to meliorate their condition by inclining them to be more friendly to us, and our citizens to be more friendly to them; if an inflexible determination to maintain peace and inviolable faith with all nations, and that system of neutrality and impartiality among the belligerent powers of Europe which has been adopted by this Government and so solemnly sanctioned by both Houses of Congress and applauded by the legislatures of the States and the public opinion, until it shall be otherwise ordained by Congress; if a personal esteem for the French nation, formed in a residence of seven years chiefly among them, and a sincere desire to preserve the friendship which has been so much for the honor and interest of both nations; if, while the conscious honor and integrity of the people of America and the internal sentiment of their own power and energies must be preserved, an earnest endeavor to investigate every just cause and remove every colorable pretense of complaint; if an intention to pursue by amicable negotiation a reparation for the injuries that have been committed on the commerce of our fellow-citizens by whatever nation, and if success can not be obtained, to lay the facts before the Legislature, that they may consider what further measures the honor and interest of the Government and its constituents demand; if a resolution to do justice as far as may depend upon me, at all times and to all nations, and maintain peace, friendship, and benevolence with all the world; if an unshaken confidence in the honor, spirit, and resources of the American people, on which I have so often hazarded my all and never been deceived; if elevated ideas of the high destinies of this country and of my own duties toward it, founded on a knowledge of the moral principles and intellectual improvements of the people deeply engraven on my mind in early life, and not obscured but exalted by experience and age; and, with humble reverence, I feel it to be my duty to add, if a veneration for the religion of a people who profess and call themselves Christians, and a fixed resolution to consider a decent respect for Christianity among the best recommendations for the public service, can enable me in any degree to comply with your wishes, it shall be my strenuous endeavor that this sagacious injunction of the two Houses shall not be without effect.

With this great example before me, with the sense and spirit, the faith and honor, the duty and interest, of the same American people pledged to support the Constitution of the United States, I entertain no doubt of its continuance in all its energy, and my mind is prepared without hesitation to lay myself under the most solemn obligations to support it to the utmost of my power.

And may that Being who is supreme over all, the Patron of Order, the Fountain of Justice, and the Protector in all ages of the world of virtuous liberty, continue His blessing upon this nation and its Government and give it all possible success and duration consistent with the ends of His providence.

The Colossus of Independence

THE INAUGURAL ADDRESS OF JOHN ADAMS

R. M. Barlow

ON THE DAY after his inauguration as the second president of the United States, John Adams wrote to his wife Abigail, "Your dearest Friend never had a more trying day than Yesterday." As the successor to George Washington, he faced a daunting challenge: to the teary-eyed crowd gathered in the chamber of the House of Representatives on March 4, 1797, it appeared that a glorious sun was setting, and one "less Splendid" was rising. Adams nevertheless observed, "Methought I heard him think Ay! I am fairly out and your fairly in! see which of Us will be happiest."[1]

For President Adams, the unhappy circumstances of 1797 included not only unfavorable comparisons to George Washington, but also a crisis in foreign policy, which had contributed to a division of the Federalists between those who would follow his leadership, and the High Federalists, who tended to look to Alexander Hamilton for guidance, as well as the emergence of the rival Republican Party. Adams had been Washington's vice president, Alexander Hamilton the secretary of the treasury, and Thomas Jefferson the secretary of state. Hamilton, though now a private citizen, held tremendous influence with Washington's—now Adams's—Cabinet, and he emphasized the advantages to the United States of commercial ties with Great Britain. Jefferson, sympathetic to the French revolutionaries, had abandoned his retirement from public life, and although acknowledged as head of the Republican Party, he was nevertheless Adams's vice president. The political chaos seemed to call for the independent executive, balancing opposing forces, whom Adams had written about in the three sprawling volumes of his *Defence of the Constitutions of the United States*.

The crisis in foreign policy centered on yet another breach in the peace between Great Britain and France. The 1789 French Revolution first appeared to be establishing a constitutional monarchy similar to that of Britain, then a French "sister" republic, even more worthy of the 1778 alliance. But President Washington instead declared the United States at peace with both powers and sent John Jay to negotiate a commercial treaty with Great Britain. Americans disagreed on their interpretation and application of the 1778 French treaties. Was the United States obligated to take an active part in the war on the side of France? Could French privateers enter American ports with their prizes and have the local French consul declare them legal captures? Was a treaty made with the French monarch still valid with a revolutionary republican government? Was the Jay Treaty simply a commercial treaty between the United States and Great Britain, or was it an unprincipled surrender to the enemy of America's French ally? Was Washington's Neutrality Proclamation a violation of the Constitution?

Two days before Adams's inauguration, the Directory, whether genuinely appalled that America had signed the Jay Treaty with Great Britain, or simply eyeing American commerce as a source of revenue—or motivated by some combination of the two—granted permission to French privateers to seize American merchant ships. Writing to his son, John Quincy, on March 31, 1797, Adams explained that his presidency was commencing with a "Misunderstanding" with France that he hoped to resolve through diplomacy without sacrificing American honor. He insisted, using large letters for emphasis, that America was not "Scared."

In preparing his Inaugural Address, Adams needed to acknowledge the status of George Washington, reassure listeners that he took the French threat to American shipping seriously, and attempt to unite the High Federalists and the Jeffersonian Republicans. At over 2,000 words, his Inaugural Address was longer than those given by his predecessor, George Washington, and his successor, Thomas Jefferson. His call for a system of neutrality appears at first glance to be support for George Washington's Neutrality Proclamation. But Adams's commitment to an independent foreign policy predated the Washington administration by more than a decade.

Accordingly, Adams's speech was an overview of American history that began with the struggle for independence during the American Revolution. By drawing attention to the overreach of the British Parliament, he suggested that the French Directory was attempting a similar tyranny. He praised the Constitution as the foundation for a successful foreign policy, made clear his appreciation for the French, but warned that political factions invited foreign meddling in American politics. By recounting the nation's history, he highlighted his own role in that history. He was the Atlas of Independence who insisted the time for reconciliation was past, the diplomat in France who refused to be cowed by the Comte de Vergennes, the representative who negotiated the Anglo-American peace treaty that ended the Revolutionary War, and the first minister to the Court of St. James who heralded a new relationship with the former mother country. The patriotic American, familiar with both courts, who had conquered them during the Revolution, was now at the helm. Adams was the revolutionary who insisted, "I will be buried in the Ocean or in any other manner sacrificed, before I will voluntarily put on the Chains of France when I am struggling to throw off those of Great Britain."[2] There was no danger that as president he would be a pawn of Great Britain, and although not as friendly to France as his vice president Thomas Jefferson, neither was he as hostile as members of his Cabinet.

Adams was unsure if his speech had been successful. Recognizing the opposition he faced, he explained to Abigail on March 9, 1797, that in both his farewell speech to the Senate and his Inaugural Address, "I was determined to say some Things, as an Appeal to Posterity. foreign nations and future times will understand them better." But two days later, the Philadelphia *Aurora General Advertiser*, normally highly critical of the Federalists, conceded that Adams's Inaugural Address was that "of a fellow citizen, who will not deign to become the President of a Party, but the President of the United States."[3] Still in the future were the failed commission to France, the French demand for a bribe which led to the XYZ affair, the new provisional army, the potential escalation of the Quasi-War with France into a full-scale war, the threat of a formal alliance between the United States and Great Britain, and his loss of the presidency.

Adams would later boast that he was the founder of the American system of neutrality, that he had "humbled" the French Directory, and that in making peace with France he had prevented a tyrannical alliance between the United States and Great Britain. But the memory of his presidency has instead been focused on the notorious Alien and Sedition Acts. The balance between defending the Union from threats foreign and domestic, while at the same respecting individual rights and freedom, remains the legacy of his administration.

Notes

1. "Letter from John Adams to Abigail Adams, 5 March 1797," Masshist.org, retrieved June 19, 2024, from https://www.masshist.org/digitaladams/archive/doc?id=L17970305ja.
2. "John Adams Autobiography, Part 2, 'Travels, and Negotiations,' 1777–1778," Masshist.org, retrieved June 19, 2024, from https://www.masshist.org/digitaladams/archive/doc?id=A2_17.
3. "Adams Papers Digital Edition—Massachusetts Historical Society," *Masshist.org*, retrieved June 19, 2024, from https://www.masshist.org/publications/adams-papers/index.php/volume/AFC12/pageid/AFC12p18.

Thomas Jefferson's First Inaugural Address

WEDNESDAY, MARCH 4, 1801

FRIENDS AND FELLOW-CITIZENS:

Called upon to undertake the duties of the first executive office of our country, I avail myself of the presence of that portion of my fellow-citizens which is here assembled to express my grateful thanks for the favor with which they have been pleased to look toward me, to declare a sincere consciousness that the task is above my talents, and that I approach it with those anxious and awful presentiments which the greatness of the charge and the weakness of my powers so justly inspire. A rising nation, spread over a wide and fruitful land, traversing all the seas with the rich productions of their industry, engaged in commerce with nations who feel power and forget right, advancing rapidly to destinies beyond the reach of mortal eye—when I contemplate these transcendent objects, and see the honor, the happiness, and the hopes of this beloved country committed to the issue and the auspices of this day, I shrink from the contemplation, and humble myself before the magnitude of the undertaking. Utterly, indeed, should I despair did not the presence of many whom I here see remind me that in the other high authorities provided by our Constitution I shall find resources of wisdom, of virtue, and of zeal on which to rely under all difficulties. To you, then, gentlemen, who are charged with the sovereign functions of legislation, and to those associated with you, I look with encouragement for that guidance and support which may enable us to steer with safety the vessel in which we are all embarked amidst the conflicting elements of a troubled world.

During the contest of opinion through which we have passed the animation of discussions and of exertions has sometimes worn an aspect which might impose on strangers unused to think freely and to speak and to write what they think; but this being now decided by the voice of the nation, announced according to the rules of the Constitution, all will, of course, arrange themselves under the will of the law, and unite in common efforts for the common good. All, too, will bear in mind this sacred principle, that though the will of the majority is in all cases to prevail, that will to be rightful must be reasonable; that the minority possess their equal rights, which equal law must protect, and to violate would be oppression. Let us, then, fellow-citizens, unite with one heart and one mind. Let us restore to social intercourse that harmony and affection without which liberty and even life itself are but dreary things. And let us reflect that, having banished from our land that religious intolerance under which mankind so long bled and suffered, we have yet gained little if we countenance a political intolerance as despotic, as wicked, and capable of as bitter and bloody persecutions. During the throes and convulsions of the ancient world, during the agonizing spasms of infuriated man, seeking through blood and slaughter his long-lost liberty, it was not wonderful that the agitation of the billows should reach even this distant and peaceful shore; that this should be more felt and feared by some and less by others, and should divide opinions as to measures of safety. But every difference of opinion is not a difference of principle. We have called by different names brethren of the same principle. We are all Republicans, we are all Federalists. If there be any among us who would wish to dissolve this Union or to change its republican form, let them stand undisturbed as monuments of the safety with which error of opinion may be tolerated where reason is left free to combat it. I know, indeed, that some honest men fear that a republican government can not be strong, that this Government is not strong enough; but would the honest patriot, in the full tide of successful experiment, abandon a government which has so far kept us free and firm on the theoretic and visionary fear that this Government, the world's best hope, may by possibility want energy to preserve itself? I trust not. I believe this, on the contrary, the strongest Government on earth. I believe it the only one where every man, at the call of the law, would fly to the standard of the law, and would meet invasions of the public order as his own personal concern. Sometimes it is said that man can not be trusted with the government of himself. Can he, then, be trusted with the government of others? Or have we found angels in the forms of kings to govern him? Let history answer this question.

Let us, then, with courage and confidence pursue our own Federal and Republican principles, our attachment to union and representative government. Kindly separated by nature and a wide ocean from the exterminating havoc of one quarter of the globe; too high-minded to endure the degradations of the others; possessing a chosen country, with room enough for our descendants to the thousandth and thousandth generation; entertaining a due sense of our equal right to the use of our own faculties, to the acquisitions of our own industry, to honor and confidence from our fellow-citizens, resulting not from birth, but from our actions and their sense of them; enlightened by a benign religion, professed, indeed, and practiced in various forms, yet all of them inculcating honesty, truth, temperance, gratitude, and the love of man; acknowledging and adoring an overruling Providence, which by all its dispensations proves that it delights in the happiness of man here and his greater happiness hereafter—with all these blessings, what more is necessary to make us a happy and a prosperous people? Still one thing more, fellow-citizens—a wise and frugal Government, which shall restrain men from injuring one another, shall leave them otherwise free to regulate their own pursuits of industry and improvement, and shall not take from the mouth of labor the bread it has earned. This is the sum of good government, and this is necessary to close the circle of our felicities.

About to enter, fellow-citizens, on the exercise of duties which comprehend everything dear and valuable to you, it is proper you should understand what I deem the essential principles of our Government, and consequently those which ought to shape its Administration. I will compress them within the narrowest compass they will bear, stating the general principle, but not all its limitations. Equal and exact justice to all men, of whatever state or persuasion, religious or political; peace, commerce, and honest friendship with all nations, entangling alliances with none; the support of the State governments in all their rights, as the most competent administrations for our domestic concerns and the surest bulwarks against antirepublican tendencies; the preservation of the General Government in its whole constitutional vigor, as the sheet anchor of our peace at home and safety abroad; a jealous care of the right of election by the people—a mild and safe corrective of abuses which are lopped by the sword of revolution where peaceable remedies are unprovided; absolute acquiescence in the decisions of the majority, the vital principle of republics, from which is no appeal but to force, the vital principle and immediate parent of despotism; a well-disciplined militia, our best reliance in peace and for the first moments of war, till regulars may relieve them; the supremacy of the civil over the military authority; economy in the public expense, that labor may be lightly burthened; the honest payment of our debts and sacred preservation of the public faith; encouragement of agriculture, and of commerce as its handmaid; the diffusion of information and arraignment of all abuses at the bar of the public reason; freedom of religion; freedom of the press, and freedom of person under the protection of the habeas corpus, and trial by juries impartially selected. These principles form the bright constellation which has gone before us and guided our steps through an age of revolution and reformation. The wisdom of our sages and blood of our heroes have been devoted to their attainment. They should be the creed of our political faith, the text of civic instruction, the touchstone by which to try the services of those we trust;

and should we wander from them in moments of error or of alarm, let us hasten to retrace our steps and to regain the road which alone leads to peace, liberty, and safety.

I repair, then, fellow-citizens, to the post you have assigned me. With experience enough in subordinate offices to have seen the difficulties of this the greatest of all, I have learnt to expect that it will rarely fall to the lot of imperfect man to retire from this station with the reputation and the favor which bring him into it. Without pretensions to that high confidence you reposed in our first and greatest revolutionary character, whose preeminent services had entitled him to the first place in his country's love and destined for him the fairest page in the volume of faithful history, I ask so much confidence only as may give firmness and effect to the legal administration of your affairs. I shall often go wrong through defect of judgment. When right, I shall often be thought wrong by those whose positions will not command a view of the whole ground. I ask your indulgence for my own errors, which will never be intentional, and your support against the errors of others, who may condemn what they would not if seen in all its parts. The approbation implied by your suffrage is a great consolation to me for the past, and my future solicitude will be to retain the good opinion of those who have bestowed it in advance, to conciliate that of others by doing them all the good in my power; and to be instrumental to the happiness and freedom of all.

Relying, then, on the patronage of your good will, I advance with obedience to the work, ready to retire from it whenever you become sensible how much better choice it is in your power to make. And may that Infinite Power which rules the destinies of the universe lead our councils to what is best, and give them a favorable issue for your peace and prosperity.

The Sage of Monticello

THE FIRST INAUGURAL ADDRESS OF THOMAS JEFFERSON

Peter S. Onuf

FEW OF THOSE who gathered in Washington, D.C., the new capitol city, on March 4, 1801, to hear Thomas Jefferson deliver his First Inaugural Address could make out what this notoriously poor public speaker had to say. But the Virginian's eloquent prose soon appeared in cool print, reassuring anxious Americans across the country that the "more perfect union" the framers of the federal Constitution had so recently constructed would survive its first great crisis. Jefferson was famous for drafting the Declaration of Independence, inspiring revolutionary patriots at war to risk everything to vindicate the new nation's claims against the former mother country. Now, as Americans retreated from the brink of anarchy and disunion, he counseled his countrymen to seek "that harmony and affection without which liberty and even life itself are but dreary things."

Over the preceding decade, deepening partisan divisions between the Federalist administrations of presidents George Washington and John Adams and Jeffersonian Republican insurgents threatened to destroy the union, unleash the "dogs of war," and reverse the Revolution's outcome. The Constitution's failure to distinguish between Electoral College votes for president and vice president in the 1800 presidential election exacerbated the crisis, producing an unexpected tie in the final count between Jefferson and Aaron Burr, his putative running mate, and throwing the choice into the House of Representatives where each state's congressional delegation would have an equal vote. (The Twelfth Amendment to the Constitution, adopted before the next presidential canvass in 1804, rectified the error, distinguishing electors' votes for president and vice president.) The 1801 impasse, finally resolved after thirty-six tallies from February 11 to 17, led to frantic negotiations as rumors spread that Jefferson's angry supporters might resort to arms if their will was thwarted in a "stolen" election. When Burr's supporters capitulated and Jefferson's inauguration was finally assured, the new president seized the opportunity to preach peace. Promising to restore the Constitution that the American people had originally ratified, he reassured his misguided partisan opponents that they would not be persecuted. In the heat of political combat, partisans exaggerated differences, failing to recognize that "every difference of opinion is not a difference of principle." After all, Jefferson famously intoned, "We are all Republicans, we are all Federalists," sharing a principled commitment to the "republican form" of government and the federal union of states. This was a message many Federalists were eager to hear. John Adams certainly had no interest in perpetuating the crisis. Though conspicuously missing from Jefferson's inaugural audience, the former president signaled acquiescence in his former friend's ascension by returning to his Massachusetts home to lick his wounds.

In his Inaugural Address, Jefferson predicted a glorious future of "peace and prosperity" for the new nation. But his prophecy would only be fulfilled if his fellow Americans reaffirmed their "attachment to union and representative government." The increasingly vicious partisan struggles of the 1790s suggested that their bold experiment in republican self-government might all too easily fail, as "the throes and convulsions of the ancient world" resulting from the French Revolutionary wars threatened to wreak havoc even on "this distant and peaceful shore." Americans must return to Revolutionary first principles, Jefferson insisted, so recognizing the fundamental difference between their peaceful new world and an old world at war, where "infuriated man" sought "his long-lost liberty... through blood and slaughter."

Jefferson was the first great exponent of American exceptionalism, situating the new nation on the cusp of the future, as "the world's best hope," and at a safe distance from Europe's "convulsions." Americans' liberties were not "long lost," the new president enjoined, but must instead be zealously preserved and defended against foreign threats. Republics had failed throughout ancient and modern history when demagogues and would-be despots exploited crises to seize power and deprive citizens of their liberties. In his Inaugural Address, the self-effacing new president sought to defuse anxieties by assuming a disarmingly modest pose. Declaring "a sincere consciousness that the task is above my talents," Jefferson juxtaposed "the greatness of the charge" to "the weakness of my powers." He would not pretend to possess the authority or capacity to exercise rule over his fellow citizens, recognizing instead that the congressmen in his audience "are charged with the sovereign functions of legislation." He was the people's humble servant, the instrument of "your good will." Just as he had given voice to the common sentiments of patriotic Americans in the Declaration of Independence, the outcome of the 1800 election was determined "by the voice of the nation, announced according to the rules of the Constitution." The success of his administration would be the people's, not his, as they arranged "themselves under the will of the law" and united "in common efforts for the common good."

Jefferson underscored his modest political persona by evoking the image of the recently deceased first president, George Washington, "our first and greatest revolutionary character, whose preeminent services had entitled him to the first place in his country's love, and destined for him the fairest page in the volume of faithful history." If Jefferson's address epitomized the exceptionalist narrative of national history, his apotheosis of Washington was his boldest rhetorical move. By focusing on the commander-in-chief's critical role in winning the war for independence, Jefferson shifted attention away from the late 1790s, when Republicans began to mobilize *against* Washington as the Federalists' leader. This was revisionist history, a willful denial of the bitter partisanship that had divided the past and future Virginian presidents. Effectively acknowledging that Washington had been the country's "savior" (as so many other Americans called him), Jefferson played a key role in fashioning an American civil religion that transcended partisan divisions. Repentant Federalists would return to the fold as they reaffirmed the tenets of the national faith. For their part, Republicans would restore Washington to his exalted position in the national pantheon. By distinguishing himself from Washington and recognizing the primacy of his former political enemy, Jefferson reassured his countrymen that he would not seize and exercise despotic power. It was something of a miracle that Washington had not succumbed to the temptation to make himself a king, instead deferring to the superior authority of the people he had led to the promised land of independence. Jefferson would never face such temptation, for the power he exercised would depend on the sanction of a united people and their representatives. "The approbation implied by your suffrage is a great consolation to me for the past," he told his fellow Americans, "and my future solicitude will be to retain the good opinion of those who have bestowed it in advance, to conciliate that of others by doing them all the good in my power; and to be instrumental to the happiness and freedom of all."

According to the "creed of our political faith" that Jefferson elaborated in his address, the people's "good opinion" could not be taken for granted. His own, often troubled experience in elected office—particularly as governor of Virginia—and as Washington's secretary of state and Adams's vice president showed how easily good citizens could divide over personalities or policy preferences. But Americans must always remind themselves of what made them a people in the first place by recurring to the first principles of republican government that the Revolutionary generation declared in 1776. "The essential principles of our Government" included "equal and exact justice to all men," "peace, commerce, and honest friendship with all nations, entangling alliances with none," and the perpetuation of the federal union, with "State governments" providing "the surest bulwarks against antirepublican tendencies" and "the General government in its whole constitutional vigor" guaranteeing "our peace at home, and safety abroad." The civil liberties citizens enjoyed were both the foundation and product of properly limited, constitutional government, a benign circularity that would sustain republican rule across the generations and spare Americans the ruinous "convulsions" of revolution and regime change that drenched European battlefields in "rivers of blood."

Americans were a "chosen" people, blessed with freedoms unprecedented in human history: "freedom of religion; freedom of the press; and freedom of person, under the protection of the habeas corpus, and trial by juries impartially selected." This "bright constellation" of principles had "guided our steps through an age of revolution and reformation," Jefferson proclaimed, and it would guarantee peace and prosperity for future generations as long as they upheld the republican faith. Americans were "enlightened by a benign religion, professed, indeed, and practiced in various forms, yet all of them inculcating honesty, truth, temperance, gratitude and the love of man; acknowledging and adoring an overruling Providence, which by all its dispensations proves that it delights in the happiness of man here, and his greater happiness hereafter." They had banished "that religious intolerance under which mankind so long bled and suffered," instead erecting the "wall of separation" between church and state that Jefferson codified in his Bill for Religious Freedom in Virginia (1786) and James Madison incorporated in the federal Bill of Rights (1791). A plurality of churches nourished a common faith in the constellation of principles that would make Americans a great and flourishing people. Faithful republicans looked beyond superficial differences in profession and practice to recognize the hand of God in their providential good fortune. But the partisan warfare of the 1790s raised the frightening specter of "a political intolerance, as despotic, as wicked, and capable of as bitter and bloody persecutions." Convinced of their own righteousness, political zealots waged a holy war against their supposed partisan enemies, exaggerating differences over policies and personalities and losing sight of the fundamental principles that inspired the patriots of 1776 and bound them to one another. Jefferson's distinction between principle and opinion thus coincided with the line he drew between the spheres of religion and politics. The "creed of our political faith" should teach us that first things (and last) transcended the evanescent passions and prejudices of political conflict. Americans should look back on the political turbulence of the recent past and be grateful that—for all the portentous rattling of sabers—they had *not* taken the fatal plunge into disunion and anarchy and a bloody war of all against all.

In his Inaugural Address, Jefferson—a deist, if not worse, according to hostile critics—deployed religious language to reassure anxious Americans that God (or "an overruling Providence") was on their side, urging them to look beyond the perilous moment. God's presence in his address, like Washington's, emphasized Jefferson's modest pretensions as he assumed the reins of power: he was the people's humble servant, pledging fealty to the republican creed and the federal union of states. The perfection and perpetuity of that union ultimately depended on the character of the American people. "Let us, then, fellow-citizens, unite with one heart and one mind" to fulfill our destiny, he prayerfully intoned: "may that infinite power, which rules the destinies of the universe, lead our councils to what is best, and give them a favorable issue for your peace and prosperity." Jefferson thus envisioned a sacredly sanctioned civil millennium, a terrestrial life everlasting for a fortunate people "possessing a chosen country, with room enough for our descendants to the thousandth and thousandth generation."

Thomas Jefferson's Second Inaugural Address

MONDAY, MARCH 4, 1805

PROCEEDING, FELLOW-CITIZENS, TO that qualification which the Constitution requires before my entrance on the charge again conferred on me, it is my duty to express the deep sense I entertain of this new proof of confidence from my fellow-citizens at large, and the zeal with which it inspires me so to conduct myself as may best satisfy their just expectations.

On taking this station on a former occasion I declared the principles on which I believed it my duty to administer the affairs of our Commonwealth. My conscience tells me I have on every occasion acted up to that declaration according to its obvious import and to the understanding of every candid mind.

In the transaction of your foreign affairs we have endeavored to cultivate the friendship of all nations, and especially of those with which we have the most important relations. We have done them justice on all occasions, favored where favor was lawful, and cherished mutual interests and intercourse on fair and equal terms. We are firmly convinced, and we act on that conviction, that with nations as with individuals our interests soundly calculated will ever be found inseparable from our moral duties, and history bears witness to the fact that a just nation is trusted on its word when recourse is had to armaments and wars to bridle others.

At home, fellow-citizens, you best know whether we have done well or ill. The suppression of unnecessary offices, of useless establishments and expenses, enabled us to discontinue our internal taxes. These, covering our land with officers and opening our doors to their intrusions, had already begun that process of domiciliary vexation which once entered is scarcely to be restrained from reaching successively every article of property and produce. If among these taxes some minor ones fell which had not been inconvenient, it was because their amount would not have paid the officers who collected them, and because, if they had any merit, the State authorities might adopt them instead of others less approved.

The remaining revenue on the consumption of foreign articles is paid chiefly by those who can afford to add foreign luxuries to domestic comforts, being collected on our seaboard and frontiers only, and, incorporated with the transactions of our mercantile citizens, it may be the pleasure and the pride of an American to ask, What farmer, what mechanic, what laborer ever sees a taxgatherer of the United States? These contributions enable us to support the current expenses of the Government, to fulfill contracts with foreign nations, to extinguish the native right of soil within our limits, to extend those limits, and to apply such a surplus to our public debts as places at a short day their final redemption, and that redemption once effected the revenue thereby liberated may, by a just repartition of it among the States and a corresponding amendment of the Constitution, be applied *in time of peace* to rivers, canals, roads, arts, manufactures, education, and other great objects within each State. *In time of war*, if injustice by ourselves or others must sometimes produce war, increased as the same revenue will be by increased population and consumption, and aided by other resources reserved for that crisis, it may meet within the year all the expenses of the year without encroaching on the rights of future generations by burthening them with the debts of the past. War will then be but a suspension of useful works, and a return to a state of peace a return to the progress of improvement.

I have said, fellow-citizens, that the income reserved had enabled us to extend our limits, but that extension may possibly pay for itself before we are called on, and in the meantime may keep down the accruing interest; in all events, it will replace the advances we shall have made. I know that the acquisition of Louisiana has been disapproved by some from a candid apprehension that the enlargement of our territory would endanger its union. But who can limit the extent to which the federative principle may operate effectively? The larger our association the less will it be shaken by local passions; and in any view is it not better that the opposite bank of the Mississippi should be settled by our own brethren and children than by strangers of another family? With which should we be most likely to live in harmony and friendly intercourse?

In matters of religion I have considered that its free exercise is placed by the Constitution independent of the powers of the General Government. I have therefore undertaken on no occasion to prescribe the religious exercises suited to it, but have left them, as the Constitution found them, under the direction and discipline of the church or state authorities acknowledged by the several religious societies.

The aboriginal inhabitants of these countries I have regarded with the commiseration their history inspires. Endowed with the faculties and the rights of men, breathing an ardent love of liberty and independence, and occupying a country which left them no desire but to be undisturbed, the stream of overflowing population from other regions directed itself on these shores; without power to divert or habits to contend against it, they have been overwhelmed by the current or driven before it; now reduced within limits too narrow for the hunter's state, humanity enjoins us to teach them agriculture and the domestic arts; to encourage them to that industry which alone can enable them to maintain their place in existence and to prepare them in time for that state of society which to bodily comforts adds the improvement of the mind and morals. We have therefore liberally furnished them with the implements of husbandry and household use; we have placed among them instructors in the arts of first necessity, and they are covered with the aegis of the law against aggressors from among ourselves.

But the endeavors to enlighten them on the fate which awaits their present course of life, to induce them to exercise their reason, follow its dictates, and change their pursuits with the change of circumstances have powerful obstacles to encounter; they are combated by the habits of their bodies, prejudices of their minds, ignorance, pride, and the influence of interested and crafty individuals among them who feel themselves something in the present order of things and fear to become nothing in any other. These persons inculcate a sanctimonious reverence for the customs of their ancestors; that whatsoever they did must be done through all time; that reason is a false guide, and to advance under its counsel in their physical, moral, or political condition is perilous innovation; that their duty is to remain as their Creator made them, ignorance being safety and knowledge full of danger; in short, my friends, among them also is seen the action and counteraction of good sense and of bigotry; they too have their antiphilosophists who find an interest in keeping things in their present state, who dread reformation, and exert all their faculties to maintain the ascendancy of habit over the duty of improving our reason and obeying its mandates.

In giving these outlines I do not mean, fellow-citizens, to arrogate to myself the merit of the measures. That is due, in the first place, to the reflecting character of our citizens at large, who, by the weight of public opinion, influence and strengthen the public measures. It is due to the sound discretion with which they select from among themselves those to whom they confide the legislative duties. It is due to the zeal and wisdom of the characters thus selected, who lay the foundations of public happiness in wholesome laws, the execution of which alone remains for others, and it is due to the able and faithful auxiliaries, whose patriotism has associated them with me in the executive functions.

During this course of administration, and in order to disturb it, the artillery of the press has been leveled against us, charged with whatsoever its licentiousness could devise or dare. These abuses of an institution so important to freedom and science are deeply to be regretted, inasmuch as they tend to lessen its usefulness and to sap its safety. They might, indeed, have been corrected by the wholesome punishments reserved to and provided by the laws of the several States against falsehood and defamation, but public duties more urgent press on the time of public servants, and the offenders have therefore been left to find their punishment in the public indignation.

Nor was it uninteresting to the world that an experiment should be fairly and fully made, whether freedom of discussion, unaided by power, is not sufficient for the propagation and protection of truth—whether a government conducting itself in the true spirit of its constitution, with zeal and purity, and doing no act which it would be unwilling the whole world should witness, can be written down by falsehood and defamation. The experiment has been tried; you have witnessed the scene; our fellow-citizens looked on, cool and collected; they saw the latent source from which these outrages proceeded; they gathered around their public functionaries, and when the Constitution called them to the decision by suffrage, they pronounced their verdict, honorable to those who had served them and consolatory to the friend of man who believes that he may be trusted with the control of his own affairs.

No inference is here intended that the laws provided by the States against false and defamatory publications should not be enforced; he who has time renders a service to public morals and public tranquillity in reforming these abuses by the salutary coercions of the law; but the experiment is noted to prove that, since truth and reason have maintained their ground against false opinions in league with false facts, the press, confined to truth, needs no other legal restraint; the public judgment will correct false reasoning and opinions on a full hearing of all parties; and no other definite line can be drawn between the inestimable liberty of the press and its demoralizing licentiousness. If there be still improprieties which this rule would not restrain, its supplement must be sought in the censorship of public opinion.

Contemplating the union of sentiment now manifested so generally as auguring harmony and happiness to our future course, I offer to our country sincere congratulations. With those, too, not yet rallied to the same point the disposition to do so is gaining strength; facts are piercing through the veil drawn over them, and our doubting brethren will at length see that the mass of their fellow-citizens with whom they can not yet resolve to act as to principles and measures, think as they think and desire what they desire; that our wish as well as theirs is that the public efforts may be directed honestly to the public good, that peace be cultivated, civil and religious liberty unassailed, law and order preserved, equality of rights maintained, and that state of property, equal or unequal, which results to every man from his own industry or that of his father's. When satisfied of these views it is not in human nature that they should not approve and support them. In the meantime let us cherish them with patient affection, let us do them justice, and more than justice, in all competitions of interest, and we need not doubt that truth, reason, and their own interests will at length prevail, will gather them into the fold of their country, and will complete that entire union of opinion which gives to a nation the blessing of harmony and the benefit of all its strength.

I shall now enter on the duties to which my fellow-citizens have again called me, and shall proceed in the spirit of those principles which they have approved. I fear not that any motives of interest may lead me astray; I am sensible of no passion which could seduce me knowingly from the path of justice, but the weaknesses of human nature and the limits of my own understanding will produce errors of judgment sometimes injurious to your interests. I shall need, therefore, all the indulgence which I have heretofore experienced from my constituents; the want of it will certainly not lessen with increasing years. I shall need, too, the favor of that Being in whose hands we are, who led our fathers, as Israel of old, from their native land and planted them in a country flowing with all the necessaries and comforts of life; who has covered our infancy with His providence and our riper years with His wisdom and power, and to whose goodness I ask you to join in supplications with me that He will so enlighten the minds of your servants, guide their councils, and prosper their measures that whatsoever they do shall result in your good, and shall secure to you the peace, friendship, and approbation of all nations.

The Man of the People

THE SECOND INAUGURAL ADDRESS OF THOMAS JEFFERSON

Annette Gordon-Reed

ON MARCH 4, 1805, when President Thomas Jefferson gave his Second Inaugural Address in the wake of his re-election to the presidency of the United States, he faced drastically different circumstances than when he famously pronounced, "we are all republicans: we are all federalists" on the occasion of his First Inaugural Address. On that day, in March 1801, those assembled to hear the newly elected president speak—in a voice so soft that many in the audience could not hear all he had to say—were well of aware of the bruising circumstances that attended his rise to the position of chief executive. After an extremely hard-hitting political battle against the incumbent John Adams, Jefferson and Aaron Burr (who was supposed to be vice president) ended up with an equal number of electoral votes. The election had been thrown to the House of Representatives. Jefferson was elected on the 36th ballot.

Jefferson's first election was notable, among other things, for being the first transfer of power between the political parties that had been formed during the country's first decade of existence—the Federalists, headed by Washington and Adams, and the Democratic-Republicans, headed by Jefferson. Jefferson later referred to his first election as the "Revolution of 1800" in which he and his fellow Democratic-Republicans, in his view, had brought the country back to the principles of 1776. The battles had not ceased. Although the Federalist press had been even more aggressive in attacking him during the run-up to his second election, he ultimately had a much easier time winning the second time around. He crushed his Federalist opponent, Charles Cotesworth Pinckney, receiving

162 electoral votes to Pinckney's 14. The Democratic-Republicans gained large majorities in the Senate and the House. So, as he gave his Second Inaugural Address, as softly as he had his First, Jefferson had every reason to feel that he was more in command of the situation than he had been four years before, a confidence that is evident in the language employed in his speech. Notes he wrote in preparation for the address show that Jefferson perfectly understood the task before him.

> The former one [the First Inaugural] was an exposition of the principles on which I thought it my duty to administer the government. the second then should naturally be a Compte rendu, or a statement of facts, shewing that I have conformed to those principles. the former was *promise*: this is *performance*.[1]

The choice of the word "performance" is interesting for two reasons. There is the substance—speaking about the things he did. But there is performance in another sense: the actual giving of the speech. Markings on the reading draft of the address show that Jefferson paid particular attention to how he was going to deliver the speech. He placed markings for when he was to speak with particular emphasis and for moments when he was to pause. And unlike his First Inaugural Address, the Second was written in a form of shorthand. So, for example, the first paragraph:

> Proceeding, fellow citizens, to that qualification which the constitution requires before my entrance on the charge again conferred on me, it is my duty to express the deep sense I entertain of this new proof of confidence from my fellow citizens at large, and the zeal with which it inspires me so to conduct myself as may best satisfy their just expectations.

was rendered:

> proceedg. f. c. to yt qualfcn ' wch ye Constnɪ reqres. befre. my entrnce. on ye charge agn. conferd. on me †
>   it is my duty t. exprss. ye deep sense I entertn. ' of ys new[2] proof of confidce. frm. my f. c. at large & ye zeal wth. whch. it inspires m. ' s. t. condct. myslf. ' as m. best satsfy yr just expectns.[3] "

In his notes about the address, Jefferson set out six areas of concentration speech, or "heads" as he termed them, and he stuck to them.

These heads are, Foreign affairs; Domestic do. viz. Taxes. Debts. Louisiana. Religion. Indians. the Press. none of these heads need any commentary but that of the Indians. this is a proper topic, not only to promote the work of humanising our citizens towards these people, but to conciliate to us the good opinion of Europe on the subject of the Indians.[4]

Although well-written, as one would expect of Jefferson, his Second Inaugural Address was not as profound or memorable as the first. That would seem natural given the circumstances, when much more was at stake. Jefferson was a known quantity by 1805. Before he was president, he had been branded a Jacobin who would bring chaos to the country. He would unleash the unbridled democracy of the mob. He would ban the Bible and confiscate it from private homes. Incest and adultery would become rampant.

Of course, none of those things happened. Instead, as Jefferson emphasized in the first paragraphs of his address, during the four years of his presidency, the country had been stable and thriving. On foreign policy, his administration had kept the United States at peace with other nations—"we have endeavored to cultivate the friendship of all nations, & especially of those with which we have the most important relations."[5] Then, on the domestic front, the government was smaller and more efficient, he said. Playing to the voters who made up his base of support, he noted that the administration had favored the end to internal taxes, relying instead on tariffs which, he felt it important to point out, largely affected "those who [could] afford to add foreign luxuries to domestic comforts." And then: "it may be the pleasure and the pride of an American to ask What farmer, what mechanic, what labourer ever sees a tax-gatherer of the United States?" He predicted that the country was on its way to being free of debt, one of his particular obsessions.

Then Jefferson turned to his most important achievement of all. He had scored a historic, diplomatic triumph that transformed the physical boundaries of the United States. The Louisiana Purchase of 1803 had doubled the size of the country and was widely popular among White Americans who believed in the goal of westward expansion. The Federalists, as Jefferson reminded without mentioning his opponents by name, had, in the main, been opposed to the deal. They feared the prospect of upsetting the balance of power as the territory potentially would bring more Western and Southern states into the Union, the sprawl endangering the viability of the Republic. Jefferson had an answer to that fear in one of the address's more memorable lines: "but who can limit the extent to which the federative principle may operate effectively?" The Purchase was of questionable enough constitutionality that Jefferson had drafted his own Amendment to the

Constitution to allow for the transaction. As time was of the essence in making the deal, however, he decided to go ahead without invoking the Amendment process. This alone made him and his party enormously popular.

After a brief mention of religion—it was not a matter for interference by the federal government—Jefferson turned to the poignant section of the address, discussing the "Aboriginals." He restated a position that he had expressed privately and in *Notes on the State of Virginia*: Native peoples had to be incorporated into the United States by a process of assimilation. They had to give up their ways of life. He scorned the idea that peoples should do things because their ancestors had done those things, a point he had made in other contexts, and he presented the triumph of the European Americans as a fait accompli:

> the stream of overflowing population from other regions directed itself on these shores. without power to divert, or habits to contend against it, they have been overwhelmed by the current, or driven before it.

There was no way, in his telling, of a different outcome.

Jefferson followed with a fairly long disquisition on the nature of the press. He had been known as a champion of press freedom, but it appears that his bruising experience between 1798 and the period before the election had given him a more jaundiced view. He spoke of the "artillery of the press" that has been used against him and his fellow Democratic-Republicans. In any event, the best guard against overreaching by the press would be the public.

> public judgment will correct false reasonings and opinions on a full hearing of all parties; and no other definite line can be drawn between the inestimable liberty of the press, and its demoralizing licentiousness. If there be still improprieties which this rule would not restrain, its supplement must be sought in the censorship of public opinion.[6]

After stating all of his administration's accomplishments, Jefferson ended on an optimistic note, indicating that he took the results to be a mandate to continue in the direction he had taken. Like most presidents who have two terms, Jefferson's second term in office would be seen as, if not a failure, a disappointment. On March 4, 1805, however, the prospects for continued success seemed clear to him.

Notes

1. MS DLC: TJ Papers, 147:25710 in TJ's hand, undated.
2. MS DLC: TJ Papers, 147:25710 in TJ's hand, undated.
3. P.J.T. T.K.
4. P.J.T. T.K.
5. TJ Second Inaugural Address, MS (DLC: TJ Papers, 147:25711–13) in TJ's hand.
6. P.J.T. T.K.

James Madison's First Inaugural Address

SATURDAY, MARCH 4, 1809

UNWILLING TO DEPART from examples of the most revered authority, I avail myself of the occasion now presented to express the profound impression made on me by the call of my country to the station to the duties of which I am about to pledge myself by the most solemn of sanctions. So distinguished a mark of confidence, proceeding from the deliberate and tranquil suffrage of a free and virtuous nation, would under any circumstances have commanded my gratitude and devotion, as well as filled me with an awful sense of the trust to be assumed. Under the various circumstances which give peculiar solemnity to the existing period, I feel that both the honor and the responsibility allotted to me are inexpressibly enhanced.

The present situation of the world is indeed without a parallel, and that of our own country full of difficulties. The pressure of these, too, is the more severely felt because they have fallen upon us at a moment when the national prosperity being at a height not before attained, the contrast resulting from the change has been rendered the more striking. Under the benign influence of our republican institutions, and the maintenance of peace with all nations whilst so many of them were engaged in bloody and wasteful wars, the fruits of a just policy were enjoyed in an unrivaled growth of our faculties and resources. Proofs of this were seen in the improvements of agriculture, in the successful enterprises of commerce, in the progress of manufacturers and useful arts, in the increase of the public revenue and the use made of it in reducing the public debt, and in the valuable works and establishments everywhere multiplying over the face of our land.

It is a precious reflection that the transition from this prosperous condition of our country to the scene which has for some time been distressing us is not chargeable on any unwarrantable views, nor, as I trust, on any involuntary errors in the public councils. Indulging no passions which trespass on the rights or the repose of other nations, it has been the true glory of the United States to cultivate peace by observing justice, and to entitle themselves to the respect of the nations at war by fulfilling their neutral obligations with the most scrupulous impartiality. If there be candor in the world, the truth of these assertions will not be questioned; posterity at least will do justice to them.

This unexceptionable course could not avail against the injustice and violence of the belligerent powers. In their rage against each other, or impelled by more direct motives, principles of retaliation have been introduced equally contrary to universal reason and acknowledged law. How long their arbitrary edicts will be continued in spite of the demonstrations that not even a pretext for them has been given by the United States, and of the fair and liberal attempt to induce a revocation of them, can not be anticipated. Assuring myself that under every vicissitude the determined spirit and united councils of the nation will be safeguards to its honor and its essential interests, I repair to the post assigned me with no other discouragement than what springs from my own inadequacy to its high duties. If I do not sink under the weight of this deep conviction it is because I find some support in a consciousness of the purposes and a confidence in the principles which I bring with me into this arduous service.

To cherish peace and friendly intercourse with all nations having correspondent dispositions; to maintain sincere neutrality toward belligerent nations; to prefer in all cases amicable discussion and reasonable accommodation of differences to a decision of them by an appeal to arms; to exclude foreign intrigues and foreign partialities, so degrading to all countries and so baneful to free ones; to foster a spirit of independence too just to invade the rights of others, too proud to surrender our own, too liberal to indulge unworthy prejudices ourselves and too elevated not to look down upon them in others; to hold the union of the States as the basis of their peace and happiness; to support the Constitution, which is the cement of the Union, as well in its limitations as in its authorities; to respect the rights and authorities reserved to the States and to the people as equally incorporated with and essential to the success of the general system; to avoid the slightest interference with the rights of conscience or the functions of religion, so wisely exempted from civil jurisdiction; to preserve in their full energy the other salutary provisions in behalf of private and personal rights, and of the freedom of the press; to observe economy in public expenditures; to liberate the public resources by an honorable discharge of the public debts; to keep within the requisite limits a standing military force, always remembering that an armed and trained militia is the firmest bulwark of republics—that without standing armies their liberty can never be in danger, nor with large ones safe; to promote by authorized means improvements friendly to agriculture, to manufactures, and to external as well as internal commerce; to favor in like manner the advancement of science and the diffusion of information as the best aliment to true liberty; to carry on the benevolent plans which have been so meritoriously applied to the conversion of our aboriginal neighbors from the degradation and wretchedness of savage life to a participation of the improvements of which the human mind and manners are susceptible in a civilized state—as far as sentiments and intentions such as these can aid the fulfillment of my duty, they will be a resource which can not fail me.

It is my good fortune, moreover, to have the path in which I am to tread lighted by examples of illustrious services successfully rendered in the most trying difficulties by those who have marched before me. Of those of my immediate predecessor it might least become me here to speak. I may, however, be pardoned for not suppressing the sympathy with which my heart is full in the rich reward he enjoys in the benedictions of a beloved country, gratefully bestowed for exalted talents zealously devoted through a long career to the advancement of its highest interest and happiness.

But the source to which I look for the aids which alone can supply my deficiencies is in the well-tried intelligence and virtue of my fellow-citizens, and in the counsels of those representing them in the other departments associated in the care of the national interests. In these my confidence will under every difficulty be best placed, next to that which we have all been encouraged to feel in the guardianship and guidance of that Almighty Being whose power regulates the destiny of nations, whose blessings have been so conspicuously dispensed to this rising Republic, and to whom we are bound to address our devout gratitude for the past, as well as our fervent supplications and best hopes for the future.

The Father of the Constitution

THE FIRST INAUGURAL ADDRESS OF JAMES MADISON

Stuart Leibiger

AT NOON ON Saturday, March 4, 1809, fifty-seven-year-old Virginian James Madison read his first—and the nation's sixth—inaugural address from a handwritten manuscript in the House of Representatives chamber in the U.S. Capitol building in Washington, D.C. "A large concourse of citizens" joined Congress to witness the speech. "Such was the interest to be present at the Inauguration that the whole area allotted to citizens in the Representative Hall was filled, and overflowing several hours before noon," reported the *National Intelligencer*. "It is computed that the number of persons surrounding the Capitol, unable to obtain admittance, exceeded ten thousand."[1]

After assuring his listeners of the profound sense of duty impressed upon him "by the call of my country" to the presidency, Madison candidly pronounced "the present situation" of the nation "full of difficulties." Yet he could not bring himself to blame the country's political, economic, and diplomatic woes on the preceding administration. That regime had been led by his good friend Thomas Jefferson, under whom he himself had been the secretary of state, overseeing the realm of foreign affairs where the country's troubles had begun.

During Jefferson's presidency, the United States had found itself caught between the belligerent nations Great Britain and France, who were locked in the bitter conflict known as the Napoleonic Wars. On the one hand, the war offered tremendous trade opportunities, as both sides eagerly sought U.S. agricultural products. But on the other hand, U.S. ships headed for either England or France were often seized and confiscated by the navy of the other side on the high seas. Jefferson's solution to the dilemma was the Embargo, passed by a compliant Republican Congress in 1807. An ill-fated attempt at economic coercion, the Embargo banned all exports from the United States until the belligerent nations stopped seizing American ships. Instead of bringing Great Britain and France to their knees in their desperation for American produce, the Embargo instead threw the United States into an economic recession. One reason for the Embargo's failure was the refusal of New England merchants to abide by it. These traders were willing to take their chances on the high seas, knowing that enough cargoes would reach their destinations to turn handsome profits despite occasional ship seizures. Determined to give his Embargo a fair trial, Jefferson tried to enforce it on the New England states by martial law. Congress's repeal of the Embargo took effect on March 4, 1809, the very day Madison took office. The administration's experiment in economic coercion had failed. It would be up to the new president, an originator of the hapless Embargo, to deal with the fallout.

Madison's First Inaugural Address thus could hardly blame the nation's troubles on his predecessor. "It is a precious reflection," declared Madison, "that the transition from this prosperous condition of our country to the scene which has for some time been distressing us is not chargeable on any unwarrantable views, nor, as I trust, on any involuntary errors in the public councils." Instead, Madison blamed the nation's misfortunes on the extreme and desperate measures of Great Britain and France. "In their rage against each other," Madison bemoaned, "principles of retaliation have been introduced equally contrary to universal reason and acknowledged law." With the unexpected failure of the Embargo, "[h]ow long their arbitrary edicts will be continued . . . can not be anticipated."

Madison's First Inaugural Address did not offer new policy proposals to deal with the crisis. Instead, it promised that the United States would "cherish peace and friendly intercourse with all nations having correspondent dispositions" and would "maintain sincere neutrality toward belligerent nations." War would be a last resort. Madison further pledged "to support the Constitution . . . in its limitations as in its authorities." Perhaps already anticipating a war with Great Britain, Madison assured that his administration would never use events as an excuse to trample personal rights and liberties enshrined in the Bill of Rights that he himself had authored. He would "avoid the slightest interference with the rights of conscience or the functions of religion," and would "preserve in their full energy the other salutary provisions in behalf of private and personal rights, and of the freedom of the press." His administration would not take advantage of the crisis to aggrandize the power of the federal government or to militarize American society by the introduction of "a standing military force" that Revolutionary-era citizens had dreaded so much as an instrument of tyranny.

In facing an uncertain future, Madison's First Inaugural Address promised that he would be guided by the "illustrious" examples of his predecessors as chief executive, including Jefferson. He would also rely on "the well-tried intelligence and virtue of my fellow-citizens" and on the support and advice of the other branches of the federal government. Finally, he would look to the "guardianship and guidance of that Almighty Being... whose blessings have been so conspicuously dispensed to this rising Republic."

After failing to halt the seizures of American ships (mainly by the British, who had established naval superiority on the Atlantic Ocean) and to stop the British practice of impressment of sailors from U.S. vessels, Madison sought a declaration of war against Great Britain in 1812. An uncharismatic leader, Madison performed disappointingly as commander in chief during the War of 1812. He failed to provide the vigorous and competent leadership of the armed forces during conflict that George Washington had once demonstrated. He could not prevent the British from invading Washington, D.C., in 1814 and burning the public buildings, including the White House. Throughout the hostilities, however, Madison scrupulously adhered to the promise articulated in his Inaugural Address to preserve and protect personal rights and liberties. President Madison, in short, led the United States through a second war for independence against Great Britain without undermining or infringing upon the nation's republican principles. In so doing, he maintained the devotion of his fellow citizens, and he could almost certainly have won a third term as president had he desired one.

James Madison is perhaps the only president whose pre-presidential career is studied more than his presidency. Yet his presidency witnessed many critical events, not the least of which was the first ever presidential request for a congressional declaration of war. Interestingly, President Madison's First Inaugural Address was not the first inaugural speech that he wrote. In 1789, as a confidential advisor to president-elect George Washington, Madison had ghostwritten a draft of the very first inaugural address. Indeed, as the Father of the Constitution and the Father of the Bill of Rights, Madison came to the presidency more well versed in American constitutionalism than any other president, qualifications amply demonstrated by his First Inaugural Address.

Note

1. "The national intelligencer and Washington advertiser. [volume] (Washington City [D.C.]) 1800–1810, March 06, 1809, Image 2," chroniclingamerica.loc.gov.

James Madison's Second Inaugural Address

THURSDAY, MARCH 4, 1813

ABOUT TO ADD the solemnity of an oath to the obligations imposed by a second call to the station in which my country heretofore placed me, I find in the presence of this respectable assembly an opportunity of publicly repeating my profound sense of so distinguished a confidence and of the responsibility united with it. The impressions on me are strengthened by such an evidence that my faithful endeavors to discharge my arduous duties have been favorably estimated, and by a consideration of the momentous period at which the trust has been renewed. From the weight and magnitude now belonging to it I should be compelled to shrink if I had less reliance on the support of an enlightened and generous people, and felt less deeply a conviction that the war with a powerful nation, which forms so prominent a feature in our situation, is stamped with that justice which invites the smiles of Heaven on the means of conducting it to a successful termination.

May we not cherish this sentiment without presumption when we reflect on the characters by which this war is distinguished?

It was not declared on the part of the United States until it had been long made on them, in reality though not in name; until arguments and expostulations had been exhausted; until a positive declaration had been received that the wrongs provoking it would not be discontinued; nor until this last appeal could no longer be delayed without breaking down the spirit of the nation, destroying all confidence in itself and in its political institutions, and either perpetuating a state of disgraceful suffering or regaining by more costly sacrifices and more severe struggles our lost rank and respect among independent powers.

On the issue of the war are staked our national sovereignty on the high seas and the security of an important class of citizens, whose occupations give the proper value to those of every other class. Not to contend for such a stake is to surrender our equality with other powers on the element common to all and to violate the sacred title which every member of the society has to its protection. I need not call into view the unlawfulness of the practice by which our mariners are forced at the will of every cruising officer from their own vessels into foreign ones, nor paint the outrages inseparable from it. The proofs are in the records of each successive Administration of our Government, and the cruel sufferings of that portion of the American people have found their way to every bosom not dead to the sympathies of human nature.

As the war was just in its origin and necessary and noble in its objects, we can reflect with a proud satisfaction that in carrying it on no principle of justice or honor, no usage of civilized nations, no precept of courtesy or humanity, have been infringed. The war has been waged on our part with scrupulous regard to all these obligations, and in a spirit of liberality which was never surpassed.

How little has been the effect of this example on the conduct of the enemy!

They have retained as prisoners of war citizens of the United States not liable to be so considered under the usages of war.

They have refused to consider as prisoners of war, and threatened to punish as traitors and deserters, persons emigrating without restraint to the United States, incorporated by naturalization into our political family, and fighting under the authority of their adopted country in open and honorable war for the maintenance of its rights and safety. Such is the avowed purpose of a Government which is in the practice of naturalizing by thousands citizens of other countries, and not only of permitting but compelling them to fight its battles against their native country.

They have not, it is true, taken into their own hands the hatchet and the knife, devoted to indiscriminate massacre, but they have let loose the savages armed with these cruel instruments; have allured them into their service, and carried them to battle by their sides, eager to glut their savage thirst with the blood of the vanquished and to finish the work of torture and death on maimed and defenseless captives. And, what was never before seen, British commanders have extorted victory over the unconquerable valor of our troops by presenting to the sympathy of their chief captives awaiting massacre from their savage associates. And now we find them, in further contempt of the modes of honorable warfare, supplying the place of a conquering force by attempts to disorganize our political society, to dismember our confederated Republic. Happily, like others, these will recoil on the authors; but they mark the degenerate counsels from which they emanate, and if they did not belong to a series of unexampled inconsistencies might excite the greater wonder as proceeding from a Government which founded the very war in which it has been so long engaged on a charge against the disorganizing and insurrectional policy of its adversary.

To render the justice of the war on our part the more conspicuous, the reluctance to commence it was followed by the earliest and strongest manifestations of a disposition to arrest its progress. The sword was scarcely out of the scabbard before the enemy was apprised of the reasonable terms on which it would be resheathed. Still more precise advances were repeated, and have been received in a spirit forbidding every reliance not placed on the military resources of the nation.

These resources are amply sufficient to bring the war to an honorable issue. Our nation is in number more than half that of the British Isles. It is composed of a brave, a free, a virtuous, and an intelligent people. Our country abounds in the necessaries, the arts, and the comforts of life. A general prosperity is visible in the public countenance. The means employed by the British cabinet to undermine it have recoiled on themselves; have given to our national faculties a more rapid development, and, draining or diverting the precious metals from British circulation and British vaults, have poured them into those of the United States. It is a propitious consideration that an unavoidable war should have found this seasonable facility for the contributions required to support it. When the public voice called for war, all knew, and still know, that without them it could not be carried on through the period which it might last, and the patriotism, the good sense, and the manly spirit of our fellow-citizens are pledges for the cheerfulness with which they will bear each his share of the common burden. To render the war short and its success sure, animated and systematic exertions alone are necessary, and the success of our arms now may long preserve our country from the necessity of another resort to them. Already have the gallant exploits of our naval heroes proved to the world our inherent capacity to maintain our rights on one element. If the reputation of our arms has been thrown under clouds on the other, presaging flashes of heroic enterprise assure us that nothing is wanting to correspondent triumphs there also but the discipline and habits which are in daily progress.

The First Wartime President

THE SECOND INAUGURAL ADDRESS OF JAMES MADISON

J. C. A. Stagg

AT NOON ON March 4, 1813, James Madison delivered his Second Inaugural Address before a concourse of congressmen, diplomats, judges, and other residents of the nation's capital. As he was drafting his remarks, the president's thoughts undoubtedly returned to the message he had sent to Congress on June 1, 1812, listing the reasons why he believed the United States should declare war against Great Britain. That message had been organized as a catalogue of the violations of American neutral rights and sovereignty committed by Great Britain after 1803. It culminated in the prediction that the national legislature would issue a declaration worthy of "the enlightened and patriotic Councils of a virtuous, a free, and powerful nation" before concluding with the hint that the international situation of the republic was so fraught with difficulties that a war against France might also be necessary.

The intervening nine months had not gone well for the Madison administration. The principal justification for the war—Great Britain's seemingly inflexible adherence to the trade restrictions embodied in the Orders in Council—had been removed in London five days after the commencement of hostilities on June 18, 1812. Worse, the United States proved to be a far less powerful nation than Madison had wished. Three invasions of the British provinces of Upper and Lower Canada had ended in embarrassing failures, with one of them resulting in the loss of Detroit and the Michigan territory to numerically inferior British forces and their Native American allies. The U.S. Army had been unable to equip and train the forces raised since the spring of 1812. Admittedly, the infant U.S. Navy had exceeded low expectations by winning three encounters at sea with British frigates, but there had been no comparable successes on the Great Lakes, which would have facilitated the operations of American land forces. Consequently, the British government was under no pressure to engage in negotiations over the grievances Madison had outlined in June. Nor had France improved its relations with the United States. Instead, Napoleon had embarked on the invasion of Russia at the very same moment the United States went to war with Great Britain. Madison had anticipated that Napoleon would win his war—thereby making Russia's British ally more amenable to ending its American war—but by early 1813 it was clear that Napoleon had sustained a massive defeat, with French imperial forces in full retreat from eastern Europe. Great Britain was now in an even stronger position vis-à-vis the United States.

This was the situation Madison faced as he entered on his second term, immediately after three difficult months with the second session of the Twelfth Congress. Congressional dissatisfaction with the conduct of the war had compelled Madison to restructure his Cabinet. The failures of the Canadian campaigns required hasty improvisations to raise and train new forces for the spring and summer of 1813. And the successes of the navy dictated a greater expansion of its forces—both for the Great Lakes and the Atlantic Ocean—to an extent that president and his Republican allies only grudgingly conceded. All of this would require significant increases in spending, but Congress balked at imposing taxes, even though it had pledged in 1812 that taxation would be required in a state of war. But over the winter of 1812–1813, Congress did no more than double the duties on imported goods, an expedient that irritated the nation's mercantile communities. Despite these difficulties, Madison had won re-election in November 1812, albeit with a reduced majority from his success in 1808. However, his critics, in his own party and in the Federalist opposition, were now more numerous and more vociferous than they had been in 1812. The next session of Congress, which Madison had already summoned for a spring meeting to address the needs of the Treasury, promised to be the most difficult the president had ever faced.

For all these reasons, Madison's second inaugural was a short document, barely 1,500 words, and it concealed more than it revealed. The president's immediate problem was: how to justify continuing a war under such unpromising circumstances, and how might the United State emerge victorious? There is no evidence that Madison ever considered ending the war; his goal remained to obtain a peace treaty that addressed all the grievances he had outlined in June 1812. But after Great Britain had lifted the Orders in Council, attention had to be focused on the next most serious grievance—the impressment of American seamen by the Royal Navy on the high seas. This had long been an intractable dispute that had not even been the subject of serious discussions since 1808. At one point,

Madison had contemplated that Great Britain and the United States might agree to forgo the employment of their nationals in their respective merchant marines, but Great Britain would never accept this, and the policy would have seriously harmed the expansion of American commerce. Even so, in February 1813 the president revived this proposal and called upon Congress to turn it into law in order to provide a firmer basis of support for the war.

The so-called Seamen's Bill had passed Congress by the end of February 1813, but it hardly accomplished Madison's goals. Certainly, many of the Federalists, all of whom had voted against war in June 1812, supported the bill, but a larger number of Republicans, including several of the strongest supporters of the war, voted against it. Their reason was that, by seeming to accept in advance Great Britain's claims that the United States should neither naturalize British subjects nor employ them on American vessels, the administration had made too great a concession to British doctrines about citizenship and sovereignty. Nevertheless, much of Madison's second inaugural was devoted to justifying the war on the grounds that it was essential to protect all American mariners from impressment, regardless of their country of origin, and particularly to safeguard British subjects who had enlisted in the American armed forces and had become prisoners of war from the threat of treason trials. Otherwise, the address said little else about the grievances Madison had cited in his June 1, 1812, message. He withdrew, to some extent, his charge that the British in Canada had incited Native Americans in the Northwest to wage war on the frontiers, and instead criticized the enemy for accepting the services of such "savage" allies. About the possibility of a war with France, Madison said nothing at all.

As Madison delivered this address, many in his audience must have suspected that Great Britain would not agree to a peace based on the Seamen's Bill. But Madison had withheld one piece of information that he believed might make a treaty possible. In September 1812, Alexander I of Russia had offered to mediate in the war between Great Britain and the United States. The emperor was allied to Great Britain in the war against France, but he also strongly sympathized with the United States in its rejection of British doctrines about maritime and neutral rights. The Russian offer had reached Washington by the end of February 1813, but Madison did not announce that he would accept it until March 8, 1813. He may have even concluded that Great Britain would accept the Russian offer. The prospect of Russian diplomatic support against Great Britain, even as French power in Europe declined, was one reason why Madison decided that the War of 1812 should be continued. Details of his other ideas about how the war might be waged were left until the first session of the Thirteenth Congress, assembled in Washington on May 24, 1813.

James Monroe's First Inaugural Address

TUESDAY, MARCH 4, 1817

I SHOULD BE destitute of feeling if I was not deeply affected by the strong proof which my fellow-citizens have given me of their confidence in calling me to the high office whose functions I am about to assume. As the expression of their good opinion of my conduct in the public service, I derive from it a gratification which those who are conscious of having done all that they could to merit it can alone feel. My sensibility is increased by a just estimate of the importance of the trust and of the nature and extent of its duties, with the proper discharge of which the highest interests of a great and free people are intimately connected. Conscious of my own deficiency, I can not enter on these duties without great anxiety for the result. From a just responsibility I will never shrink, calculating with confidence that in my best efforts to promote the public welfare my motives will always be duly appreciated and my conduct be viewed with that candor and indulgence which I have experienced in other stations.

In commencing the duties of the chief executive office it has been the practice of the distinguished men who have gone before me to explain the principles which would govern them in their respective Administrations. In following their venerated example my attention is naturally drawn to the great causes which have contributed in a principal degree to produce the present happy condition of the United States. They will best explain the nature of our duties and shed much light on the policy which ought to be pursued in future.

From the commencement of our Revolution to the present day almost forty years have elapsed, and from the establishment of this Constitution twenty-eight. Through this whole term the Government has been what may emphatically be called self-government. And what has been the effect? To whatever object we turn our attention, whether it relates to our foreign or domestic concerns, we find abundant cause to felicitate ourselves in the excellence of our institutions. During a period fraught with difficulties and marked by very extraordinary events the United States have flourished beyond example. Their citizens individually have been happy and the nation prosperous.

Under this Constitution our commerce has been wisely regulated with foreign nations and between the States; new States have been admitted into our Union; our territory has been enlarged by fair and honorable treaty, and with great advantage to the original States; the States, respectively protected by the National Government under a mild, parental system against foreign dangers, and enjoying within their separate spheres, by a wise partition of power, a just proportion of the sovereignty, have improved their police, extended their settlements, and attained a strength and maturity which are the best proofs of wholesome laws well administered. And if we look to the condition of individuals what a proud spectacle does it exhibit! On whom has oppression fallen in any quarter of our Union? Who has been deprived of any right of person or property? Who restrained from offering his vows in the mode which he prefers to the Divine Author of his being? It is well known that all these blessings have been enjoyed in their fullest extent; and I add with peculiar satisfaction that there has been no example of a capital punishment being inflicted on anyone for the crime of high treason.

Some who might admit the competency of our Government to these beneficent duties might doubt it in trials which put to the test its strength and efficiency as a member of the great community of nations. Here too experience has afforded us the most satisfactory proof in its favor. Just as this Constitution was put into action several of the principal States of Europe had become much agitated and some of them seriously convulsed. Destructive wars ensued, which have of late only been terminated. In the course of these conflicts the United States received great injury from several of the parties. It was their interest to stand aloof from the contest, to demand justice from the party committing the injury, and to cultivate by a fair and honorable conduct the friendship of all. War became at length inevitable, and the result has shown that our Government is equal to that, the greatest of trials, under the most unfavorable circumstances. Of the virtue of the people and of the heroic exploits of the Army, the Navy, and the militia I need not speak.

Such, then, is the happy Government under which we live—a Government adequate to every purpose for which the social compact is formed; a Government elective in all its branches, under which every citizen may by his merit obtain the highest trust recognized by the Constitution; which contains within it no cause of discord, none to put at variance one portion of the community with another; a

Government which protects every citizen in the full enjoyment of his rights, and is able to protect the nation against injustice from foreign powers.

Other considerations of the highest importance admonish us to cherish our Union and to cling to the Government which supports it. Fortunate as we are in our political institutions, we have not been less so in other circumstances on which our prosperity and happiness essentially depend. Situated within the temperate zone, and extending through many degrees of latitude along the Atlantic, the United States enjoy all the varieties of climate, and every production incident to that portion of the globe. Penetrating internally to the Great Lakes and beyond the sources of the great rivers which communicate through our whole interior, no country was ever happier with respect to its domain. Blessed, too, with a fertile soil, our produce has always been very abundant, leaving, even in years the least favorable, a surplus for the wants of our fellow-men in other countries. Such is our peculiar felicity that there is not a part of our Union that is not particularly interested in preserving it. The great agricultural interest of the nation prospers under its protection. Local interests are not less fostered by it. Our fellow-citizens of the North engaged in navigation find great encouragement in being made the favored carriers of the vast productions of the other portions of the United States, while the inhabitants of these are amply recompensed, in their turn, by the nursery for seamen and naval force thus formed and reared up for the support of our common rights. Our manufactures find a generous encouragement by the policy which patronizes domestic industry, and the surplus of our produce a steady and profitable market by local wants in less-favored parts at home.

Such, then, being the highly favored condition of our country, it is the interest of every citizen to maintain it. What are the dangers which menace us? If any exist they ought to be ascertained and guarded against.

In explaining my sentiments on this subject it may be asked, What raised us to the present happy state? How did we accomplish the Revolution? How remedy the defects of the first instrument of our Union, by infusing into the National Government sufficient power for national purposes, without impairing the just rights of the States or affecting those of individuals? How sustain and pass with glory through the late war? The Government has been in the hands of the people. To the people, therefore, and to the faithful and able depositaries of their trust is the credit due. Had the people of the United States been educated in different principles, had they been less intelligent, less independent, or less virtuous, can it be believed that we should have maintained the same steady and consistent career or been blessed with the same success? While, then, the constituent body retains its present sound and healthful state everything will be safe. They will choose competent and faithful representatives for every department. It is only when the people become ignorant and corrupt, when they degenerate into a populace, that they are incapable of exercising the sovereignty. Usurpation is then an easy attainment, and an usurper soon found. The people themselves become the willing instruments of their own debasement and ruin. Let us, then, look to the great cause, and endeavor to preserve it in full force. Let us by all wise and constitutional measures promote intelligence among the people as the best means of preserving our liberties.

Dangers from abroad are not less deserving of attention. Experiencing the fortune of other nations, the United States may be again involved in war, and it may in that event be the object of the adverse party to overset our Government, to break our Union, and demolish us as a nation. Our distance from Europe and the just, moderate, and pacific policy of our Government may form some security against these dangers, but they ought to be anticipated and guarded against. Many of our citizens are engaged in commerce and navigation, and all of them are in a certain degree dependent on their prosperous state. Many are engaged in the fisheries. These interests are exposed to invasion in the wars between other powers, and we should disregard the faithful admonition of experience if we did not expect it. We must support our rights or lose our character, and with it, perhaps, our liberties. A people who fail to do it can scarcely be said to hold a place among independent nations. National honor is national property of the highest value. The sentiment in the mind of every citizen is national strength. It ought therefore to be cherished.

To secure us against these dangers our coast and inland frontiers should be fortified, our Army and Navy, regulated upon just principles as to the force of each, be kept in perfect order, and our militia be placed on the best practicable footing. To put our extensive coast in such a state of defense as to secure our cities and interior from invasion will be attended with expense, but the work when finished will be permanent, and it is fair to presume that a single campaign of invasion by a naval force superior to our own, aided by a few thousand land troops, would expose us to greater expense, without taking into the estimate the loss of property and distress of our citizens, than would be sufficient for this great work. Our land and naval forces should be moderate, but adequate to the necessary purposes—the former to garrison and preserve our fortifications and to meet the first invasions of a foreign foe, and, while constituting the elements of a greater force, to preserve the science as well as all the necessary implements of war in a state to be brought into activity in the event of war; the latter, retained within the limits proper in a state of peace, might aid in maintaining the neutrality of the United States with dignity in the wars of other powers and in saving the property of their citizens from spoliation. In time of war, with the enlargement of which the great naval resources of the country render it susceptible, and which should be duly fostered in time of peace, it would contribute essentially, both as an auxiliary of defense and as a powerful engine of annoyance, to diminish the calamities of war and to bring the war to a speedy and honorable termination.

But it ought always to be held prominently in view that the safety of these States and of everything dear to a free people must depend in an eminent degree on the militia. Invasions may be made too formidable to be resisted by any land and naval force which it would comport either with the principles of our Government or the circumstances of the United States to maintain. In such cases recourse must be had to the great body of the people, and in a manner to produce the best effect. It is of the highest importance, therefore, that they be so organized and trained as to be prepared for any emergency. The arrangement should be such as to put at the command of the Government the ardent patriotism and youthful vigor of the country. If formed on equal and just principles, it can not be oppressive. It is the crisis which makes the pressure, and not the laws which provide a remedy for it. This arrangement should be formed, too, in time of peace, to be the better prepared for war. With such an organization of such a people the United States have nothing to dread from foreign invasion. At its approach an overwhelming force of gallant men might always be put in motion.

Other interests of high importance will claim attention, among which the improvement of our country by roads and canals, proceeding always with a constitutional sanction, holds a distinguished place. By thus facilitating the intercourse between the States we shall add much to the convenience and comfort of our fellow-citizens, much to the ornament of the country, and, what is of greater importance, we shall shorten distances, and, by making each part more accessible to and dependent on the other, we shall bind the Union more closely together. Nature has done so much for us by intersecting the country with so many great rivers, bays, and lakes, approaching from distant points so near to each other, that the inducement to complete the work seems to be peculiarly strong. A more interesting spectacle was perhaps never seen than is exhibited within the limits of the United States—a territory so vast and advantageously situated, containing objects so grand, so useful, so happily connected in all their parts!

Our manufacturers will likewise require the systematic and fostering care of the Government. Possessing as we do all the raw materials, the fruit of our own soil and industry, we ought not to depend in the degree we have done on supplies from other countries. While we are thus dependent the sudden event of war, unsought and unexpected, can not fail to plunge us into the most serious difficulties. It is important, too, that the capital which nourishes our manufacturers should be domestic, as its influence in that case instead of exhausting, as it may do in foreign hands, would be felt advantageously on agriculture and every other branch of industry. Equally important is it to provide at home a market for our raw materials, as by extending the competition it will enhance the price and protect the cultivator against the casualties incident to foreign markets.

With the Indian tribes it is our duty to cultivate friendly relations and to act with kindness and liberality in all our transactions. Equally proper is it to persevere in our efforts to extend to them the advantages of civilization.

The great amount of our revenue and the flourishing state of the Treasury are a full proof of the competency of the national resources for any emergency, as they are of the willingness of our fellow-citizens to bear the burdens which the public necessities require. The vast amount of vacant lands, the value of which daily augments, forms an additional resource of great extent and duration. These resources, besides accomplishing every other necessary purpose, put it completely in the power of the United States to discharge the national debt at an early period. Peace is the best time for improvement and preparation of every kind; it is in peace that our commerce flourishes most, that taxes are most easily paid, and that the revenue is most productive.

The Executive is charged officially in the Departments under it with the disbursement of the public money, and is responsible for the faithful application of it to the purposes for which it is raised. The Legislature is the watchful guardian over the public purse. It is its duty to see that the disbursement has been honestly made. To meet the requisite responsibility every facility should be afforded to the Executive to enable it to bring the public agents intrusted with the public money strictly and promptly to account. Nothing should be presumed against them; but if, with the requisite facilities, the public money is suffered to lie long and uselessly in their hands, they will not be the only defaulters, nor will the demoralizing effect be confined to them. It will evince a relaxation and want of tone in the Administration which will be felt by the whole community. I shall do all I can to secure economy and fidelity in this important branch of the Administration, and I doubt not that the Legislature will perform its duty with equal zeal. A thorough examination should be regularly made, and I will promote it.

It is particularly gratifying to me to enter on the discharge of these duties at a time when the United States are blessed with peace. It is a state most consistent with their prosperity and happiness. It will be my sincere desire to preserve it, so far as depends on the Executive, on just principles with all nations, claiming nothing unreasonable of any and rendering to each what is its due.

Equally gratifying is it to witness the increased harmony of opinion which pervades our Union. Discord does not belong to our system. Union is recommended as well by the free and benign principles of our Government, extending its blessings to every individual, as by the other eminent advantages attending it. The American people have encountered together great dangers and sustained severe trials with success. They constitute one great family with a common interest. Experience has enlightened us on some questions of essential importance to the country. The progress has been slow, dictated by a just reflection and a faithful regard to every interest connected with it. To promote this harmony in accord with the principles of our republican Government and in a manner to give them the most complete effect, and to advance in all other respects the best interests of our Union, will be the object of my constant and zealous exertions.

Never did a government commence under auspices so favorable, nor ever was success so complete. If we look to the history of other nations, ancient or modern, we find no example of a growth so rapid, so gigantic, of a people so prosperous and happy. In contemplating what we have still to perform, the heart of every citizen must expand with joy when he reflects how near our Government has approached to perfection; that in respect to it we have no essential improvement to make; that the great object is to preserve it in the essential principles and features which characterize it, and that that is to be done by preserving the virtue and enlightening the minds of the people; and as a security against foreign dangers to adopt such arrangements as are indispensable to the support of our independence, our rights and liberties. If we persevere in the career in which we have advanced so far and in the path already traced, we can not fail, under the favor of a gracious Providence, to attain the high destiny which seems to await us.

In the Administrations of the illustrious men who have preceded me in this high station, with some of whom I have been connected by the closest ties from early life, examples are presented which will always be found highly instructive and useful to their successors. From these I shall endeavor to derive all the advantages which they may afford. Of my immediate predecessor, under whom so important a portion of this great and successful experiment has been made, I shall be pardoned for expressing my earnest wishes that he may long enjoy in his retirement the affections of a grateful country, the best reward of exalted talents and the most faithful and meritorious service. Relying on the aid to be derived from the other departments of the Government, I enter on the trust to which I have been called by the suffrages of my fellow-citizens with my fervent prayers to the Almighty that He will be graciously pleased to continue to us that protection which He has already so conspicuously displayed in our favor.

The Era of Good Feelings

THE FIRST INAUGURAL ADDRESS OF JAMES MONROE

Daniel F. Preston

JAMES MONROE ASSUMED the reins of government during a period of peace and prosperity. The European war that had begun in the early 1790s and persisted until 1815 and that had ensnared the United States and led to the War of 1812 was at last ended. The American economy, which had been badly shaken by the years of maritime disruption and war, was showing a remarkable recovery, exemplified by the steady stream of revenue from land sales, import tariffs, and excise taxes flowing into the national treasury. To be certain, there were grave crises lurking just beyond the horizon, but in March 1817 a bright future beckoned.

When Monroe turned to address the crowd attending the ceremony—the first inauguration to be held outdoors—the new president began his remarks by examining the causes of the "present happy condition" of the country. For Monroe, the explanation could be summed up in one word: republicanism. The strength and prosperity of the United States flowed from an adherence to the principles of self-government championed during the American Revolution and enunciated in the federal Constitution as well as in the constitutions of the various states. Republicanism—a system of popularly elected representative and constitutional government free of the trappings of monarchy, hereditary aristocracy, and established religion—was Monroe's political credo from the days of the American Revolution until his death in 1831.

How, Monroe asked rhetorically, can we explain the success of the American experiment in elective government in the face of wide-ranging skepticism about the practicability of such a form of government and the failure of other attempts throughout history to establish such a system? During a period "fraught with difficulties" the United States had "flourished beyond example." The citizens were happy; the nation prosperous; territorial boundaries had been expanded and new states admitted; the states themselves, protected by the national government from foreign aggression, enjoyed sovereignty in their separate spheres and effectively governed themselves. How was this done? "How did we accomplish the Revolution? . . . How sustain, and pass with glory through the late war?" The president had a ready answer: "The Government has been in the hands of the people." To the people, with their intelligence, their independence, and their virtue, "is the credit due."

Monroe encapsulated his absolute belief in the political virtue of the American people in just a few sentences. He went into much greater detail, however, in an unused draft of the message. The English heritage of representative government and the semi-independent status of the British American colonies imbued the American people with a love of republicanism. It gave them the fortitude and courage to fight for and win their independence. It gave them the understanding and temperament to form republican governments and the intelligence and virtue to sustain them. As long as the American people remained true to the principles of the Revolution and the Constitution, they could confront and overcome any challenge, domestic or foreign, that arose. "While the constituent body retains its present sound and healthful state," he said in his address, "everything will be safe." There being no crisis of any proportion worth noting, the American people had only two major tasks at hand: to preserve the liberty and advantages they enjoyed under their republican government and to further develop the prosperity of the nation.

And yet, for all his faith in the American people, he still warned about complacency. Without proper vigilance the people may become "ignorant and corrupt . . . the willing instruments of their own debasement and ruin." "Usurpation is then an easy attainment," he warned, "and an usurper soon found." To prevent such a situation, he vaguely suggested that Congress, "by all wise and constitutional measures," create a system of academies "as the best means of preserving our liberties," a hint that he stated more explicitly in his first annual message to Congress in December 1817, by urging a constitutional amendment that would grant "a right in Congress to institute seminaries of learning, for the all important purpose, of diffusing knowledge among our fellow citizens, throughout the United States."

Nor should the American people be complacent about peace. The United States had been caught unprepared for war in 1812, and although the Americans had fought the war to an honorable termination, Monroe knew how perilously close the country had come to disaster. He was adamant that this must not happen again. The possibility of war in the future should not be discounted, and with an enemy determined to "overset our Government, to break our Union and demolish us as a nation." The key to national defense was, of course, a well-regulated army and navy, moderate in size, but "adequate to the necessary purposes" of defense. Also, a system of fortifications was needed to defend the nation's extensive coastline, a measure that Monroe had urged at least as early as 1805. Finally, there was the militia, the central bulwark of defense in any republic. The new president had been an advocate for a strong national defense throughout his public career, but like many of his generation he harbored a fear that a large professional army, detached from the daily concerns of the people, could become an instrument of tyranny. A standing army was certainly necessary to meet any immediate danger, but the great body of any defensive force should be embodied in the militia. Monroe's experience as governor of Virginia and as secretary of war made him well aware of the inadequacies of the militia, and he now insisted, as he had done in the past, that this people's army be "organized and trained as to be prepared for any emergency."

Monroe went on to note that the United States was particularly blessed in its geographic location, occupying a portion of the globe that produced a great variety of valuable crops and natural resources. "No country was ever happier with respect to its domain," he wrote, especially in terms of agriculture. The United States possessed soil so fertile that there had always been a surplus for export, even at the times of the poorest harvests. This benefited not only the growers, but also the merchants and seamen who carried the agricultural bounty to other countries. The United States was home to a vast overseas carrying trade, a trade so critical that British interference with it led to the declaration of war in 1812. Monroe was well aware of the importance of foreign trade to the economic wealth of the nation, and both as secretary of state and president sought commercial treaties that not only secured advantageous trade agreements with the European powers but also expanded American trade into new markets. At the same time, he hoped to expand the American economy at home, not only by bringing new land into cultivation but also by encouraging the development of manufacturing. The United States possessed the necessary raw materials and capital and "ought not to depend in the degree we have done" on foreign countries for finished goods. This beneficial economic independence could be achieved with "the systematic and fostering care of the Government."

Monroe ventured onto more controversial ground when he urged the passage of a constitutional amendment granting the national government authority to construct a network of roads and canals. Most Americans acknowledged that such a system was needed and, being national in scope, that it ought to be undertaken by the national government. But they disagreed whether the government possessed the constitutional authority to do so. Monroe was one of the doubters and favored the expedient of a constitutional amendment specifically granting the power. But he had no doubt of the necessity or benefit of such a network. Not only would it add to the "convenience and comfort" of the people, but by shortening distances and making the various parts of the country "more accessible to and dependent on the other," it would "bind the Union more closely together."

This brought the president to the other basic tenet of his political creed—the absolute necessity of the union of the states. Monroe believed that the state governments bore the responsibility of protecting the liberty and promoting the welfare of their citizens. But he also believed that they were not strong enough individually or regionally to do this. They must unite in a continental union to protect the republic from all threats, domestic and foreign. Monroe told his audience that he was gratified by the harmony that pervaded the nation. "Discord does not belong to our system." Unity had carried the American people through past trials, it would continue to promote prosperity and happiness. The American people "constitute one great family with a common interest." "To promote this harmony, in accord with the principles of our republican Government and in a manner to give them the most complete effect, and to advance in all other respects the best interests of our Union," Monroe promised, "will be the object of my constant and zealous exertions."

James Monroe's Second Inaugural Address

MONDAY, MARCH 5, 1821

FELLOW-CITIZENS:
I shall not attempt to describe the grateful emotions which the new and very distinguished proof of the confidence of my fellow-citizens, evinced by my reelection to this high trust, has excited in my bosom. The approbation which it announces of my conduct in the preceding term affords me a consolation which I shall profoundly feel through life. The general accord with which it has been expressed adds to the great and never-ceasing obligations which it imposes. To merit the continuance of this good opinion, and to carry it with me into my retirement as the solace of advancing years, will be the object of my most zealous and unceasing efforts.

Having no pretensions to the high and commanding claims of my predecessors, whose names are so much more conspicuously identified with our Revolution, and who contributed so preeminently to promote its success, I consider myself rather as the instrument than the cause of the union which has prevailed in the late election. In surmounting, in favor of my humble pretensions, the difficulties which so often produce division in like occurrences, it is obvious that other powerful causes, indicating the great strength and stability of our Union, have essentially contributed to draw you together. That these powerful causes exist, and that they are permanent, is my fixed opinion; that they may produce a like accord in all questions touching, however remotely, the liberty, prosperity, and happiness of our country will always be the object of my most fervent prayers to the Supreme Author of All Good.

In a government which is founded by the people, who possess exclusively the sovereignty, it seems proper that the person who may be placed by their suffrages in this high trust should declare on commencing its duties the principles on which he intends to conduct the Administration. If the person thus elected has served the preceding term, an opportunity is afforded him to review its principal occurrences and to give such further explanation respecting them as in his judgment may be useful to his constituents. The events of one year have influence on those of another, and, in like manner, of a preceding on the succeeding Administration. The movements of a great nation are connected in all their parts. If errors have been committed they ought to be corrected; if the policy is sound it ought to be supported. It is by a thorough knowledge of the whole subject that our fellow-citizens are enabled to judge correctly of the past and to give a proper direction to the future.

Just before the commencement of the last term the United States had concluded a war with a very powerful nation on conditions equal and honorable to both parties. The events of that war are too recent and too deeply impressed on the memory of all to require a development from me. Our commerce had been in a great measure driven from the sea, our Atlantic and inland frontiers were invaded in almost every part; the waste of life along our coast and on some parts of our inland frontiers, to the defense of which our gallant and patriotic citizens were called, was immense, in addition to which not less than $120,000,000 were added at its end to the public debt.

As soon as the war had terminated, the nation, admonished by its events, resolved to place itself in a situation which should be better calculated to prevent the recurrence of a like evil, and, in case it should recur, to mitigate its calamities. With this view, after reducing our land force to the basis of a peace establishment, which has been further modified since, provision was made for the construction of fortifications at proper points through the whole extent of our coast and such an augmentation of our naval force as should be well adapted to both purposes. The laws making this provision were passed in 1815 and 1816, and it has been since the constant effort of the Executive to carry them into effect.

The advantage of these fortifications and of an augmented naval force in the extent contemplated, in a point of economy, has been fully illustrated by a report of the Board of Engineers and Naval Commissioners lately communicated to Congress, by which it appears that in an invasion by 20,000 men, with a correspondent naval force, in a campaign of six months only, the whole expense of the construction of the works would be defrayed by the difference in the sum necessary to maintain the force which would be adequate to our defense with the aid of those works and that which would be incurred without them. The reason of this difference is obvious. If fortifications are judiciously placed on our great inlets, as distant from our cities as circumstances will permit, they will form the only points of attack, and the enemy will be detained there by a small regular force a sufficient time to enable our militia to collect and repair to that on which the attack is made. A force adequate to the enemy, collected at that single point, with suitable preparation for such others as might be menaced, is all that would be requisite. But if there were no fortifications, then the enemy might go where he pleased, and, changing his position and sailing from place to place, our force must be called out and spread in vast numbers along the whole coast and on both sides of every bay and river as high up in each as it might be navigable for ships of war. By these fortifications, supported by our Navy, to which they would afford like support, we should present to other powers an armed front from St. Croix to the Sabine, which would protect in the event of war our whole coast and interior from invasion; and even in the wars of other powers, in which we were neutral, they would be found eminently useful, as, by keeping their public ships at a distance from our cities, peace and order in them would be preserved and the Government be protected from insult.

It need scarcely be remarked that these measures have not been resorted to in a spirit of hostility to other powers. Such a disposition does not exist toward any power. Peace and good will have been, and will hereafter be, cultivated with all, and by the most faithful regard to justice. They have been dictated by a love of peace, of economy, and an earnest desire to save the lives of our fellow-citizens from that destruction and our country from that devastation which are inseparable from war when it finds us unprepared for it. It is believed, and experience has shown, that such a preparation is the best expedient that can be resorted to prevent war. I add with much pleasure that considerable progress has already been made in these measures of defense, and that they will be completed in a few years, considering the great extent and importance of the object, if the plan be zealously and steadily persevered in.

The conduct of the Government in what relates to foreign powers is always an object of the highest importance to the nation. Its agriculture, commerce, manufactures, fisheries, revenue, in short, its peace, may all be affected by it. Attention is therefore due to this subject.

At the period adverted to the powers of Europe, after having been engaged in long and destructive wars with each other, had concluded a peace, which happily still exists. Our peace with the power with whom we had been engaged had also been concluded. The war between Spain and the colonies in South America, which had commenced many years before, was then the only conflict that remained unsettled. This being a contest between different parts of the same community, in which other powers had not interfered, was not affected by their accommodations.

This contest was considered at an early stage by my predecessor a civil war in which the parties were entitled to equal rights in our ports. This decision, the first made by any power, being formed on great consideration of the comparative strength and resources of the parties, the length of time, and successful opposition made by the colonies, and of all other circumstances on which it ought to depend, was in strict accord with the law of nations. Congress has invariably acted on this principle, having made no change in our relations with either party. Our attitude has therefore been that of neutrality between them, which has been maintained by the Government with the strictest impartiality. No aid has been afforded to either, nor has any privilege been enjoyed by the one which has not been equally open to the other party, and every exertion has been made in its power to enforce the execution of the laws prohibiting illegal equipments with equal rigor against both.

By this equality between the parties their public vessels have been received in our ports on the same footing; they have enjoyed an equal right to purchase and export arms, munitions of war, and every other supply, the exportation of all articles whatever being permitted under laws which were passed long before the commencement of the contest; our citizens have traded equally with both, and their commerce with each has been alike protected by the Government.

Respecting the attitude which it may be proper for the United States to maintain hereafter between the parties, I have no hesitation in stating it as my opinion that the neutrality heretofore observed should still be adhered to. From the change in the Government of Spain and the negotiation now depending, invited by the Cortes and accepted by the colonies, it may be presumed, that their differences will be settled on the terms proposed by the colonies. Should the war be continued, the United States, regarding its occurrences, will always have it in their power to adopt such measures respecting it as their honor and interest may require.

Shortly after the general peace a band of adventurers took advantage of this conflict and of the facility which it afforded to establish a system of buccaneering in the neighboring seas, to the great annoyance of the commerce of the United States, and, as was represented, of that of other powers. Of this spirit and of its injurious bearing on the United States strong proofs were afforded by the establishment at Amelia Island, and the purposes to which it was made instrumental by this band in 1817, and by the occurrences which took place in other parts of Florida in 1818, the details of which in both instances are too well known to require to be now recited. I am satisfied had a less decisive course been adopted that the worst consequences would have resulted from it. We have seen that these checks, decisive as they were, were not sufficient to crush that piratical spirit. Many culprits brought within our limits have been condemned to suffer death, the punishment due to that atrocious crime. The decisions of upright and enlightened tribunals fall equally on all whose crimes subject them, by a fair interpretation of the law, to its censure. It belongs to the Executive not to suffer the executions under these decisions to transcend the great purpose for which punishment is necessary. The full benefit of example being secured, policy as well as humanity equally forbids that they should be carried further. I have acted on this principle, pardoning those who appear to have been led astray by ignorance of the criminality of the acts they had committed, and suffering the law to take effect on those only in whose favor no extenuating circumstances could be urged.

Great confidence is entertained that the late treaty with Spain, which has been ratified by both the parties, and the ratifications whereof have been exchanged, has placed the relations of the two countries on a basis of permanent friendship. The provision made by it for such of our citizens as have claims on Spain of the character described will, it is presumed, be very satisfactory to them, and the boundary which is established between the territories of the parties westward of the Mississippi, heretofore in dispute, has, it is thought, been settled on conditions just and advantageous to both. But to the acquisition of Florida too much importance can not be attached. It secures to the United States a territory important in itself, and whose importance is much increased by its bearing on many of the highest interests of the Union. It opens to several of the neighboring States a free passage to the ocean, through the Province ceded, by several rivers, having their sources high up within their limits. It secures us against all future annoyance from powerful Indian tribes. It gives us several excellent harbors in the Gulf of Mexico for ships of war of the largest size. It covers by its position in the Gulf the Mississippi and other great waters within our extended limits, and thereby enables the United States to afford complete protection to the vast and very valuable productions of our whole Western country, which find a market through those streams.

By a treaty with the British Government, bearing date on the 20th of October, 1818, the convention regulating the commerce between the United States and Great Britain, concluded on the 3d of July, 1815, which was about expiring, was revived and continued for the term of ten years from the time of its expiration. By that treaty, also, the differences which had arisen under the treaty of Ghent respecting the right claimed by the United States for their citizens to take and cure fish on the coast of His Britannic Majesty's dominions in America, with other differences on important interests, were adjusted to the satisfaction of both parties. No agreement has yet been entered into respecting the commerce between the United States and the British dominions in the West Indies and on this continent. The restraints imposed on that commerce by Great Britain, and reciprocated by the United States on a principle of defense, continue still in force.

The negotiation with France for the regulation of the commercial relations between the two countries, which in the course of the last summer had been commenced at Paris, has since been transferred to this city, and will be pursued on the part of the United States in the spirit of conciliation, and with an earnest desire that it may terminate in an arrangement satisfactory to both parties.

Our relations with the Barbary Powers are preserved in the same state and by the same means that were employed when I came into this office. As early as 1801 it was found necessary to send a squadron into the Mediterranean for the protection of our commerce, and no period has intervened, a short term excepted, when it was thought advisable to withdraw it. The great interests which the United States have in the Pacific, in commerce and in the fisheries, have also made it necessary to maintain a naval force there. In disposing of this force in both instances the most effectual measures in our power have been taken, without interfering with its other duties, for the suppression of the slave trade and of piracy in the neighboring seas.

The situation of the United States in regard to their resources, the extent of their revenue, and the facility with which it is raised affords a most gratifying spectacle. The payment of nearly $67,000,000 of the public debt, with the great progress made in measures of defense and in other improvements of various kinds since the late war, are conclusive proofs of this extraordinary prosperity, especially when it is recollected that these expenditures have been defrayed without a burthen on the people, the direct tax and excise having been repealed soon after the conclusion of the late war, and the revenue applied to these great objects having been raised in a manner not to be felt. Our great resources therefore remain untouched for any purpose which may affect the vital interests of the nation. For all such purposes they are inexhaustible. They are more especially to be found in the virtue, patriotism, and intelligence of our fellow-citizens, and in the devotion with which they would yield up by any just measure of taxation all their property in support of the rights and honor of their country.

Under the present depression of prices, affecting all the productions of the country and every branch of industry, proceeding from causes explained on a former occasion, the revenue has considerably diminished, the effect of which has been to compel Congress either to abandon these great measures of defense or to resort to loans or internal taxes to supply the deficiency. On the presumption that this depression and the deficiency in the revenue arising from it would be temporary, loans were authorized for the demands of the last and present year. Anxious to relieve my fellow-citizens in 1817 from every burthen which could be dispensed with, and the state of the Treasury permitting it, I recommended the repeal of the internal taxes, knowing that such relief was then peculiarly necessary in consequence of the great exertions made in the late war. I made that recommendation under a pledge that should the public exigencies require a recurrence to them at any time while I remained in this trust, I would with equal promptitude perform the duty which would then be alike incumbent on me. By the experiment now making it will be seen by the next session of Congress whether the revenue shall have been so augmented as to be adequate to all these necessary purposes. Should the deficiency still continue, and especially should it be probable that it would be permanent, the course to be pursued appears to me to be obvious. I am satisfied that under certain circumstances loans may be resorted to with great advantage. I am equally well satisfied, as a general rule, that the demands of the current year, especially in time of peace, should be provided for by the revenue of that year.

I have never dreaded, nor have I ever shunned, in any situation in which I have been placed making appeals to the virtue and patriotism of my fellow-citizens, well knowing that they could never be made in vain, especially in times of great emergency or for purposes of high national importance. Independently of the exigency of the case, many considerations of great weight urge a policy having in view a provision of revenue to meet to a certain extent the demands of the nation, without relying altogether on the precarious resource of foreign commerce. I am satisfied that internal duties and excises, with corresponding imposts on foreign articles of the same kind, would, without imposing any serious burdens on the people, enhance the price of produce, promote our manufactures, and augment the revenue, at the same time that they made it more secure and permanent.

The care of the Indian tribes within our limits has long been an essential part of our system, but, unfortunately, it has not been executed in a manner to accomplish all the objects intended by it. We have treated them as independent nations, without their having any substantial pretensions to that rank. The distinction has flattered their pride, retarded their improvement, and in many instances paved the way to their destruction. The progress of our settlements westward, supported as they are by a dense population, has constantly driven them back, with almost the total sacrifice of the lands which they have been compelled to abandon. They have claims on the magnanimity and, I may add, on the justice of this nation which we must all feel. We should become their real benefactors; we should perform the office of their Great Father, the endearing title which they emphatically give to the Chief Magistrate of our Union. Their sovereignty over vast territories should cease, in lieu of which the right of soil should be secured to each individual and his posterity in competent portions; and for the territory thus ceded by each tribe some reasonable equivalent should be granted, to be vested in permanent funds for the support of civil government over them and for the education of their children, for their instruction in the arts of husbandry, and to provide sustenance for them until they could provide it for themselves. My earnest hope is that Congress will digest some plan, founded on these principles, with such improvements as their wisdom may suggest, and carry it into effect as soon as it may be practicable.

Europe is again unsettled and the prospect of war increasing. Should the flame light up in any quarter, how far it may extend it is impossible to foresee. It is our peculiar felicity to be altogether unconnected with the causes which produce this menacing aspect elsewhere. With every power we are in perfect amity, and it is our interest to remain so if it be practicable on just conditions. I see no reasonable cause to apprehend variance with any power, unless it proceed from a violation of our maritime rights. In these contests, should they occur, and to whatever extent they may be carried, we shall be neutral; but as a neutral power we have rights which it is our duty to maintain. For like injuries it will be incumbent on us to seek redress in a spirit of amity, in full confidence that, injuring none, none would knowingly injure us. For more imminent dangers we should be prepared, and it should always be recollected that such preparation adapted to the circumstances and sanctioned by the judgment and wishes of our constituents can not fail to have a good effect in averting dangers of every kind. We should recollect also that the season of peace is best adapted to these preparations.

If we turn our attention, fellow-citizens, more immediately to the internal concerns of our country, and more especially to those on which its future welfare depends, we have every reason to anticipate the happiest results. It is now rather more than forty-four years since we declared our independence, and thirty-seven since it was acknowledged. The talents and virtues which were displayed in that great struggle were a sure presage of all that has since followed. A people who were able to surmount in their infant state such great perils would be more competent as they rose into manhood to repel any which they might meet in their progress. Their physical strength would be more adequate to foreign danger, and the practice of self-government, aided by the light of experience, could not fail to produce an effect equally salutary on all those questions connected with the internal organization. These favorable anticipations have been realized.

In our whole system, national and State, we have shunned all the defects which unceasingly preyed on the vitals and destroyed the ancient Republics. In them there were distinct orders, a nobility and a people, or the people governed in one assembly. Thus, in the one instance there was a perpetual conflict between the orders in society for the ascendency, in which the victory of either terminated in the overthrow of the government and the ruin of the state; in the other, in which the people governed in a body, and whose dominions seldom exceeded the dimensions of a county in one of our States, a tumultuous and disorderly movement permitted only a transitory existence. In this great nation there is but one order, that of the people, whose power, by a peculiarly happy improvement of the representative principle, is transferred from them, without impairing in the slightest degree their sovereignty, to bodies of their own creation, and to persons elected by themselves, in the full extent necessary for all the purposes of free, enlightened and efficient government. The whole system is elective, the complete sovereignty being in the people, and every officer in every department deriving his authority from and being responsible to them for his conduct.

Our career has corresponded with this great outline. Perfection in our organization could not have been expected in the outset either in the National or State Governments or in tracing the line between their respective powers. But no serious conflict has arisen, nor any contest but such as are managed by argument and by a fair appeal to the good sense of the people, and many of the defects which experience had clearly demonstrated in both Governments have been remedied. By steadily pursuing this course in this spirit there is every reason to believe that our system will soon attain the highest degree of perfection of which human institutions are capable, and that the movement in all its branches will exhibit such a degree of order and harmony as to command the admiration and respect of the civilized world.

Our physical attainments have not been less eminent. Twenty-five years ago the river Mississippi was shut up and our Western brethren had no outlet for their commerce. What has been the progress since that time? The river has not only become the property of the United States from its source to the ocean, with all its tributary streams (with the exception of the upper part of the Red River only), but Louisiana, with a fair and liberal boundary on the western side and the Floridas on the eastern, have been ceded to us. The United States now enjoy the complete and uninterrupted sovereignty over the whole territory from St. Croix to the Sabine. New States, settled from among ourselves in this and in other parts, have been admitted into our Union in equal participation in the national sovereignty with the original States. Our population has augmented in an astonishing degree and extended in every direction. We now, fellow-citizens, comprise within our limits the dimensions and faculties of a great power under a Government possessing all the energies of any government ever known to the Old World, with an utter incapacity to oppress the people.

Entering with these views the office which I have just solemnly sworn to execute with fidelity and to the utmost of my ability, I derive great satisfaction from a knowledge that I shall be assisted in the several Departments by the very enlightened and upright citizens from whom I have received so much aid in the preceding term. With full confidence in the continuance of that candor and generous indulgence from my fellow-citizens at large which I have heretofore experienced, and with a firm reliance on the protection of Almighty God, I shall forthwith commence the duties of the high trust to which you have called me.

The Last Cocked Hat

THE SECOND INAUGURAL ADDRESS OF JAMES MONROE

Sandra Moats

JAMES MONROE'S SECOND inauguration as president in 1821 proved to be unusual in several respects. With the congressionally mandated date of March 4th falling on a Sunday, Monroe delayed his inauguration until Monday, March 5, in deference to religious observances. (The inaugurations of 1849, 1877, and 1917 also occurred on March 5 for the same reason.) Monroe's path to a second term was even more remarkable: he ran unopposed, the only president other than George Washington to enjoy such a distinction. His lack of a presidential opponent underscored the political crossroads the nation confronted in 1820. The once robust Federalist party no longer enjoyed a national following. Meanwhile, younger members of Monroe's Democratic-Republican party, lacking the stature and prominence of the founding generation, waited in the wings for their shot at the presidency. Monroe's Second Inaugural Address anticipated this political watershed as he reviewed his first-term accomplishments and largely avoided making bold policy pronouncements for the future.

Speaking to his "Fellow Citizens," Monroe began his Inaugural Address by situating his presidency within the larger context of the republican ideas and the sovereign citizens whose "confidence" made his second term possible. He reminded his audience that the American government was "founded by the people, who possess exclusively the sovereignty." He also honored his presidential predecessors, "whose names are so much more conspicuously identified with our Revolution." Instead, Monroe saw himself "rather as the instrument than the cause of the union." He renewed his commitment to the United States' founding principles of "liberty, prosperity, and happiness." With the nation's sovereign citizens entrusting Monroe with a second term as president, he believed he owed his "constituents" a "review" of the "principal occurrences" of his first term and "further explanation" of his "judgment." This overview guided the content and organization of his 1821 Inaugural Address.

As Monroe discussed his first-term accomplishments and their future ramifications, he emphasized foreign affairs. He explained to his audience: "The conduct of the Government ... to foreign powers is an always an object of the highest importance to the nation." Other issues such as the nation's "agriculture, commerce, manufactures, fisheries, revenue, in short, its peace, may all be affected by it." For this reason, "attention is therefore due to this subject" of international affairs.

Of course, the most significant issue in foreign affairs was the recently concluded War of 1812 with Great Britain. Trading disputes in the Atlantic, particularly British impressment of American sailors, provided the principal motivation for this war. Monroe reminded his audience that "the events of that war are too recent and too deeply impressed on the memory of all to require a development from me." Instead, Monroe focused on the war's hefty price tag of $120 million, as well as the lessons from the war: the need to build fortifications to defend the nation's Atlantic coastline and to raise a navy capable of supporting and protecting these military facilities. With these defenses being constructed, Monroe also reported that more than half of the war debt, about $67 million, had been paid.

Monroe then turned his attention to the warfare occurring between Spain and its colonies in South America. Despite the geographical proximity of these conflicts to the United States, Monroe reiterated that these disputes were "a contest between different parts of the same community" and did not concern the United States. Instead, he renewed the nation's long-standing commitment to neutrality, an approach that had begun with George Washington's Neutrality Proclamation of 1793. American neutrality emphasized friendly trading relations with all nations, even those at war, along with a steadfast avoidance of political or diplomatic alliances that would entangle the United States in unnecessary warfare. Monroe explained how this principle worked in practice: "by this equality between the parties their public vessels have been received in our ports on the same footing; they have enjoyed an equal right to purchase and export arms, munitions of war, and every other supply ... permitted under laws." Nonetheless, Monroe left open the possibility "to adopt such measures" as needed, if the warfare in South America continued.

Closer to home, Monroe discussed the unauthorized invasion of Spanish Florida by a "band of adventurers" in 1817–1818. Known officially as the First Seminole War, General Andrew Jackson had led this assault against Spanish authorities, Florida's Seminole tribe, and even two British officers. Despite the diplomatic embarrassment of Jackson's escapades, his successful attack exposed Spain's weaknesses in Florida (and elsewhere) and paved the way for the Transcontinental Treaty of 1819. Although Monroe did not mention Jackson by name in his Inaugural Address, he did highlight the importance of the 1819 treaty: "Great confidence is entertained that the late treaty with Spain . . . has placed the relations of the two countries on a basis of permanent friendship." This landmark treaty resulted in the legal acquisition of Florida as well as a clarification of the nation's western boundary along the vast Louisiana territory, acquired from France in 1803. In 1818, the United States had also concluded a treaty with Britain affirming the northern boundary of the United States at the 49th parallel.

As he discussed the state of European affairs in 1821, Monroe could not have seen that the Napoleonic Wars between Britain and France during the 1810s, as well as Spain's attenuation as a power, would produce an important diplomatic opportunity for the United States. Nonetheless, several years later, Monroe and his able secretary of state, John Quincy Adams, recognized a diplomatic opportunity and issued the landmark "Monroe Doctrine" in 1823. A bold statement of solidarity between the United States and its "sister republics" in South America, the Monroe Doctrine declared that the Western Hemisphere was closed to further European colonization. And despite an official stance of neutrality, the United States would view any new colonial encroachments as a threat to its well-being.

Although receiving much less attention than foreign affairs, Monroe's Inaugural Address highlighted two domestic issues. One was the economic downturn known as the Panic of 1819, in which Americans experienced the loss of jobs, homes, and lands. To alleviate the financial burden on struggling Americans, Monroe had recommended the lowering of taxes. The second domestic issue concerned Native Americans and, unlike other parts of the address, represented a dramatic change in policy rather than a reflection of past accomplishments. Monroe explained: "We have treated them as independent nations, without their having any substantial pretensions to that rank." Instead, he recommended "the education of their children, for their instruction in the arts of husbandry [farming], and to provide sustenance for them until they could provide it themselves." In recommending that Congress consider these proposals, Monroe was advocating what would become known as an "assimilationist" approach. Notably absent from his discussion of domestic matters was the Missouri controversy of 1819–1820, in which this territory hoped to become the nation's twelfth slave state. Although the Missouri Compromise of 1820 resolved this crisis, the specter of slavery threatened the delicate compromises that held the young republic together.

Generally regarded as the last of the "founding father" presidents, Monroe had no obvious successor. Although a younger generation eagerly sought the reins of power, none of them possessed the national following or stature of the nation's first five presidents. Without a revolutionary war to fight or a republican government to build, younger politicians such as Andrew Jackson, Henry Clay, and William Crawford would need to find new ways to distinguish themselves. Not surprisingly, the election to succeed Monroe ended inconclusively, with none of the four candidates receiving enough electoral votes to be elected outright. The 1824 election was resolved in the U.S. Congress through a compromise that resulted in John Quincy Adams, the son of a "founding father," becoming the nation's sixth president. Over the next decade, a new set of political parties would be established to support a new group of politicians and a new style of politics. As the nation inaugurated Adams on March 4, 1825, they also said goodbye to a president whose career and achievements embodied the nation's founding era.

John Quincy Adams's Inaugural Address

FRIDAY, MARCH 4, 1825

IN COMPLIANCE WITH an usage coeval with the existence of our Federal Constitution, and sanctioned by the example of my predecessors in the career upon which I am about to enter, I appear, my fellow-citizens, in your presence and in that of Heaven to bind myself by the solemnities of religious obligation to the faithful performance of the duties allotted to me in the station to which I have been called.

In unfolding to my countrymen the principles by which I shall be governed in the fulfillment of those duties my first resort will be to that Constitution which I shall swear to the best of my ability to preserve, protect, and defend. That revered instrument enumerates the powers and prescribes the duties of the Executive Magistrate, and in its first words declares the purposes to which these and the whole action of the Government instituted by it should be invariably and sacredly devoted—to form a more perfect union, establish justice, insure domestic tranquillity, provide for the common defense, promote the general welfare, and secure the blessings of liberty to the people of this Union in their successive generations. Since the adoption of this social compact one of these generations has passed away. It is the work of our forefathers. Administered by some of the most eminent men who contributed to its formation, through a most eventful period in the annals of the world, and through all the vicissitudes of peace and war incidental to the condition of associated man, it has not disappointed the hopes and aspirations of those illustrious benefactors of their age and nation. It has promoted the lasting welfare of that country so dear to us all; it has to an extent far beyond the ordinary lot of humanity secured the freedom and happiness of this people. We now receive it as a precious inheritance from those to whom we are indebted for its establishment, doubly bound by the examples which they have left us and by the blessings which we have enjoyed as the fruits of their labors to transmit the same unimpaired to the succeeding generation.

In the compass of thirty-six years since this great national covenant was instituted a body of laws enacted under its authority and in conformity with its provisions has unfolded its powers and carried into practical operation its effective energies. Subordinate departments have distributed the executive functions in their various relations to foreign affairs, to the revenue and expenditures, and to the military force of the Union by land and sea. A coordinate department of the judiciary has expounded the Constitution and the laws, settling in harmonious coincidence with the legislative will numerous weighty questions of construction which the imperfection of human language had rendered unavoidable. The year of jubilee since the first formation of our Union has just elapsed; that of the declaration of our independence is at hand. The consummation of both was effected by this Constitution.

Since that period a population of four millions has multiplied to twelve. A territory bounded by the Mississippi has been extended from sea to sea. New States have been admitted to the Union in numbers nearly equal to those of the first Confederation. Treaties of peace, amity, and commerce have been concluded with the principal dominions of the earth. The people of other nations, inhabitants of regions acquired not by conquest, but by compact, have been united with us in the participation of our rights and duties, of our burdens and blessings. The forest has fallen by the ax of our woodsmen; the soil has been made to teem by the tillage of our farmers; our commerce has whitened every ocean. The dominion of man over physical nature has been extended by the invention of our artists. Liberty and law have marched hand in hand. All the purposes of human association have been accomplished as effectively as under any other government on the globe, and at a cost little exceeding in a whole generation the expenditure of other nations in a single year.

Such is the unexaggerated picture of our condition under a Constitution founded upon the republican principle of equal rights. To admit that this picture has its shades is but to say that it is still the condition of men upon earth. From evil—physical, moral, and political—it is not our claim to be exempt. We have suffered sometimes by the visitation of Heaven through disease; often by the wrongs and injustice of other nations, even to the extremities of war; and, lastly, by dissensions among ourselves—dissensions perhaps inseparable from the enjoyment of freedom, but which have more than once appeared to threaten the dissolution of the Union, and with it the overthrow of all the enjoyments of our present lot and all our earthly hopes of the future. The causes of these dissensions have been various, founded upon differences of speculation in the theory of republican government; upon conflicting views of policy in our relations with foreign nations; upon jealousies of partial and sectional interests, aggravated by prejudices and prepossessions which strangers to each other are ever apt to entertain.

It is a source of gratification and of encouragement to me to observe that the great result of this experiment upon the theory of human rights has at the close of that generation by which it was formed been crowned with success equal to the most sanguine expectations of its founders. Union, justice, tranquillity, the common defense, the general welfare, and the blessings of liberty—all have been promoted by the Government under which we have lived. Standing at this point of time, looking back to that generation which has gone by and forward to that which is advancing, we may at once indulge in grateful exultation and in cheering hope. From the experience of the past we derive instructive lessons for the future. Of the two great political parties which have divided the opinions and feelings of our country, the candid and the just will now admit that both have contributed splendid talents, spotless integrity, ardent patriotism, and disinterested sacrifices to the formation and administration of this Government, and that both have required a liberal indulgence for a portion of human infirmity and error. The revolutionary wars of Europe, commencing precisely at the moment when the Government of the United States first went into operation under this Constitution, excited a collision of sentiments and of sympathies which kindled all the passions and imbittered the conflict of parties till the nation was involved in war and the Union was shaken to its center. This time of trial embraced a period of five and twenty years, during which the policy of the Union in its relations with Europe constituted the principal basis of our political divisions and the most arduous part of the action of our Federal Government. With the catastrophe in which the wars of the French Revolution terminated, and our own subsequent peace with Great Britain, this baneful weed of party strife was uprooted. From that time no difference of principle, connected either with the theory of government or with our intercourse with foreign nations, has existed or been called forth in force sufficient to sustain a continued combination of parties or to give more than wholesome animation to public sentiment or legislative debate. Our political creed is, without a dissenting voice that can be heard, that the will of the people is the source and the happiness of the people the end of all legitimate government upon earth; that the best security for the beneficence and the best guaranty against the abuse of power consists in the freedom, the purity, and the frequency of popular elections; that the General Government of the Union and the separate governments of the States are all sovereignties of limited powers, fellow-servants of the same masters, uncontrolled within their respective spheres, uncontrollable by encroachments upon each other; that the firmest security of peace is the preparation during peace of the defenses of war; that a rigorous economy and accountability of public expenditures should guard against the aggravation and alleviate when possible the burden of taxation; that the military should be kept in strict subordination to the civil power; that the freedom of the press and of religious opinion should be inviolate; that the policy of our country is peace and the ark of our salvation union are articles of faith upon which we are all now agreed. If there have been those who doubted whether a confederated representative democracy were a government competent to the wise and orderly management of the common concerns of a mighty nation, those doubts have been dispelled; if there have been projects of partial confederacies to be erected upon the ruins of the Union, they have been scattered to the winds; if there have been dangerous attachments to one foreign nation and antipathies against another, they have been extinguished. Ten years of peace, at home and abroad, have assuaged the animosities of political contention and blended into harmony the most discordant elements of public opinion. There still remains one effort of magnanimity, one sacrifice of prejudice and passion, to be made by the individuals throughout the nation who have heretofore followed the standards of political party. It is that of discarding every remnant of rancor against each other, of embracing as countrymen and friends, and of yielding to talents and virtue alone that confidence which in times of contention for principle was bestowed only upon those who bore the badge of party communion.

The collisions of party spirit which originate in speculative opinions or in different views of administrative policy are in their nature transitory. Those which are founded on geographical divisions, adverse interests of soil, climate, and modes of domestic life are more permanent, and therefore, perhaps, more dangerous. It is this which gives inestimable value to the character of our Government, at once federal and national. It holds out to us a perpetual admonition to preserve alike and with equal anxiety the rights of each individual State in its own government and the rights of the whole nation in that of the Union. Whatsoever is of domestic concernment, unconnected with the other members of the Union or with foreign lands, belongs exclusively to the administration of the State governments. Whatsoever directly involves the rights and interests of the federative fraternity or of foreign powers is of the resort of this General Government. The duties of both are obvious in the general principle, though sometimes perplexed with difficulties in the detail. To respect the rights of the State governments is the inviolable duty of that of the Union; the government of every State will feel its own obligation to respect and preserve the rights of the whole. The prejudices everywhere too commonly entertained against distant strangers are worn away, and the jealousies of jarring interests are allayed by the composition and functions of the great national councils annually assembled from all quarters of the Union at this place. Here the distinguished men from every section of our country, while meeting to deliberate upon the great interests of those by whom they are deputed, learn to estimate the talents and do justice to the virtues of each other. The harmony of the nation is promoted and the whole Union is knit together by the sentiments of mutual respect, the habits of social intercourse, and the ties of personal friendship formed between the representatives of its several parts in the performance of their service at this metropolis.

Passing from this general review of the purposes and injunctions of the Federal Constitution and their results as indicating the first traces of the path of duty in the discharge of my public trust, I turn to the Administration of my immediate predecessor as the second. It has passed away in a period of profound peace, how much to the satisfaction of our country and to the honor of our country's name is known to you all. The great features of its policy, in general concurrence with the will of the Legislature, have been to cherish peace while preparing for defensive war; to yield exact justice to other nations and maintain the rights of our own; to cherish the principles of freedom and of equal rights wherever they were proclaimed; to discharge with all possible promptitude the national debt; to reduce within the narrowest limits of efficiency the military force; to improve the organization and discipline of the Army; to provide and sustain a school of military science; to extend equal protection to all the great interests of the nation; to promote the civilization of the Indian tribes, and to proceed in the great system of internal improvements within the limits of the constitutional power of the Union. Under the pledge of these promises, made by that eminent citizen at the time of his first induction to this office, in his career of eight years the internal taxes have been repealed; sixty millions of the public debt have been discharged; provision has been made for the comfort and relief of the aged and indigent among the surviving warriors of the Revolution; the regular armed force has been reduced and its constitution revised and perfected; the accountability for the expenditure of public moneys has been made more effective; the Floridas have been peaceably acquired, and our boundary has been extended to the Pacific Ocean; the independence of the southern nations of this hemisphere has been recognized, and recommended by example and by counsel to the potentates of Europe; progress has been made in the defense of the country by fortifications and the increase of the Navy, toward the effectual suppression of the African traffic in slaves, in alluring the aboriginal hunters of our land to the cultivation of the soil and of the mind, in exploring the interior regions of the Union, and in preparing by scientific researches and surveys for the further application of our national resources to the internal improvement of our country.

In this brief outline of the promise and performance of my immediate predecessor the line of duty for his successor is clearly delineated. To pursue to their consummation those purposes of improvement in our common condition instituted or recommended by him will embrace the whole sphere of my obligations. To the topic of internal improvement, emphatically urged by him at his inauguration, I recur with peculiar satisfaction. It is that from which I am convinced that the unborn millions of our posterity who are in future ages to people this continent will derive their most fervent gratitude to the founders of the Union; that in which the beneficent action of its Government will be most deeply felt and acknowledged. The magnificence and splendor of their public works are among the imperishable glories of the ancient republics. The roads and aqueducts of Rome have been the admiration of all after ages, and have survived thousands of years after all her conquests have been swallowed up in despotism or become the spoil of barbarians. Some diversity of opinion has prevailed with regard to the powers of Congress for legislation upon objects of this nature. The most respectful deference is due to doubts originating in pure patriotism and sustained by venerated authority. But nearly twenty years have passed since the construction of the first national road was commenced. The authority for its construction was then unquestioned. To how many thousands of our countrymen has it proved a benefit? To what single individual has it ever proved an injury? Repeated, liberal, and candid discussions in the Legislature have conciliated the sentiments and approximated the opinions of enlightened minds upon the question of constitutional power. I can not but hope that by the same process of friendly, patient, and persevering deliberation all constitutional objections will ultimately be removed. The extent and limitation of the powers of the General Government in relation to this transcendently important interest will be settled and acknowledged to the common satisfaction of all, and every speculative scruple will be solved by a practical public blessing.

Fellow-citizens, you are acquainted with the peculiar circumstances of the recent election, which have resulted in affording me the opportunity of addressing you at this time. You have heard the exposition of the principles which will direct me in the fulfillment of the high and solemn trust imposed upon me in this station. Less possessed of your confidence in advance than any of my predecessors, I am deeply conscious of the prospect that I shall stand more and oftener in need of your indulgence. Intentions upright and pure, a heart devoted to the welfare of our country, and the unceasing application of all the faculties allotted to me to her service are all the pledges that I can give for the faithful performance of the arduous duties I am to undertake. To the guidance of the legislative councils, to the assistance of the executive and subordinate departments, to the friendly cooperation of the respective State governments, to the candid and liberal support of the people so far as it may be deserved by honest industry and zeal, I shall look for whatever success may attend my public service; and knowing that "except the Lord keep the city the watchman waketh but in vain," with fervent supplications for His favor, to His overruling providence I commit with humble but fearless confidence my own fate and the future destinies of my country.

The Corrupt Bargain

THE INAUGURAL ADDRESS OF JOHN QUINCY ADAMS

C. James Taylor

NO PERSON CAME to the presidency with a better resume then John Quincy Adams. A native of Massachusetts, like his father, President John Adams, he was a nationalist. He spent most of his adult life in public service, as a senator, a diplomat in several European capitals, and as secretary of state for almost eight years. In his limited time as a private citizen he practiced law and held a professorship at Harvard. Adams enjoyed lifelong interests in education, science, and the arts. The presidency, the ultimate capstone for most American political careers, proved to be merely an interlude for him. After a brief post-presidential sabbatical, he returned to public life as a congressman.

Adams carefully prepared his Inaugural Address and sent a copy to the press two days before the event. Late on the eve of his inauguration, he received and corrected the proof copy that would appear in a special edition of the *National Intelligencer* the next day. According to his diary, he had two sleepless nights before delivering the address. Adding to the natural anxiety of the day, his wife was ill. She did not attend the ceremony.

He launched the address with a brief overview of the growth and success of the nation since the ratification of the Constitution. A territory once bounded by the Mississippi River now "extended from sea to sea." The new lands were not taken through conquest, but acquired by treaty or purchase. Rather than subservient colonial status, the people in the new territories participated in the same rights and duties as citizens in the original states. Such was "our condition under a Constitution founded upon the republican principle of equal rights."

However, he noted that "From evil—physical, moral, and political—it is not our claim to be exempt." Almost at the moment of its founding, the nation suffered "a collision of sentiments and sympathies which kindled all the passions and imbittered the conflict of parties." Sectional differences and disagreements over the proper response to the French Revolution and subsequent European wars created a twenty-five-year period of political unrest, which ended with the War of 1812 and the presidency of James Monroe. Now that political calm seemed to have returned, Adams didn't use the popular term "Era of Good Feelings," but did recognize that "this baneful weed of party strife was uprooted." Understanding what had brought the country to this relatively tranquil point, Americans could "indulge in grateful exultation and in cheering hope."

He reviewed the "promise and performance" of the Monroe administration and stated that "to pursue their consummation . . . will embrace the whole sphere of my obligations." In foreign affairs, he highlighted the peaceful expansion of the national boundaries and recognition of the independence of countries in the Southern Hemisphere from European colonial control. In the domestic realm he listed reduction of the national debt, reorganization of the postwar army, improvements in the nation's fortifications and navy, suppression of the African slave trade, and the encouragement of the Native American population to evolve from hunters to farmers as accomplishments during Monroe's two terms. Internal improvements "emphatically urged by him [Monroe] at his inauguration" but still lagging were the issue Adams embraced in his address. He acknowledged that "some diversity of opinion has prevailed with regard to the powers of Congress for legislation upon subjects of this nature." He offered "the most respectful deference" to those who held constitutional objections to federally funded internal improvements. But the benefits of these public works, he predicted, would mean that "all constitutional objections will ultimately be removed." He offered Roman roads and aqueducts as examples of the lasting importance of a nation's investment in internal improvements. As a nationalist, he noted that interstate communication and transportation would be essential elements in reducing sectionalism.

He concluded the address by recognizing that he owed his position to "the peculiar circumstances of the recent election." He had finished second to Andrew Jackson in both the popular and electoral votes. Because the vote was divided among four candidates, no one received the necessary majority and the decision fell to the House of Representatives, where Adams emerged the victor. In the days leading to the vote in the House, he received warnings and threats of organized opposition and even civil war if Jackson failed to gain the majority, according to his diary entry of January 29, 1825. After the vote, Jackson supporters condemned the apparent collusion between Adams and the fourth-place finisher, Henry Clay, as a "corrupt bargain." Adams appealed to his auditors that "less possessed of your confidence in advance than any of my predecessors," he needed their "indulgence."

The address for the most part sought recognition of the Americans' common history and recent apparent tranquility during the Monroe administration. By extolling the nation's founders, "those illustrious benefactors of their age," he appealed to all the people. The address was conciliatory and suited to the moment. He would attempt to avoid all sectional and partisan conflict. In this he would fail. A second party system would evolve during his administration. Where he did succeed, at least moderately, was in pushing forward with the internal improvements. However, his commitment to internal improvements further angered the Jacksonians and intensified the growing partisanship.

If Adams had been elected with less controversy, the address certainly would have been more forceful and specific. His December 6, 1825, annual address to Congress is more often cited and recognized as representative of his vision for the nation. Among other things, he called for additional reciprocal agreements with European countries to improve commerce. He noted that the United States had accepted an invitation to a congress of American countries to be held in Central America. He listed advances being made in "surveying, marking and laying out roads" throughout the states and territories, including a continuation of the Cumberland road. In this address Adams called for a national university, a national astronomical observatory, and government-supported exploration of the Northwest coast. The partisan animosity that grew out of the contested election and caused him to be cautious in his Inaugural Address never subsided during his term.

Andrew Jackson's First Inaugural Address

WEDNESDAY, MARCH 4, 1829

FELLOW-CITIZENS:

About to undertake the arduous duties that I have been appointed to perform by the choice of a free people, I avail myself of this customary and solemn occasion to express the gratitude which their confidence inspires and to acknowledge the accountability which my situation enjoins. While the magnitude of their interests convinces me that no thanks can be adequate to the honor they have conferred, it admonishes me that the best return I can make is the zealous dedication of my humble abilities to their service and their good.

As the instrument of the Federal Constitution it will devolve on me for a stated period to execute the laws of the United States, to superintend their foreign and their confederate relations, to manage their revenue, to command their forces, and, by communications to the Legislature, to watch over and to promote their interests generally. And the principles of action by which I shall endeavor to accomplish this circle of duties it is now proper for me briefly to explain.

In administering the laws of Congress I shall keep steadily in view the limitations as well as the extent of the Executive power, trusting thereby to discharge the functions of my office without transcending its authority. With foreign nations it will be my study to preserve peace and to cultivate friendship on fair and honorable terms, and in the adjustment of any differences that may exist or arise to exhibit the forbearance becoming a powerful nation rather than the sensibility belonging to a gallant people.

In such measures as I may be called on to pursue in regard to the rights of the separate States I hope to be animated by a proper respect for those sovereign members of our Union, taking care not to confound the powers they have reserved to themselves with those they have granted to the Confederacy.

The management of the public revenue—that searching operation in all governments—is among the most delicate and important trusts in ours, and it will, of course, demand no inconsiderable share of my official solicitude. Under every aspect in which it can be considered it would appear that advantage must result from the observance of a strict and faithful economy. This I shall aim at the more anxiously both because it will facilitate the extinguishment of the national debt, the unnecessary duration of which is incompatible with real independence, and because it will counteract that tendency to public and private profligacy which a profuse expenditure of money by the Government is but too apt to engender. Powerful auxiliaries to the attainment of this desirable end are to be found in the regulations provided by the wisdom of Congress for the specific appropriation of public money and the prompt accountability of public officers.

With regard to a proper selection of the subjects of impost with a view to revenue, it would seem to me that the spirit of equity, caution, and compromise in which the Constitution was formed requires that the great interests of agriculture, commerce, and manufactures should be equally favored, and that perhaps the only exception to this rule should consist in the peculiar encouragement of any products of either of them that may be found essential to our national independence.

Internal improvement and the diffusion of knowledge, so far as they can be promoted by the constitutional acts of the Federal Government, are of high importance.

Considering standing armies as dangerous to free governments in time of peace, I shall not seek to enlarge our present establishment, nor disregard that salutary lesson of political experience which teaches that the military should be held subordinate to the civil power. The gradual increase of our Navy, whose flag has displayed in distant climes our skill in navigation and our fame in arms; the preservation of our forts, arsenals, and dockyards, and the introduction of progressive improvements in the discipline and science of both branches of our military service are so plainly prescribed by prudence that I should be excused for omitting their mention sooner than for enlarging on their importance. But the bulwark of our defense is the national militia, which in the present state of our intelligence and population must render us invincible. As long as our Government is administered for the good of the people, and is regulated by their will; as long as it secures to us the rights of person and of property, liberty of conscience and of the press, it will be worth defending; and so long as it is worth defending a patriotic militia will cover it with an impenetrable aegis. Partial injuries and occasional mortifications we may be subjected to, but a million of armed freemen, possessed of the means of war, can never be conquered by a foreign foe. To any just system, therefore, calculated to strengthen this natural safeguard of the country I shall cheerfully lend all the aid in my power.

It will be my sincere and constant desire to observe toward the Indian tribes within our limits a just and liberal policy, and to give that humane and considerate attention to their rights and their wants which is consistent with the habits of our Government and the feelings of our people.

The recent demonstration of public sentiment inscribes on the list of Executive duties, in characters too legible to be overlooked, the task of *reform*, which will require particularly the correction of those abuses that have brought the patronage of the Federal Government into conflict with the freedom of elections, and the counteraction of those causes which have disturbed the rightful course of appointment and have placed or continued power in unfaithful or incompetent hands.

In the performance of a task thus generally delineated I shall endeavor to select men whose diligence and talents will insure in their respective stations able and faithful cooperation, depending for the advancement of the public service more on the integrity and zeal of the public officers than on their numbers.

A diffidence, perhaps too just, in my own qualifications will teach me to look with reverence to the examples of public virtue left by my illustrious predecessors, and with veneration to the lights that flow from the mind that founded and the mind that reformed our system. The same diffidence induces me to hope for instruction and aid from the coordinate branches of the Government, and for the indulgence and support of my fellow-citizens generally. And a firm reliance on the goodness of that Power whose providence mercifully protected our national infancy, and has since upheld our liberties in various vicissitudes, encourages me to offer up my ardent supplications that He will continue to make our beloved country the object of His divine care and gracious benediction.

Calm before the Storm

THE FIRST INAUGURAL ADDRESS OF ANDREW JACKSON

Harry L. Watson

SHORT, VAGUE, AND almost inaudible, Andrew Jackson's first Inaugural Address belied the general's stormy personality and the tumultuous path that took him to the White House in 1829. Humbly born and mostly self-taught, Jackson came to the presidency with a victorious military record but limited experience in civilian government and a vivid reputation for flouting established laws, procedures, and authorities. His winning presidential campaign had stirred an uproar of lies, distortions, and bitter recriminations, and his administration followed an equally stormy path that featured discharges of experienced civil servants, forced removal of American Indians, a threatened civil war with South Carolina, doom for a national transportation policy, a "Bank War" that destroyed the nation's largest financial institution, and a revival of cutthroat political partisanship. Nevertheless, Jackson betrayed few signs of these developments when he addressed the nation on March 4, 1829.

A Tennessee lawyer, planter, and frontier land speculator, Jackson became major general of the state militia and won national renown when his forces overwhelmed the British and the Creek Indians in the War of 1812. Postwar clashes with the federal judiciary and civilian Army leadership did nothing to dampen his reputation for decisive, winning action, and they paved the way for his first presidential run in 1824. In that contest, Jackson won the most votes against a field of prominent but unexciting figures from James Monroe's incumbent administration, but he still lacked the required majority. For the second time in the young republic's history, the House of Representatives had to choose a winner from the finalists.

Their choice had been John Quincy Adams, the second-place finisher and son of former president John Adams. Burdened by a chilly, distant personality, the younger Adams was a Harvard graduate and a former member of its faculty. He had grown up in foreign courts where his father served as a U.S. diplomat, and he ran on his distinguished record as the incumbent secretary of state. By contrast, established leaders scorned Jackson as a mere "military chieftain" with dictatorial potential but no polish, education, or civilian accomplishments. When Adams, the brilliant but privileged insider, seemed to pay for his victory by naming House Speaker Henry Clay as the next secretary of state, with an inside track to follow him as president, Washington exploded with charges of corruption. Incensed Jackson supporters denounced Washington schemers for violating "the will of the people" and vowed to vindicate democracy with a Jackson-Adams rematch four years later.

In keeping with Jackson's rough-hewn image, Adams elitism, and widespread resentment of the last election's outcome, Jackson's 1828 campaign embodied a populist spirit that glorified the ascendancy of ordinary white male Americans over the eighteenth-century Framers. Sadly, however, the campaign also revealed democracy's ugly side, with scurrilous demagogy on both sides and few policy debates. This time, Jackson reaped the benefits of calculated chaos, routed Adams, and drew massive crowds to Washington to celebrate his triumph. As he faced the throng who gathered to witness his oath-taking before the Capitol's East Portico, however, Jackson seems to have understood that calm reassurance might yield political benefits, and he sought to quiet fears that a frontier strongman might wreck the republic. Behind his bland platitudes, however, signs lurked of coming controversies.

Jackson began by thanking the American people for their trust, pledging his fidelity to their welfare, and offering to explain his guiding principles. First came a promise to respect the Constitution's limits and the rights of the states. It was a loaded pledge. John Quincy Adams had come to grief by calling for a vast program of federally funded "internal improvements," or roads, canals, and other expensive public works that defied public opinion and current interpretations of the Constitution. "Were we to slumber in indolence," he had asked, "or fold up our arms and proclaim to the world that we are palsied by the will of our constituents, would it not be to cast away the bounties of Providence and doom ourselves to perpetual inferiority?" In a single sentence, Adams thus tied a radical expansion of federal powers to fiscal extravagance, intellectual snobbery, disregard of the Constitution, and contempt for the democratic process. Rejoicing at the New Englander's blunder, Jacksonians gleefully swatted down his dreams and denounced them as extravagant and unconstitutional. Southern congressmen felt these concerns more than most. As recently as 1819 and 1820. Congress had nearly exploded over a proposal to ban slavery from the new state of Missouri, so any move to expand federal powers worried nervous slaveholders. Determined to preserve the brutal system of racial exploitation, one warned frankly, "if Congress can make canals, they can with more propriety emancipate."

Like other Southern leaders, Andrew Jackson was a very large slaveholder himself and would never tolerate attacks on the system. A promise to respect both the opportunities and limitations of executive power thus became the first substantive promise in his Inaugural Address, followed by support for states' rights. There was no hint that Jackson would eventually call himself "the sole representative of the American people," claiming a right to override Congress and confirming his enemies' worst fears of his dictatorial impulses.

The new president turned next to fiscal matters. Hoping to extinguish the national debt, he pledged "a strict and faithful economy" in public spending and then turned to the tricky subject of taxation. Ever since its creation, the federal government had depended on tariffs or import taxes as a major source of revenue. In addition, Northern states increasingly demanded high tariffs to give their nascent industries a price advantage over foreign competitors. Southerners vehemently opposed such plans, convinced that tariffs would only aid manufacturers at their expense since slavery supposedly prevented an industrial South. Eventually, South Carolina decided that using tariffs to favor one economic sector over another was unconstitutional and attempted to block the policy by "nullifying" or canceling the federal tariff within its borders. In 1832–1833, an infuriated Andrew Jackson would quash this violation of majority rule and his own authority, but he gave no warning at his inauguration. There he only favored protection for military suppliers and vowed to settle all other tariff disagreements through compromise. Jackson took a similar approach to internal improvements, President Adams's signature issue. He would later brand federal funding for most transportation projects as unconstitutional, but his Inaugural Address ducked this question and only acknowledged the "high importance" of internal improvements and education, *if* pursued by constitutional means.

As president, two of Jackson's most controversial policies were his stances on presidential appointments and on Native Americans, but here, too, he revealed little about these plans. Prefiguring modern attacks on the "deep state" and the Washington "swamp," Jackson had vowed an overhaul of the small federal bureaucracy, which was filled, he believed, with Adams supporters and corrupt incompetents. His address pledged unspecified reforms, which took the form of mass dismissals of suspected Adams supporters. Though Jackson promised replacements with "diligence and talents," he demanded their unshakable loyalty as well. The president called this policy "rotation in office" and saw it as a democratic improvement over long-term appointments. Ever since, others have condemned it as the "spoils system." Despite Jacksonian protests over alleged corruption by Adams and Clay, rewarding party activists with public office and using their help at re-election time became a fixture of nineteenth-century politics.

Regarding Indians, Jackson and his frontier supporters passionately coveted the fertile lands still occupied by Native peoples east of the Mississippi. At the time of his inauguration, the president was already planning to seize these territories and force the tribes westward, but he also kept these intentions quiet and only promised a "just and liberal" Indian policy. Jackson told himself that separation would benefit whites and Indians alike, but the death toll on the "Trail of Tears" would tell otherwise. Jackson also said nothing about his plans for the Bank of the United States, the nation's largest financial institution, but his later campaign to destroy it became the biggest controversy of his administration.

The new president concluded predictably by invoking God's blessing and the example of his predecessors. His Inaugural Address had hinted at disputes that lay ahead without revealing his intentions. In time, however, Andrew Jackson's policies became so controversial that his enemies formed an opposition political party to resist him, calling themselves the Whigs. Organized in the Democratic Party, the president's supporters fought them relentlessly to the eve of the Civil War, and American politics has featured two-party competition ever since. It became the most enduring legacy of Andrew Jackson's soothing Inaugural Address.

Andrew Jackson's Second Inaugural Address

MONDAY, MARCH 4, 1833

FELLOW-CITIZENS:

The will of the American people, expressed through their unsolicited suffrages, calls me before you to pass through the solemnities preparatory to taking upon myself the duties of President of the United States, for another term. For their approbation of my public conduct, through a period which has not been without its difficulties, and for this renewed expression of their confidence in my good intentions, I am at a loss for terms adequate to the expression of my gratitude. It shall be displayed, to the extent of my humble abilities, in continued efforts so to administer the Government, as to preserve their liberty and promote their happiness.

So many events have occurred within the last four years, which have necessarily called forth, sometimes under circumstances the most delicate and painful, my views of the principles and policy which ought to be pursued by the General Government, that I need, on this occasion, but allude to a few leading considerations, connected with some of them.

The foreign policy adopted by our Government soon after the formation of our present Constitution, and very generally pursued by successive administrations, has been crowned with almost complete success, and has elevated our character among the nations of the earth. To do justice to all, and submit to wrong from none, has been, during my administration, its governing maxim; and so happy has been its results, that we are not only at peace with all the world, but have few causes of controversy, and those of minor importance, remaining unadjusted.

In the domestic policy of this Government, there are two objects which especially deserve the attention of the people and their Representatives, and which have been, and will continue to be, the subjects of my increasing solicitude. They are the preservation of the rights of the several States, and the integrity of the Union.

These great objects are necessarily connected, and can only be attained by an enlightened exercise of the powers of each within its appropriate sphere, in conformity with the public will constitutionally expressed. To this end, it becomes the duty of all to yield a ready and patriotic submission to the laws constitutionally enacted, and thereby promote and strengthen a proper confidence in those institutions of the several States and of the United States which the people themselves have ordained for their own government.

My experience in public concerns, and the observation of a life somewhat advanced, confirm the opinions long since imbibed by me, that the destruction of our State governments or the annihilation of their control over the local concerns of the people, would lead directly to revolution and anarchy, and finally to despotism and military domination. In proportion, therefore, as the general government encroaches upon the rights of the States, in the same proportion does it impair its own power and detract from its ability to fulfil the purposes of its creation. Solemnly impressed with these considerations, my countrymen will ever find me ready to exercise my constitutional powers in arresting measures which may directly or indirectly encroach upon the rights of the States, or tend to consolidate all political power in the General Government.

But of equal, and indeed of incalculable importance is the union of these States, and the sacred duty of all to contribute to its preservation by a liberal support of the General Government in the exercise of its just powers. You have been wisely admonished to "accustom yourselves to think and speak of the Union as of the palladium of your political safety and prosperity, watching for its preservation with jealous anxiety, discountenancing whatever may suggest even a suspicion that it can in any event be abandoned, and indignantly frowning upon the first dawning of any attempt to alienate any portion of our country from the rest, or to enfeeble the sacred ties which now link together the various parts." Without union our independence and liberty would never have been achieved— without union they can never can be maintained. Divided into twenty-four, or even a smaller number of separate communities, we shall see our internal trade burdened with numberless restraints and exactions; communication between distant points and sections obstructed, or cut off; our sons made soldiers to deluge with blood the fields they now till in peace; the mass of our people borne down and impoverished by taxes to support armies and navies; and military leaders at the head of their victorious legions becoming our law-givers and judges. The loss of liberty, of all good government, of peace, plenty and happiness, must inevitably follow a dissolution of the Union. In supporting it, therefore, we support all that is dear to the freeman and the philanthropist.

The time at which I stand before you is full of interest. The eyes of all nations are fixed on our republic. The event of the existing crisis will be decisive in the opinion of mankind of the practicability of our federal system of government. Great is the stake placed in our hands: great is the responsibility which must rest upon the people of the United States. Let us realize the importance of the attitude in which we stand before the world. Let us exercise forbearance and firmness. Let us extricate our country from the dangers which surround it, and learn wisdom from the lessons they inculcate.

Deeply impressed with the truth of these observations, and under the obligation of that solemn oath which I am about to take, I shall continue to exert all my faculties to maintain the just powers of the Constitution, and to transmit unimpaired to posterity the blessings of our federal Union. At the same time, it will be my aim to inculcate by my official acts, the necessity of exercising, by the General Government, those powers only that are clearly delegated; to encourage simplicity and economy in the expenditures of the Government; to raise no more money from the people than may be requisite for these objects, and in a manner that will best promote the interests of all classes of the community, and of all portions of the Union. Constantly bearing in mind that, in entering into society "individuals must give up a share of liberty to preserve the rest," it will be my desire so to discharge my duties as to foster, with our brethren in all parts of the country, a spirit of liberal concession and compromise; and, by reconciling our fellow citizens to those partial sacrifices which they must unavoidably make, for the preservation of a greater good, to recommend our invaluable Government and Union to the confidence and affections of the American people.

Finally, it is my most fervent prayer, to that Almighty Being before whom I now stand, and who has kept us in his hands from the infancy of our Republic to the present day, that he will so overrule all my intentions and actions, and inspire the hearts of my fellow-citizens, that we may be preserved from dangers of all kinds, and continue forever a UNITED AND HAPPY PEOPLE.

Old Hickory

THE SECOND INAUGURAL ADDRESS OF ANDREW JACKSON

Thomas Coens

ON MARCH 4, 1833, shortly after twelve noon, Andrew Jackson took the oath of office for the second time in the Capitol's Hall of Representatives. The ceremony had been slated for the Capitol's East Portico, but a recent snowfall and sub-freezing temperatures forced the event indoors. The Hall's tight quarters limited spectators, but there was room enough to accommodate Jackson's Cabinet, Supreme Court judges, senators and congressmen, foreign ministers, and Washington, D.C.'s mayor, as well as what the newspapers called a sizable "concourse of ladies and citizens." Standing before the Speaker's chair and flanked to his left by newly elected Vice President Martin Van Buren and to his right by his nephew and private secretary Andrew Jackson Donelson, Jackson delivered his Second Inaugural "in an audible and firm voice." The address was cheered by the audience, after which Supreme Court Chief Justice John Marshall approached Jackson and administered him the presidential oath.

Jackson began his address by thanking his countrymen for his re-election and the "renewed expression of their confidence in my good intentions," and concluded with a "fervent prayer, to that Almighty Being before whom I now stand, and who has kept us in his hands from the infancy of our Republic to the present day." In between, Jackson devoted almost the entirety of his Second Inaugural to outlining, in very general terms, what he considered the "two objects which especially deserve the attention of the people," namely, "the preservation of the rights of the several States, and the integrity of the Union." On the one hand, Jackson emphasized the importance of safeguarding the constitutionally protected prerogatives of state governments. The "destruction of our State governments," Jackson warned, "or the annihilation of their control over the local concerns of the people, would lead directly to revolution and anarchy, and finally to despotism and military domination." At the same time, Jackson encouraged Americans to cherish the federal Union and to give "a liberal support of the General Government in the exercise of its just powers." "Without union our independence and liberty would never have been achieved," Jackson reminded Americans, and hollowing out of the authority of the federal government risked economic chaos, constant strife and bickering, civil war, and ultimately "loss of liberty."

Perhaps the most notable feature of Jackson's Second Inaugural was how short it was. At 1,176 words, only seven inaugural addresses have been shorter, and one of those was Jackson's first, given in 1829. Virtually everyone who heard or read the address and commented upon it noted its slimness. John Quincy Adams, who was not present at the ceremony but received a firsthand report, described it as "brief and full of smooth professions," while fellow diarist Philip Hone noted that it was "well done, not too long."[1] By contemporary as well as modern standards, Old Hickory was a rather infrequent public speaker, and it is not a stretch to suggest that the brevity of Jackson's two inaugurals was no accident. Despite his reputation as the father of "Jacksonian Democracy," with all its boisterous electioneering, Jackson rarely appealed to voters in person, and he limited his communications with the public to written exchanges published in newspapers, and, as president, to State Papers and messages to Congress. This was in keeping with the patrician practices of his predecessors, but Jackson's aversion to public speaking and self-promotion went beyond even theirs. In fact, other than remarks he delivered at an 1833 monument cornerstone-laying ceremony honoring George Washington's mother, Jackson did not once formally address a public audience during his eight years as president.

The other noticeable thing about Jackson's Second Inaugural is how lacking it was in specific references to concrete events or policies. Newspapers opposed to Jackson complained, with some justification, that it contained "no allusion to debatable matter" and was filled with "generalities and non-committals" with which "none will be found to disagree." It is not true, however, that Jackson's address had nothing to say about the important issues of the day, even if what he said was stated so obliquely as to require listeners to read between the lines. As with many a presidential inaugural, Jackson's second addressed contemporary political conflicts without mentioning them by name.

Near the end of his inaugural, Jackson dropped several hints that his reflections on states' rights and federal power were not to be taken as abstract musings, but as commentary on recent events and his handling of them. In the address's third to last paragraph, Jackson referred to the "existing crisis" and the "dangers which surround" the country, and he expressed his hope that the nation could pass through them by exercising "forbearance and firmness." The "crisis" facing the country, as Jackson's audience would have immediately known, was nullification. In November 1832, a South Carolina convention, claiming to act in the name of that state's people, declared void, or "nullified," two federal laws raising tariff rates on imports, measures the convention believed to be unconstitutional and unfair on the grounds that they made Southerners pay more for imports while getting less for their agricultural exports. The South Carolina convention also warned that the State would secede from the Union if an attempt was made to enforce those laws within South Carolina's borders. Jackson met South Carolina's provocation with a fiery December 1832 proclamation denouncing nullification and secession as unconstitutional and reckless. The means to defuse the crisis, however, came from Congress, which during the 1832–1833 session passed a so-called Compromise tariff law that gradually reduced rates over the coming years until they came down to levels thought to be acceptable to Southerners. Jackson had signed the measure into law only two days earlier, and whether South Carolina would back down—it did, more or less—was on inauguration day yet unknown.

Four drafts of Jackson's Second Inaugural survive in the Library of Congress's collection of Jackson Papers, and an examination of those drafts reveals that the decision to address nullification with kid gloves, or at least indirectly, had been internally debated by Jackson and his aides during the address's drafting process. Jackson's first draft, written out in his own hand, reads like a slightly shorter, slightly less eloquent version of the final address. Jackson's "Kitchen Cabinet" advisor Amos Kendall took Jackson's first draft and lengthened and revised it. As the former Kentucky newspaper editor was wont to do, Kendall added to Jackson's draft a fair measure of piquancy and punch. Kendall's revision castigated nullifiers as "misguided men," suffering from "madness or delusion," and had Jackson dramatically vow to *preserve the union of these states although it may cost me my life.* Jackson's dutifully copied over Kendall's provocative comments into a third draft, but they were removed in the final draft executed by his nephew and secretary Andrew Jackson Donelson. Who was responsible for doing so is not known; given the rapid and peaceful abatement of the nullification crisis in the weeks following, it is no doubt best that they were.

Also lurking beneath the generalizations of Jackson's Second Inaugural was Old Hickory's famous "War" against the Bank of the United States. Jackson had won re-election in 1832 over opponent Henry Clay by campaigning under the banner of his 1832 veto of legislation rechartering the Bank of the United States, a semi-private, semi-public institution Jackson felt to be unconstitutional, aristocratic, and dangerous. With his Bank veto as the unmistakable subtext, Jackson in his Second Inaugural touted his willingness to "exercise my constitutional powers in arresting measures which may directly or indirectly encroach upon the rights of the States, or tend to consolidate all political power in the General Government."

Seen this way, Jackson's Second Inaugural can be read as a justification of his dual decisions, made during his first term, to wage war against the Bank and against nullification. The two, each in their own way, violated his middle-of-the-road approach to states' rights and federal power: the Bank was born of federal overreach and threatened to overawe the states and state-chartered banks; while nullification took states' rights too far, diminishing the legitimate powers of the federal government and jeopardizing the very existence of the Union.

It is fair, however, to ask whether this is an accurate description of how Jackson really operated. Did Jackson go after the Bank and after nullification because of his constitutional scruples, or were constitutional scruples invoked as plausible cover for other, more decisive motivations? Critics of Jackson, both then and in the years since, have caricatured Jackson as someone who "shot from the hip" and made decisions not on the basis of political principles, but to indulge personal vendettas and fits of pique. Jackson's first serious biographer (and not much of a fan), James Parton, famously wrote in 1860 that Jackson was at heart "a fighting man, and little more than a fighting man . . . [he hated] nullification much, but Calhoun more . . . the bank much, but Biddle more. He was a thorough-going human fighting-cock."[2] Documentary evidence, much of it only unearthed in the past few decades by editors of Jackson's presidential papers, suggests that Parton's take on Jackson is largely incorrect. Jackson began drafting closely reasoned arguments against the Bank's constitutionality early in his first term, and he was heavily involved in drafting the parts of his 1832 nullification proclamation that denounced secession. Such evidence does not forbid us from wondering whether Jackson's constitutional scruples were ultimately good rather than real reasons for his actions, but it is simply not true that Jackson acted impulsively or made important decisions during bouts of rage.

At the same time, it would be a mistake to suggest that Jackson's middle-of-the-road approach to questions of federal power is an ideological Rosetta Stone capable of explaining all of his actions as president, during either his first or second presidential terms. Jackson, after all, had during his first term allowed the State of Georgia to effectively nullify federal treaties and laws protecting the Cherokees on the grounds that the federal government was powerless to intervene. Conversely, Jackson was not shy about exercising dubious federal powers under the right circumstances, as when he recommended curbing free speech by outlawing the circulation of abolitionist materials in the mail. All of this, however, only goes to show that Jackson's Second Inaugural Address, like all inaugural addresses, was first and foremost a political document, one that sought to mold public perceptions and, in doing so, inevitably smoothed away some of the rough edges in Jackson's record.

Notes

1. Philip Hone, *The Diary of Philip Hone, 1828–1851* (Allan Nevins, Ed.), Vol. 1 (New York: Dodd, Mead and Company, 1927) 89.
2. James Parton, *Life of Andrew Jackson*, Vol. 3 (New York: Mason Bros, 1861), 695.

Martin Van Buren's Inaugural Address

SATURDAY, MARCH 4, 1837

FELLOW-CITIZENS:

The practice of all my predecessors imposes on me an obligation I cheerfully fulfill—to accompany the first and solemn act of my public trust with an avowal of the principles that will guide me in performing it and an expression of my feelings on assuming a charge so responsible and vast. In imitating their example I tread in the footsteps of illustrious men, whose superiors it is our happiness to believe are not found on the executive calendar of any country. Among them we recognize the earliest and firmest pillars of the Republic—those by whom our national independence was first declared, him who above all others contributed to establish it on the field of battle, and those whose expanded intellect and patriotism constructed, improved, and perfected the inestimable institutions under which we live. If such men in the position I now occupy felt themselves overwhelmed by a sense of gratitude for this the highest of all marks of their country's confidence, and by a consciousness of their inability adequately to discharge the duties of an office so difficult and exalted, how much more must these considerations affect one who can rely on no such claims for favor or forbearance! Unlike all who have preceded me, the Revolution that gave us existence as one people was achieved at the period of my birth; and whilst I contemplate with grateful reverence that memorable event, I feel that I belong to a later age and that I may not expect my countrymen to weigh my actions with the same kind and partial hand.

So sensibly, fellow-citizens, do these circumstances press themselves upon me that I should not dare to enter upon my path of duty did I not look for the generous aid of those who will be associated with me in the various and coordinate branches of the Government; did I not repose with unwavering reliance on the patriotism, the intelligence, and the kindness of a people who never yet deserted a public servant honestly laboring their cause; and, above all, did I not permit myself humbly to hope for the sustaining support of an ever-watchful and beneficent Providence.

To the confidence and consolation derived from these sources it would be ungrateful not to add those which spring from our present fortunate condition. Though not altogether exempt from embarrassments that disturb our tranquillity at home and threaten it abroad, yet in all the attributes of a great, happy, and flourishing people we stand without a parallel in the world. Abroad we enjoy the respect and, with scarcely an exception, the friendship of every nation; at home, while our Government quietly but efficiently performs the sole legitimate end of political institutions—in doing the greatest good to the greatest number—we present an aggregate of human prosperity surely not elsewhere to be found.

How imperious, then, is the obligation imposed upon every citizen, in his own sphere of action, whether limited or extended, to exert himself in perpetuating a condition of things so singularly happy! All the lessons of history and experience must be lost upon us if we are content to trust alone to the peculiar advantages we happen to possess. Position and climate and the bounteous resources that nature has scattered with so liberal a hand—even the diffused intelligence and elevated character of our people—will avail us nothing if we fail sacredly to uphold those political institutions that were wisely and deliberately formed with reference to every circumstance that could preserve or might endanger the blessings we enjoy. The thoughtful framers of our Constitution legislated for our country as they found it. Looking upon it with the eyes of statesmen and patriots, they saw all the sources of rapid and wonderful prosperity; but they saw also that various habits, opinions, and institutions peculiar to the various portions of so vast a region were deeply fixed. Distinct sovereignties were in actual existence, whose cordial union was essential to the welfare and happiness of all. Between many of them there was, at least to some extent, a real diversity of interests, liable to be exaggerated through sinister designs; they differed in size, in population, in wealth, and in actual and prospective resources and power; they varied in the character of their industry and staple productions, and [in some] existed domestic institutions which, unwisely disturbed, might endanger the harmony of the whole. Most carefully were all these circumstances weighed, and the foundations of the new Government laid upon principles of reciprocal concession and equitable compromise. The jealousies which the smaller States might entertain of the power of the rest were allayed by a rule of representation confessedly unequal at the time, and designed forever to remain so. A natural fear that the broad scope of general legislation might bear upon and unwisely control particular interests was counteracted by limits strictly drawn around the action of the Federal authority, and to the people and the States was left unimpaired their sovereign power over the innumerable subjects embraced in the internal government of a just republic, excepting such only as necessarily appertain to the concerns of the whole confederacy or its intercourse as a united community with the other nations of the world.

This provident forecast has been verified by time. Half a century, teeming with extraordinary events, and elsewhere producing astonishing results, has passed along, but on our institutions it has left no injurious mark. From a small community we have risen to a people powerful in numbers and in strength; but with our increase has gone hand in hand the progress of just principles. The privileges, civil and religious, of the humblest individual are still sacredly protected at home, and while the valor and fortitude of our people have removed far from us the slightest apprehension of foreign power, they have not yet induced us in a single instance to forget what is right. Our commerce has been extended to the remotest nations; the value and even nature of our productions have been greatly changed; a wide difference has arisen in the relative wealth and resources of every portion of our country; yet the spirit of mutual regard and of faithful adherence to existing compacts has continued to prevail in our councils and never long been absent from our conduct. We have learned by experience a fruitful lesson—that an implicit and undeviating adherence to the principles on which we set out can carry us prosperously onward through all the conflicts of circumstances and vicissitudes inseparable from the lapse of years.

The success that has thus attended our great experiment is in itself a sufficient cause for gratitude, on account of the happiness it has actually conferred and the example it has unanswerably given. But to me, my fellow-citizens, looking forward to the far-distant future with ardent prayers and confiding hopes, this retrospect presents a ground for still deeper delight. It impresses on my mind a firm belief that the perpetuity of our institutions depends upon ourselves; that if we maintain the principles on which they were established they are destined to confer their benefits on countless generations yet to come, and that America will present to every friend of mankind the cheering proof that a popular government, wisely formed, is wanting in no element of endurance or strength. Fifty years ago its rapid failure was boldly predicted. Latent and uncontrollable causes of dissolution were supposed to exist even by the wise and good, and not only did unfriendly or speculative theorists anticipate for us the fate of past republics, but the fears of many an honest patriot overbalanced his sanguine hopes. Look back on these forebodings, not hastily but reluctantly made, and see how in every instance they have completely failed.

An imperfect experience during the struggles of the Revolution was supposed to warrant the belief that the people would not bear the taxation requisite to discharge an immense public debt already incurred and to pay the necessary expenses of the Government. The cost of two wars has been paid, not only without a murmur, but with unequaled alacrity. No one is now left to doubt that every burden will be cheerfully borne that may be necessary to sustain our civil institutions or guard our honor or welfare. Indeed, all experience has shown that the willingness of the people to contribute to these ends in cases of emergency has uniformly outrun the confidence of their representatives.

In the early stages of the new Government, when all felt the imposing influence as they recognized the unequaled services of the first President, it was a common sentiment that the great weight of his character could alone bind the discordant materials of our Government together and save us from the violence of contending factions. Since his death nearly forty years are gone. Party exasperation has been often carried to its highest point; the virtue and fortitude of the people have sometimes been greatly tried; yet our system, purified and enhanced in value by all it has encountered, still preserves its spirit of free and fearless discussion, blended with unimpaired fraternal feeling.

The capacity of the people for self-government, and their willingness, from a high sense of duty and without those exhibitions of coercive power so generally employed in other countries, to submit to all needful restraints and exactions of municipal law, have also been favorably exemplified in the history of the American States. Occasionally, it is true, the ardor of public sentiment, outrunning the regular progress of the judicial tribunals or seeking to reach cases not denounced as criminal by the existing law, has displayed itself in a manner calculated to give pain to the friends of free government and to encourage the hopes of those who wish for its overthrow. These occurrences, however, have been far less frequent in our country than in any other of equal population on the globe, and with the diffusion of intelligence it may well be hoped that they will constantly diminish in frequency and violence. The generous patriotism and sound common sense of the great mass of our fellow-citizens will assuredly in time produce this result; for as every assumption of illegal power not only wounds the majesty of the law, but furnishes a pretext for abridging the liberties of the people, the latter have the most direct and permanent interest in preserving the landmarks of social order and maintaining on all occasions the inviolability of those constitutional and legal provisions which they themselves have made.

In a supposed unfitness of our institutions for those hostile emergencies which no country can always avoid their friends found a fruitful source of apprehension, their enemies of hope. While they foresaw less promptness of action than in governments differently formed, they overlooked the far more important consideration that with us war could never be the result of individual or irresponsible will, but must be a measure of redress for injuries sustained, voluntarily resorted to by those who were to bear the necessary sacrifice, who would consequently feel an individual interest in the contest, and whose energy would be commensurate with the difficulties to be encountered. Actual events have proved their error; the last war, far from impairing, gave new confidence to our Government, and amid recent apprehensions of a similar conflict we saw that the energies of our country would not be wanting in ample season to vindicate its rights. We may not possess, as we should not desire to possess, the extended and ever-ready military organization of other nations; we may occasionally suffer in the outset for the want of it; but among ourselves all doubt upon this great point has ceased, while a salutary experience will prevent a contrary opinion from inviting aggression from abroad.

Certain danger was foretold from the extension of our territory, the multiplication of States, and the increase of population. Our system was supposed to be adapted only to boundaries comparatively narrow. These have been widened beyond conjecture; the members of our Confederacy are already doubled, and the numbers of our people are incredibly augmented. The alleged causes of danger have long surpassed anticipation, but none of the consequences have followed. The power and influence of the Republic have arisen to a height obvious to all mankind; respect for its authority was not more apparent at its ancient than it is at its present limits; new and inexhaustible sources of general prosperity have been opened; the effects of distance have been averted by the inventive genius of our people, developed and fostered by the spirit of our institutions; and the enlarged variety and amount of interests, productions, and pursuits have strengthened the chain of mutual dependence and formed a circle of mutual benefits too apparent ever to be overlooked.

In justly balancing the powers of the Federal and State authorities difficulties nearly insurmountable arose at the outset, and subsequent collisions were deemed inevitable. Amid these it was scarcely believed possible that a scheme of government so complex in construction could remain uninjured. From time to time embarrassments have certainly occurred; but how just is the confidence of future safety imparted by the knowledge that each in succession has been happily removed! Overlooking partial and temporary evils as inseparable from the practical operation of all human institutions, and looking only to the general result, every patriot has reason to be satisfied. While the Federal Government has successfully performed its appropriate functions in relation to foreign affairs and concerns evidently national, that of every State has remarkably improved in protecting and developing local interests and individual welfare; and if the vibrations of authority have occasionally tended too much toward one or the other, it is unquestionably certain that the ultimate operation of the entire system has been to strengthen all the existing institutions and to elevate our whole country in prosperity and renown.

The last, perhaps the greatest, of the prominent sources of discord and disaster supposed to lurk in our political condition was the institution of domestic slavery. Our forefathers were deeply impressed with the delicacy of this subject, and they treated it with a forbearance so evidently wise that in spite of every sinister foreboding it never until the present period disturbed the tranquillity of our common country. Such a result is sufficient evidence of the justice and the patriotism of their course; it is evidence not to be mistaken that an adherence to it can prevent all embarrassment from this as well as from every other anticipated cause of difficulty or danger. Have not recent events made it obvious to the slightest reflection that the least deviation from this spirit of forbearance is injurious to every interest, that of humanity included? Amidst the violence of excited passions this generous and fraternal feeling has been sometimes disregarded; and standing as I now do before my countrymen, in this high place of honor and of trust, I can not refrain from anxiously invoking my fellow-citizens never to be deaf to its dictates. Perceiving before my election the deep interest this subject was beginning to excite, I believed it a solemn duty fully to make known my sentiments in regard to it, and now, when every motive for misrepresentation has passed away, I trust that they will be candidly weighed and understood. At least they will be my standard of conduct in the path before me. I then declared that if the desire of those of my countrymen who were favorable to my election was gratified "I must go into the Presidential chair the inflexible and uncompromising opponent of every attempt on the part of Congress to abolish slavery in the District of Columbia against the wishes of the slaveholding States, and also with a determination equally decided to resist the slightest interference with it in the States where it exists." I submitted also to my fellow-citizens, with fullness and frankness, the reasons which led me to this determination. The result authorizes me to believe that they have been approved and are confided in by a majority of the people of the United States, including those whom they most immediately affect. It now only remains to add that no bill conflicting with these views can ever receive my constitutional sanction. These opinions have been adopted in the firm belief that they are in accordance with the spirit that actuated the venerated fathers of the Republic, and that succeeding experience has proved them to be humane, patriotic, expedient, honorable, and just. If the agitation of this subject was intended to reach the stability of our institutions, enough has occurred to show that it has signally failed, and that in this as in every other instance the apprehensions of the timid and the hopes of the wicked for the destruction of our Government are again destined to be disappointed. Here and there, indeed, scenes of dangerous excitement have occurred, terrifying instances of local violence have been witnessed, and a reckless disregard of the consequences of their conduct has exposed individuals to popular indignation; but neither masses of the people nor sections of the country have been swerved from their devotion to the bond of union and the principles it has made sacred. It will be ever thus. Such attempts at dangerous agitation may periodically return, but with each the object will be better understood. That predominating affection for our political system which prevails throughout our territorial limits, that calm and enlightened judgment which ultimately governs our people as one vast body, will always be at hand to resist and control every effort, foreign or domestic, which aims or would lead to overthrow our institutions.

What can be more gratifying than such a retrospect as this? We look back on obstacles avoided and dangers overcome, on expectations more than realized and prosperity perfectly secured. To the hopes of the hostile, the fears of the timid, and the doubts of the anxious actual experience has given the conclusive reply. We have seen time gradually dispel every unfavorable foreboding and our Constitution surmount every adverse circumstance dreaded at the outset as beyond control. Present excitement will at all times magnify present dangers, but true philosophy must teach us that none more threatening than the past can remain to be overcome; and we ought (for we have just reason) to entertain an abiding confidence in the stability of our institutions and an entire conviction that if administered in the true form, character, and spirit in which they were established they are abundantly adequate to preserve to us and our children the rich blessings already derived from them, to make our beloved land for a thousand generations that chosen spot where happiness springs from a perfect equality of political rights.

For myself, therefore, I desire to declare that the principle that will govern me in the high duty to which my country calls me is a strict adherence to the letter and spirit of the Constitution as it was designed by those who framed it. Looking back to it as a sacred instrument carefully and not easily framed; remembering that it was throughout a work of concession and compromise; viewing it as limited to national objects; regarding it as leaving to the people and the States all power not explicitly parted with, I shall endeavor to preserve, protect, and defend it by anxiously referring to its provision for direction in every action. To matters of domestic concernment which it has intrusted to the Federal Government and to such as relate to our intercourse with foreign nations I shall zealously devote myself; beyond those limits I shall never pass.

To enter on this occasion into a further or more minute exposition of my views on the various questions of domestic policy would be as obtrusive as it is probably unexpected. Before the suffrages of my countrymen were conferred upon me I submitted to them, with great precision, my opinions on all the most prominent of these subjects. Those opinions I shall endeavor to carry out with my utmost ability.

Our course of foreign policy has been so uniform and intelligible as to constitute a rule of Executive conduct which leaves little to my discretion, unless, indeed, I were willing to run counter to the lights of experience and the known opinions of my constituents. We sedulously cultivate the friendship of all nations as the conditions most compatible with our welfare and the principles of our Government. We decline alliances as adverse to our peace. We desire commercial relations on equal terms, being ever willing to give a fair equivalent for advantages received. We endeavor to conduct our intercourse with openness and sincerity, promptly avowing our objects and seeking to establish that mutual frankness which is as beneficial in the dealings of nations as of men. We have no disposition and we disclaim all right to meddle in disputes, whether internal or foreign, that may molest other countries, regarding them in their actual state as social communities, and preserving a strict neutrality in all their controversies. Well knowing the tried valor of our people and our exhaustless resources, we neither anticipate nor fear any designed aggression; and in the consciousness of our own just conduct we feel a security that we shall never be called upon to exert our determination never to permit an invasion of our rights without punishment or redress.

In approaching, then, in the presence of my assembled countrymen, to make the solemn promise that yet remains, and to pledge myself that I will faithfully execute the office I am about to fill, I bring with me a settled purpose to maintain the institutions of my country, which I trust will atone for the errors I commit.

In receiving from the people the sacred trust twice confided to my illustrious predecessor, and which he has discharged so faithfully and so well, I know that I can not expect to perform the arduous task with equal ability and success. But united as I have been in his counsels, a daily witness of his exclusive and unsurpassed devotion to his country's welfare, agreeing with him in sentiments which his countrymen have warmly supported, and permitted to partake largely of his confidence, I may hope that somewhat of the same cheering approbation will be found to attend upon my path. For him I but express with my own the wishes of all, that he may yet long live to enjoy the brilliant evening of his well-spent life; and for myself, conscious of but one desire, faithfully to serve my country, I throw myself without fear on its justice and its kindness. Beyond that I only look to the gracious protection of the Divine Being whose strengthening support I humbly solicit, and whom I fervently pray to look down upon us all. May it be among the dispensations of His providence to bless our beloved country with honors and with length of days. May her ways be ways of pleasantness and all her paths be peace!

The Little Magician

THE INAUGURAL ADDRESS OF MARTIN VAN BUREN

Michael J. Gerhardt

AMERICA'S SEVENTH PRESIDENT, Andrew Jackson, was a hard act to follow, especially for the man who succeeded him, Martin Van Buren. Jackson led the popular vote all three times he ran for the presidency (1824, 1828, 1832). While not all Americans loved Jackson, he had a humble background, was anti-elitist, championed the common man against rapacious big businesses, and was the first president to stand firmly against secession. Stubborn to a fault, Jackson issued a directive in the final year of his presidency that prohibited the use of paper money in the purchase of federal lands. In his first few weeks in office, Van Buren watched helplessly as Jackson's move provoked foreclosures and bank failures, which led to the nation's first great depression.

Whereas Jackson manifested the toughness he wished to embody, Van Buren was well known for his wiliness and penchant for compromise. When Jackson reshuffled his Cabinet to rid it of those who felt allegiance to his first vice president, John Calhoun, Van Buren agreed to relinquish his position as secretary of state in favor of serving as the minister to Great Britain. But, when Calhoun cast the tie-breaking vote to reject Van Buren's nomination as minister to Great Britain, Van Buren instantly became a martyr for Jackson's cause. Jackson picked him as his running mate in the 1832 election, and Jackson paved the way for Van Buren to win the party's nomination in 1836 and the ensuing presidential election of 1836.

The scene of Van Buren's inaugural on March 4, 1837, delighted Jackson. Swearing in his chosen successor was Chief Justice Roger Taney, Jackson's longtime adviser, whom Jackson had helped to secure the post after the Senate had rejected his nominations for treasury secretary and associate justice on the Court. While the ceremony was a triumph for Jackson, it was not for Van Buren, who could take pride in becoming the first native-born American to become president, but had the challenge on that day to demonstrate both his commitment to Jackson's policies and popular support *and* his own toughness to fight, as Jackson did, big business, an overreaching federal government, and secession.

Van Buren's Inaugural Address demonstrated that he was no Jackson. Whereas his predecessor spoke plainly and directly, Van Buren spoke formally and cautiously, ever mindful of the traps he had to avoid ahead. Van Buren had not been formally educated, but he had the presence of a man who overcompensated for his humble beginnings. Looking back on that day, long-time Jackson ally Senator Thomas Hart Benton aptly observed, "For once, the rising son was eclipsed by the setting son."

The first sentence of Van Buren's Inaugural Address gave an indication of where Van Buren was going—nearly eight lines long when put down in writing. He "cheerfully" agreed to "fulfill" the obligation set by his predecessors of delivering an inaugural, a sentiment he took forty-nine words to express. He went downhill from there, abandoning any pretense of being the verbal pugilist that Jackson was. Instead, he launched into a long disquisition—comprising twelve of the addresses' eighteen long paragraphs—underscoring his humility by retelling the story of America up until that moment. The longest paragraph of the entire address is the thirteenth, which addressed "the institution of domestic slavery." Van Buren recounted some of the country's early history in wrestling with that problem before he explained his "solemn duty" as a candidate to have "declared that if the desire of those of my countrymen who were favorable to my election was gratified 'I must go into the Presidential chair the inflexible and uncompromising opponent of every attempt on the part of Congress to abolish slavery in the District of Columbia against the wishes of the slaveholding states, and also with a determination equally decided to resist the slightest interference with it in the States where it exists.'" This is Van Buren taking a strong stand: he was more lawyer than politician in trying to soften flashpoints of disagreement by using the least incendiary rhetoric he could to make his points. This kind of talk was classic Van Buren, trying mightily to please his audience while committing himself to a policy unpleasing to many. Van Buren placed these remarks roughly in the middle of his address, thus making it nearly impossible to reassure the very people he wanted to reassure. They wanted bluster and boldness but they got the opposite—calmly worded bromides, long disquisitions on history, and reluctance to showcase his strongest stand.

This paragraph continues to nearly the end of his speech, when he finally spoke directly to the audience before him and those reading the address later: "For myself, therefore, I desire to declare that the principle that will govern me in the high duty to which my country calls me is a strict adherence to the letter and spirit of the Constitution as it was designed by those who framed it." "I shall endeavor," he added later in the same long paragraph (after recounting the origins of the Constitution), "to preserve, protect, and defend it anxiously referring to its direction in every action. To matters of domestic concernment which it has intrusted to the Federal Government and to such as relate to our intercourse with foreign nations I shall zealously devote myself; beyond those limits I shall never pass." Van Buren echoed Jackson's commitment to what has become known as original meaning as the touchstone of constitutional law.

Van Buren was pronouncing how he would govern and interpret the nation's preeminent governing document, but he was also repeating himself and failing to frame anything memorable in his rhetoric. Van Buren of course was entitled as the duly elected president to speak in his own voice, but it was not a voice that convinced anyone that he was a man of the people like Jackson. The verbiage confirmed his image as a clever politician that one had to watch carefully to keep in check.

After two long paragraphs about his approach to foreign policy (declaring he had little "discretion" to deviate from Jackson's "uniform and intelligible" foreign policy), Van Buren arrived at his last two paragraphs. He concluded the first of these with his promise "to bring with me a settled purpose to maintain the institutions of my country, which I trust will atone for the errors I commit." The more protestations of humility he made, the less tough he sounded and the more like a regular politician whom Jackson's followers detested. Jacksonians did not want any career politicians but instead a man who shared their experiences and values as common folk. Van Buren had come into the presidency as a career politician; he sounded and looked like one. Having been out of the country for a year before he became vice president in 1836, he was not a familiar face or presence to most Americans, but, through his inaugural, he was reminding everyone that he was exactly what his critics charged—a career politician more interested in helping himself than in helping others, especially those who needed the government to stand with them against the big businesses that were gouging them.

Most of the last paragraph was devoted to reminding Americans that he had served under Jackson for many years and was "a daily witness of his exclusive and unsurpassed devotion to his country's welfare, agreeing with him in sentiments which his countrymen have warmly supported, and permitted to partake largely of his confidence." He praised Jackson further and then the nation before "throw[ing] myself without fear on its justice and its kindness" and looking for guidance to Jackson and the "Divine Being whose strengthening support I humbly solicit."

The address sounded many of the right notes for Van Buren, but it sowed more doubts than confidence that Van Buren could ever be as tough as Jackson in opposing the forces preying on the common people who were his supporters. Van Buren served his country for many years—as a senator, as the attorney general and governor of New York, as secretary of state, minister to Great Britain, and as president. His résumé, loyalty to Jackson, and humility could not save him from political disaster when, just weeks after his address, the nation confronted its first great depression. The crisis required boldness, imagination, and empathy, but Van Buren was not the man who could deliver these when he needed to, and he lost re-election in 1840.

William Henry Harrison's Inaugural Address

THURSDAY, MARCH 4, 1841

CALLED FROM A retirement which I had supposed was to continue for the residue of my life to fill the chief executive office of this great and free nation, I appear before you, fellow-citizens, to take the oaths which the Constitution prescribes as a necessary qualification for the performance of its duties; and in obedience to a custom coeval with our Government and what I believe to be your expectations I proceed to present to you a summary of the principles which will govern me in the discharge of the duties which I shall be called upon to perform.

It was the remark of a Roman consul in an early period of that celebrated Republic that a most striking contrast was observable in the conduct of candidates for offices of power and trust before and after obtaining them, they seldom carrying out in the latter case the pledges and promises made in the former. However much the world may have improved in many respects in the lapse of upward of two thousand years since the remark was made by the virtuous and indignant Roman, I fear that a strict examination of the annals of some of the modern elective governments would develop similar instances of violated confidence.

Although the fiat of the people has gone forth proclaiming me the Chief Magistrate of this glorious Union, nothing upon their part remaining to be done, it may be thought that a motive may exist to keep up the delusion under which they may be supposed to have acted in relation to my principles and opinions; and perhaps there may be some in this assembly who have come here either prepared to condemn those I shall now deliver, or, approving them, to doubt the sincerity with which they are now uttered. But the lapse of a few months will confirm or dispel their fears. The outline of principles to govern and measures to be adopted by an Administration not yet begun will soon be exchanged for immutable history, and I shall stand either exonerated by my countrymen or classed with the mass of those who promised that they might deceive and flattered with the intention to betray. However strong may be my present purpose to realize the expectations of a magnanimous and confiding people, I too well understand the dangerous temptations to which I shall be exposed from the magnitude of the power which it has been the pleasure of the people to commit to my hands not to place my chief confidence upon the aid of that Almighty Power which has hitherto protected me and enabled me to bring to favorable issues other important but still greatly inferior trusts heretofore confided to me by my country.

The broad foundation upon which our Constitution rests being the people—a breath of theirs having made, as a breath can unmake, change, or modify it—it can be assigned to none of the great divisions of government but to that of democracy. If such is its theory, those who are called upon to administer it must recognize as its leading principle the duty of shaping their measures so as to produce the greatest good to the greatest number. But with these broad admissions, if we would compare the sovereignty acknowledged to exist in the mass of our people with the power claimed by other sovereignties, even by those which have been considered most purely democratic, we shall find a most essential difference. All others lay claim to power limited only by their own will. The majority of our citizens, on the contrary, possess a sovereignty with an amount of power precisely equal to that which has been granted to them by the parties to the national compact, and nothing beyond. We admit of no government by divine right, believing that so far as power is concerned the Beneficent Creator has made no distinction amongst men; that all are upon an equality, and that the only legitimate right to govern is an express grant of power from the governed. The Constitution of the United States is the instrument containing this grant of power to the several departments composing the Government. On an examination of that instrument it will be found to contain declarations of power granted and of power withheld. The latter is also susceptible of division into power which the majority had the right to grant, but which they do not think proper to intrust to their agents, and that which they could not have granted, not being possessed by themselves. In other words, there are certain rights possessed by each individual American citizen which in his compact with the others he has never surrendered. Some of them, indeed, he is unable to surrender, being, in the language of our system, unalienable. The boasted privilege of a Roman citizen was to him a shield only against a petty provincial ruler, whilst the proud democrat of Athens would console himself under a sentence of death for a supposed violation of the national faith—which no one understood and which at times was the subject of the mockery of all—or the banishment from his home, his family, and his country with or without an alleged cause, that it was the act not of a single tyrant or hated aristocracy, but of his assembled countrymen. Far different is the power of our sovereignty. It can interfere with no one's faith, prescribe forms of worship for no one's observance, inflict no punishment but after well-ascertained guilt, the result of investigation under rules prescribed by the Constitution itself. These precious privileges, and those scarcely less important of giving expression to his thoughts and opinions, either by writing or speaking, unrestrained but by the liability for injury to others, and that of a full participation in all the advantages which flow from the Government, the acknowledged property of all, the American citizen derives from no charter granted by his fellow-man. He claims them because he is himself a man, fashioned by the same Almighty hand as the rest of his species and entitled to a full share of the blessings with which He has endowed them. Notwithstanding the limited sovereignty possessed by the people of the United States and the restricted grant of power to the Government which they have adopted, enough has been given to accomplish all the objects for which it was created. It has been found powerful in war, and hitherto justice has been administered, and intimate union effected, domestic tranquillity preserved, and personal liberty secured to the citizen. As was to be expected, however, from the defect of language and the necessarily sententious manner in which the Constitution is written, disputes have arisen as to the amount of power which it has actually granted or was intended to grant.

This is more particularly the case in relation to that part of the instrument which treats of the legislative branch, and not only as regards the exercise of powers claimed under a general clause giving that body the authority to pass all laws necessary to carry into effect the specified powers, but in relation to the latter also. It is, however, consolatory to reflect that *most* of the instances of alleged departure from the letter or spirit of the Constitution have ultimately received the sanction of a majority of the people. And the fact that many of our statesmen most distinguished for talent and patriotism have been at one time or other of their political career on both sides of each of the most warmly disputed questions forces upon us the inference that the errors, if errors there were, are attributable to the intrinsic difficulty in many instances of ascertaining the intentions of the framers of the Constitution rather than the influence of any sinister or unpatriotic motive. But the great danger to our institutions does not appear to me to be in a usurpation by the Government of power not granted by the people, but by the accumulation in one of the departments of that which was assigned to others. Limited as are the powers which have been granted, still enough have been granted to constitute a despotism if concentrated in one of the departments. This danger is greatly heightened, as it has been always observable that men are less jealous of encroachments of one department upon another than upon their own reserved rights. When the Constitution of the United States first came from the hands of the Convention which formed it, many of the sternest republicans of the day were alarmed at the extent of the power which had been granted to the Federal Government, and more particularly of that portion which had been assigned to the executive branch. There were in it features which appeared not to be in harmony with their ideas of a simple representative democracy or republic, and knowing the tendency of power to increase itself, particularly when exercised by a single individual, predictions were made that at no very remote period the Government would terminate in virtual monarchy. It would not become me to say that the fears of these patriots have been already realized; but as I sincerely believe that the tendency of measures and of men's opinions for some years past has been in that direction, it is, I conceive, strictly proper that I should take this occasion to repeat the assurances I have heretofore given of my determination to arrest the progress of that tendency if it really exists and restore the Government to its pristine health and vigor, as far as this can be effected by any legitimate exercise of the power placed in my hands.

I proceed to state in as summary a manner as I can my opinion of the sources of the evils which have been so extensively complained of and the correctives which may be applied. Some of the former are unquestionably to be found in the defects of the Constitution; others, in my judgment, are attributable to a misconstruction of some of its provisions. Of the former is the eligibility of the same individual to a second term of the Presidency. The sagacious mind of Mr. Jefferson early saw and lamented this error, and attempts have been made, hitherto without success, to apply the amendatory power of the States to its correction. As, however, one mode of correction is in the power of every President, and consequently in mine, it would be useless, and perhaps invidious, to enumerate the evils of which, in the opinion of many of our fellow-citizens, this error of the sages who framed the Constitution may have been the source and the bitter fruits which we are still to gather from it if it continues to disfigure our system. It may be observed, however, as a general remark, that republics can commit no greater error than to adopt or continue any feature in their systems of government which may be calculated to create or increase the lover of power in the bosoms of those to whom necessity obliges them to commit the management of their affairs; and surely nothing is more likely to produce such a state of mind than the long continuance of an office of high trust. Nothing can be more corrupting, nothing more destructive of all those noble feelings which belong to the character of a devoted republican patriot. When this corrupting passion once takes possession of the human mind, like the love of gold it becomes insatiable. It is the never-dying worm in his bosom, grows with his growth and strengthens with the declining years of its victim. If this is true, it is the part of wisdom for a republic to limit the service of that officer at least to whom she has intrusted the management of her foreign relations, the execution of her laws, and the command of her armies and navies to a period so short as to prevent his forgetting that he is the accountable agent, not the principal; the servant, not the master. Until an amendment of the Constitution can be effected public opinion may secure the desired object. I give my aid to it by renewing the pledge heretofore given that under no circumstances will I consent to serve a second term.

But if there is danger to public liberty from the acknowledged defects of the Constitution in the want of limit to the continuance of the Executive power in the same hands, there is, I apprehend, not much less from a misconstruction of that instrument as it regards the powers actually given. I can not conceive that by a fair construction any or either of its provisions would be found to constitute the President a part of the legislative power. It can not be claimed from the power to recommend, since, although enjoined as a duty upon him, it is a privilege which he holds in common with every other citizen; and although there may be something more of confidence in the propriety of the measures recommended in the one case than in the other, in the obligations of ultimate decision there can be no difference. In the language of the Constitution, "all the legislative powers" which it grants "are vested in the Congress of the United States." It would be a solecism in language to say that any portion of these is not included in the whole.

It may be said, indeed, that the Constitution has given to the Executive the power to annul the acts of the legislative body by refusing to them his assent. So a similar power has necessarily resulted from that instrument to the judiciary, and yet the judiciary forms no part of the Legislature. There is, it is true, this difference between these grants of power: The Executive can put his negative upon the acts of the Legislature for other cause than that of want of conformity to the Constitution, whilst the judiciary can only declare void those which violate that instrument. But the decision of the judiciary is final in such a case, whereas in every instance where the veto of the Executive is applied it may be overcome by a vote of two-thirds of both Houses of Congress. The negative upon the acts of the legislative by the executive authority, and that in the hands of one individual, would seem to be an incongruity in our system. Like some others of a similar character, however, it appears to be highly expedient, and if used only with the forbearance and in the spirit which was intended by its authors it may be productive of great good and be found one of the best safeguards to the Union. At the period of the formation of the Constitution the principle does not appear to have enjoyed much favor in the State governments. It existed but in two, and in one of these there was a plural executive. If we would search for the motives which operated upon the purely patriotic and enlightened assembly which framed the Constitution for the adoption of a provision so apparently repugnant to the leading democratic principle that the majority should govern, we must reject the idea that they anticipated from it any benefit to the ordinary course of legislation. They knew too well the high degree of intelligence which existed among the people and the enlightened character of the State legislatures not to have the fullest confidence that the two bodies elected by them would be worthy representatives of such constituents, and, of course, that they would require no aid in conceiving and maturing the measures which the circumstances of the country might require. And it is preposterous to suppose that a thought could for a moment have been entertained that the President, placed at the capital, in the center of the country, could better understand the wants and wishes of the people than their own immediate representatives, who spend a part of every year among them, living with them, often laboring with them, and bound to them by the triple tie of interest, duty, and affection. To assist or control Congress, then, in its ordinary legislation could not, I conceive, have been the motive for conferring the veto power on the President. This argument acquires additional force from the fact of its never having been thus used by the first six Presidents—and two of them were members of the Convention, one presiding over its deliberations and the other bearing a larger share in consummating the labors of that august body than any other person. But if bills were never returned to Congress by either of the Presidents above referred to upon the ground of their being inexpedient or not as well adapted as they might be to the wants of the people, the veto was applied upon that of want of conformity to the Constitution or because errors had been committed from a too hasty enactment.

There is another ground for the adoption of the veto principle, which had probably more influence in recommending it to the Convention than any other. I refer to the security which it gives to the just and equitable action of the Legislature upon all parts of the Union. It could not but have occurred to the Convention that in a country so extensive, embracing so great a variety of soil and climate, and consequently of products, and which from the same causes must ever exhibit a great difference in the amount of the population of its various sections, calling for a great diversity in the employments of the people, that the legislation of the majority might not always justly regard the rights and interests of the minority, and that acts of this character might be passed under an express grant by the words of the Constitution, and therefore not within the competency of the judiciary to declare void; that however enlightened and patriotic they might suppose from past experience the members of Congress might be, and however largely partaking, in the general, of the liberal feelings of the people, it was impossible to expect that bodies so constituted should not sometimes be controlled by local interests and sectional feelings. It was proper, therefore, to provide some umpire from whose situation and mode of appointment more independence and freedom from such influences might be expected. Such a one was afforded by the executive department constituted by the Constitution. A person elected to that high office, having his constituents in every section, State, and subdivision of the Union, must consider himself bound by the most solemn sanctions to guard, protect, and defend the rights of all and of every portion, great or small, from the injustice and oppression of the rest. I consider the veto power, therefore, given by the Constitution to the Executive of the United States solely as a conservative power, to be used only, first, to protect the Constitution from violation; secondly, the people from the effects of hasty legislation where their will has been probably disregarded or not well understood, and, thirdly, to prevent the effects of combinations violative of the rights of minorities. In reference to the second of these objects I may observe that I consider it the right and privilege of the people to decide disputed points of the Constitution arising from the general grant of power to Congress to carry into effect the powers expressly given; and I believe with Mr. Madison that "repeated recognitions under varied circumstances in acts of the legislative, executive, and judicial branches of the Government, accompanied by indications in different modes of the concurrence of the general will of the nation," as affording to the President sufficient authority for his considering such disputed points as settled.

Upward of half a century has elapsed since the adoption of the present form of government. It would be an object more highly desirable than the gratification of the curiosity of speculative statesmen if its precise situation could be ascertained, a fair exhibit made of the operations of each of its departments, of the powers which they respectively claim and exercise, of the collisions which have occurred between them or between the whole Government and those of the States or either of them. We could then compare our actual condition after fifty years' trial of our system with what it was in the commencement of its operations and ascertain whether the predictions of the patriots who opposed its adoption or the confident hopes of its advocates have been best realized. The great dread of the former seems to have been that the reserved powers of the States would be absorbed by those of the Federal Government and a consolidated power established, leaving to the States the shadow only of that independent action for which they had so zealously contended and on the preservation of which they relied as the last hope of liberty. Without denying that the result to which they looked with so much apprehension is in the way of being realized, it is obvious that they did not clearly see the mode of its accomplishment. The General Government has seized upon none of the reserved rights of the States. As far as any open warfare may have gone, the State authorities have amply maintained their rights. To a casual observer our system presents no appearance of discord between the different members which compose it. Even the addition of many new ones has produced no jarring. They move in their respective orbits in perfect harmony with the central head and with each other. But there is still an undercurrent at work by which, if not seasonably checked, the worst apprehensions of our antifederal patriots will be realized, and not only will the State authorities be overshadowed by the great increase of power in the executive department of the General Government, but the character of that Government, if not its designation, be essentially and radically changed. This state of things has been in part effected by causes inherent in the Constitution and in part by the never-failing tendency of political power to increase itself. By making the President the sole distributer of all the patronage of the Government the framers of the Constitution do not appear to have anticipated at how short a period it would become a formidable instrument to control the free operations of the State governments. Of trifling importance at first, it had early in Mr. Jefferson's Administration become so powerful as to create great alarm in the mind of that patriot from the potent influence it might exert in controlling the freedom of the elective franchise. If such could have then been the effects of its influence, how much greater must be the danger at this time, quadrupled in amount as it certainly is and more completely under the control of the Executive will than their construction of their powers allowed or the forbearing characters of all the early Presidents permitted them to make. But it is not by the extent of its patronage alone that the executive department has become dangerous, but by the use which it appears may be made of the appointing power to bring under its control the whole revenues of the country. The Constitution has declared it to be the duty of the President to see that the laws are executed, and it makes him the Commander in Chief of the Armies and Navy of the United States. If the opinion of the most approved writers upon that species of mixed government which in modern Europe is termed *monarchy* in contradistinction to *despotism* is correct, there was wanting no other addition to the powers of our Chief Magistrate to stamp a monarchical character on our Government but the control of the public finances; and to me it appears strange indeed that anyone should doubt that the entire control which the President possesses over the officers who have the custody of the public money, by the power of removal with or without cause, does, for all mischievous purposes at least, virtually subject the treasure also to his disposal. The first Roman Emperor, in his attempt to seize the sacred treasure, silenced the opposition of the officer to whose charge it had been committed by a significant allusion to his sword. By a selection of political instruments for the care of the public money a reference to their commissions by a President would be quite as effectual an argument as that of Caesar to the Roman knight. I am not insensible of the great difficulty that exists in drawing a proper plan for the safe-keeping and disbursement of the public revenues, and I know the importance which has been attached by men of great abilities and patriotism to the divorce, as it is called, of the Treasury from the banking institutions. It is not the divorce which is complained of, but the unhallowed union of the Treasury with the executive department, which has created such extensive alarm. To this danger to our republican institutions and that created by the influence given to the Executive through the instrumentality of the Federal officers I propose to apply all the remedies which may be at my command. It was certainly a great error in the framers of the Constitution not to have made the officer at the head of the Treasury Department entirely independent of the Executive. He should at least have been removable only upon the demand of the popular branch of the Legislature. I have determined never to remove a Secretary of the Treasury without communicating all the circumstances attending such removal to both Houses of Congress.

The influence of the Executive in controlling the freedom of the elective franchise through the medium of the public officers can be effectually checked by renewing the prohibition published by Mr. Jefferson forbidding their interference in elections further than giving their own votes, and their own independence secured by an assurance of perfect immunity in exercising this sacred privilege of freemen under the dictates of their own unbiased judgments. Never with my consent shall an officer of the people, compensated for his services out of their pockets, become the pliant instrument of Executive will.

There is no part of the means placed in the hands of the Executive which might be used with greater effect for unhallowed purposes than the control of the public press. The maxim which our ancestors derived from the mother country that "the freedom of the press is the great bulwark of civil and religious liberty" is one of the most precious legacies which they have left us. We have learned, too, from our own as well as the experience of other countries, that golden shackles, by whomsoever or by whatever pretense imposed, are as fatal to it as the iron bonds of despotism. The presses in the necessary employment of the Government should never be used "to clear the guilty or to varnish crime." A decent and manly examination of the acts of the Government should be not only tolerated, but encouraged.

Upon another occasion I have given my opinion at some length upon the impropriety of Executive interference in the legislation of Congress—that the article in the Constitution making it the duty of the President to communicate information and authorizing him to recommend measures was not intended to make him the source in legislation, and, in particular, that he should never be looked to for schemes of finance. It would be very strange, indeed, that the Constitution should have strictly forbidden one branch of the Legislature from interfering in the origination of such bills and that it should be considered proper that an altogether different department of the Government should be permitted to do so. Some of our best political maxims and opinions have been drawn from our parent isle. There are others, however, which can not be introduced in our system without singular incongruity and the production of much mischief, and this I conceive to be one. No matter in which of the houses of Parliament a bill may originate nor by whom introduced—a minister or a member of the opposition—by the fiction of law, or rather of constitutional principle, the sovereign is supposed to have prepared it agreeably to his will and then submitted it to Parliament for their advice and consent. Now the very reverse is the case here, not only with regard to the principle, but the forms prescribed by the Constitution. The principle certainly assigns to the only body constituted by the Constitution (the legislative body) the power to make laws, and the forms even direct that the enactment should be ascribed to them. The Senate, in relation to revenue bills, have the right to propose amendments, and so has the Executive by the power given him to return them to the House of Representatives with his objections. It is in his power also to propose amendments in the existing revenue laws, suggested by his observations upon their defective or injurious operation. But the delicate duty of devising schemes of revenue should be left where the Constitution has placed it—with the immediate representatives of the people. For similar reasons the mode of keeping the public treasure should be prescribed by them, and the further removed it may be from the control of the Executive the more wholesome the arrangement and the more in accordance with republican principle.

Connected with this subject is the character of the currency. The idea of making it exclusively metallic, however well intended, appears to me to be fraught with more fatal consequences than any other scheme having no relation to the personal rights of the citizens that has ever been devised. If any single scheme could produce the effect of arresting at once that mutation of condition by which thousands of our most indigent fellow-citizens by their industry and enterprise are raised to the possession of wealth, that is the one. If there is one measure better calculated than another to produce that state of things so much deprecated by all true republicans, by which the rich are daily adding to their hoards and the poor sinking deeper into penury, it is an exclusive metallic currency. Or if there is a process by which the character of the country for generosity and nobleness of feeling may be destroyed by the great increase and necessary toleration of usury, it is an exclusive metallic currency.

Amongst the other duties of a delicate character which the President is called upon to perform is the supervision of the government of the Territories of the United States. Those of them which are destined to become members of our great political family are compensated by their rapid progress from infancy to manhood for the partial and temporary deprivation of their political rights. It is in this District only where American citizens are to be found who under a settled policy are deprived of many important political privileges without any inspiring hope as to the future. Their only consolation under circumstances of such deprivation is that of the devoted exterior guards of a camp—that their sufferings secure tranquillity and safety within. Are there any of their countrymen, who would subject them to greater sacrifices, to any other humiliations than those essentially necessary to the security of the object for which they were thus separated from their fellow-citizens? Are their rights alone not to be guaranteed by the application of those great principles upon which all our constitutions are founded? We are told by the greatest of British orators and statesmen that at the commencement of the War of the Revolution the most stupid men in England spoke of "their American subjects." Are there, indeed, citizens of any of our States who have dreamed *of their subjects* in the District of Columbia? Such dreams can never be realized by any agency of mine. The people of the District of Columbia are not the subjects of the people of the States, but free American citizens. Being in the latter condition when the Constitution was formed, no words used in that instrument could have been intended to deprive them of that character. If there is anything in the great principle of unalienable rights so emphatically insisted upon in our Declaration of Independence, they could neither make nor the United States accept a surrender of their liberties and become the *subjects*—in other words, the slaves—of their former fellow-citizens. If this be true—and it will scarcely be denied by anyone who has a correct idea of his own rights as an American citizen—the grant to Congress of exclusive jurisdiction in the District of Columbia can be interpreted, so far as respects the aggregate people of the United States, as meaning nothing more than to allow to Congress the controlling power necessary to afford a free and safe exercise of the functions assigned to the General Government by the Constitution. In all other respects the legislation of Congress should be adapted to their peculiar position and wants and be conformable with their deliberate opinions of their own interests.

I have spoken of the necessity of keeping the respective departments of the Government, as well as all the other authorities of our country, within their appropriate orbits. This is a matter of difficulty in some cases, as the powers which they respectively claim are often not defined by any distinct lines. Mischievous, however, in their tendencies as collisions of this kind may be, those which arise between the respective communities which for certain purposes compose one nation are much more so, for no such nation can long exist without the careful culture of those feelings of confidence and affection which are the effective bonds to union between free and confederated states. Strong as is the tie of interest, it has been often found ineffectual. Men blinded by their passions have been known to adopt measures for their country in direct opposition to all the suggestions of policy. The alternative, then, is to destroy or keep down a bad passion by creating and fostering a good one, and this seems to be the corner stone upon which our American political architects have reared the fabric of our Government. The cement which was to bind it and perpetuate its existence was the affectionate attachment between all its members. To insure the continuance of this feeling, produced at first by a community of dangers, of sufferings, and of interests, the advantages of each were made accessible to all. No participation in any good possessed by any member of our extensive Confederacy, except in domestic government, was withheld from the citizen of any other member. By a process attended with no difficulty, no delay, no expense but that of removal, the citizen of one might become the citizen of any other, and successively of the whole. The lines, too, separating powers to be exercised by the citizens of one State from those of another seem to be so distinctly drawn as to leave no room for misunderstanding. The citizens of each State unite in their persons all the privileges which that character confers and all that they may claim as citizens of the United States, but in no case can the same persons at the same time act as the citizen of two separate States, and *he is therefore positively precluded from any interference with the reserved powers of any State but that of which he is for the time being a citizen*. He may, indeed, offer to the citizens of other States his advice as to their management, and the form in which it is tendered is left to his own discretion and sense of propriety. It may be observed, however, that organized associations of citizens requiring compliance with their wishes too much resemble the *recommendations* of Athens to her allies, supported by an armed and powerful fleet. It was, indeed, to the ambition of the leading States of Greece to control the domestic concerns of the others that the destruction of that celebrated Confederacy, and subsequently of all its members, is mainly to be attributed, and it is owing to the absence of that spirit that the Helvetic Confederacy has for so many years been preserved. Never has there been seen in the institutions of the separate members of any confederacy more elements of discord. In the principles and forms of government and religion, as well as in the circumstances of the several Cantons, so marked a discrepancy was observable as to promise anything but harmony in their intercourse or permanency in their alliance, and yet for ages neither has been interrupted. Content with the positive benefits which their union produced, with the independence and safety from foreign aggression which it secured, these sagacious people respected the institutions of each other, however repugnant to their own principles and prejudices.

Our Confederacy, fellow-citizens, can only be preserved by the same forbearance. Our citizens must be content with the exercise of the powers with which the Constitution clothes them. The attempt of those of one State to control the domestic institutions of another can only result in feelings of distrust and jealousy, the certain harbingers of disunion, violence, and civil war, and the ultimate destruction of our free institutions. Our Confederacy is perfectly illustrated by the terms and principles governing a common copartnership. There is a fund of power to be exercised under the direction of the joint councils of the allied members, but that which has been reserved by the individual members is intangible by the common Government or the individual members composing it. To attempt it finds no support in the principles of our Constitution.

It should be our constant and earnest endeavor mutually to cultivate a spirit of concord and harmony among the various parts of our Confederacy. Experience has abundantly taught us that the agitation by citizens of one part of the Union of a subject not confided to the General Government, but exclusively under the guardianship of the local authorities, is productive of no other consequences than bitterness, alienation, discord, and injury to the very cause which is intended to be advanced. Of all the great interests which appertain to our country, that of union—cordial, confiding, fraternal union—is by far the most important, since it is the only true and sure guaranty of all others.

In consequence of the embarrassed state of business and the currency, some of the States may meet with difficulty in their financial concerns. However deeply we may regret anything imprudent or excessive in the engagements into which States have entered for purposes of their own, it does not become us to disparage the States governments, nor to discourage them from making proper efforts for their own relief. On the contrary, it is our duty to encourage them to the extent of our constitutional authority to apply their best means and cheerfully to make all necessary sacrifices and submit to all necessary burdens to fulfill their engagements and maintain their credit, for the character and credit of the several States form a part of the character and credit of the whole country. The resources of the country are abundant, the enterprise and activity of our people proverbial, and we may well hope that wise legislation and prudent administration by the respective governments, each acting within its own sphere, will restore former prosperity.

Unpleasant and even dangerous as collisions may sometimes be between the constituted authorities of the citizens of our country in relation to the lines which separate their respective jurisdictions, the results can be of no vital injury to our institutions if that ardent patriotism, that devoted attachment to liberty, that spirit of moderation and forbearance for which our countrymen were once distinguished, continue to be cherished. If this continues to be the ruling passion of our souls, the weaker feeling of the mistaken enthusiast will be corrected, the Utopian dreams of the scheming politician dissipated, and the complicated intrigues of the demagogue rendered harmless. The spirit of liberty is the sovereign balm for every injury which our institutions may receive. On the contrary, no care that can be used in the construction of our Government, no division of powers, no distribution of checks in its several departments, will prove effectual to keep us a free people if this spirit is suffered to decay; and decay it will without constant nurture. To the neglect of this duty the best historians agree in attributing the ruin of all the republics with whose existence and fall their writings have made us acquainted. The same causes will ever produce the same effects, and as long as the love of power is a dominant passion of the human bosom, and as long as the understandings of men can be warped and their affections changed by operations upon their passions and prejudices, so long will the liberties of a people depend on their own constant attention to its preservation. The danger to all well-established free governments arises from the unwillingness of the people to believe in its existence or from the influence of designing men diverting their attention from the quarter whence it approaches to a source from which it can never come. This is the old trick of those who would usurp the government of their country. In the name of democracy they speak, warning the people against the influence of wealth and the danger of aristocracy. History, ancient and modern, is full of such examples. Caesar became the master of the Roman people and the senate under the pretense of supporting the democratic claims of the former against the aristocracy of the latter; Cromwell, in the character of protector of the liberties of the people, became the dictator of England, and Bolivar possessed himself of unlimited power with the title of his country's liberator. There is, on the contrary, no instance on record of an extensive and well-established republic being changed into an aristocracy. The tendencies of all such governments in their decline is to monarchy, and the antagonist principle to liberty there is the spirit of faction—a spirit which assumes the character and in times of great excitement imposes itself upon the people as the genuine spirit of freedom, and, like the false Christs whose coming was foretold by the Savior, seeks to, and were it possible would, impose upon the true and most faithful disciples of liberty. It is in periods like this that it behooves the people to be most watchful of those to whom they have intrusted power. And although there is at times much difficulty in distinguishing the false from the true spirit, a calm and dispassionate investigation will detect the counterfeit, as well by the character of its operations as the results that are produced. The true spirit of liberty, although devoted, persevering, bold, and uncompromising in principle, that secured is mild and tolerant and scrupulous as to the means it employs, whilst the spirit of party, assuming to be that of liberty, is harsh, vindictive, and intolerant, and totally reckless as to the character of the allies which it brings to the aid of its cause. When the genuine spirit of liberty animates the body of a people to a thorough examination of their affairs, it leads to the excision of every excrescence which may have fastened itself upon any of the departments of the government, and restores the system to its pristine health and beauty. But the reign of an intolerant spirit of party amongst a free people seldom fails to result in a dangerous accession to the executive power introduced and established amidst unusual professions of devotion to democracy.

The foregoing remarks relate almost exclusively to matters connected with our domestic concerns. It may be proper, however, that I should give some indications to my fellow-citizens of my proposed course of conduct in the management of our foreign relations. I assure them, therefore, that it is my intention to use every means in my power to preserve the friendly intercourse which now so happily subsists with every foreign nation, and that although, of course, not well informed as to the state of pending negotiations with any of them, I see in the personal characters of the sovereigns, as well as in the mutual interests of our own and of the governments with which our relations are most intimate, a pleasing guaranty that the harmony so important to the interests of their subjects as well as of our citizens will not be interrupted by the advancement of any claim or pretension upon their part to which our honor would not permit us to yield. Long the defender of my country's rights in the field, I trust that my fellow-citizens will not see in my earnest desire to preserve peace with foreign powers any indication that their rights will ever be sacrificed or the honor of the nation tarnished by any admission on the part of their Chief Magistrate unworthy of their former glory. In our intercourse with our aboriginal neighbors the same liberality and justice which marked the course prescribed to me by two of my illustrious predecessors when acting under their direction in the discharge of the duties of superintendent and commissioner shall be strictly observed. I can conceive of no more sublime spectacle, none more likely to propitiate an impartial and common Creator, than a rigid adherence to the principles of justice on the part of a powerful nation in its transactions with a weaker and uncivilized people whom circumstances have placed at its disposal.

Before concluding, fellow-citizens, I must say something to you on the subject of the parties at this time existing in our country. To me it appears perfectly clear that the interest of that country requires that the violence of the spirit by which those parties are at this time governed must be greatly mitigated, if not entirely extinguished, or consequences will ensue which are appalling to be thought of.

If parties in a republic are necessary to secure a degree of vigilance sufficient to keep the public functionaries within the bounds of law and duty, at that point their usefulness ends. Beyond that they become destructive of public virtue, the parent of a spirit antagonist to that of liberty, and eventually its inevitable conqueror. We have examples of republics where the love of country and of liberty at one time were the dominant passions of the whole mass of citizens, and yet, with the continuance of the name and forms of free government, not a vestige of these qualities remaining in the bosoms of any one of its citizens. It was the beautiful remark of a distinguished English writer that "in the Roman senate Octavius had a party and Anthony a party, but the Commonwealth had none." Yet the senate continued to meet in the temple of liberty to talk of the sacredness and beauty of the Commonwealth and gaze at the statues of the elder Brutus and of the Curtii and Decii, and the people assembled in the forum, not, as in the days of Camillus and the Scipios, to cast their free votes for annual magistrates or pass upon the acts of the senate, but to receive from the hands of the leaders of the respective parties their share of the spoils and to shout for one or the other, as those collected in Gaul or Egypt and the lesser Asia would furnish the larger dividend. The spirit of liberty had fled, and, avoiding the abodes of civilized man, had sought protection in the wilds of Scythia or Scandinavia; and so under the operation of the same causes and influences it will fly from our Capitol and our forums. A calamity so awful, not only to our country, but to the world, must be deprecated by every patriot and every tendency to a state of things likely to produce it immediately checked. Such a tendency has existed—does exist. Always the friend of my countrymen, never their flatterer, it becomes my duty to say to them from this high place to which their partiality has exalted me that there exists in the land a spirit hostile to their best interests—hostile to liberty itself. It is a spirit contracted in its views, selfish in its objects. It looks to the aggrandizement of a few even to the destruction of the interests of the whole. The entire remedy is with the people. Something, however, may be effected by the means which they have placed in my hands. It is union that we want, not of a party for the sake of that party, but a union of the whole country for the sake of the whole country, for the defense of its interests and its honor against foreign aggression, for the defense of those principles for which our ancestors so gloriously contended. As far as it depends upon me it shall be accomplished. All the influence that I possess shall be exerted to prevent the formation at least of an Executive party in the halls of the legislative body. I wish for the support of no member of that body to any measure of mine that does not satisfy his judgment and his sense of duty to those from whom he holds his appointment, nor any confidence in advance from the people but that asked for by Mr. Jefferson, "to give firmness and effect to the legal administration of their affairs."

I deem the present occasion sufficiently important and solemn to justify me in expressing to my fellow-citizens a profound reverence for the Christian religion and a thorough conviction that sound morals, religious liberty, and a just sense of religious responsibility are essentially connected with all true and lasting happiness; and to that good Being who has blessed us by the gifts of civil and religious freedom, who watched over and prospered the labors of our fathers and has hitherto preserved to us institutions far exceeding in excellence those of any other people, let us unite in fervently commending every interest of our beloved country in all future time.

Fellow-citizens, being fully invested with that high office to which the partiality of my countrymen has called me, I now take an affectionate leave of you. You will bear with you to your homes the remembrance of the pledge I have this day given to discharge all the high duties of my exalted station according to the best of my ability, and I shall enter upon their performance with entire confidence in the support of a just and generous people.

Old Tippecanoe

THE INAUGURAL ADDRESS OF WILLIAM HENRY HARRISON

Daniel Walker Howe

THE 3RD OF March, 1841, was bitter cold in Washington, D.C. William Henry Harrison, having been chosen ninth president of the United States in the election of 1840, was due to take the oath of office and assume its duties. Harrison had been depicted during the campaign as a simple old man, content to read while sipping hard cider in the garden of a log cabin. This image had been created as satire by his Jacksonian Democrat opponents, but then was preempted by his Whig Party supporters, who found it helped Harrison win over some Jacksonian voters. The incoming president was eager to move away from this humble characterization toward a more presidential one, closer to his own self-image. Accordingly, he had composed a dignified and very elaborate address for his inauguration, only slightly edited by the learned orator Daniel Webster (whom Harrison had already selected to be his secretary of state). Defying the cold, the new incumbent refused to wear an overcoat while delivering his lengthy oration, even though, at sixty-eight, he was the oldest president inaugurated (before sixty-nine-year-old Ronald Reagan in 1981). The old man (by the standards of the age) caught the fatal chill that led to pneumonia. As president, he of course received the best medical care on offer—which, in an era of medical blood-letting, made his condition worse. Harrison's address remains the longest one ever delivered at a presidential inauguration, heralding, ironically, the shortest term ever served by an American president. Harrison died exactly one month after delivering this speech.

Harrison conceived his Inaugural Address as a repudiation of the strong presidency that the Democratic Party of Andrew Jackson and his designated heir

Martin Van Buren had introduced. Presidential power had been the major issue debated in the campaign of 1840. The Whig Party to which Harrison belonged had taken its name from an English political party that resisted the executive power of the king. Still a major party in 1840, the UK Whigs had been responsible for both reapportioning the House of Commons and freeing the slaves in the British Empire. A prominent feature of the new American Whig Party was the hostile portrayal of Andrew Jackson as a would-be monarch, "King Andrew the First." Sometimes called the "country party" tradition, such resistance to executive power had been a recurring theme in both colonial and English political tradition during and before the American Revolution. This attitude retained sufficient appeal among the American electorate for the Whigs to invoke it successfully in the election of 1840. Meanwhile, in a variety of locations rewriting their state constitutions at the time, the Whigs consistently favored restricting the executive power of the governors.

The biggest factor in determining the outcome of the election, however, had actually been the Financial Panic of 1839, which the electorate blamed on the incumbent administration, as electorates always do in hard times. Harrison had beaten Van Buren 234 to 60 in the Electoral College. He could look forward to a Congress with comfortable Whig majorities of seven in the Senate and thirty-one in the House. Under the circumstances, one might expect that Harrison would be looking forward to a glorious triumph and exercising relatively unchecked power. In his Inaugural Address, however, he took an altogether different stance: assuring his audience that he would carefully restrict his own presidential powers, in keeping with his party's campaign commitment.

Harrison promised "a summary of the principles which will govern me" as president. All too often, in both ancient and modern times, he noted, officeholders neglect promises made before election once they have secured power. (Classical allusions were consistent with the dignified image the speaker wished to present; Harrison had studied classics at Hampton-Sydney College in Virginia before turning to his military career.) The age cherished public speaking as an art form, and Harrison intended to lay his claim to its prestige. Yet the grammatical structure of his oration, with its long and complex sentences, does not seem very well suited to a large audience out of doors. At first it may have seemed to listeners that the incoming president prioritized constitutional theory over practical matters, but Harrison soon gave his constitutional interpretation specific relevance. Declaring that he regretted the Constitution had permitted presidents to run for re-election, Harrison promised at the outset that he himself would not do so. Everyone in the audience would have immediately interpreted this as a reproach directed at both Andrew Jackson and Martin Van Buren, whose attempted re-election Harrison had just defeated.

The speaker immediately turned his attention to another power the Constitution had bestowed on the federal chief executive: to veto acts of Congress. At that time, the veto power seemed much more drastic and unusual than it does to us. None of the first six presidents had ever invoked it. The veto was closely associated with Andrew Jackson's decision to use it to nullify congressional renewal of the Charter of the Second Bank of the United States. Harrison took the position that legislative power belonged to the houses of Congress, and the executive branch should not normally interfere with it. In the final analysis, however, he reluctantly conceded that the existence of a veto power was legitimate to help guard against abuse of the Constitution by Congress.

Harrison next complained about the president's power to appoint all employees of the federal government. Andrew Jackson had turned this labor force (mostly postal employees in those days) into a huge source of political power by purging employees who were not active members of his party and filling their places with loyal Jacksonian Democrats. No civil service then restrained the president's discretion in appointments. Harrison's legitimate protest against such abuse of executive power was only gradually implemented during the late decades of the nineteenth century by the creation of the civil service. Another of Harrison's complaints, that Jackson tried to interfere with freedom of the press in order to favor periodicals that supported the Democratic Party, did not identify a specific remedy and did not lead to any particular action.

Harrison expressed disapproval of congressional attempts to interfere with the governance of the District of Columbia. He was undoubtedly referring to proposals to abolish slavery in the District, although he never mentioned the word "slavery." Such proposals often included financial compensation for slave owners, but even so were bitterly resented and opposed by slavery's advocates throughout the South. Harrison had consistently supported slavery during his long service as a governor in the Northwest Territories, and on this issue he did not draw a distinction between his position and the well-known pro-slavery stance of Jackson and his Democratic Party. On the subject of relations with the American Indians, however, Harrison did draw such a distinction. Opposition to Jackson's and Van Buren's drastic program of "Indian Removal" had been strong among Whigs. Earlier in 1840, Harrison had published a sympathetic history of the Northwestern tribes, and in his Inaugural Address he called for "liberality and justice" in dealing with "our aboriginal neighbors."

To summarize and conflate his moral precepts, Harrison deplored political partisanship. "The reign of an intolerant spirit of party amongst a free people seldom fails to result in a dangerous accession to the executive power," he warned. Clearly, Harrison identified political partisanship with Andrew Jackson and his followers, but not with his own Whig followers. "All the influence that I possess,"

President Harrison promised, "shall be exerted to prevent the formation at least of an Executive party in the halls of the legislative body." How this principle could have been followed in practice the American people never had a chance to witness. Harrison's sudden and surprising death left the White House in the control of his vice president, John Tyler. (Vice presidents succeeding to the presidency upon their predecessor's death do not have an opportunity to deliver an inaugural address.) Tyler disagreed with the congressional Whigs about recreating a Bank of the United States and vetoed their efforts to charter one. Tyler would have liked to create a party of his own, or to enlist the Democrats behind him, but never succeeded in either project. From our own point of view, Harrison's election led to what historians have called "the second party system," a two-party system of Whigs and Democrats, rather than the no-party system to which Harrison himself had aspired.

John Tyler's Address upon Assuming the Office of President of the United States

FRIDAY, APRIL 9, 1841

TO THE PEOPLE of the United States
Fellow-Citizens:
Before my arrival at the seat of Government the painful communication was made to you by the officers presiding over the several Departments of the deeply regretted death of William Henry Harrison, late President of the United States. Upon him you had conferred your suffrages for the first office in your gift, and had selected him as your chosen instrument to correct and reform all such errors and abuses as had manifested themselves from time to time in the practical operation of the Government. While standing at the threshold of this great work he has by the dispensation of an all-wise Providence been removed from amongst us, and by the provisions of the Constitution the efforts to be directed to the accomplishing of this vitally important task have devolved upon myself. This same occurrence has subjected the wisdom and sufficiency of our institutions to a new test. For the first time in our history the person elected to the Vice-Presidency of the United States, by the happening of a contingency provided for in the Constitution, has had devolved upon him the Presidential office. The spirit of faction, which is directly opposed to the spirit of a lofty patriotism, may find in this occasion for assaults upon my Administration; and in succeeding, under circumstances so sudden and unexpected and to responsibilities so greatly augmented, to the administration of public affairs I shall place in the intelligence and patriotism of the people my only sure reliance. My earnest prayer shall be constantly addressed to the all-wise and all-powerful Being who made me, and by whose dispensation

I am called to the high office of President of this Confederacy, understandingly to carry out the principles of that Constitution which I have sworn "to protect, preserve, and defend."

The usual opportunity which is afforded to a Chief Magistrate upon his induction to office of presenting to his countrymen an exposition of the policy which would guide his Administration, in the form of an inaugural address, not having, under the peculiar circumstances which have brought me to the discharge of the high duties of President of the United States, been afforded to me, a brief exposition of the principles which will govern me in the general course of my administration of public affairs would seem to be due as well to myself as to you.

In regard to foreign nations, the groundwork of my policy will be justice on our part to all, submitting to injustice from none. While I shall sedulously cultivate the relations of peace and amity with one and all, it will be my most imperative duty to see that the honor of the country shall sustain no blemish. With a view to this, the condition of our military defenses will become a matter of anxious solicitude. The Army, which has in other days covered itself with renown, and the Navy, not inappropriately termed the right arm of the public defense, which has spread a light of glory over the American standard in all the waters of the earth, should be rendered replete with efficiency.

In view of the fact, well avouched by history, that the tendency of all human institutions is to concentrate power in the hands of a single man, and that their ultimate downfall has proceeded from this cause, I deem it of the most essential importance that a complete separation should take place between the sword and the purse. No matter where or how the public moneys shall be deposited, so long as the President can exert the power of appointing and removing at his pleasure the agents selected for their custody the Commander in Chief of the Army and Navy is in fact the treasurer. A permanent and radical change should therefore be decreed. The patronage incident to the Presidential office, already great, is constantly increasing. Such increase is destined to keep pace with the growth of our population, until, without a figure of speech, an army of officeholders may be spread over the land. The unrestrained power exerted by a selfishly ambitious man in order either to perpetuate his authority or to hand it over to some favorite as his successor may lead to the employment of all the means within his control to accomplish his object. The right to remove from office, while subjected to no just restraint, is inevitably destined to produce a spirit of crouching servility with the official corps, which, in order to uphold the hand which feeds them, would lead to direct and active interference in the elections, both State and Federal, thereby subjecting the course of State legislation to the dictation of the chief executive officer and making the will of that officer absolute and supreme. I will at a proper time invoke the action of Congress upon this subject, and shall readily acquiesce in the adoption of all proper measures which are calculated to arrest these evils, so full of danger in their tendency. I will remove no incumbent from office who has faithfully and honestly acquitted himself of the duties of his office, except in such cases where such officer has been guilty of an active partisanship or by secret means—the less manly, and therefore the more objectionable—has given his official influence to the purposes of party, thereby bringing the patronage of the Government in conflict with the freedom of elections. Numerous removals may become necessary under this rule. These will be made by me through no acerbity of feeling—I have had no cause to cherish or indulge unkind feelings toward any—but my conduct will be regulated by a profound sense of what is due to the country and its institutions; nor shall I neglect to apply the same unbending rule to those of my own appointment. Freedom of opinion will be tolerated, the full enjoyment of the right of suffrage will be maintained as the birthright of every American citizen; but I say emphatically to the official corps, "Thus far and no farther." I have dwelt the longer upon this subject because removals from office are likely often to arise, and I would have my countrymen to understand the principle of the Executive action.

In all public expenditures the most rigid economy should be resorted to, and, as one of its results, a public debt in time of peace be sedulously avoided. A wise and patriotic constituency will never object to the imposition of necessary burdens for useful ends, and true wisdom dictates the resort to such means in order to supply deficiencies in the revenue, rather than to those doubtful expedients which, ultimating in a public debt, serve to embarrass the resources of the country and to lessen its ability to meet any great emergency which may arise. All sinecures should be abolished. The appropriations should be direct and explicit, so as to leave as limited a share of discretion to the disbursing agents as may be found compatible with the public service. A strict responsibility on the part of all the agents of the Government should be maintained and peculation or defalcation visited with immediate expulsion from office and the most condign punishment.

The public interest also demands that if any war has existed between the Government and the currency it shall cease. Measures of a financial character now having the sanction of legal enactment shall be faithfully enforced until repealed by the legislative authority. But I owe it to myself to declare that I regard existing enactments as unwise and impolitic and in a high degree oppressive. I shall promptly give my sanction to any constitutional measure which, originating in Congress, shall have for its object the restoration of a sound circulating medium, so essentially necessary to give confidence in all the transactions of life, to secure to industry its just and adequate rewards, and to reestablish the public prosperity. In deciding upon the adaptation of any such measure to the end proposed, as well as its conformity to the Constitution, I shall resort to the fathers of the great republican school for advice and instruction, to be drawn from their sage views of our system of government and the light of their ever-glorious example.

The institutions under which we live, my countrymen, secure each person in the perfect enjoyment of all his rights. The spectacle is exhibited to the world of a government deriving its powers from the consent of the governed and having imparted to it only so much power as is necessary for its successful operation. Those who are charged with its administration should carefully abstain from all attempts to enlarge the range of powers thus granted to the several departments of the Government other than by an appeal to the people for additional grants, lest by so doing they disturb that balance which the patriots and statesmen who framed the Constitution designed to establish between the Federal Government and the States composing the Union. The observance of these rules is enjoined upon us by that feeling of reverence and affection which finds a place in the heart of every patriot for the preservation of union and the blessings of union—for the good of our children and our children's children through countless generations. An opposite course could not fail to generate factions intent upon the gratification of their selfish ends, to give birth to local and sectional jealousies, and to ultimate either in breaking asunder the bonds of union or in building up a central system which would inevitably end in a bloody scepter and an iron crown.

In conclusion I beg you to be assured that I shall exert myself to carry the foregoing principles into practice during my administration of the Government, and, confiding in the protecting care of an everwatchful and overruling Providence, it shall be my first and highest duty to preserve unimpaired the free institutions under which we live and transmit them to those who shall succeed me in their full force and vigor.

The President without a Party
JOHN TYLER'S ADDRESS UPON ASSUMING THE OFFICE OF PRESIDENT OF THE UNITED STATES

Christopher J. Leahy

JOHN TYLER'S ACCESSION to the presidency marked the first time in American history that a vice president took over the nation's highest office because of the death of the incumbent—in this case, William Henry Harrison. Upon Harrison's passing on Palm Sunday, April 4, 1841, his cabinet dispatched two messengers to Tyler's home in Williamsburg, Virginia, with instructions to bring the vice president back to Washington, where he could take the reins of the government. Arriving in the capital around 4:00 a.m. on Tuesday, April 6, Tyler checked into a suite at Brown's Indian Queen Hotel. Fully aware that Harrison's death had created a potentially dangerous constitutional crisis, and imbued with a sense of the historical significance of the moment, Tyler took steps to ensure that he established himself as president of the United States. Later that morning, he took the oath of office in the parlor of the hotel and immediately made clear that he was in charge. "I am the President," he declared, "and I shall be held responsible for my administration."[1]

Three days later, Tyler took another step to establish himself as chief executive when he delivered what amounted to an inaugural address before a small audience at the Capitol. Not nearly as long as a typical inaugural address, and unaccompanied by the traditional pomp and ceremony of a normal inauguration, Tyler's remarks focused on three areas—foreign affairs, the federal government's patronage system, and financial matters—and also included a summary statement of his political principles. Tyler believed that the American people deserved to hear from him and he wanted to lay out some general plans of public policy. He also aimed to reassure the nation that, despite the calamity of Harrison's death, the government would continue to function smoothly and without interruption.

As he prepared a rough draft of his address, Tyler included a section that renounced his desire to seek a presidential term in his own right in 1844. Before leaving Williamsburg to travel to Washington, he spoke briefly with his neighbor and friend, Nathaniel Beverley Tucker. Tucker, a professor at the nearby College of William and Mary, advised Tyler to assert from the start that he would merely serve out the reminder of Harrison's term and retire. Tucker recognized that, despite Tyler's nomination and election to the vice presidency as a Whig in November 1840, his long-standing political principles of states' rights, strict construction of the Constitution, and limited federal power did not comport with the nationalist-oriented ideology of the mainstream of the party. Tucker worried that leading Whigs such as Senator Henry Clay, in command of a newly won majority, would seek to dominate Tyler and force him to accept the party's entire agenda. Moreover, the opposition Democrats might attempt to exploit this potentially difficult relationship between the new president and Congress, which would tear Tyler "in pieces as by wild horses" if he appeared overly ambitious. In Tucker's view, disclaiming a desire to stand for election in 1844 would allow Tyler to govern while other contenders for the presidency—including Clay—jockeyed for position. Tyler could thus adopt the pose of a disinterested statesman who would act only for the good of the nation.[2]

Tucker underestimated Tyler's ambition. The statement disavowing a second term did not survive revisions to the address. The new president intended to seek his own term in 1844. In fact, the best way to read the majority of Tyler's Inaugural Address is to interpret it as the opening salvo in his own campaign for the White House, though he made no overt statement in the address announcing his intentions. Not content with being remembered only as the man who had replaced William Henry Harrison, Tyler began to lay the groundwork for his campaign mere days after taking office.

The section covering foreign affairs was the most cursory of the address but nevertheless imparted a strong message. Tyler had been briefed by Secretary of State Daniel Webster on the progress of the case against Alexander McLeod, a Canadian who had been indicted for murder and arson by the State of New York for his role in the destruction of the *Caroline* in December 1837. The *Caroline* was an American steamer that conveyed supplies to Canadian rebels who were defying British authority in the area around Niagara Falls. McLeod had allegedly aided a contingent of British soldiers who boarded the ship with the intention of putting an end to the ongoing insurrection. In the melee that ensued, an American named Amos Durfee had been killed—shot through the head with a musket ball. McLeod had bragged of his role in the so-called *Caroline* affair and faced the death penalty if a jury in New York found him guilty of his alleged crimes. Britain had made clear to the U.S. government that such an outcome could result in war, because, as a Canadian, McLeod was a British subject. Furthermore, Whitehall maintained that McLeod's actions had been undertaken as a military necessity and with the concurrence of military authorities in Canada. The general statement in Tyler's inaugural address that asserted his desire to "sedulously cultivate the relations of peace and amity with one and all" alluded to the tensions between the United States and Britain over McLeod's fate. Tyler further made clear, however, that "the honor" of his country "shall sustain no blemish" on his watch. What he had done with this statement was adopt a firm posture toward Britain that he hoped would buy him time to work behind the scenes to secure a not-guilty verdict for McLeod in a New York court. With the aid of Webster, he succeeded. Moreover, he and the secretary of state accomplished a tremendous feat in 1842 when they secured the Webster-Ashburton Treaty with Britain, a pact that, among other things, settled a long-standing border dispute between Maine and Canada.

Domestic political circumstances influenced the remainder of Tyler's inaugural address. He paid lip service to the Whig argument that Democratic Presidents Andrew Jackson and Martin Van Buren had abused the federal patronage, or "spoils system," by appointing and removing officeholders based solely on their partisanship. He decried the practice and even suggested he would be willing to work with the Whig congressional majority to remedy the "evils" inherent in the system.

He did not mean it. In fact, Tyler contradicted himself and used his inaugural address to put the Whigs on notice that he would not hesitate to remove appointed officials who sought to advance the party's agenda at the expense of his administration. He signaled his willingness to act on behalf of his own political interests through patronage if circumstances demanded it. Tyler evidently intended to attempt to build a political base for himself using the presidential power to appoint and remove officeholders. Far from taking the advice of his friend Tucker and declaring he would not seek a term of his own in 1844, the new president was laying the groundwork for his political advancement. And he intended to head the Whigs off if they interfered with his overriding goal of winning the presidency in his own right.

With a similar objective in mind, Tyler also addressed the state of the nation's finances. The effects of an economic depression, known to history as the Panic of 1837, lingered as Tyler assumed the presidency. Indeed, Henry Clay had persuaded President Harrison to call a special session of Congress for the summer of 1841 so that the Whig majority could take steps to alleviate the country's financial woes. Tyler was not keen on the special session but recognized astutely that Clay and his comrades intended to repeal President Van Buren's ineffective Independent Treasury, which had hampered the nation's currency system, and charter a new national bank as the signature feature of their economic recovery program. Tyler favored repeal of the Independent Treasury, but would not cede control of the process to create an appropriate financial institution to Clay. He asserted his willingness to sign "any constitutional measure" the Congress devised that would provide for the "restoration of a sound circulating medium."

But therein lay the rub. Tyler proclaimed that he would follow the example of "the fathers of the great republican school"—Jefferson and Madison—as he determined the constitutionality of the bank the Whigs were sure to create during the special session. As president, he retained the veto power and would be the ultimate arbiter of whether such a bank passed constitutional muster. This portion of the address served to remind the American people as well as the Whigs of his long-standing political principles. Without calling it by name, Tyler returned here to the compact theory of government spelled out in the Kentucky and Virginia Resolutions, authored by those republican fathers in 1798, that he believed properly articulated the "balance" between the federal government and the states. He could not have made any clearer his intention to abide by the states' rights, strict construction, limited government ideology that had guided him throughout his long career in politics. With this section of the inaugural, he thus set the stage for the inevitable clash with the Whig majority that would result in his banishment from their ranks as he became a president without a party.

Notes

1. Christopher J. Leahy, *President without a Party: The Life of John Tyler* (Baton Rouge: Louisiana State University Press, 2020), 132.
2. Leahy, *President without a Party*, 127.

James K. Polk's Inaugural Address

TUESDAY, MARCH 4, 1845

FELLOW-CITIZENS:

Without solicitation on my part, I have been chosen by the free and voluntary suffrages of my countrymen to the most honorable and most responsible office on earth. I am deeply impressed with gratitude for the confidence reposed in me. Honored with this distinguished consideration at an earlier period of life than any of my predecessors, I can not disguise the diffidence with which I am about to enter on the discharge of my official duties.

If the more aged and experienced men who have filled the office of President of the United States even in the infancy of the Republic distrusted their ability to discharge the duties of that exalted station, what ought not to be the apprehensions of one so much younger and less endowed now that our domain extends from ocean to ocean, that our people have so greatly increased in numbers, and at a time when so great diversity of opinion prevails in regard to the principles and policy which should characterize the administration of our Government? Well may the boldest fear and the wisest tremble when incurring responsibilities on which may depend our country's peace and prosperity, and in some degree the hopes and happiness of the whole human family.

In assuming responsibilities so vast I fervently invoke the aid of that Almighty Ruler of the Universe in whose hands are the destinies of nations and of men to guard this Heaven-favored land against the mischiefs which without His guidance might arise from an unwise public policy. With a firm reliance upon the wisdom of Omnipotence to sustain and direct me in the path of duty which I am appointed to pursue, I stand in the presence of this assembled multitude of my countrymen to take upon myself the solemn obligation "to the best of my ability to preserve, protect, and defend the Constitution of the United States."

A concise enumeration of the principles which will guide me in the administrative policy of the Government is not only in accordance with the examples set me by all my predecessors, but is eminently befitting the occasion.

The Constitution itself, plainly written as it is, the safeguard of our federative compact, the offspring of concession and compromise, binding together in the bonds of peace and union this great and increasing family of free and independent States, will be the chart by which I shall be directed.

It will be my first care to administer the Government in the true spirit of that instrument, and to assume no powers not expressly granted or clearly implied in its terms. The Government of the United States is one of delegated and limited powers, and it is by a strict adherence to the clearly granted powers and by abstaining from the exercise of doubtful or unauthorized implied powers that we have the only sure guaranty against the recurrence of those unfortunate collisions between the Federal and State authorities which have occasionally so much disturbed the harmony of our system and even threatened the perpetuity of our glorious Union.

"To the States, respectively, or to the people" have been reserved "the powers not delegated to the United States by the Constitution nor prohibited by it to the States." Each State is a complete sovereignty within the sphere of its reserved powers. The Government of the Union, acting within the sphere of its delegated authority, is also a complete sovereignty. While the General Government should abstain from the exercise of authority not clearly delegated to it, the States should be equally careful that in the maintenance of their rights they do not overstep the limits of powers reserved to them. One of the most distinguished of my predecessors attached deserved importance to "the support of the State governments in all their rights, as the most competent administration for our domestic concerns and the surest bulwark against antirepublican tendencies," and to the "preservation of the General Government in its whole constitutional vigor, as the sheet anchor of our peace at home and safety abroad."

To the Government of the United States has been intrusted the exclusive management of our foreign affairs. Beyond that it wields a few general enumerated powers. It does not force reform on the States. It leaves individuals, over whom it casts its protecting influence, entirely free to improve their own condition by the legitimate exercise of all their mental and physical powers. It is a common protector of each and all the States; of every man who lives upon our soil, whether of native or foreign birth; of every religious sect, in their worship of the Almighty according to the dictates of their own conscience; of every shade of opinion, and the most free inquiry; of every art, trade, and occupation consistent with the laws of the States. And we rejoice in the general happiness, prosperity, and advancement of our country, which have been the offspring of freedom, and not of power.

This most admirable and wisest system of well-regulated self-government among men ever devised by human minds has been tested by its successful operation for more than half a century, and if preserved from the usurpations of the Federal Government on the one hand and the exercise by the States of powers not reserved to them on the other, will, I fervently hope and believe, endure for ages to come and dispense the blessings of civil and religious liberty to distant generations. To effect objects so dear to every patriot I shall devote myself with anxious solicitude. It will be my desire to guard against that most fruitful source of danger to the harmonious action of our system which consists in substituting the mere discretion and caprice of the Executive or of majorities in the legislative department of the Government for powers which have been withheld from the Federal Government by the Constitution. By the theory of our Government majorities rule, but this right is not an arbitrary or unlimited one. It is a right to be exercised in subordination to the Constitution and in conformity to it. One great object of the Constitution was to restrain majorities from oppressing minorities or encroaching upon their just rights. Minorities have a right to appeal to the Constitution as a shield against such oppression.

That the blessings of liberty which our Constitution secures may be enjoyed alike by minorities and majorities, the Executive has been wisely invested with a qualified veto upon the acts of the Legislature. It is a negative power, and is conservative in its character. It arrests for the time hasty, inconsiderate, or unconstitutional legislation, invites reconsideration, and transfers questions at issue between the legislative and executive departments to the tribunal of the people. Like all other powers, it is subject to be abused. When judiciously and properly exercised, the Constitution itself may be saved from infraction and the rights of all preserved and protected.

The inestimable value of our Federal Union is felt and acknowledged by all. By this system of united and confederated States our people are permitted collectively and individually to seek their own happiness in their own way, and the consequences have been most auspicious. Since the Union was formed the number of the States has increased from thirteen to twenty-eight; two of these have taken their position as members of the Confederacy within the last week. Our population has increased from three to twenty millions. New communities and States are seeking protection under its aegis, and multitudes from the Old World are flocking to our shores to participate in its blessings. Beneath its benign sway peace and prosperity prevail. Freed from the burdens and miseries of war, our trade and intercourse have extended throughout the world. Mind, no longer tasked in devising means to accomplish or resist schemes of ambition, usurpation, or conquest, is devoting itself to man's true interests in developing his faculties and powers and the capacity of nature to minister to his enjoyments. Genius is free to announce its inventions and discoveries, and the hand is free to accomplish whatever the head conceives not incompatible with the rights of a fellow-being. All distinctions of birth or of rank have been abolished. All citizens, whether native or adopted, are placed upon terms of precise equality. All are entitled to equal rights and equal protection. No union exists between church and state, and perfect freedom of opinion is guaranteed to all sects and creeds.

These are some of the blessings secured to our happy land by our Federal Union. To perpetuate them it is our sacred duty to preserve it. Who shall assign limits to the achievements of free minds and free hands under the protection of this glorious Union? No treason to mankind since the organization of society would be equal in atrocity to that of him who would lift his hand to destroy it. He would overthrow the noblest structure of human wisdom, which protects himself and his fellow-man. He would stop the progress of free government and involve his country either in anarchy or despotism. He would extinguish the fire of liberty, which warms and animates the hearts of happy millions and invites all the nations of the earth to imitate our example. If he say that error and wrong are committed in the administration of the Government, let him remember that nothing human can be perfect, and that under no other system of government revealed by Heaven or devised by man has reason been allowed so free and broad a scope to combat error. Has the sword of despots proved to be a safer or surer instrument of reform in government than enlightened reason? Does he expect to find among the ruins of this Union a happier abode for our swarming millions than they now have under it? Every lover of his country must shudder at the thought of the possibility of its dissolution, and will be ready to adopt the patriotic sentiment, "Our Federal Union—it must be preserved." To preserve it the compromises which alone enabled our fathers to form a common constitution for the government and protection of so many States and distinct communities, of such diversified habits, interests, and domestic institutions, must be sacredly and religiously observed. Any attempt to disturb or destroy these compromises, being terms of the compact of union, can lead to none other than the most ruinous and disastrous consequences.

It is a source of deep regret that in some sections of our country misguided persons have occasionally indulged in schemes and agitations whose object is the destruction of domestic institutions existing in other sections—institutions which existed at the adoption of the Constitution and were recognized and protected by it. All must see that if it were possible for them to be successful in attaining their object the dissolution of the Union and the consequent destruction of our happy form of government must speedily follow.

I am happy to believe that at every period of our existence as a nation there has existed, and continues to exist, among the great mass of our people a devotion to the Union of the States which will shield and protect it against the moral treason of any who would seriously contemplate its destruction. To secure a continuance of that devotion the compromises of the Constitution must not only be preserved, but sectional jealousies and heartburnings must be discountenanced, and all should remember that they are members of the same political family, having a common destiny. To increase the attachment of our people to the Union, our laws should be just. Any policy which shall tend to favor monopolies or the peculiar interests of sections or classes must operate to the prejudice of the interest of their fellow-citizens, and should be avoided. If the compromises of the Constitution be preserved, if sectional jealousies and heartburnings be discountenanced, if our laws be just and the Government be practically administered strictly within the limits of power prescribed to it, we may discard all apprehensions for the safety of the Union.

With these views of the nature, character, and objects of the Government and the value of the Union, I shall steadily oppose the creation of those institutions and systems which in their nature tend to pervert it from its legitimate purposes and make it the instrument of sections, classes, and individuals. We need no national banks or other extraneous institutions planted around the Government to control or strengthen it in opposition to the will of its authors. Experience has taught us how unnecessary they are as auxiliaries of the public authorities—how impotent for good and how powerful for mischief.

Ours was intended to be a plain and frugal government, and I shall regard it to be my duty to recommend to Congress and, as far as the Executive is concerned, to enforce by all the means within my power the strictest economy in the expenditure of the public money which may be compatible with the public interests.

A national debt has become almost an institution of European monarchies. It is viewed in some of them as an essential prop to existing governments. Melancholy is the condition of that people whose government can be sustained only by a system which periodically transfers large amounts from the labor of the many to the coffers of the few. Such a system is incompatible with the ends for which our republican Government was instituted. Under a wise policy the debts contracted in our Revolution and during the War of 1812 have been happily extinguished. By a judicious application of the revenues not required for other necessary purposes, it is not doubted that the debt which has grown out of the circumstances of the last few years may be speedily paid off.

I congratulate my fellow-citizens on the entire restoration of the credit of the General Government of the Union and that of many of the States. Happy would it be for the indebted States if they were freed from their liabilities, many of which were incautiously contracted. Although the Government of the Union is neither in a legal nor a moral sense bound for the debts of the States, and it would be a violation of our compact of union to assume them, yet we can not but feel a deep interest in seeing all the States meet their public liabilities and pay off their just debts at the earliest practicable period. That they will do so as soon as it can be done without imposing too heavy burdens on their citizens there is no reason to doubt. The sound moral and honorable feeling of the people of the indebted States can not be questioned, and we are happy to perceive a settled disposition on their part, as their ability returns after a season of unexampled pecuniary embarrassment, to pay off all just demands and to acquiesce in any reasonable measures to accomplish that object.

One of the difficulties which we have had to encounter in the practical administration of the Government consists in the adjustment of our revenue laws and the levy of the taxes necessary for the support of Government. In the general proposition that no more money shall be collected than the necessities of an economical administration shall require all parties seem to acquiesce. Nor does there seem to be any material difference of opinion as to the absence of right in the Government to tax one section of country, or one class of citizens, or one occupation, for the mere profit of another. "Justice and sound policy forbid the Federal Government to foster one branch of industry to the detriment of another, or to cherish the interests of one portion to the injury of another portion of our common country." I have heretofore declared to my fellow-citizens that "in my judgment it is the duty of the Government to extend, as far as it may be practicable to do so, by its revenue laws and all other means within its power, fair and just protection to all of the great interests of the whole Union, embracing agriculture, manufactures, the mechanic arts, commerce, and navigation." I have also declared my opinion to be "in favor of a tariff for revenue," and that "in adjusting the details of such a tariff I have sanctioned such moderate discriminating duties as would produce the amount of revenue needed and at the same time afford reasonable incidental protection to our home industry," and that I was "opposed to a tariff for protection merely, and not for revenue."

The power "to lay and collect taxes, duties, imposts, and excises" was an indispensable one to be conferred on the Federal Government, which without it would possess no means of providing for its own support. In executing this power by levying a tariff of duties for the support of Government, the raising of *revenue* should be the *object* and *protection* the *incident*. To reverse this principle and make *protection* the *object* and *revenue* the *incident* would be to inflict manifest injustice upon all other than the protected interests. In levying duties for revenue it is doubtless proper to make such discriminations within the *revenue principle* as will afford incidental protection to our home interests. Within the revenue limit there is a discretion to discriminate; beyond that limit the rightful exercise of the power is not conceded. The incidental protection afforded to our home interests by discriminations within the revenue range it is believed will be ample. In making discriminations all our home interests should as far as practicable be equally protected. The largest portion of our people are agriculturists. Others are employed in manufactures, commerce, navigation, and the mechanic arts. They are all engaged in their respective pursuits, and their joint labors constitute the national or home industry. To tax one branch of this home industry for the benefit of another would be unjust. No one of these interests can rightfully claim an advantage over the others, or to be enriched by impoverishing the others. All are equally entitled to the fostering care and protection of the Government. In exercising a sound discretion in levying discriminating duties within the limit prescribed, care should be taken that it be done in a manner not to benefit the wealthy few at the expense of the toiling millions by taxing *lowest* the luxuries of life, or articles of superior quality and high price, which can only be consumed by the wealthy, and *highest* the necessaries of life, or articles of coarse quality and low price, which the poor and great mass of our people must consume. The burdens of government should as far as practicable be distributed justly and equally among all classes of our population. These general views, long entertained on this subject, I have deemed it proper to reiterate. It is a subject upon which conflicting interests of sections and occupations are supposed to exist, and a spirit of mutual concession and compromise in adjusting its details should be cherished by every part of our widespread country as the only means of preserving harmony and a cheerful acquiescence of all in the operation of our revenue laws. Our patriotic citizens in every part of the Union will readily submit to the payment of such taxes as shall be needed for the support of their Government, whether in peace or in war, if they are so levied as to distribute the burdens as equally as possible among them.

The Republic of Texas has made known her desire to come into our Union, to form a part of our Confederacy and enjoy with us the blessings of liberty secured and guaranteed by our Constitution. Texas was once a part of our country—was unwisely ceded away to a foreign power—is now independent, and possesses an undoubted right to dispose of a part or the whole of her territory and to merge her sovereignty as a separate and independent state in ours. I congratulate my country that by an act of the late Congress of the United States the assent of this Government has been given to the reunion, and it only remains for the two countries to agree upon the terms to consummate an object so important to both.

I regard the question of annexation as belonging exclusively to the United States and Texas. They are independent powers competent to contract, and foreign nations have no right to interfere with them or to take exceptions to their reunion. Foreign powers do not seem to appreciate the true character of our Government. Our Union is a confederation of independent States, whose policy is peace with each other and all the world. To enlarge its limits is to extend the dominions of peace over additional territories and increasing millions. The world has nothing to fear from military ambition in our Government. While the Chief Magistrate and the popular branch of Congress are elected for short terms by the suffrages of those millions who must in their own persons bear all the burdens and miseries of war, our Government can not be otherwise than pacific. Foreign powers should therefore look on the annexation of Texas to the United States not as the conquest of a nation seeking to extend her dominions by arms and violence, but as the peaceful acquisition of a territory once her own, by adding another member to our confederation, with the consent of that member, thereby diminishing the chances of war and opening to them new and ever-increasing markets for their products.

To Texas the reunion is important, because the strong protecting arm of our Government would be extended over her, and the vast resources of her fertile soil and genial climate would be speedily developed, while the safety of New Orleans and of our whole southwestern frontier against hostile aggression, as well as the interests of the whole Union, would be promoted by it.

In the earlier stages of our national existence the opinion prevailed with some that our system of confederated States could not operate successfully over an extended territory, and serious objections have at different times been made to the enlargement of our boundaries. These objections were earnestly urged when we acquired Louisiana. Experience has shown that they were not well founded. The title of numerous Indian tribes to vast tracts of country has been extinguished; new States have been admitted into the Union; new Territories have been created and our jurisdiction and laws extended over them. As our population has expanded, the Union has been cemented and strengthened. As our boundaries have been enlarged and our agricultural population has been spread over a large surface, our federative system has acquired additional strength and security. It may well be doubted whether it would not be in greater danger of overthrow if our present population were confined to the comparatively narrow limits of the original thirteen States than it is now that they are sparsely settled over a more expanded territory. It is confidently believed that our system may be safely extended to the utmost bounds of our territorial limits, and that as it shall be extended the bonds of our Union, so far from being weakened, will become stronger.

None can fail to see the danger to our safety and future peace if Texas remains an independent state or becomes an ally or dependency of some foreign nation more powerful than herself. Is there one among our citizens who would not prefer perpetual peace with Texas to occasional wars, which so often occur between bordering independent nations? Is there one who would not prefer free intercourse with her to high duties on all our products and manufactures which enter her ports or cross her frontiers? Is there one who would not prefer an unrestricted communication with her citizens to the frontier obstructions which must occur if she remains out of the Union? Whatever is good or evil in the local institutions of Texas will remain her own whether annexed to the United States or not. None of the present States will be responsible for them any more than they are for the local institutions of each other. They have confederated together for certain specified objects. Upon the same principle that they would refuse to form a perpetual union with Texas because of her local institutions our forefathers would have been prevented from forming our present Union. Perceiving no valid objection to the measure and many reasons for its adoption vitally affecting the peace, the safety, and the prosperity of both countries, I shall on the broad principle which formed the basis and produced the adoption of our Constitution, and not in any narrow spirit of sectional policy, endeavor by all constitutional, honorable, and appropriate means to consummate the expressed will of the people and Government of the United States by the reannexation of Texas to our Union at the earliest practicable period.

Nor will it become in a less degree my duty to assert and maintain by all constitutional means the right of the United States to that portion of our territory which lies beyond the Rocky Mountains. Our title to the country of the Oregon is "clear and unquestionable," and already are our people preparing to perfect that title by occupying it with their wives and children. But eighty years ago our population was confined on the west by the ridge of the Alleghanies. Within that period—within the lifetime, I might say, of some of my hearers—our people, increasing to many millions, have filled the eastern valley of the Mississippi, adventurously ascended the Missouri to its headsprings, and are already engaged in establishing the blessings of self-government in valleys of which the rivers flow to the Pacific. The world beholds the peaceful triumphs of the industry of our emigrants. To us belongs the duty of protecting them adequately wherever they may be upon our soil. The jurisdiction of our laws and the benefits of our republican institutions should be extended over them in the distant regions which they have selected for their homes. The increasing facilities of intercourse will easily bring the States, of which the formation in that part of our territory can not be long delayed, within the sphere of our federative Union. In the meantime every obligation imposed by treaty or conventional stipulations should be sacredly respected.

In the management of our foreign relations it will be my aim to observe a careful respect for the rights of other nations, while our own will be the subject of constant watchfulness. Equal and exact justice should characterize all our intercourse with foreign countries. All alliances having a tendency to jeopard the welfare and honor of our country or sacrifice any one of the national interests will be studiously avoided, and yet no opportunity will be lost to cultivate a favorable understanding with foreign governments by which our navigation and commerce may be extended and the ample products of our fertile soil, as well as the manufactures of our skillful artisans, find a ready market and remunerating prices in foreign countries.

In taking "care that the laws be faithfully executed," a strict performance of duty will be exacted from all public officers. From those officers, especially, who are charged with the collection and disbursement of the public revenue will prompt and rigid accountability be required. Any culpable failure or delay on their part to account for the moneys intrusted to them at the times and in the manner required by law will in every instance terminate the official connection of such defaulting officer with the Government.

Although in our country the Chief Magistrate must almost of necessity be chosen by a party and stand pledged to its principles and measures, yet in his official action he should not be the President of a part only, but of the whole people of the United States. While he executes the laws with an impartial hand, shrinks from no proper responsibility, and faithfully carries out in the executive department of the Government the principles and policy of those who have chosen him, he should not be unmindful that our fellow-citizens who have differed with him in opinion are entitled to the full and free exercise of their opinions and judgments, and that the rights of all are entitled to respect and regard.

Confidently relying upon the aid and assistance of the coordinate departments of the Government in conducting our public affairs, I enter upon the discharge of the high duties which have been assigned me by the people, again humbly supplicating that Divine Being who has watched over and protected our beloved country from its infancy to the present hour to continue His gracious benedictions upon us, that we may continue to be a prosperous and happy people.

Dark Horse

THE INAUGURAL ADDRESS OF JAMES K. POLK

Walter R. Borneman

THE AMERICA OF the 1840s flexed its expansionist muscles. Railroads spread out from East Coast cities. Steamboats plied the Mississippi River and its tributaries. Beyond the Mississippi, the western half of the continent beckoned. To many Americans, coming out of the country's worst depression to date (the Panic of 1837), the wide-open lands of the West—though partially occupied by Native Americans, Mexican nationals, and British subjects—offered a relief valve and the hope of better times.

Settlers poured into the newly independent Republic of Texas; wagon trains rolled up the Platte River toward the Oregon country; and a few opportunists poked around the Mexican province of California. John Tyler, having become president upon the death of William Henry Harrison in 1841, wanted a term of his own but found little support from anyone.

Expansionist fervor aside, the two leading candidates for their party's 1844 nominations, Henry Clay of the Whigs and Martin Van Buren of the Democrats, publicly stated that the annexation of Texas favored by Tyler might lead to war with Mexico and should not be undertaken. Andrew Jackson, hero of the battle of New Orleans and occupant of the White House for two tumultuous terms, became furious. Jackson felt betrayed by Van Buren, his vice president whom he had championed to succeed him in 1836.

Jackson summoned another protégé, James K. Polk, a former seven-term congressman, speaker of the U.S. House of Representatives, and governor of Tennessee. Jackson had long coveted Texas, but despite characterizations as a saber rattler, he had never taken affirmative steps to bring it into the union. In the final year of his life, "Old Hickory" lectured Polk that he must win the presidency and accomplish the task.

It took Polk nine ballots and ample political arm-twisting to win the Democratic nomination in Baltimore. Despite the Whigs' dismissive chant of "Who is James K. Polk?" Polk's credentials made him one of the most seasoned and informed politicians of the era. A "dark horse" he definitely was not. In part to counter Henry Clay's one-term pledge, but also to coalesce support among Democratic contenders who could look to their own chances four years hence, Polk pledged to be a one-term president. Whatever his goals, he would accomplish them in four years.

It proved a tight electoral contest. But for 5,000 votes in New York State, Henry Clay would have given the inaugural address that James. K. Polk delivered on March 4, 1845. Clay would have focused on federally funded internal improvements, extended an olive branch toward Mexico and Great Britain in foreign affairs, and, to the extent possible, toned down the drumbeat of westward expansion.

Polk's vision was more sweeping. According to Polk's secretary of the navy and would-be biographer, George Bancroft, Polk summarized his inaugural address when he confided to Bancroft "the four great measures" of his administration. First, the joint occupation of Oregon with Great Britain had to be settled; second, the American continent must be rounded out by the acquisition of California from Mexico; third, the protectionist tariff burdening Southern states had to be reduced to a revenue basis; and finally, an independent treasury had to be established.

But what about Texas? Lame duck president John Tyler was as much in favor of acquiring Texas as Andrew Jackson and James K. Polk. After considerable intrigue and political maneuvering, on the last full day of his administration Tyler dispatched a message to all Texans that the United States stood ready and willing to admit the Lone Star Republic into the Union as the twenty-eighth state. Tyler didn't wait for his successor to make good on Texas.

Rather than being surprised or upset by Tyler's last-minute act, Polk embraced it as he stepped to the podium to deliver his inaugural address. Even if Texas had not yet assented, the new president left no doubt about his view of its status to the United States. Polk counted the number of states at twenty-eight and noted "two of these"—referring to Florida and Texas—"have taken their position as members . . . within the last week."

Before embracing Texas, Polk acknowledged his relative youth and professed to be "honored with this distinguished consideration [the presidency] at an earlier period of life than any of my predecessors." He also gave strong measure to his model of constitutional government. It would be his "first care" to administer the government in the spirit of the Constitution, and he urged "strict adherence to the clearly granted powers" and abstention from the exercise of any "doubtful or unauthorized implied powers."

If there were those who viewed him as a Southerner first, Polk left no doubt that he was cut from Old Hickory's cloth. "Every lover of his country must shudder at the thought of the possibility of its dissolution," the Young Hickory proclaimed, "and will be ready to adopt the patriotic sentiment, 'Our Federal Union—it must be preserved.'"

Polk further declared, "All citizens, whether native or adopted, are placed upon terms of precise equality. All are entitled to equal rights and equal protection." Yet, in espousing this Jacksonian triumph of the common man, Polk failed to count the slaves he owned among that number.

Indeed, Polk defended the institution of slavery without mentioning it by name. "It is a source of deep regret," Polk continued, "that in some sections of our country misguided persons have occasionally indulged in schemes and agitations whose object is the destruction of domestic institutions existing in other sections—institutions which existed at the adoption of the Constitution and were recognized and protected by it."

Polk's other domestic views were consistent with his "four great measures" and the planks of the Democratic Platform. "We need no national banks," he said, or federal involvement in internal improvements. And almost verbatim, Polk repeated the careful wording of his tariff letter during the campaign—"a tariff for revenue" with just enough incidental protection to appease the North.

The second half of Polk's inaugural was devoted to foreign affairs, *expansionist* affairs, one concludes. Even as the Constitution did not "force reform on the States," in Polk's view, it had entrusted "the exclusive management of our foreign affairs" to the federal government. His prior words about implied powers aside, Polk would make the most of it.

He espoused long-stated but dubious annexationist views that Texas had once been "a part of our country." It had been "unwisely ceded away to a foreign power," but was now independent and had the sovereign right to become a state. Congratulating neither Tyler nor Congress, Polk instead chose to congratulate "my country" that Texas was finally on the road to reunion.

Polk went on to warn that the question of annexation belonged exclusively to the United States and Texas. It was not the concern of Great Britain or France, and it was certainly not the concern of Mexico. Polk asserted that he would act just as dutifully against Great Britain to maintain the right of the United States to the whole of Oregon as he would against Mexico vis-à-vis Texas.

With the British ambassador in the crowd, Polk repeated the pledge of the Democratic platform: "Our title to the country of the Oregon is 'clear and unquestionable' and already are our people preparing to perfect that title by occupying it with their wives and children." This was no military operation, Polk maintained, but "the peaceful triumphs of the industry of our emigrants." And to us, the president concluded, "belongs the duty of protecting them adequately wherever they may be upon our soil."

With that, cannon thundered and the rain-soaked crowd escorted the Polks down Pennsylvania Avenue to a reception at the White House. James was forty-nine, the youngest person yet to assume the presidency and a full decade younger than the average age of his predecessors. His wife, Sarah, was forty-one. Together they made a striking and energetic couple who signaled the passing of the torch to the next generation in a way that would not again reverberate so sharply until 1961.

James K. Polk did not hesitate in the coming four years to expand the powers of the presidency—particularly infringing on Congress's right to declare war—to extend the Texas border, push the British out of Oregon, and wrestle California and what became the states of the American Southwest from Mexico. He accomplished his goals and died within months of completing his one term.

Zachary Taylor's Inaugural Address

MONDAY, MARCH 5, 1849

ELECTED BY THE American people to the highest office known to our laws, I appear here to take the oath prescribed by the Constitution, and, in compliance with a time-honored custom, to address those who are now assembled.

The confidence and respect shown by my countrymen in calling me to be the Chief Magistrate of a Republic holding a high rank among the nations of the earth have inspired me with feelings of the most profound gratitude; but when I reflect that the acceptance of the office which their partiality has bestowed imposes the discharge of the most arduous duties and involves the weightiest obligations, I am conscious that the position which I have been called to fill, though sufficient to satisfy the loftiest ambition, is surrounded by fearful responsibilities. Happily, however, in the performance of my new duties I shall not be without able cooperation. The legislative and judicial branches of the Government present prominent examples of distinguished civil attainments and matured experience, and it shall be my endeavor to call to my assistance in the Executive Departments individuals whose talents, integrity, and purity of character will furnish ample guaranties for the faithful and honorable performance of the trusts to be committed to their charge. With such aids and an honest purpose to do whatever is right, I hope to execute diligently, impartially, and for the best interests of the country the manifold duties devolved upon me.

In the discharge of these duties my guide will be the Constitution, which I this day swear to "preserve, protect, and defend." For the interpretation of that instrument I shall look to the decisions of the judicial tribunals established by its authority and to the practice of the Government under the earlier Presidents, who had so large a share in its formation. To the example of those illustrious patriots I shall always defer with reverence, and especially to his example who was by so many titles "the Father of his Country."

To command the Army and Navy of the United States; with the advice and consent of the Senate, to make treaties and to appoint ambassadors and other officers; to give to Congress information of the state of the Union and recommend such measures as he shall judge to be necessary; and to take care that the laws shall be faithfully executed—these are the most important functions intrusted to the President by the Constitution, and it may be expected that I shall briefly indicate the principles which will control me in their execution.

Chosen by the body of the people under the assurance that my Administration would be devoted to the welfare of the whole country, and not to the support of any particular section or merely local interest, I this day renew the declarations I have heretofore made and proclaim my fixed determination to maintain to the extent of my ability the Government in its original purity and to adopt as the basis of my public policy those great republican doctrines which constitute the strength of our national existence.

In reference to the Army and Navy, lately employed with so much distinction on active service, care shall be taken to insure the highest condition of efficiency, and in furtherance of that object the military and naval schools, sustained by the liberality of Congress, shall receive the special attention of the Executive.

As American freemen we can not but sympathize in all efforts to extend the blessings of civil and political liberty, but at the same time we are warned by the admonitions of history and the voice of our own beloved Washington to abstain from entangling alliances with foreign nations. In all disputes between conflicting governments it is our interest not less than our duty to remain strictly neutral, while our geographical position, the genius of our institutions and our people, the advancing spirit of civilization, and, above all, the dictates of religion direct us to the cultivation of peaceful and friendly relations with all other powers. It is to be hoped that no international question can now arise which a government confident in its own strength and resolved to protect its own just rights may not settle by wise negotiation; and it eminently becomes a government like our own, founded on the morality and intelligence of its citizens and upheld by their affections, to exhaust every resort of honorable diplomacy before appealing to arms. In the conduct of our foreign relations I shall conform to these views, as I believe them essential to the best interests and the true honor of the country.

The appointing power vested in the President imposes delicate and onerous duties. So far as it is possible to be informed, I shall make honesty, capacity, and fidelity indispensable prerequisites to the bestowal of office, and the absence of either of these qualities shall be deemed sufficient cause for removal.

It shall be my study to recommend such constitutional measures to Congress as may be necessary and proper to secure encouragement and protection to the great interests of agriculture, commerce, and manufactures, to improve our rivers and harbors, to provide for the speedy extinguishment of the public debt, to enforce a strict accountability on the part of all officers of the Government and the utmost economy in all public expenditures; but it is for the wisdom of Congress itself, in which all legislative powers are vested by the Constitution, to regulate these and other matters of domestic policy. I shall look with confidence to the enlightened patriotism of that body to adopt such measures of conciliation as may harmonize conflicting interests and tend to perpetuate that Union which should be the paramount object of our hopes and affections. In any action calculated to promote an object so near the heart of everyone who truly loves his country I will zealously unite with the coordinate branches of the Government.

In conclusion I congratulate you, my fellow-citizens, upon the high state of prosperity to which the goodness of Divine Providence has conducted our common country. Let us invoke a continuance of the same protecting care which has led us from small beginnings to the eminence we this day occupy, and let us seek to deserve that continuance by prudence and moderation in our councils, by well-directed attempts to assuage the bitterness which too often marks unavoidable differences of opinion, by the promulgation and practice of just and liberal principles, and by an enlarged patriotism, which shall acknowledge no limits but those of our own widespread Republic.

Old Rough and Ready

THE INAUGURAL ADDRESS OF ZACHARY TAYLOR

Michael F. Holt

ZACHARY TAYLOR'S PLATITUDE-FILLED Inaugural Address was the shortest by any president in American history. His personal background largely accounts for its brevity and its patriotic paeans. But the few concrete items also reflect the campaign run for him before and after the Whig party's national convention nominated him in June 1848, as well as the major issues that shaped that election.

The first sentence of Taylor's address suggests that he considered it a necessary but unwelcome obligation. The inaugural may well have been the first public speech he ever had to make. Taylor was not a politician. He had never sought or held a civilian public office, attended a party meeting, or even voted prior to November 1848. Rather, he was a career army officer who commanded the American troops in northern Mexico during the first year of the Mexican-American War. The seemingly miraculous victory of his heavily outnumbered army at Buena Vista in February 1847 injected him into the presidential race. His fame and popularity simply exploded as news of his triumph spread eastward from the Mississippi Valley to the Atlantic coast, and by May 1847 savvy politicos predicted that he was certain to be the next president.

His early backers, like Taylor himself, presented him not as a Whig, but as a "No Party" or "People's" candidate who would not be beholden to any party's principles if elected president. This apparent contempt for traditional Whig programs and Taylor's willingness before and even after Whigs nominated him to accept non-Whig nominations outraged established Whig leaders who vowed they would never support anyone but an identifiable Whig.

Party regulars' hostility to Taylor forced him and his most trusted advisors to compose two public letters attesting to his Whig credentials, one in April six weeks before the Whigs' national convention and one in September, six weeks before election day. Known as the Allison letters, they accurately previewed the inaugural he gave in March 1849. Then, too, he tried to reassure suspicious Whigs that he deserved their trust. In the first Allison letter, Taylor identified himself as "a Whig but not an ultra Whig" even while adding his intention "to act independent of party domination" if elected. Then came a muted pledge of Whig allegiance. From the start of the Mexican War under Democratic President James K. Polk, Whigs blasted it as an unconscionable act of aggression aimed at grabbing land from a weak neighbor. In the first Allison letter, therefore, Taylor condemned aggressive wars of conquest and called for magnanimity toward the defeated Mexicans. This language augured Taylor's words about foreign policy in his inaugural. His promise to "exhaust every resort of honorable diplomacy before appealing to arms" was a thinly concealed shaft at Polk's actions inciting the Mexican War. This was straight Whig doctrine.

Even more important, in the first and second Allison letters, just as in his inaugural message, Taylor embraced the fundamental Whig principle that it was Congress's duty, not the president's, to set domestic policies regarding tariffs, internal improvements, currency, and the like and that he would never veto congressional legislation unless it were clearly unconstitutional. This idea of the supremacy of Congress over the executive branch had been the founding rationale for the Whig party when it organized against Andrew Jackson in the 1830s.

Yet when Taylor said in his Inaugural Address that "I shall look with confidence to the enlightened patriotism of that body [Congress] to adopt such measures of conciliation as may harmonize conflicting interests and tend to perpetuate that Union which should be the paramount object of our hopes and affections," he referred to far more than the proper relationship between the executive and legislative branches. Instead, he pointed obliquely to the sectional quarrel over slavery expansion that had dominated the election of 1848 and that remained unsettled as of March 1849. By the fall of 1847, in fact, Taylor had privately written that this escalating sectional conflict over slavery's possible extension was the gravest threat to the Union since the adoption of the Constitution. His inaugural words about perpetuating the Union were not mere platitudes. To this old soldier, they were heartfelt, as his subsequent actions as president emphatically made clear.

From the moment the war started in May 1846, Northerners, many of them Whigs, denounced it as a Democratic plot to seize Mexican land so that Southerners could extend slavery west of Texas. In part to refute that charge, in August 1846 a Pennsylvania Democrat introduced an amendment to a bill in the House of Representatives that would bar slavery from any land taken from

Mexico as a result of the war. This so-called Wilmot Proviso passed the House, where free-state members outnumbered slave-state members, on a strict sectional vote. Northerners supported it. Southerners vehemently opposed it because it denied slaveholders the right to enter national territories on an equal basis with Northern non-slaveholders. The amended bill died in the Senate, and the Wilmot Proviso never passed Congress. But it continually came to a vote in subsequent sessions of Congress, always polarizing the Northern and Southern members of both the Whig and Democratic parties against each other. The longer it did so, the more tempers frayed. By mid-1847, Northern state legislatures were instructing their U.S. senators to impose the Proviso on any land taken from Mexico, while growing numbers of Southern state legislatures threatened to secede from the Union should the Proviso ever be enacted into law. This was the crisis that so disturbed Taylor a year before his election.

To restore unity across sectional lines in 1847, both Whigs and Democrats sought alternative policies to the Proviso for dealing with the slavery extension issue. Democrats did so with a formula called popular sovereignty. This called for Congress to forgo any action concerning slavery in territories and instead allow the actual settlers in them to decide whether to admit or prohibit slavery. A major proponent of this formula, Michigan Senator Lewis Cass, was the Democratic presidential candidate in 1848, and in that campaign he pledged that he would veto the Proviso should it ever pass Congress. Throughout 1847, when the acquisition of Mexican territory was still hypothetical, Northern and Southern Whigs united behind an insistence that no territory whatsoever be seized from Mexico. Ratification of the Treaty of Guadalupe-Hidalgo and with it the huge Mexican Cession in March 1848 ended that dodge. Now Whigs had to face their party's sectional polarization over slavery extension head on.

That fact mightily influenced Taylor's nomination, even while making it more controversial. On the one hand, the loss of the anti-war, anti-expansion issues while Democrats could claim credit for almost doubling the size of the country convinced a majority of Whigs at their national convention that the party needed to run a military hero to have any chance of winning the election. On the other hand, it deepened the hostility to Taylor by Northerners who loathed the prospect of slavery's further western extension. It was not just that Taylor gave no public support to Northern Whigs' demand that slavery be prohibited from the Mexican Cession by congressional law. A resident of Baton Rouge, Louisiana, Taylor owned over a hundred slaves who worked plantations in Louisiana and Mississippi. To most Northern Whigs, this fact made Taylor seem a certain loser in their states. Hence, his eventual nomination appalled them.

Whigs' selection of a large slaveholder and Democrats' nomination of a man who pledged to veto the Proviso prompted the most fervent anti-slavery men in both parties to bolt to a new Free Soil party that would capture 14 percent of the North's popular vote in 1848. Eliminating the rationale for this new party, one of the "conflicting interests" he mentioned, was thus one of the achievements Taylor hinted at in his Inaugural Address.

In the 1848 campaign Whigs brazenly ran a two-faced campaign. In the South they promised that Taylor as a slaveholder and fellow Southerner would never allow the insulting Wilmot Proviso to become law. In the North, by contrast, Whig campaigners seized on Taylor's pledge not to veto congressional legislation. The best way to stop slavery's extension, they avowed, much to the frustration of Free Soil campaigners, was to elect a Northern Whig majority to Congress. They would pass the Proviso, and Taylor, quite unlike Lewis Cass, would sign it into law.

Whigs' doubled-faced tactic worked in 1848. Taylor carried seven of fifteen Northern states and eight of fifteen slave states. Free Soil incursions into both major parties' ranks varied from state to state. They helped Whigs carry New York while giving Ohio to Cass. But the dodge worked only because Congress had as yet failed to do anything about organizing territories in the newly acquired Mexican Cession upon which Congress might impose the Proviso. Nor was Congress able to do so in the short session between Taylor's election and his inauguration, even though Whigs were desperate to spare Taylor from having to make a decision that would give the lie to what Whig campaigners in one section or the other had promised he would do.

Although Taylor had told a confidant that he would sign the Proviso should Congress ever enact it, few people knew what he intended to do when he delivered his brief Inaugural Address. Despite his professed confidence about Congress's ability to find a mutually satisfactory solution for slavery extension, he and his administration quickly decided to bypass Congress altogether by avoiding any formal organization of territorial governments upon which Congress might act. Instead, they tried to have California and New Mexico immediately enter the Union as states, without any territorial phase whatsoever. This solution, he promised in another rare public speech, would render any need for a Free Soil party moot. However sensible it was, the plan failed. But Taylor had died on July 9, 1850, before Congress replaced it with the famous Compromise of 1850 for the Mexican Cession.

Millard Fillmore's Announcement to Congress of the Death of President Taylor

WEDNESDAY, JULY 10, 1850

FELLOW-CITIZENS OF THE Senate and House of Representatives:
I have to perform the melancholy duty of announcing to you that it has pleased Almighty God to remove from this life Zachary Taylor, late President of the United States. He deceased last evening at the hour of half-past 10 o'clock, in the midst of his family and surrounded by affectionate friends, calmly and in the full possession of all his faculties. Among his last words were these, which he uttered with emphatic distinctness:

> I have always done my duty. I am ready to die. My only regret is for the friends I leave behind me.

Having announced to you, fellow-citizens, this most afflicting bereavement, and assuring you that it has penetrated no heart with deeper grief than mine, it remains for me to say that I propose this day at 12 o'clock, in the Hall of the House of Representatives, in the presence of both Houses of Congress, to take the oath prescribed by the Constitution, to enable me to enter on the execution of the office which this event has devolved on me.

Millard Fillmore's First Annual Message

MONDAY, DECEMBER 2, 1850

FELLOW-CITIZENS OF THE Senate and of the House of Representatives:
Being suddenly called in the midst of the last session of Congress by a painful dispensation of Divine Providence to the responsible station which I now hold, I contented myself with such communications to the Legislature as the exigency of the moment seemed to require. The country was shrouded in mourning for the loss of its venerable Chief Magistrate and all hearts were penetrated with grief. Neither the time nor the occasion appeared to require or to justify on my part any general expression of political opinions or any announcement of the principles which would govern me in the discharge of the duties to the performance of which I had been so unexpectedly called. I trust, therefore, that it may not be deemed inappropriate if I avail myself of this opportunity of the reassembling of Congress to make known my sentiments in a general manner in regard to the policy which ought to be pursued by the Government both in its intercourse with foreign nations and its management and administration of internal affairs.

Nations, like individuals in a state of nature, are equal and independent, possessing certain rights and owing certain duties to each other, arising from their necessary and unavoidable relations; which rights and duties there is no common human authority to protect and enforce. Still, they are rights and duties, binding in morals, in conscience, and in honor, although there is no tribunal to which an injured party can appeal but the disinterested judgment of mankind, and ultimately the arbitrament of the sword.

Among the acknowledged rights of nations is that which each possesses of establishing that form of government which it may deem most conducive to the happiness and prosperity of its own citizens, of changing that form as circumstances may require, and of managing its internal affairs according to its own will. The people of the United States claim this right for themselves, and they readily concede it to others. Hence it becomes an imperative duty not to interfere in the government or internal policy of other nations; and although we may sympathize with the unfortunate or the oppressed everywhere in their struggles for freedom, our principles forbid us from taking any part in such foreign contests. We make no wars to promote or to prevent successions to thrones, to maintain any theory of a balance of power, or to suppress the actual government which any country chooses to establish for itself. We instigate no revolutions, nor suffer any hostile military expeditions to be fitted out in the United States to invade the territory or provinces of a friendly nation. The great law of morality ought to have a national as well as a personal and individual application. We should act toward other nations as we wish them to act toward us, and justice and conscience should form the rule of conduct between governments, instead of mere power, self interest, or the desire of aggrandizement. To maintain a strict neutrality in foreign wars, to cultivate friendly relations, to reciprocate every noble and generous act, and to perform punctually and scrupulously every treaty obligation—these are the duties which we owe to other states, and by the performance of which we best entitle ourselves to like treatment from them; or, if that, in any case, be refused, we can enforce our own rights with justice and a clear conscience.

In our domestic policy the Constitution will be my guide, and in questions of doubt I shall look for its interpretation to the judicial decisions of that tribunal which was established to expound it and to the usage of the Government, sanctioned by the acquiescence of the country. I regard all its provisions as equally binding. In all its parts it is the will of the people expressed in the most solemn form, and the constituted authorities are but agents to carry that will into effect. Every power which it has granted is to be exercised for the public good; but no pretense of utility, no honest conviction, even, of what might be expedient, can justify the assumption of any power not granted. The powers conferred upon the Government and their distribution to the several departments are as clearly expressed in that sacred instrument as the imperfection of human language will allow, and I deem it my first duty not to question its wisdom, add to its provisions, evade its requirements, or nullify its commands.

Upon you, fellow-citizens, as the representatives of the States and the people, is wisely devolved the legislative power. I shall comply with my duty in laying before you from time to time any information calculated to enable you to discharge your high and responsible trust for the benefit of our common constituents.

My opinions will be frankly expressed upon the leading subjects of legislation; and if—which I do not anticipate—any act should pass the two Houses of Congress which should appear to me unconstitutional, or an encroachment on the just powers of other departments, or with provisions hastily adopted and likely to produce consequences injurious and unforeseen, I should not shrink from the duty of returning it to you, with my reasons, for your further consideration. Beyond the due performance of these constitutional obligations, both my respect for the Legislature and my sense of propriety will restrain me from any attempt to control or influence your proceedings. With you is the power, the honor, and the responsibility of the legislation of the country.

The Government of the United States is a limited Government. It is confined to the exercise of powers expressly granted and such others as may be necessary for carrying those powers into effect; and it is at all times an especial duty to guard against any infringement on the just rights of the States. Over the objects and subjects intrusted to Congress its legislative authority is supreme. But here that authority ceases, and every citizen who truly loves the Constitution and desires the continuance of its existence and its blessings will resolutely and firmly resist any interference in those domestic affairs which the Constitution has clearly and unequivocally left to the exclusive authority of the States. And every such citizen will also deprecate useless irritation among the several members of the Union and all reproach and crimination tending to alienate one portion of the country from another. The beauty of our system of government consists, and its safety and durability must consist, in avoiding mutual collisions and encroachments and in the regular separate action of all, while each is revolving in its own distinct orbit.

The Constitution has made it the duty of the President to take care that the laws be faithfully executed. In a government like ours, in which all laws are passed by a majority of the representatives of the people, and these representatives are chosen for such short periods that any injurious or obnoxious law can very soon be repealed, it would appear unlikely that any great numbers should be found ready to resist the execution of the laws. But it must be borne in mind that the country is extensive; that there may be local interests or prejudices rendering a law odious in one part which is not so in another, and that the thoughtless and inconsiderate, misled by their passions or their imaginations, may be induced madly to resist such laws as they disapprove. Such persons should recollect that without law there can be no real practical liberty; that when law is trampled under foot tyranny rules, whether it appears in the form of a military despotism or of popular violence. The law is the only sure protection of the weak and the only efficient restraint upon the strong. When impartially and faithfully administered, none is beneath its protection and none above its control. You, gentlemen, and the country may be assured that to the utmost of my ability and to the extent of the power vested in me I shall at all times and in all places take care that the laws be faithfully executed. In the discharge of this duty, solemnly imposed upon me by the Constitution and by my oath of office, I shall shrink from no responsibility, and shall endeavor to meet events as they may arise with firmness, as well as with prudence and discretion.

The appointing power is one of the most delicate with which the Executive is invested. I regard it as a sacred trust, to be exercised with the sole view of advancing the prosperity and happiness of the people. It shall be my effort to elevate the standard of official employment by selecting for places of importance individuals fitted for the posts to which they are assigned by their known integrity, talents, and virtues. In so extensive a country, with so great a population, and where few persons appointed to office can be known to the appointing power, mistakes will sometimes unavoidably happen and unfortunate appointments be made notwithstanding the greatest care. In such cases the power of removal may be properly exercised; and neglect of duty or malfeasance in office will be no more tolerated in individuals appointed by myself than in those appointed by others.

I am happy in being able to say that no unfavorable change in our foreign relations has taken place since the message at the opening of the last session of Congress. We are at peace with all nations and we enjoy in an eminent degree the blessings of that peace in a prosperous and growing commerce and in all the forms of amicable national intercourse. The unexampled growth of the country, the present amount of its population, and its ample means of self-protection assure for it the respect of all nations, while it is trusted that its character for justice and a regard to the rights of other States will cause that respect to be readily and cheerfully paid.

A convention was negotiated between the United States and Great Britain in April last for facilitating and protecting the construction of a ship canal between the Atlantic and Pacific oceans and for other purposes. The instrument has since been ratified by the contracting parties, the exchange of ratifications has been effected, and proclamation thereof has been duly made.

In addition to the stipulations contained in this convention, two other objects remain to be accomplished between the contracting powers: First. The designation and establishment of a free port at each end of the canal.

Second. An agreement fixing the distance from the shore within which belligerent maritime operations shall not be carried on. On these points there is little doubt that the two Governments will come to an understanding.

The company of citizens of the United States who have acquired from the State of Nicaragua the privilege of constructing a ship canal between the two oceans through the territory of that State have made progress in their preliminary arrangements. The treaty between the United States and Great Britain of the 19th of April last, above referred to, being now in operation, it is to be hoped that the guaranties which it offers will be sufficient to secure the completion of the work with all practicable expedition. It is obvious that this result would be indefinitely postponed if any other than peaceful measures for the purpose of harmonizing conflicting claims to territory in that quarter should be adopted. It will consequently be my endeavor to cause any further negotiations on the part of this Government which may be requisite for this purpose to be so conducted as to bring them to a speedy and successful close.

Some unavoidable delay has occurred, arising from distance and the difficulty of intercourse between this Government and that of Nicaragua, but as intelligence has just been received of the appointment of an envoy extraordinary and minister plenipotentiary of that Government to reside at Washington, whose arrival may soon be expected, it is hoped that no further impediments will be experienced in the prompt transaction of business between the two Governments.

Citizens of the United States have undertaken the connection of the two oceans by means of a railroad across the Isthmus of Tehuantepec, under grants of the Mexican Government to a citizen of that Republic. It is understood that a thorough survey of the course of the communication is in preparation, and there is every reason to expect that it will be prosecuted with characteristic energy, especially when that Government shall have consented to such stipulations with the Government of the United States as may be necessary to impart a feeling of security to those who may embark their property in the enterprise. Negotiations are pending for the accomplishment of that object, and a hope is confidently entertained that when the Government of Mexico shall become duly sensible of the advantages which that country can not fail to derive from the work, and learn that the Government of the United States desires that the right of sovereignty of Mexico in the Isthmus shall remain unimpaired, the stipulations referred to will be agreed to with alacrity.

By the last advices from Mexico it would appear, however, that that Government entertains strong objections to some of the stipulations which the parties concerned in the project of the railroad deem necessary for their protection and security. Further consideration, it is to be hoped, or some modification of terms, may yet reconcile the differences existing between the two Governments in this respect.

Fresh instructions have recently been given to the minister of the United States in Mexico, who is prosecuting the subject with promptitude and ability.

Although the negotiations with Portugal for the payment of claims of citizens of the United States against that Government have not yet resulted in a formal treaty, yet a proposition, made by the Government of Portugal for the final adjustment and payment of those claims, has recently been accepted on the part of the United States. It gives me pleasure to say that Mr. Clay, to whom the negotiation on the part of the United States had been intrusted, discharged the duties of his appointment with ability and discretion, acting always within the instructions of his Government.

It is expected that a regular convention will be immediately negotiated for carrying the agreement between the two Governments into effect. The commissioner appointed under the act of Congress for carrying into effect the convention with Brazil of the 27th of January, 1849, has entered upon the performance of the duties imposed upon him by that act. It is hoped that those duties may be completed within the time which it prescribes. The documents, however, which the Imperial Government, by the third article of the convention, stipulates to furnish to the Government of the United States have not yet been received. As it is presumed that those documents will be essential for the correct disposition of the claims, it may become necessary for Congress to extend the period limited for the duration of the commission. The sum stipulated by the fourth article of the convention to be paid to this Government has been received.

The collection in the ports of the United States of discriminating duties upon the vessels of Chili and their cargoes has been suspended, pursuant to the provisions of the act of Congress of the 24th of May, 1828. It is to be hoped that this measure will impart a fresh impulse to the commerce between the two countries, which of late, and especially since our acquisition of California, has, to the mutual advantage of the parties, been much augmented.

Peruvian guano has become so desirable an article to the agricultural interest of the United States that it is the duty of the Government to employ all the means properly in its power for the purpose of causing that article to be imported into the country at a reasonable price. Nothing will be omitted on my part toward accomplishing this desirable end. I am persuaded that in removing any restraints on this traffic the Peruvian Government will promote its own best interests, while it will afford a proof of a friendly disposition toward this country, which will be duly appreciated.

The treaty between the United States and His Majesty the King of the Hawaiian Islands, which has recently been made public, will, it is believed, have a beneficial effect upon the relations between the two countries.

The relations between those parts of the island of St. Domingo which were formerly colonies of Spain and France, respectively, are still in an unsettled condition. The proximity of that island to the United States and the delicate questions involved in the existing controversy there render it desirable that it should be permanently and speedily adjusted. The interests of humanity and of general commerce also demand this; and as intimations of the same sentiment have been received from other governments, it is hoped that some plan may soon be devised to effect the object in a manner likely to give general satisfaction. The Government of the United States will not fail, by the exercise of all proper friendly offices, to do all in its power to put an end to the destructive war which has raged between the different parts of the island and to secure to them both the benefits of peace and commerce.

I refer you to the report of the Secretary of the Treasury for a detailed statement of the finances.

The total receipts into the Treasury for the year ending 30th of June last were $47,421,748.90. The total expenditures during the same period were $43,002,168.90. The public debt has been reduced since the last annual report from the Treasury Department $495,276.79.

By the nineteenth section of the act of 28th January, 1847, the proceeds of the sales of the public lands were pledged for the interest and principal of the public debt. The great amount of those lands subsequently granted by Congress for military bounties will, it is believed, very nearly supply the public demand for several years to come, and but little reliance can, therefore, be placed on that hitherto fruitful source of revenue. Aside from the permanent annual expenditures, which have necessarily largely increased, a portion of the public debt, amounting to $8,075,986.59, must be provided for within the next two fiscal years. It is most desirable that these accruing demands should be met without resorting to new loans.

All experience has demonstrated the wisdom and policy of raising a large portion of revenue for the support of Government from duties on goods imported. The power to lay these duties is unquestionable, and its chief object, of course, is to replenish the Treasury. But if in doing this an incidental advantage may be gained by encouraging the industry of our own citizens, it is our duty to avail ourselves of that advantage.

A duty laid upon an article which can not be produced in this country, such as tea or coffee, adds to the cost of the article, and is chiefly or wholly paid by the consumer. But a duty laid upon an article which may be produced here stimulates the skill and industry of our own country to produce the same article, which is brought into the market in competition with the foreign article, and the importer is thus compelled to reduce his price to that at which the domestic article can be sold, thereby throwing a part of the duty upon the producer of the foreign article. The continuance of this process creates the skill and invites the capital which finally enable us to produce the article much cheaper than it could have been procured from abroad, thereby benefiting both the producer and the consumer at home. The consequence of this is that the artisan and the agriculturist are brought together, each affords a ready market for the produce of the other, the whole country becomes prosperous, and the ability to produce every necessary of life renders us independent in war as well as in peace.

A high tariff can never be permanent. It will cause dissatisfaction, and will be changed. It excludes competition, and thereby invites the investment of capital in manufactures to such excess that when changed it brings distress, bankruptcy, and ruin upon all who have been misled by its faithless protection. What the manufacturer wants is uniformity and permanency, that he may feel a confidence that he is not to be ruined by sudden exchanges. But to make a tariff uniform and permanent it is not only necessary that the laws should not be altered, but that the duty should not fluctuate. To effect this all duties should be specific wherever the nature of the article is such as to admit of it. Ad valorem duties fluctuate with the price and offer strong temptations to fraud and perjury. Specific duties, on the contrary, are equal and uniform in all ports and at all times, and offer a strong inducement to the importer to bring the best article, as he pays no more duty upon that than upon one of inferior quality. I therefore strongly recommend a modification of the present tariff, which has prostrated some of our most important and necessary manufactures, and that specific duties be imposed sufficient to raise the requisite revenue, making such discriminations in favor of the industrial pursuits of our own country as to encourage home production without excluding foreign competition. It is also important that an unfortunate provision in the present tariff, which imposes a much higher duty upon the raw material that enters into our manufactures than upon the manufactured article, should be remedied.

The papers accompanying the report of the Secretary of the Treasury will disclose frauds attempted upon the revenue, in variety and amount so great as to justify the conclusion that it is impossible under any system of ad valorem duties levied upon the foreign cost or value of the article to secure an honest observance and an effectual administration of the laws. The fraudulent devices to evade the law which have been detected by the vigilance of the appraisers leave no room to doubt that similar impositions not discovered, to a large amount, have been successfully practiced since the enactment of the law now in force. This state of things has already had a prejudicial influence upon those engaged in foreign commerce. It has a tendency to drive the honest trader from the business of importing and to throw that important branch of employment into the hands of unscrupulous and dishonest men, who are alike regardless of law and the obligations of an oath. By these means the plain intentions of Congress, as expressed in the law, are daily defeated. Every motive of policy and duty, therefore, impels me to ask the earnest attention of Congress to this subject. If Congress should deem it unwise to attempt any important changes in the system of levying duties at this session, it will become indispensable to the protection of the revenue that such remedies as in the judgment of Congress may mitigate the evils complained of should be at once applied.

As before stated, specific duties would, in my opinion, afford the most perfect remedy for this evil; but if you should not concur in this view, then, as a partial remedy, I beg leave respectfully to recommend that instead of taking the invoice of the article abroad as a means of determining its value here, the correctness of which invoice it is in many cases impossible to verify, the law be so changed as to require a home valuation or appraisal, to be regulated in such manner as to give, as far as practicable, uniformity in the several ports.

There being no mint in California, I am informed that the laborers in the mines are compelled to dispose of their gold dust at a large discount. This appears to me to be a heavy and unjust tax upon the labor of those employed in extracting this precious metal, and I doubt not you will be disposed at the earliest period possible to relieve them from it by the establishment of a mint. In the meantime, as an assayer's office is established there, I would respectfully submit for your consideration the propriety of authorizing gold bullion which has been assayed and stamped to be received in payment of Government dues. I can not conceive that the Treasury would suffer any loss by such a provision, which will at once raise bullion to its par value, and thereby save (if I am rightly informed) many millions of dollars to the laborers which are now paid in brokerage to convert this precious metal into available funds. This discount upon their hard earnings is a heavy tax, and every effort should be made by the Government to relieve them from so great a burden.

More than three-fourths of our population are engaged in the cultivation of the soil. The commercial, manufacturing, and navigating interests are all to a great extent dependent on the agricultural. It is therefore the most important interest of the nation, and has a just claim to the fostering care and protection of the Government so far as they can be extended consistently with the provisions of the Constitution. As this can not be done by the ordinary modes of legislation, I respectfully recommend the establishment of an agricultural bureau, to be charged with the duty of giving to this leading branch of American industry the encouragement which it so well deserves. In view of the immense mineral resources of our country, provision should also be made for the employment of a competent mineralogist and chemist, who should be required, under the direction of the head of the bureau, to collect specimens of the various minerals of our country and to ascertain by careful analysis their respective elements and properties and their adaptation to useful purposes. He should also be required to examine and report upon the qualities of different soils and the manures best calculated to improve their productiveness. By publishing the results of such experiments, with suitable explanations, and by the collection and distribution of rare seeds and plants, with instructions as to the best system of cultivation, much may be done to promote this great national interest.

In compliance with the act of Congress passed on the 23d of May, 1850, providing, among other things, for taking the Seventh Census, a superintendent was appointed and all other measures adopted which were deemed necessary to insure the prompt and faithful performance of that duty. The appropriation already made will, it is believed, be sufficient to defray the whole expense of the work, but further legislation may be necessary in regard to the compensation of some of the marshals of the Territories. It will also be proper to make provision by law at an early day for the publication of such abstracts of the returns as the public interests may require.

The unprecedented growth of our territories on the Pacific in wealth and population and the consequent increase of their social and commercial relations with the Atlantic States seem to render it the duty of the Government to use all its constitutional power to improve the means of intercourse with them. The importance of opening "a line of communication, the best and most expeditious of which the nature of the country will admit," between the Valley of the Mississippi and the Pacific was brought to your notice by my predecessor in his annual message; and as the reasons which he presented in favor of the measure still exist in full force, I beg leave to call your attention to them and to repeat the recommendations then made by him.

The uncertainty which exists in regard to the validity of land titles in California is a subject which demands your early consideration. Large bodies of land in that State are claimed under grants said to have been made by authority of the Spanish and Mexican Governments. Many of these have not been perfected, others have been revoked, and some are believed to be fraudulent. But until they shall have been judicially investigated they will continue to retard the settlement and improvement of the country. I therefore respectfully recommend that provision be made by law for the appointment of commissioners to examine all such claims with a view to their final adjustment.

I also beg leave to call your attention to the propriety of extending at an early day our system of land laws, with such modifications as may be necessary, over the State of California and the Territories of Utah and New Mexico. The mineral lands of California will, of course, form an exception to any general system which may be adopted. Various methods of disposing of them have been suggested. I was at first inclined to favor the system of leasing, as it seemed to promise the largest revenue to the Government and to afford the best security against monopolies; but further reflection and our experience in leasing the lead mines and selling lands upon credit have brought my mind to the conclusion that there would be great difficulty in collecting the rents, and that the relation of debtor and creditor between the citizens and the Government would be attended with many mischievous consequences. I therefore recommend that instead of retaining the mineral lands under the permanent control of the Government they be divided into small parcels and sold, under such restrictions as to quantity and time as will insure the best price and guard most effectually against combinations of capitalists to obtain monopolies.

The annexation of Texas and the acquisition of California and New Mexico have given increased importance to our Indian relations. The various tribes brought under our jurisdiction by these enlargements of our boundaries are estimated to embrace a population of 124,000. Texas and New Mexico are surrounded by powerful tribes of Indians, who are a source of constant terror and annoyance to the inhabitants. Separating into small predatory bands, and always mounted, they overrun the country, devastating farms, destroying crops, driving off whole herds of cattle, and occasionally murdering the inhabitants or carrying them into captivity. The great roads leading into the country are infested with them, whereby traveling is rendered extremely dangerous and immigration is almost entirely arrested. The Mexican frontier, which by the eleventh article of the treaty of Guadalupe Hidalgo we are bound to protect against the Indians within our border, is exposed to these incursions equally with our own. The military force stationed in that country, although forming a large proportion of the Army, is represented as entirely inadequate to our own protection and the fulfillment of our treaty stipulations with Mexico. The principal deficiency is in cavalry, and I recommend that Congress should, at as early a period as practicable, provide for the raising of one or more regiments of mounted men.

For further suggestions on this subject and others connected with our domestic interests and the defense of our frontier, I refer you to the reports of the Secretary of the Interior and of the Secretary of War.

I commend also to your favorable consideration the suggestion contained in the last-mentioned report and in the letter of the General in Chief relative to the establishment of an asylum for the relief of disabled and destitute soldiers. This subject appeals so strongly to your sympathies that it would be superfluous in me to say anything more than barely to express my cordial approbation of the proposed object.

The Navy continues to give protection to our commerce and other national interests in the different quarters of the globe, and, with the exception of a single steamer on the Northern lakes, the vessels in commission are distributed in six different squadrons.

The report of the head of that Department will exhibit the services of these squadrons and of the several vessels employed in each during the past year. It is a source of gratification that, while they have been constantly prepared for any hostile emergency, they have everywhere met with the respect and courtesy due as well to the dignity as to the peaceful dispositions and just purposes of the nation.

The two brigantines accepted by the Government from a generous citizen of New York and placed under the command of an officer of the Navy to proceed to the Arctic Seas in quest of the British commander Sir John Franklin and his companions, in compliance with the act of Congress approved in May last, had when last heard from penetrated into a high northern latitude; but the success of this noble and humane enterprise is yet uncertain.

I invite your attention to the view of our present naval establishment and resources presented in the report of the Secretary of the Navy, and the suggestions therein made for its improvement, together with the naval policy recommended for the security of our Pacific Coast and the protection and extension of our commerce with eastern Asia. Our facilities for a larger participation in the trade of the East, by means of our recent settlements on the shores of the Pacific, are too obvious to be overlooked or disregarded.

The questions in relation to rank in the Army and Navy and relative rank between officers of the two branches of the service, presented to the Executive by certain resolutions of the House of Representatives at the last session of Congress, have been submitted to a board of officers in each branch of the service, and their report may be expected at an early day.

I also earnestly recommend the enactment of a law authorizing officers of the Army and Navy to be retired from the service when incompetent for its vigorous and active duties, taking care to make suitable provision for those who have faithfully served their country and awarding distinctions by retaining in appropriate commands those who have been particularly conspicuous for gallantry and good conduct. While the obligation of the country to maintain and honor those who, to the exclusion of other pursuits, have devoted themselves to its arduous service is acknowledged, this obligation should not be permitted to interfere with the efficiency of the service itself.

I am gratified in being able to state that the estimates of expenditure for the Navy in the ensuing year are less by more than $1,000,000 than those of the present, excepting the appropriation which may become necessary for the construction of a dock on the coast of the Pacific, propositions for which are now being considered and on which a special report may be expected early in your present session.

There is an evident justness in the suggestion of the same report that appropriations for the naval service proper should be separated from those for fixed and permanent objects, such as building docks and navy yards and the fixtures attached, and from the extraordinary objects under the care of the Department which, however important, are not essentially naval.

A revision of the code for the government of the Navy seems to require the immediate consideration of Congress. Its system of crimes and punishments had undergone no change for half a century until the last session, though its defects have been often and ably pointed out; and the abolition of a particular species of corporal punishment, which then took place, without providing any substitute, has left the service in a state of defectiveness which calls for prompt correction. I therefore recommend that the whole subject be revised without delay and such a system established for the enforcement of discipline as shall be at once humane and effectual.

The accompanying report of the Postmaster-General presents a satisfactory view of the operations and condition of that Department. At the close of the last fiscal year the length of the inland mail routes in the United States (not embracing the service in Oregon and California) was 178,672 miles, the annual transportation thereon 46,541,423 miles, and the annual cost of such transportation $2,724,426. The increase of the annual transportation over that of the preceding year was 3,997,354 miles and the increase in cost was $342,440. The number of post-offices in the United States on the 1st day of July last was 18,417, being an increase of 1,670 during the preceding year.

The gross revenues of the Department for the fiscal year ending June 30, 1850, amounted to $5,552,971.48, including the annual appropriation of $200,000 for the franked matter of the Departments and excluding the foreign postages collected for and payable to the British Government.

The expenditures for the same period were $5,212,953.43, leaving a balance of revenue over expenditures of $340,018.05.

I am happy to find that the fiscal condition of the Department is such as to justify the Postmaster-General in recommending the reduction of our inland letter postage to 3 cents the single letter when prepaid and 5 cents when not prepaid. He also recommends that the prepaid rate shall be reduced to 2 cents whenever the revenues of the Department, after the reduction, shall exceed its expenditures by more than 5 per cent for two consecutive years; that the postage upon California and other letters sent by our ocean steamers shall be much reduced, and that the rates of postage on newspapers, pamphlets, periodicals, and other printed matter shall be modified and some reduction thereon made.

It can not be doubted that the proposed reductions will for the present diminish the revenues of the Department. It is believed that the deficiency, after the surplus already accumulated shall be exhausted, may be almost wholly met either by abolishing the existing privileges of sending free matter through the mails or by paying out of the Treasury to the Post-Office Department a sum equivalent to the postage of which it is deprived by such privileges. The last is supposed to be the preferable mode, and will, if not entirely, so nearly supply that deficiency as to make any further appropriation that may be found necessary so inconsiderable as to form no obstacle to the proposed reductions.

I entertain no doubt of the authority of Congress to make appropriations for leading objects in that class of public works comprising what are usually called works of internal improvement. This authority I suppose to be derived chiefly from the power of regulating commerce with foreign nations and among the States and the power of laying and collecting imposts. Where commerce is to be carried on and imposts collected there must be ports and harbors as well as wharves and custom-houses. If ships laden with valuable cargoes approach the shore or sail along the coast, light-houses are necessary at suitable points for the protection of life and property. Other facilities and securities for commerce and navigation are hardly less important; and those clauses of the Constitution, therefore, to which I have referred have received from the origin of the Government a liberal and beneficial construction. Not only have light-houses, buoys, and beacons been established and floating lights maintained, but harbors have been cleared and improved, piers constructed, and even breakwaters for the safety of shipping and sea walls to protect harbors from being filled up and rendered useless by the action of the ocean, have been erected at very great expense. And this construction of the Constitution appears the more reasonable from the consideration that if these works, of such evident importance and utility, are not to be accomplished by Congress they can not be accomplished at all. By the adoption of the Constitution the several States voluntarily parted with the power of collecting duties of imposts in their own ports, and it is not to be expected that they should raise money by internal taxation, direct or indirect, for the benefit of that commerce the revenues derived from which do not, either in whole or in part, go into their own treasuries. Nor do I perceive any difference between the power of Congress to make appropriations for objects of this kind on the ocean and the power to make appropriations for similar objects on lakes and rivers, wherever they are large enough to bear on their waters an extensive traffic. The magnificent Mississippi and its tributaries and the vast lakes of the North and Northwest appear to me to fall within the exercise of the power as justly and as clearly as the ocean and the Gulf of Mexico. It is a mistake to regard expenditures judiciously made for these objects as expenditures for local purposes. The position or sight of the work is necessarily local, but its utility is general. A ship canal around the Falls of St. Mary of less than a mile in length, though local in its construction, would yet be national in its purpose and its benefits, as it would remove the only obstruction to a navigation of more than 1,000 miles, affecting several States, as well as our commercial relations with Canada. So, too, the breakwater at the mouth of the Delaware is erected, not for the exclusive benefit of the States bordering on the bay and river of that name, but for that of the whole coastwise navigation of the United States and, to a considerable extent, also of foreign commerce. If a ship be lost on the bar at the entrance of a Southern port for want of sufficient depth of water, it is very likely to be a Northern ship; and if a steamboat be sunk in any part of the Mississippi on account of its channel not having been properly cleared of obstructions, it may be a boat belonging to either of eight or ten States. I may add, as somewhat remarkable, that among all the thirty-one States there is none that is not to a greater or less extent bounded on the ocean, or the Gulf of Mexico, or one of the Great Lakes, or some navigable river.

In fulfilling our constitutional duties, fellow-citizens, on this subject, as in carrying into effect all other powers conferred by the Constitution, we should consider ourselves as deliberating and acting for one and the same country, and bear constantly in mind that our regard and our duty are due not to a particular part only, but to the whole.

I therefore recommend that appropriations be made for completing such works as have been already begun and for commencing such others as may seem to the wisdom of Congress to be of public and general importance.

The difficulties and delays incident to the settlement of private claims by Congress amount in many cases to a denial of justice. There is reason to apprehend that many unfortunate creditors of the Government have thereby been unavoidably ruined. Congress has so much business of a public character that it is impossible it should give much attention to mere private claims, and their accumulation is now so great that many claimants must despair of ever being able to obtain a hearing. It may well be doubted whether Congress, from the nature of its organization, is properly constituted to decide upon such cases. It is impossible that each member should examine the merits of every claim on which he is compelled to vote, and it is preposterous to ask a judge to decide a case which he has never heard. Such decisions may, and frequently must, do injustice either to the claimant or the Government, and I perceive no better remedy for this growing evil than the establishment of some tribunal to adjudicate upon such claims.

I beg leave, therefore, most respectfully to recommend that provision be made by law for the appointment of a commission to settle all private claims against the United States; and as an ex parte hearing must in all contested cases be very unsatisfactory, I also recommend the appointment of a solicitor, whose duty it shall be to represent the Government before such commission and protect it against all illegal, fraudulent, or unjust claims which may be presented for their adjudication. This District, which has neither voice nor vote in your deliberations, looks to you for protection and aid, and I commend all its wants to your favorable consideration, with a full confidence that you will meet them not only with justice, but with liberality. It should be borne in mind that in this city, laid out by Washington and consecrated by his name, is located the Capitol of our nation, the emblem of our Union and the symbol of our greatness. Here also are situated all the public buildings necessary for the use of the Government, and all these are exempt from taxation. It should be the pride of Americans to render this place attractive to the people of the whole Republic and convenient and safe for the transaction of the public business and the preservation of the public records. The Government should therefore bear a liberal proportion of the burdens of all necessary and useful improvements. And as nothing could contribute more to the health, comfort, and safety of the city and the security of the public buildings and records than an abundant supply of pure water, I respectfully recommend that you make such provisions for obtaining the same as in your wisdom you may deem proper.

The act, passed at your last session, making certain propositions to Texas for settling the disputed boundary between that State and the Territory of New Mexico was, immediately on its passage, transmitted by express to the governor of Texas, to be laid by him before the general assembly for its agreement thereto. Its receipt was duly acknowledged, but no official information has yet been received of the action of the general assembly thereon. It may, however, be very soon expected, as, by the terms of the propositions submitted they were to have been acted upon on or before the first day of the present month.

It was hardly to have been expected that the series of measures passed at your last session with the view of healing the sectional differences which had sprung from the slavery and territorial questions should at once have realized their beneficent purpose. All mutual concession in the nature of a compromise must necessarily be unwelcome to men of extreme opinions. And though without such concessions our Constitution could not have been formed, and can not be permanently sustained, yet we have seen them made the subject of bitter controversy in both sections of the Republic. It required many months of discussion and deliberation to secure the concurrence of a majority of Congress in their favor. It would be strange if they had been received with immediate approbation by people and States prejudiced and heated by the exciting controversies of their representatives. I believe those measures to have been required by the circumstances and condition of the country. I believe they were necessary to allay asperities and animosities that were rapidly alienating one section of the country from another and destroying those fraternal sentiments which are the strongest supports of the Constitution. They were adopted in the spirit of conciliation and for the purpose of conciliation. I believe that a great majority of our fellow citizens sympathize in that spirit and that purpose, and in the main approve and are prepared in all respects to sustain these enactments. I can not doubt that the American people, bound together by kindred blood and common traditions, still cherish a paramount regard for the Union of their fathers, and that they are ready to rebuke any attempt to violate its integrity, to disturb the compromises on which it is based, or to resist the laws which have been enacted under its authority.

The series of measures to which I have alluded are regarded by me as a settlement in principle and substance—a final settlement of the dangerous and exciting subjects which they embraced. Most of these subjects, indeed, are beyond your reach, as the legislation which disposed of them was in its character final and irrevocable. It may be presumed from the opposition which they all encountered that none of those measures was free from imperfections, but in their mutual dependence and connection they formed a system of compromise the most conciliatory and best for the entire country that could be obtained from conflicting sectional interests and opinions.

For this reason I recommend your adherence to the adjustment established by those measures until time and experience shall demonstrate the necessity of further legislation to guard against evasion or abuse.

By that adjustment we have been rescued from the wide and boundless agitation that surrounded us, and have a firm, distinct, and legal ground to rest upon. And the occasion, I trust, will justify me in exhorting my countrymen to rally upon and maintain that ground as the best, if not the only, means of restoring peace and quiet to the country and maintaining inviolate the integrity of the Union.

And now, fellow-citizens, I can not bring this communication to a close without invoking you to join me in humble and devout thanks to the Great Ruler of Nations for the multiplied blessings which He has graciously bestowed upon us. His hand, so often visible in our preservation, has stayed the pestilence, saved us from foreign wars and domestic disturbances, and scattered plenty throughout the land.

Our liberties, religions and civil, have been maintained, the fountains of knowledge have all been kept open, and means of happiness widely spread and generally enjoyed greater than have fallen to the lot of any other nation. And while deeply penetrated with gratitude for the past, let us hope that His all-wise providence will so guide our counsels as that they shall result in giving satisfaction to our constituents, securing the peace of the country, and adding new strength to the united Government under which we live.

A Strict Constitutionalist

MILLARD FILLMORE'S FIRST ANNUAL MESSAGE

Claude Welch

RANKINGS OF AMERICAN presidents generally place Millard Fillmore toward the bottom. Critics consider his approval of the Compromise of 1850 a major flaw. In fairness to him, we must recognize the delicate balance struck in this legislation. The most infamous part, the Fugitive Slave Act, formed part of a broader package of five bills. The Compromise temporarily defused a political confrontation between slave and free states that had existed since the republic's establishment. On the positive side, various bills in the Compromise abolished slavery in the District of Columbia. California, Texas, and other territories acquired during the Mexican-American War became full-fledged states. Arguably, four positive actions, one negative.

Fillmore, a largely self-educated individual, prized caution, lawyerly and above all constitutionally sanctioned actions. His first major address to Congress, delivered December 2, 1850, may likely be one of the longest speeches ever delivered by a president to this body. The ninth president, William Henry Harrison, took an hour and 45 minutes to deliver his close to 8,500-word inaugural oration. He died thirty-one days later, hence gaining the dubious distinction of serving the shortest term in American history. Fillmore, the thirteenth president, remained in the presidency for two years and thirty-seven days. He came close to Harrison's record, with an annual address of more than 8,300 words.

A political chasm existed between Taylor and Fillmore, Fillmore having been selected largely for geographic balance. Neither gave remarks filled with quotable quotes, unlike some of the other addresses examined in this book. Fillmore's speech was ponderous, filled with long, complex sentences. Consider the following: "I trust, therefore, that it may not be deemed inappropriate if I avail myself of this opportunity of the reassembling of Congress to make known my sentiments in a general manner in regard to the policy which ought to be pursued by the Government both in its intercourse with foreign nations and its management and administration of internal affairs."

Fillmore broke with the expansionist policies of his predecessor James K. Polk, saying, "We make no wars to promote or to prevent successions to thrones, to maintain any theory of a balance of power, or to suppress the actual government which any country chooses to establish for itself." In his first annual address to Congress, Fillmore also praised the treaty reached by the United States with Great Britain, "facilitating and protecting the construction of a ship canal between the Atlantic and Pacific oceans and for other purposes." No, the passageway would not be located across the Isthmus of Panama, but across Nicaragua. On the other hand, Fillmore subsequently authorized Commodore Matthew Perry's 1853 expedition to Japan, a clear exercise in gunboat diplomacy.

The thirteenth president personally opposed slavery. However, as chief executive, he believed himself bound to support the "peculiar institution." As he stated, "In our domestic policy the Constitution will be my guide, and in questions of doubt I shall look for its interpretation to the judicial decisions of that tribunal which was established to expound it and to the usage of the Government, sanctioned by the acquiescence of the country." Further, Fillmore pledged to "deprecate useless irritation among the several members of the Union and all reproach and crimination tending to alienate one portion of the country from another." Implicitly, he showed himself willing to remain within the broad tradition demonstrated by the renowned Whig leader Daniel Webster. According to Fillmore, "without law there can be no real practical liberty; that when law is trampled under foot tyranny rules, whether it appears in the form of a military despotism or of popular violence."

The infamous Dred Scott decision followed seven years later.

Fillmore was the last of the Whig presidents, having been preceded by the aforementioned Harrison and Zachary Taylor. In terms of internal policy, the Whigs favored high tariffs to protect nascent domestic industries. As Fillmore stated, "All experience has demonstrated the wisdom and policy of raising a large portion of revenue for the support of Government from duties on goods imported. The power to lay these duties is unquestionable, and its chief object, of course, is to replenish the Treasury. But if in doing this an incidental advantage may be gained by encouraging the industry of our own citizens, it is our duty to avail ourselves of that advantage."

Fillmore foreshadowed the 1862 creation of the Department of Agriculture, proposing "the establishment of an agricultural bureau, to be charged with the duty of giving to this leading branch of American industry the encouragement which it so well deserves." He also recommended "the employment of a competent mineralogist and chemist . . . [who would analyze] their respective elements and properties and their adaptation to useful purposes . . . and examine and report upon the qualities of different soils and the manures best calculated to improve their productiveness." Fillmore further echoed Taylor's 1848 recommendation to open "'a line of communication, the best and most expeditious of which the nature of the country will admit,' between the Valley of the Mississippi and the Pacific."

The Mexican-American War resulted in the incorporation of numerous Native Americans. Fillmore alluded to this dramatic change thus: "Texas and New Mexico are surrounded by powerful tribes of Indians, who are a source of constant terror and annoyance to the inhabitants. Separating into small predatory bands, and always mounted, they overrun the country, devastating farms, destroying crops, driving off whole herds of cattle, and occasionally murdering the inhabitants or carrying them into captivity."

Internationally, Fillmore stressed facilitating imports of guano. "Peruvian guano has become so desirable an article to the agricultural interest of the United States that it is the duty of the Government to employ all the means properly in its power for the purpose of causing that article to be imported into the country at a reasonable price." He called upon Spain and Great Britain to settle their boundary dispute in Hispaniola, which he called "St. Domingo." "The proximity of that island to the United States and the delicate questions involved in the existing controversy there render it desirable that it should be permanently and speedily adjusted."

Fillmore concluded his address with a final plea for reason. In his view, "It was hardly to have been expected that the series of measures passed at your last session with the view of healing the sectional differences which had sprung from the slavery and territorial questions should at once have realized their beneficent purpose. All mutual concession in the nature of a compromise must necessarily be unwelcome to men of extreme opinions."

What lessons can one draw from this brief analysis of a single speech?

First, Fillmore saw his role as chief executive as one constrained by the Constitution, Acts of Congress, and major judicial decisions. As a largely self-educated lawyer who had received little formal schooling, he firmly defended the constraints imposed by the other branches of government.

Fillmore likewise did not stray from Whig orthodoxy. His support for significant domestic infrastructure improvements and industrial development, funded by tariff walls, remained constant. Third, he viewed America's international role as largely an outgrowth of domestic policies, as experienced by the stress upon guano imports or his concern about Hispaniola, where boundary disputes threatened U.S. interests.

Finally, and most significant in the view of later historians, Fillmore "failed" largely due to one of the five bills contained in the Compromise of 1850. I would advance a contrary view, despite the fact that millions of slaves continued to experience the travails of the "peculiar institution" for several years more. During the interim between the Compromise and the outburst of the Civil War, the North's industrial strength and population dominance grew. It entered the conflict even stronger than its Confederate adversary. Did the objective—additional years of peace—justify the means? That is a question that readers of this chapter, and other parts of the publication, must weigh for every president. What they said in their inaugural addresses should be judged in terms of the words of the various chief executives relative to their subsequent records and to the verdict rendered later by history.

Franklin Pierce's Inaugural Address

FRIDAY, MARCH 4, 1853

MY COUNTRYMEN:

It is a relief to feel that no heart but my own can know the personal regret and bitter sorrow over which I have been borne to a position so suitable for others rather than desirable for myself.

The circumstances under which I have been called for a limited period to preside over the destinies of the Republic fill me with a profound sense of responsibility, but with nothing like shrinking apprehension. I repair to the post assigned me not as to one sought, but in obedience to the unsolicited expression of your will, answerable only for a fearless, faithful, and diligent exercise of my best powers. I ought to be, and am, truly grateful for the rare manifestation of the nation's confidence; but this, so far from lightening my obligations, only adds to their weight. You have summoned me in my weakness; you must sustain me by your strength. When looking for the fulfillment of reasonable requirements, you will not be unmindful of the great changes which have occurred, even within the last quarter of a century, and the consequent augmentation and complexity of duties imposed in the administration both of your home and foreign affairs.

Whether the elements of inherent force in the Republic have kept pace with its unparalleled progression in territory, population, and wealth has been the subject of earnest thought and discussion on both sides of the ocean. Less than sixty-four years ago the Father of his Country made "the" then "recent accession of the important State of North Carolina to the Constitution of the United States" one of the subjects of his special congratulation. At that moment, however, when the agitation consequent upon the Revolutionary struggle had hardly subsided, when we were just emerging from the weakness and embarrassments of the Confederation, there was an evident consciousness of vigor equal to the great mission so wisely and bravely fulfilled by our fathers. It was not a presumptuous assurance, but a calm faith, springing from a clear view of the sources of power in a government constituted like ours. It is no paradox to say that although comparatively weak the new-born nation was intrinsically strong. Inconsiderable in population and apparent resources, it was upheld by a broad and intelligent comprehension of rights and an all-pervading purpose to maintain them, stronger than armaments. It came from the furnace of the Revolution, tempered to the necessities of the times. The thoughts of the men of that day were as practical as their sentiments were patriotic. They wasted no portion of their energies upon idle and delusive speculations, but with a firm and fearless step advanced beyond the governmental landmarks which had hitherto circumscribed the limits of human freedom and planted their standard, where it has stood against dangers which have threatened from abroad, and internal agitation, which has at times fearfully menaced at home. They proved themselves equal to the solution of the great problem, to understand which their minds had been illuminated by the dawning lights of the Revolution. The object sought was not a thing dreamed of; it was a thing realized. They had exhibited not only the power to achieve, but, what all history affirms to be so much more unusual, the capacity to maintain. The oppressed throughout the world from that day to the present have turned their eyes hitherward, not to find those lights extinguished or to fear lest they should wane, but to be constantly cheered by their steady and increasing radiance.

In this our country has, in my judgment, thus far fulfilled its highest duty to suffering humanity. It has spoken and will continue to speak, not only by its words, but by its acts, the language of sympathy, encouragement, and hope to those who earnestly listen to tones which pronounce for the largest rational liberty. But after all, the most animating encouragement and potent appeal for freedom will be its own history—its trials and its triumphs. Preeminently, the power of our advocacy reposes in our example; but no example, be it remembered, can be powerful for lasting good, whatever apparent advantages may be gained, which is not based upon eternal principles of right and justice. Our fathers decided for themselves, both upon the hour to declare and the hour to strike. They were their own judges of the circumstances under which it became them to pledge to each other "their lives, their fortunes, and their sacred honor" for the acquisition of the priceless inheritance transmitted to us. The energy with which that great conflict was opened and, under the guidance of a manifest and beneficent Providence the uncomplaining endurance with which it was prosecuted to its consummation were only surpassed by the wisdom and patriotic spirit of concession which characterized all the counsels of the early fathers.

One of the most impressive evidences of that wisdom is to be found in the fact that the actual working of our system has dispelled a degree of solicitude which at the outset disturbed bold hearts and far-reaching intellects. The apprehension of dangers from extended territory, multiplied States, accumulated wealth, and augmented population has proved to be unfounded. The stars upon your banner have become nearly threefold their original number; your densely populated possessions skirt the shores of the two great oceans; and yet this vast increase of people and territory has not only shown itself compatible with the harmonious action of the States and Federal Government in their respective constitutional spheres, but has afforded an additional guaranty of the strength and integrity of both.

With an experience thus suggestive and cheering, the policy of my Administration will not be controlled by any timid forebodings of evil from expansion. Indeed, it is not to be disguised that our attitude as a nation and our position on the globe render the acquisition of certain possessions not within our jurisdiction eminently important for our protection, if not in the future essential for the preservation of the rights of commerce and the peace of the world. Should they be obtained, it will be through no grasping spirit, but with a view to obvious national interest and security, and in a manner entirely consistent with the strictest observance of national faith. We have nothing in our history or position to invite aggression; we have everything to beckon us to the cultivation of relations of peace and amity with all nations. Purposes, therefore, at once just and pacific will be significantly marked in the conduct of our foreign affairs. I intend that my Administration shall leave no blot upon our fair record, and trust I may safely give the assurance that no act within the legitimate scope of my constitutional control will be tolerated on the part of any portion of our citizens which can not challenge a ready justification before the tribunal of the civilized world. An Administration would be unworthy of confidence at home or respect abroad should it cease to be influenced by the conviction that no apparent advantage can be purchased at a price so dear as that of national wrong or dishonor. It is not your privilege as a nation to speak of a distant past. The striking incidents of your history, replete with instruction and furnishing abundant grounds for hopeful confidence, are comprised in a period comparatively brief. But if your past is limited, your future is boundless. Its obligations throng the unexplored pathway of advancement, and will be limitless as duration. Hence a sound and comprehensive policy should embrace not less the distant future than the urgent present.

The great objects of our pursuit as a people are best to be attained by peace, and are entirely consistent with the tranquillity and interests of the rest of mankind. With the neighboring nations upon our continent we should cultivate kindly and fraternal relations. We can desire nothing in regard to them so much as to see them consolidate their strength and pursue the paths of prosperity and happiness. If in the course of their growth we should open new channels of trade and create additional facilities for friendly intercourse, the benefits realized will be equal and mutual. Of the complicated European systems of national polity we have heretofore been independent. From their wars, their tumults, and anxieties we have been, happily, almost entirely exempt. Whilst these are confined to the nations which gave them existence, and within their legitimate jurisdiction, they can not affect us except as they appeal to our sympathies in the cause of human freedom and universal advancement. But the vast interests of commerce are common to all mankind, and the advantages of trade and international intercourse must always present a noble field for the moral influence of a great people.

With these views firmly and honestly carried out, we have a right to expect, and shall under all circumstances require, prompt reciprocity. The rights which belong to us as a nation are not alone to be regarded, but those which pertain to every citizen in his individual capacity, at home and abroad, must be sacredly maintained. So long as he can discern every star in its place upon that ensign, without wealth to purchase for him preferment or title to secure for him place, it will be his privilege, and must be his acknowledged right, to stand unabashed even in the presence of princes, with a proud consciousness that he is himself one of a nation of sovereigns and that he can not in legitimate pursuit wander so far from home that the agent whom he shall leave behind in the place which I now occupy will not see that no rude hand of power or tyrannical passion is laid upon him with impunity. He must realize that upon every sea and on every soil where our enterprise may rightfully seek the protection of our flag American citizenship is an inviolable panoply for the security of American rights. And in this connection it can hardly be necessary to reaffirm a principle which should now be regarded as fundamental. The rights, security, and repose of this Confederacy reject the idea of interference or colonization on this side of the ocean by any foreign power beyond present jurisdiction as utterly inadmissible.

The opportunities of observation furnished by my brief experience as a soldier confirmed in my own mind the opinion, entertained and acted upon by others from the formation of the Government, that the maintenance of large standing armies in our country would be not only dangerous, but unnecessary. They also illustrated the importance—I might well say the absolute necessity—of the military science and practical skill furnished in such an eminent degree by the institution which has made your Army what it is, under the discipline and instruction of officers not more distinguished for their solid attainments, gallantry, and devotion to the public service than for unobtrusive bearing and high moral tone. The Army as organized must be the nucleus around which in every time of need the strength of your military power, the sure bulwark of your defense—a national militia—may be readily formed into a well-disciplined and efficient organization. And the skill and self-devotion of the Navy assure you that you may take the performance of the past as a pledge for the future, and may confidently expect that the flag which has waved its untarnished folds over every sea will still float in undiminished honor. But these, like many other subjects, will be appropriately brought at a future time to the attention of the coordinate branches of the Government, to which I shall always look with profound respect and with trustful confidence that they will accord to me the aid and support which I shall so much need and which their experience and wisdom will readily suggest.

In the administration of domestic affairs you expect a devoted integrity in the public service and an observance of rigid economy in all departments, so marked as never justly to be questioned. If this reasonable expectation be not realized, I frankly confess that one of your leading hopes is doomed to disappointment, and that my efforts in a very important particular must result in a humiliating failure. Offices can be properly regarded only in the light of aids for the accomplishment of these objects, and as occupancy can confer no prerogative nor importunate desire for preferment any claim, the public interest imperatively demands that they be considered with sole reference to the duties to be performed. Good citizens may well claim the protection of good laws and the benign influence of good government, but a claim for office is what the people of a republic should never recognize. No reasonable man of any party will expect the Administration to be so regardless of its responsibility and of the obvious elements of success as to retain persons known to be under the influence of political hostility and partisan prejudice in positions which will require not only severe labor, but cordial cooperation. Having no implied engagements to ratify, no rewards to bestow, no resentments to remember, and no personal wishes to consult in selections for official station, I shall fulfill this difficult and delicate trust, admitting no motive as worthy either of my character or position which does not contemplate an efficient discharge of duty and the best interests of my country. I acknowledge my obligations to the masses of my countrymen, and to them alone. Higher objects than personal aggrandizement gave direction and energy to their exertions in the late canvass, and they shall not be disappointed. They require at my hands diligence, integrity, and capacity wherever there are duties to be performed. Without these qualities in their public servants, more stringent laws for the prevention or punishment of fraud, negligence, and peculation will be vain. With them they will be unnecessary.

But these are not the only points to which you look for vigilant watchfulness. The dangers of a concentration of all power in the general government of a confederacy so vast as ours are too obvious to be disregarded. You have a right, therefore, to expect your agents in every department to regard strictly the limits imposed upon them by the Constitution of the United States. The great scheme of our constitutional liberty rests upon a proper distribution of power between the State and Federal authorities, and experience has shown that the harmony and happiness of our people must depend upon a just discrimination between the separate rights and responsibilities of the States and your common rights and obligations under the General Government; and here, in my opinion, are the considerations which should form the true basis of future concord in regard to the questions which have most seriously disturbed public tranquillity. If the Federal Government will confine itself to the exercise of powers clearly granted by the Constitution, it can hardly happen that its action upon any question should endanger the institutions of the States or interfere with their right to manage matters strictly domestic according to the will of their own people.

In expressing briefly my views upon an important subject rich has recently agitated the nation to almost a fearful degree, I am moved by no other impulse than a most earnest desire for the perpetuation of that Union which has made us what we are, showering upon us blessings and conferring a power and influence which our fathers could hardly have anticipated, even with their most sanguine hopes directed to a far-off future. The sentiments I now announce were not unknown before the expression of the voice which called me here. My own position upon this subject was clear and unequivocal, upon the record of my words and my acts, and it is only recurred to at this time because silence might perhaps be misconstrued. With the Union my best and dearest earthly hopes are entwined. Without it what are we individually or collectively? What becomes of the noblest field ever opened for the advancement of our race in religion, in government, in the arts, and in all that dignifies and adorns mankind? From that radiant constellation which both illumines our own way and points out to struggling nations their course, let but a single star be lost, and, if these be not utter darkness, the luster of the whole is dimmed. Do my countrymen need any assurance that such a catastrophe is not to overtake them while I possess the power to stay it? It is with me an earnest and vital belief that as the Union has been the source, under Providence, of our prosperity to this time, so it is the surest pledge of a continuance of the blessings we have enjoyed, and which we are sacredly bound to transmit undiminished to our children. The field of calm and free discussion in our country is open, and will always be so, but never has been and never can be traversed for good in a spirit of sectionalism and uncharitableness. The founders of the Republic dealt with things as they were presented to them, in a spirit of self-sacrificing patriotism, and, as time has proved, with a comprehensive wisdom which it will always be safe for us to consult. Every measure tending to strengthen the fraternal feelings of all the members of our Union has had my heartfelt approbation. To every theory of society or government, whether the offspring of feverish ambition or of morbid enthusiasm, calculated to dissolve the bonds of law and affection which unite us, I shall interpose a ready and stern resistance. I believe that involuntary servitude, as it exists in different States of this

Confederacy, is recognized by the Constitution. I believe that it stands like any other admitted right, and that the States where it exists are entitled to efficient remedies to enforce the constitutional provisions. I hold that the laws of 1850, commonly called the "compromise measures," are strictly constitutional and to be unhesitatingly carried into effect. I believe that the constituted authorities of this Republic are bound to regard the rights of the South in this respect as they would view any other legal and constitutional right, and that the laws to enforce them should be respected and obeyed, not with a reluctance encouraged by abstract opinions as to their propriety in a different state of society, but cheerfully and according to the decisions of the tribunal to which their exposition belongs. Such have been, and are, my convictions, and upon them I shall act. I fervently hope that the question is at rest, and that no sectional or ambitious or fanatical excitement may again threaten the durability of our institutions or obscure the light of our prosperity.

But let not the foundation of our hope rest upon man's wisdom. It will not be sufficient that sectional prejudices find no place in the public deliberations. It will not be sufficient that the rash counsels of human passion are rejected. It must be felt that there is no national security but in the nation's humble, acknowledged dependence upon God and His overruling providence.

We have been carried in safety through a perilous crisis. Wise counsels, like those which gave us the Constitution, prevailed to uphold it. Let the period be remembered as an admonition, and not as an encouragement, in any section of the Union, to make experiments where experiments are fraught with such fearful hazard. Let it be impressed upon all hearts that, beautiful as our fabric is, no earthly power or wisdom could ever reunite its broken fragments. Standing, as I do, almost within view of the green slopes of Monticello, and, as it were, within reach of the tomb of Washington, with all the cherished memories of the past gathering around me like so many eloquent voices of exhortation from heaven, I can express no better hope for my country than that the kind Providence which smiled upon our fathers may enable their children to preserve the blessings they have inherited.

Handsome Frank

THE INAUGURAL ADDRESS OF FRANKLIN PIERCE

Peter A. Wallner

AFTER A CAMPAIGN of mutual innuendo and charges by both candidates, on November 2, 1852, Franklin Pierce was elected fourteenth president of the United States by a landslide. Pierce won twenty-one of the twenty-seven states that then constituted the Union. His opponent was the Whig candidate, Winfield Scott, who would serve as the commander of the Army throughout Pierce's term despite not getting along with Pierce's choice for secretary of war, Jefferson Davis. Nonetheless, he was able to choose a Cabinet, led by Davis and Secretary of State William L. Marcy, which stayed together for the next four years—the first time in U.S. history that a Cabinet remained intact for an entire presidential term, with no resignations. As Pierce's secretary, Sidney Webster, wrote, "The elements of that Cabinet were such that, if left without a controlling chief, it would have broken asunder in a week." What kept them together was their mutual respect, even fondness, for Pierce.

Less than two months before the inauguration, the event was marred by the death of the Pierce's only surviving child, eleven-year-old Benny, in a train wreck. Pierce was unable to choose his Cabinet until after the funeral, and Jane Pierce, who was always unstable mentally, was totally unable to resolve his death with her very fundamentalist religious views. Jane's cousin wrote at the time, "you cannot but tremble for one who is always so depressed and now has such bitter cause." There was concern that Jane would not rally to become a comfort to her husband in time for the inauguration, and, in fact, this was the case. The inaugural ball was canceled. She stayed in Baltimore with friends, and on March 2, her husband traveled to the city to read his Inaugural Address to Jane. She seemed completely uninterested in the address and insisted that politics be forgotten for the moment. Instead, he left abruptly, and Jane was unable to share her feelings with him and to give him a lock of his son's hair, which she hoped he would keep near him on Inauguration Day.

Inauguration Day was a cold, raw March day with light snow falling as Pierce prepared for the ceremonies. The procession to the Capitol began at City Hall and marched to Willard's Hotel, where President Fillmore joined the parade in an open carriage. It was noon when Pierce left the hotel and climbed into the carriage next to the president. The two men rode down Pennsylvania Avenue, in the barouche, accompanied by Senators Bright and Hamlin. All the way down the Avenue, Pierce stood up in the carriage bare-headed and waved to the people gathered on both sides. There were an estimated 70,000 visitors in the city for the inauguration. Vice President–elect William Rufus DeVane King was in Cuba in a vain attempt to restore his health; he suffered from tuberculosis and would die shortly after the inauguration. The preliminary ceremony of the swearing-in of the vice president was dispensed with, and Senator Bright led Pierce from the chamber to the east front of the Capitol, where he took the oath of office from Chief Justice Roger B. Taney. Pierce also broke precedent by affirming rather than swearing to uphold the Constitution.

The nation's youngest president to that date turned and faced the crowd of some 15,000 who stood before him. In the confident manner of the "easy lawyer and speaker," he began to address the crowd. Pierce spoke for the next thirty minutes entirely from memory. Though he kept the document by his side, he delivered his Inaugural Address without it. He began with a statement he had added to the speech that morning, speaking of the recent death of his son: "My Countrymen. It is a relief to feel that no heart but my own can know the personal regret and bitter sorrow over which I have been borne to a position so suitable for others rather than desirable for myself." The address was an eloquent summary of all that Jacksonian democracy stood for. While it did not propose a specific agenda, the speech was generally praised by the press. The politically neutral *Baltimore Sun* wrote, "No similar document, that we remember, met with such general favor." On reading the speech, H. R. French, a judge in New Hampshire, wrote, "The inaugural is first rate and pleases all parties. He has a wonderful gift of propriety in all his acts, and words, and writing. I should have written about such address as that had I been President."

Fillmore accompanied the new president back to the White House and then took his leave. The new president received guests throughout the rest of the day. He stood for hours shaking hands with all comers before finally making his way upstairs to the family quarters. Since the Fillmores had not moved out completely, due to the illness of Mrs. Fillmore, the new president had to make do by assigning one room to his secretary, Sidney Webster, and retired to the other room.

James Buchanan's Inaugural Address

WEDNESDAY, MARCH 4, 1857

FELLOW-CITIZENS:

I appear before you this day to take the solemn oath "that I will faithfully execute the office of President of the United States and will to the best of my ability preserve, protect, and defend the Constitution of the United States."

In entering upon this great office I must humbly invoke the God of our fathers for wisdom and firmness to execute its high and responsible duties in such a manner as to restore harmony and ancient friendship among the people of the several States and to preserve our free institutions throughout many generations. Convinced that I owe my election to the inherent love for the Constitution and the Union which still animates the hearts of the American people, let me earnestly ask their powerful support in sustaining all just measures calculated to perpetuate these, the richest political blessings which Heaven has ever bestowed upon any nation. Having determined not to become a candidate for reelection, I shall have no motive to influence my conduct in administering the Government except the desire ably and faithfully to serve my country and to live in grateful memory of my countrymen.

We have recently passed through a Presidential contest in which the passions of our fellow-citizens were excited to the highest degree by questions of deep and vital importance; but when the people proclaimed their will the tempest at once subsided and all was calm.

The voice of the majority, speaking in the manner prescribed by the Constitution, was heard, and instant submission followed. Our own country could alone have exhibited so grand and striking a spectacle of the capacity of man for self-government.

What a happy conception, then, was it for Congress to apply this simple rule, that the will of the majority shall govern, to the settlement of the question of domestic slavery in the Territories! Congress is neither "to legislate slavery into any Territory or State nor to exclude it therefrom, but to leave the people thereof perfectly free to form and regulate their domestic institutions in their own way, subject only to the Constitution of the United States."

As a natural consequence, Congress has also prescribed that when the Territory of Kansas shall be admitted as a State it "shall be received into the Union with or without slavery, as their constitution may prescribe at the time of their admission."

A difference of opinion has arisen in regard to the point of time when the people of a Territory shall decide this question for themselves.

This is, happily, a matter of but little practical importance. Besides, it is a judicial question, which legitimately belongs to the Supreme Court of the United States, before whom it is now pending, and will, it is understood, be speedily and finally settled. To their decision, in common with all good citizens, I shall cheerfully submit, whatever this may be, though it has ever been my individual opinion that under the Nebraska-Kansas act the appropriate period will be when the number of actual residents in the Territory shall justify the formation of a constitution with a view to its admission as a State into the Union. But be this as it may, it is the imperative and indispensable duty of the Government of the United States to secure to every resident inhabitant the free and independent expression of his opinion by his vote. This sacred right of each individual must be preserved. That being accomplished, nothing can be fairer than to leave the people of a Territory free from all foreign interference to decide their own destiny for themselves, subject only to the Constitution of the United States.

The whole Territorial question being thus settled upon the principle of popular sovereignty—a principle as ancient as free government itself—everything of a practical nature has been decided. No other question remains for adjustment, because all agree that under the Constitution slavery in the States is beyond the reach of any human power except that of the respective States themselves wherein it exists. May we not, then, hope that the long agitation on this subject is approaching its end, and that the geographical parties to which it has given birth, so much dreaded by the Father of his Country, will speedily become extinct? Most happy will it be for the country when the public mind shall be diverted from this question to others of more pressing and practical importance. Throughout the whole progress of this agitation, which has scarcely known any intermission for more than twenty years, whilst it has been productive of no positive good to any human being it has been the prolific source of great evils to the master, to the slave, and to the whole country. It has alienated and estranged the people of the sister States from each other, and has even seriously endangered the very existence of the Union. Nor has the danger yet entirely ceased. Under our system there is a remedy for all mere political evils in the sound sense and sober judgment of the people. Time is a great corrective. Political subjects which but a few years ago excited and exasperated the public mind have passed away and are now nearly forgotten. But this question of domestic slavery is of far graver importance than any mere political question, because should the agitation continue it may eventually endanger the personal safety of a large portion of our countrymen where the institution exists. In that event no form of government, however admirable in itself and however productive of material benefits, can compensate for the loss of peace and domestic security around the family altar. Let every Union-loving man, therefore, exert his best influence to suppress this agitation, which since the recent legislation of Congress is without any legitimate object.

It is an evil omen of the times that men have undertaken to calculate the mere material value of the Union. Reasoned estimates have been presented of the pecuniary profits and local advantages which would result to different States and sections from its dissolution and of the comparative injuries which such an event would inflict on other States and sections. Even descending to this low and narrow view of the mighty question, all such calculations are at fault. The bare reference to a single consideration will be conclusive on this point. We at present enjoy a free trade throughout our extensive and expanding country such as the world has never witnessed. This trade is conducted on railroads and canals, on noble rivers and arms of the sea, which bind together the North and the South, the East and the West, of our Confederacy. Annihilate this trade, arrest its free progress by the geographical lines of jealous and hostile States, and you destroy the prosperity and onward march of the whole and every part and involve all in one common ruin. But such considerations, important as they are in themselves, sink into insignificance when we reflect on the terrific evils which would result from disunion to every portion of the Confederacy—to the North, not more than to the South, to the East not more than to the West. These I shall not attempt to portray, because I feel an humble confidence that the kind Providence which inspired our fathers with wisdom to frame the most perfect form of government and union ever devised by man will not suffer it to perish until it shall have been peacefully instrumental by its example in the extension of civil and religious liberty throughout the world.

Next in importance to the maintenance of the Constitution and the Union is the duty of preserving the Government free from the taint or even the suspicion of corruption. Public virtue is the vital spirit of republics, and history proves that when this has decayed and the love of money has usurped its place, although the forms of free government may remain for a season, the substance has departed forever.

Our present financial condition is without a parallel in history. No nation has ever before been embarrassed from too large a surplus in its treasury. This almost necessarily gives birth to extravagant legislation. It produces wild schemes of expenditure and begets a race of speculators and jobbers, whose ingenuity is exerted in contriving and promoting expedients to obtain public money. The purity of official agents, whether rightfully or wrongfully, is suspected, and the character of the government suffers in the estimation of the people. This is in itself a very great evil.

The natural mode of relief from this embarrassment is to appropriate the surplus in the Treasury to great national objects for which a clear warrant can be found in the Constitution. Among these I might mention the extinguishment of the public debt, a reasonable increase of the Navy, which is at present inadequate to the protection of our vast tonnage afloat, now greater than that of any other nation, as well as to the defense of our extended seacoast.

It is beyond all question the true principle that no more revenue ought to be collected from the people than the amount necessary to defray the expenses of a wise, economical, and efficient administration of the Government. To reach this point it was necessary to resort to a modification of the tariff, and this has, I trust, been accomplished in such a manner as to do as little injury as may have been practicable to our domestic manufactures, especially those necessary for the defense of the country. Any discrimination against a particular branch for the purpose of benefiting favored corporations, individuals, or interests would have been unjust to the rest of the community and inconsistent with that spirit of fairness and equality which ought to govern in the adjustment of a revenue tariff.

But the squandering of the public money sinks into comparative insignificance as a temptation to corruption when compared with the squandering of the public lands.

No nation in the tide of time has ever been blessed with so rich and noble an inheritance as we enjoy in the public lands. In administering this important trust, whilst it may be wise to grant portions of them for the improvement of the remainder, yet we should never forget that it is our cardinal policy to reserve these lands, as much as may be, for actual settlers, and this at moderate prices. We shall thus not only best promote the prosperity of the new States and Territories, by furnishing them a hardy and independent race of honest and industrious citizens, but shall secure homes for our children and our children's children, as well as for those exiles from foreign shores who may seek in this country to improve their condition and to enjoy the blessings of civil and religious liberty. Such emigrants have done much to promote the growth and prosperity of the country. They have proved faithful both in peace and in war. After becoming citizens they are entitled, under the Constitution and laws, to be placed on a perfect equality with native-born citizens, and in this character they should ever be kindly recognized.

The Federal Constitution is a grant from the States to Congress of certain specific powers, and the question whether this grant should be liberally or strictly construed has more or less divided political parties from the beginning. Without entering into the argument, I desire to state at the commencement of my Administration that long experience and observation have convinced me that a strict construction of the powers of the Government is the only true, as well as the only safe, theory of the Constitution. Whenever in our past history doubtful powers have been exercised by Congress, these have never failed to produce injurious and unhappy consequences. Many such instances might be adduced if this were the proper occasion. Neither is it necessary for the public service to strain the language of the Constitution, because all the great and useful powers required for a successful administration of the Government, both in peace and in war, have been granted, either in express terms or by the plainest implication.

Whilst deeply convinced of these truths, I yet consider it clear that under the war-making power Congress may appropriate money toward the construction of a military road when this is absolutely necessary for the defense of any State or Territory of the Union against foreign invasion. Under the Constitution Congress has power "to declare war," "to raise and support armies," "to provide and maintain a navy," and to call forth the militia to "repel invasions." Thus endowed, in an ample manner, with the war-making power, the corresponding duty is required that "the United States shall protect each of them [the States] against invasion." Now, how is it possible to afford this protection to California and our Pacific possessions except by means of a military road through the Territories of the United States, over which men and munitions of war may be speedily transported from the Atlantic States to meet and to repel the invader? In the event of a war with a naval power much stronger than our own we should then have no other available access to the Pacific Coast, because such a power would instantly close the route across the isthmus of Central America. It is impossible to conceive that whilst the Constitution has expressly required Congress to defend all the States it should yet deny to them, by any fair construction, the only possible means by which one of these States can be defended. Besides, the Government, ever since its origin, has been in the constant practice of constructing military roads. It might also be wise to consider whether the love for the Union which now animates our fellow-citizens on the Pacific Coast may not be impaired by our neglect or refusal to provide for them, in their remote and isolated condition, the only means by which the power of the States on this side of the Rocky Mountains can reach them in sufficient time to "protect" them "against invasion." I forbear for the present from expressing an opinion as to the wisest and most economical mode in which the

Government can lend its aid in accomplishing this great and necessary work. I believe that many of the difficulties in the way, which now appear formidable, will in a great degree vanish as soon as the nearest and best route shall have been satisfactorily ascertained.

It may be proper that on this occasion I should make some brief remarks in regard to our rights and duties as a member of the great family of nations. In our intercourse with them there are some plain principles, approved by our own experience, from which we should never depart. We ought to cultivate peace, commerce, and friendship with all nations, and this not merely as the best means of promoting our own material interests, but in a spirit of Christian benevolence toward our fellow-men, wherever their lot may be cast. Our diplomacy should be direct and frank, neither seeking to obtain more nor accepting less than is our due. We ought to cherish a sacred regard for the independence of all nations, and never attempt to interfere in the domestic concerns of any unless this shall be imperatively required by the great law of self-preservation. To avoid entangling alliances has been a maxim of our policy ever since the days of Washington, and its wisdom's no one will attempt to dispute. In short, we ought to do justice in a kindly spirit to all nations and require justice from them in return.

It is our glory that whilst other nations have extended their dominions by the sword we have never acquired any territory except by fair purchase or, as in the case of Texas, by the voluntary determination of a brave, kindred, and independent people to blend their destinies with our own. Even our acquisitions from Mexico form no exception. Unwilling to take advantage of the fortune of war against a sister republic, we purchased these possessions under the treaty of peace for a sum which was considered at the time a fair equivalent. Our past history forbids that we shall in the future acquire territory unless this be sanctioned by the laws of justice and honor. Acting on this principle, no nation will have a right to interfere or to complain if in the progress of events we shall still further extend our possessions. Hitherto in all our acquisitions the people, under the protection of the American flag, have enjoyed civil and religious liberty, as well as equal and just laws, and have been contented, prosperous, and happy. Their trade with the rest of the world has rapidly increased, and thus every commercial nation has shared largely in their successful progress.

I shall now proceed to take the oath prescribed by the Constitution, whilst humbly invoking the blessing of Divine Providence on this great people.

Doughface

THE INAUGURAL ADDRESS OF JAMES BUCHANAN

Jean H. Baker

PROMPTLY AT NOON on the pleasant sunny day of March 4, 1857, James Buchanan, soon to take the oath of office as the fifteenth president of the United States, began his Inaugural Address to a distinguished audience of congressmen, judges, diplomats, and residents of the District of Columbia. At sixty-five he was older than all but one of his predecessors, and his snow-white hair, stooped shoulders, and reedy voice suggested as much. Few actually heard what Buchanan had to say in an address of nearly 3,000 words; rather, it would reach Americans in its printed version published in the nation's newspapers. Buchanan was not feeling well. Since his arrival in Washington he had been suffering from the dysentery associated with the National Hotel where he was staying before moving into the White House. Still, the moment was a time of personal affirmation. After a long career in public service, he had reached the pinnacle of his ambitions.

Born in Franklin County, Pennsylvania, in 1791, Buchanan had begun his career in the Pennsylvania state legislature. He had served five terms in the U.S. Congress from 1821 to 1831. In 1834 he had been elected to the U.S. Senate, where he served two terms. In addition, he had foreign policy experience, having served as U.S. minister to Russia and, more recently, to the Court of St. James in Great Britain. And he had served in James Polk's cabinet as secretary of state. There was no one in the United States who could boast of such a distinguished public career.

A loyal Democrat, Buchanan was popular in the South for his positions against the Republicans, members of the newly formed party whom he considered agitators. He had often taken the side of the South on issues relating to slavery. In historical terms he represented a "doughface," that is, a Northern man who supported Southern interests, especially as they related to slavery. Some Americans called him "Old Public Functionary," but his service gave him confidence that he could solve the existential threat to the United States of what to do about slavery in the territories.

Buchanan began his address with what became staples for American inaugural addresses. He repeated the presidential oath of office; he invoked God's help and, a fervent exponent of American exceptionalism, he proclaimed the United States as the nation with the greatest "capacity of man for self-government." In an unusual aside, he promised he would not run again, though no one expected him to.

After these platitudes, Buchanan addressed the issue of slavery in the territories west of Missouri and Iowa, an area known as Kansas and Nebraska, that awaited organization. In 1854 new legislation supported by Illinois Senator Stephen Douglas upended the previous arrangement in the Missouri Compromise that banned slavery in the region. Instead the Kansas Nebraska Act introduced the concept of popular sovereignty; the people, not Congress, should decide about slavery through their representatives in the territorial legislature.

Buchanan had been in London when the controversial Kansas Nebraska Act accelerated the process of party decay and led to the formation of the Republican party. Despite Northern opposition, Buchanan now saluted the arrangement as "a happy conception," an acknowledgment of the self-government and the will of the majority that he saw as essential aspects of American greatness. In his address he took the Southern position that Congress could not prohibit slavery during the territorial phase of preparation for statehood. Only when citizens were drafting a constitution could slavery be prohibited by their votes. In any case, Buchanan insisted that the Supreme Court would settle this issue: "to their decision ... I shall cheerfully submit."

Buchanan referred here to the Dred Scott case, which after years had reached the Supreme Court. What he did not say is that he already knew its outcome. In fact, he had helped frame the decision. In an act of extraordinary impropriety as president-elect, Buchanan had put pressure on his friend, Justice Robert Grier of Pennsylvania, to join with the Southern judges to embrace a broad-ranging judicial decision that would end controversies over the extension of slavery into the western territories.

Two days after Buchanan's inauguration the U.S. Supreme Court in *Dred Scott v. Sanford* ruled that Blacks had no rights of federal citizenship and that the Missouri Compromise, by prohibiting slavery in a part of national territory, was unconstitutional. Slavery was nationalized; the newly emerging Republican party's most important platform was overturned. Buchanan's intervention had played a significant role in this accommodation to Southern interests.

From Buchanan's point of view, the decision emboldened him to believe that he would be the chief executive who put to rest "this agitation": "May we not, then, hope that the long agitation on this subject is approaching its end, and that the geographical parties [by which he meant the Republicans] to which it has given birth... will speedily become extinct?" Having dealt with the most divisive issue of his time in four paragraphs, Buchanan moved on to other matters in the rest of his speech. But as president he soon learned that the Dred Scott decision, rather than creating the sectional harmony he anticipated, had only deepened the sectional divide in the nation. Kansas became a flash point, and with little sensitivity to Northern positions, Buchanan's pro-Southern handling of its governance doomed his presidency.

Having dispensed with the issue of slavery in the territories, Buchanan next celebrated the familiar principles of mid-century rhetoric—the Constitution and Union. The nation's economic success came from its large free-trading area "conducted on railroads and canals, on noble rivers and arms of the sea, which bind together the North and the South, the East and West." So successful was this financial union that there was a surplus in the U.S. Treasury that the president-elect proposed could be used to pay down the public debt and shore up the U.S. Navy as well as the nation's seacoast defenses. Among the blessings of America, he asserted, was its vast inheritance of public lands. In an obvious slap at the rival nativist political party, the Know Nothings or American party, Buchanan saluted the contributions of "those exiles from foreign shores... who have done so much to promote the growth and prosperity of the nation" by settling on western lands.

As a self-avowed strict constitutionalist, Buchanan nevertheless promoted the importance of a military road across the territories to the Pacific. And he spent as much of his speech on justifying such an extension of constitutional authority as he had on the issue of slavery in the territories. In fact, during his presidency he would have little time or energy to promote such a road.

Finally, drawing on his experience as a minister abroad, Buchanan offered his thoughts on diplomacy. It should be "direct and frank" and conducted in a spirit of "Christian benevolence," avoiding the entangling alliances that President Jefferson had warned about. In the final paragraph of his Inaugural Address, Buchanan offered an astounding review of previous American foreign policy. Americans, he said, had never extended their control over the continent by force. Rather, their territorial expansion had come through "fair purchase." He did not consider any dispossession of the Native Americans, and as for the recent acquisitions in Mexico, they had come through purchase in a peace treaty.

After this, James Buchanan took the oath of office. His Inaugural Address had included some boilerplate concerns of the Democratic party, such as strict construction of the Constitution and support of immigration and territorial expansion. But his address also previewed a split in the party as Buchanan embraced Southern interests in the matter of slavery in the territories. Expecting that the courts had solved the issue, he expected his presidency to deal with other matters. But his inaugural forecast proved incorrect as the United States drifted toward civil war, in part because as president, James Buchanan failed to consider the legitimate interests of the North.

Abraham Lincoln's First Inaugural Address

MONDAY, MARCH 4, 1861

FELLOW-CITIZENS OF the United States:

In compliance with a custom as old as the Government itself, I appear before you to address you briefly and to take in your presence the oath prescribed by the Constitution of the United States to be taken by the President "before he enters on the execution of this office."

I do not consider it necessary at present for me to discuss those matters of administration about which there is no special anxiety or excitement.

Apprehension seems to exist among the people of the Southern States that by the accession of a Republican Administration their property and their peace and personal security are to be endangered. There has never been any reasonable cause for such apprehension. Indeed, the most ample evidence to the contrary has all the while existed and been open to their inspection. It is found in nearly all the published speeches of him who now addresses you. I do but quote from one of those speeches when I declare that—

> I have no purpose, directly or indirectly, to interfere with the institution of slavery in the States where it exists. I believe I have no lawful right to do so, and I have no inclination to do so.

Those who nominated and elected me did so with full knowledge that I had made this and many similar declarations and had never recanted them; and more than this, they placed in the platform for my acceptance, and as a law to themselves and to me, the clear and emphatic resolution which I now read:

Resolved, That the maintenance inviolate of the rights of the States, and especially the right of each State to order and control its own domestic institutions according to its own judgment exclusively, is essential to that balance of power on which the perfection and endurance of our political fabric depend; and we denounce the lawless invasion by armed force of the soil of any State or Territory, no matter what pretext, as among the gravest of crimes.

I now reiterate these sentiments, and in doing so I only press upon the public attention the most conclusive evidence of which the case is susceptible that the property, peace, and security of no section are to be in any wise endangered by the now incoming Administration. I add, too, that all the protection which, consistently with the Constitution and the laws, can be given will be cheerfully given to all the States when lawfully demanded, for whatever cause—as cheerfully to one section as to another.

There is much controversy about the delivering up of fugitives from service or labor. The clause I now read is as plainly written in the Constitution as any other of its provisions:

No person held to service or labor in one State, under the laws thereof, escaping into another, shall in consequence of any law or regulation therein be discharged from such service or labor, but shall be delivered up on claim of the party to whom such service or labor may be due.

It is scarcely questioned that this provision was intended by those who made it for the reclaiming of what we call fugitive slaves; and the intention of the lawgiver is the law. All members of Congress swear their support to the whole Constitution—to this provision as much as to any other. To the proposition, then, that slaves whose cases come within the terms of this clause "shall be delivered up" their oaths are unanimous. Now, if they would make the effort in good temper, could they not with nearly equal unanimity frame and pass a law by means of which to keep good that unanimous oath?

There is some difference of opinion whether this clause should be enforced by national or by State authority, but surely that difference is not a very material one. If the slave is to be surrendered, it can be of but little consequence to him or to others by which authority it is done. And should anyone in any case be content that his oath shall go unkept on a merely unsubstantial controversy as to *how* it shall be kept?

Again: In any law upon this subject ought not all the safeguards of liberty known in civilized and humane jurisprudence to be introduced, so that a free man be not in any case surrendered as a slave? And might it not be well at the same time to provide by law for the enforcement of that clause in the Constitution which guarantees that "the citizens of each State shall be entitled to all privileges and immunities of citizens in the several States"?

I take the official oath to-day with no mental reservations and with no purpose to construe the Constitution or laws by any hypercritical rules; and while I do not choose now to specify particular acts of Congress as proper to be enforced, I do suggest that it will be much safer for all, both in official and private stations, to conform to and abide by all those acts which stand unrepealed than to violate any of them trusting to find impunity in having them held to be unconstitutional.

It is seventy-two years since the first inauguration of a President under our National Constitution. During that period fifteen different and greatly distinguished citizens have in succession administered the executive branch of the Government. They have conducted it through many perils, and generally with great success. Yet, with all this scope of precedent, I now enter upon the same task for the brief constitutional term of four years under great and peculiar difficulty. A disruption of the Federal Union, heretofore only menaced, is now formidably attempted.

I hold that in contemplation of universal law and of the Constitution the Union of these States is perpetual. Perpetuity is implied, if not expressed, in the fundamental law of all national governments. It is safe to assert that no government proper ever had a provision in its organic law for its own termination. Continue to execute all the express provisions of our National Constitution, and the Union will endure forever, it being impossible to destroy it except by some action not provided for in the instrument itself.

Again: If the United States be not a government proper, but an association of States in the nature of contract merely, can it, as a contract, be peaceably unmade by less than all the parties who made it? One party to a contract may violate it—break it, so to speak—but does it not require all to lawfully rescind it?

Descending from these general principles, we find the proposition that in legal contemplation the Union is perpetual confirmed by the history of the Union itself. The Union is much older than the Constitution. It was formed, in fact, by the Articles of Association in 1774. It was matured and continued by the Declaration of Independence in 1776. It was further matured, and the faith of all the then thirteen States expressly plighted and engaged that it should be perpetual, by the Articles of Confederation in 1778. And finally, in 1787, one of the declared objects for ordaining and establishing the Constitution was "*to form a more perfect Union.*"

But if destruction of the Union by one or by a part only of the States be lawfully possible, the Union is *less* perfect than before the Constitution, having lost the vital element of perpetuity.

It follows from these views that no State upon its own mere motion can lawfully get out of the Union; that *resolves* and *ordinances* to that effect are legally void, and that acts of violence within any State or States against the authority of the United States are insurrectionary or revolutionary, according to circumstances.

I therefore consider that in view of the Constitution and the laws the Union is unbroken, and to the extent of my ability I shall take care, as the Constitution itself expressly enjoins upon me, that the laws of the Union be faithfully executed in all the States. Doing this I deem to be only a simple duty on my part, and I shall perform it so far as practicable unless my rightful masters, the American people, shall withhold the requisite means or in some authoritative manner direct the contrary. I trust this will not be regarded as a menace, but only as the declared purpose of the Union that it *will* constitutionally defend and maintain itself.

In doing this there needs to be no bloodshed or violence, and there shall be none unless it be forced upon the national authority. The power confided to me will be used to hold, occupy, and possess the property and places belonging to the Government and to collect the duties and imposts; but beyond what may be necessary for these objects, there will be no invasion, no using of force against or among the people anywhere. Where hostility to the United States in any interior locality shall be so great and universal as to prevent competent resident citizens from holding the Federal offices, there will be no attempt to force obnoxious strangers among the people for that object. While the strict legal right may exist in the Government to enforce the exercise of these offices, the attempt to do so would be so irritating and so nearly impracticable withal that I deem it better to forego for the time the uses of such offices.

The mails, unless repelled, will continue to be furnished in all parts of the Union. So far as possible the people everywhere shall have that sense of perfect security which is most favorable to calm thought and reflection. The course here indicated will be followed unless current events and experience shall show a modification or change to be proper, and in every case and exigency my best discretion will be exercised, according to circumstances actually existing and with a view and a hope of a peaceful solution of the national troubles and the restoration of fraternal sympathies and affections.

That there are persons in one section or another who seek to destroy the Union at all events and are glad of any pretext to do it I will neither affirm nor deny; but if there be such, I need address no word to them. To those, however, who really love the Union may I not speak?

Before entering upon so grave a matter as the destruction of our national fabric, with all its benefits, its memories, and its hopes, would it not be wise to ascertain precisely why we do it? Will you hazard so desperate a step while there is any possibility that any portion of the ills you fly from have no real existence? Will you, while the certain ills you fly to are greater than all the real ones you fly from, will you risk the commission of so fearful a mistake?

All profess to be content in the Union if all constitutional rights can be maintained. Is it true, then, that any right plainly written in the Constitution has been denied? I think not. Happily, the human mind is so constituted that no party can reach to the audacity of doing this. Think, if you can, of a single instance in which a plainly written provision of the Constitution has ever been denied. If by the mere force of numbers a majority should deprive a minority of any clearly written constitutional right, it might in a moral point of view justify revolution; certainly would if such right were a vital one. But such is not our case. All the vital rights of minorities and of individuals are so plainly assured to them by affirmations and negations, guarantees and prohibitions, in the Constitution that controversies never arise concerning them. But no organic law can ever be framed with a provision specifically applicable to every question which may occur in practical administration. No foresight can anticipate nor any document of reasonable length contain express provisions for all possible questions. Shall fugitives from labor be surrendered by national or by State authority? The Constitution does not expressly say. *May* Congress prohibit slavery in the Territories? The Constitution does not expressly say. *Must* Congress protect slavery in the Territories? The Constitution does not expressly say.

From questions of this class spring all our constitutional controversies, and we divide upon them into majorities and minorities. If the minority will not acquiesce, the majority must, or the Government must cease. There is no other alternative, for continuing the Government is acquiescence on one side or the other. If a minority in such case will secede rather than acquiesce, they make a precedent which in turn will divide and ruin them, for a minority of their own will secede from them whenever a majority refuses to be controlled by such minority. For instance, why may not any portion of a new confederacy a year or two hence arbitrarily secede again, precisely as portions of the present Union now claim to secede from it? All who cherish disunion sentiments are now being educated to the exact temper of doing this.

Is there such perfect identity of interests among the States to compose a new union as to produce harmony only and prevent renewed secession?

Plainly the central idea of secession is the essence of anarchy. A majority held in restraint by constitutional checks and limitations, and always changing easily with deliberate changes of popular opinions and sentiments, is the only true sovereign of a free people. Whoever rejects it does of necessity fly to anarchy or to despotism. Unanimity is impossible. The rule of a minority, as a permanent arrangement, is wholly inadmissible; so that, rejecting the majority principle, anarchy or despotism in some form is all that is left.

I do not forget the position assumed by some that constitutional questions are to be decided by the Supreme Court, nor do I deny that such decisions must be binding in any case upon the parties to a suit as to the object of that suit, while they are also entitled to very high respect and consideration in all parallel cases by all other departments of the Government. And while it is obviously possible that such decision may be erroneous in any given case, still the evil effect following it, being limited to that particular case, with the chance that it may be overruled and never become a precedent for other cases, can better be borne than could the evils of a different practice. At the same time, the candid citizen must confess that if the policy of the Government upon vital questions affecting the whole people is to be irrevocably fixed by decisions of the Supreme Court, the instant they are made in ordinary litigation between parties in personal actions the people will have ceased to be their own rulers, having to that extent practically resigned their Government into the hands of that eminent tribunal. Nor is there in this view any assault upon the court or the judges. It is a duty from which they may not shrink to decide cases properly brought before them, and it is no fault of theirs if others seek to turn their decisions to political purposes.

One section of our country believes slavery is *right* and ought to be extended, while the other believes it is *wrong* and ought not to be extended. This is the only substantial dispute. The fugitive-slave clause of the Constitution and the law for the suppression of the foreign slave trade are each as well enforced, perhaps, as any law can ever be in a community where the moral sense of the people imperfectly supports the law itself. The great body of the people abide by the dry legal obligation in both cases, and a few break over in each. This, I think, can not be perfectly cured, and it would be worse in both cases *after* the separation of the sections than before. The foreign slave trade, now imperfectly suppressed, would be ultimately revived without restriction in one section, while fugitive slaves, now only partially surrendered, would not be surrendered at all by the other.

Physically speaking, we can not separate. We can not remove our respective sections from each other nor build an impassable wall between them. A husband and wife may be divorced and go out of the presence and beyond the reach of each other, but the different parts of our country can not do this. They can not but remain face to face, and intercourse, either amicable or hostile, must continue between them. Is it possible, then, to make that intercourse more advantageous or more satisfactory *after* separation than *before*? Can aliens make treaties easier than friends can make laws? Can treaties be more faithfully enforced between aliens than laws can among friends? Suppose you go to war, you can not fight always; and when, after much loss on both sides and no gain on either, you cease fighting, the identical old questions, as to terms of intercourse, are again upon you.

This country, with its institutions, belongs to the people who inhabit it. Whenever they shall grow weary of the existing Government, they can exercise their *constitutional* right of amending it or their *revolutionary* right to dismember or overthrow it. I can not be ignorant of the fact that many worthy and patriotic citizens are desirous of having the National Constitution amended. While I make no recommendation of amendments, I fully recognize the rightful authority of the people over the whole subject, to be exercised in either of the modes prescribed in the instrument itself; and I should, under existing circumstances, favor rather than oppose a fair opportunity being afforded the people to act upon it. I will venture to add that to me the convention mode seems preferable, in that it allows amendments to originate with the people themselves, instead of only permitting them to take or reject propositions originated by others, not especially chosen for the purpose, and which might not be precisely such as they would wish to either accept or refuse. I understand a proposed amendment to the Constitution—which amendment, however, I have not seen—has passed Congress, to the effect that the Federal Government shall never interfere with the domestic institutions of the States, including that of persons held to service. To avoid misconstruction of what I have said, I depart from my purpose not to speak of particular amendments so far as to say that, holding such a provision to now be implied constitutional law, I have no objection to its being made express and irrevocable.

The Chief Magistrate derives all his authority from the people, and they have conferred none upon him to fix terms for the separation of the States. The people themselves can do this also if they choose, but the Executive as such has nothing to do with it. His duty is to administer the present Government as it came to his hands and to transmit it unimpaired by him to his successor.

Why should there not be a patient confidence in the ultimate justice of the people? Is there any better or equal hope in the world? In our present differences, is either party without faith of being in the right? If the Almighty Ruler of Nations, with His eternal truth and justice, be on your side of the North, or on yours of the South, that truth and that justice will surely prevail by the judgment of this great tribunal of the American people.

By the frame of the Government under which we live this same people have wisely given their public servants but little power for mischief, and have with equal wisdom provided for the return of that little to their own hands at very short intervals. While the people retain their virtue and vigilance no Administration by any extreme of wickedness or folly can very seriously injure the Government in the short space of four years.

My countrymen, one and all, think calmly and *well* upon this whole subject. Nothing valuable can be lost by taking time. If there be an object to *hurry* any of you in hot haste to a step which you would never take *deliberately*, that object will be frustrated by taking time; but no good object can be frustrated by it. Such of you as are now dissatisfied still have the old Constitution unimpaired, and, on the sensitive point, the laws of your own framing under it; while the new Administration will have no immediate power, if it would, to change either. If it were admitted that you who are dissatisfied hold the right side in the dispute, there still is no single good reason for precipitate action. Intelligence, patriotism, Christianity, and a firm reliance on Him who has never yet forsaken this favored land are still competent to adjust in the best way all our present difficulty.

In *your* hands, my dissatisfied fellow-countrymen, and not in *mine*, is the momentous issue of civil war. The Government will not assail *you*. You can have no conflict without being yourselves the aggressors. *You* have no oath registered in heaven to destroy the Government, while *I* shall have the most solemn one to "preserve, protect, and defend it."

I am loath to close. We are not enemies, but friends. We must not be enemies. Though passion may have strained it must not break our bonds of affection. The mystic chords of memory, stretching from every battlefield and patriot grave to every living heart and hearthstone all over this broad land, will yet swell the chorus of the Union, when again touched, as surely they will be, by the better angels of our nature.

Trying to Stave off War

THE FIRST INAUGURAL ADDRESS OF ABRAHAM LINCOLN

David S. Reynolds

ABRAHAM LINCOLN DELIVERED his First Inaugural Address during the worst crisis in American history. Between November 6, 1860, when Lincoln won the presidency in a four-man race, and March 4, 1861, when he gave the Inaugural Address, seven Southern states seceded from the Union and formed what they called a separate nation, the Confederate States of America, with its own constitution, president, and legislature. The Inaugural Address, Lincoln knew, must be very cautiously worded. It must affirm the federal government's resolve to save the Union without pushing the South so hard that reunion became impossible.

In the Inaugural Address, Lincoln repeated several points he had made in previous speeches: secession was impossible, because a minority cannot overrule the majority; the North would not invade the South without provocation; his administration would leave slavery alone where it existed and would enforce the Fugitive Slave Act as long as the suspected runaways received due process.

Lincoln's answer to Southerners who used states' rights to defend secession was that there is a "universal law," or "organic law," that is "the fundamental law of all national governments."[1]

No nation, he pointed out, was formed with its own destruction in mind. Perpetuity was the goal of any nation. "It is safe to assert," he said, "that no government proper, ever had a provision in its organic law for its own termination."[2] In America, Lincoln said, national consolidation originated with the Articles of Association (1774), was made perpetual by the Declaration of Independence (1776) and the Articles of Confederation (1781), and then was codified by the

Constitution (1787). The Constitution proclaimed that the aim of the people of the United States was "to form a more perfect union." Secession, which creates a Union that is "less perfect than before," was thus "absurd."

While emphasizing the broader law of nations, Lincoln in the inaugural did not lose sight of the moral law that motivated him and other anti-slavery reformers. He said, "One section [of the nation] believes slavery is right, and ought to be extended, while the other believes it is wrong, and ought not to be extended."[3]

To subvert the South's position, he deployed clever rhetorical weapons. "Physically speaking," he said, "we cannot separate. We cannot remove our respective sections from each other, nor build an impassable wall between them." The continent—the very earth itself—bound the parts of the nation together. Separation violated the law of nature.

He fused religion with democracy: "If the Almighty Ruler of nations, with his eternal truth and justice, be on our side, or on yours, that truth and that justice will surely prevail, by the judgment of this great tribunal, the American people." The North and the South, he was saying, each believed that its view was supported by God. Which side was correct must be finally decided by the "great tribunal": the people. In the 1860 election, the people had decided against slavery. In democratic America, the people's judgment was equivalent to God's judgment.

Lincoln named two great dangers to the nation: despotism and anarchy. Despotism would result from an overbearing federal government that ignored the constitutional rights of states or individuals. Anarchy, on the other hand, resulted from secession, or an overemphasis of states' rights. "Plainly," Lincoln declared, "the central idea of secession, is the essence of anarchy."[4] If a group of states separates from the Union, why cannot one or two states, by the same principle, separate from the newly formed confederacy? Other divisions would follow. Centrifugalism would reign.

A respect for majority rule, Lincoln argued, can hold the sections of the nation together. "Whoever rejects it," he declared, "does, of necessity, fly to anarchy or despotism."[4]

Lincoln had worked on the address for several weeks prior to March 4 and had distributed it among friends for their comments. Two, Orville Browning and William Seward, softened his tone. Browning thought Lincoln's declared intention to "reclaim" U.S. forts taken over by the rebels made the federal government sound too aggressive. Lincoln removed the word, saying, more mildly, that the federal power would be used "to hold, occupy, and possess the property, and places belonging to the government, and to collect the duties and imposts."[5] Seward suggested thirty-three changes, twenty-seven of which Lincoln accepted, some in modified form. By far the most important was Seward's suggestion to replace the militant closing line of the original, in which Lincoln left the question of "peace, or a sword" up to the South, with a charitable final paragraph that, in Lincoln's reworking, became one of the most memorable passages in American oratory.

Here is Seward's version of the paragraph:

> I close. We are not we must not be aliens or enemies but ["countrym" deleted] fellow countrymen and brethren. Although passion has strained our bonds of affection too hardly they must not ["be broken they will not" deleted], I am sure they will not be broken. The mystic chords which proceeding from ["every ba" deleted] so many battle fields and ["patriot" deleted] so many patriot graves ["bind" deleted] pass through all the hearts and ["hearths" deleted] all the hearths in this broad continent of ours will yet ["harmon" deleted] again harmonize in their ancient music when ["touched as they surely" deleted] breathed upon ["again" deleted] by the ["better angel" deleted] guardian angel of the nation.[6]

Here is Lincoln:

> I am loath to close. We are not enemies, but friends. We must not be enemies. Though passion may have strained, it must not break our bonds of affection. The mystic chords of memory, stre[t]ching from every battlefield, and patriot grave, to every living heart and hearthstone, all over this broad land, will yet swell the chorus of the Union, when again touched, as surely they will be, by the better angels of our nature.[7]

Besides streamlining Seward's bumpy language, Lincoln emphatically called for national unity on the basis of common culture. The "mystic chords" connecting the dead with the living evoked spiritualism, the influential movement that deeply affected Mary Todd Lincoln and millions of other Americans. The connecting "chords" would remind many of Lincoln's hearers of the electromagnetic forces that were then thought to form a "spiritual telegraph" between the living and the dead. The joining of every "patriot grave" to "every living heart and hearthstone" drew from other sources of cultural unity: the shared worship of the founding generation, which negated sectional categories, and the imagery found in popular domestic literature. "This broad land" utilized political ecology in its suggestion of the American continent. "The chorus of union" referenced music, which Lincoln considered a key unifying cultural force. "The better angels of our nature" not only humanized Seward's rather distant "guardian angel of the nation," but also drew from what was a common trope in sentimental literature of that era: the angelic nature of good people.

Lincoln's revised version of Seward's paragraph was a culturally representative passage, offered to a divided nation in what was a massive rhetorical effort to repair the Union. The effort failed. Although Northern journalists generally saw the inaugural as a sensible, compassionate peace offering, Southerners took it as coercive declaration by a Black Republican president. Within eight weeks of giving the speech, Lincoln was presiding over a war that would last for four years and would cost some 750,000 American lives. His masterly language could not stave off bloody civil war.

Notes

1. *The Collected Works of Abraham Lincoln*. Edited by Roy P. Basler, Lloyd A. Dunlap, and Marion Dolores Pratt. 8 vols. (New Brunswick, NJ: Rutgers University Press, 1953–1955), 4: 264. Hereafter cited as CW.
2. CW 4: 264. The remaining quotations in this paragraph are from CW 4: 253.
3. CW 4: 268–269.
4. CW 4: 268.
5. CW 4: 268.
6. CW 4: 268.
7. CW 4: 262–63. The next block quotation is from CW 4: 271.

Abraham Lincoln's Second Inaugural Address

SATURDAY, MARCH 4, 1865

FELLOW-COUNTRYMEN:

At this second appearing to take the oath of the Presidential office there is less occasion for an extended address than there was at the first. Then a statement somewhat in detail of a course to be pursued seemed fitting and proper. Now, at the expiration of four years, during which public declarations have been constantly called forth on every point and phase of the great contest which still absorbs the attention and engrosses the energies of the nation, little that is new could be presented. The progress of our arms, upon which all else chiefly depends, is as well known to the public as to myself, and it is, I trust, reasonably satisfactory and encouraging to all. With high hope for the future, no prediction in regard to it is ventured.

On the occasion corresponding to this four years ago all thoughts were anxiously directed to an impending civil war. All dreaded it, all sought to avert it. While the inaugural address was being delivered from this place, devoted altogether to *saving* the Union without war, urgent agents were in the city seeking to *destroy* it without war—seeking to dissolve the Union and divide effects by negotiation. Both parties deprecated war, but one of them would *make* war rather than let the nation survive, and the other would *accept* war rather than let it perish, and the war came.

One-eighth of the whole population were colored slaves, not distributed generally over the Union, but localized in the southern part of it. These slaves constituted a peculiar and powerful interest. All knew that this interest was somehow the cause of the war. To strengthen, perpetuate, and extend this interest was the object for which the insurgents would rend the Union even by war, while the

Government claimed no right to do more than to restrict the territorial enlargement of it. Neither party expected for the war the magnitude or the duration which it has already attained. Neither anticipated that the *cause* of the conflict might cease with or even before the conflict itself should cease. Each looked for an easier triumph, and a result less fundamental and astounding. Both read the same Bible and pray to the same God, and each invokes His aid against the other. It may seem strange that any men should dare to ask a just God's assistance in wringing their bread from the sweat of other men's faces, but let us judge not, that we be not judged. The prayers of both could not be answered. That of neither has been answered fully. The Almighty has His own purposes. "Woe unto the world because of offenses; for it must needs be that offenses come, but woe to that man by whom the offense cometh." If we shall suppose that American slavery is one of those offenses which, in the providence of God, must needs come, but which, having continued through His appointed time, He now wills to remove, and that He gives to both North and South this terrible war as the woe due to those by whom the offense came, shall we discern therein any departure from those divine attributes which the believers in a living God always ascribe to Him? Fondly do we hope, fervently do we pray, that this mighty scourge of war may speedily pass away. Yet, if God wills that it continue until all the wealth piled by the bondsman's two hundred and fifty years of unrequited toil shall be sunk, and until every drop of blood drawn with the lash shall be paid by another drawn with the sword, as was said three thousand years ago, so still it must be said "the judgments of the Lord are true and righteous altogether."

With malice toward none, with charity for all, with firmness in the right as God gives us to see the right, let us strive on to finish the work we are in, to bind up the nation's wounds, to care for him who shall have borne the battle and for his widow and his orphan, to do all which may achieve and cherish a just and lasting peace among ourselves and with all nations.

The Great Uniter

THE SECOND INAUGURAL ADDRESS OF ABRAHAM LINCOLN

Richard John Carwardine

ON THE MORNING of Saturday, March 4, 1865, Abraham Lincoln emerged from the Capitol building to address some 30,000 people gathered for the inauguration of his second term. For the first time on such an occasion, his audience included thousands of African Americans. To music and cheers, he took his place on the platform. As he took the oath of office, the sun burst through the clouds: a symbol, it seemed to many, of divine approval and the recent turn in the nation's fortunes.

Four years earlier, at his first inauguration, Lincoln had appeared vigorous; now he had, as one reporter put it, the look of a man "on whom sorrow and care have done their worst." Yet he had reason to be buoyant. The war had entered its final phase. The political outlook, too, was encouraging. Vindicated by his re-election, Lincoln had successfully set about driving an emancipation amendment through Congress. Electoral triumph, military progress, and the death spasms of slavery gave Lincoln a greater sense of presidential authority than he had previously enjoyed.

Delivered in a strong, clear voice, Lincoln's speech bespoke a powerful self-confidence. A fraction over 700 words, it was the shortest Inaugural Address in the history of the Republic. It began with a flat, matter-of-fact introduction: an extended review of political and military progress was unnecessary, he said, since the events were well-known to all. By contrast, each of the three succeeding paragraphs was rich in concentrated meaning and striking rhetoric.

The first summarized the process by which the nation had fallen into war. It is notable for Lincoln's broad even-handedness. He located the war's origins in a dispute over the Union. One side wanted to save it, the other to destroy it. Although "destroy" is a not a neutral term, Lincoln does not assign blame for the armed conflict: "all sought to avert it.... Both parties deprecated war."

The next paragraph—the longest—moved on from a summary narrative of the coming of war to a causal explanation of the conflict. Southern slavery "constituted a peculiar and powerful interest. All knew that this interest was somehow the cause of the war. To strengthen, perpetuate, and extend this interest was the object for which the insurgents would rend the Union even by war, while the Government claimed no right to do more than to restrict the territorial enlargement of it." The war, Lincoln reflected, had developed into a struggle whose dimensions and duration "neither party expected.... Each looked for an easier triumph, and a result less fundamental and astounding."

Then followed a sentence that launched the speech in a direction that few expected: "Both [parties] read the same Bible and pray to the same God, and each invokes His aid against the other." The religious turn makes the speech unique among presidential inaugural addresses. Successive generations have marveled at the depth of Lincoln's theology, especially about God's will and His divine judgment on the American nation. In this address he mentions God fourteen times, quotes four times from Scripture, and talks about prayer on three occasions.

As historian Douglas Wilson has shown, the president grew increasingly ambitious in the themes he sought to convey in his wartime public utterances. With a Union victory now likely, he sought a way of conveying that the war had been about the violation of the inalienable rights set out in the Declaration of Independence, and that complicity in the offense of slaveholding was not confined to the Confederacy.

Delivering this hard message, Lincoln judged, could be best achieved through religious language and ideas familiar to an audience that comprised mostly Protestant Christians and among whom he was viewed as a man of faith—as "a sort of half way clergyman," as one admirer put it. They would not have been surprised by the tenor of the speech, nor Lincoln's appeal to the book of Genesis and Jesus's sermon on the Mount: "It may seem strange that any men should dare to ask a just God's assistance in wringing their bread from the sweat of other men's faces, but let us judge not, that we be not judged."

Lincoln here used a well-known oratorical technique: emphasizing something by purporting not to intend it. Although he implies that the "strange" stance of slaveholders was a form of hypocrisy, this was less a sly dig at the South than a prelude to a statement that formed the theological center of the speech: "The prayers of both [contending sides] could not be answered. That of neither has been answered fully. The Almighty has His own purposes."

By these means Lincoln prepared his audience for a wrenching passage that implicated both North and South in the sin of slavery. "The bondsman's two hundred and fifty years of unrequited toil" was an offense against "a living God" who had to be recognized as a force in human affairs. If it were God's will that "the scourge of war" should continue, "until all the wealth piled by the bondsman's two hundred and fifty years of unrequited toil shall be sunk, and until every drop of blood drawn with the lash shall be paid by another drawn with the sword, as was said three thousand years ago, so still it must be said 'the judgments of the Lord are true and righteous altogether'" (Psalm 19).

This national complicity in the sin of slavery opened the way for Lincoln's memorable concluding paragraph, the core political purpose of his speech. Here he echoed the words of Malachi, invoking God's judgment against the oppressors of the widow and the fatherless:

> With malice toward none, with charity for all, with firmness in the right as God gives us to see the right, let us strive on to finish the work we are in, to bind up the nation's wounds, to care for him who shall have borne the battle and for his widow and his orphan, to do all which may achieve and cherish a just and lasting peace among ourselves and with all nations.

Lincoln was a kindly man, who by his own estimate probably had "too little" of the feeling of personal resentment. He saw the irony that, as someone who did not bear a grudge, he had found himself at the center of so profound a conflict.

The address was designed to prepare the way for a postwar reconciliatory reconstruction incumbent on the whole nation. The institution described as "peculiar" to the South owed its introduction and continued existence to the whole nation's moral deficiencies. At no point does Lincoln call the South "the enemy," "rebels," or even "Confederates"; his language is inclusive. He understood that the self-righteousness that had inflected wartime Unionism would not serve the nation well in peacetime.

The president's shocking assassination deprived the nation of a Lincolnian scheme of reconstruction, so we can only speculate on what would have constituted a course that he wanted to see shaped by "firmness in the right as God gives us to see the right." On April 11, four days before his death, he addressed a crowd that had gathered outside the White House to celebrate the Confederate surrender at Appomattox. We may see this speech as Lincoln's opening position in a debate with Congress. He declared his preference that the vote be conferred on two categories of African Americans: "the very intelligent, and ... those who serve our cause as soldiers." Was this a step toward the radical minority who wanted full suffrage for freedmen and the confiscation of rebels' land? We cannot know for certain, since in the crowd there was one who was determined the president should not have the opportunity to act. John Wilkes Booth took Lincoln's words to be heralds of a world turned upside down.

Frederick Douglass, invited by Lincoln to the White House reception after the ceremony, told the president that the address was "a sacred effort." Lincoln was undoubtedly pleased. But he was aware, too, of the risk he had run in delivering a speech that broke so completely with public expectations. It was in both its religion and its politics a startling, challenging, and potentially transformative document. Lincoln fully understood this. He wrote to a fellow Republican:

> I expect the [inaugural address] to wear as well as—perhaps better than—any thing I have produced; but I believe it is not immediately popular. Men are not flattered by being shown that there has been a difference of purpose between the Almighty and them. To deny it, however, in this case, is to deny that there is a God governing the world. It is a truth which I thought needed to be told; and as whatever of humiliation there is in it, falls most directly on myself, I thought others might afford for me to tell it.[1]

Note

1. "Collected Works of Abraham Lincoln. Volume 8 [Sept. 12, 1864–Apr. 14, 1865, undated, appendices]" in the digital collection *Collected Works of Abraham Lincoln*, University of Michigan Library Digital Collections, accessed June 19, 2024, https://name.umdl.umich.edu/lincoln8.

Andrew Johnson's Address upon Assuming the Office of President of the United States

MONDAY, APRIL 15, 1865

GENTLEMEN: I MUST be permitted to say that I have been almost overwhelmed by the announcement of the sad event which has so recently occurred. I feel incompetent to perform duties so important and responsible as those which have been so unexpectedly thrown upon me. As to an indication of any policy which may be pursued by me in the administration of the Government, I have to say that that must be left for development as the Administration progresses. The message or declaration must be made by the acts as they transpire. The only assurance that I can now give of the future is reference to the past. The course which I have taken in the past in connection with this rebellion must be regarded as a guaranty of the future. My past public life, which has been long and laborious, has been founded, as I in good conscience believe, upon a great principle of right, which lies at the basis of all things. The best energies of my life have been spent in endeavoring to establish and perpetuate the principles of free government, and I believe that the Government in passing through its present perils will settle down upon principles consonant with popular rights more permanent and enduring than heretofore. I must be permitted to say, if I understand the feelings of my own heart, that I have long labored to ameliorate and elevate the condition of the great mass of the American people. Toil and an honest advocacy of the great principles of free government have been my lot. Duties have been mine; consequences are God's. This has been the foundation of my political creed, and I feel that in the end the Government will triumph and that these great principles will be permanently established.

In conclusion, gentlemen, let me say that I want your encouragement and countenance. I shall ask and rely upon you and others in carrying the Government through its present perils. I feel in making this request that it will be heartily responded to by you and all other patriots and lovers of the rights and interests of a free people.

On Opposite Ends

ANDREW JOHNSON'S ADDRESS UPON ASSUMING THE
OFFICE OF PRESIDENT OF THE UNITED STATES

Michael Les Benedict

IT WAS ONE of the worst days in American history. Abraham Lincoln had been shot the night before. Vice President Andrew Johnson had been targeted as well, but the assassin had lost his nerve. Johnson had rushed to Lincoln's side, but he soon left. He did not want to look like he was hovering in anticipation of the worst, which clearly was coming. He returned to the hotel room where he had been lodging since arriving in Washington for his inauguration, which had not gone well. Sick and feverish after his long trip to the capital, he had fortified himself with whiskey, no more than usually braced him, but too much for someone who was ill. He had been unsteady, disorganized. He had slurred his words. Lincoln took it calmly, but others had been shocked. Mortified, Johnson had retreated to the estate of his friend Frank Blair, Sr. He had only recently returned to the hotel. Now, he knew he would become president. He awaited the dreaded notification.

Members of Lincoln's cabinet, a few senators and representatives, Johnson's friend Frank Blair, and his son Montgomery silently filed into Johnson's room. Chief Justice Salmon P. Chase somberly administered the oath of office specified in the Constitution. Johnson repeated it gravely, "very distinctively and impressively," to the relief of any who worried he might repeat the earlier fiasco. "May God support, guide, and bless you," Chase said earnestly.[1]

Johnson had no time to prepare a speech. His response was only 360 words—a few more than Washington had said at his second inauguration and a bit longer than Millard Fillmore's statement following the death of President Zachary

Taylor. He was not prepared to say anything about the most pressing matter before him—the mode of restoring the Confederate states to the Union. That "must be left for development as the Administration progresses." He could only point to what he had done in the past as the best guarantee of the future. He had worked all his life to do what was right, "to establish and perpetuate the principles of free government." He had always worked to secure the "popular rights" of "the great mass of the American people." "This has been the foundation of my political creed," he said.

Johnson had harkened to the basic myths of American political identity—"free government" and "popular rights." But rarely has a statement of public principle been so vague. The only way to guess how Johnson would apply such general principles was to take his advice and look at what he had said and done.

Johnson had not said much in Congress. He had seemed a typical pro-slavery Southern senator, blasting abolitionists and warning Northerners to respect Southern rights. But he had never taken up reams of paper like other Southerners to define his notion of slaveholders' rights. He agreed that Congress could not exclude slavery from the territories, but he had not been outspoken against or in favor of Stephen A. Douglas's idea of leaving the matter to settlers in the territories. Nor had he endorsed Jefferson Davis's demand that Congress establish a slave code in the territories. He had spent most of his energy trying to pass a law giving homesteads to western settlers—a concrete manifestation of his concern for ordinary Americans.

He never questioned slavery before the war, but he had stood for the interests of yeoman farmers against those of large planters and cotton merchants. He reflected the views of his strongest constituency—the hill-country farmers of East Tennessee. Like them, he was inclined to fight for Southern rights within the Union. After Lincoln's election in November 1860, most Southern opponents of secession claimed to favor delay until all Southerners could cooperate to resist clearly intolerable Northern demands. Johnson scorned such equivocations. He would defend the Union until Northerners took concrete actions against slavery. He was sure his eastern Tennessee constituents felt the same. When other Southern senators resigned from the Senate as their states seceded, Johnson was the only one who remained, promising to hang the traitors if he got the chance. At the same time, he coauthored the congressional resolution declaring that the war was to preserve the Union and nothing more.

After federal troops occupied central and western Tennessee, President Lincoln appointed Johnson military governor, with the assignment of organizing loyal Tennesseans to establish a government that adhered to the Union. In that capacity, Johnson had exercised sweeping authority. From the beginning, he knew he had to break down the disloyalty that blocked the establishment of a loyal government. "Traitors should be punished and treason crushed," he declared when he arrived.[2] He repeated that mantra again and again. He vacated municipal offices and appointed loyal replacements, jailed and exiled those who refused to take loyalty oaths, and forced disloyal newspapers to close. He demanded a stricter loyalty oath than Lincoln required. Conservative unionists organized to oppose his draconian measures. Radical unionists organized to back him. When Lincoln finally made emancipation a war issue, Johnson and his radical unionists endorsed him. But he was not very sympathetic to the former slaves; abolition of slavery would free the white masses from the despotism of slaveholding aristocrats, he argued. He required that the courts treat former slaves as "free persons of color," not as citizens.[3]

Johnson had toured the North delivering fiery Union speeches and endorsing emancipation. Lincoln and the Republicans saw him as a symbol of the loyal South, and a Democrat as well. Desperate to create a cluster of Southern loyalists upon which to build loyal states, Lincoln and other party leaders seized on Johnson as a representative example, nominating him as their vice presidential candidate on what they called the Union ticket. By nominating him, Johnson had said, the Union party affirmed "that the rebellious States are still in the Union, that their loyal citizens are still citizens of the United States."[4] It was a crucial question. No matter what the government of a state did, those who remained loyal to the Union remained American citizens, with the rights of American citizens.

A radical Republican like Ohio's Senator Benjamin F. Wade should have foreseen the problem. Like many radical Republicans, Wade thought secession had disrupted Southern governments and their relations with the federal Union. They would not be entitled to restoration until Congress said they were. That meant that their citizens, even those who had remained loyal to the Union, were not entitled to representation in Congress. Along with Representative Henry Winter Davies, Wade had authored a reconstruction bill that reflected that understanding. He was furious when Lincoln refused to sign it. What Wade saw in Johnson's record was that he was more determined than Lincoln to keep Southern government out of the hands of traitors. "Johnson, we have faith in you," Wade told him as he took office. "There will be no trouble now in running the government."[5]

It turned out that Republicans had misjudged him. He had always insisted that loyal citizens had retained all their rights despite the treason of their state governments. Johnson's denunciations of the disloyal, his arrests, had always been designed to coerce loyalty. He had allowed exiles to return once they took the required oaths; he had let traitors out of jail. During the war, few had taken up his blandishments. They would not betray allies who were still fighting for Southern rights. But once the war ended, that consideration evaporated. Johnson did require leading Confederates to seek individual pardons from him personally, rather than simply take a loyalty oath. But, to his amazed gratification, nearly all applied. All that remained was to re-establish loyal governments and let the revitalized states resume their places in the Union, with their now loyal citizens once again represented in Congress. Ratify the Thirteenth Amendment abolishing slavery, amend state constitutions to do the same, nullify the secession ordinances, and repudiate the debts incurred to sustain the rebellion, he demanded. Those actions would demonstrate renewed loyalty. That the restored states would decide the status of the freed slaves did not trouble him in the least. This program would restore the republican self-government to which he had dedicated his career. In a society without slaves, the masses whose interests he had always championed would be free of a slaveholding aristocracy. It became clear that he had never included Black southerners among "the great mass of the American people." The "American people" were white, and racial equality threatened their interests.

Through the years of turmoil that followed, Johnson always believed he was staying true to the principles he had articulated in his brief address upon taking office. The Republicans who broke with him, including most of the radical Unionists in Tennessee, violated the principles undergirding popular government. In his view, keeping Southern states out of the Union in a fanatic effort to protect the rights of freed slaves was a flagrant violation of constitutional democracy. Sure of his ideals, he would fight the Republicans as vigorously and as vehemently as he had fought the secessionists.

Notes

1. Hans L. Trefousse, *Andrew Johnson: A Biography* (New York: W. W. Norton, 1989), 196–197.
2. Speech in Nashville, March 13, 1862, in *The Papers of Andrew Johnson*, ed. Leroy P. Graf and Ralph W. Haskins (Knoxville: University of Tennessee Press, 1967–2000), 5: 203.
3. Paul H. Bergeron, *Andrew Johnson's Civil War and Reconstruction* (Knoxville: University of Tennessee Press, 2011), 54.
4. Trefousse, *Johnson*, 181.
5. Trefousse, *Johnson*, 199.

Ulysses S. Grant's First Inaugural Address

THURSDAY, MARCH 4, 1869

CITIZENS OF THE *United States:*

Your suffrages having elected me to the office of President of the United States, I have, in conformity to the Constitution of our country, taken the oath of office prescribed therein. I have taken this oath without mental reservation and with the determination to do to the best of my ability all that is required of me. The responsibilities of the position I feel, but accept them without fear. The office has come to me unsought; I commence its duties untrammeled. I bring to it a conscious desire and determination to fill it to the best of my ability to the satisfaction of the people.

On all leading questions agitating the public mind I will always express my views to Congress and urge them according to my judgment, and when I think it advisable will exercise the constitutional privilege of interposing a veto to defeat measures which I oppose; but all laws will be faithfully executed, whether they meet my approval or not.

I shall on all subjects have a policy to recommend, but none to enforce against the will of the people. Laws are to govern all alike—those opposed as well as those who favor them. I know no method to secure the repeal of bad or obnoxious laws so effective as their stringent execution.

The country having just emerged from a great rebellion, many questions will come before it for settlement in the next four years which preceding Administrations have never had to deal with. In meeting these it is desirable that they should be approached calmly, without prejudice, hate, or sectional pride, remembering that the greatest good to the greatest number is the object to be attained.

This requires security of person, property, and free religious and political opinion in every part of our common country, without regard to local prejudice. All laws to secure these ends will receive my best efforts for their enforcement.

A great debt has been contracted in securing to us and our posterity the Union. The payment of this, principal and interest, as well as the return to a specie basis as soon as it can be accomplished without material detriment to the debtor class or to the country at large, must be provided for. To protect the national honor, every dollar of Government indebtedness should be paid in gold, unless otherwise expressly stipulated in the contract. Let it be understood that no repudiator of one farthing of our public debt will be trusted in public place, and it will go far toward strengthening a credit which ought to be the best in the world, and will ultimately enable us to replace the debt with bonds bearing less interest than we now pay. To this should be added a faithful collection of the revenue, a strict accountability to the Treasury for every dollar collected, and the greatest practicable retrenchment in expenditure in every department of Government.

When we compare the paying capacity of the country now, with the ten States in poverty from the effects of war, but soon to emerge, I trust, into greater prosperity than ever before, with its paying capacity twenty-five years ago, and calculate what it probably will be twenty-five years hence, who can doubt the feasibility of paying every dollar then with more ease than we now pay for useless luxuries? Why, it looks as though Providence had bestowed upon us a strong box in the precious metals locked up in the sterile mountains of the far West, and which we are now forging the key to unlock, to meet the very contingency that is now upon us.

Ultimately it may be necessary to insure the facilities to reach these riches, and it may be necessary also that the General Government should give its aid to secure this access; but that should only be when a dollar of obligation to pay secures precisely the same sort of dollar to use now, and not before. Whilst the question of specie payments is in abeyance the prudent business man is careful about contracting debts payable in the distant future. The nation should follow the same rule. A prostrate commerce is to be rebuilt and all industries encouraged.

The young men of the country—those who from their age must be its rulers twenty-five years hence—have a peculiar interest in maintaining the national honor. A moment's reflection as to what will be our commanding influence among the nations of the earth in their day, if they are only true to themselves, should inspire them with national pride. All divisions—geographical, political, and religious—can join in this common sentiment. How the public debt is to be paid or specie payments resumed is not so important as that a plan should be adopted and acquiesced in. A united determination to do is worth more than divided counsels upon the method of doing. Legislation upon this subject may not be necessary now, nor even advisable, but it will be when the civil law is more fully restored in all parts of the country and trade resumes its wonted channels.

It will be my endeavor to execute all laws in good faith, to collect all revenues assessed, and to have them properly accounted for and economically disbursed. I will to the best of my ability appoint to office those only who will carry out this design.

In regard to foreign policy, I would deal with nations as equitable law requires individuals to deal with each other, and I would protect the law-abiding citizen, whether of native or foreign birth, wherever his rights are jeopardized or the flag of our country floats. I would respect the rights of all nations, demanding equal respect for our own. If others depart from this rule in their dealings with us, we may be compelled to follow their precedent.

The proper treatment of the original occupants of this land—the Indians—is one deserving of careful study. I will favor any course toward them which tends to their civilization and ultimate citizenship.

The question of suffrage is one which is likely to agitate the public so long as a portion of the citizens of the nation are excluded from its privileges in any State. It seems to me very desirable that this question should be settled now, and I entertain the hope and express the desire that it may be by the ratification of the fifteenth article of amendment to the Constitution.

In conclusion I ask patient forbearance one toward another throughout the land, and a determined effort on the part of every citizen to do his share toward cementing a happy union; and I ask the prayers of the nation to Almighty God in behalf of this consummation.

The Hero as President

THE FIRST INAUGURAL ADDRESS OF
ULYSSES S. GRANT

Joan Waugh

THURSDAY, MARCH 4, 1869, dawned cold and cloudy. Citizens had already been pouring into Washington, D.C., to witness the inauguration ceremony of the eighteenth president of the United States, Republican Ulysses S. Grant. The crowds viewed a parade featuring thousands of marching soldiers and, despite the weather, were in a festive mood. Roughly 50,000 citizens gathered at noon to watch Chief Justice Salmon Chase administer the oath of office to the forty-three-year-old Grant on the east portico of the Capitol building. Unaccustomed to public speaking, President Grant read his brief handwritten speech of 1,127 words to the expectant crowd, who strained to hear his softly spoken words. Grant's famous campaign slogan, "Let Us Have Peace," stated his desire for the country's peaceful reconciliation and promised to help secure it "calmly, without prejudice, hate, or sectional pride." While offering the olive branch to the ex-Confederates, General, now President, Grant also made plain that the United States' victory in the Civil War was to be secured on Northern terms. That meant restoring the rights and privileges of citizenship of white Southerners, but also protecting the rights and establishing the citizenship of the freed people. He affirmed, "This requires security of person, property, and free religious and political opinion in every part of our common country, without regard to local prejudice," adding: "All laws to secure these ends will receive my best efforts for their enforcement."

Indeed, 1868 was the first presidential campaign in which the issues of Reconstruction predominated, mirroring an intense debate among Americans over the struggle for the meaning of the Civil War: Was it primarily about saving the Union with a focus on restoring white harmony, or was it about ensuring the fruits of emancipation and racial justice? Could both be accommodated? After briefly mentioning his other major goals for the country—building a prosperous economy, paying down the war debt, accomplishing Indian reform, earning prestige on the international stage, and passing the Fifteenth Amendment that would grant suffrage for Black men—Grant made his case for healing the bitterness of wartime animosities. He began this part of his speech by asserting, "The country having just emerged from a great rebellion, many questions will come before it for settlement in the next four years which preceding Administrations have never had to deal with," then calling for all citizens to meet those questions, "calmly, without prejudice, hate or sectional pride, remembering that the greatest good to the greatest number is the object to be attained."

More prosaic than poetic, Grant's First Inaugural Address offered a clear and pleasing pledge to reunify the broken nation inspired by the principles of Abraham Lincoln's Republican party—Union, free labor for all, economic progress, and American security abroad. Neither the press nor the people expected the "silent" general to suddenly emerge as a great orator, yet praise for the address was nearly universal, the *New York Times* declaring that Grant "said it strongly and well."[1] The newly sworn-in president might have assumed that he had a mandate from Northern voters to rise above politics to heal the country. Yet his inaugural remarks indicate that he expected to meet some resistance. A brief examination of the contest that preceded the inaugural festivities will shed light on the challenges beyond the election.

The search for a Republican candidate took place against the backdrop of President Andrew Johnson's impeachment trial. In February 1868, the House of Representatives voted to impeach the nominally Republican Johnson, failing by one vote to win the necessary Senate majority needed for removal. Moderate Republicans thus gained traction over the selection process as the party prepared for the 1868 presidential election. Worried that none of the current crop of politicians held the national stature to secure the nomination, Republican leaders turned to the popular Union hero Grant. As general, he had planned and executed military campaigns, presided over occupation of the Southern population and territory, and formulated and implemented policies and practices that constituted wartime reconstruction. After the Appomattox surrender, he remained a powerful presence, serving as general-in-chief and overseeing the military part of Reconstruction policy for President Johnson. He, perhaps as much as anyone in the United States, had an investment in helping to establish a permanent and solid peace between North and South.

The majority of Republicans viewed Grant as a solid moderate. He had backed congressional reconstruction without embracing radical proposals of land redistribution or immediate social equality between the races, although he pledged support for both the Fourteenth (passed 1866, ratified 1868) and Fifteenth Amendments. The fact that he was not a career politician did not seem to matter. In fact, it might have been a plus to the voter, part of the generation who lived through a period of extraordinary political turmoil. No ordinary candidate exuded the strength, the authority, and the power of Grant; no other candidate held the reputation or the successes. No other candidate's legacy was more at stake. He was the obvious, inevitable choice for the Republican party.

The ensuing Republican campaign and its candidate sought to unify a divided, diverse country around the symbols of nationhood—the founding fathers, the flag, religion, economic opportunity, and above all, the shared sacrifice of the Civil War. Following tradition, Grant stayed at his home in Galena, Illinois, where he received groups of supporters. A few years later, he described the stakes for the 1868 campaign: "I believed that if a democratic president was elected there would be little chance for those who fought for the Union."[2] The Democratic party accused the Republicans—"the Radical party"—of violating the constitutional rights of the Southern states and of subjecting them to "military despotism." Their Democratic platform, while accepting emancipation, blamed Republicans of planning to elevate the interests of the freed people above those of the white population. Party leaders, such as their presidential candidate, Horatio Seymour of New York, attacked Grant as an uncouth, simple-minded, unprincipled, "Negro-loving" tyrant. As Republicans marched in parades, Democrats taunted them with signs proclaiming "Grant the Butcher" and "Grant the Drunkard," the latter referring to his alleged weakness for alcohol.

The Republicans returned fire, but highlighted a positive message, emphasizing their role as the party that saved the Union, freed the slaves, and was peacefully reforming the South. Republican operatives in the former Confederate states targeted enfranchised freedmen with educational political pamphlets, provided Black and white speakers with "Grant badges" to distribute, started political clubs, and organized barbecues and other political entertainments. Violence entered directly into electoral politics, with white supremacists launching terrorist attacks in every Southern state. Houses, churches, schools, printing offices, and political clubrooms were attacked and sometimes destroyed. The lame-duck Johnson administration did nothing to stop this terror in which hundreds of Black and white Republicans were killed.

When election day, November 3, arrived and the votes were tabulated, Grant scored a comfortable, but not a smashing, victory in the popular vote, 53 percent to Seymour's 47 percent, while winning by a landslide in the Electoral College, 214 to 80. The majority of electoral votes (157) came from states free of slavery before the Civil War; Seymour carried just three of them. Some 78 percent of the electorate participated, including, for the first time in American history, an estimated 400,000–500,000 Black men.

No man other than George Washington came to the office with such high expectations as those that accompanied Ulysses S. Grant to his swearing-in ceremonies. Some Democrats worried aloud that Grant's election meant that "militarism" would dominate government policy, but most Republicans thought his victory meant redemption for the Union cause for which so many had fought and died and sacrificed since 1861. They would agree with the judgment offered up by the influential journal *Harper's Weekly* describing the election as the "final interpretation of the war."[3]

Ulysses S. Grant's First Inaugural Address prepared the country for his coming administration. He, and it, would be charged with, and judged by, implementing the Republican-dominated, interracial governments already present in most of the ex-Confederate States. Concluding, President Grant asked for a "patient forbearance one toward another throughout the land, and a determined effort on the part of every citizen to do his share toward cementing a happy union," adding, "and I ask the prayers of the nation to Almighty God in behalf of this consummation."

Notes

1. *New York Times,* March 5, 1869.
2. John Y. Simon, ed., *The Papers of Ulysses S. Grant: June 1, 1871–January 31, 1872,* Vol. 22 (Carbondale: Southern Illinois University Press, n.d.), 31.
3. *Harper's Weekly,* November 21, 1868.

Ulysses S. Grant's Second Inaugural Address

TUESDAY, MARCH 4, 1873

FELLOW-CITIZENS:
Under Providence I have been called a second time to act as Executive over this great nation. It has been my endeavor in the past to maintain all the laws, and, so far as lay in my power, to act for the best interests of the whole people. My best efforts will be given in the same direction in the future, aided, I trust, by my four years' experience in the office.

When my first term of the office of Chief Executive began, the country had not recovered from the effects of a great internal revolution, and three of the former States of the Union had not been restored to their Federal relations.

It seemed to me wise that no new questions should be raised so long as that condition of affairs existed. Therefore the past four years, so far as I could control events, have been consumed in the effort to restore harmony, public credit, commerce, and all the arts of peace and progress. It is my firm conviction that the civilized world is tending toward republicanism, or government by the people through their chosen representatives, and that our own great Republic is destined to be the guiding star to all others.

Under our Republic we support an army less than that of any European power of any standing and a navy less than that of either of at least five of them. There could be no extension of territory on the continent which would call for an increase of this force, but rather might such extension enable us to diminish it.

The theory of government changes with general progress. Now that the telegraph is made available for communicating thought, together with rapid transit by steam, all parts of a continent are made contiguous for all purposes of government, and communication between the extreme limits of the country made easier than it was throughout the old thirteen States at the beginning of our national existence.

The effects of the late civil strife have been to free the slave and make him a citizen. Yet he is not possessed of the civil rights which citizenship should carry with it. This is wrong, and should be corrected. To this correction I stand committed, so far as Executive influence can avail.

Social equality is not a subject to be legislated upon, nor shall I ask that anything be done to advance the social status of the colored man, except to give him a fair chance to develop what there is good in him, give him access to the schools, and when he travels let him feel assured that his conduct will regulate the treatment and fare he will receive.

The States lately at war with the General Government are now happily rehabilitated, and no Executive control is exercised in any one of them that would not be exercised in any other State under like circumstances.

In the first year of the past Administration the proposition came up for the admission of Santo Domingo as a Territory of the Union. It was not a question of my seeking, but was a proposition from the people of Santo Domingo, and which I entertained. I believe now, as I did then, that it was for the best interest of this country, for the people of Santo Domingo, and all concerned that the proposition should be received favorably. It was, however, rejected constitutionally, and therefore the subject was never brought up again by me.

In future, while I hold my present office, the subject of acquisition of territory must have the support of the people before I will recommend any proposition looking to such acquisition. I say here, however, that I do not share in the apprehension held by many as to the danger of governments becoming weakened and destroyed by reason of their extension of territory. Commerce, education, and rapid transit of thought and matter by telegraph and steam have changed all this. Rather do I believe that our Great Maker is preparing the world, in His own good time, to become one nation, speaking one language, and when armies and navies will be no longer required.

My efforts in the future will be directed to the restoration of good feeling between the different sections of our common country; to the restoration of our currency to a fixed value as compared with the world's standard of values— gold—and, if possible, to a par with it; to the construction of cheap routes of transit throughout the land, to the end that the products of all may find a market and leave a living remuneration to the producer; to the maintenance of friendly relations with all our neighbors and with distant nations; to the reestablishment of our commerce and share in the carrying trade upon the ocean; to the encouragement of such manufacturing industries as can be economically pursued in this country, to the end that the exports of home products and industries may pay for our imports—the only sure method of returning to and permanently maintaining a specie basis; to the elevation of labor; and, by a humane course, to bring the aborigines of the country under the benign influences of education and civilization. It is either this or war of extermination. Wars of extermination, engaged in by people pursuing commerce and all industrial pursuits, are expensive even against the weakest people, and are demoralizing and wicked. Our superiority of strength and advantages of civilization should make us lenient toward the Indian. The wrong inflicted upon him should be taken into account and the balance placed to his credit. The moral view of the question should be considered and the question asked, Can not the Indian be made a useful and productive member of society by proper teaching and treatment? If the effort is made in good faith, we will stand better before the civilized nations of the earth and in our own consciences for having made it.

All these things are not to be accomplished by one individual, but they will receive my support and such recommendations to Congress as will in my judgment best serve to carry them into effect. I beg your support and encouragement.

It has been, and is, my earnest desire to correct abuses that have grown up in the civil service of the country. To secure this reformation rules regulating methods of appointment and promotions were established and have been tried. My efforts for such reformation shall be continued to the best of my judgment. The spirit of the rules adopted will be maintained.

I acknowledge before this assemblage, representing, as it does, every section of our country, the obligation I am under to my countrymen for the great honor they have conferred on me by returning me to the highest office within their gift, and the further obligation resting on me to render to them the best services within my power. This I promise, looking forward with the greatest anxiety to the day when I shall be released from responsibilities that at times are almost overwhelming, and from which I have scarcely had a respite since the eventful firing upon Fort Sumter, in April, 1861, to the present day. My services were then tendered and accepted under the first call for troops growing out of that event.

I did not ask for place or position, and was entirely without influence or the acquaintance of persons of influence, but was resolved to perform my part in a struggle threatening the very existence of the nation. I performed a conscientious duty, without asking promotion or command, and without a revengeful feeling toward any section or individual.

Notwithstanding this, throughout the war, and from my candidacy for my present office in 1868 to the close of the last Presidential campaign, I have been the subject of abuse and slander scarcely ever equaled in political history, which to-day I feel that I can afford to disregard in view of your verdict, which I gratefully accept as my vindication.

"Errors of Judgement, Not of Intent"

THE SECOND INAUGURAL ADDRESS OF ULYSSES S. GRANT

John F. Marszalek

ULYSSES S. GRANT was both the commanding general of the Union Army, 1861–1865, and president of the United States, 1869–1877. Since President Abraham Lincoln was assassinated in 1865, and his successor, Andrew Johnson, the vice president, was impeached in 1868, U. S. Grant became the nation's most famous politician. From the time of Andrew Jackson (1829–1837) to the presidency of Woodrow Wilson (1913–1921), U. S. Grant was the only American for nearly a century to hold two terms in office as president.

Grant was easily elected in 1868 and then re-elected in 1872. In the 1868 election, the Republicans met in Chicago and easily nominated Grant as their standard bearer, with Schuyler Colfax, of South Bend, Indiana, as his running mate. Grant won 26 of 34 states with an electoral victory of 214 to 80. His popular vote victory was only slightly more than 306,000 out of 5,715,000. It was the newly enfranchised Blacks who elected him with a vote of over 500,000 in his favor.

In the election of 1872, the Republicans met in Philadelphia and chose their ticket of Grant for president and Henry Wilson of Massachusetts for vice president. This time Grant won 286 to 66 electoral votes over Democrat Horace Greeley. A number of third parties siphoned off just a few votes. In this election, too, Grant won by 763,000 popular votes. Ironically, Greeley died on November 29, 1868, and Wilson died in 1875. Therefore, Grant served most of his second term without a vice president.

When Grant ran and took office in 1869, he inherited many problems: Reconstruction, Greenbacks, Black Friday (or the attempt to corner the gold market), the Ku Klux Klan, Civil Service Reform, the New York City Tweed Ring, the Liberal Republican Movement, the issue of Santo Domingo, and the Credit Mobilier (with Vice President Schuyler Colfax involved). Despite these first-term difficulties, Grant ran again and won once more in 1873. This time he faced the "Crime of 1873" or the Coinage Act, making gold, not silver, the monetary standard; the "Salary Grab," or doubling the president's salary (which was repealed in January 1874); the Panic of 1873; the Whiskey Ring; the impeachment of Secretary of War William Belknap; the disputed Hayes-Tilden presidential election of 1877; Custer's Last Stand; and a variety of Indian problems.

Grant thus had to deal with numerous post–Civil War problems and was often cited as being corrupt and running a corrupt administration. Although he never was implicated in any wrongdoing, his second inauguration proved to be more difficult than the first.

Grant's second inauguration was one of the coldest in American history, with driving winds and the temperature near zero degrees. The weather was as horrible as it might be. Spectators lined up in the middle of Pennsylvania Avenue, standing on street car tracks with people and carriages traveling along the northern side of the avenue. Marchers tried to take advantage of the recent street improvements but still suffered wind-blown dirt in their faces. People took advantage of every piece of warm clothes they could wear, hoping to gain some protection against the temperature and the wind. Still the event was festive; every building was draped with majestic cloth and bunting.

The most impressive part of the entire day was the parade, which consisted of marching bands and military units, some 12,000 people in all. Even African Americans were included. Some of the marchers, for example, West Point cadets and Annapolis midshipmen, suffered severe frostbite. U. S. Grant joined the parade march from the White House, along Pennsylvania Avenue, wearing a thick overcoat, and riding in an open carriage pulled by four magnificent horses. Men and women cheered when they saw Grant, and a young boy, all wrapped in warm clothes, briefly ran alongside the carriage, yelling "Hurrah for Grant." When the president reached the Capitol, he mounted the inaugural stand on the east side. At precisely 12:30 p.m. Salmon P. Chase, the chief justice of the Supreme Court, swore Grant in, and the president gave his inaugural speech. Few could hear him because of the howling wind. A photographer set up a tower and took as many pictures as he could. The crowd seemed pleased with his effort.

His speech was not long, and the frozen audience must have been happy that Grant kept his rhetoric relatively brief. He wrote his own speech, and his thoughts at that time were obvious. He was pleased to have won re-election. He was also happy that he could say something positive about the aftermath of the Civil War, even though he recognized that three former states had not yet been returned into the Union. He was overconfident when he indicated that all was going well within the United States during his first term, but he went too far when he insisted that the world was moving inexorably toward "republicanism" and that the United States was "destined to be the guiding star to all others." He was obviously happy that the telegraph and steam power were pushing the nation into a union never before enjoyed.

Then, however, he quickly switched to the major problem that the nation was still suffering. Black people did not yet enjoy their rightful social equality. He did not want to overemphasize this phenomenon, although he did want to give the Black man a "fair chance to develop what there is good in him, give him access to the schools, and when he travels let him feel assured that his conduct will regulate the treatment and fare he will receive." The amazing fact was that Grant was saying these words in 1873, long before the nation was ready to guarantee such rights to Black people. And, he was proud that no federal force was being used on any of the former rebellious states.

In this speech, too, President Grant indicated that he would continue to support gold as the monetary standard and support international trade linking the world together. And, he clearly believed that the American Indian "be made a useful and productive member of society by proper teaching and treatment." He hoped, too, that civil service reform would be made an essential part of the nation's future.

The second-term president wanted everyone within the sound of his voice (and because of the wind, few fit into this category) to know that he appreciated that the nation had given him the honor of its leadership. He promised that he would always do his best, and he wanted everyone to realize that he never asked for any "place or position" and that he would never be "vengeful" toward the South or any individual within it. He promised, too, never to ask for "promotion or command."

Finally, Grant reminded his listeners: "I have been the subject of abuse and slander scarcely ever equaled in political history." But being the beneficiary of the nation's good feelings as expressed in this presidency, he believed firmly that, "in view of your verdict... I gratefully accept [this honor] as my vindication."

In short, therefore, U. S. Grant, in giving his Second Inaugural Address, indicated his willingness to serve another term in office and to continue his good work for the benefit of the nation. The cold did not deter his great plans for the future, but it was certainly a bad omen for his second term.

Rutherford B. Hayes's Inaugural Address

MONDAY, MARCH 5, 1877

FELLOW-CITIZENS:

We have assembled to repeat the public ceremonial, begun by Washington, observed by all my predecessors, and now a time-honored custom, which marks the commencement of a new term of the Presidential office. Called to the duties of this great trust, I proceed, in compliance with usage, to announce some of the leading principles, on the subjects that now chiefly engage the public attention, by which it is my desire to be guided in the discharge of those duties. I shall not undertake to lay down irrevocably principles or measures of administration, but rather to speak of the motives which should animate us, and to suggest certain important ends to be attained in accordance with our institutions and essential to the welfare of our country.

At the outset of the discussions which preceded the recent Presidential election it seemed to me fitting that I should fully make known my sentiments in regard to several of the important questions which then appeared to demand the consideration of the country. Following the example, and in part adopting the language, of one of my predecessors, I wish now, when every motive for misrepresentation has passed away, to repeat what was said before the election, trusting that my countrymen will candidly weigh and understand it, and that they will feel assured that the sentiments declared in accepting the nomination for the Presidency will be the standard of my conduct in the path before me, charged, as I now am, with the grave and difficult task of carrying them out in the practical administration of the Government so far as depends, under the Constitution and laws on the Chief Executive of the nation.

The permanent pacification of the country upon such principles and by such measures as will secure the complete protection of all its citizens in the free enjoyment of all their constitutional rights is now the one subject in our public affairs which all thoughtful and patriotic citizens regard as of supreme importance.

Many of the calamitous efforts of the tremendous revolution which has passed over the Southern States still remain. The immeasurable benefits which will surely follow, sooner or later, the hearty and generous acceptance of the legitimate results of that revolution have not yet been realized. Difficult and embarrassing questions meet us at the threshold of this subject. The people of those States are still impoverished, and the inestimable blessing of wise, honest, and peaceful local self-government is not fully enjoyed. Whatever difference of opinion may exist as to the cause of this condition of things, the fact is clear that in the progress of events the time has come when such government is the imperative necessity required by all the varied interests, public and private, of those States. But it must not be forgotten that only a local government which recognizes and maintains inviolate the rights of all is a true self-government.

With respect to the two distinct races whose peculiar relations to each other have brought upon us the deplorable complications and perplexities which exist in those States, it must be a government which guards the interests of both races carefully and equally. It must be a government which submits loyally and heartily to the Constitution and the laws—the laws of the nation and the laws of the States themselves—accepting and obeying faithfully the whole Constitution as it is.

Resting upon this sure and substantial foundation, the superstructure of beneficent local governments can be built up, and not otherwise. In furtherance of such obedience to the letter and the spirit of the Constitution, and in behalf of all that its attainment implies, all so-called party interests lose their apparent importance, and party lines may well be permitted to fade into insignificance. The question we have to consider for the immediate welfare of those States of the Union is the question of government or no government; of social order and all the peaceful industries and the happiness that belongs to it, or a return to barbarism. It is a question in which every citizen of the nation is deeply interested, and with respect to which we ought not to be, in a partisan sense, either Republicans or Democrats, but fellow-citizens and fellow-men, to whom the interests of a common country and a common humanity are dear.

The sweeping revolution of the entire labor system of a large portion of our country and the advance of 4,000,000 people from a condition of servitude to that of citizenship, upon an equal footing with their former masters, could not occur without presenting problems of the gravest moment, to be dealt with by the emancipated race, by their former masters, and by the General Government, the author of the act of emancipation. That it was a wise, just, and providential act, fraught with good for all concerned, is not generally conceded throughout the country. That a moral obligation rests upon the National Government to employ its constitutional power and influence to establish the rights of the people it has emancipated, and to protect them in the enjoyment of those rights when they are infringed or assailed, is also generally admitted.

The evils which afflict the Southern States can only be removed or remedied by the united and harmonious efforts of both races, actuated by motives of mutual sympathy and regard; and while in duty bound and fully determined to protect the rights of all by every constitutional means at the disposal of my Administration, I am sincerely anxious to use every legitimate influence in favor of honest and efficient local *self*-government as the true resource of those States for the promotion of the contentment and prosperity of their citizens. In the effort I shall make to accomplish this purpose I ask the cordial cooperation of all who cherish an interest in the welfare of the country, trusting that party ties and the prejudice of race will be freely surrendered in behalf of the great purpose to be accomplished. In the important work of restoring the South it is not the political situation alone that merits attention. The material development of that section of the country has been arrested by the social and political revolution through which it has passed, and now needs and deserves the considerate care of the National Government within the just limits prescribed by the Constitution and wise public economy.

But at the basis of all prosperity, for that as well as for every other part of the country, lies the improvement of the intellectual and moral condition of the people. Universal suffrage should rest upon universal education. To this end, liberal and permanent provision should be made for the support of free schools by the State governments, and, if need be, supplemented by legitimate aid from national authority.

Let me assure my countrymen of the Southern States that it is my earnest desire to regard and promote their truest interest—the interests of the white and of the colored people both and equally—and to put forth my best efforts in behalf of a civil policy which will forever wipe out in our political affairs the color line and the distinction between North and South, to the end that we may have not merely a united North or a united South, but a united country.

I ask the attention of the public to the paramount necessity of reform in our civil service—a reform not merely as to certain abuses and practices of so-called official patronage which have come to have the sanction of usage in the several Departments of our Government, but a change in the system of appointment itself; a reform that shall be thorough, radical, and complete; a return to the principles and practices of the founders of the Government. They neither expected nor desired from public officers any partisan service. They meant that public officers should owe their whole service to the Government and to the people. They meant that the officer should be secure in his tenure as long as his personal character remained untarnished and the performance of his duties satisfactory. They held that appointments to office were not to be made nor expected merely as rewards for partisan services, nor merely on the nomination of members of Congress, as being entitled in any respect to the control of such appointments.

The fact that both the great political parties of the country, in declaring their principles prior to the election, gave a prominent place to the subject of reform of our civil service, recognizing and strongly urging its necessity, in terms almost identical in their specific import with those I have here employed, must be accepted as a conclusive argument in behalf of these measures. It must be regarded as the expression of the united voice and will of the whole country upon this subject, and both political parties are virtually pledged to give it their unreserved support.

The President of the United States of necessity owes his election to office to the suffrage and zealous labors of a political party, the members of which cherish with ardor and regard as of essential importance the principles of their party organization; but he should strive to be always mindful of the fact that he serves his party best who serves the country best.

In furtherance of the reform we seek, and in other important respects a change of great importance, I recommend an amendment to the Constitution prescribing a term of six years for the Presidential office and forbidding a reelection.

With respect to the financial condition of the country, I shall not attempt an extended history of the embarrassment and prostration which we have suffered during the past three years. The depression in all our varied commercial and manufacturing interests throughout the country, which began in September, 1873, still continues. It is very gratifying, however, to be able to say that there are indications all around us of a coming change to prosperous times.

Upon the currency question, intimately connected, as it is, with this topic, I may be permitted to repeat here the statement made in my letter of acceptance, that in my judgment the feeling of uncertainty inseparable from an irredeemable paper currency, with its fluctuation of values, is one of the greatest obstacles to a return to prosperous times. The only safe paper currency is one which rests upon a coin basis and is at all times and promptly convertible into coin.

I adhere to the views heretofore expressed by me in favor of Congressional legislation in behalf of an early resumption of specie payments, and I am satisfied not only that this is wise, but that the interests, as well as the public sentiment, of the country imperatively demand it.

Passing from these remarks upon the condition of our own country to consider our relations with other lands, we are reminded by the international complications abroad, threatening the peace of Europe, that our traditional rule of noninterference in the affairs of foreign nations has proved of great value in past times and ought to be strictly observed.

The policy inaugurated by my honored predecessor, President Grant, of submitting to arbitration grave questions in dispute between ourselves and foreign powers points to a new, and incomparably the best, instrumentality for the preservation of peace, and will, as I believe, become a beneficent example of the course to be pursued in similar emergencies by other nations.

If, unhappily, questions of difference should at any time during the period of my Administration arise between the United States and any foreign government, it will certainly be my disposition and my hope to aid in their settlement in the same peaceful and honorable way, thus securing to our country the great blessings of peace and mutual good offices with all the nations of the world.

Fellow-citizens, we have reached the close of a political contest marked by the excitement which usually attends the contests between great political parties whose members espouse and advocate with earnest faith their respective creeds. The circumstances were, perhaps, in no respect extraordinary save in the closeness and the consequent uncertainty of the result.

For the first time in the history of the country it has been deemed best, in view of the peculiar circumstances of the case, that the objections and questions in dispute with reference to the counting of the electoral votes should be referred to the decision of a tribunal appointed for this purpose.

That tribunal—established by law for this sole purpose; its members, all of them, men of long-established reputation for integrity and intelligence, and, with the exception of those who are also members of the supreme judiciary, chosen equally from both political parties; its deliberations enlightened by the research and the arguments of able counsel—was entitled to the fullest confidence of the American people. Its decisions have been patiently waited for, and accepted as legally conclusive by the general judgment of the public. For the present, opinion will widely vary as to the wisdom of the several conclusions announced by that tribunal. This is to be anticipated in every instance where matters of dispute are made the subject of arbitration under the forms of law. Human judgment is never unerring, and is rarely regarded as otherwise than wrong by the unsuccessful party in the contest.

The fact that two great political parties have in this way settled a dispute in regard to which good men differ as to the facts and the law no less than as to the proper course to be pursued in solving the question in controversy is an occasion for general rejoicing.

Upon one point there is entire unanimity in public sentiment—that conflicting claims to the Presidency must be amicably and peaceably adjusted, and that when so adjusted the general acquiescence of the nation ought surely to follow.

It has been reserved for a government of the people, where the right of suffrage is universal, to give to the world the first example in history of a great nation, in the midst of the struggle of opposing parties for power, hushing its party tumults to yield the issue of the contest to adjustment according to the forms of law.

Looking for the guidance of that Divine Hand by which the destinies of nations and individuals are shaped, I call upon you, Senators, Representatives, judges, fellow-citizens, here and everywhere, to unite with me in an earnest effort to secure to our country the blessings, not only of material prosperity, but of justice, peace, and union—a union depending not upon the constraint of force, but upon the loving devotion of a free people; "and that all things may be so ordered and settled upon the best and surest foundations that peace and happiness, truth and justice, religion and piety, may be established among us for all generations."

The End of Reconstruction

THE INAUGURAL ADDRESS OF RUTHERFORD B. HAYES

Dustin McLochlin

WHEN RUTHERFORD B. Hayes gave his Inaugural Address on March 5, 1877, it was only three days removed from Congress confirming his victory over his opponent, Samuel Tilden of New York. For four months the two parties fought over the returns, which initially appeared to show a clear victory for Tilden. But Republicans noticed that, if Hayes carried the three close Southern states of Louisiana, Florida, and South Carolina, he would win the election by one electoral vote.

Once the Republican party halted the results, both parties sent delegates to the three states in question to find evidence for their side's victory. Predictably, both determined their candidate had won. To break this stalemate, Congress created an Electoral Commission of fifteen members. The Democratic party supported this in heavier numbers because they hoped the deciding member of the commission would be David Davis, whom they believed would side with their party. But he resigned the court and the deciding spot went to Joseph Bradley, who sided with the Republicans. Upon looking at all of the state returns, the Commission voted strictly down party lines and determined that Hayes was the victor.

Partly because of the drama that surrounded Hayes's confirmation, Chief Justice Morrison Waite, through the direction of Ulysses S. Grant, swore Hayes into the presidency two days early in the White House, on March 3. Hayes's public inauguration on March 5, therefore, was truly ceremonial.

Since the Civil War ended, the major political topic was Reconstruction, and this election year had been no different. But, by the time of Hayes's inauguration, the Reconstruction project had been ongoing for nearly twelve years, and the continued presence of federal troops in the South became increasingly tenuous as Southern states were readmitted into the Union, culminating in the seating of Georgia Senator Jonah Hill in February 1871. Despite the formal reintroduction of all of the rebellious Southern states, the use of Union troops remained in a limbo of questionable constitutional legality. The true tenuousness of this continued presence led to many climactic moments, including in Louisiana when the Army moved to defend the Republican governor from a Democratic coup in 1874. Public opinion seemed to teeter between the federal government upholding state democratic institutions and allowing states to run their own affairs (which was a tacit acceptance of white dominance and disenfranchisement of Black men). If the federal government no longer had the will of the people to oversee the actions of Southern states, then a new course needed to be charted. It was in this milieu that Hayes took the office, and his speech reflects this understanding.

A strong adherent to his interpretation of the Constitution, Hayes felt it was time the South was allowed "local self-government," especially now that the nation had passed the Thirteenth, Fourteenth, and Fifteenth Amendments. We can see his insistence on the South abiding by those amendments as well as the rest of the Constitution when he argues for "accepting and obeying faithfully the *whole* Constitution as it is" (emphasis mine). His focus on the Constitution is especially purposeful here since he says "Constitution" or "constitutional" seven times in his section on the South, only using the word two other times throughout the rest of his speech. But his hope for Southern adherence to these amendments was of little use without some plan for long-term sustainability. And, for Hayes, it was in the belief that the division along party lines in the South was based upon the racial question. He felt that once "bayonet rule" came to an end, then people would vote on other concerns. Southern former-Whigs who had more in common with the Republicans would, thus, abandon their Democratic allegiance and provide a larger umbrella of voters for the Republican party in the South. Implicit in this plan was a further assumption that a Southern Black man would also be free to vote Democratic if he felt it aligned with his beliefs; thus Southern white men would not feel compelled to terrorize these potential voters.

Hayes was attempting to chart a new course that was doomed to failure. Perhaps Hayes was naïve, or he was accepting a course and hoped for the best, despite his limited options. Regardless, to historians, this election and the outcome in South Carolina and Louisiana would be an ending point to Reconstruction.

While the gravity of the racial question in the post–Civil War was the most pressing, and needed to be addressed directly, all of Hayes's subsequent policy statements fed into his path forward beyond Reconstruction policies. First, through Civil Service reform, Hayes hoped to find an avenue for bridging the gap between the North and South (and, therefore, Republican and Democrat). He called for a "thorough, radical, and complete" reform and felt on solid ground with this because "both the great political parties ... gave a prominent place to the subject of reform of our civil service." It is in this context that he made the statement that resonated the most with the nation, proclaiming "he serves his party best who serves the country best." This line, mostly borrowed from his eventual Secretary of the Interior Carl Schurz, highlighted that reform was not a partisan issue, and that serving your country was a better means of upholding the honorability of your party, not attempting to maintain its dominance through political appointment. And a means to combat this political machinery was perhaps through an amendment to change presidential appointments to a single, six-year term. Hayes had pledged a single term in his nomination letter, and this one-term pronouncement was an argument that, in his opinion, presidential first terms were merely used as a vehicle to establish enough of a machine for re-election.

Charting a course of civil service reform was not without its perils within his own party. Politicians like Roscoe Conkling of New York made a career working with the machine politics system. In fact, Conkling was a prominent name to potentially unseat James Blaine of Maine, the front runner for the Republican nomination in 1876. Only through the split between Conkling and Blaine supporters did Hayes even ascend to the nomination since many Conkling supporters would rather take their chances with the unknown Hayes than accept Blaine. When Hayes made his intentions clear on civil service, Conkling only halfheartedly supported Hayes over Tilden.

While civil service reform undoubtedly created rifts within the Republican party, which Hayes might want to avoid, his stance on the economy had the potential of creating rifts within the Democratic party, in which Hayes hoped. The economic panic, which started in 1873, showed signs of recovery by 1877, but discussing his belief in the elimination of "irredeemable paper currency" showed that he was attempting to win over the "hard money" element of the Democratic party who were most likely to be former Whigs. In fact, the Democratic ticket included the hard money Tilden and the "soft money" vice presidential nominee Thomas Hendricks.

Hayes makes room for one more policy announcement before his closing remarks. But this pronouncement is much more a conciliatory note to Grant and his wing of the party than Hayes laying out his foreign policy objectives. While the statement itself says little other than Hayes's intention to continue Grant's policy of "submitting to arbitration grave questions in dispute," Hayes had made a number of choices in his nomination letter that were seen as direct rebukes to Grant and his administration. His civil service pledge could be seen as an attack on Grant and his connection to Roscoe Conkling's wing of the Republican party, and his call for a single term came after a time when many thought Grant would attempt a third term (which he did the following election). Hayes knew he needed to embrace Grant, and hopefully his wing, at some level during his Inaugural Address.

All of this was unquestionably in the backdrop of the dubious way in which Hayes was confirmed as the president, and Hayes had to make some mention. Playing the role of the conciliator, Hayes calls for everyone to move forward from the decision made by the Electoral Commission (he calls it the "tribunal"). In this discussion we see many conciliatory statements given to Democrats, and Southerners, that perhaps the Electoral Commission did err in its judgment. And, while we can commend Hayes for sympathizing with the opposing party for its differing view on the outcome, we should also commend him for understanding the peaceful transfer of power and pointing out that, regardless of the outcome, there needs to be a general "acquiescence" to the outcome, even if individuals may not like Hayes. This acceptance of democracy above personal ambition was an important element of this contentious outcome.

James A. Garfield's Inaugural Address

FRIDAY, MARCH 4, 1881

FELLOW-CITIZENS:

We stand to-day upon an eminence which overlooks a hundred years of national life—a century crowded with perils, but crowned with the triumphs of liberty and law. Before continuing the onward march let us pause on this height for a moment to strengthen our faith and renew our hope by a glance at the pathway along which our people have traveled.

It is now three days more than a hundred years since the adoption of the first written constitution of the United States—the Articles of Confederation and Perpetual Union. The new Republic was then beset with danger on every hand. It had not conquered a place in the family of nations. The decisive battle of the war for independence, whose centennial anniversary will soon be gratefully celebrated at Yorktown, had not yet been fought. The colonists were struggling not only against the armies of a great nation, but against the settled opinions of mankind; for the world did not then believe that the supreme authority of government could be safely intrusted to the guardianship of the people themselves.

We can not overestimate the fervent love of liberty, the intelligent courage, and the sum of common sense with which our fathers made the great experiment of self-government. When they found, after a short trial, that the confederacy of States, was too weak to meet the necessities of a vigorous and expanding republic, they boldly set it aside, and in its stead established a National Union, founded directly upon the will of the people, endowed with full power of self-preservation and ample authority for the accomplishment of its great object.

Under this Constitution the boundaries of freedom have been enlarged, the foundations of order and peace have been strengthened, and the growth of our people in all the better elements of national life has indicated the wisdom of the founders and given new hope to their descendants. Under this Constitution our people long ago made themselves safe against danger from without and secured for their mariners and flag equality of rights on all the seas. Under this Constitution twenty-five States have been added to the Union, with constitutions and laws, framed and enforced by their own citizens, to secure the manifold blessings of local self-government.

The jurisdiction of this Constitution now covers an area fifty times greater than that of the original thirteen States and a population twenty times greater than that of 1780.

The supreme trial of the Constitution came at last under the tremendous pressure of civil war. We ourselves are witnesses that the Union emerged from the blood and fire of that conflict purified and made stronger for all the beneficent purposes of good government.

And now, at the close of this first century of growth, with the inspirations of its history in their hearts, our people have lately reviewed the condition of the nation, passed judgment upon the conduct and opinions of political parties, and have registered their will concerning the future administration of the Government. To interpret and to execute that will in accordance with the Constitution is the paramount duty of the Executive.

Even from this brief review it is manifest that the nation is resolutely facing to the front, resolved to employ its best energies in developing the great possibilities of the future. Sacredly preserving whatever has been gained to liberty and good government during the century, our people are determined to leave behind them all those bitter controversies concerning things which have been irrevocably settled, and the further discussion of which can only stir up strife and delay the onward march.

The supremacy of the nation and its laws should be no longer a subject of debate. That discussion, which for half a century threatened the existence of the Union, was closed at last in the high court of war by a decree from which there is no appeal—that the Constitution and the laws made in pursuance thereof are and shall continue to be the supreme law of the land, binding alike upon the States and the people. This decree does not disturb the autonomy of the States nor interfere with any of their necessary rights of local self-government, but it does fix and establish the permanent supremacy of the Union.

The will of the nation, speaking with the voice of battle and through the amended Constitution, has fulfilled the great promise of 1776 by proclaiming "liberty throughout the land to all the inhabitants thereof."

The elevation of the negro race from slavery to the full rights of citizenship is the most important political change we have known since the adoption of the Constitution of 1787. No thoughtful man can fail to appreciate its beneficent effect upon our institutions and people. It has freed us from the perpetual danger of war and dissolution. It has added immensely to the moral and industrial forces of our people. It has liberated the master as well as the slave from a relation which wronged and enfeebled both. It has surrendered to their own guardianship the manhood of more than 5,000,000 people, and has opened to each one of them a career of freedom and usefulness. It has given new inspiration to the power of self-help in both races by making labor more honorable to the one and more necessary to the other. The influence of this force will grow greater and bear richer fruit with the coming years.

No doubt this great change has caused serious disturbance to our Southern communities. This is to be deplored, though it was perhaps unavoidable. But those who resisted the change should remember that under our institutions there was no middle ground for the negro race between slavery and equal citizenship. There can be no permanent disfranchised peasantry in the United States. Freedom can never yield its fullness of blessings so long as the law or its administration places the smallest obstacle in the pathway of any virtuous citizen.

The emancipated race has already made remarkable progress. With unquestioning devotion to the Union, with a patience and gentleness not born of fear, they have "followed the light as God gave them to see the light." They are rapidly laying the material foundations of self-support, widening their circle of intelligence, and beginning to enjoy the blessings that gather around the homes of the industrious poor. They deserve the generous encouragement of all good men. So far as my authority can lawfully extend they shall enjoy the full and equal protection of the Constitution and the laws.

The free enjoyment of equal suffrage is still in question, and a frank statement of the issue may aid its solution. It is alleged that in many communities negro citizens are practically denied the freedom of the ballot. In so far as the truth of this allegation is admitted, it is answered that in many places honest local government is impossible if the mass of uneducated negroes are allowed to vote. These are grave allegations. So far as the latter is true, it is the only palliation that can be offered for opposing the freedom of the ballot. Bad local government is certainly a great evil, which ought to be prevented; but to violate the freedom and sanctities of the suffrage is more than an evil. It is a crime which, if persisted in, will destroy the Government itself. Suicide is not a remedy. If in other lands it be high treason to compass the death of the king, it shall be counted no less a crime here to strangle our sovereign power and stifle its voice.

It has been said that unsettled questions have no pity for the repose of nations. It should be said with the utmost emphasis that this question of the suffrage will never give repose or safety to the States or to the nation until each, within its own jurisdiction, makes and keeps the ballot free and pure by the strong sanctions of the law.

But the danger which arises from ignorance in the voter can not be denied. It covers a field far wider than that of negro suffrage and the present condition of the race. It is a danger that lurks and hides in the sources and fountains of power in every state. We have no standard by which to measure the disaster that may be brought upon us by ignorance and vice in the citizens when joined to corruption and fraud in the suffrage.

The voters of the Union, who make and unmake constitutions, and upon whose will hang the destinies of our governments, can transmit their supreme authority to no successors save the coming generation of voters, who are the sole heirs of sovereign power. If that generation comes to its inheritance blinded by ignorance and corrupted by vice, the fall of the Republic will be certain and remediless.

The census has already sounded the alarm in the appalling figures which mark how dangerously high the tide of illiteracy has risen among our voters and their children.

To the South this question is of supreme importance. But the responsibility for the existence of slavery did not rest upon the South alone. The nation itself is responsible for the extension of the suffrage, and is under special obligations to aid in removing the illiteracy which it has added to the voting population. For the North and South alike there is but one remedy. All the constitutional power of the nation and of the States and all the volunteer forces of the people should be surrendered to meet this danger by the savory influence of universal education.

It is the high privilege and sacred duty of those now living to educate their successors and fit them, by intelligence and virtue, for the inheritance which awaits them.

In this beneficent work sections and races should be forgotten and partisanship should be unknown. Let our people find a new meaning in the divine oracle which declares that "a little child shall lead them," for our own little children will soon control the destinies of the Republic.

My countrymen, we do not now differ in our judgment concerning the controversies of past generations, and fifty years hence our children will not be divided in their opinions concerning our controversies. They will surely bless their fathers and their fathers' God that the Union was preserved, that slavery was overthrown, and that both races were made equal before the law. We may hasten or we may retard, but we can not prevent, the final reconciliation. Is it not possible for us now to make a truce with time by anticipating and accepting its inevitable verdict?

Enterprises of the highest importance to our moral and material well-being unite us and offer ample employment of our best powers. Let all our people, leaving behind them the battlefields of dead issues, move forward and in their strength of liberty and the restored Union win the grander victories of peace.

The prosperity which now prevails is without parallel in our history. Fruitful seasons have done much to secure it, but they have not done all. The preservation of the public credit and the resumption of specie payments, so successfully attained by the Administration of my predecessors, have enabled our people to secure the blessings which the seasons brought.

By the experience of commercial nations in all ages it has been found that gold and silver afford the only safe foundation for a monetary system. Confusion has recently been created by variations in the relative value of the two metals, but I confidently believe that arrangements can be made between the leading commercial nations which will secure the general use of both metals. Congress should provide that the compulsory coinage of silver now required by law may not disturb our monetary system by driving either metal out of circulation. If possible, such an adjustment should be made that the purchasing power of every coined dollar will be exactly equal to its debt-paying power in all the markets of the world.

The chief duty of the National Government in connection with the currency of the country is to coin money and declare its value. Grave doubts have been entertained whether Congress is authorized by the Constitution to make any form of paper money legal tender. The present issue of United States notes has been sustained by the necessities of war; but such paper should depend for its value and currency upon its convenience in use and its prompt redemption in coin at the will of the holder, and not upon its compulsory circulation. These notes are not money, but promises to pay money. If the holders demand it, the promise should be kept.

The refunding of the national debt at a lower rate of interest should be accomplished without compelling the withdrawal of the national-bank notes, and thus disturbing the business of the country.

I venture to refer to the position I have occupied on financial questions during a long service in Congress, and to say that time and experience have strengthened the opinions I have so often expressed on these subjects.

The finances of the Government shall suffer no detriment which it may be possible for my Administration to prevent.

The interests of agriculture deserve more attention from the Government than they have yet received. The farms of the United States afford homes and employment for more than one-half our people, and furnish much the largest part of all our exports. As the Government lights our coasts for the protection of mariners and the benefit of commerce, so it should give to the tillers of the soil the best lights of practical science and experience.

Our manufacturers are rapidly making us industrially independent, and are opening to capital and labor new and profitable fields of employment. Their steady and healthy growth should still be matured. Our facilities for transportation should be promoted by the continued improvement of our harbors and great interior waterways and by the increase of our tonnage on the ocean.

The development of the world's commerce has led to an urgent demand for shortening the great sea voyage around Cape Horn by constructing ship canals or railways across the isthmus which unites the continents. Various plans to this end have been suggested and will need consideration, but none of them has been sufficiently matured to warrant the United States in extending pecuniary aid. The subject, however, is one which will immediately engage the attention of the Government with a view to a thorough protection to American interests. We will urge no narrow policy nor seek peculiar or exclusive privileges in any commercial route; but, in the language of my predecessor, I believe it to be the right "and duty of the United States to assert and maintain such supervision and authority over any interoceanic canal across the isthmus that connects North and South America as will protect our national interest."

The Constitution guarantees absolute religious freedom. Congress is prohibited from making any law respecting an establishment of religion or prohibiting the free exercise thereof. The Territories of the United States are subject to the direct legislative authority of Congress, and hence the General Government is responsible for any violation of the Constitution in any of them. It is therefore a reproach to the Government that in the most populous of the Territories the constitutional guaranty is not enjoyed by the people and the authority of Congress is set at naught. The Mormon Church not only offends the moral sense of manhood by sanctioning polygamy, but prevents the administration of justice through ordinary instrumentalities of law.

In my judgment it is the duty of Congress, while respecting to the uttermost the conscientious convictions and religious scruples of every citizen, to prohibit within its jurisdiction all criminal practices, especially of that class which destroy the family relations and endanger social order. Nor can any ecclesiastical organization be safely permitted to usurp in the smallest degree the functions and powers of the National Government.

The civil service can never be placed on a satisfactory basis until it is regulated by law. For the good of the service itself, for the protection of those who are intrusted with the appointing power against the waste of time and obstruction to the public business caused by the inordinate pressure for place, and for the protection of incumbents against intrigue and wrong, I shall at the proper time ask Congress to fix the tenure of the minor offices of the several Executive

Departments and prescribe the grounds upon which removals shall be made during the terms for which incumbents have been appointed.

Finally, acting always within the authority and limitations of the Constitution, invading neither the rights of the States nor the reserved rights of the people, it will be the purpose of my Administration to maintain the authority of the nation in all places within its jurisdiction; to enforce obedience to all the laws of the Union in the interests of the people; to demand rigid economy in all the expenditures of the Government, and to require the honest and faithful service of all executive officers, remembering that the offices were created, not for the benefit of incumbents or their supporters, but for the service of the Government.

And now, fellow-citizens, I am about to assume the great trust which you have committed to my hands. I appeal to you for that earnest and thoughtful support which makes this Government in fact, as it is in law, a government of the people.

I shall greatly rely upon the wisdom and patriotism of Congress and of those who may share with me the responsibilities and duties of administration, and, above all, upon our efforts to promote the welfare of this great people and their Government I reverently invoke the support and blessings of Almighty God.

The Preacher President

THE INAUGURAL ADDRESS OF JAMES A. GARFIELD

Charles W. Calhoun

WHEN THE REPUBLICAN party tapped James A. Garfield for president in 1880, observers labeled him a dark horse nominee, but he had long occupied a place in the front rank of American politicians. Through seventeen years in Congress, he had positioned himself as an eloquent advocate of Republican doctrine, and, not unreasonably, he anticipated that a deadlocked national convention might turn to him. He was right. A prolonged struggle between supporters of former president Ulysses S. Grant and those of Maine Senator James G. Blaine ended when Blaine delegates swung to Garfield. Eventually the party closed ranks, and he went on to victory in November. He was the only Republican from 1876 to 1892 to win a popular-vote plurality over his Democratic opponent.

Few presidents have approached preparing an inaugural with greater intellectual strengths than Garfield's. Educated at Williams College, he had been a professor of ancient languages, ordained minister, college president, lawyer, and Ohio state senator—all before he turned thirty, at which age he became a general in the United States army. A scholar of politics, he carried on a lively correspondence with professors, literary figures, and leading political economists. He labored long hours in researching and writing his speeches and essays, taking breaks to read his favorite Roman poets in Latin.

It is remarkable, then, that when Garfield set about writing his address, he fell into an almost crippling hesitation. After his fashion, he launched the task by studying all his predecessors' speeches, but as the weeks went by, his usual scholarly self-discipline abandoned him. He put no words to paper and allowed himself to be distracted by tedious consultations regarding patronage and other political matters. His procrastination was not entirely out of character, for at key points in his career Garfield had suffered spasms of indecision. Rather than being inspired by previous inaugural addresses, he considered them, except for Lincoln's, "dreary reading" and feared that "mine will be also." Daunted by the responsibility of framing the most important utterance of his life, he grumbled that the inaugural genre had "so many limitations" that it left "little freedom in its composition." More than once he considered giving no address at all. Three days before the inauguration he finally had a draft, but was "so much dissatisfied with it" that he started all over again. He did not complete the speech until 2:30 in the morning of March 4, 1881, the day of its delivery.

In the end, Garfield fell back on a personal model for his address—the public letter he had issued accepting the Republican presidential nomination. In that campaign letter he had discussed the central issues confronting the American people, and he now reprised those questions in roughly the same order. He aimed to cultivate favor with both the Grant wing of his party, which emphasized continued support for civil rights, and the Blaine wing, which stressed economic issues. Eschewing high-flown rhetoric, he presented a clear exposition of the state of the Republic and where he wanted to take it.

Garfield began his address with a reverent yet monitory review of the Republic's progress through the previous century. At the outset, he observed, the American Revolution represented not merely a violent withdrawal from the British Empire but the initiation of a "great experiment of self-government," which formed the new nation's quintessence. The American revolutionaries defied not only "the armies of a great nation," but also "the settled opinions of mankind" in battling for the radical principle that "the supreme authority of government could be safely intrusted to the guardianship of the people themselves." After a halting start, the Articles of Confederation gave way to the Constitution, establishing "a National Union, founded directly upon the will of the people." Yet, despite the nation's growth and success, doubts about the durability of its democratic project persisted, until the Civil War brought "the supreme trial of the Constitution."

Although the war's outcome secured the Union's permanency, sixteen years after Appomattox, American democracy still remained contested. Garfield expressed the anxiety felt by many citizens, especially Republicans, that the nation could not finally secure the promise of the Founders' design as long as it was held hostage by men who placed white supremacy above admitting Blacks to participation in self-government. "There can be no permanent disfranchised peasantry in the United States," he declared. "To violate the freedom and sanctities of the suffrage is more than an evil. It is a crime which, if persisted in, will destroy the Government itself. Suicide is not a remedy."

Still, Garfield suggested no revival of military Reconstruction, which neither Congress nor the nation would sanction. Conceding the validity of complaints about the ignorance of Black voters, he favored not denying them suffrage but instead improving their capacity for citizenship by a thorough program of education. But, he said, the problem of voter ignorance extended beyond the South. Decrying a rising "tide of illiteracy" in the country, he called for "all the constitutional power of the nation and of the States" to "meet this danger by the savory influence of universal education." Again, he stressed the precariousness of the democratic experiment, warning that if the next "generation comes to its inheritance blinded by ignorance and corrupted by vice, the fall of the Republic will be certain and remediless."

Turning to economic questions, Garfield hailed the nation's prosperity after a half decade of depression in the 1870s. He attributed the good fortune not only to bountiful harvests, but also to government policies for the preservation of the public credit and the resumption of the payment of specie for greenback paper dollars issued during the Civil War. Subscribing to prevailing financial orthodoxy, he saw gold and silver as the "only safe foundation for a monetary system." Paper notes such as the greenbacks were only "promises to pay money" and must be held at par with specie. Like gold, silver possessed intrinsic value, but its safe use as money depended on its coinage in equivalence with gold, preferably at a ratio set by international agreement. Garfield also called for refinancing the national debt at a lower interest rate.

As an economic nationalist, Garfield favored an expanded role for government in fostering prosperity. For farmers, he advocated programs to provide "the best lights of practical science and experience." Over the years Garfield had shown less enthusiasm than many Republicans had displayed on behalf of a high tariff to protect American industry from foreign competition. The Republican campaign in 1880 had placed great emphasis on that policy, but Garfield omitted any specific mention of it in his address. Instead he saluted the nation's burgeoning manufacturers and said simply that their "steady and healthy growth should still be matured." The vagueness of this locution in the passive voice suggested Garfield's lingering affinity for freer trade and offered scant encouragement to his party's protectionist wing.

In the interest of expanding trade, Garfield advocated improvement of harbors and interior waterways and support to revitalize the American merchant fleet. He also favored further consideration of plans for a Central American ship canal and asserted that any such waterway should remain under American "supervision and authority."

Since its first national platform in 1856, the Republican party had decried polygamy, condemning it, like slavery, as a "relic of barbarism." This issue centered in the Utah Territory, where adherents to the Mormon Church predominated. Garfield acknowledged the Constitution's guarantee of "absolute religious freedom," but he asserted that Congress had the duty to prohibit in areas under its jurisdiction "all criminal practices," especially those that "destroy the family relations and endanger social order." Again he warned of danger to America's democratic experiment, denouncing the Mormon Church's exclusionary political practices in the territory. No "ecclesiastical organization," he insisted, could "be safely permitted to usurp in the smallest degree the functions and powers of the National Government."

Finally, Garfield turned to civil service reform, an issue that had roiled politics for more than a decade. President Grant had first instituted a reform program in the early 1870s, but Congress had never confirmed it through legislation. Without statute law, Garfield argued, the civil service could "never be placed on a satisfactory basis." But he did not call for a legislated mandate for competitive exams for appointments. Instead he promised to ask Congress to prescribe the term-lengths for minor offices as well as the grounds for legitimate dismissal, thus hoping to protect upright civil servants from arbitrary removal for political reasons. As matters turned out, the most significant achievement of Garfield's brief term came with his successful assertion of the power of the president to appoint officials despite the objection of state party bosses.

Though hardly a masterpiece, Garfield's address won general praise. One Republican newspaper said his "admirable" speech justified the people's "high confidence" in him. Yet, the paper added, "it still remains for him to show whether he possesses the rare tact, the patience, and the practical statesmanship to get things done."[1]

Four months later an assassin's bullet denied him the chance.

Note

1. "Uinta Chieftain March 12, 1881—Wyoming Digital Newspaper Collection," wyomingnewspapers.org, retrieved June 19, 2024, from https://wyomingnewspapers.org/?a=d&d=WYUUCH18810312-01.1.3&e=-------en-20--1--img-txIN%7ctxCO%7ctxTA--------0------.

Chester A. Arthur's Address upon Assuming the Office of President of the United States

THURSDAY, SEPTEMBER 22, 1881

FOR THE FOURTH time in the history of the Republic its Chief Magistrate has been removed by death. All hearts are filled with grief and horror at the hideous crime which has darkened our land, and the memory of the murdered President, his protracted sufferings, his unyielding fortitude, the example and achievements of his life, and the pathos of his death will forever illumine the pages of our history.

For the fourth time the officer elected by the people and ordained by the Constitution to fill a vacancy so created is called to assume the Executive chair. The wisdom of our fathers, foreseeing even the most dire possibilities, made sure that the Government should never be imperiled because of the uncertainty of human life. Men may die, but the fabrics of our free institutions remain unshaken. No higher or more assuring proof could exist of the strength and permanence of popular government than the fact that though the chosen of the people be struck down his constitutional successor is peacefully installed without shock or strain except the sorrow which mourns the bereavement. All the noble aspirations of my lamented predecessor which found expression in his life, the measures devised and suggested during his brief Administration to correct abuses, to enforce economy, to advance prosperity, and to promote the general welfare, to insure domestic security and maintain friendly and honorable relations with the nations of the earth, will be garnered in the hearts of the people; and it will be my earnest endeavor to profit, and to see that the nation shall profit, by his example and experience.

Prosperity blesses our country. Our fiscal policy is fixed by law, is well grounded and generally approved. No threatening issue mars our foreign intercourse, and the wisdom, integrity, and thrift of our people may be trusted to continue undisturbed the present assured career of peace, tranquilly, and welfare. The gloom and anxiety which have enshrouded the country must make repose especially welcome now. No demand for speedy legislation has been heard; no adequate occasion is apparent for an unusual session of Congress. The Constitution defines the functions and powers of the executive as clearly as those of either of the other two departments of the Government, and he must answer for the just exercise of the discretion it permits and the performance of the duties it imposes. Summoned to these high duties and responsibilities and profoundly conscious of their magnitude and gravity, I assume the trust imposed by the Constitution, relying for aid on divine guidance and the virtue, patriotism, and intelligence of the American people.

"Chet Arthur? President of the United States? Good God!"

CHESTER A. ARTHUR'S ADDRESS UPON ASSUMING THE OFFICE OF PRESIDENT OF THE UNITED STATES

Walter Nugent

AS THE ELECTION of 1880 drew near, the Republicans—dominant in presidential elections since 1860 but not lately in congressional contests—were divided into two large factions: the Stalwarts and the Half-Breeds. The Stalwarts hoped to nominate former president Ulysses S. Grant, whom they believed was a sure winner. But Grant had already served two full terms (1869–1877), and he was diffident about running again. The Half-Breeds were eager to capture both the nomination and the election. Grant's delegate votes stalled on the thirty-fourth ballot. The leader of the Half-Breeds, Senator James G. Blaine of Maine, was in second place but could not pull into the lead. The nomination soon went to a dark horse, long-term congressman James A. Garfield of Ohio.

The convention, for party unity's sake, then turned to a Stalwart for the vice presidential nomination: Chester Alan Arthur of New York, an ally of Stalwart leader Senator Roscoe Conkling. Arthur was a Vermont-born New York City lawyer, known for his high-fashion dandified attire. He had also been a solid Republican since the late 1850s and was noted for two cases in which he successfully defended African Americans, one a woman prevented from riding on the city's public transit and the other a slave who claimed freedom after his owner brought him to New York. In 1871, President Grant appointed Arthur the Collector of the Port of New York, the most lucrative patronage job in the federal system, overseeing a staff of a thousand at the Customs House. Arthur held this position until President Hayes, in a burst of reform zeal (which Arthur was then scarcely noted for), fired him in 1878. But by 1880, Hayes was without much influence, and Arthur was a Conkling ally. In the presidential election, Garfield and Arthur squeaked by the Democratic candidates, General Winfield Scott Hancock and Indiana congressman William English, by only 33,000 votes out of 8.86 million cast.

Garfield and Arthur swore their oaths of office on March 4, 1881. Garfield filled his cabinet with party leaders and faithful, with the eminent Blaine as secretary of state. But not quite four months later, on July 2, Charles Guiteau, who has gone down in history as "a disappointed office seeker," shot Garfield in the back and arm. The president lingered two and a half months. Physicians, as yet unaware of antisepsis, tried to dig out the bullet, but gave Garfield blood poisoning which, together with a weakened heart and other problems, killed him on September 19. Garfield had had little time to accomplish much. He had advocated civil service reform, but that and other ideas had to await his successor. Arthur took the presidential oath at his New York residence in the wee hours of the next day. He would serve out nearly a full term until March 1885.

Arthur did not have a formal inauguration nor a true inaugural address. But he did transmit his "Address upon Assuming the Office of President" almost immediately, on September 22, 1881. Hardly any of it touched on policy or gave an indication of any legislation he might propose. As the document shows, Arthur promised to "profit by his [Garfield's] example and experience" and strive "to correct abuses, to enforce economy, to advance prosperity, and to promote the general welfare, to insure domestic security and maintain friendly and honorable relations with the nations of the earth." Hardly radical, even anodyne. His aim, evidently, was to reassure the people that the road ahead would be smooth. "No demand for speedy legislation has been heard," no "unusual session of Congress" is occasioned.

Nonetheless, Arthur and his administration did achieve a number of things, which together form a more activist federal government—not a lot more, but visibly more—than the Hayes administration that preceded his. In less than three months after taking over, the entrepreneurial Blaine resigned, leaving foreign policy more clearly in Arthur's hands. Nearly all of Garfield's Cabinet members would be replaced within a year. In early 1882, Congress passed two acts that restricted rights rather than extending them: in March 1882, the Edmunds Act, outlawing polygamy, an anti-Mormon measure; and in May 1882, the Chinese Exclusion Act, cutting off migration from China for ten years. (Arthur had vetoed a bill a few days earlier because its exclusion period was twenty years, but he signed the revised one. In 1892 and later, exclusion would be extended permanently.)

In the fall of 1882, Congress argued about civil service reform. The issue had come up in Hayes's time, and pressure mounted for some form of action. First the Senate, and then the House, passed the Pendleton Civil Service Act in late 1882, and Arthur signed it into law on January 16, 1883. It is the one achievement for which the Arthur administration is best—or at all—known, mentioned in virtually every subsequent textbook of post–Civil War American history. Many have remarked on the apparent incongruity of Arthur, a preeminent spoilsman of the 1870s, signing the first broad act to limit or replace the spoils system with competitive merit examinations for holding office.

The spring of 1883 also brought a revision of the tariff, though levels changed very little as interests competed for protection. The act became known as the "mongrel tariff," and it finally passed in December. Arthur also signed a generous bill to expand appropriations for the U.S. Navy, which he regarded as under strength. In so doing, he built a reputation as an expansionist, if not an imperialist. Another naval bill the next year cemented that reputation. So did the United States' acquisition in 1884 of Pearl Harbor, in Hawaii, as a coaling station for American vessels.

Under Arthur's watch, the United States in 1884 became a signatory to the international treaty establishing standard time, with a line running through the Greenwich Observatory in London as the "prime meridian." In pre-railroad days, time zones were unknown and unnecessary. But by the 1880s, different railroad lines had run on different schedules, with sometimes lethal results. The standardization of time, into four zones across the United States, was an essential safety measure and an achievement of the Arthur years. The final significant legislation signed by Arthur was the Foran Act, outlawing contract labor, in February 1885.

Did his actions conform to, or reflect, his initial address? Vague as those were, he could hardly have missed. The Pendleton Civil Service Act did correct abuses, the tariff could be claimed to have advanced prosperity, and the naval appropriations ensured security, in its way.

By early 1885, Arthur had unsuccessfully sought renomination. Blaine became the Republican candidate for president in the 1884 election, only to be defeated by the Democrat, New York governor Grover Cleveland, by about as narrow a margin as Garfield and Arthur had managed in 1880.

Arthur's nearly four years in office were certainly not devoid of achievements, and the Pendleton Act was by no means the only one. Arthur became president only sixteen years after the end of the Civil War, and he left the office only sixteen years before the accession of Theodore Roosevelt and the onset of full-blown Progressive reform. In Arthur's day, Jim Crow had not yet grown into its full malign maturity, but already many Ku Klux Klan atrocities and other terrorism were wreaked upon the former slaves. The Army and settlers continued to push back Indians from their tribal lands. Civil War issues and loyalties persisted strongly, in the South, in Supreme Court decisions, and in the election of former Confederates to Congress and other offices. On the other hand, looking forward, the Arthur presidency produced glimmerings of the kind of reforms that would soon mark the full-blown Progressive Era. Historians have traditionally called the years from the Civil War to World War I "the Gilded Age and Progressive Era," but were they so different, stodgy, and corrupt on the early side, enlightened and filled with reform on the later? It's not quite that simple. Many changes that we might think of as "progressive" really began in the so-called Gilded Age, the 1870s through the 1890s. But some of the actions of Arthur and the Congresses of his day give off more than a whiff of "Progressivism." The more restrictive and, by today's standards, illiberal side of Progressivism was manifest in the Chinese Exclusion Act and the Edmunds Anti-Polygamy law. Yet the more liberal kind of Progressivism was at the core of the Pendleton Civil Service Act, and the imperialism of Theodore Roosevelt was of a kind with Arthur's naval upgrading and the franchise on Pearl Harbor.

All in all, Arthur and his administration compiled not a bad record of achievements in those three and a half years, starting with the shock of Garfield's assassination. It was an honorable and incorrupt record. Throughout those years, Arthur suffered from Bright's disease—the modern name is glomerulonephritis—and he died of it about a year after he left the White House.

Grover Cleveland's First Inaugural Address

WEDNESDAY, MARCH 4, 1885

FELLOW-CITIZENS:

In the presence of this vast assemblage of my countrymen I am about to supplement and seal by the oath which I shall take the manifestation of the will of a great and free people. In the exercise of their power and right of self-government they have committed to one of their fellow-citizens a supreme and sacred trust, and he here consecrates himself to their service.

This impressive ceremony adds little to the solemn sense of responsibility with which I contemplate the duty I owe to all the people of the land. Nothing can relieve me from anxiety lest by any act of mine their interests may suffer, and nothing is needed to strengthen my resolution to engage every faculty and effort in the promotion of their welfare.

Amid the din of party strife the people's choice was made, but its attendant circumstances have demonstrated anew the strength and safety of a government by the people. In each succeeding year it more clearly appears that our democratic principle needs no apology, and that in its fearless and faithful application is to be found the surest guaranty of good government.

But the best results in the operation of a government wherein every citizen has a share largely depend upon a proper limitation of purely partisan zeal and effort and a correct appreciation of the time when the heat of the partisan should be merged in the patriotism of the citizen.

To-day the executive branch of the Government is transferred to new keeping. But this is still the Government of all the people, and it should be none the less an object of their affectionate solicitude. At this hour the animosities of political strife, the bitterness of partisan defeat, and the exultation of partisan triumph should be supplanted by an ungrudging acquiescence in the popular will and a sober, conscientious concern for the general weal. Moreover, if from this hour we cheerfully and honestly abandon all sectional prejudice and distrust, and determine, with manly confidence in one another, to work out harmoniously the achievements of our national destiny, we shall deserve to realize all the benefits which our happy form of government can bestow.

On this auspicious occasion we may well renew the pledge of our devotion to the Constitution, which, launched by the founders of the Republic and consecrated by their prayers and patriotic devotion, has for almost a century borne the hopes and the aspirations of a great people through prosperity and peace and through the shock of foreign conflicts and the perils of domestic strife and vicissitudes.

By the Father of his Country our Constitution was commended for adoption as "the result of a spirit of amity and mutual concession." In that same spirit it should be administered, in order to promote the lasting welfare of the country and to secure the full measure of its priceless benefits to us and to those who will succeed to the blessings of our national life. The large variety of diverse and competing interests subject to Federal control, persistently seeking the recognition of their claims, need give us no fear that "the greatest good to the greatest number" will fail to be accomplished if in the halls of national legislation that spirit of amity and mutual concession shall prevail in which the Constitution had its birth. If this involves the surrender or postponement of private interests and the abandonment of local advantages, compensation will be found in the assurance that the common interest is subserved and the general welfare advanced.

In the discharge of my official duty I shall endeavor to be guided by a just and unstrained construction of the Constitution, a careful observance of the distinction between the powers granted to the Federal Government and those reserved to the States or to the people, and by a cautious appreciation of those functions which by the Constitution and laws have been especially assigned to the executive branch of the Government.

But he who takes the oath today to preserve, protect, and defend the Constitution of the United States only assumes the solemn obligation which every patriotic citizen—on the farm, in the workshop, in the busy marts of trade, and everywhere—should share with him. The Constitution which prescribes his oath, my countrymen, is yours; the Government you have chosen him to administer for a time is yours; the suffrage which executes the will of freemen is yours; the laws and the entire scheme of our civil rule, from the town meeting to the State capitals and the national capital, is yours. Your every voter, as surely as your Chief Magistrate, under the same high sanction, though in a different sphere, exercises a public trust. Nor is this all. Every citizen owes to the country a vigilant watch and close scrutiny of its public servants and a fair and reasonable estimate of their fidelity and usefulness. Thus is the people's will impressed upon the whole framework of our civil polity—municipal, State, and Federal; and this is the price of our liberty and the inspiration of our faith in the Republic.

It is the duty of those serving the people in public place to closely limit public expenditures to the actual needs of the Government economically administered, because this bounds the right of the Government to exact tribute from the earnings of labor or the property of the citizen, and because public extravagance begets extravagance among the people. We should never be ashamed of the simplicity and prudential economies which are best suited to the operation of a republican form of government and most compatible with the mission of the American people. Those who are selected for a limited time to manage public affairs are still of the people, and may do much by their example to encourage, consistently with the dignity of their official functions, that plain way of life which among their fellow-citizens aids integrity and promotes thrift and prosperity.

The genius of our institutions, the needs of our people in their home life, and the attention which is demanded for the settlement and development of the resources of our vast territory dictate the scrupulous avoidance of any departure from that foreign policy commended by the history, the traditions, and the prosperity of our Republic. It is the policy of independence, favored by our position and defended by our known love of justice and by our power. It is the policy of peace suitable to our interests. It is the policy of neutrality, rejecting any share in foreign broils and ambitions upon other continents and repelling their intrusion here. It is the policy of Monroe and of Washington and Jefferson—"Peace, commerce, and honest friendship with all nations; entangling alliance with none."

A due regard for the interests and prosperity of all the people demands that our finances shall be established upon such a sound and sensible basis as shall secure the safety and confidence of business interests and make the wage of labor sure and steady, and that our system of revenue shall be so adjusted as to relieve the people of unnecessary taxation, having a due regard to the interests of capital invested and workingmen employed in American industries, and preventing the accumulation of a surplus in the Treasury to tempt extravagance and waste.

Care for the property of the nation and for the needs of future settlers requires that the public domain should be protected from purloining schemes and unlawful occupation.

The conscience of the people demands that the Indians within our boundaries shall be fairly and honestly treated as wards of the Government and their education and civilization promoted with a view to their ultimate citizenship, and that polygamy in the Territories, destructive of the family relation and offensive to the moral sense of the civilized world, shall be repressed.

The laws should be rigidly enforced which prohibit the immigration of a servile class to compete with American labor, with no intention of acquiring citizenship, and bringing with them and retaining habits and customs repugnant to our civilization.

The people demand reform in the administration of the Government and the application of business principles to public affairs. As a means to this end, civil-service reform should be in good faith enforced. Our citizens have the right to protection from the incompetency of public employees who hold their places solely as the reward of partisan service, and from the corrupting influence of those who promise and the vicious methods of those who expect such rewards; and those who worthily seek public employment have the right to insist that merit and competency shall be recognized instead of party subserviency or the surrender of honest political belief.

In the administration of a government pledged to do equal and exact justice to all men there should be no pretext for anxiety touching the protection of the freedmen in their rights or their security in the enjoyment of their privileges under the Constitution and its amendments. All discussion as to their fitness for the place accorded to them as American citizens is idle and unprofitable except as it suggests the necessity for their improvement. The fact that they are citizens entitles them to all the rights due to that relation and charges them with all its duties, obligations, and responsibilities.

These topics and the constant and ever-varying wants of an active and enterprising population may well receive the attention and the patriotic endeavor of all who make and execute the Federal law. Our duties are practical and call for industrious application, an intelligent perception of the claims of public office, and, above all, a firm determination, by united action, to secure to all the people of the land the full benefits of the best form of government ever vouchsafed to man. And let us not trust to human effort alone, but humbly acknowledging the power and goodness of Almighty God, who presides over the destiny of nations, and who has at all times been revealed in our country's history, let us invoke His aid and His blessings upon our labors.

"A Fine Man, a Grand Man"

THE FIRST INAUGURAL ADDRESS OF GROVER CLEVELAND

Mark W. Summers

PROSY AND FREE from a single memorable phrase, Cleveland's First Inaugural Address was strikingly short: a thousand words less than Garfield's, and 1,500 fewer than Benjamin Harrison's. Perhaps that was because, rather than reading it, he memorized the whole thing and spoke it, hands clasped behind his back, like an elocution student delivering a discourse. "God, what a magnificent gambler," one Republican senator burst out.[1]

There was nothing of the gambler in "the faithful plodder"[2] who succeeded Chester Alan Arthur that March, nor in his style. His labored public documents expressed a duty-driven, sober workaholic, who had learned composition from his clergyman father and as a Buffalo lawyer had always been picked to write up obituary resolutions.[3] The first Democrat elected president since before the Civil War, Cleveland was well aware of how uneasily the Republican half of America greeted the change in the White House. Its congressional delegation bulging with "Rebel brigadiers," the Democratic party was notoriously the home for Confederate diehards and violent white supremacists. They had made a "Solid South" by intimidation and fraud and, as far as their enemies were concerned, had won only by preventing a free, fair count in the one-time slave states. Associated as the Democratic party was with Tammany Hall's scrofulous political machine, with Irish Catholicism, and with wide-open saloons, the Rev. Samuel D. Burchard blurted out what many believed and many others feared, that Democratic ascendancy meant a win for "rum, Romanism, and rebellion." As New York's reform governor and a man whose political career really began a generation after the Civil War, Cleveland had won the presidential nomination because of how little he seemed to fit that stereotype. But could the leader of a party feared as sectional and agrarian be trusted with the nation's industrial interests? Or would he follow so many of his fellow members in the South and West in supporting a currency supply inflated with the issue of additional silver coinage and a cut in the high protective tariff that would put factory workers at the mercy of low-earners' goods from overseas? Might his party even reopen the postwar settlement to restore what they had once boasted was "a white man's government"?

For that reassurance, Grover Cleveland did not need a long address—quite the reverse. Unlike his predecessor and successor, he would propose no laundry list of desirable legislation. Specifics were sure to stir controversy. In any case, Democrats leaned toward a cheap government that did as little as possible. Instead, the incoming president concentrated on setting a tone of safe, guarded reform under an executive determined neither to dictate to Congress nor to revolutionize the way things worked already. There would be no power-grabs like those that brought the last Democrat in the White House, Andrew Johnson, before the Senate on impeachment charges—no ambitions like those that Democrats had imputed to Ulysses S. Grant as a "Caesar" in the making. The president would maintain the 1883 Pendleton civil service law, with its hedges against any partisan scouring of the federal officeholders and its emphasis on the rewarding of merit, but not propose to widen its coverage. Unlike James Garfield, he would give no hint of tinkering with the monetary system, certainly not toward giving silver the same status as gold.[4] As for the protective tariff, Cleveland went no further than to urge that the revenue system be changed to prevent so much of the nation's money supply being locked up in Treasury vaults beyond what the government could spend and to hint that any alterations should guard the interests of industry and wage-earners.

Indeed, from the inaugural, one might easily conclude that Cleveland saw his office as purely administrative. Policy, apparently, was all Congress's doing, and the chief executive would show "a cautious appreciation of [his] functions." The promise to limit public spending might have meant nothing at all. Presidents always promised to see that the people's taxes got spent responsibly and were held to the bare minimum needed. Cleveland meant it, though. Unlike Garfield, he looked askance at any national aid to public education; unlike Benjamin Harrison, he did not couple his thrifty sentiments with an endorsement of money to dredge rivers and harbors and subsidize the country's merchant marine. Listeners could not know that the new president would go out of his way to veto bills providing relief to drought-stricken ranchers, private claims, and, most controversially, 228 individual pension bills for Union veterans whose claims he found undeserving.[5]

Nor could they know that within three years, Cleveland had realized that, when it came to the tariff, Congress had a gift for doing nothing (quite aggressively and at endless length) and that a presidential initiative must push them toward serious downward reform. Then he showed his other side, in one newspaper's words, rushing at big things "as unhesitatingly as a rock out of a catapult at a plate glass window, smashing them all to pieces."[6] (But then, if they had known that before the 1884 election, Cleveland certainly would have lost. That was why he had dodged the issue, while the Democratic platform faced both ways at once.)

At the same time, Cleveland needed to reassure Republicans that the change in the White House did not mean a Democratic ascendancy. There would be, as the Boston *Advertiser* remarked, "no backward look," no "undoing."[7] The election proved that whoever took power, the republic was in no danger. Elected by one party, the president saw himself as custodian for all the people, regardless of section or race. That his opponents allowed a smooth transition, he hinted, showed the excellence of free government—and to Democrats with bitter memories of the so-called stolen election of 1876, may have been the gentlest of swipes at another year when the apparent losers played nowhere near so fair a game. His appeal for an end to rancor between North and South brought the loudest cheer of any in the audience. Some saw it as a rebuke to the Republican "bloody shirt" rhetoric, branding its opponents as once and future traitors; others saw it as a commitment to let the Reconstruction settlement stand, and Cleveland nailed down that impression by affirming that, however bitter past disputes had been, the emancipation and extension of rights to the freedpeople were no longer in dispute. Famous for a statement put into his mouth by another, Cleveland's main point in his inaugural was to assert that public office was, indeed, a public trust, and not only for officers elected nationally, but at every level of government.

Government "is a matter of practical acts and not of glittering generalities," the Philadelphia *Press* complained, "and when we look through what President Cleveland says to see what he will do, we do not find it."[8] A fair complaint, though in retrospect, vague phrases would take on weight as ponderous as the incumbent's own. He had been conspicuously silent about appointing officers on merit alone, as civil service reformers wanted. Sure enough, most Republicans whose fixed term ended would have Democrats replacing them.[9] In the South, that meant that the many Black postmasters had white successors, even if Cleveland showed himself reasonably liberal for a member of his party in occasionally nominating an African American for a prominent patronage position (which made smart politics with a Republican Senate uncomfortable about drawing the white line tighter than a Democratic president did). The mainstream press did not notice how, unlike his predecessor and successor, Cleveland spent no sentences denouncing the suppression of the Black vote in the South. In any case, they very likely expected that the federal enforcement laws, giving nominal protection to non-white voters, would fall into what the president would have called "innocuous desuetude"—as indeed they did.[10] The Democratic South could proceed toward wiping out any opposition party without the least hindrance from Washington.

For labor, Cleveland offered no help, beyond calling for sterner enforcement of laws to keep "a servile class . . . retaining habits and customs repugnant to our civilization" from settling in America. Nobody doubted who he meant: the Chinese, excluded under an 1882 law for ten years. The new administration would try to make the ban permanent and to prevent those who left the United States from re-entering it. Other immigrants the president had no word against. Any literacy or property requirement for newcomers would have cut deep into Democratic constituencies. So, not surprisingly, when Congress put through a literacy test, Cleveland would veto it.[11]

Cleveland's inaugural did give hints of where his administration meant to go. On foreign policy, he called for an American presence friendly to all, allied to none. There would be no talk of countering foreign designs on the Western Hemisphere or negotiating commercial treaties. The emphasis on restraint may have been hinting at what a contrast he would be to the man he beat for president, James G. Blaine, whose aggressiveness in promoting American hemispheric influence earned him (not all that fairly) the nickname "Jingo Jim." It certainly meant that the recently negotiated treaty looking to the building of an isthmian canal was no better than waste paper; by choosing the treaty's fiercest enemy, Senator Thomas F. Bayard, for secretary of state, Cleveland made that doubly sure.[12]

Cleveland also spoke of the need for action against the land-grabbers out west. It was a promise his administration kept. Even some of his most generous campaign contributors found themselves forced to surrender lands claimed and forfeited because the conditions of the grants had gone unfulfilled.[13] The president's assertion that Native Americans should be protected and helped toward full citizenship found its realization in moves to drive squatters off their land. In 1887, the Dawes Severalty Act—aiming, however defectively, toward integrating the tribes into white society—had Cleveland's support, though he rightly worried that it would strip the nation's wards of too much of their property too quickly, however benevolently the proceeds from selling it were used.[14]

"Ah, sure, he's the greatest man I ever saw," one visitor to the White House exclaimed. "He's a fine man—a grand man. *He wouldn't promise to do one d—d thing I asked him!*"[15] The country could have done worse than Cleveland in his first term. And it did—in his second—for Cleveland's conscience left him with no flexibility about his principles. "Had he started out in 1893 with the deliberate purpose of killing off all of the few great men in the Democratic party and then destroying it beyond hope of repair, he could not have succeeded more admirably," a reporter commented later.[16] But already, could one sense how confined the Democratic party's concept of reform was? Conscientious, clean government Americans would get. To one partisan who chided him for slowness in advancing "the principles of the Democratic party," Cleveland snapped, "I suppose you mean that I should appoint two horse-thieves a day, instead of one."[17] Nor was it necessarily a bad thing to be, in another associate's words, "the kind of man who would rather do something badly for himself than to have somebody else do it well."[18] Administrative restraint and modest promises cautiously carried out all gave the country a sense of security that it preferred and the Democrats the respectable reputation that they needed. But the problems of a country rapidly being transformed by a globalizing economy, by industrial power, and the untrammeled authority of those whose aim was democracy and had the shotguns to deliver it fatal rounds may have needed the boldness that a Cleveland could not give. Gilded Age America may not have been the gainer by a system where the president promised scarcely more than to be a good caretaker.

Notes

1. Allan Nevins, *Grover Cleveland: A Study in Courage* (New York: Dodd, Mead, 1932), 206.
2. A description by his friend and close associate, Congressman William L. Wilson. Festus P. Summers, ed., *The Cabinet Diary of William L. Wilson* (Chapel Hill: University of North Carolina Press, 1957), 245.
3. Chauncey M. Depew, *My Memories of Eighty Years* (New York and London: Charles Scribner's Sons, 1922), 128.
4. Nevins, *Grover Cleveland: A Study in Courage*, 203–204, 266–277.
5. Nevins, *Grover Cleveland: A Study in Courage*, 326–332; Richard E. Welch, Jr., *The Presidencies of Grover Cleveland* (Lawrence: University Press of Kansas, 1988), 62–63. Less publicity attended the 1,871 that he allowed to pass.
6. *Brooklyn Daily Eagle*, November 8, 1888.
7. *New York Times*, March 6, 1885.
8. *New York Times*, March 6, 1885.
9. Nevins, *Grover Cleveland: A Study in Courage*, 246–252.
10. Welch, *The Presidencies of Grover Cleveland*, 65–67.
11. Welch, *The Presidencies of Grover Cleveland*, 71–73.
12. Nevins, *Grover Cleveland: A Study in Courage*, 205.
13. Nevins, *Grover Cleveland: A Study in Courage*, 223–228, 359–361.
14. Nevins, *Grover Cleveland: A Study in Courage*, 228–30, 357–359; Welch, *The Presidencies of Grover Cleveland*, 69–71.

15. Harry T. Peck, *Twenty Years of the Republic* (New York: Dodd, Mead & Company, 1919), 304.
16. O. O. Stealey, *Twenty Years in the Press Gallery* (New York: Publishers Printing Company, 1906), 28.
17. Peck, *Twenty Years of the Republic*, 78.
18. George F. Parker, *Recollections of Grover Cleveland* (New York: The Century Company, 1909), 340–341.

Benjamin Harrison's Inaugural Address

MONDAY, MARCH 4, 1889

FELLOW-CITIZENS:

There is no constitutional or legal requirement that the President shall take the oath of office in the presence of the people, but there is so manifest an appropriateness in the public induction to office of the chief executive officer of the nation that from the beginning of the Government the people, to whose service the official oath consecrates the officer, have been called to witness the solemn ceremonial. The oath taken in the presence of the people becomes a mutual covenant. The officer covenants to serve the whole body of the people by a faithful execution of the laws, so that they may be the unfailing defense and security of those who respect and observe them, and that neither wealth, station, nor the power of combinations shall be able to evade their just penalties or to wrest them from a beneficent public purpose to serve the ends of cruelty or selfishness.

My promise is spoken; yours unspoken, but not the less real and solemn. The people of every State have here their representatives. Surely I do not misinterpret the spirit of the occasion when I assume that the whole body of the people covenant with me and with each other to-day to support and defend the Constitution and the Union of the States, to yield willing obedience to all the laws and each to every other citizen his equal civil and political rights. Entering thus solemnly into covenant with each other, we may reverently invoke and confidently expect the favor and help of Almighty God—that He will give to me wisdom, strength, and fidelity, and to our people a spirit of fraternity and a love of righteousness and peace.

This occasion derives peculiar interest from the fact that the Presidential term which begins this day is the twenty-sixth under our Constitution. The first inauguration of President Washington took place in New York, where Congress was then sitting, on the 30th day of April, 1789, having been deferred by reason of delays attending the organization of the Congress and the canvass of the electoral vote. Our people have already worthily observed the centennials of the Declaration of Independence, of the battle of Yorktown, and of the adoption of the Constitution, and will shortly celebrate in New York the institution of the second great department of our constitutional scheme of government. When the centennial of the institution of the judicial department, by the organization of the Supreme Court, shall have been suitably observed, as I trust it will be, our nation will have fully entered its second century.

I will not attempt to note the marvelous and in great part happy contrasts between our country as it steps over the threshold into its second century of organized existence under the Constitution and that weak but wisely ordered young nation that looked undauntedly down the first century, when all its years stretched out before it.

Our people will not fail at this time to recall the incidents which accompanied the institution of government under the Constitution, or to find inspiration and guidance in the teachings and example of Washington and his great associates, and hope and courage in the contrast which thirty-eight populous and prosperous States offer to the thirteen States, weak in everything except courage and the love of liberty, that then fringed our Atlantic seaboard.

The Territory of Dakota has now a population greater than any of the original States (except Virginia) and greater than the aggregate of five of the smaller States in 1790. The center of population when our national capital was located was east of Baltimore, and it was argued by many well-informed persons that it would move eastward rather than westward; yet in 1880 it was found to be near Cincinnati, and the new census about to be taken will show another stride to the westward. That which was the body has come to be only the rich fringe of the nation's robe. But our growth has not been limited to territory, population and aggregate wealth, marvelous as it has been in each of those directions. The masses of our people are better fed, clothed, and housed than their fathers were. The facilities for popular education have been vastly enlarged and more generally diffused.

The virtues of courage and patriotism have given recent proof of their continued presence and increasing power in the hearts and over the lives of our people. The influences of religion have been multiplied and strengthened. The sweet offices of charity have greatly increased. The virtue of temperance is held in higher estimation. We have not attained an ideal condition. Not all of our people are happy and prosperous; not all of them are virtuous and law-abiding. But on the whole the opportunities offered to the individual to secure the comforts of life are better than are found elsewhere and largely better than they were here one hundred years ago.

The surrender of a large measure of sovereignty to the General Government, effected by the adoption of the Constitution, was not accomplished until the suggestions of reason were strongly reenforced by the more imperative voice of experience. The divergent interests of peace speedily demanded a "more perfect union." The merchant, the shipmaster, and the manufacturer discovered and disclosed to our statesmen and to the people that commercial emancipation must be added to the political freedom which had been so bravely won. The commercial policy of the mother country had not relaxed any of its hard and oppressive features. To hold in check the development of our commercial marine, to prevent or retard the establishment and growth of manufactures in the States, and so to secure the American market for their shops and the carrying trade for their ships, was the policy of European statesmen, and was pursued with the most selfish vigor.

Petitions poured in upon Congress urging the imposition of discriminating duties that should encourage the production of needed things at home. The patriotism of the people, which no longer found a field of exercise in war, was energetically directed to the duty of equipping the young Republic for the defense of its independence by making its people self-dependent. Societies for the promotion of home manufactures and for encouraging the use of domestics in the dress of the people were organized in many of the States. The revival at the end of the century of the same patriotic interest in the preservation and development of domestic industries and the defense of our working people against injurious foreign competition is an incident worthy of attention. It is not a departure but a return that we have witnessed. The protective policy had then its opponents. The argument was made, as now, that its benefits inured to particular classes or sections.

If the question became in any sense or at any time sectional, it was only because slavery existed in some of the States. But for this there was no reason why the cotton-producing States should not have led or walked abreast with the New England States in the production of cotton fabrics. There was this reason only why the States that divide with Pennsylvania the mineral treasures of the great southeastern and central mountain ranges should have been so tardy in bringing to the smelting furnace and to the mill the coal and iron from their near opposing hillsides. Mill fires were lighted at the funeral pile of slavery. The Emancipation Proclamation was heard in the depths of the earth as well as in the sky; men were made free, and material things became our better servants.

The sectional element has happily been eliminated from the tariff discussion. We have no longer States that are necessarily only planting States. None are excluded from achieving that diversification of pursuits among the people which brings wealth and contentment. The cotton plantation will not be less valuable when the product is spun in the country town by operatives whose necessities call for diversified crops and create a home demand for garden and agricultural products. Every new mine, furnace, and factory is an extension of the productive capacity of the State more real and valuable than added territory.

Shall the prejudices and paralysis of slavery continue to hang upon the skirts of progress? How long will those who rejoice that slavery no longer exists cherish or tolerate the incapacities it put upon their communities? I look hopefully to the continuance of our protective system and to the consequent development of manufacturing and mining enterprises in the States hitherto wholly given to agriculture as a potent influence in the perfect unification of our people. The men who have invested their capital in these enterprises, the farmers who have felt the benefit of their neighborhood, and the men who work in shop or field will not fail to find and to defend a community of interest.

Is it not quite possible that the farmers and the promoters of the great mining and manufacturing enterprises which have recently been established in the South may yet find that the free ballot of the workingman, without distinction of race, is needed for their defense as well as for his own? I do not doubt that if those men in the South who now accept the tariff views of Clay and the constitutional expositions of Webster would courageously avow and defend their real convictions they would not find it difficult, by friendly instruction and cooperation, to make the black man their efficient and safe ally, not only in establishing correct principles in our national administration, but in preserving for their local communities the benefits of social order and economical and honest government. At least until the good offices of kindness and education have been fairly tried the contrary conclusion can not be plausibly urged.

I have altogether rejected the suggestion of a special Executive policy for any section of our country. It is the duty of the Executive to administer and enforce in the methods and by the instrumentalities pointed out and provided by the Constitution all the laws enacted by Congress. These laws are general and their administration should be uniform and equal. As a citizen may not elect what laws he will obey, neither may the Executive eject which he will enforce. The duty to obey and to execute embraces the Constitution in its entirety and the whole code of laws enacted under it. The evil example of permitting individuals, corporations, or communities to nullify the laws because they cross some selfish or local interest or prejudices is full of danger, not only to the nation at large, but much more to those who use this pernicious expedient to escape their just obligations or to obtain an unjust advantage over others. They will presently themselves be compelled to appeal to the law for protection, and those who would use the law as a defense must not deny that use of it to others.

If our great corporations would more scrupulously observe their legal limitations and duties, they would have less cause to complain of the unlawful limitations of their rights or of violent interference with their operations. The community that by concert, open or secret, among its citizens denies to a portion of its members their plain rights under the law has severed the only safe bond of social order and prosperity. The evil works from a bad center both ways. It demoralizes those who practice it and destroys the faith of those who suffer by it in the efficiency of the law as a safe protector. The man in whose breast that faith has been darkened is naturally the subject of dangerous and uncanny suggestions. Those who use unlawful methods, if moved by no higher motive than the selfishness that prompted them, may well stop and inquire what is to be the end of this.

An unlawful expedient can not become a permanent condition of government. If the educated and influential classes in a community either practice or connive at the systematic violation of laws that seem to them to cross their convenience, what can they expect when the lesson that convenience or a supposed class interest is a sufficient cause for lawlessness has been well learned by the ignorant classes? A community where law is the rule of conduct and where courts, not mobs, execute its penalties is the only attractive field for business investments and honest labor.

Our naturalization laws should be so amended as to make the inquiry into the character and good disposition of persons applying for citizenship more careful and searching. Our existing laws have been in their administration an unimpressive and often an unintelligible form. We accept the man as a citizen without any knowledge of his fitness, and he assumes the duties of citizenship without any knowledge as to what they are. The privileges of American citizenship are so great and its duties so grave that we may well insist upon a good knowledge of every person applying for citizenship and a good knowledge by him of our institutions. We should not cease to be hospitable to immigration, but we should cease to be careless as to the character of it. There are men of all races, even the best, whose coming is necessarily a burden upon our public revenues or a threat to social order. These should be identified and excluded.

We have happily maintained a policy of avoiding all interference with European affairs. We have been only interested spectators of their contentions in diplomacy and in war, ready to use our friendly offices to promote peace, but never obtruding our advice and never attempting unfairly to coin the distresses of other powers into commercial advantage to ourselves. We have a just right to expect that our European policy will be the American policy of European courts.

It is so manifestly incompatible with those precautions for our peace and safety which all the great powers habitually observe and enforce in matters affecting them that a shorter waterway between our eastern and western seaboards should be dominated by any European Government that we may confidently expect that such a purpose will not be entertained by any friendly power.

We shall in the future, as in the past, use every endeavor to maintain and enlarge our friendly relations with all the great powers, but they will not expect us to look kindly upon any project that would leave us subject to the dangers of a hostile observation or environment. We have not sought to dominate or to absorb any of our weaker neighbors, but rather to aid and encourage them to establish free and stable governments resting upon the consent of their own people. We have a clear right to expect, therefore, that no European Government will seek to establish colonial dependencies upon the territory of these independent American States. That which a sense of justice restrains us from seeking they may be reasonably expected willingly to forego.

It must not be assumed, however, that our interests are so exclusively American that our entire inattention to any events that may transpire elsewhere can be taken for granted. Our citizens domiciled for purposes of trade in all countries and in many of the islands of the sea demand and will have our adequate care in their personal and commercial rights. The necessities of our Navy require convenient coaling stations and dock and harbor privileges. These and other trading privileges we will feel free to obtain only by means that do not in any degree partake of coercion, however feeble the government from which we ask such concessions. But having fairly obtained them by methods and for purposes entirely consistent with the most friendly disposition toward all other powers, our consent will be necessary to any modification or impairment of the concession.

We shall neither fail to respect the flag of any friendly nation or the just rights of its citizens, nor to exact the like treatment for our own. Calmness, justice, and consideration should characterize our diplomacy. The offices of an intelligent diplomacy or of friendly arbitration in proper cases should be adequate to the peaceful adjustment of all international difficulties. By such methods we will make our contribution to the world's peace, which no nation values more highly, and avoid the opprobrium which must fall upon the nation that ruthlessly breaks it.

The duty devolved by law upon the President to nominate and, by and with the advice and consent of the Senate, to appoint all public officers whose appointment is not otherwise provided for in the Constitution or by act of Congress has become very burdensome and its wise and efficient discharge full of difficulty. The civil list is so large that a personal knowledge of any large number of the applicants is impossible. The President must rely upon the representations of others, and these are often made inconsiderately and without any just sense of responsibility. I have a right, I think, to insist that those who volunteer or are invited to give advice as to appointments shall exercise consideration and fidelity.

A high sense of duty and an ambition to improve the service should characterize all public officers.

There are many ways in which the convenience and comfort of those who have business with our public offices may be promoted by a thoughtful and obliging officer, and I shall expect those whom I may appoint to justify their selection by a conspicuous efficiency in the discharge of their duties. Honorable party service will certainly not be esteemed by me a disqualification for public office, but it will in no case be allowed to serve as a shield of official negligence, incompetency, or delinquency. It is entirely creditable to seek public office by proper methods and with proper motives, and all applicants will be treated with consideration; but I shall need, and the heads of Departments will need, time for inquiry and deliberation. Persistent importunity will not, therefore, be the best support of an application for office. Heads of Departments, bureaus, and all other public officers having any duty connected therewith will be expected to enforce the civil-service law fully and without evasion. Beyond this obvious duty I hope to do something more to advance the reform of the civil service. The ideal, or even my own ideal, I shall probably not attain. Retrospect will be a safer basis of judgment than promises. We shall not, however, I am sure, be able to put our civil service upon a nonpartisan basis until we have secured an incumbency that fair-minded men of the opposition will approve for impartiality and integrity. As the number of such in the civil list is increased removals from office will diminish.

While a Treasury surplus is not the greatest evil, it is a serious evil. Our revenue should be ample to meet the ordinary annual demands upon our Treasury, with a sufficient margin for those extraordinary but scarcely less imperative demands which arise now and then. Expenditure should always be made with economy and only upon public necessity. Wastefulness, profligacy, or favoritism in public expenditures is criminal. But there is nothing in the condition of our country or of our people to suggest that anything presently necessary to the public prosperity, security, or honor should be unduly postponed.

It will be the duty of Congress wisely to forecast and estimate these extraordinary demands, and, having added them to our ordinary expenditures, to so adjust our revenue laws that no considerable annual surplus will remain. We will fortunately be able to apply to the redemption of the public debt any small and unforeseen excess of revenue. This is better than to reduce our income below our necessary expenditures, with the resulting choice between another change of our revenue laws and an increase of the public debt. It is quite possible, I am sure, to effect the necessary reduction in our revenues without breaking down our protective tariff or seriously injuring any domestic industry.

The construction of a sufficient number of modern war ships and of their necessary armament should progress as rapidly as is consistent with care and perfection in plans and workmanship. The spirit, courage, and skill of our naval officers and seamen have many times in our history given to weak ships and inefficient guns a rating greatly beyond that of the naval list. That they will again do so upon occasion I do not doubt; but they ought not, by premeditation or neglect, to be left to the risks and exigencies of an unequal combat. We should encourage the establishment of American steamship lines. The exchanges of commerce demand stated, reliable, and rapid means of communication, and until these are provided the development of our trade with the States lying south of us is impossible.

Our pension laws should give more adequate and discriminating relief to the Union soldiers and sailors and to their widows and orphans. Such occasions as this should remind us that we owe everything to their valor and sacrifice.

It is a subject of congratulation that there is a near prospect of the admission into the Union of the Dakotas and Montana and Washington Territories. This act of justice has been unreasonably delayed in the case of some of them. The people who have settled these Territories are intelligent, enterprising, and patriotic, and the accession of these new States will add strength to the nation. It is due to the settlers in the Territories who have availed themselves of the invitations of our land laws to make homes upon the public domain that their titles should be speedily adjusted and their honest entries confirmed by patent.

It is very gratifying to observe the general interest now being manifested in the reform of our election laws. Those who have been for years calling attention to the pressing necessity of throwing about the ballot box and about the elector further safeguards, in order that our elections might not only be free and pure, but might clearly appear to be so, will welcome the accession of any who did not so soon discover the need of reform. The National Congress has not as yet taken control of elections in that case over which the Constitution gives it jurisdiction, but has accepted and adopted the election laws of the several States, provided penalties for their violation and a method of supervision. Only the inefficiency of the State laws or an unfair partisan administration of them could suggest a departure from this policy.

It was clearly, however, in the contemplation of the framers of the Constitution that such an exigency might arise, and provision was wisely made for it. The freedom of the ballot is a condition of our national life, and no power vested in Congress or in the Executive to secure or perpetuate it should remain unused upon occasion. The people of all the Congressional districts have an equal interest that the election in each shall truly express the views and wishes of a majority of the qualified electors residing within it. The results of such elections are not local, and the insistence of electors residing in other districts that they shall be pure and free does not savor at all of impertinence.

If in any of the States the public security is thought to be threatened by ignorance among the electors, the obvious remedy is education. The sympathy and help of our people will not be withheld from any community struggling with special embarrassments or difficulties connected with the suffrage if the remedies proposed proceed upon lawful lines and are promoted by just and honorable methods. How shall those who practice election frauds recover that respect for the sanctity of the ballot which is the first condition and obligation of good citizenship? The man who has come to regard the ballot box as a juggler's hat has renounced his allegiance.

Let us exalt patriotism and moderate our party contentions. Let those who would die for the flag on the field of battle give a better proof of their patriotism and a higher glory to their country by promoting fraternity and justice. A party success that is achieved by unfair methods or by practices that partake of revolution is hurtful and evanescent even from a party standpoint. We should hold our differing opinions in mutual respect, and, having submitted them to the arbitrament of the ballot, should accept an adverse judgment with the same respect that we would have demanded of our opponents if the decision had been in our favor.

No other people have a government more worthy of their respect and love or a land so magnificent in extent, so pleasant to look upon, and so full of generous suggestion to enterprise and labor. God has placed upon our head a diadem and has laid at our feet power and wealth beyond definition or calculation. But we must not forget that we take these gifts upon the condition that justice and mercy shall hold the reins of power and that the upward avenues of hope shall be free to all the people.

I do not mistrust the future. Dangers have been in frequent ambush along our path, but we have uncovered and vanquished them all. Passion has swept some of our communities, but only to give us a new demonstration that the great body of our people are stable, patriotic, and law-abiding. No political party can long pursue advantage at the expense of public honor or by rude and indecent methods without protest and fatal disaffection in its own body. The peaceful agencies of commerce are more fully revealing the necessary unity of all our communities, and the increasing intercourse of our people is promoting mutual respect. We shall find unalloyed pleasure in the revelation which our next census will make of the swift development of the great resources of some of the States. Each State will bring its generous contribution to the great aggregate of the nation's increase. And when the harvests from the fields, the cattle from the hills, and the ores of the earth shall have been weighed, counted, and valued, we will turn from them all to crown with the highest honor the State that has most promoted education, virtue, justice, and patriotism among its people.

Little Ben

THE INAUGURAL ADDRESS OF BENJAMIN HARRISON

Allan B. Spetter

BENJAMIN HARRISON, THE only grandson of a president, William Henry Harrison, to serve as president as well, understood the difficult position he faced almost from the moment he took office. He took the oath of office one hundred years after George Washington did so on April 30, 1789, in New York City. Harrison would be the "centennial president" and would be compared unfavorably to Washington.

Furthermore, Harrison had not won the popular vote. No individual would envy Harrison's situation. Harrison, however, spoke confidently about what the nation had accomplished over the past century and about the unlimited possibilities of the nation's future. Harrison began by reviewing the remarkable movement of Americans into the vast spaces of the Great Plains in the quarter-century since the end of the Civil War.

He pointed out that the Dakota Territory, so large that it would be split in half and admitted to the Union as two separate states in 1889, had a larger population, estimated at between 150,000 and 200,000, than all but one, Virginia, of the thirteen original states according to the census of 1790. (Virginia's population of almost 750,000 in the census of 1790 included almost 300,000 slaves).

Harrison, who fought with distinction in the Civil War and rose to the rank of brigadier general, emphasized that the end of slavery provided the South with the opportunity to participate in the tremendous growth of the nation's industrial economy. He asked, rather eloquently, "Shall the prejudices and paralysis of slavery continue to hang upon the skirts of progress?" He called for an improved pension program for Union soldiers and sailors and their widows and orphans. Congress would respond with the Dependent Pension Act of 1890.

It has been said that Harrison tried to do more for the civil rights of African Americans than any president in the thirty-five years between Lincoln and Teddy Roosevelt. He appealed to the men of the South to realize that a free ballot would benefit both whites and African Americans. He expressed the continuing belief of Republicans of that era that the men who had invested to build an industrial economy in the South would accept the Black man as an ally in that effort.

Harrison devoted much of the rest of his Inaugural Address to his vision of the United States becoming a "great power." To begin with, he made a very strong statement about any future canal linking the Atlantic and Pacific oceans. He said: "It is so manifestly incompatible with the precautions for our peace and safety . . . that a shorter waterway between our eastern and western seaboards should be dominated by any European Government."

He went on to explain the foundations of what has been called the "new empire" of the United States. Harrison said: "the necessities of our Navy require convenient coaling stations and dock and harbor privileges." Harrison engaged in a drawn-out attempt to acquire a naval base in Haiti that would protect the Atlantic side of any future canal. Although he believed that Haiti had promised to turn over the base, he could not make the decision to use force.

Harrison tried to take the first steps toward creation of an American empire. Some scholars have suggested that the Pacific and the Asian continent should not be considered the Far East from the American perspective but the "Far west." He reached out into the Pacific and agreed to share control of the Samoan islands with Germany. He attempted to annex Hawaii but would be thwarted by Grover Cleveland, the next president and an ardent anti-imperialist.

Harrison supported an ill-fated attempt by private interests to build a canal across Nicaragua as an alternative to a canal across Panama that would be under the control of French private interests. He realized that a canal and naval bases required a modern navy. Construction of the first modern warships built of steel began in the 1880s, but that handful of ships consisted only of cruisers of varying size and two vessels described as second-class battleships.

Harrison and his closest friend, Secretary of the Navy Benjamin Franklin Tracy, would oversee a giant leap forward for American naval power. Tracy waged an unrelenting campaign to persuade Congress to approve construction of the first three real battleships, the *Indiana*, the *Massachusetts*, and the *Oregon* in 1890. Of more than 10,000 tons displacement, the ships would be dubbed "coastline" battleships to indicate their defensive purpose.

By 1892, however, Congress would approve construction of the first "seagoing" battleship, the mighty *Iowa*, of 11,400 tons displacement. Congress also approved construction of several larger cruisers. Construction material moved forward from steel to armor. Tracy had lamented that the United States had only the twelfth most powerful navy in the world. Harrison and Tracy put the nation on the path toward becoming the sixth largest naval power in the world.

The nation seemed to fill in dramatically by the 1890s. Six new states entered the Union in 1889–1890: North Dakota and South Dakota, Idaho, Wyoming, Montana, and Washington, more than in any other administration. Legendary historian Frederick Jackson Turner would declare in an essay written in 1893 that, according to the census of 1890, the frontier had disappeared. Some Americans believed that there could be a new frontier, however, in the Pacific and even on the Asian continent.

Harrison did his best to further that idea. He may have been a bit premature. If he had won a second term, the United States almost certainly would have annexed Hawaii before 1898. Near the end of his Inaugural Address, Harrison stated confidently, "I do not mistrust the future." His aggressive foreign policy initiatives prepared the United States for the challenges of the twentieth century.

Neither Harrison nor any of his contemporaries could have imagined that the economy would plunge into the second worst depression in the nation's history shortly after Harrison left office in 1893. The depression almost certainly resulted from too rapid an expansion of the railroad system and the continuing overproduction of the agricultural sector. The economy would hit bottom in 1894 and slowly recover between 1895 and 1897.

Grover Cleveland's Second Inaugural Address

SATURDAY, MARCH 4, 1893

MY FELLOW-CITIZENS:

In obedience of the mandate of my countrymen I am about to dedicate myself to their service under the sanction of a solemn oath. Deeply moved by the expression of confidence and personal attachment which has called me to this service, I am sure my gratitude can make no better return than the pledge I now give before God and these witnesses of unreserved and complete devotion to the interests and welfare of those who have honored me.

I deem it fitting on this occasion, while indicating the opinion I hold concerning public questions of present importance, to also briefly refer to the existence of certain conditions and tendencies among our people which seem to menace the integrity and usefulness of their Government.

While every American citizen must contemplate with the utmost pride and enthusiasm the growth and expansion of our country, the sufficiency of our institutions to stand against the rudest shocks of violence, the wonderful thrift and enterprise of our people, and the demonstrated superiority of our free government, it behooves us to constantly watch for every symptom of insidious infirmity that threatens our national vigor.

The strong man who in the confidence of sturdy health courts the sternest activities of life and rejoices in the hardihood of constant labor may still have lurking near his vitals the unheeded disease that dooms him to sudden collapse.

It can not be doubted that our stupendous achievements as a people and our country's robust strength have given rise to heedlessness of those laws governing our national health which we can no more evade than human life can escape the laws of God and nature.

Manifestly nothing is more vital to our supremacy as a nation and to the beneficent purposes of our Government than a sound and stable currency. Its exposure to degradation should at once arouse to activity the most enlightened statesmanship, and the danger of depreciation in the purchasing power of the wages paid to toil should furnish the strongest incentive to prompt and conservative precaution.

In dealing with our present embarrassing situation as related to this subject we will be wise if we temper our confidence and faith in our national strength and resources with the frank concession that even these will not permit us to defy with impunity the inexorable laws of finance and trade. At the same time, in our efforts to adjust differences of opinion we should be free from intolerance or passion, and our judgments should be unmoved by alluring phrases and unvexed by selfish interests.

I am confident that such an approach to the subject will result in prudent and effective remedial legislation. In the meantime, so far as the executive branch of the Government can intervene, none of the powers with which it is invested will be withheld when their exercise is deemed necessary to maintain our national credit or avert financial disaster.

Closely related to the exaggerated confidence in our country's greatness which tends to a disregard of the rules of national safety, another danger confronts us not less serious. I refer to the prevalence of a popular disposition to expect from the operation of the Government especial and direct individual advantages.

The verdict of our voters which condemned the injustice of maintaining protection for protection's sake enjoins upon the people's servants the duty of exposing and destroying the brood of kindred evils which are the unwholesome progeny of paternalism. This is the bane of republican institutions and the constant peril of our government by the people. It degrades to the purposes of wily craft the plan of rule our fathers established and bequeathed to us as an object of our love and veneration. It perverts the patriotic sentiments of our countrymen and tempts them to pitiful calculation of the sordid gain to be derived from their Government's maintenance. It undermines the self-reliance of our people and substitutes in its place dependence upon governmental favoritism. It stifles the spirit of true Americanism and stupefies every ennobling trait of American citizenship.

The lessons of paternalism ought to be unlearned and the better lesson taught that while the people should patriotically and cheerfully support their Government its functions do not include the support of the people.

The acceptance of this principle leads to a refusal of bounties and subsidies, which burden the labor and thrift of a portion of our citizens to aid ill-advised or languishing enterprises in which they have no concern. It leads also to a challenge of wild and reckless pension expenditure, which overleaps the bounds of grateful recognition of patriotic service and prostitutes to vicious uses the people's prompt and generous impulse to aid those disabled in their country's defense.

Every thoughtful American must realize the importance of checking at its beginning any tendency in public or private station to regard frugality and economy as virtues which we may safely outgrow. The toleration of this idea results in the waste of the people's money by their chosen servants and encourages prodigality and extravagance in the home life of our countrymen.

Under our scheme of government the waste of public money is a crime against the citizen, and the contempt of our people for economy and frugality in their personal affairs deplorably saps the strength and sturdiness of our national character.

It is a plain dictate of honesty and good government that public expenditures should be limited by public necessity, and that this should be measured by the rules of strict economy; and it is equally clear that frugality among the people is the best guaranty of a contented and strong support of free institutions.

One mode of the misappropriation of public funds is avoided when appointments to office, instead of being the rewards of partisan activity, are awarded to those whose efficiency promises a fair return of work for the compensation paid to them. To secure the fitness and competency of appointees to office and remove from political action the demoralizing madness for spoils, civil-service reform has found a place in our public policy and laws. The benefits already gained through this instrumentality and the further usefulness it promises entitle it to the hearty support and encouragement of all who desire to see our public service well performed or who hope for the elevation of political sentiment and the purification of political methods.

The existence of immense aggregations of kindred enterprises and combinations of business interests formed for the purpose of limiting production and fixing prices is inconsistent with the fair field which ought to be open to every independent activity. Legitimate strife in business should not be superseded by an enforced concession to the demands of combinations that have the power to destroy, nor should the people to be served lose the benefit of cheapness which usually results from wholesome competition. These aggregations and combinations frequently constitute conspiracies against the interests of the people, and in all their phases they are unnatural and opposed to our American sense of fairness. To the extent that they can be reached and restrained by Federal power the General Government should relieve our citizens from their interference and exactions.

Loyalty to the principles upon which our Government rests positively demands that the equality before the law which it guarantees to every citizen should be justly and in good faith conceded in all parts of the land. The enjoyment of this right follows the badge of citizenship wherever found, and, unimpaired by race or color, it appeals for recognition to American manliness and fairness.

Our relations with the Indians located within our border impose upon us responsibilities we can not escape. Humanity and consistency require us to treat them with forbearance and in our dealings with them to honestly and considerately regard their rights and interests. Every effort should be made to lead them, through the paths of civilization and education, to self-supporting and independent citizenship. In the meantime, as the nation's wards, they should be promptly defended against the cupidity of designing men and shielded from every influence or temptation that retards their advancement.

The people of the United States have decreed that on this day the control of their Government in its legislative and executive branches shall be given to a political party pledged in the most positive terms to the accomplishment of tariff reform. They have thus determined in favor of a more just and equitable system of Federal taxation. The agents they have chosen to carry out their purposes are bound by their promises not less than by the command of their masters to devote themselves unremittingly to this service.

While there should be no surrender of principle, our task must be undertaken wisely and without heedless vindictiveness. Our mission is not punishment, but the rectification of wrong. If in lifting burdens from the daily life of our people we reduce inordinate and unequal advantages too long enjoyed, this is but a necessary incident of our return to right and justice. If we exact from unwilling minds acquiescence in the theory of an honest distribution of the fund of the governmental beneficence treasured up for all, we but insist upon a principle which underlies our free institutions. When we tear aside the delusions and misconceptions which have blinded our countrymen to their condition under vicious tariff laws, we but show them how far they have been led away from the paths of contentment and prosperity. When we proclaim that the necessity for revenue to support the Government furnishes the only justification for taxing the people, we announce a truth so plain that its denial would seem to indicate the extent to which judgment may be influenced by familiarity with perversions of the taxing power. And when we seek to reinstate the self-confidence and business enterprise of our citizens by discrediting an abject dependence upon governmental favor, we strive to stimulate those elements of American character which support the hope of American achievement.

Anxiety for the redemption of the pledges which my party has made and solicitude for the complete justification of the trust the people have reposed in us constrain me to remind those with whom I am to cooperate that we can succeed in doing the work which has been especially set before us only by the most sincere, harmonious, and disinterested effort. Even if insuperable obstacles and opposition prevent the consummation of our task, we shall hardly be excused; and if failure can be traced to our fault or neglect we may be sure the people will hold us to a swift and exacting accountability.

The oath I now take to preserve, protect, and defend the Constitution of the United States not only impressively defines the great responsibility I assume, but suggests obedience to constitutional commands as the rule by which my official conduct must be guided. I shall to the best of my ability and within my sphere of duty preserve the Constitution by loyally protecting every grant of Federal power it contains, by defending all its restraints when attacked by impatience and restlessness, and by enforcing its limitations and reservations in favor of the States and the people.

Fully impressed with the gravity of the duties that confront me and mindful of my weakness, I should be appalled if it were my lot to bear unaided the responsibilities which await me. I am, however, saved from discouragement when I remember that I shall have the support and the counsel and cooperation of wise and patriotic men who will stand at my side in Cabinet places or will represent the people in their legislative halls.

I find also much comfort in remembering that my countrymen are just and generous and in the assurance that they will not condemn those who by sincere devotion to their service deserve their forbearance and approval.

Above all, I know there is a Supreme Being who rules the affairs of men and whose goodness and mercy have always followed the American people, and I know He will not turn from us now if we humbly and reverently seek His powerful aid.

Grover the Good

THE SECOND INAUGURAL ADDRESS OF GROVER CLEVELAND

Matthew Algeo

WHEN I THINK of Grover Cleveland's Second Inaugural Address on March 4, 1893—which, to be honest, isn't very often—I imagine myself standing in the crowd on the east side of the Capitol, shivering in the cold, snow swirling. Looking up at burly Cleveland bundled in his big black overcoat, standing at the front of the wooden stage erected at the bottom of the steps, the dome rising up above him in the gloomy gray sky, I strain to hear his oration. Cleveland was one of the most famous public speakers of his age, with a booming voice befitting his large size. He once gave a speech to twenty thousand people at the old Madison Square Garden and it was said that every single one of them could hear every single word.

But even a bellowing Grover Cleveland cannot overcome Mother Nature on this winter day, and, without the benefit of artificial amplification, his Second Inaugural Address is swallowed up by the howling wind, audible only to those seated closest to him on the stage. Out among the throng huddled on the frozen lawn, Cleveland cannot be heard.

This is too bad, because, as long-winded Gilded Age inaugural addresses go, Cleveland's second wasn't too bad.

A little background: Cleveland was the first and so far only president to win back the office after losing it. So March 4, 1893, really should have been a triumphant day for him—what a comeback!—but, alas, it was not an auspicious time to assume the presidency. Cleveland inherited a mess from Benjamin Harrison. The country was on the brink of an economic catastrophe that would come to be known as the Panic of 1893, the worst depression in the nation's history until the Great Depression. The Reading Railroad had just gone bankrupt, the stock market was crashing, and unemployment and hunger were rising. So, in his second inaugural, Cleveland attempts to calm fears. He delicately refers to the crumbling economy as "our present embarrassing situation" and promises to do everything in his power to "avert financial disaster." He reassures the public that "prudent and effective remedial legislation" will address the crisis.

At the same time, however, Cleveland warns the people that they should expect little in the way of direct support from the federal government, saying: "The lessons of paternalism ought to be unlearned and the better lesson taught that while the people should patriotically and cheerfully support their Government its functions do not include the support of the people." This was one of Grover Cleveland's mantras. There would be no government handouts. Americans would have to fend for themselves.

Several other themes emerge in the address, some of which sound archaic today: a disdain for tariffs, a commitment to "sound money," opposition to "wild and reckless" pensions for Civil War veterans. But a few themes still resonate. Cleveland was a Democrat—the only Democrat elected between Buchanan and Wilson, in fact—and the Democrats, in the South at least, were the party of white supremacy. But Cleveland—who was from Buffalo—pointedly includes in the address a call for civil rights for African Americans.

"Loyalty to the principles upon which our Government rests positively demands that the equality before the law which it guarantees to every citizen should be justly and in good faith conceded in all parts of the land," he says. "The enjoyment of this right follows the badge of citizenship wherever found, and, unimpaired by race or color, it appeals for recognition to American manliness and fairness."

Cleveland also calls for the fair treatment of Native Americans, though in tones that sound a lot like the "paternalism" he earlier disdained. "Every effort should be made to lead them, through the paths of civilization and education, to self-supporting and independent citizenship," he says. "In the meantime, as the nation's wards, they should be promptly defended against the cupidity of designing men and shielded from every influence or temptation that retards their advancement."

Cleveland was conservative—as that term was understood at the time—but he clearly did not believe in frugality when it came to words. A lawyer by training and profession, Cleveland wrote in a style that might charitably be described as cumbersome. Hence this paragraph, in which Cleveland uses seventy-six words to say, in effect, I have a lot of work ahead of me, but I'll have plenty of help:

> Fully impressed with the gravity of the duties that confront me and mindful of my weakness, I should be appalled if it were my lot to bear unaided the responsibilities which await me. I am, however, saved from discouragement when I remember that I shall have the support and the counsel and cooperation of wise and patriotic men who will stand at my side in Cabinet places or will represent the people in their legislative halls.

There's something else in the speech that, in retrospect, is especially striking. At one point, Cleveland likens the looming financial crisis to an unseen malady:

> The strong man who in the confidence of sturdy health courts the sternest activities of life and rejoices in the hardihood of constant labor may still have lurking near his vitals the unheeded disease that dooms him to sudden collapse.

Just weeks later, Cleveland himself would discover lurking near his vitals a disease that threatened him to sudden collapse: a cancerous growth on the roof of his mouth. The tumor would be removed in a secret operation on a friend's yacht in early July.

Cleveland's father was a Presbyterian minister, and Cleveland inherited his faith (if not his sobriety). He ends his Second Inaugural with a call for God's blessing:

> Above all, I know there is a Supreme Being who rules the affairs of men and whose goodness and mercy have always followed the American people, and I know He will not turn from us now if we humbly and reverently seek His powerful aid.

Much of Cleveland's second term would be consumed by political disputes, sectional rivalries, and labor strife. His refusal to initiate bold government programs to counteract the effects of the depression did nothing to endear him to a public weary of the misery. He did not run for a third term in 1896. By then he was so unpopular that even his own party had repudiated him. At the Democratic convention in Chicago that year, delegates hurled more insults at Cleveland than at the Republican presidential nominee, William McKinley.

Grover Cleveland never wavered from his principles, and he paid the price.

William McKinley's First Inaugural Address

THURSDAY, MARCH 4, 1897

FELLOW-CITIZENS:

In obedience to the will of the people, and in their presence, by the authority vested in me by this oath, I assume the arduous and responsible duties of President of the United States, relying upon the support of my countrymen and invoking the guidance of Almighty God. Our faith teaches that there is no safer reliance than upon the God of our fathers, who has so singularly favored the American people in every national trial, and who will not forsake us so long as we obey His commandments and walk humbly in His footsteps.

The responsibilities of the high trust to which I have been called—always of grave importance—are augmented by the prevailing business conditions entailing idleness upon willing labor and loss to useful enterprises. The country is suffering from industrial disturbances from which speedy relief must be had. Our financial system needs some revision; our money is all good now, but its value must not further be threatened. It should all be put upon an enduring basis, not subject to easy attack, nor its stability to doubt or dispute. Our currency should continue under the supervision of the Government. The several forms of our paper money offer, in my judgment, a constant embarrassment to the Government and a safe balance in the Treasury. Therefore I believe it necessary to devise a system which, without diminishing the circulating medium or offering a premium for its contraction, will present a remedy for those arrangements which, temporary in their nature, might well in the years of our prosperity have been displaced by wiser provisions. With adequate revenue secured, but not until then, we can enter upon such changes in our fiscal laws as will, while insuring safety and volume to our money, no longer impose upon the Government the necessity of maintaining so large a gold reserve, with its attendant and inevitable temptations to speculation. Most of our financial laws are the outgrowth of experience and trial, and should not be amended without investigation and demonstration of the wisdom of the proposed changes. We must be both "sure we are right" and "make haste slowly." If, therefore, Congress, in its wisdom, shall deem it expedient to create a commission to take under early consideration the revision of our coinage, banking and currency laws, and give them that exhaustive, careful and dispassionate examination that their importance demands, I shall cordially concur in such action. If such power is vested in the President, it is my purpose to appoint a commission of prominent, well-informed citizens of different parties, who will command public confidence, both on account of their ability and special fitness for the work. Business experience and public training may thus be combined, and the patriotic zeal of the friends of the country be so directed that such a report will be made as to receive the support of all parties, and our finances cease to be the subject of mere partisan contention. The experiment is, at all events, worth a trial, and, in my opinion, it can but prove beneficial to the entire country.

The question of international bimetallism will have early and earnest attention. It will be my constant endeavor to secure it by co-operation with the other great commercial powers of the world. Until that condition is realized when the parity between our gold and silver money springs from and is supported by the relative value of the two metals, the value of the silver already coined and of that which may hereafter be coined, must be kept constantly at par with gold by every resource at our command. The credit of the Government, the integrity of its currency, and the inviolability of its obligations must be preserved. This was the commanding verdict of the people, and it will not be unheeded.

Economy is demanded in every branch of the Government at all times, but especially in periods, like the present, of depression in business and distress among the people. The severest economy must be observed in all public expenditures, and extravagance stopped wherever it is found, and prevented wherever in the future it may be developed. If the revenues are to remain as now, the only relief that can come must be from decreased expenditures. But the present must not become the permanent condition of the Government. It has been our uniform practice to retire, not increase our outstanding obligations, and this policy must again be resumed and vigorously enforced. Our revenues should always be large enough to meet with ease and promptness not only our current needs and the principal and interest of the public debt, but to make proper and liberal provision for that most deserving body of public creditors, the soldiers and sailors and the widows and orphans who are the pensioners of the United States.

The Government should not be permitted to run behind or increase its debt in times like the present. Suitably to provide against this is the mandate of duty—the certain and easy remedy for most of our financial difficulties. A deficiency is inevitable so long as the expenditures of the Government exceed its receipts. It can only be met by loans or an increased revenue. While a large annual surplus of revenue may invite waste and extravagance, inadequate revenue creates distrust and undermines public and private credit. Neither should be encouraged. Between more loans and more revenue there ought to be but one opinion. We should have more revenue, and that without delay, hindrance, or postponement. A surplus in the Treasury created by loans is not a permanent or safe reliance. It will suffice while it lasts, but it can not last long while the outlays of the Government are greater than its receipts, as has been the case during the past two years. Nor must it be forgotten that however much such loans may temporarily relieve the situation, the Government is still indebted for the amount of the surplus thus accrued, which it must ultimately pay, while its ability to pay is not strengthened, but weakened by a continued deficit. Loans are imperative in great emergencies to preserve the Government or its credit, but a failure to supply needed revenue in time of peace for the maintenance of either has no justification.

The best way for the Government to maintain its credit is to pay as it goes—not by resorting to loans, but by keeping out of debt—through an adequate income secured by a system of taxation, external or internal, or both. It is the settled policy of the Government, pursued from the beginning and practiced by all parties and Administrations, to raise the bulk of our revenue from taxes upon foreign productions entering the United States for sale and consumption, and avoiding, for the most part, every form of direct taxation, except in time of war. The country is clearly opposed to any needless additions to the subject of internal taxation, and is committed by its latest popular utterance to the system of tariff taxation. There can be no misunderstanding, either, about the principle upon which this tariff taxation shall be levied. Nothing has ever been made plainer at a general election than that the controlling principle in the raising of revenue from duties on imports is zealous care for American interests and American labor. The people have declared that such legislation should be had as will give ample protection and encouragement to the industries and the development of our country. It is, therefore, earnestly hoped and expected that Congress will, at the earliest practicable moment, enact revenue legislation that shall be fair, reasonable, conservative, and just, and which, while supplying sufficient revenue for public purposes, will still be signally beneficial and helpful to every section and every enterprise of the people. To this policy we are all, of whatever party, firmly bound by the voice of the people—a power vastly more potential than the expression of any political platform. The paramount duty of Congress is to stop deficiencies by the restoration of that protective legislation which has always been the firmest prop of the Treasury. The passage of such a law or laws would strengthen the credit of the Government both at home and abroad, and go far toward stopping the drain upon the gold reserve held for the redemption of our currency, which has been heavy and well-nigh constant for several years.

In the revision of the tariff especial attention should be given to the re-enactment and extension of the reciprocity principle of the law of 1890, under which so great a stimulus was given to our foreign trade in new and advantageous markets for our surplus agricultural and manufactured products. The brief trial given this legislation amply justifies a further experiment and additional discretionary power in the making of commercial treaties, the end in view always to be the opening up of new markets for the products of our country, by granting concessions to the products of other lands that we need and cannot produce ourselves, and which do not involve any loss of labor to our own people, but tend to increase their employment.

The depression of the past four years has fallen with especial severity upon the great body of toilers of the country, and upon none more than the holders of small farms. Agriculture has languished and labor suffered. The revival of manufacturing will be a relief to both. No portion of our population is more devoted to the institution of free government nor more loyal in their support, while none bears more cheerfully or fully its proper share in the maintenance of the Government or is better entitled to its wise and liberal care and protection. Legislation helpful to producers is beneficial to all. The depressed condition of industry on the farm and in the mine and factory has lessened the ability of the people to meet the demands upon them, and they rightfully expect that not only a system of revenue shall be established that will secure the largest income with the least burden, but that every means will be taken to decrease, rather than increase, our public expenditures. Business conditions are not the most promising. It will take time to restore the prosperity of former years. If we cannot promptly attain it, we can resolutely turn our faces in that direction and aid its return by friendly legislation. However troublesome the situation may appear, Congress will not, I am sure, be found lacking in disposition or ability to relieve it as far as legislation can do so. The restoration of confidence and the revival of business, which men of all parties so much desire, depend more largely upon the prompt, energetic, and intelligent action of Congress than upon any other single agency affecting the situation.

It is inspiring, too, to remember that no great emergency in the one hundred and eight years of our eventful national life has ever arisen that has not been met with wisdom and courage by the American people, with fidelity to their best interests and highest destiny, and to the honor of the American name. These years of glorious history have exalted mankind and advanced the cause of freedom throughout the world, and immeasurably strengthened the precious free institutions which we enjoy. The people love and will sustain these institutions. The great essential to our happiness and prosperity is that we adhere to the principles upon which the Government was established and insist upon their faithful observance. Equality of rights must prevail, and our laws be always and everywhere respected and obeyed. We may have failed in the discharge of our full duty as citizens of the great Republic, but it is consoling and encouraging to realize that free speech, a free press, free thought, free schools, the free and unmolested right of religious liberty and worship, and free and fair elections are dearer and more universally enjoyed to-day than ever before. These guaranties must be sacredly preserved and wisely strengthened. The constituted authorities must be cheerfully and vigorously upheld. Lynchings must not be tolerated in a great and civilized country like the United States; courts, not mobs, must execute the penalties of the law. The preservation of public order, the right of discussion, the integrity of courts, and the orderly administration of justice must continue forever the rock of safety upon which our Government securely rests.

One of the lessons taught by the late election, which all can rejoice in, is that the citizens of the United States are both law-respecting and law-abiding people, not easily swerved from the path of patriotism and honor. This is in entire accord with the genius of our institutions, and but emphasizes the advantages of inculcating even a greater love for law and order in the future. Immunity should be granted to none who violate the laws, whether individuals, corporations, or communities; and as the Constitution imposes upon the President the duty of both its own execution, and of the statutes enacted in pursuance of its provisions, I shall endeavor carefully to carry them into effect. The declaration of the party now restored to power has been in the past that of "opposition to all combinations of capital organized in trusts, or otherwise, to control arbitrarily the condition of trade among our citizens," and it has supported "such legislation as will prevent the execution of all schemes to oppress the people by undue charges on their supplies, or by unjust rates for the transportation of their products to the market." This purpose will be steadily pursued, both by the enforcement of the laws now in existence and the recommendation and support of such new statutes as may be necessary to carry it into effect.

Our naturalization and immigration laws should be further improved to the constant promotion of a safer, a better, and a higher citizenship. A grave peril to the Republic would be a citizenship too ignorant to understand or too vicious to appreciate the great value and beneficence of our institutions and laws, and against all who come here to make war upon them our gates must be promptly and tightly closed. Nor must we be unmindful of the need of improvement among our own citizens, but with the zeal of our forefathers encourage the spread of knowledge and free education. Illiteracy must be banished from the land if we shall attain that high destiny as the foremost of the enlightened nations of the world which, under Providence, we ought to achieve.

Reforms in the civil service must go on; but the changes should be real and genuine, not perfunctory, or prompted by a zeal in behalf of any party simply because it happens to be in power. As a member of Congress I voted and spoke in favor of the present law, and I shall attempt its enforcement in the spirit in which it was enacted. The purpose in view was to secure the most efficient service of the best men who would accept appointment under the Government, retaining faithful and devoted public servants in office, but shielding none, under the authority of any rule or custom, who are inefficient, incompetent, or unworthy. The best interests of the country demand this, and the people heartily approve the law wherever and whenever it has been thus administrated.

Congress should give prompt attention to the restoration of our American merchant marine, once the pride of the seas in all the great ocean highways of commerce. To my mind, few more important subjects so imperatively demand its intelligent consideration. The United States has progressed with marvelous rapidity in every field of enterprise and endeavor until we have become foremost in nearly all the great lines of inland trade, commerce, and industry. Yet, while this is true, our American merchant marine has been steadily declining until it is now lower, both in the percentage of tonnage and the number of vessels employed, than it was prior to the Civil War. Commendable progress has been made of late years in the upbuilding of the American Navy, but we must supplement these efforts by providing as a proper consort for it a merchant marine amply sufficient for our own carrying trade to foreign countries. The question is one that appeals both to our business necessities and the patriotic aspirations of a great people.

It has been the policy of the United States since the foundation of the Government to cultivate relations of peace and amity with all the nations of the world, and this accords with my conception of our duty now. We have cherished the policy of non-interference with affairs of foreign governments wisely inaugurated by Washington, keeping ourselves free from entanglement, either as allies or foes, content to leave undisturbed with them the settlement of their own domestic concerns. It will be our aim to pursue a firm and dignified foreign policy, which shall be just, impartial, ever watchful of our national honor, and always insisting upon the enforcement of the lawful rights of American citizens everywhere. Our diplomacy should seek nothing more and accept nothing less than is due us. We want no wars of conquest; we must avoid the temptation of territorial aggression. War should never be entered upon until every agency of peace has failed; peace is preferable to war in almost every contingency. Arbitration is the true method of settlement of international as well as local or individual differences. It was recognized as the best means of adjustment of differences between employers and employees by the Forty-ninth Congress, in 1886, and its application was extended to our diplomatic relations by the unanimous concurrence of the Senate and House of the Fifty-first Congress in 1890. The latter resolution was accepted as the basis of negotiations with us by the British House of Commons in 1893, and upon our invitation a treaty of arbitration between the United States and Great Britain was signed at Washington and transmitted to the Senate for its ratification in January last. Since this treaty is clearly the result of our own initiative; since it has been recognized as the leading feature of our foreign policy throughout our entire national history—the adjustment of difficulties by judicial methods rather than force of arms—and since it presents to the world the glorious example of reason and peace, not passion and war, controlling the relations between two of the greatest nations in the world, an example certain to be followed by others, I respectfully urge the early action of the Senate thereon, not merely as a matter of policy, but as a duty to mankind. The importance and moral influence of the ratification of such a treaty can hardly be overestimated in the cause of advancing civilization. It may well engage the best thought of the statesmen and people of every country, and I cannot but consider it fortunate that it was reserved to the United States to have the leadership in so grand a work.

It has been the uniform practice of each President to avoid, as far as possible, the convening of Congress in extraordinary session. It is an example which, under ordinary circumstances and in the absence of a public necessity, is to be commended. But a failure to convene the representatives of the people in Congress in extra session when it involves neglect of a public duty places the responsibility of such neglect upon the Executive himself. The condition of the public Treasury, as has been indicated, demands the immediate consideration of Congress. It alone has the power to provide revenues for the Government. Not to convene it under such circumstances I can view in no other sense than the neglect of a plain duty. I do not sympathize with the sentiment that Congress in session is dangerous to our general business interests. Its members are the agents of the people, and their presence at the seat of Government in the execution of the sovereign will should not operate as an injury, but a benefit. There could be no better time to put the Government upon a sound financial and economic basis than now. The people have only recently voted that this should be done, and nothing is more binding upon the agents of their will than the obligation of immediate action. It has always seemed to me that the postponement of the meeting of Congress until more than a year after it has been chosen deprived Congress too often of the inspiration of the popular will and the country of the corresponding benefits. It is evident, therefore, that to postpone action in the presence of so great a necessity would be unwise on the part of the Executive because unjust to the interests of the people. Our action now will be freer from mere partisan consideration than if the question of tariff revision was postponed until the regular session of Congress. We are nearly two years from a Congressional election, and politics cannot so greatly distract us as if such contest was immediately pending. We can approach the problem calmly and patriotically, without fearing its effect upon an early election.

Our fellow-citizens who may disagree with us upon the character of this legislation prefer to have the question settled now, even against their preconceived views, and perhaps settled so reasonably, as I trust and believe it will be, as to insure great permanence, than to have further uncertainty menacing the vast and varied business interests of the United States. Again, whatever action Congress may take will be given a fair opportunity for trial before the people are called to pass judgment upon it, and this I consider a great essential to the rightful and lasting settlement of the question. In view of these considerations, I shall deem it my duty as President to convene Congress in extraordinary session on Monday, the 15th day of March, 1897.

In conclusion, I congratulate the country upon the fraternal spirit of the people and the manifestations of good will everywhere so apparent. The recent election not only most fortunately demonstrated the obliteration of sectional or geographical lines, but to some extent also the prejudices which for years have distracted our councils and marred our true greatness as a nation. The triumph of the people, whose verdict is carried into effect today, is not the triumph of one section, nor wholly of one party, but of all sections and all the people. The North and the South no longer divide on the old lines, but upon principles and policies; and in this fact surely every lover of the country can find cause for true felicitation.

Let us rejoice in and cultivate this spirit; it is ennobling and will be both a gain and a blessing to our beloved country. It will be my constant aim to do nothing, and permit nothing to be done, that will arrest or disturb this growing sentiment of unity and cooperation, this revival of esteem and affiliation which now animates so many thousands in both the old antagonistic sections, but I shall cheerfully do everything possible to promote and increase it.

Let me again repeat the words of the oath administered by the Chief Justice which, in their respective spheres, so far as applicable, I would have all my countrymen observe: "I will faithfully execute the office of President of the United States, and will, to the best of my ability, preserve, protect, and defend the Constitution of the United States." This is the obligation I have reverently taken before the Lord Most High. To keep it will be my single purpose, my constant prayer; and I shall confidently rely upon the forbearance and assistance of all the people in the discharge of my solemn responsibilities.

The Front Porch Campaign

THE FIRST INAUGURAL ADDRESS OF
WILLIAM MCKINLEY

Christopher Capozzola

WILLIAM MCKINLEY STEPPED to the podium on the east front of the U.S. Capitol building in Washington, unfolded his handwritten speech, and addressed the crowd of 40,000 who had gathered that sunny March afternoon to watch the fifty-four-year-old Civil War veteran take the presidential oath of office. McKinley spoke during the depths of the worst economic downturn America had experienced in its history; four decades later, people would talk about the "Great Depression" to distinguish it from the one that followed the Panic of 1893. The last inaugural address of the nineteenth century looked backward, promising Americans the restoration of a better past. But as Thomas Edison's newly invented "kinetoscope" recorded the inauguration—the first ever captured on film—the day's events signaled the impending arrival of a modern, industrial, outward-looking, media-drenched age: the twentieth century.

William McKinley knew how to win an election. By 1896, he was an experienced former member of Congress, a popular governor of Ohio, and a natural at the glad-handing style and smoke-filled rooms of Republican party politics. Born in 1843, McKinley saw combat during the Civil War (long after he retired his uniform, people still called him "the Major") and built a successful legal career in Canton, Ohio, where he married Ida Saxton, who suffered medical problems throughout her husband's career. In 1876, the young lawyer won election to the U.S. House of Representatives and served fourteen years in Washington before taking the governor's seat in Columbus in 1892.

Both Republicans and Democrats considered McKinley just a little more moderate than the rest of the GOP. They were right to think so. As a rookie congressman, he had voted for a compromise currency policy known as "bimetallism," which would protect the gold standard that bankers loved while allowing for a modest increase in the quantity of silver-backed currency, a move that could help working families make ends meet. The Major also pushed through the McKinley Tariff of 1890, which raised tariffs on imports (helping American business) and permitted the negotiation of reciprocal trade deals to sell American factory goods abroad (aiding workers). McKinley trod a middle path in cultural conflicts as well. As Ohio's governor, McKinley had taken a modest stand against the nativist American Protective Association and the tide of anti-immigrant politics that swept the nation during the Panic of 1893.

After cruising to victory in the Republican nomination contest, McKinley faced a formidable opponent in William Jennings Bryan, a former Nebraska congressman. "The Great Commoner" electrified the Democratic convention in Chicago on July 9, 1896, with a speech that rallied delegates to a platform of free silver, intoning that "you shall not crucify mankind upon a cross of gold." Bryan raised the stakes of the election and, in the midst of a national depression, put economic policy on the ballot.

By all accounts, Bryan had the upper hand on the campaign trail. A political outsider, he had youth, energy, oratorical skills, and a bold financial platform. And, thanks to Jim Crow laws and Election Day violence that had been steadily disfranchising African American voters in the South, the Democrats had a near-lock on the 112 electoral votes of the former Confederacy. But McKinley had an appealingly moderate image, strong support in the Northeast and the cities, and knew the American people were tired of the Democratic party that had given them eight (non-consecutive) years of President Grover Cleveland—a man who did little to relieve the depression and made no effort to appeal to ordinary voters. McKinley sat on a huge campaign war chest (despite McKinley's slogan of "the people against the bosses," wealthy industrialists were fully on his side), and he had a shrewd campaign manager, Mark Hanna, to steward it.

While Bryan took to the rails for a grueling whistle-stop campaign, McKinley ran a quiet "front porch" effort that invited thousands of onlookers to his home in Canton, Ohio. (The maneuver also spared Ida McKinley the exhaustion that travel would have required.) On the issues, McKinley promised to bury the hatchet of the Civil War, hoping that sectional unity could pick off one or two states from the Solid South. Sensing the public's hesitation about Bryan's free silver crusade, and under pressure from party bosses, McKinley veered toward a more conservative embrace of the gold standard. His running mate, New Jersey Governor Garret Hobart, brought an Eastern, industrial, big-money balance to the ticket. At a time of social upheaval and economic crisis, McKinley was the electorate's safe choice, and he won an easy victory of 271 electoral votes to 176 for Bryan.

Four months later, McKinley arrived in Washington. On the night before the inauguration, in a mood that he recalled as one of "settled sadness and sincerity," McKinley dined with the outgoing president, Grover Cleveland, who warned his Republican successor that war loomed in Venezuela or Cuba. The next morning, dressed in an American-made woolen suit, McKinley traveled to Capitol Hill and took the oath of office from Chief Justice Melville Fuller. Economic issues had determined the election, and the "depression in business and distress among the people" likewise dominated McKinley's address. The new president acknowledged the crisis that had bankrupted so many (including, nearly, McKinley himself), promising to end the "prevailing business conditions entailing idleness upon willing labor and loss to useful enterprises." No friend of organized labor, though, McKinley warned of "industrial disturbances," or strikes, "from which speedy relief must be had." The new president endorsed the tariff—calling it "settled policy... pursued from the beginning and practiced by all parties"—and called for Congress to meet in special session to increase tariff rates, which, in July 1897, they promptly did. Seeking to thread a moderate needle on the currency question, McKinley reiterated his call for an international conference to consider bimetallism, promising that such a commission would have "early and earnest attention" from his administration. In office, McKinley quickly abandoned that aim and fully embraced the gold standard, enshrining it in law in March 1900.

Taking his oath on a Bible presented to him by the bishops of the African Methodist Episcopal Church, a reminder of the war for racial equality that was rapidly fading from living memory, McKinley embodied the contradictions of white Republicans' thinking on race. At a time when racist violence was at a national peak, McKinley asserted that "[l]ynchings must not be tolerated in a great and civilized country like the United States." But he did not push matters too far, observing in his address that the election "demonstrated the obliteration of sectional or geographical lines." Reaching out a hand of friendship to his former Confederate foes, while remaining largely silent on the aspirations of African Americans, McKinley proclaimed that "[t]he North and the South no longer divide on the old lines."

On other political issues of the day, McKinley promised moderation. He called for reform of business trusts—though in no particularly detailed way—and endorsed civil service reform and the care of Civil War veterans, "that most deserving body of public creditors." He urged reform of immigration and citizenship laws but insisted that to anarchists "our gates must be promptly and tightly closed," a policy that would have done nothing to stop the American-born anarchist Leon Czolgosz, who assassinated McKinley in 1901.

In foreign affairs, the new president once again looked backward to reassure the American people. "We have cherished the policy of non-interference with affairs of foreign governments wisely inaugurated by [George] Washington." McKinley suggested that the new administration wanted none of the headaches that had plagued his predecessor: no aim of annexing the Hawaiian Kingdom (overthrown with participation by U.S. troops in 1893); no wish for conflict with Britain over Venezuela (which had nearly brought the two nations to war in 1895); no interest in meddling in the Cuban war of independence. There was no sign of the future to come, as foreign affairs quickly displaced domestic issues during McKinley's first term: the acquisition of Spain's colonial empire, the brutal suppression of a nationalist independence movement in the Philippines, and the announcement of the Open Door Policy in China. Quite the opposite: "We want no wars of conquest," McKinley insisted. "[W]e must avoid the temptation of territorial aggression."

The national press praised the "peaceful, dignified, and practical temper" of McKinley's address, while that same day William Jennings Bryan offered the press a statement of his own political views, not-so-subtly foreshadowing his plan to challenge McKinley four years later. McKinley's Inaugural Address marked the beginning of decades of Republican dominance in the White House. As Americans watched aging Civil War veterans march, as they heard farmers cry out against an urban industrial economy, as political leaders brushed away the political claims of African Americans at home or of Cubans abroad, the United States stood at the end of a passing era, with a president poised to lead them into the twentieth century. On that afternoon in Washington, Thomas Edison's cameras were there to capture it.

William McKinley's Second Inaugural Address

MONDAY, MARCH 4, 1901

MY FELLOW-CITIZENS:

When we assembled here on the 4th of March, 1897, there was great anxiety with regard to our currency and credit. None exists now. Then our Treasury receipts were inadequate to meet the current obligations of the Government. Now they are sufficient for all public needs, and we have a surplus instead of a deficit. Then I felt constrained to convene the Congress in extraordinary session to devise revenues to pay the ordinary expenses of the Government. Now I have the satisfaction to announce that the Congress just closed has reduced taxation in the sum of $41,000,000. Then there was deep solicitude because of the long depression in our manufacturing, mining, agricultural, and mercantile industries and the consequent distress of our laboring population. Now every avenue of production is crowded with activity, labor is well employed, and American products find good markets at home and abroad.

Our diversified productions, however, are increasing in such unprecedented volume as to admonish us of the necessity of still further enlarging our foreign markets by broader commercial relations. For this purpose reciprocal trade arrangements with other nations should in liberal spirit be carefully cultivated and promoted.

The national verdict of 1896 has for the most part been executed. Whatever remains unfulfilled is a continuing obligation resting with undiminished force upon the Executive and the Congress. But fortunate as our condition is, its permanence can only be assured by sound business methods and strict economy in national administration and legislation. We should not permit our great prosperity to lead us to reckless ventures in business or profligacy in public expenditures.

While the Congress determines the objects and the sum of appropriations, the officials of the executive departments are responsible for honest and faithful disbursement, and it should be their constant care to avoid waste and extravagance.

Honesty, capacity, and industry are nowhere more indispensable than in public employment. These should be fundamental requisites to original appointment and the surest guaranties against removal.

Four years ago we stood on the brink of war without the people knowing it and without any preparation or effort at preparation for the impending peril. I did all that in honor could be done to avert the war, but without avail. It became inevitable; and the Congress at its first regular session, without party division, provided money in anticipation of the crisis and in preparation to meet it. It came. The result was signally favorable to American arms and in the highest degree honorable to the Government. It imposed upon us obligations from which we cannot escape and from which it would be dishonorable to seek escape. We are now at peace with the world, and it is my fervent prayer that if differences arise between us and other powers they may be settled by peaceful arbitration and that hereafter we may be spared the horrors of war.

Intrusted by the people for a second time with the office of President, I enter upon its administration appreciating the great responsibilities which attach to this renewed honor and commission, promising unreserved devotion on my part to their faithful discharge and reverently invoking for my guidance the direction and favor of Almighty God. I should shrink from the duties this day assumed if I did not feel that in their performance I should have the co-operation of the wise and patriotic men of all parties. It encourages me for the great task which I now undertake to believe that those who voluntarily committed to me the trust imposed upon the Chief Executive of the Republic will give to me generous support in my duties to "preserve, protect, and defend, the Constitution of the United States" and to "care that the laws be faithfully executed." The national purpose is indicated through a national election. It is the constitutional method of ascertaining the public will. When once it is registered it is a law to us all, and faithful observance should follow its decrees.

Strong hearts and helpful hands are needed, and, fortunately, we have them in every part of our beloved country. We are reunited. Sectionalism has disappeared. Division on public questions can no longer be traced by the war maps of 1861. These old differences less and less disturb the judgment. Existing problems demand the thought and quicken the conscience of the country, and the responsibility for their presence, as well as for their righteous settlement, rests upon us all—no more upon me than upon you. There are some national questions in the solution of which patriotism should exclude partisanship. Magnifying their difficulties will not take them off our hands nor facilitate their adjustment. Distrust of the capacity, integrity, and high purposes of the American people will not be an inspiring theme for future political contests. Dark pictures and gloomy forebodings are worse than useless. These only becloud, they do not help to point the way of safety and honor. "Hope maketh not ashamed." The prophets of evil were not the builders of the Republic, nor in its crises since have they saved or served it. The faith of the fathers was a mighty force in its creation, and the faith of their descendants has wrought its progress and furnished its defenders. They are obstructionists who despair, and who would destroy confidence in the ability of our people to solve wisely and for civilization the mighty problems resting upon them. The American people, intrenched in freedom at home, take their love for it with them wherever they go, and they reject as mistaken and unworthy the doctrine that we lose our own liberties by securing the enduring foundations of liberty to others. Our institutions will not deteriorate by extension, and our sense of justice will not abate under tropic suns in distant seas. As heretofore, so hereafter will the nation demonstrate its fitness to administer any new estate which events devolve upon it, and in the fear of God will "take occasion by the hand and make the bounds of freedom wider yet." If there are those among us who would make our way more difficult, we must not be disheartened, but the more earnestly dedicate ourselves to the task upon which we have rightly entered. The path of progress is seldom smooth. New things are often found hard to do. Our fathers found them so. We find them so. They are inconvenient. They cost us something. But are we not made better for the effort and sacrifice, and are not those we serve lifted up and blessed?

We will be consoled, too, with the fact that opposition has confronted every onward movement of the Republic from its opening hour until now, but without success. The Republic has marched on and on, and its step has exalted freedom and humanity. We are undergoing the same ordeal as did our predecessors nearly a century ago. We are following the course they blazed. They triumphed. Will their successors falter and plead organic impotency in the nation? Surely after 125 years of achievement for mankind we will not now surrender our equality with other powers on matters fundamental and essential to nationality. With no such purpose was the nation created. In no such spirit has it developed its full and independent sovereignty. We adhere to the principle of equality among ourselves, and by no act of ours will we assign to ourselves a subordinate rank in the family of nations.

My fellow-citizens, the public events of the past four years have gone into history. They are too near to justify recital. Some of them were unforeseen; many of them momentous and far-reaching in their consequences to ourselves and our relations with the rest of the world. The part which the United States bore so honorably in the thrilling scenes in China, while new to American life, has been in harmony with its true spirit and best traditions, and in dealing with the results its policy will be that of moderation and fairness.

We face at this moment a most important question that of the future relations of the United States and Cuba. With our near neighbors we must remain close friends. The declaration of the purposes of this Government in the resolution of April 20, 1898, must be made good. Ever since the evacuation of the island by the army of Spain, the Executive, with all practicable speed, has been assisting its people in the successive steps necessary to the establishment of a free and independent government prepared to assume and perform the obligations of international law which now rest upon the United States under the treaty of Paris. The convention elected by the people to frame a constitution is approaching the completion of its labors. The transfer of American control to the new government is of such great importance, involving an obligation resulting from our intervention and the treaty of peace, that I am glad to be advised by the recent act of Congress of the policy which the legislative branch of the Government deems essential to the best interests of Cuba and the United States. The principles which led to our intervention require that the fundamental law upon which the new government rests should be adapted to secure a government capable of performing the duties and discharging the functions of a separate nation, of observing its international obligations of protecting life and property, insuring order, safety, and liberty, and conforming to the established and historical policy of the United States in its relation to Cuba.

The peace which we are pledged to leave to the Cuban people must carry with it the guaranties of permanence. We became sponsors for the pacification of the island, and we remain accountable to the Cubans, no less than to our own country and people, for the reconstruction of Cuba as a free commonwealth on abiding foundations of right, justice, liberty, and assured order. Our enfranchisement of the people will not be completed until free Cuba shall "be a reality, not a name; a perfect entity, not a hasty experiment bearing within itself the elements of failure."

While the treaty of peace with Spain was ratified on the 6th of February, 1899, and ratifications were exchanged nearly two years ago, the Congress has indicated no form of government for the Philippine Islands. It has, however, provided an army to enable the Executive to suppress insurrection, restore peace, give security to the inhabitants, and establish the authority of the United States throughout the archipelago. It has authorized the organization of native troops as auxiliary to the regular force. It has been advised from time to time of the acts of the military and naval officers in the islands, of my action in appointing civil commissions, of the instructions with which they were charged, of their duties and powers, of their recommendations, and of their several acts under executive commission, together with the very complete general information they have submitted. These reports fully set forth the conditions, past and present, in the islands, and the instructions clearly show the principles which will guide the Executive until the Congress shall, as it is required to do by the treaty, determine "the civil rights and political status of the native inhabitants." The Congress having added the sanction of its authority to the powers already possessed and exercised by the Executive under the Constitution, thereby leaving with the Executive the responsibility for the government of the Philippines, I shall continue the efforts already begun until order shall be restored throughout the islands, and as fast as conditions permit will establish local governments, in the formation of which the full co-operation of the people has been already invited, and when established will encourage the people to administer them. The settled purpose, long ago proclaimed, to afford the inhabitants of the islands self-government as fast as they were ready for it will be pursued with earnestness and fidelity. Already something has been accomplished in this direction. The Government's representatives, civil and military, are doing faithful and noble work in their mission of emancipation and merit the approval and support of their countrymen. The most liberal terms of amnesty have already been communicated to the insurgents, and the way is still open for those who have raised their arms against the Government for honorable submission to its authority. Our countrymen should not be deceived. We are not waging war against the inhabitants of the Philippine Islands. A portion of them are making war against the United States. By far the greater part of the inhabitants recognize American sovereignty and welcome it as a guaranty of order and of security for life, property, liberty, freedom of conscience, and the pursuit of happiness. To them full protection will be given. They shall not be abandoned. We will not leave the destiny of the loyal millions the islands to the disloyal thousands who are in rebellion against the United States. Order under civil institutions will come as soon as those who now break the peace shall keep it. Force will not be needed or used when those who make war against us shall make it no more. May it end without further bloodshed, and there be ushered in the reign of peace to be made permanent by a government of liberty under law!

The Imperial Presidency

THE SECOND INAUGURAL ADDRESS OF WILLIAM MCKINLEY

Christopher McKnight Nichols

IN THE CAMPAIGN leading up to his first term, William McKinley often spoke of his hope to focus on pressing domestic issues such as the economic recession that began with the Panic of 1893, the politics and economics of the gold standard and bimetallism, and protective tariffs. However, that was not to be. Currency, the economy, and tariffs were significant factors in his first term, but McKinley was mostly consumed with foreign relations—including the United States' first war with a European nation in over eighty years.

A popular rebellion in Cuba, one of many over the past generation, heightened tensions with Spain and exploded when the USS *Maine* did, sinking in Havana harbor in February 1898; this helped to precipitate war in April of that year, not just in the Caribbean but also in the Pacific. In the aftermath, the United States annexed Hawaii, Puerto Rico, and Guam, and also acquired the Philippines and protection over Cuba. One result of such actions is that the nation became embroiled in a deadly counterinsurgency war in the Philippines against the very same revolutionaries the United States had come to fight with against Spain. The struggle continued through the election of 1900, until the second war in the Philippines formally ended in 1902, although resistance by Filipinos continued. Thus, the politics of the presidential election in 1900 and for a second term revolved largely around foreign policy concerns.

McKinley's resounding "rematch" victory came over William Jennings Bryan, a "fusion" candidate of the Democratic and Populist parties, who ran with vice presidential nominee Adlai Stevenson. McKinley was on the ticket with war hero

"Rough Rider" New York Governor Theodore Roosevelt because Vice President Garret Hobart died in November 1899, making him the sixth vice president to die in office. McKinley garnered nearly a million more votes than Bryan, carrying twenty-eight states (292 electoral college votes) to Bryan's seventeen states (155 electoral college votes), most of which were in the "solid" Democratic South. The rapid victory in what came to be known as the Spanish American War, combined with an economic recovery, helped propel McKinley and the Republicans to a sweeping victory in November 1900. After wins in the Senate and some losses in the House during the midterm elections of 1898, the 1900 campaign centered simply on "prestige abroad and prosperity at home" and the slogan of "four more years of the full dinner pail." It was highly effective. Republicans starting with the inauguration in 1901 held the "trifecta" of power—controlling the White House, the Senate, and the House of Representatives. In short, election for a second term at a moment like this amounted to a mandate. McKinley's second inaugural therefore focused largely on foreign policy successes and areas remaining to be not simply addressed but resolved, while also touching on the major economic and revenue progress made in his first term. He also hinted at changes to tariff and tax policies that he hoped to achieve, as well as additional international relations goals, all of which McKinley could not see to conclusion because he was assassinated in September 1901.

In just the second ever filmed presidential inaugural address, William McKinley paraded to the Capitol on Monday, March 4, 1901. It was an overcast day with clouds and rain overnight. It was dry during the procession to the Capitol, and temperatures reached a relatively balmy mid-to-upper 40s by noon. Light rain returned throughout the ceremony that day, but McKinley and those in the audience continued undeterred. With the economy heating up and a successful war against Spain, leading to new territorial acquisitions and the promise of new markets abroad, the future seemed bright for the president, the Republican party, and the nation.

"When we assembled here on the 4th of March, 1897," began McKinley from a stage in front of the Capitol festooned with flags and surrounded by an enormous crowd, "there was great anxiety with regard to our currency and credit. None exists now," he proudly declared.

As with most inaugural addresses, McKinley outlined the current state of the United States. He noted with satisfaction the many successes of his first term. In particular, he mentioned settling issues related to currency (by staying on the gold standard), securing more tax revenue, increasing production, and enlarging and enhancing markets at home and abroad. The essence of that message was epitomized by his statement that the "national verdict of 1896 has for the most part been executed."

So, what next? McKinley noted that in his new term he would adhere to what had worked well in the past one, namely "sound business methods and strict economy in national administration and legislation" without becoming "reckless." In other words, the people could count on McKinley and the Republicans to continue delivering business-oriented policies to seek more prosperity, limit appropriations, and avoid "waste and extravagance." He pushed for more reciprocal treaties with other nations to keep promoting prosperity.

Another element of his speech was emblematic of the times and of tensions in the Republican party. What had been the so-called party of Lincoln was beginning to fracture regarding how to grapple with rising Jim Crow segregation, atrocities against Black people, and the role of Democrats in building up systematic disfranchisement in the American South. Yet, in the seventh paragraph, in the middle of the speech, McKinley paused to reflect on the major challenges of the nineteenth century and to declare them overcome. "Sectionalism," he asserted, "has disappeared." His campaign and the 1900 Electoral College map undermines such a claim. Nevertheless, McKinley laid out a case for unity, in essence agreeing to the end of Reconstruction and not making any strong proposals for racial justice legislation at the federal level. He avoided explicit discussion of racist injustices, such as rampant lynching and acts of violence, and the active purging of Southern voting rolls of African Americans, themselves stalwart Republican voters. "Division on public questions," he said, "can no longer be traced by the war maps of 1861." As in the campaign of 1900, McKinley argued for sectional harmony; he connected prosperity and national greatness to expansion abroad. In the Inaugural he implicitly linked the challenges of ensuring equal protection after the end of slavery given entrenched racism to the advance of American democracy abroad. McKinley tried to ameliorate the concerns of critics by arguing that "our institutions will not deteriorate by extension, and our sense of justice will not abate under tropic suns in distant seas." But such assertions rang hollow to persecuted Black Americans rapidly losing hard-fought citizenship rights, as well as to those now subject to U.S. rule in the Caribbean and the Pacific.

In keeping with that emphasis on "extension," much of his speech focused on the foreign policies that helped to cement McKinley's reputation. Noting that the United States "stood on the brink of war" four years earlier, he first made clear that he did his best to avoid war, but when conflict became "inevitable," a bipartisan Congress brought the nation to war, and only reluctantly. The result, he triumphantly declared, was an honorable course of action and victory. He boldly clarified that the United States had no interest in ruling Cuba and he assured domestic and international audiences that the United States would be a benign protector of the Cuban people (unlike the Spanish). While some in his party and across the nation hoped the United States might eventually annex Cuba, and others were adamantly opposed to remaining there, even as protectors, in the speech McKinley laid out his vision of U.S. objectives: to help get the Cuban people "with all practicable speed" through the appropriate stages to establish "a free and independent government."

McKinley also hinted at a national first at the intersection of commerce, diplomacy, and military policy when he mentioned "thrilling scenes in China." The United States issued what are now known as the "Open Door Notes" in 1899 and 1900, making a worldwide claim that American goods and businesses would not be prevented from accessing markets in China. To buttress the Open Door pronouncement, in a historic first, McKinley had deployed U.S. Marines and naval forces to fight, for the first time alongside the militaries of major powers (European and Japanese), in China, to rescue their citizens and agents, and defend the foreign legation district in Beijing, during the Boxer Rebellion (1899–1901).

McKinley concluded the speech by addressing an area of uncertainty. He expressed his hopes for a peaceful resolution to the ongoing insurgency in the Philippines and articulated a vision much at odds with events on the ground at home and abroad. A robust group known as the Anti-Imperialist League had formed in June 1898 to oppose U.S. expansionism. They particularly rejected the U.S. annexation and rule of the Philippines. Their ranks were remarkably heterogeneous, making the League the most diverse large foreign policy lobby in U.S. history. Among others, it included Mark Twain, Andrew Carnegie, William James, Grover Cleveland, Jane Addams, Samuel Gompers, and W. E. B. Du Bois. In the campaign of 1900 and at the time of the Inaugural Address, these anti-imperialists pushed back against U.S. occupation policies in the Philippines, deeming them an anti-democratic, imperialist project unbecoming of a republican nation born in a revolutionary struggle to achieve self-rule. They asked: "Is the U.S. a republic or an empire?" In his campaign, William Jennings Bryan echoed aspects of their critique of McKinley's expansionist policies of ruling peoples "against their will," but the war was popular, patriotism and nationalism were potent, and the charges did not stick. Still, the facts were difficult to contest. In 1899 U.S. troops had turned on the very Filipino revolutionaries they had fought alongside and the first democratic government that they had formed. In McKinley's Inaugural Address, however, he dismissed this criticism. The United States was "not waging war against the inhabitants of the Philippines Island . . . [rather] a portion of them are making war against the United States." He concluded his Inaugural Address by laying out key American aims in the Philippines: pledging to support and protect the Islands and its peoples, acquired through the Treaty of Paris with Spain (signed December 1898, ratified February 1899), to end the bloodshed, to guarantee "order" as well as "security for life, property, liberty, freedom of conscience, and the pursuit of happiness."

A "civilizing" mission was the central cog in the ideological machine of American expansionism, as McKinley and fellow Republican advocates of a "large policy" of U.S. expansionism, such as Massachusetts Senator Henry Cabot Lodge, Roosevelt, and future president William Howard Taft, saw it. Taft, handpicked by McKinley, was then serving as head of the First Philippine Commission (running the government), soon to be U.S. Civil Governor of the Philippines, advocated a paternalist project of "tutoring" those in the Philippines (as well as Cuba and Puerto Rico) through varied civilizational stages to develop their ability to build up and maintain what McKinley called in the speech a "government of liberty." At McKinley's instruction, Taft aimed to create new civil society institutions, representative government, and public education in the Philippines similar to American models.

Many Filipinos, including much of the leadership of the revolutionary armies that had been seeking freedom against Spain, did not see shifting to the "protection" of the United States as a tolerable culmination of their efforts; they continued to fight against those they perceived as a new occupation army, through a series of losses that resulted in a peace treaty in July 1902. In the course of this conflict, both sides committed heinous acts, and the United States adopted widely despised techniques of interrogation, such as waterboarding and forced population control, grouping people into camps, as the Spanish had. Ultimately, the United States lost far more in the war in the Philippines than with Spain (nearly 5,000 U.S. troops, with Philippine casualties and famine killing as many as 200,000, by some estimates). Sporadic hostilities against the United States continued for over a decade. The islands did not achieve independent self-rule until 1946.

McKinley's speech was hailed as a success. One headline read "Chief Champion of Prosperity Inaugurated for a Second Term." The presence of foreign diplomats newly recognizing the United States' international power in the wake of the war with Spain was widely noted in contemporary accounts. The media recounted the cheers and approval that McKinley received from the crowds that had gathered despite the rain and overcast day.

Though McKinley did not have the great charisma of his vice president and successor, Theodore Roosevelt, he was affable and well aware of the importance of his speeches and messages. In his first term, with help from arch-strategist and Ohio Republican Senator Mark Hanna and several exceptional aides, McKinley built up the White House's first ever real press operations team. As several scholars have observed, he was essential in the "modernization of presidential press relations."[1] McKinley held press conferences, offered scoops to favored journalists, provided dedicated office space to correspondents in the White House, and established routines for monitoring the press and releasing statements, including enforcement against journalists and news outlets publishing information before it was agreed they do so. Notably, McKinley as commander in chief built a "war room" to manage the conflicts in the Caribbean and Pacific in near-real time via telegraph and telegram, heralding a new era and the dawn of the "imperial presidency," which set the stage for the Roosevelt presidency's masterful efforts at public relations.

Where was McKinley headed? From his speech it seems clear that balancing and streamlining federal government operations, promoting business while keeping an eye on individual opportunities, enhancing domestic production, and advancing foreign market access were key areas where McKinley hoped to take the nation over the next four years.

It is impossible to know what might have happened if McKinley had not been assassinated in September 1901 at the Buffalo, New York, Pan-American Exposition by anarchist Leon Czolgosz. Shot twice in the abdomen on September 6, McKinley had a modest recovery and then lingered as gangrene set in, dying in the early morning on September 14. He was the third president to be assassinated, all in under forty years (including Abraham Lincoln in 1865 and James Garfield in 1881). His killing by a self-professed, unrepentant anarchist, in an era of labor unrest, hyper-nationalism, and Americanism, following a "splendid little war" (as John Hay famously put it), shook the nation. In turn, the McKinley assassination helped to consolidate federal power and propelled anti-radical sentiment and police action.

Nevertheless, McKinley's inaugural speech provides some clues as to the aims he might have pursued. In that address and subsequent speeches before his death, he hinted at the desire to push for reductions in tariffs (as opposed to some 1900 campaign pledges, such as support for the highly restrictive 1897 Dingley Tariff) and to advocate for more reciprocal and bilateral trade deals. He had the credibility and support to have accomplished such aims given his success in championing the major tariff increase (some as high as 49 percent) in 1890 that bore his name: "the McKinley Tariff." Roosevelt, in contrast, was uninterested in promulgating major tariff changes. Some historians suggest that much of what happened under Roosevelt would have happened under McKinley, such as the Panama Canal, moderate anti-corporate lawsuits and trust-busting efforts, and the settlement of boundary issues with Canada.

On the other hand, Theodore Roosevelt's policies of pushing for conservation and national parks, his "square deal" approach to the federal government as central mediator in business-labor disputes, U.S. mediation in the Russo-Japanese War, and perhaps some of his later progressive reform tendencies appear less likely under a full McKinley second term. Roosevelt, for example, welcomed Booker T. Washington to the White House almost immediately upon becoming president, in October 1901, a gesture in keeping with Lincoln's invitation to Frederick Douglass in 1863. This caused great consternation from Southern whites, but Roosevelt held his ground. One cannot imagine McKinley doing so.

After McKinley died, Roosevelt, in his first address to Congress, vowed that government must do more to clean up industrial America; to protect individuals, workers, women, and children; to limit working hours; and to prevent the exploitation of natural resources. He also pushed to keep out immigrants who, he argued, would not be exemplary citizens (by this he was rejecting radicals like Czolgosz). He also proposed building up the army and particularly the navy to help spread U.S. ideals and commerce worldwide and to solidify the nation's position as a world power. At the very least, had McKinley lived, some of the most radical of these policies would have been put off until a possible Roosevelt presidency, which could not have happened until the election of 1904. That said, fellow Republicans were calmed by the relative lack of radicalism from the immensely popular and head-strong Roosevelt, something that they had feared when he joined the ticket in 1900.

In turn, had McKinley served two terms and so had Roosevelt, then the ruptures of the Republican party and the contested four-way election of 1912 likely would not have happened. The election of 1912 drove a wedge between incumbent William Howard Taft and his former mentor and ally Roosevelt, who split off from the Republicans and started his own party, the Progressive Party (colloquially known as the "Bull Moose Party" because Roosevelt proclaimed he felt strong as a "bull moose" even after his defeat at the GOP convention by Taft). The internecine 1912 Republican struggle was what made room for Democrat Woodrow Wilson to pull out a narrow victory, aided also by the remarkable showing of Socialist Eugene Debs. Such observations suggest another astonishing counterfactual: Roosevelt in a third term or, more likely, Taft in his first term, not Wilson, might well have been president during World War I. Given Taft and Roosevelt's advocacy of intervention in the war and a League to Enforce Peace, it is entirely possible that Taft or Roosevelt might have led the nation into the Great War sometime after summer 1914 and before April 1917, when a confluence of factors pushed Wilson to declare war as an "associate power" aiming to "make the world safe for democracy." How might the war have been different had the United States intervened in 1915 or 1916? What might that have meant for the Bolshevik Revolution? The dissolution of the Russian, Ottoman, Austro-Hungarian, German, and other empires? How might a Taft (or Roosevelt) and U.S.-led international organization have been part of the peace-making? The possibilities are endless and the results unknowable.

Note

1. Stephen Ponder, "The President Makes News: William McKinley and the First Presidential Press Corps, 1897–1901," *Presidential Studies Quarterly*, 24 (1994): 823–836.

Theodore Roosevelt's Inaugural Address

SATURDAY, MARCH 4, 1905

MY FELLOW-CITIZENS,

No people on earth have more cause to be thankful than ours, and this is said reverently, in no spirit of boastfulness in our own strength, but with gratitude to the Giver of Good who has blessed us with the conditions which have enabled us to achieve so large a measure of well-being and of happiness. To us as a people it has been granted to lay the foundations of our national life in a new continent. We are the heirs of the ages, and yet we have had to pay few of the penalties which in old countries are exacted by the dead hand of a bygone civilization. We have not been obliged to fight for our existence against any alien race; and yet our life has called for the vigor and effort without which the manlier and hardier virtues wither away. Under such conditions it would be our own fault if we failed; and the success which we have had in the past, the success which we confidently believe the future will bring, should cause in us no feeling of vainglory, but rather a deep and abiding realization of all which life has offered us; a full acknowledgment of the responsibility which is ours; and a fixed determination to show that under a free government a mighty people can thrive best, alike as regards the things of the body and the things of the soul.

Much has been given to us, and much will rightfully be expected from us. We have duties to others and duties to ourselves; and we can shirk neither. We have become a great nation, forced by the fact of its greatness into relations with the other nations of the earth, and we must behave as beseems a people with such responsibilities. Toward all other nations, large and small, our attitude must be one of cordial and sincere friendship. We must show not only in our words but in our deeds that we are earnestly desirous of securing their good will by acting toward them in a spirit of just and generous recognition of all their rights. But justice and generosity in a nation, as in an individual, count most when shown not by the weak but by the strong. While ever careful to refrain from wrongdoing others, we must be no less insistent that we are not wronged ourselves. We wish peace; but we wish the peace of justice, the peace of righteousness. We wish it because we think it is right and not because we are afraid. No weak nation that acts manfully and justly should ever have cause to fear us, and no strong power should ever be able to single us out as a subject for insolent aggression.

Our relations with the other powers of the world are important; but still more important are our relations among ourselves. Such growth in wealth, in population, and in power as this nation has seen during the century and a quarter of its national life is inevitably accompanied by a like growth in the problems which are ever before every nation that rises to greatness. Power invariably means both responsibility and danger. Our forefathers faced certain perils which we have outgrown. We now face other perils the very existence of which it was impossible that they should foresee. Modern life is both complex and intense, and the tremendous changes wrought by the extraordinary industrial development of the last half century are felt in every fiber of our social and political being. Never before have men tried so vast and formidable an experiment as that of administering the affairs of a continent under the forms of a democratic republic. The conditions which have told for our marvelous material well-being, which have developed to a very high degree our energy, self-reliance, and individual initiative, have also brought the care and anxiety inseparable from the accumulation of great wealth in industrial centers. Upon the success of our experiment much depends; not only as regards our own welfare, but as regards the welfare of mankind. If we fail, the cause of free self-government throughout the world will rock to its foundations; and therefore our responsibility is heavy, to ourselves, to the world as it is to-day, and to the generations yet unborn. There is no good reason why we should fear the future, but there is every reason why we should face it seriously, neither hiding from ourselves the gravity of the problems before us nor fearing to approach these problems with the unbending, unflinching purpose to solve them aright.

Yet, after all, though the problems are new, though the tasks set before us differ from the tasks set before our fathers who founded and preserved this Republic, the spirit in which these tasks must be undertaken and these problems faced, if our duty is to be well done, remains essentially unchanged. We know that self-government is difficult. We know that no people needs such high traits of character as that people which seeks to govern its affairs aright through the freely expressed will of the freemen who compose it. But we have faith that we shall not prove false to the memories of the men of the mighty past. They did their work, they left us the splendid heritage we now enjoy. We in our turn have an assured confidence that we shall be able to leave this heritage unwasted and enlarged to our children and our children's children. To do so we must show, not merely in great crises, but in the everyday affairs of life, the qualities of practical intelligence, of courage, of hardihood and endurance, and above all the power of devotion to a lofty ideal, which made great the men who founded this Republic in the days of Washington, which made great the men who preserved this Republic in the days of Abraham Lincoln.

The Bully Pulpit

THE INAUGURAL ADDRESS OF THEODORE ROOSEVELT

Jean M. Yarbrough

ALTHOUGH THEODORE ROOSEVELT served as president of the United States for seven and a half years, he delivered only one Inaugural Address in 1905. Roosevelt had been tapped to serve as William McKinley's running mate in 1900, and after McKinley's assassination in September of the following year, Roosevelt ascended to the presidency. He was then forty-two years old, making him the youngest person ever to serve in that office. During his first term, Roosevelt was determined not to antagonize the Republican party power brokers, so as not to jeopardize his nomination for a second term. To that end, he retained the slain president's Cabinet and hewed to his policies. But when in 1904 he won a landslide re-election, Roosevelt felt free to chart his own course.

Several things stand out about Roosevelt's 1905 Inaugural Address. First, he wrote it himself. It was not until the Harding administration that presidents began to employ others to help them compose their speeches. Second, for someone whose previous Annual Messages ran to fifty or more pages and who in campaign mode was never at a loss for words, his Inaugural Address is surprisingly short. The entire address consists of four paragraphs, each with its distinctive theme.

The theme of the first paragraph is American exceptionalism, ending with a challenge. As others before Roosevelt had noted, America was singularly blessed in laying the foundations for its experiment in republican self-government on a new and fertile continent. Unlike the nations of Europe, which had been compelled to fight against "alien races" for their very existence, the United States faced no such mortal foes. In his histories, Roosevelt had celebrated the triumphs of his countrymen over the Mexicans to the south and the French to the north, as well as their victories over the Native American tribes. But compared to the Europeans, none of these contests posed existential challenges to American survival.

Americans were also exceptional because they could profit from the accumulated wisdom of the ages, but they were not weighed down by "the dead hand of a bygone civilization." This last point is telling because, although Roosevelt had praised the work of the more nationalist Founding Fathers and would continue to do so, he would find himself during his second term (and afterward) on a collision course with the principles of liberal republicanism they embraced. In this respect, Roosevelt sounded like no one as much as Thomas Jefferson, who also had inveighed against "mortmain," insisting that "the earth belongs to the living" and that constitutions should be remade every generation to take into account the progressive character of political science. Yet, Roosevelt "cordially despised" the third president because in his view Jefferson's policies had simultaneously provoked the British into attack and left the United States defenseless against it. As he had explained in his well-received first book, *The Naval War of 1812*, Jefferson's reliance on citizen-militias and a defensive naval fleet had led the fledgling nation to the brink of disaster. Only in recent years had the United States begun to recover from the disastrous effect that Jefferson's policies and misguided theories had foisted upon the new republic. Despite these egregious errors, Americans had prevailed and were now poised to take their rightful place on the world stage. The challenge facing the country at the beginning of a new century was whether America could show to the world that a free government could provide for both "the things of the body and the things of the soul."

This last phrase speaks to one of the twenty-sixth president's most enduring themes. As a rising Republican reformer, Roosevelt had inveighed against the crass vulgarity of the Gilded Age. "Purely commercial ideals," he warned in an 1895 essay, were "mean and sordid," producing timid and fearful men "incapable of the thrill of generous emotion" and lacking in the capacity for heroism and greatness. "American Ideals," he insisted, must rest on "nobler grounds" than "mere business expediency."[1] Although his Inaugural Address had referred only vaguely to the "things of the soul," Roosevelt's aim was to turn Americans away from their preoccupation with rights, especially the soft and easy enjoyment of the property rights of the wealthy, and to reorient them to their duties. Righteousness, rather than rights, would speak to these loftier spiritual needs. As his British friend, Arthur Lee Hamilton, wrote in his introduction to Roosevelt's biography of Oliver Cromwell, Roosevelt was "essentially a preacher," who "was not ashamed to invoke the Sword of the Lord and of Gideon."[2] But in keeping with the teachings of the Social Gospel, Roosevelt directed his energies toward combating the vulgar materialism of America's commercial ideals and fighting for a "Square Deal" for America's working men and women.

From this opening, Roosevelt moved on to foreign affairs, warning that a great nation could not afford to "shirk" its duties or shrink from its responsibilities. His policies aimed at the lofty ideal of national greatness, which required both military might and the cultivation of the manly virtues. In this address, Roosevelt confined himself to the articulation of general principles, expressing his desire for "cordial and sincere friendship" toward all nations. But in the background, his audience no doubt recalled a number of crises that arose during Roosevelt's first term that hit close to home. One of the key issues that emerged early in his presidency involved the application of the Monroe Doctrine. When faced with a crisis in the Dominican Republic, he announced what became known as the Roosevelt Corollary to the Monroe Doctrine. Whereas the original doctrine had opposed territorial aggrandizement by non-American powers, under the Roosevelt Corollary, the United States would do what it would not allow the Europeans to do: intervene in the domestic politics of other American nations to keep Europeans out. This, Roosevelt suggested, was as much to recognize the rights of our weaker southern neighbors as it was to make sure that our own interests were not threatened. "We wish peace; but we wish the peace of justice, the peace of righteousness." His noble sentiments, however, may have been belied by his bullying treatment of Colombia in obtaining the territory on which he later oversaw construction of the Panama Canal. Looking beyond the New World of North and South America, Roosevelt's national greatness agenda ran into trouble in the Philippines. Not all Americans were reconciled to the idea of their democratic republic extending its empire over foreign and faraway peoples.

Roosevelt then turned to domestic affairs, observing that the problems Americans faced in his day could not possibly have been foreseen by "our forefathers." When the authors of *The Federalist* defended the large democratic republic, they never imagined "administering the affairs of a continent." The advent of the Industrial Revolution following the Civil War encouraged Americans to apply their initiative, energy, and self-reliance to improve their standard of living. But, he implied, the vast wealth and power generated by that revolution also produced "care and anxiety" that the architects of the commercial republic had not anticipated. Echoing the sentiments of one of his heroes, Abraham Lincoln, he warned that upon the success of the American experiment hinged not only the welfare of his countrymen, but also the "welfare of mankind," and not only for today, but for "generations yet unborn." He counseled resolve and confidence but offered no specific policies.

In his final paragraph, Roosevelt returned to the theme that the problems confronting his generation were entirely novel. He urged Americans to face up to them in the same "spirit" that their forefathers had brought to their problems. In particular, he singled out "the qualities of practical intelligence, of courage, of hardihood, and endurance, and above all the power of devotion to a lofty ideal." What he did not say is that he was devoted to preserving and advancing the same *ideals* as our forefathers, that is, to the protection of each individual's inalienable rights to life, liberty, and the pursuit of happiness, secured by an energetic but limited federal government. In his second term, Roosevelt would demonstrate through his policies and pronouncements that the lofty goal to which he aspired was in fact quite far removed from the ideals of the Founders he claimed most to admire.

Notes

1. Theodore Roosevelt, *American Ideals and Other Essays, Social and Political*, Vol. 1 (Philadelphia: Gebbie and Company, 1903).
2. *Proof of Oliver Cromwell*, Sagamore Hill National Historic Site, Theodore Roosevelt Digital Library. Dickinson State University, [June 1923?], https://www.theodorerooseveltcenter.org/Research/Digital-Library/Record?libID=0279599.

William Howard Taft's Inaugural Address

THURSDAY, MARCH 4, 1909

MY FELLOW-CITIZENS:

Anyone who has taken the oath I have just taken must feel a heavy weight of responsibility. If not, he has no conception of the powers and duties of the office upon which he is about to enter, or he is lacking in a proper sense of the obligation which the oath imposes.

The office of an inaugural address is to give a summary outline of the main policies of the new administration, so far as they can be anticipated. I have had the honor to be one of the advisers of my distinguished predecessor, and as such, to hold up his hands in the reforms he has initiated. I should be untrue to myself, to my promises and to the declarations of the party platform upon which I was elected to office, if I did not make the maintenance and enforcement of those reforms a most important feature of my administration. They were directed to the suppression of the lawlessness and abuses of power of the great combinations of capital invested in railroads and in industrial enterprises carrying on interstate commerce. The steps which my predecessor took and the legislation passed on his recommendation have accomplished much, have caused a general halt in the vicious policies which created popular alarm, and have brought about in the business affected, a much higher regard for existing law.

To render the reforms lasting, however, and to secure at the same time freedom from alarm on the part of those pursuing proper and progressive business methods, further legislative and executive action are needed. Relief of the railroads from certain restrictions of the antitrust law have been urged by my predecessor and will be urged by me. On the other hand, the administration is pledged to legislation looking to a proper federal supervision and restriction to prevent excessive issues of bonds and stock by companies owning and operating interstate commerce railroads.

Then too a reorganization of the Department of Justice, of the Bureau of Corporations in the Department of Commerce and Labor, and of the Interstate Commerce Commission, looking to effective cooperation of these agencies, is needed to secure a more rapid and certain enforcement of the laws affecting interstate railroads and industrial combinations.

I hope to be able to submit, at the first regular session of the incoming Congress, in December next, definite suggestions in respect to the needed amendments to the antitrust and the interstate commerce law, and the changes required in the executive departments concerned in their enforcement.

It is believed that with the changes to be recommended, American business can be assured of that measure of stability and certainty in respect to those things that may be done and those that are prohibited, which is essential to the life and growth of all business. Such a plan must include the right of the people to avail themselves of those methods of combining capital and effort deemed necessary to reach the highest degree of economic efficiency, at the same time differentiating between combinations based upon legitimate economic reasons and those formed with the intent of creating monopolies and artificially controlling prices.

The work of formulating into practical shape such changes is creative work of the highest order, and requires all the deliberation possible in the interval. I believe that the amendments to be proposed are just as necessary in the protection of legitimate business as in the clinching of the reforms which properly bear the name of my predecessor.

A matter of most pressing importance is the revision of the tariff. In accordance with the promises of the platform upon which I was elected, I shall call Congress into extra session, to meet on the 15th day of March, in order that consideration may be at once given to a bill revising the Dingley Act. This should secure an adequate revenue and adjust the duties in such a manner as to afford to labor and to all industries in this country, whether of the farm, mine or factory, protection by tariff equal to the difference between the cost of production abroad and the cost of production here, and have a provision which shall put into force, upon executive determination of certain facts, a higher or maximum tariff against those countries whose trade policy toward us equitably requires such discrimination. It is thought that there has been such a change in conditions since the enactment of the Dingley Act, drafted on a similarly protective principle, that the measure of the tariff above stated will permit the reduction of rates in certain schedules and will require the advancement of few, if any.

The proposal to revise the tariff made in such an authoritative way as to lead the business community to count upon it necessarily halts all those branches of business directly affected; and as these are most important, it disturbs the whole business of the country. It is imperatively necessary, therefore, that a tariff bill be drawn in good faith in accordance with promises made before the election by the party in power, and as promptly passed as due consideration will permit. It is not that the tariff is more important in the long run than the perfecting of the reforms in respect to antitrust legislation and interstate commerce regulation, but the need for action when the revision of the tariff has been determined upon is more immediate to avoid embarrassment of business. To secure the needed speed in the passage of the tariff bill, it would seem wise to attempt no other legislation at the extra session. I venture this as a suggestion only, for the course to be taken by Congress, upon the call of the Executive, is wholly within its discretion.

In the making of a tariff bill, the prime motive is taxation, and the securing thereby of a revenue. Due largely to the business depression which followed the financial panic of 1907, the revenue from customs and other sources has decreased to such an extent that the expenditures for the current fiscal year will exceed the receipts by $100,000,000. It is imperative that such a deficit shall not continue, and the framers of the tariff bill must of course have in mind the total revenues likely to be produced by it, and so arrange the duties as to secure an adequate income. Should it be impossible to do so by import duties, new kinds of taxation must be adopted, and among these I recommend a graduated inheritance tax as correct in principle and as certain and easy of collection.

The obligation on the part of those responsible for the expenditures made to carry on the Government, to be as economical as possible, and to make the burden of taxation as light as possible, is plain, and should be affirmed in every declaration of government policy. This is especially true when we are face to face with a heavy deficit. But when the desire to win the popular approval leads to the cutting off of expenditures really needed to make the Government effective and to enable it to accomplish its proper objects, the result is as much to be condemned as the waste of government funds in unnecessary expenditure. The scope of a modern government in what it can and ought to accomplish for its people, has been widened far beyond the principles laid down by the old "laissez faire" school of political writers, and this widening has met popular approval.

In the Department of Agriculture, the use of scientific experiments on a large scale, and the spread of information derived from them for the improvement of general agriculture, must go on.

The importance of supervising business of great railways and industrial combinations, and the necessary investigation and prosecution of unlawful business methods are another necessary tax upon Government which did not exist half a century ago.

The putting into force of laws which shall secure the conservation of our resources, so far as they may be within the jurisdiction of the Federal Government, including the most important work of saving and restoring our forests, and the great improvement of waterways, are all proper government functions which must involve large expenditure if properly performed. While some of them, like the reclamation of arid lands, are made to pay for themselves, others are of such an indirect benefit that this cannot be expected of them. A permanent improvement, like the Panama Canal, should be treated as a distinct enterprise, and should be paid for by the proceeds of bonds, the issue of which will distribute its cost between the present and future generations in accordance with the benefits derived. It may well be submitted to the serious consideration of Congress whether the deepening and control of the channel of a great river system, like that of the Ohio or of the Mississippi, when definite and practical plans for the enterprise have been approved and determined upon, should not be provided for in the same way.

Then, too, there are expenditures of Government absolutely necessary if our country is to maintain its proper place among the nations of the world, and is to exercise its proper influence in defense of its own trade interests, in the maintenance of traditional American policy against the colonization of European monarchies in this hemisphere, and in the promotion of peace and international morality. I refer to the cost of maintaining a proper Army, a proper Navy, and suitable fortifications upon the mainland of the United States and in its dependencies.

We should have an Army so organized, and so officered, as to be capable in time of emergency, in cooperation with the National Militia and under the provisions of a proper national volunteer law, rapidly to expand into a force sufficient to resist all probable invasion from abroad and to furnish a respectable expeditionary force, if necessary, in the maintenance of our traditional American policy which bears the name of President Monroe.

Our fortifications are yet in a state of only partial completeness, and the number of men to man them is insufficient. In a few years, however, the usual annual appropriations for our coast defenses both on the mainland and in the dependencies, will make them sufficient to resist all direct attack, and by that time we may hope that the men to man them will be provided as a necessary adjunct. The distance of our shores from Europe and Asia of course reduces the necessity for maintaining under arms a great army, but it does not take away the requirement of mere prudence—that we should have an army sufficiently large and so constituted as to form a nucleus out of which a suitable force can quickly grow.

What has been said of the army may be affirmed in even a more emphatic way, of the Navy. A modern navy cannot be improvised. It must be built and in existence when the emergency arises which calls for its use and operation. My distinguished predecessor has in many speeches and messages set out with great force and striking language the necessity for maintaining a strong navy commensurate with the coast line, the governmental resources and the foreign trade of our Nation; and I wish to reiterate all the reasons which he has presented in favor of the policy of maintaining a strong navy as the best conservator of our peace with other nations, and the best means of securing respect for the assertion of our rights, the defense of our interests and the exercise of our influence in international matters.

Our international policy is always to promote peace. We shall enter into any war with a full consciousness of the awful consequences that it always entails, whether successful or not, and we, of course, shall make every effort consistent with national honor and the highest national interest, to avoid a resort to arms. We favor every instrumentality, like that of the Hague Tribunal and arbitration treaties made with a view to its use in all international controversies, in order to maintain peace and to avoid war. But we should be blind to existing conditions and should allow ourselves to become foolish idealists, if we did not realize that with all the nations of the world armed and prepared for war, we must be ourselves in a similar condition, in order to prevent other nations from taking advantage of us and of our inability to defend our interests and assert our rights with a strong hand.

In the international controversies that are likely to arise in the Orient, growing out of the question of the open door and other issues, the United States can maintain her interests intact and can secure respect for her just demands. She will not be able to do so, however, if it is understood that she never intends to back up her assertion of right and her defense of her interest by anything but mere verbal protest and diplomatic note. For these reasons the expenses of the army and navy and of coast defenses should always be considered as something which the Government must pay for, and they should not be cut off through mere consideration of economy. Our Government is able to afford a suitable army and a suitable navy. It may maintain them without the slightest danger to the Republic or the cause of free institutions, and fear of additional taxation ought not to change a proper policy in this regard.

The policy of the United States in the Spanish War, and since, has given it a position of influence among the nations that it never had before, and should be constantly exerted to securing to its bona fide citizens, whether native or naturalized, respect for them as such in foreign countries. We should make every effort to prevent humiliating and degrading prohibition against any of our citizens wishing temporarily to sojourn in foreign countries because of race or religion.

The admission of Asiatic immigrants who cannot be amalgamated with our population has been made the subject either of prohibitory clauses in our treaties and statutes or of strict administrative regulation secured by diplomatic negotiation. I sincerely hope that we may continue to minimize the evils likely to arise from such immigration without unnecessary friction and by mutual concessions between self-respecting governments. Meantime we must take every precaution to prevent, or failing that, to punish outbursts of race feeling among our people against foreigners of whatever nationality who have by our grant a treaty right to pursue lawful business here and to be protected against lawless assault or injury.

This leads me to point out a serious defect in the present federal jurisdiction, which ought to be remedied at once. Having assured to other countries by treaty the protection of our laws for such of their subjects or citizens as we permit to come within our jurisdiction, we now leave to a state or a city, not under the control of the Federal Government, the duty of performing our international obligations in this respect. By proper legislation we may, and ought to, place in the hands of the Federal Executive the means of enforcing the treaty rights of such aliens in the courts of the Federal Government. It puts our Government in a pusillanimous position to make definite engagements to protect aliens and then to excuse the failure to perform those engagements by an explanation that the duty to keep them is in States or cities, not within our control. If we would promise we must put ourselves in a position to perform our promise. We cannot permit the possible failure of justice due to local prejudice in any State or municipal government to expose us to the risk of a war which might be avoided if federal jurisdiction was asserted by suitable legislation by Congress and carried out by proper proceedings instituted by the Executive, in the courts of the National Government.

One of the reforms to be carried out during the incoming administration is a change of our monetary and banking laws, so as to secure greater elasticity in the forms of currency available for trade, and to prevent the limitations of law from operating to increase the embarrassment of a financial panic. The monetary commission, lately appointed, is giving full consideration to existing conditions and to all proposed remedies and will doubtless suggest one that will meet the requirements of business and of public interest.

We may hope that the report will embody neither the narrow dew of those who believe that the sole purpose of the new system should be to secure a large return on banking capital or of those who would have greater expansion of currency with little regard to provisions for its immediate redemption or ultimate security. There is no subject of economic discussion so intricate and so likely to evoke differing views and dogmatic statements as this one. The commission in studying the general influence of currency on business and of business on currency, have wisely extended their investigations in European banking and monetary methods. The information that they have derived from such experts as they have found abroad will undoubtedly be found helpful in the solution of the difficult problem they have in hand.

The incoming Congress should promptly fulfill the promise of the Republican platform and pass a proper postal savings bank bill. It will not be unwise or excessive paternalism. The promise to repay by the Government will furnish an inducement to savings deposits which private enterprise can not supply and at such a low rate of interest as not to withdraw custom from existing banks. It will substantially increase the funds available for investment as capital in useful enterprises. It will furnish absolute security which makes the proposed scheme of government guaranty of deposits so alluring, without its pernicious results.

I sincerely hope that the incoming Congress will be alive, as it should be, to the importance of our foreign trade and of encouraging it in every way feasible. The possibility of increasing this trade in the Orient, in the Philippines, and in South America are known to everyone who has given the matter attention. The direct effect of free trade between this country and the Philippines will be marked upon our sales of cottons, agricultural machinery, and other manufactures. The necessity of the establishment of direct lines of steamers between North and South America has been brought to the attention of Congress by my predecessor, and by Mr. Root before and after his noteworthy visit to that continent, and I sincerely hope that Congress may be induced to see the wisdom of a tentative effort to establish such lines by the use of mail subsidies.

The importance of the part which the Departments of Agriculture and of Commerce and Labor may play in ridding the markets of Europe of prohibitions and discriminations against the importation of our products, is fully understood, and it is hoped that the use of the maximum and minimum feature of our tariff law to be soon passed will be effective to remove many of those restrictions.

The Panama Canal will have a most important bearing upon the trade between the eastern and far western sections of our country, and will greatly increase the facilities for transportation between the eastern and the western seaboard, and may possibly revolutionize the transcontinental rates with respect to bulky merchandise. It will also have a most beneficial effect to increase the trade between the eastern seaboard of the United States and the western coast of South America, and indeed with some of the important ports on the east coast of South America reached by rail from the west coast.

The work on the canal is making most satisfactory progress. The type of the canal as a lock canal was fixed by Congress after a full consideration of the conflicting reports of the majority and minority of the consulting board, and after the recommendation of the War Department and the Executive upon those reports. Recent suggestion that something had occurred on the Isthmus to make the lock type of the canal less feasible than it was supposed to be when the reports were made and the policy determined, led to a visit to the Isthmus of a board of competent engineers to examine the Gatun Dam and locks, which are the key of the lock type. The report of that board shows nothing has occurred in the nature of newly revealed evidence which should change the views once formed in the original discussion. The construction will go on under a most effective organization controlled by Colonel Goethals and his fellow army engineers associated with him, and will certainly be completed early in the next administration, if not before.

Some type of canal must be constructed. The lock type has been selected. We are all in favor of having it built as promptly as possible. We must not now, therefore, keep up a fire in the rear of the agents whom we have authorized to do our work on the Isthmus. We must hold up their hands, and speaking for the incoming administration, I wish to say that I propose to devote all the energy possible and under my control, to the pushing of this work on the plans which have been adopted, and to stand behind the men who are doing faithful, hard work to bring about the early completion of this, the greatest constructive enterprise of modern times.

The governments of our dependencies in Puerto Rico and the Philippines are progressing as favorably as could be desired. The prosperity of Puerto Rico continues unabated. The business conditions in the Philippines are not all that we could wish them to be, but with the passage of the new tariff bill permitting free trade between the United States and the Archipelago, with such limitations on sugar and tobacco as shall prevent injury to the domestic interests in those products, we can count on an improvement in business conditions in the Philippines and the development of a mutually profitable trade between this country and the islands. Meantime our Government in each dependency is upholding the traditions of civil liberty and increasing popular control which might be expected under American auspices. The work which we are doing there redounds to our credit as a nation.

I look forward with hope to increasing the already good feeling between the South and the other sections of the country. My chief purpose is not to effect a change in the electoral vote of the Southern states. That is a secondary consideration. What I look forward to, is an increase in the tolerance of political views of all kinds and their advocacy throughout the South, and the existence of a respectable political opposition in every State; even more than this, to an increased feeling on the part of all the people in the South that this Government is their Government, and that its officers in their states are their officers.

The consideration of this question can not however be complete and full without reference to the negro race, its progress and its present condition. The 13th Amendment secured them freedom; the 14th Amendment due process of law, protection of property, and the pursuit of happiness; and the 15th Amendment attempted to secure the negro against any deprivation of the privilege to vote because he was a negro. The 13th and 14th Amendments have been generally enforced and have secured the objects for which they are intended. While the 15th Amendment has not been generally observed in the past, it ought to be observed, and the tendency of Southern legislation today is toward the enactment of electoral qualifications which shall square with that amendment. Of course, the mere adoption of a constitutional law is only one step in the right direction. It must be fairly and justly enforced as well. In time both will come. Hence it is clear to all that the domination of an ignorant, irresponsible element can be prevented by constitutional laws which shall exclude from voting both negroes and whites not having education or other qualifications thought to be necessary for a proper electorate. The danger of the control of an ignorant electorate has therefore passed. With this change, the interest which many of the Southern white citizens take in the welfare of the negroes has increased. The colored men must base their hope on the results of their own industry, self-restraint, thrift, and business success, as well as upon the aid and comfort and sympathy which they may receive from their white neighbors of the South.

There was a time when Northerners who sympathized with the negro in his necessary struggle for better conditions sought to give him the suffrage as a protection, and to enforce its exercise against the prevailing sentiment of the South. The movement proved to be a failure. What remains is the 15th Amendment to the Constitution and the right to have statutes of States specifying qualifications for electors subjected to the test of compliance with that amendment. This is a great protection to the negro. It never will be repealed, and it never ought to be repealed. If it had not passed, it might be difficult now to adopt it; but with it in our fundamental law, the policy of Southern legislation must and will tend to obey it, and so long as the statutes of the States meet the test of this amendment and are not otherwise in conflict with the Constitution and laws of the United States, it is not the disposition or within the province of the Federal Government to interfere with the regulation by Southern states of their domestic affairs. There is in the South a stronger feeling than ever among the intelligent, well-to-do and influential element in favor of the industrial education of the negro and the encouragement of the race to make themselves useful members of the community. The progress which the negro has made in the last fifty years from slavery, when its statistics are reviewed is marvelous, and it furnishes every reason to hope that in the next twenty-five years a still greater improvement in his condition as a productive member of society, on the farm, and in the shop, and in other occupations may come.

The negroes are now Americans. Their ancestors came here years ago against their will, and this is their only country and their only flag. They have shown themselves anxious to live for it and to die for it. Encountering the race feeling against them, subjected at times to cruel injustice growing out of it, they may well have our profound sympathy and aid in the struggle they are making. We are charged with the sacred duty of making their path as smooth and easy as we can. Any recognition of their distinguished men, any appointment to office from among their number, is properly taken as an encouragement and an appreciation of their progress, and this just policy should be pursued when suitable occasion offers.

But it may well admit of doubt whether, in the case of any race, an appointment of one of their number to a local office in a community in which the race feeling is so widespread and acute as to interfere with the ease and facility with which the local government business can be done by the appointee, is of sufficient benefit by way of encouragement to the race to outweigh the recurrence and increase of race feeling which such an appointment is likely to engender. Therefore the Executive in recognizing the negro race by appointments must exercise a careful discretion not thereby to do it more harm than good. On the other hand, we must be careful not to encourage the mere pretense of race feeling manufactured in the interest of individual political ambition.

Personally, I have not the slightest race prejudice or feeling, and recognition of its existence only awakens in my heart a deeper sympathy for those who have to bear it or suffer from it, and I question the wisdom of a policy which is likely to increase it. Meantime, if nothing is done to prevent it, a better feeling between the negroes and the whites in the South will continue to grow, and more and more of the white people will come to realize that the future of the South is to be much benefited by the industrial and intellectual progress of the negro. The exercise of political franchises by those of this race who are intelligent and well to do will be acquiesced in, and the right to vote will be withheld only from the ignorant and irresponsible of both races.

There is one other matter to which I shall refer. It was made the subject of great controversy during the election, and calls for at least a passing reference now. My distinguished predecessor has given much attention to the cause of labor with whose struggle for better things he has shown the sincerest sympathy. At his instance, Congress has passed the bill fixing the liability of interstate carriers to their employees for injury sustained in the course of employment, abolishing the rule of fellow-servant and the common law rule as to contributory negligence, and substituting therefor the so-called rule of "comparative negligence." It has also passed a law fixing the compensation of government employees for injuries sustained in the employ of the Government through the negligence of the superior. It has also passed a model child-labor law for the District of Columbia. In previous administrations an arbitration law for interstate commerce railroads and their employees, and laws for the application of safety devices to save the lives and limbs of employees of interstate railroads had been passed. Additional legislation of this kind was passed by the outgoing Congress.

I wish to say that insofar as I can I hope to promote the enactment of further legislation of this character. I am strongly convinced that the Government should make itself as responsible to employees injured in its employ as an interstate-railway corporation is made responsible by federal law to its employees; and I shall be glad, whenever any additional reasonable safety device can be invented to reduce the loss of life and limb among railway employees, to urge Congress to require its adoption by interstate railways.

Another labor question has arisen which has awakened the most excited discussion. That is in respect to the power of the Federal courts to issue injunctions in industrial disputes. As to that, my convictions are fixed. Take away from the courts, if it could be taken away, the power to issue injunctions in labor disputes, and it would create a privileged class among the laborers and save the lawless among their number from a most needful remedy available to all men for the protection of their business against lawless invasion. The proposition that business is not a property or pecuniary right which can be protected by equitable injunction is utterly without foundation in precedent or reason. The proposition is usually linked with one to make the secondary boycott lawful. Such a proposition is at variance with the American instinct and will find no support, in my judgment, when submitted to the American people. The secondary boycott is an instrument of tyranny, and ought not to be made legitimate.

The issue of a temporary restraining order without notice has in several instances been abused by its inconsiderate exercise, and to remedy this, the platform upon which I was elected recommends the formulation in a statute of the conditions under which such a temporary restraining order ought to issue. A statute can and ought to be framed to embody the best modern practice, and can bring the subject so closely to the attention of the court as to make abuses of the process unlikely in the future. The American people, if I understand them, insist that the authority of the courts shall be sustained, and are opposed to any change in the procedure by which the powers of a court may be weakened and the fearless and effective administration of justice be interfered with.

Having thus reviewed the questions likely to recur during my administration, and having expressed in a summary way the position which I expect to take in recommendations to Congress and in my conduct as an Executive, I invoke the considerate sympathy and support of my fellow-citizens and the aid of the Almighty God in the discharge of my responsible duties.

Between Giants

THE INAUGURAL ADDRESS OF WILLIAM HOWARD TAFT

Jonathan Lurie

MARCH 4, 1909, found Washington, D.C., in the grip of a horrific blizzard, so severe that Taft's inauguration was shifted inside to the Senate Chamber. The night before, Taft and his wife had stayed at the White House as the guests of outgoing President Theodore Roosevelt, amid an atmosphere replete with apparent tension between the two men. It was, apparently, the first night for the incoming president and the last for the outgoing chief executive, who for the remainder of his life appears never to have returned to the Executive Mansion. In the wake of his triumphant re-election in 1904, Roosevelt had pledged that under no conditions would he accept re-nomination for a second full term in 1908.

During much of Roosevelt's tenure after 1904, Taft served in the Cabinet as his secretary of war. From 1900 until he joined the Roosevelt Cabinet, he had been in the Philippines, where he ultimately became the governing general. Admittedly a close friend of Roosevelt, Taft declined two offers from him of appointment to the Supreme Court, insisting that he needed to remain in his post on the Archipelago. By 1904, however, Roosevelt persuaded him to return home, even as popular commentary began to link Taft to the presidency, as his chosen successor in the 1908 election. By any measure a tough act to follow, Roosevelt had been a dynamic, effective, and skillful political figure, adept at making use of "the bully pulpit." But Taft was a very different public figure. Conservative in outlook, ponderous and deliberative (if not phlegmatic) in manner, he never was at home in politics. With the exception of a successful 1888 campaign for a judicial seat in Ohio, all of his numerous offices had come to him through appointment rather than election. Politics had no appeal for him. Indeed, "politics, when I am in it, makes me sick." Given a nomination he had not really desired, Taft gamely campaigned in the fall of 1908, always with a concerned Roosevelt cajoling, critiquing, and commenting in the background. He need not have worried, as Taft ended up with more than a million-vote majority over William Jennings Bryan.

As Roosevelt's term wound down, from his Cabinet post as secretary of war Taft observed that increasingly the president became enamored with progressive causes, such as conservation, matters of public health, and anti-trust regulation. Working with the well-established conservative Republican congressional leadership, throughout his tenure, Roosevelt had not hesitated to use the issue of tariff reform as a bargaining chip. In return for cooperation in getting other regulatory legislation passed, he made sure that tariff reform somehow never received presidential attention. As president-elect, Taft had to decide how far he would emulate Roosevelt's neo-progressive policies, which had tended to split the GOP, as the 1908 election came and went. The answer emerged in his Inaugural Address, delivered before a packed Senate chamber whose guests included the former president.

Speaking for about an hour, Taft immediately distanced himself from Roosevelt, even though he repeatedly lauded the former president's accomplishments. Taft promised to call Congress into special session specifically to confront the tariff issue, with the result (hopefully) of the "reduction of rates in certain schedules [plus] . . . the advancement of few, if any." Pointing to a projected million-dollar federal deficit, he added that if import duties (tariffs) do not secure an adequate income, "new kinds of taxation must be adopted, and among these I recommend a graduated inheritance tax." Before the ensuing congressional battle over the tariff had ended, Taft would propose three new constitutional amendments, dealing with direct election of senators, the franchise for women, and a graduated income tax. All would be adopted. The "scope of a modern government," added Taft, "has been widened far beyond the principles laid down by the old 'laissez faire' school of political writers, and this widening has met with popular approval."

Taft emphasized the accomplishments of Roosevelt even as he repeatedly called for "further legislative and executive action." He believed "that the amendments to be proposed are just as necessary in the protection of legitimate business as in the clinching of the reforms which properly bear the name of my predecessor." If his address thus far had reflected some aspects of progressive thought, its remainder revealed more conservative nuances. Thus Taft referred to the admission of Asiatic immigrants "who cannot be amalgamated with our population" and hoped that "we may continue to minimize the evils likely to arise from such immigration without unnecessary friction." Further, he devoted an unusual amount of space—more than any other topic covered in his address—to the South and the issue of racial integration.

In 1909, there could be no doubt concerning two salient facts in American political life: (a) that in terms of national politics the South voted a solid Democratic bloc, and (b) that especially in the first decade of the twentieth century, racial discrimination was widespread throughout the United States, not just in the South. Taft did not seek "to effect a change in the electoral vote of the Southern states," as much as "an increase in the tolerance of political views of all kinds and their advocacy throughout the South." In other words, a viable Republican party presence. As to the Fifteenth Amendment that supposedly protected the "negro race" from "any deprivation of the privilege to vote," it "never will be repealed and it never ought to be repealed," even though "if it had not passed, it might be difficult now to adopt it." Nevertheless, it is now within our fundamental law, and "so long as the statutes of the States meet the test of this amendment, ... it is not within the province of the Federal Government to interfere with the regulation by Southern States of their domestic affairs."

Appointment of a Black to federal office, however, represented a far different matter. In a single convoluted sentence, Taft revealed his innate racial bias. "It may well admit of doubt whether, in the case of any race, an appointment of one of their own to a local office in a community in which the race feeling is so widespread and acute as to interfere with the ease and facility with which the local government business can be done . . . is of sufficient benefit . . . to outweigh the recurrence and increase of race feeling which such an appointment is likely to engender." Further, while it seems outlandish today, in 1909 Taft could believe that "the exercise of political franchises by those of this race who are intelligent and well to do will be acquiesced in, and the right to vote will be withheld only from the ignorant and irresponsible of both races." In the meantime, echoing Booker T. Washington, Taft hoped that "a still greater improvement [of the Blacks] on the farm, and in the shop, and in other occupations may come."

Finally, Taft noted and strongly rejected the current progressive proposals to restrict the power of the federal courts to issue injunctions in industrial labor disputes. "As to that, my convictions are fixed." Such action "would create a privileged class among the laborers and save the lawless among their number from a most needful remedy available to all men for the protection of their business against lawless invasion." Indeed, "the proposition that business is not a property or pecuniary right which can be protected by equitable injunction is utterly without foundation in precedent or reason." The secondary boycott, against which injunctive relief was often directed, "is an instrument of tyranny, and ought not to be made legitimate."

As has generally been true of his presidency, Taft's Inaugural Address has not fared particularly well at the hands of historians who, finding much to praise in the tenure of Theodore Roosevelt, jump immediately to that of Woodrow Wilson and his "New Freedom." Again, Roosevelt would have been a hard act to follow for any successor, and all the more so for Taft, who differed so markedly from TR in his approach to politics. "I cannot be more aggressive than my nature makes me.... If the people don't like that kind of man then they have got to take another."[1] His address pointed to the forthcoming and tragic triumph of segregation throughout the South, as well as the inability of organized labor to withstand pressure from the federal courts. As an indicator of what was to come, his inaugural speech was all too accurate, On the other hand, Taft's administration had some positive results that were mentioned, albeit all but barely hinted at, in the address. Taken in its entirety, the Taft Inaugural Address reflected both the prejudices of his time and the potential for change within its context.

Note

1. Pringle Papers, August 11, 1908.

Woodrow Wilson's First Inaugural Address

TUESDAY, MARCH 4, 1913

THERE HAS BEEN a change of government. It began two years ago, when the House of Representatives became Democratic by a decisive majority. It has now been completed. The Senate about to assemble will also be Democratic. The offices of President and Vice President have been put into the hands of Democrats. What does the change mean? That is the question that is uppermost in our minds to-day. That is the question I am going to try to answer, in order, if I may, to interpret the occasion.

It means much more than the mere success of a party. The success of a party means little except when the nation is using that party for a large and definite purpose. No one can mistake the purpose for which the nation now seeks to use the Democratic Party. It seeks to use it to interpret a change in its own plans and point of view. Some old things with which we had grown familiar, and which had begun to creep into the very habit of our thought and of our lives, have altered their aspect as we have latterly looked critically upon them, with fresh, awakened eyes; have dropped their disguises and shown themselves alien and sinister. Some new things, as we look frankly upon them, willing to comprehend their real character, have come to assume the aspect of things long believed in and familiar, stuff of our own convictions. We have been refreshed by a new insight into our own life.

We see that in many things that life is very great. It is incomparably great in its material aspects, in its body of wealth, in the diversity and sweep of its energy, in the industries which have been conceived and built up by the genius of individual men and the limitless enterprise of groups of men. It is great, also, very great, in its moral force. Nowhere else in the world have noble men and women exhibited in more striking forms the beauty and the energy of sympathy and helpfulness and counsel in their efforts to rectify wrong, alleviate suffering, and set the weak in the way of strength and hope. We have built up, moreover, a great system of government, which has stood through a long age as in many respects a model for those who seek to set liberty upon foundations that will endure against fortuitous change, against storm and accident. Our life contains every great thing, and contains it in rich abundance.

But the evil has come with the good, and much fine gold has been corroded. With riches has come inexcusable waste. We have squandered a great part of what we might have used, and have not stopped to conserve the exceeding bounty of nature, without which our genius for enterprise would have been worthless and impotent, scorning to be careful, shamefully prodigal as well as admirably efficient. We have been proud of our industrial achievements, but we have not hitherto stopped thoughtfully enough to count the human cost, the cost of lives snuffed out, of energies overtaxed and broken, the fearful physical and spiritual cost to the men and women and children upon whom the dead weight and burden of it all has fallen pitilessly the years through. The groans and agony of it all had not yet reached our ears, the solemn, moving undertone of our life, coming up out of the mines and factories, and out of every home where the struggle had its intimate and familiar seat. With the great Government went many deep secret things which we too long delayed to look into and scrutinize with candid, fearless eyes. The great Government we loved has too often been made use of for private and selfish purposes, and those who used it had forgotten the people.

At last a vision has been vouchsafed us of our life as a whole. We see the bad with the good, the debased and decadent with the sound and vital. With this vision we approach new affairs. Our duty is to cleanse, to reconsider, to restore, to correct the evil without impairing the good, to purify and humanize every process of our common life without weakening or sentimentalizing it. There has been something crude and heartless and unfeeling in our haste to succeed and be great. Our thought has been "Let every man look out for himself, let every generation look out for itself," while we reared giant machinery which made it impossible that any but those who stood at the levers of control should have a chance to look out for themselves. We had not forgotten our morals. We remembered well enough that we had set up a polity which was meant to serve the humblest as well as the most powerful, with an eye single to the standards of justice and fair play, and remembered it with pride. But we were very heedless and in a hurry to be great.

We have come now to the sober second thought. The scales of heedlessness have fallen from our eyes. We have made up our minds to square every process of our national life again with the standards we so proudly set up at the beginning and have always carried at our hearts. Our work is a work of restoration.

We have itemized with some degree of particularity the things that ought to be altered and here are some of the chief items: A tariff which cuts us off from our proper part in the commerce of the world, violates the just principles of taxation, and makes the Government a facile instrument in the hand of private interests; a banking and currency system based upon the necessity of the Government to sell its bonds fifty years ago and perfectly adapted to concentrating cash and restricting credits; an industrial system which, take it on all its sides, financial as well as administrative, holds capital in leading strings, restricts the liberties and limits the opportunities of labor, and exploits without renewing or conserving the natural resources of the country; a body of agricultural activities never yet given the efficiency of great business undertakings or served as it should be through the instrumentality of science taken directly to the farm, or afforded the facilities of credit best suited to its practical needs; water courses undeveloped, waste places unreclaimed, forests untended, fast disappearing without plan or prospect of renewal, unregarded waste heaps at every mine. We have studied as perhaps no other nation has the most effective means of production, but we have not studied cost or economy as we should either as organizers of industry, as statesmen, or as individuals.

Nor have we studied and perfected the means by which government may be put at the service of humanity, in safeguarding the health of the Nation, the health of its men and its women and its children, as well as their rights in the struggle for existence. This is no sentimental duty. The firm basis of government is justice, not pity. These are matters of justice. There can be no equality or opportunity, the first essential of justice in the body politic, if men and women and children be not shielded in their lives, their very vitality, from the consequences of great industrial and social processes which they can not alter, control, or singly cope with. Society must see to it that it does not itself crush or weaken or damage its own constituent parts. The first duty of law is to keep sound the society it serves. Sanitary laws, pure food laws, and laws determining conditions of labor which individuals are powerless to determine for themselves are intimate parts of the very business of justice and legal efficiency.

These are some of the things we ought to do, and not leave the others undone, the old-fashioned, never-to-be-neglected, fundamental safeguarding of property and of individual right. This is the high enterprise of the new day: to lift everything that concerns our life as a Nation to the light that shines from the hearthfire of every man's conscience and vision of the right. It is inconceivable that we should do this as partisans; it is inconceivable we should do it in ignorance of the facts as they are or in blind haste. We shall restore, not destroy. We shall deal with our economic system as it is and as it may be modified, not as it might be if we had a clean sheet of paper to write upon; and step by step we shall make it what it should be, in the spirit of those who question their own wisdom and seek counsel and knowledge, not shallow self-satisfaction or the excitement of excursions whither they can not tell. Justice, and only justice, shall always be our motto.

And yet it will be no cool process of mere science. The Nation has been deeply stirred, stirred by a solemn passion, stirred by the knowledge of wrong, of ideals lost, of government too often debauched and made an instrument of evil. The feelings with which we face this new age of right and opportunity sweep across our heartstrings like some air out of God's own presence, where justice and mercy are reconciled and the judge and the brother are one. We know our task to be no mere task of politics but a task which shall search us through and through, whether we be able to understand our time and the need of our people, whether we be indeed their spokesmen and interpreters, whether we have the pure heart to comprehend and the rectified will to choose our high course of action.

This is not a day of triumph; it is a day of dedication. Here muster, not the forces of party, but the forces of humanity. Men's hearts wait upon us; men's lives hang in the balance; men's hopes call upon us to say what we will do. Who shall live up to the great trust? Who dares fail to try? I summon all honest men, all patriotic, all forward-looking men, to my side. God helping me, I will not fail them, if they will but counsel and sustain me!

The Schoolmaster

THE FIRST INAUGURAL ADDRESS OF WOODROW WILSON

Robert A. Enholm

WOODROW WILSON IS the most consequential American president in the period between Abraham Lincoln and Franklin D. Roosevelt.

Why should we re-examine President Woodrow Wilson's First Inaugural Address? Why do we study history at all? Is it to help explain how we got to the present? Is it to help us understand human nature? Is it to expand our range of experiences and help us to imagine the possibilities of our lives and of society?

In fact, events and personalities from history are constantly re-evaluated and reinterpreted in light of prevailing concerns and understandings. Thus one cannot discuss President Woodrow Wilson today without acknowledging that he has become a symbol of the white supremacy that prevailed in and defined his era. An analysis of Wilson's First Inaugural Address written ten years ago might not have mentioned his racism, and an analysis written in the future might find another point about Wilson's life to highlight.

So, what are we to say about Woodrow Wilson? In what ways was he merely emblematic of his times? What ideas did he advance that constituted what we today might call "progress"? What events from his biography surprise us or cause us to reconsider our opinion of him, or even to reconsider our opinions about ourselves?

Perhaps what history provides is context. A century after Wilson's death in 1923, our world is very different from his own. How did his thinking and his decisions affect us for good and ill? How did he, raised as a child during the American Civil War, grow to understand and address the changing world he inhabited?

How do we grow to understand and address our changing world? In reading his First Inaugural Address, what can we see there, what is missing, and what can we learn?

Before turning to Woodrow Wilson's First Inaugural Address, a brief biography will provide some perspective. Wilson was born in 1856 in Staunton, Virginia, and was raised during the American Civil War and Reconstruction Period in Augusta, Georgia, and Columbia, South Carolina. Wilson was the son, grandson, son-in-law, and nephew of Presbyterian ministers and theologians. Like some American presidents, all four of his grandparents were born outside of the United States. His ancestors were Scottish, English, and Irish.

Wilson attended college for a year at Davidson College, in North Carolina, before transferring to the College of New Jersey (later to become Princeton University). Wilson studied law at the University of Virginia and received his master's degree and PhD at Johns Hopkins University in Baltimore. After teaching briefly at Bryn Mawr College (in Pennsylvania) and Wesleyan University (in Connecticut), he joined the faculty at Princeton University in 1890, where he would spend the rest of his academic career. Wilson was considered an excellent orator and was a prominent and popular professor at Princeton. In 1902 he became Princeton's president.

As Wilson was wrapping up his graduate academic work, in 1885 he married Ellen Axson. Sadly, she would die of a kidney disease as First Lady in the White House in 1914. They had three daughters, born in the 1890s.

Wilson's rise in politics was as improbable as it was unprecedented. He went from university president in 1910, to governor of New Jersey, for two years, to election as president of the United States in 1912. William Jennings Bryan had been the Democratic party nominee in three of the four most recent presidential elections. At the 1912 Democratic party convention, Wilson did not receive the nomination until the 46th ballot. Bryan eventually supported Wilson at the convention and was appointed secretary of state in Wilson's initial Cabinet.

The 1912 presidential election was one of the wildest and most unusual in American history. Wilson competed against William Howard Taft, the incumbent president, Theodore Roosevelt, the former president, and Eugene V. Debs, the perennial Socialist party candidate. Wilson won an Electoral College landslide (435 out of 531) with only 42 percent of the popular vote. Wilson won because he was well-spoken, a novel figure in American politics, a Northern governor with Southern roots, and he supported policies that were progressive for his time.

Wilson was the first elected Democrat president since Grover Cleveland in 1892 and was the first Southern-born president since the Civil War. He was (and remains) the only president to have earned a PhD. In the 1912 election, as

Wilson mentions in his First Inaugural Address, his Democratic party retained control of the House of Representatives and gained control of the Senate. When Wilson took office in 1913, there were several Civil War veterans (Union and Confederate) in the Congress.

Re-examining President Woodrow Wilson's First Inaugural Address today, we notice several things. First, he uses his lofty oratory to elevate our thinking. The hallmark of Woodrow Wilson's rhetoric was his exhortation to great ideals and his invocation of universal principles. Wilson begins by acknowledging the success of the Democratic party, but he immediately pivots to say that his aims transcend partisanship and serve national goals, even humanity itself. "The success of a party means little except when the nation is using that party for a large and definite purpose." The invocation of higher principles is, of course, seen later in Wilson's speeches in support of the League of Nations. At his First Inauguration he exclaims, "This is not a day of triumph; it is a day of dedication. Here muster, not the forces of party, but the force of humanity."

Second, Wilson sets forth a list of practical goals that he intends to achieve. Sometimes in history the most remarkable innovations are accepted and become so ordinary that the innovation becomes obscured. This may be true of Wilson's exercise of presidential leadership. He consciously brings to the Congress an agenda of desired actions. In his speech he alludes disparagingly to the tariff system which underpinned the finances of the federal government. The Sixteenth Amendment to the Constitution had recently been ratified (after the November election and before the March Inauguration), enabling a reduction in tariffs whose revenue to support the federal government would be replaced by revenue from a newly approved progressive federal income tax. The tariff reduction would help the economy, and the burden of a progressive tax would be carried principally by the wealthy. The Revenue Act of 1913 was Wilson's first order of business for the new Congress, and its passage fulfilled a long-held wish of progressive Democrats.

Similarly, Wilson disparaged the current "banking and currency system," and before the end of his first year in office, Wilson would push through Congress the Federal Reserve Act, which established a national bank in the United States for the first time in over seventy years. The Federal Reserve System remains the foundation of the American banking system today.

In his Inaugural Address, Wilson also targets the "industrial system," and during his first term as president, Wilson oversaw the passage of both the Clayton Antitrust Act and the Federal Trade Commission Act to strengthen federal regulation of anticompetitive business practices and to help trade unions. The Federal Farm Loan Act and the National Park Service Act, both enacted in 1916, are also anticipated in Wilson's Inaugural Address. Wilson's first term in office achieved the greatest outpouring of progressive federal legislation until the New Deal a generation later.

The final observation to be made about Wilson's First Inaugural Address is that it is animated by progressivism, a movement in both Republican and Democratic politics in this era associated with good government, antitrust, conservation of natural resources, efficiency, workers' rights, and product safety. In the progressive tradition, Wilson is not calling for revolution. He identifies and criticizes shortcomings of capitalism, but he reassures, "Our work is a work of restoration." Wilson did not have the advantages of communicating by television or radio. He spoke and wrote in relatively long and complex sentences that lent themselves to being read in newspapers. The progressive spirit is evident: "There can be no equality or opportunity, the first essential of justice in the body politic, if men and women and children be not shielded in their lives, their very vitality, from the consequences of great industrial and social processes which they can not alter, control, or singly cope with."

So, what did Woodrow Wilson overlook? A century later, we have the advantage of being able to look back and see what Wilson did not say at his First Inauguration. This takes us into the realm of subjective or normative history (if there is such a realm). We can look back and consider what we think Wilson's concerns should have been. To a great extent we must allow figures in history to be of their own time. The broader question might be: to what extent can political leaders get ahead of their people? There are many examples in history of leaders who did things that were unpopular and yet have come to be regarded as farsighted. There are many other leaders who failed for being "ahead of their time." What did Wilson fail to foresee?

Obvious oversights by Wilson would include international issues. Today Wilson is well known for leading the United States through the First World War and thereafter for leading the establishment of the League of Nations, for which he would receive the Nobel Peace Prize in 1919. But in 1913 the thunderclap that would be the eruption of the First World War was not foreseen.

Similarly, Wilson is silent about the growing suffragist movement that would lead in less than seven years, during his second term, to the adoption of the Nineteenth Amendment to the Constitution, securing for women the federal constitutional right to vote. Wilson came into office skeptical of the wisdom of a federal constitutional amendment on the subject. He supported state laws favoring women's suffrage, and in 1915 voted as a citizen for such a law in his home state of New Jersey (it did not pass). Over the course of his presidency, seeing the sacrifices American women made for the war and receiving lobbying attention from suffragists, Wilson evolved and ultimately gave decisive support to the Nineteenth Amendment.

But from a modern point of view, Wilson's greatest oversight in his First Inaugural Address is his silence on the plight of Black people and the segregation and racism that prevailed in his time. Those who study the Progressive Era recognize and regret that progressivism in this era did not embrace racial justice. American history includes decades of racial segregation, institutionalized racism, Jim Crow laws, and racial discrimination. Students of history may wish that President Wilson had possessed and exhibited more enlightened views on race, but the fact is that he did not. This reveals much about him and his contemporaries.

Few in 1913 America were expecting Woodrow Wilson to make progress in dismantling the white supremacy that characterized and dominated so many institutions at this time. The problem of racism was much bigger than any single president. And unfortunately, most Americans did not recognize it as a problem at all.

Some modern observers will accept as sufficient to understand Wilson's racism an explanation that Wilson was from the South. History commands us to see that Wilson's unenlightened views on race were held more broadly in early twentieth-century America, even among educated, religious, and socially prominent people, in all regions of the country.

Over the past several years, historians have drawn their attention to Woodrow Wilson, the racism of his administration, and particularly his perpetuation of and acquiescence to segregation. That scholarship is too voluminous and fast-developing to be summarized here. The problem of racism in America challenges historians. Those who study this era do not want to suggest that they approve of the prevailing racism and do not want their writings to be interpreted as justifications for racism or apologies for those who perpetuated it. On the other hand, to speak plainly about this era is to describe a time when racial discrimination of the rankest sort, including segregation, was tolerated, accepted, and commonplace.

What can be said is that Wilson did not publicly display the hostile racist animus that was exhibited by many of his contemporaries. But it is clear that Wilson acquiesced to the racist activities and segregation practices of his subordinates, including several Cabinet members. Wilson, like much of America, was blind to the problem. It remains the task of historians to explain why. History can help us imagine the challenges that faced civil rights advocates in an era before "civil rights" was even broadly recognized as a term.

Woodrow Wilson's Second Inaugural Address

MONDAY, MARCH 5, 1917

MY FELLOW CITIZENS:

The four years which have elapsed since last I stood in this place have been crowded with counsel and action of the most vital interest and consequence. Perhaps no equal period in our history has been so fruitful of important reforms in our economic and industrial life or so full of significant changes in the spirit and purpose of our political action. We have sought very thoughtfully to set our house in order, correct the grosser errors and abuses of our industrial life, liberate and quicken the processes of our national genius and energy, and lift our politics to a broader view of the people's essential interests.

It is a record of singular variety and singular distinction. But I shall not attempt to review it. It speaks for itself and will be of increasing influence as the years go by. This is not the time for retrospect. It is time rather to speak our thoughts and purposes concerning the present and the immediate future.

Although we have centered counsel and action with such unusual concentration and success upon the great problems of domestic legislation to which we addressed ourselves four years ago, other matters have more and more forced themselves upon our attention—matters lying outside our own life as a nation and over which we had no control, but which, despite our wish to keep free of them, have drawn us more and more irresistibly into their own current and influence.

It has been impossible to avoid them. They have affected the life of the whole world. They have shaken men everywhere with a passion and an apprehension they never knew before. It has been hard to preserve calm counsel while the thought of our own people swayed this way and that under their influence.

We are a composite and cosmopolitan people. We are of the blood of all the nations that are at war. The currents of our thoughts as well as the currents of our trade run quick at all seasons back and forth between us and them. The war inevitably set its mark from the first alike upon our minds, our industries, our commerce, our politics and our social action. To be indifferent to it, or independent of it, was out of the question.

And yet all the while we have been conscious that we were not part of it. In that consciousness, despite many divisions, we have drawn closer together. We have been deeply wronged upon the seas, but we have not wished to wrong or injure in return; have retained throughout the consciousness of standing in some sort apart, intent upon an interest that transcended the immediate issues of the war itself.

As some of the injuries done us have become intolerable we have still been clear that we wished nothing for ourselves that we were not ready to demand for all mankind—fair dealing, justice, the freedom to live and to be at ease against organized wrong.

It is in this spirit and with this thought that we have grown more and more aware, more and more certain that the part we wished to play was the part of those who mean to vindicate and fortify peace. We have been obliged to arm ourselves to make good our claim to a certain minimum of right and of freedom of action. We stand firm in armed neutrality since it seems that in no other way we can demonstrate what it is we insist upon and cannot forget. We may even be drawn on, by circumstances, not by our own purpose or desire, to a more active assertion of our rights as we see them and a more immediate association with the great struggle itself. But nothing will alter our thought or our purpose. They are too clear to be obscured. They are too deeply rooted in the principles of our national life to be altered. We desire neither conquest nor advantage. We wish nothing that can be had only at the cost of another people. We always professed unselfish purpose and we covet the opportunity to prove our professions are sincere.

There are many things still to be done at home, to clarify our own politics and add new vitality to the industrial processes of our own life, and we shall do them as time and opportunity serve, but we realize that the greatest things that remain to be done must be done with the whole world for stage and in cooperation with the wide and universal forces of mankind, and we are making our spirits ready for those things.

We are provincials no longer. The tragic events of the thirty months of vital turmoil through which we have just passed have made us citizens of the world. There can be no turning back. Our own fortunes as a nation are involved whether we would have it so or not.

And yet we are not the less Americans on that account. We shall be the more American if we but remain true to the principles in which we have been bred. They are not the principles of a province or of a single continent. We have known and boasted all along that they were the principles of a liberated mankind. These, therefore, are the things we shall stand for, whether in war or in peace:

That all nations are equally interested in the peace of the world and in the political stability of free peoples, and equally responsible for their maintenance; that the essential principle of peace is the actual equality of nations in all matters of right or privilege; that peace cannot securely or justly rest upon an armed balance of power; that governments derive all their just powers from the consent of the governed and that no other powers should be supported by the common thought, purpose or power of the family of nations; that the seas should be equally free and safe for the use of all peoples, under rules set up by common agreement and consent, and that, so far as practicable, they should be accessible to all upon equal terms; that national armaments shall be limited to the necessities of national order and domestic safety; that the community of interest and of power upon which peace must henceforth depend imposes upon each nation the duty of seeing to it that all influences proceeding from its own citizens meant to encourage or assist revolution in other states should be sternly and effectually suppressed and prevented.

I need not argue these principles to you, my fellow countrymen; they are your own part and parcel of your own thinking and your own motives in affairs. They spring up native amongst us. Upon this as a platform of purpose and of action we can stand together. And it is imperative that we should stand together. We are being forged into a new unity amidst the fires that now blaze throughout the world. In their ardent heat we shall, in God's Providence, let us hope, be purged of faction and division, purified of the errant humors of party and of private interest, and shall stand forth in the days to come with a new dignity of national pride and spirit. Let each man see to it that the dedication is in his own heart, the high purpose of the nation in his own mind, ruler of his own will and desire.

I stand here and have taken the high and solemn oath to which you have been audience because the people of the United States have chosen me for this august delegation of power and have by their gracious judgment named me their leader in affairs.

I know now what the task means. I realize to the full the responsibility which it involves. I pray God I may be given the wisdom and the prudence to do my duty in the true spirit of this great people. I am their servant and can succeed only as they sustain and guide me by their confidence and their counsel. The thing I shall count upon, the thing without which neither counsel nor action will avail, is the unity of America—an America united in feeling, in purpose and in its vision of duty, of opportunity and of service.

We are to beware of all men who would turn the tasks and the necessities of the nation to their own private profit or use them for the building up of private power.

United alike in the conception of our duty and in the high resolve to perform it in the face of all men, let us dedicate ourselves to the great task to which we must now set our hand. For myself I beg your tolerance, your countenance and your united aid.

The shadows that now lie dark upon our path will soon be dispelled, and we shall walk with the light all about us if we be but true to ourselves—to ourselves as we have wished to be known in the counsels of the world and in the thought of all those who love liberty and justice and the right exalted.

The Eve of War

THE SECOND INAUGURAL ADDRESS OF WOODROW WILSON

John Milton Cooper, Jr.

For if the trumpet give an uncertain sound, who shall prepare himself for the battle?
—FIRST CORINTHIANS 14:8, King James & Geneva Bible

AS THE SON, grandson, nephew, and later son-in-law of Presbyterian ministers, Woodrow Wilson would have heard and read those words many times. As a practiced orator and scrupulous stylist, Wilson would never have spoken in that fashion. Yet that was what he did when he delivered his Second Inaugural Address on March 5, 1917. He did that because he believed he had no choice.

Wilson's first words hinted at the kind of address he would rather have given. "The four years which have elapsed since last I stood in this place have been crowded with counsel and action of the most vital interest and consequence. Perhaps no equal period in our history has been so fruitful of important reforms in our economic and industrial life or so full of significant changes in the spirit and purpose of our political action." At the risk of bragging, the president could fairly point to the consequential, sometimes monumental domestic legislation he and his party had enacted during those years. More than anything else, those achievements had secured his re-election, to become the first Democrat since Andrew Jackson to win a second consecutive term. But, as he immediately conceded, he could not dwell on those accomplishments because "other matters have more and more forced themselves upon our attention—matters lying outside our own life as a nation and over which we had no control."

Wilson meant foreign affairs, specifically the titanic conflict raging across the Atlantic. A few days after he was first elected in 1912, he had remarked to a friend, "It would be an irony of fate if my administration had to deal chiefly with foreign problems; for all my preparation has been in domestic matters."[1] Even before the outbreak of the world war in 1914, "foreign problems," particularly the revolution in Mexico, had intruded on his time and attention. The sinking of the *Lusitania* in May 1915 by a German submarine had brought the war in Europe home to Americans, and it had required Wilson to become more of a diplomatist. It was remarkable that he was still able to accomplish as much as he did at home. Even more remarkably, through a combination of patient and daring diplomacy and luck, he got the Germans to rein in their submarines, thereby lifting the threat of being drawn into the war. The president and his party did play the peace card in the 1916 election, with the slogan "He Kept Us Out of War," but by the time the campaign got underway that appeal referred more to Mexico than to Europe.

This happy state of affairs came to an abrupt end only a month before the inauguration when the Germans unleashed their submarines. "We have been deeply wronged upon the seas, but we have not wished to wrong or injure in return; have retained throughout the consciousness of standing . . . apart, intent upon an interest that transcended the immediate issues of the war itself."

What hurt Wilson most about this German move, even more than having to set aside his domestic program, was that he had been seeking to end the war and begin to build a new international order. As soon as he knew he had won another term, he had mounted a peace offensive. First, he had dispatched a public call to the belligerents, asking them to state their aims, with a view toward mediating the conflict. Then, just over a week before the Germans' submarine move, he had gone before the Senate to unveil his vision of a non-punitive, brokered peace, which he called "peace without victory," to be guaranteed by a league of nations with enforcement powers, which the United States would join. This was Wilson's fondest wish, to become peacemaker-in-chief to the world.

Now, the Germans had blasted that hope. Arming American merchant ships was his present policy. Yet, he conceded, "We may even be drawn on, by circumstances, not by our purpose or desire, to a more active assertion of our rights as we see them and a more immediate association with the great struggle itself." Whether or not that came to pass, there was no way to evade involvement with what was happening on and across the seas. "We are provincials no longer. The tragical events of the thirty months of vital turmoil through which we have just passed have made us citizens of the world. There can be no turning back. Our own fortunes as a nation are involved whether we would have it so or not."

Wilson insisted that America must remain true to the vision he had so recently laid out of a just and lasting peace. He elaborated on a set of propositions he had sketched in his "peace without victory" address: equality of nations, great and small; an end to the balance of power; governments based on consent of the governed; freedom of the seas; limitation of armaments; mutual non-interference in internal affairs. Less than a year later, Wilson would reiterate these ideas and tie them to specific territorial matters in his Fourteen Points. But that would come only when he spoke as the leader of a belligerent nation, who was arrogating to himself the leadership of an armed coalition.

Despite his previous warning in the Inaugural Address, Wilson did not propose to go down the road to war yet. "I pray God I may be given the wisdom and prudence to do my duty in the true spirit of this great people. . . . The shadows that now lie dark upon our path will soon be dispelled, and we shall walk with the light all about us if we can be but true to ourselves—to ourselves as we have wished to be known in the counsels of the world and in the thought of all those who love liberty and justice and the right exalted." Noble ideals and soaring rhetoric—qualities for which Wilson was already renowned and would become still more famous—but there was no escaping the uncertain sound from the trumpet he was sounding in this Inaugural Address.

The sound was uncertain because his mind was likewise uncertain. Wilson would spend another month watching events unfold, reassessing the practicality of armed neutrality, questioning how he could best pursue the kind of peace and world order he envisioned—done mostly in solitary, thoughtful, prayerful, agonizing reflection—before he decided what to do next. Ultimately, he would choose war, and he would do it in the spirit he had shown in this address. In his eloquent speech to Congress on April 2, 1917, he would point again to the propositions he had laid down in the Inaugural Address, and he would proclaim, "The world must be made for democracy." That sentence would often be misquoted because many wanted to see Wilson's decision as a clarion call to a crusade. The note he sounded was not a resounding blare; it was a careful, sometimes muted call to fight for something beyond military victory. It was a call to take up the task of building a more just and peaceful world. His trumpet's sound would have mixed notes, but it would no longer be uncertain.

Note

1. Edward Grant Conklin, interview by RSB, June 3, 1925, RSBP, box 104.

Warren G. Harding's Inaugural Address

FRIDAY, MARCH 4, 1921

MY COUNTRYMEN:

When one surveys the world about him after the great storm, noting the marks of destruction and yet rejoicing in the ruggedness of the things which withstood it, if he is an American he breathes the clarified atmosphere with a strange mingling of regret and new hope. We have seen a world passion spend its fury, but we contemplate our Republic unshaken, and hold our civilization secure. Liberty—liberty within the law—and civilization are inseparable, and though both were threatened we find them now secure; and there comes to Americans the profound assurance that our representative government is the highest expression and surest guaranty of both.

Standing in this presence, mindful of the solemnity of this occasion, feeling the emotions which no one may know until he senses the great weight of responsibility for himself, I must utter my belief in the divine inspiration of the Founding Fathers. Surely there must have been God's intent in the making of this new-world Republic. Ours is an organic law which had but one ambiguity, and we saw that effaced in a baptism of sacrifice and blood, with union maintained, the Nation supreme, and its concord inspiring. We have seen the world rivet its hopeful gaze on the great truths on which the founders wrought. We have seen civil, human, and religious liberty verified and glorified. In the beginning the Old World scoffed at our experiment; today our foundations of political and social belief stand unshaken, a precious inheritance to ourselves, an inspiring example of freedom and civilization to all mankind. Let us express renewed and strengthened devotion, in grateful reverence for the immortal beginning, and utter our confidence in the supreme fulfillment.

The recorded progress of our Republic, materially and spiritually, in itself proves the wisdom of the inherited policy of noninvolvement in Old World affairs. Confident of our ability to work out our own destiny, and jealously guarding our right to do so, we seek no part in directing the destinies of the Old World. We do not mean to be entangled. We will accept no responsibility except as our own conscience and judgment, in each instance, may determine.

Our eyes never will be blind to a developing menace, our ears never deaf to the call of civilization. We recognize the new order in the world, with the closer contacts which progress has wrought. We sense the call of the human heart for fellowship, fraternity, and cooperation. We crave friendship and harbor no hate. But America, our America, the America built on the foundation laid by the inspired fathers, can be a party to no permanent military alliance. It can enter into no political commitments, nor assume any economic obligations which will subject our decisions to any other than our own authority.

I am sure our own people will not misunderstand, nor will the world misconstrue. We have no thought to impede the paths to closer relationship. We wish to promote understanding. We want to do our part in making offensive warfare so hateful that Governments and peoples who resort to it must prove the righteousness of their cause or stand as outlaws before the bar of civilization.

We are ready to associate ourselves with the nations of the world, great and small, for conference, for counsel; to seek the expressed views of world opinion; to recommend a way to approximate disarmament and relieve the crushing burdens of military and naval establishments. We elect to participate in suggesting plans for mediation, conciliation, and arbitration, and would gladly join in that expressed conscience of progress, which seeks to clarify and write the laws of international relationship, and establish a world court for the disposition of such justiciable questions as nations are agreed to submit thereto. In expressing aspirations, in seeking practical plans, in translating humanity's new concept of righteousness and justice and its hatred of war into recommended action we are ready most heartily to unite, but every commitment must be made in the exercise of our national sovereignty. Since freedom impelled, and independence inspired, and nationality exalted, a world supergovernment is contrary to everything we cherish and can have no sanction by our Republic. This is not selfishness, it is sanctity. It is not aloofness, it is security. It is not suspicion of others, it is patriotic adherence to the things which made us what we are.

Today, better than ever before, we know the aspirations of humankind, and share them. We have come to a new realization of our place in the world and a new appraisal of our Nation by the world. The unselfishness of these United States is a thing proven; our devotion to peace for ourselves and for the world is well established; our concern for preserved civilization has had its impassioned and heroic expression. There was no American failure to resist the attempted reversion of civilization; there will be no failure today or tomorrow.

The success of our popular government rests wholly upon the correct interpretation of the deliberate, intelligent, dependable popular will of America. In a deliberate questioning of a suggested change of national policy, where internationality was to supersede nationality, we turned to a referendum, to the American people. There was ample discussion, and there is a public mandate in manifest understanding.

America is ready to encourage, eager to initiate, anxious to participate in any seemly program likely to lessen the probability of war, and promote that brotherhood of mankind which must be God's highest conception of human relationship. Because we cherish ideals of justice and peace, because we appraise international comity and helpful relationship no less highly than any people of the world, we aspire to a high place in the moral leadership of civilization, and we hold a maintained America, the proven Republic, the unshaken temple of representative democracy, to be not only an inspiration and example, but the highest agency of strengthening good will and promoting accord on both continents.

Mankind needs a world-wide benediction of understanding. It is needed among individuals, among peoples, among governments, and it will inaugurate an era of good feeling to make the birth of a new order. In such understanding men will strive confidently for the promotion of their better relationships and nations will promote the comities so essential to peace.

We must understand that ties of trade bind nations in closest intimacy, and none may receive except as he gives. We have not strengthened ours in accordance with our resources or our genius, notably on our own continent, where a galaxy of Republics reflects the glory of new-world democracy, but in the new order of finance and trade we mean to promote enlarged activities and seek expanded confidence.

Perhaps we can make no more helpful contribution by example than prove a Republic's capacity to emerge from the wreckage of war. While the world's embittered travail did not leave us devastated lands nor desolated cities, left no gaping wounds, no breast with hate, it did involve us in the delirium of expenditure, in expanded currency and credits, in unbalanced industry, in unspeakable waste, and disturbed relationships. While it uncovered our portion of hateful selfishness at home, it also revealed the heart of America as sound and fearless, and beating in confidence unfailing.

Amid it all we have riveted the gaze of all civilization to the unselfishness and the righteousness of representative democracy, where our freedom never has made offensive warfare, never has sought territorial aggrandizement through force, never has turned to the arbitrament of arms until reason has been exhausted. When the Governments of the earth shall have established a freedom like our own and shall have sanctioned the pursuit of peace as we have practiced it, I believe the last sorrow and the final sacrifice of international warfare will have been written.

Let me speak to the maimed and wounded soldiers who are present today, and through them convey to their comrades the gratitude of the Republic for their sacrifices in its defense. A generous country will never forget the services you rendered, and you may hope for a policy under Government that will relieve any maimed successors from taking your places on another such occasion as this.

Our supreme task is the resumption of our onward, normal way. Reconstruction, readjustment, restoration all these must follow. I would like to hasten them. If it will lighten the spirit and add to the resolution with which we take up the task, let me repeat for our Nation, we shall give no people just cause to make war upon us; we hold no national prejudices; we entertain no spirit of revenge; we do not hate; we do not covet; we dream of no conquest, nor boast of armed prowess.

If, despite this attitude, war is again forced upon us, I earnestly hope a way may be found which will unify our individual and collective strength and consecrate all America, materially and spiritually, body and soul, to national defense. I can vision the ideal republic, where every man and woman is called under the flag for assignment to duty for whatever service, military or civic, the individual is best fitted; where we may call to universal service every plant, agency, or facility, all in the sublime sacrifice for country, and not one penny of war profit shall inure to the benefit of private individual, corporation, or combination, but all above the normal shall flow into the defense chest of the Nation. There is something inherently wrong, something out of accord with the ideals of representative democracy, when one portion of our citizenship turns its activities to private gain amid defensive war while another is fighting, sacrificing, or dying for national preservation.

Out of such universal service will come a new unity of spirit and purpose, a new confidence and consecration, which would make our defense impregnable, our triumph assured. Then we should have little or no disorganization of our economic, industrial, and commercial systems at home, no staggering war debts, no swollen fortunes to flout the sacrifices of our soldiers, no excuse for sedition, no pitiable slackerism, no outrage of treason. Envy and jealousy would have no soil for their menacing development, and revolution would be without the passion which engenders it.

A regret for the mistakes of yesterday must not, however, blind us to the tasks of today. War never left such an aftermath. There has been staggering loss of life and measureless wastage of materials. Nations are still groping for return to stable ways. Discouraging indebtedness confronts us like all the war-torn nations, and these obligations must be provided for. No civilization can survive repudiation.

We can reduce the abnormal expenditures, and we will. We can strike at war taxation, and we must. We must face the grim necessity, with full knowledge that the task is to be solved, and we must proceed with a full realization that no statute enacted by man can repeal the inexorable laws of nature. Our most dangerous tendency is to expect too much of government, and at the same time do for it too little. We contemplate the immediate task of putting our public household in order. We need a rigid and yet sane economy, combined with fiscal justice, and it must be attended by individual prudence and thrift, which are so essential to this trying hour and reassuring for the future.

The business world reflects the disturbance of war's reaction. Herein flows the lifeblood of material existence. The economic mechanism is intricate and its parts interdependent, and has suffered the shocks and jars incident to abnormal demands, credit inflations, and price upheavals. The normal balances have been impaired, the channels of distribution have been clogged, the relations of labor and management have been strained. We must seek the readjustment with care and courage. Our people must give and take. Prices must reflect the receding fever of war activities. Perhaps we never shall know the old levels of wages again, because war invariably readjusts compensations, and the necessaries of life will show their inseparable relationship, but we must strive for normalcy to reach stability. All the penalties will not be light, nor evenly distributed. There is no way of making them so. There is no instant step from disorder to order. We must face a condition of grim reality, charge off our losses and start afresh. It is the oldest lesson of civilization. I would like government to do all it can to mitigate; then, in understanding, in mutuality of interest, in concern for the common good, our tasks will be solved. No altered system will work a miracle. Any wild experiment will only add to the confusion. Our best assurance lies in efficient administration of our proven system.

The forward course of the business cycle is unmistakable. Peoples are turning from destruction to production. Industry has sensed the changed order and our own people are turning to resume their normal, onward way. The call is for productive America to go on. I know that Congress and the Administration will favor every wise Government policy to aid the resumption and encourage continued progress.

I speak for administrative efficiency, for lightened tax burdens, for sound commercial practices, for adequate credit facilities, for sympathetic concern for all agricultural problems, for the omission of unnecessary interference of Government with business, for an end to Government's experiment in business, and for more efficient business in Government administration. With all of this must attend a mindfulness of the human side of all activities, so that social, industrial, and economic justice will be squared with the purposes of a righteous people.

With the nation-wide induction of womanhood into our political life, we may count upon her intuitions, her refinements, her intelligence, and her influence to exalt the social order. We count upon her exercise of the full privileges and the performance of the duties of citizenship to speed the attainment of the highest state.

I wish for an America no less alert in guarding against dangers from within than it is watchful against enemies from without. Our fundamental law recognizes no class, no group, no section; there must be none in legislation or administration. The supreme inspiration is the common weal. Humanity hungers for international peace, and we crave it with all mankind. My most reverent prayer for America is for industrial peace, with its rewards, widely and generally distributed, amid the inspirations of equal opportunity. No one justly may deny the equality of opportunity which made us what we are. We have mistaken unpreparedness to embrace it to be a challenge of the reality, and due concern for making all citizens fit for participation will give added strength of citizenship and magnify our achievement.

If revolution insists upon overturning established order, let other peoples make the tragic experiment. There is no place for it in America. When World War threatened civilization we pledged our resources and our lives to its preservation, and when revolution threatens we unfurl the flag of law and order and renew our consecration. Ours is a constitutional freedom where the popular will is the law supreme and minorities are sacredly protected. Our revisions, reformations, and evolutions reflect a deliberate judgment and an orderly progress, and we mean to cure our ills, but never destroy or permit destruction by force.

I had rather submit our industrial controversies to the conference table in advance than to a settlement table after conflict and suffering. The earth is thirsting for the cup of good will, understanding is its fountain source. I would like to acclaim an era of good feeling amid dependable prosperity and all the blessings which attend.

It has been proved again and again that we cannot, while throwing our markets open to the world, maintain American standards of living and opportunity, and hold our industrial eminence in such unequal competition. There is a luring fallacy in the theory of banished barriers of trade, but preserved American standards require our higher production costs to be reflected in our tariffs on imports. Today, as never before, when peoples are seeking trade restoration and expansion, we must adjust our tariffs to the new order. We seek participation in the world's exchanges, because therein lies our way to widened influence and the triumphs of peace. We know full well we cannot sell where we do not buy, and we cannot sell successfully where we do not carry. Opportunity is calling not alone for the restoration, but for a new era in production, transportation and trade. We shall answer it best by meeting the demand of a surpassing home market, by promoting self-reliance in production, and by bidding enterprise, genius, and efficiency to carry our cargoes in American bottoms to the marts of the world.

We would not have an America living within and for herself alone, but we would have her self-reliant, independent, and ever nobler, stronger, and richer. Believing in our higher standards, reared through constitutional liberty and maintained opportunity, we invite the world to the same heights. But pride in things wrought is no reflex of a completed task. Common welfare is the goal of our national endeavor. Wealth is not inimical to welfare; it ought to be its friendliest agency. There never can be equality of rewards or possessions so long as the human plan contains varied talents and differing degrees of industry and thrift, but ours ought to be a country free from the great blotches of distressed poverty. We ought to find a way to guard against the perils and penalties of unemployment. We want an America of homes, illumined with hope and happiness, where mothers, freed from the necessity for long hours of toil beyond their own doors, may preside as befits the hearthstone of American citizenship. We want the cradle of American childhood rocked under conditions so wholesome and so hopeful that no blight may touch it in its development, and we want to provide that no selfish interest, no material necessity, no lack of opportunity shall prevent the gaining of that education so essential to best citizenship.

There is no short cut to the making of these ideals into glad realities. The world has witnessed again and again the futility and the mischief of ill-considered remedies for social and economic disorders. But we are mindful today as never before of the friction of modern industrialism, and we must learn its causes and reduce its evil consequences by sober and tested methods. Where genius has made for great possibilities, justice and happiness must be reflected in a greater common welfare.

Service is the supreme commitment of life. I would rejoice to acclaim the era of the Golden Rule and crown it with the autocracy of service. I pledge an administration wherein all the agencies of Government are called to serve, and ever promote an understanding of Government purely as an expression of the popular will.

One cannot stand in this presence and be unmindful of the tremendous responsibility. The world upheaval has added heavily to our tasks. But with the realization comes the surge of high resolve, and there is reassurance in belief in the God-given destiny of our Republic. If I felt that there is to be sole responsibility in the Executive for the America of tomorrow I should shrink from the burden.

But here are a hundred millions, with common concern and shared responsibility, answerable to God and country. The Republic summons them to their duty, and I invite cooperation.

I accept my part with single-mindedness of purpose and humility of spirit, and implore the favor and guidance of God in His Heaven. With these I am unafraid, and confidently face the future.

I have taken the solemn oath of office on that passage of Holy Writ wherein it is asked: "What doth the Lord require of thee but to do justly, and to love mercy, and to walk humbly with thy God?" This I plight to God and country.

Return to Normalcy

THE INAUGURAL ADDRESS OF WARREN G. HARDING

James D. Robenalt

"MANKIND NEEDS A ... benediction of understanding," Warren Harding said on March 4, 1921, when he was sworn in as the nation's twenty-ninth president. "It is needed among individuals, among peoples, among governments, and it will inaugurate an era of good feeling to make the birth of a new order."

When he assumed the presidency, nothing was more important than the blessing of peace and the birth of a new order in a world torn apart by a monstrous, barbaric war and rocked by an extraordinarily deadly pandemic. Harding understood that grave threats remained—resumption of war, famine and starvation, worldwide Bolshevik revolution, economic collapse, and the advent of costly and endless weapons races. The disruption had been incalculable—tens of millions died in the war, and fifty to a hundred million perished from the Spanish flu (675,000 in the United States alone).

For the United States, these forces of chaos had been met by a leaderless national government. President Woodrow Wilson, the man who headed the executive branch, had suffered a series of debilitating strokes in September and October 1919 as he stumped the country in a desperate attempt to gain acceptance of his view of a new order—the League of Nations. His strokes left Wilson incapable of performing his job, at first physically and later emotionally. His hovering spouse, Edith Wilson, allowed few visitors to his sickroom, and his condition was largely blinded to the American public.

Thus, for nearly a year and a half before Harding's inauguration, things were allowed to drift aimlessly in what was perhaps one of the most precarious times of humankind. The economy was supercharged from the war and it hit overdrive in the year following the end of the war, but then collapsed in the spring of 1920. Soldiers returning from Europe could not find jobs. Rapid inflation was followed by ruinous deflation. War taxes weighed down the economy that had to survive to save the world, prostrate from its war indebtedness.

Harding took the oath on the East Portico of the Capitol at 1:18 p.m. "under a brilliant sky and in a keen atmosphere," recorded the *New York Times*.[1] Woodrow Wilson rode with Harding from the White House to the Capitol, but then turned back, lacking the strength to witness the swearing-in of his successor. He was driven inauspiciously to his new home on S Street. Chief Justice Edward D. White, black-capped and gowned, a massive man, administered the oath on a Bible used by George Washington in his First Inaugural. Harding had it opened to Micah 6:8, his favorite verse: "What does the LORD require of thee but to do justly and to love mercy and to walk humbly with your God?"

This was the first inaugural where an electronic amplification system was employed, with speakers hidden under a huge flag in the roof of a kiosk of Corinthian architecture built on the Capitol steps for the ceremony. In previous inaugurals, one had to be within shouting distance to hear the speaker. On this day, a large crowd could hear Harding's words in resonant tones echoing in front of the speaker's platform.

They cheered for certain lines, mainly those directed against the League of Nations and in favor of national sovereignty. "A world supergovernment is contrary to everything we cherish and can have no sanction by our Republic," he said, drawing heavy applause according to the *Times*.

But Harding surprised many with his speech. While he sought to protect America's sovereignty and any decision to use its power, he was solicitous of those who believed that the United States had a sacred mission in the world. America might avoid unnecessary "entanglements" with other nations of the world, but it would not remain aloof.

He built on the theme that the United States alone was the guiding example of a representative form of government, one that had selflessly thrown itself into a war to end what had devolved into a ferocious contest that threatened civilization itself. "In the beginning the Old World scoffed at our experiment," he said. "Today our foundations of political and social belief stand unshaken, a precious inheritance to ourselves, an inspiring example of freedom and civilization to all mankind."

He warned that the United States, while it would allow no other governments to decide its fate, would not shrink from challenges to the international order: "We want to do our part in making offensive warfare so hateful that Governments and peoples who resort to it must prove the righteousness of their cause or stand as outlaws before the bar of civilization."

These warnings delivered, he turned to higher calls for associations among nations, a code word that made reservationists and irreconcilables in his party edgy. "We are ready to associate ourselves," he declared, "with the nations of the world, great and small, for conference, for counsel; to seek the expressed views of world opinion; to recommend a way to approximate disarmament and relieve the crushing burdens of military and naval establishments."

Disarmament in fact would be one of the great achievements of his administration. The Washington Naval Conference he called in 1921, resulting in the world's first arms limitation treaty, would lead to his nomination for the Nobel Peace Prize (unawarded in 1923 after he died, as Nobel rules discouraged posthumous honors).

As importantly, he recommended the United States join the World Court, a suggestion that never came to pass because of deep isolationist sentiment in the country.

Having addressed international concerns, Harding turned to his plans for the United States, recognizing that, unless America put its house in order, the world could never recover from the war wreckage; indeed, events could have turned to revolution and anarchy. This task of reconstruction, he warned, was complicated and would not be easy. Burdens would fall unfairly on some. He sought cooperation of all, management and labor. "Our people must give and take," he pleaded.

Two areas required immediate attention: reducing government expenditures and taxes. He avowed: "We can reduce the abnormal expenditures, and we will. We can strike at war taxation, and we must." To accomplish these complex tasks, Harding insisted that the government had to be placed on a budget for the first time. He would create the first Bureau of the Budget, today the Office of Management and Budget. He spoke, he said, for "administrative efficiency, for lightened tax burdens, for sound commercial practices, for adequate credit facilities."

His tactics worked. After a worsening period economically, the United States recovered and helped undergird some precious measure of economic stability in the world.

He welcomed women, who had voted for the first time in federal elections in 1920, into their rightful place as citizens. He addressed wounded veterans brought over from Walter Reed Hospital. "A generous country will never forget the services you rendered," he said. His administration would create the first Veterans' Bureau (today the Department of Veterans Affairs) to care for those wounded and maimed in the war.

He even winked at a sort of New Deal concern for the unemployed and those in poverty. "Wealth is not inimical to welfare," he observed, "it ought to be its friendliest agency." He explained: "There can never be equality of rewards or possessions so long as the human plan contains varied talents and differing degrees of industry and thrift, but ours ought to be a country free from the blotches of distressed poverty."

Presaging Franklin Roosevelt, he pondered, "We ought to find a way to guard against the perils and penalties of unemployment."

He concluded, thirty-seven minutes after he began, by imploring "the favor and guidance of God in His Heaven." Knowing his task too great for any one man, he took comfort in the fact that a hundred million Americans would share his responsibility.

Returning to Micah, "to act justly, and to love mercy, and to walk humbly with thy God," Warren Harding ended by promising, in an old-fashioned way, "This I plight to God and country." As he left the inaugural platform, the Marine Band, in scarlet coats and bright blue trousers, played a stanza of "America."

Note

1. *New York Times*, March 5, 1921.

Calvin Coolidge's Inaugural Address

WEDNESDAY, MARCH 4, 1925

MY COUNTRYMEN:

No one can contemplate current conditions without finding much that is satisfying and still more that is encouraging. Our own country is leading the world in the general readjustment to the results of the great conflict. Many of its burdens will bear heavily upon us for years, and the secondary and indirect effects we must expect to experience for some time. But we are beginning to comprehend more definitely what course should be pursued, what remedies ought to be applied, what actions should be taken for our deliverance, and are clearly manifesting a determined will faithfully and conscientiously to adopt these methods of relief.

Already we have sufficiently rearranged our domestic affairs so that confidence has returned, business has revived, and we appear to be entering an era of prosperity which is gradually reaching into every part of the Nation. Realizing that we can not live unto ourselves alone, we have contributed of our resources and our counsel to the relief of the suffering and the settlement of the disputes among the European nations. Because of what America is and what America has done, a firmer courage, a higher hope, inspires the heart of all humanity.

These results have not occurred by mere chance. They have been secured by a constant and enlightened effort marked by many sacrifices and extending over many generations. We can not continue these brilliant successes in the future, unless we continue to learn from the past. It is necessary to keep the former experiences of our country both at home and abroad continually before us, if we are to have any science of government. If we wish to erect new structures, we must have a definite knowledge of the old foundations. We must realize that human nature is about the most constant thing in the universe and that the essentials of human relationship do not change. We must frequently take our bearings from these fixed stars of our political firmament if we expect to hold a true course.

If we examine carefully what we have done, we can determine the more accurately what we can do.

We stand at the opening of the one hundred and fiftieth year since our national consciousness first asserted itself by unmistakable action with an array of force. The old sentiment of detached and dependent colonies disappeared in the new sentiment of a united and independent Nation. Men began to discard the narrow confines of a local charter for the broader opportunities of a national constitution. Under the eternal urge of freedom we became an independent Nation. A little less than 50 years later that freedom and independence were reasserted in the face of all the world, and guarded, supported, and secured by the Monroe doctrine.

The narrow fringe of States along the Atlantic seaboard advanced its frontiers across the hills and plains of an intervening continent until it passed down the golden slope to the Pacific. We made freedom a birthright. We extended our domain over distant islands in order to safeguard our own interests and accepted the consequent obligation to bestow justice and liberty upon less favored peoples. In the defense of our own ideals and in the general cause of liberty we entered the Great War. When victory had been fully secured, we withdrew to our own shores unrecompensed save in the consciousness of duty done.

Throughout all these experiences we have enlarged our freedom, we have strengthened our independence. We have been, and propose to be, more and more American. We believe that we can best serve our own country and most successfully discharge our obligations to humanity by continuing to be openly and candidly, intensely and scrupulously, American. If we have any heritage, it has been that. If we have any destiny, we have found it in that direction.

But if we wish to continue to be distinctively American, we must continue to make that term comprehensive enough to embrace the legitimate desires of a civilized and enlightened people determined in all their relations to pursue a conscientious and religious life. We can not permit ourselves to be narrowed and dwarfed by slogans and phrases. It is not the adjective, but the substantive, which is of real importance. It is not the name of the action, but the result of the action, which is the chief concern. It will be well not to be too much disturbed by the thought of either isolation or entanglement of pacifists and militarists. The physical configuration of the earth has separated us from all of the Old World, but the common brotherhood of man, the highest law of all our being, has united us by inseparable bonds with all humanity. Our country represents nothing but peaceful intentions toward all the earth, but it ought not to fail to maintain such a military force as comports with the dignity and security of a great people. It ought to be a balanced force, intensely modern, capable of defense by sea and land, beneath the surface and in the air. But it should be so conducted that all the world may see in it, not a menace, but an instrument of security and peace.

This Nation believes thoroughly in an honorable peace under which the rights of its citizens are to be everywhere protected. It has never found that the necessary enjoyment of such a peace could be maintained only by a great and threatening array of arms. In common with other nations, it is now more determined than ever to promote peace through friendliness and good will, through mutual understandings and mutual forbearance. We have never practiced the policy of competitive armaments. We have recently committed ourselves by covenants with the other great nations to a limitation of our sea power. As one result of this, our Navy ranks larger, in comparison, than it ever did before. Removing the burden of expense and jealousy, which must always accrue from a keen rivalry, is one of the most effective methods of diminishing that unreasonable hysteria and misunderstanding which are the most potent means of fomenting war. This policy represents a new departure in the world. It is a thought, an ideal, which has led to an entirely new line of action. It will not be easy to maintain. Some never move from their old position, some are constantly slipping back to the old ways of thought and the old action of seizing a musket and relying on force. America has taken the lead in this new direction, and that lead America must continue to hold. If we expect others to rely on our fairness and justice we must show that we rely on their fairness and justice.

If we are to judge by past experience, there is much to be hoped for in international relations from frequent conferences and consultations. We have before us the beneficial results of the Washington conference and the various consultations recently held upon European affairs, some of which were in response to our suggestions and in some of which we were active participants. Even the failures can not but be accounted useful and an immeasurable advance over threatened or actual warfare. I am strongly in favor of continuation of this policy, whenever conditions are such that there is even a promise that practical and favorable results might be secured.

In conformity with the principle that a display of reason rather than a threat of force should be the determining factor in the intercourse among nations, we have long advocated the peaceful settlement of disputes by methods of arbitration and have negotiated many treaties to secure that result. The same considerations should lead to our adherence to the Permanent Court of International Justice. Where great principles are involved, where great movements are under way which promise much for the welfare of humanity by reason of the very fact that many other nations have given such movements their actual support, we ought not to withhold our own sanction because of any small and inessential difference, but only upon the ground of the most important and compelling fundamental reasons. We can not barter away our independence or our sovereignty, but we ought to engage in no refinements of logic, no sophistries, and no subterfuges, to argue away the undoubted duty of this country by reason of the might of its numbers, the power of its resources, and its position of leadership in the world, actively and comprehensively to signify its approval and to bear its full share of their responsibility of a candid and disinterested attempt at the establishment of a tribunal for the administration of even-handed justice between nation and nation. The weight of our enormous influence must be cast upon the side of a reign not of force but of law and trial, not by battle but by reason.

We have never any wish to interfere in the political conditions of any other countries. Especially are we determined not to become implicated in the political controversies of the Old World. With a great deal of hesitation, we have responded to appeals for help to maintain order, protect life and property, and establish responsible government in some of the small countries of the Western Hemisphere. Our private citizens have advanced large sums of money to assist in the necessary financing and relief of the Old World. We have not failed, nor shall we fail to respond, whenever necessary to mitigate human suffering and assist in the rehabilitation of distressed nations. These, too, are requirements which must be met by reason of our vast powers and the place we hold in the world.

Some of the best thought of mankind has long been seeking for a formula for permanent peace. Undoubtedly the clarification of the principles of international law would be helpful, and the efforts of scholars to prepare such a work for adoption by the various nations should have our sympathy and support. Much may be hoped for from the earnest studies of those who advocate the outlawing of aggressive war. But all these plans and preparations, these treaties and covenants, will not of themselves be adequate. One of the greatest dangers to peace lies in the economic pressure to which people find themselves subjected. One of the most practical things to be done in the world is to seek arrangements under which such pressure may be removed, so that opportunity may be renewed and hope may be revived. There must be some assurance that effort and endeavor will be followed by success and prosperity. In the making and financing of such adjustments there is not only an opportunity, but a real duty, for America to respond with her counsel and her resources. Conditions must be provided under which people can make a living and work out of their difficulties. But there is another element, more important than all, without which there can not be the slightest hope of a permanent peace. That element lies in the heart of humanity. Unless the desire for peace be cherished there, unless this fundamental and only natural source of brotherly love be cultivated to its highest degree, all artificial efforts will be in vain. Peace will come when there is realization that only under a reign of law, based on righteousness and supported by the religious conviction of the brotherhood of man, can there be any hope of a complete and satisfying life. Parchment will fail, the sword will fail, it is only the spiritual nature of man that can be triumphant.

It seems altogether probable that we can contribute most to these important objects by maintaining our position of political detachment and independence. We are not identified with any Old World interests. This position should be made more and more clear in our relations with all foreign countries. We are at peace with all of them. Our program is never to oppress, but always to assist. But while we do justice to others, we must require that justice be done to us. With us a treaty of peace means peace, and a treaty of amity means amity. We have made great contributions to the settlement of contentious differences in both Europe and Asia. But there is a very definite point beyond which we can not go. We can only help those who help themselves. Mindful of these limitations, the one great duty that stands out requires us to use our enormous powers to trim the balance of the world.

While we can look with a great deal of pleasure upon what we have done abroad, we must remember that our continued success in that direction depends upon what we do at home. Since its very outset, it has been found necessary to conduct our Government by means of political parties. That system would not have survived from generation to generation if it had not been fundamentally sound and provided the best instrumentality's for the most complete expression of the popular will. It is not necessary to claim that it has always worked perfectly. It is enough to know that nothing better has been devised. No one would deny that there should be full and free expression and an opportunity for independence of action within the party. There is no salvation in a narrow and bigoted partisanship. But if there is to be responsible party government, the party label must be something more than a mere device for securing office. Unless those who are elected under the same party designation are willing to assume sufficient responsibility and exhibit sufficient loyalty and coherence, so that they can cooperate with each other in the support of the broad general principles, of the party platform, the election is merely a mockery, no decision is made at the polls, and there is no representation of the popular will. Common honesty and good faith with the people who support a party at the polls require that party, when it enters office, to assume the control of that portion of the Government to which it has been elected. Any other course is bad faith and a violation of the party pledges.

When the country has bestowed its confidence upon a party by making it a majority in the Congress, it has a right to expect such unity of action as will make the party majority an effective instrument of government. This Administration has come into power with a very clear and definite mandate from the people. The expression of the popular will in favor of maintaining our constitutional guarantees was overwhelming and decisive. There was a manifestation of such faith in the integrity of the courts that we can consider that issue rejected for some time to come. Likewise, the policy of public ownership of railroads and certain electric utilities met with unmistakable defeat. The people declared that they wanted their rights to have not a political but a judicial determination, and their independence and freedom continued and supported by having the ownership and control of their property, not in the Government, but in their own hands. As they always do when they have a fair chance, the people demonstrated that they are sound and are determined to have a sound government.

When we turn from what was rejected to inquire what was accepted, the policy that stands out with the greatest clearness is that of economy in public expenditure with reduction and reform of taxation. The principle involved in this effort is that of conservation. The resources of this country are almost beyond computation. No mind can comprehend them. But the cost of our combined governments is likewise almost beyond definition. Not only those who are now making their tax returns, but those who meet the enhanced cost of existence in their monthly bills, know by hard experience what this great burden is and what it does. No matter what others may want, these people want a drastic economy. They are opposed to waste. They know that extravagance lengthens the hours and diminishes the rewards of their labor. I favor the policy of economy, not because I wish to save money, but because I wish to save people. The men and women of this country who toil are the ones who bear the cost of the Government. Every dollar that we carelessly waste means that their life will be so much the more meager. Every dollar that we prudently save means that their life will be so much the more abundant. Economy is idealism in its most practical form.

If extravagance were not reflected in taxation, and through taxation both directly and indirectly injuriously affecting the people, it would not be of so much consequence. The wisest and soundest method of solving our tax problem is through economy. Fortunately, of all the great nations this country is best in a position to adopt that simple remedy. We do not any longer need wartime revenues. The collection of any taxes which are not absolutely required, which do not beyond reasonable doubt contribute to the public welfare, is only a species of legalized larceny. Under this republic the rewards of industry belong to those who earn them. The only constitutional tax is the tax which ministers to public necessity. The property of the country belongs to the people of the country. Their title is absolute. They do not support any privileged class; they do not need to maintain great military forces; they ought not to be burdened with a great array of public employees. They are not required to make any contribution to Government expenditures except that which they voluntarily assess upon themselves through the action of their own representatives. Whenever taxes become burdensome a remedy can be applied by the people; but if they do not act for themselves, no one can be very successful in acting for them.

The time is arriving when we can have further tax reduction, when, unless we wish to hamper the people in their right to earn a living, we must have tax reform. The method of raising revenue ought not to impede the transaction of business; it ought to encourage it. I am opposed to extremely high rates, because they produce little or no revenue, because they are bad for the country, and, finally, because they are wrong. We can not finance the country, we can not improve social conditions, through any system of injustice, even if we attempt to inflict it upon the rich. Those who suffer the most harm will be the poor. This country believes in prosperity. It is absurd to suppose that it is envious of those who are already prosperous. The wise and correct course to follow in taxation and all other economic legislation is not to destroy those who have already secured success but to create conditions under which every one will have a better chance to be successful. The verdict of the country has been given on this question. That verdict stands. We shall do well to heed it.

These questions involve moral issues. We need not concern ourselves much about the rights of property if we will faithfully observe the rights of persons. Under our institutions their rights are supreme. It is not property but the right to hold property, both great and small, which our Constitution guarantees. All owners of property are charged with a service. These rights and duties have been revealed, through the conscience of society, to have a divine sanction. The very stability of our society rests upon production and conservation. For individuals or for governments to waste and squander their resources is to deny these rights and disregard these obligations. The result of economic dissipation to a nation is always moral decay.

These policies of better international understandings, greater economy, and lower taxes have contributed largely to peaceful and prosperous industrial relations. Under the helpful influences of restrictive immigration and a protective tariff, employment is plentiful, the rate of pay is high, and wage earners are in a state of contentment seldom before seen. Our transportation systems have been gradually recovering and have been able to meet all the requirements of the service. Agriculture has been very slow in reviving, but the price of cereals at last indicates that the day of its deliverance is at hand.

We are not without our problems, but our most important problem is not to secure new advantages but to maintain those which we already possess. Our system of government made up of three separate and independent departments, our divided sovereignty composed of Nation and State, the matchless wisdom that is enshrined in our Constitution, all these need constant effort and tireless vigilance for their protection and support.

In a republic the first rule for the guidance of the citizen is obedience to law. Under a despotism the law may be imposed upon the subject. He has no voice in its making, no influence in its administration, it does not represent him. Under a free government the citizen makes his own laws, chooses his own administrators, which do represent him. Those who want their rights respected under the Constitution and the law ought to set the example themselves of observing the Constitution and the law. While there may be those of high intelligence who violate the law at times, the barbarian and the defective always violate it. Those who disregard the rules of society are not exhibiting a superior intelligence, are not promoting freedom and independence, are not following the path of civilization, but are displaying the traits of ignorance, of servitude, of savagery, and treading the way that leads back to the jungle.

The essence of a republic is representative government. Our Congress represents the people and the States. In all legislative affairs it is the natural collaborator with the President. In spite of all the criticism which often falls to its lot, I do not hesitate to say that there is no more independent and effective legislative body in the world. It is, and should be, jealous of its prerogative. I welcome its cooperation, and expect to share with it not only the responsibility, but the credit, for our common effort to secure beneficial legislation.

These are some of the principles which America represents. We have not by any means put them fully into practice, but we have strongly signified our belief in them. The encouraging feature of our country is not that it has reached its destination, but that it has overwhelmingly expressed its determination to proceed in the right direction. It is true that we could, with profit, be less sectional and more national in our thought. It would be well if we could replace much that is only a false and ignorant prejudice with a true and enlightened pride of race. But the last election showed that appeals to class and nationality had little effect. We were all found loyal to a common citizenship. The fundamental precept of liberty is toleration. We can not permit any inquisition either within or without the law or apply any religious test to the holding of office. The mind of America must be forever free.

It is in such contemplations, my fellow countrymen, which are not exhaustive but only representative, that I find ample warrant for satisfaction and encouragement. We should not let the much that is to do obscure the much which has been done. The past and present show faith and hope and courage fully justified. Here stands our country, an example of tranquillity at home, a patron of tranquillity abroad. Here stands its Government, aware of its might but obedient to its conscience. Here it will continue to stand, seeking peace and prosperity, solicitous for the welfare of the wage earner, promoting enterprise, developing waterways and natural resources, attentive to the intuitive counsel of womanhood, encouraging education, desiring the advancement of religion, supporting the cause of justice and honor among the nations. America seeks no earthly empire built on blood and force. No ambition, no temptation, lures her to thought of foreign dominions. The legions which she sends forth are armed, not with the sword, but with the cross. The higher state to which she seeks the allegiance of all mankind is not of human, but of divine origin. She cherishes no purpose save to merit the favor of Almighty God.

Cool Cal

THE INAUGURAL ADDRESS OF CALVIN COOLIDGE

Amity Shlaes

HOW A CITIZEN becomes president can tell us much about the presidency that follows. In the case of Calvin Coolidge, that "becoming" was unusual. Coolidge didn't win an election to become president. He became president rather because of a tragic event: the death of President Warren Harding in August 1923. Coolidge, then vice president, happened to be vacationing in the hilly village where he was born, Plymouth Notch, Vermont. His father John woke him in the middle of the night to tell him the awful news. His father, a notary, was the only legal authority present at the moment. Yet, everyone in the small house understood the importance of a quick swearing-in. Each minute they delayed was a minute that the United States went without a president. Coolidge dressed and said a prayer. He consulted by telephone with Washington on what he might do. There was no time to dress up in tuxes, or gowns. At 2:47 a.m., Coolidge's father swore the president into office using the family Bible under a kerosene light. Only a few people witnessed the events of that historic night: Mrs. Coolidge, a local congressman, and a newspaper man.

The next day the Coolidges boarded the train in Rutland and traveled south to Washington so that Coolidge might take the greatest office in the land. Coolidge gave no real speech. Out of respect for the law—but not conceding that the inauguration in Plymouth was invalid—Coolidge was sworn in once again in Washington. But the Homestead Inauguration of America's thirtieth president was so special that to this day each August the Coolidge Foundation and the State of Vermont gather a small crowd to re-enact it at Plymouth Notch. Coolidge descendants often play the roles of the new president or Mrs. Coolidge.

In 1924, Coolidge won election in his own right—and with a powerful mandate. He delivered his first and only presidential Inaugural Address at the usual March ceremony. The themes he emphasized in that address were the very same the astute observer could have picked up at that initial, improvised inauguration in Plymouth.

The first of these themes is the importance of the divisions of government—not only the three branches in Washington, but also the division of government between Washington and the states. Coolidge understood that the tension between the centralized and the local was, as he put it, evidence of "matchless wisdom that is enshrined in our Constitution." Just as on that night in Plymouth, America must always balance the needs of the nation with respect for the local authority, even if that authority is a mere notary. America's constitutional structures, Coolidge said in 1925, "need constant effort and tireless vigilance for their protection and support." National government, as he liked to refer to it, became tyranny if it did not "faithfully observe the rights of persons. Under our institutions their rights are supreme." Those rights include the right to hold property. But individuals also had duties. Coolidge also recalled: "All owners of property are charged with a service."

In his Washington inaugural, Coolidge also emphasized another preoccupation of that Plymouth night: "obedience to law." Coolidge elaborated: "Those who want their rights respected under the Constitution and the law ought to set the example themselves of observing the Constitution and the law." Further, Coolidge added that "those who disregard the rules of society are not exhibiting a superior intelligence, are not promoting freedom and independence, are not following the path of civilization."

What must the American government do to respect its citizens? Coolidge laid that out in his inaugural of 1925 as well. For Coolidge, that respect was best shown when government restrains itself and leaves Americans to lead their own lives. Toleration was a key principle. Though we all may feel differently on important issues, "the fundamental precept of liberty is toleration." Free speech and free thought are important for "the mind of America must be forever free."

The best way for the government to do that, Coolidge said, was to practice "economy in public expenditure with reduction and reform of taxation." Tax policy sounded mundane, Coolidge said, but it was not. The government should collect only enough revenue to meet "public necessity." Federal spending amounting to more than that was "legalized larceny." The president elaborated: "I favor the policy of economy, not because I wish to save money, but because I wish to save people. The men and women of this country who toil are the ones who bear the cost of Government."

A final theme of Coolidge's Inaugural Address was religious faith. The American empire, he said, was not one of "blood and force." America's strength, the president said, was to lead by example. "The higher state to which she seeks the allegiance of all mankind is not of human, but of divine origin."

What to make of Coolidge's words, at once so familiar and so strange in our current context? At a time when our nation seems so very imperfect, and differences almost insurmountable, Coolidge can offer consolation. America has lofty principles, but it can be imperfect, just as the makeshift inauguration of 1923 was imperfect. "The encouraging feature of our country," Coolidge said in 1925, "is not that it has reached its destination"—it hadn't then, just as it has not now. Rather what mattered was that "it has overwhelmingly expressed its determination to proceed in the right direction." Let us express such determination today.

Herbert Hoover's Inaugural Address

MONDAY, MARCH 4, 1929

MY COUNTRYMEN:

This occasion is not alone the administration of the most sacred oath which can be assumed by an American citizen. It is a dedication and consecration under God to the highest office in service of our people. I assume this trust in the humility of knowledge that only through the guidance of Almighty Providence can I hope to discharge its ever-increasing burdens.

It is in keeping with tradition throughout our history that I should express simply and directly the opinions which I hold concerning some of the matters of present importance.

Our Progress

If we survey the situation of our Nation both at home and abroad, we find many satisfactions; we find some causes for concern. We have emerged from the losses of the Great War and the reconstruction following it with increased virility and strength. From this strength we have contributed to the recovery and progress of the world. What America has done has given renewed hope and courage to all who have faith in government by the people. In the large view, we have reached a higher degree of comfort and security than ever existed before in the history of the world. Through liberation from widespread poverty we have reached a higher degree of individual freedom than ever before. The devotion to and concern for our institutions are deep and sincere. We are steadily building a new race—a new civilization great in its own attainments. The influence and high purposes of our Nation are respected among the peoples of the world. We aspire to distinction in the world, but to a distinction based upon confidence in our sense of justice as well as our accomplishments within our own borders and in our own lives. For wise guidance in this great period of recovery the Nation is deeply indebted to Calvin Coolidge.

But all this majestic advance should not obscure the constant dangers from which self-government must be safeguarded. The strong man must at all times be alert to the attack of insidious disease.

The Failure of Our System of Criminal Justice

The most malign of all these dangers today is disregard and disobedience of law. Crime is increasing. Confidence in rigid and speedy justice is decreasing. I am not prepared to believe that this indicates any decay in the moral fiber of the American people. I am not prepared to believe that it indicates an impotence of the Federal Government to enforce its laws.

It is only in part due to the additional burdens imposed upon our judicial system by the 18th Amendment. The problem is much wider than that. Many influences had increasingly complicated and weakened our law enforcement organization long before the adoption of the 18th Amendment.

To reestablish the vigor and effectiveness of law enforcement we must critically consider the entire Federal machinery of justice, the redistribution of its functions, the simplification of its procedure, the provision of additional special tribunals, the better selection of juries, and the more effective organization of our agencies of investigation and prosecution that justice may be sure and that it may be swift. While the authority of the Federal Government extends to but part of our vast system of national, State, and local justice, yet the standards which the Federal Government establishes have the most profound influence upon the whole structure.

We are fortunate in the ability and integrity of our Federal judges and attorneys. But the system which these officers are called upon to administer is in many respects ill adapted to present-day conditions. Its intricate and involved rules of procedure have become the refuge of both big and little criminals. There is a belief abroad that by invoking technicalities, subterfuge, and delay, the ends of justice may be thwarted by those who can pay the cost.

Reform, reorganization and strengthening of our whole judicial and enforcement system, both in civil and criminal sides, have been advocated for years by statesmen, judges, and bar associations. First steps toward that end should not longer be delayed. Rigid and expeditious justice is the first safeguard of freedom, the basis of all ordered liberty, the vital force of progress. It must not come to be in our Republic that it can be defeated by the indifference of the citizens, by exploitation of the delays and entanglements of the law, or by combinations of criminals. Justice must not fail because the agencies of enforcement are either delinquent or inefficiently organized. To consider these evils, to find their remedy, is the most sore necessity of our times.

Enforcement of the 18th Amendment

Of the undoubted abuses which have grown up under the 18th Amendment, part are due to the causes I have just mentioned; but part are due to the failure of some States to accept their share of responsibility for concurrent enforcement and to the failure of many State and local officials to accept the obligation under their oath of office zealously to enforce the laws. With the failures from these many causes has come a dangerous expansion in the criminal elements who have found enlarged opportunities in dealing in illegal liquor.

But a large responsibility rests directly upon our citizens. There would be little traffic in illegal liquor if only criminals patronized it. We must awake to the fact that this patronage from large numbers of law-abiding citizens is supplying the rewards and stimulating crime.

I have been selected by you to execute and enforce the laws of the country. I propose to do so to the extent of my own abilities, but the measure of success that the Government shall attain will depend upon the moral support which you, as citizens, extend. The duty of citizens to support the laws of the land is coequal with the duty of their Government to enforce the laws which exist. No greater national service can be given by men and women of good will—who, I know, are not unmindful of the responsibilities of citizenship—than that they should, by their example, assist in stamping out crime and outlawry by refusing participation in and condemning all transactions with illegal liquor. Our whole system of self-government will crumble either if officials elect what laws they will enforce or citizens elect what laws they will support. The worst evil of disregard for some law is that it destroys respect for all law. For our citizens to patronize the violation of a particular law on the ground that they are opposed to it is destructive of the very basis of all that protection of life, of homes and property which they rightly claim under other laws. If citizens do not like a law, their duty as honest men and women is to discourage its violation; their right is openly to work for its repeal.

To those of criminal mind there can be no appeal but vigorous enforcement of the law. Fortunately they are but a small percentage of our people. Their activities must be stopped.

A National Investigation

I propose to appoint a national commission for a searching investigation of the whole structure of our Federal system of jurisprudence, to include the method of enforcement of the 18th Amendment and the causes of abuse under it. Its purpose will be to make such recommendations for reorganization of the administration of Federal laws and court procedure as may be found desirable. In the meantime it is essential that a large part of the enforcement activities be transferred from the Treasury Department to the Department of Justice as a beginning of more effective organization.

The Relation of Government to Business

The election has again confirmed the determination of the American people that regulation of private enterprise and not Government ownership or operation is the course rightly to be pursued in our relation to business. In recent years we have established a differentiation in the whole method of business regulation between the industries which produce and distribute commodities on the one hand and public utilities on the other. In the former, our laws insist upon effective competition; in the latter, because we substantially confer a monopoly by limiting competition, we must regulate their services and rates. The rigid enforcement of the laws applicable to both groups is the very base of equal opportunity and freedom from domination for all our people, and it is just as essential for the stability and prosperity of business itself as for the protection of the public at large. Such regulation should be extended by the Federal Government within the limitations of the Constitution and only when the individual States are without power to protect their citizens through their own authority. On the other hand, we should be fearless when the authority rests only in the Federal Government.

Cooperation by the Government

The larger purpose of our economic thought should be to establish more firmly stability and security of business and employment and thereby remove poverty still further from our borders. Our people have in recent years developed a newfound capacity for cooperation among themselves to effect high purposes in public welfare. It is an advance toward the highest conception of self-government. Self-government does not and should not imply the use of political agencies alone. Progress is born of cooperation in the community—not from governmental restraints. The Government should assist and encourage these movements of collective self-help by itself cooperating with them. Business has by cooperation made great progress in the advancement of service, in stability, in regularity of employment and in the correction of its own abuses. Such progress, however, can continue only so long as business manifests its respect for law.

There is an equally important field of cooperation by the Federal Government with the multitude of agencies, State, municipal and private, in the systematic development of those processes which directly affect public health, recreation, education, and the home. We have need further to perfect the means by which Government can be adapted to human service.

Education

Although education is primarily a responsibility of the States and local communities, and rightly so, yet the Nation as a whole is vitally concerned in its development everywhere to the highest standards and to complete universality. Self-government can succeed only through an instructed electorate. Our objective is not simply to overcome illiteracy. The Nation has marched far beyond that. The more complex the problems of the Nation become, the greater is the need for more and more advanced instruction. Moreover, as our numbers increase and as our life expands with science and invention, we must discover more and more leaders for every walk of life. We can not hope to succeed in directing this increasingly complex civilization unless we can draw all the talent of leadership from the whole people. One civilization after another has been wrecked upon the attempt to secure sufficient leadership from a single group or class. If we would prevent the growth of class distinctions and would constantly refresh our leadership with the ideals of our people, we must draw constantly from the general mass. The full opportunity for every boy and girl to rise through the selective processes of education can alone secure to us this leadership.

Public Health

In public health the discoveries of science have opened a new era. Many sections of our country and many groups of our citizens suffer from diseases the eradication of which are mere matters of administration and moderate expenditure. Public health service should be as fully organized and as universally incorporated into our governmental system as is public education. The returns are a thousand fold in economic benefits, and infinitely more in reduction of suffering and promotion of human happiness.

World Peace

The United States fully accepts the profound truth that our own progress, prosperity, and peace are interlocked with the progress, prosperity, and peace of all humanity. The whole world is at peace. The dangers to a continuation of this peace today are largely the fear and suspicion which still haunt the world. No suspicion or fear can be rightly directed toward our country.

Those who have a true understanding of America know that we have no desire for territorial expansion, for economic or other domination of other peoples. Such purposes are repugnant to our ideals of human freedom. Our form of government is ill adapted to the responsibilities which inevitably follow permanent limitation of the independence of other peoples. Superficial observers seem to find no destiny for our abounding increase in population, in wealth and power except that of imperialism. They fail to see that the American people are engrossed in the building for themselves of a new economic system, a new social system, a new political system—all of which are characterized by aspirations of freedom of opportunity and thereby are the negation of imperialism. They fail to realize that because of our abounding prosperity our youth are pressing more and more into our institutions of learning; that our people are seeking a larger vision through art, literature, science, and travel; that they are moving toward stronger moral and spiritual life—that from these things our sympathies are broadening beyond the bounds of our Nation and race toward their true expression in a real brotherhood of man. They fail to see that the idealism of America will lead it to no narrow or selfish channel, but inspire it to do its full share as a nation toward the advancement of civilization. It will do that not by mere declaration but by taking a practical part in supporting all useful international undertakings. We not only desire peace with the world, but to see peace maintained throughout the world. We wish to advance the reign of justice and reason toward the extinction of force.

The recent treaty for the renunciation of war as an instrument of national policy sets an advanced standard in our conception of the relations of nations. Its acceptance should pave the way to greater limitation of armament, the offer of which we sincerely extend to the world. But its full realization also implies a greater and greater perfection in the instrumentalities for pacific settlement of controversies between nations. In the creation and use of these instrumentalities we should support every sound method of conciliation, arbitration, and judicial settlement. American statesmen were among the first to propose and they have constantly urged upon the world, the establishment of a tribunal for the settlement of controversies of a justiciable character. The Permanent Court of International Justice in its major purpose is thus peculiarly identified with American ideals and with American statesmanship. No more potent instrumentality for this purpose has ever been conceived and no other is practicable of establishment. The reservations placed upon our adherence should not be misinterpreted. The United States seeks by these reservations no special privilege or advantage but only to clarify our relation to advisory opinions and other matters which are subsidiary to the major purpose of the court. The way should, and I believe will, be found by which we may take our proper place in a movement so fundamental to the progress of peace.

Our people have determined that we should make no political engagements such as membership in the League of Nations, which may commit us in advance as a nation to become involved in the settlements of controversies between other countries. They adhere to the belief that the independence of America from such obligations increases its ability and availability for service in all fields of human progress.

I have lately returned from a journey among our sister Republics of the Western Hemisphere. I have received unbounded hospitality and courtesy as their expression of friendliness to our country. We are held by particular bonds of sympathy and common interest with them. They are each of them building a racial character and a culture which is an impressive contribution to human progress. We wish only for the maintenance of their independence, the growth of their stability, and their prosperity. While we have had wars in the Western Hemisphere, yet on the whole the record is in encouraging contrast with that of other parts of the world. Fortunately the New World is largely free from the inheritances of fear and distrust which have so troubled the Old World. We should keep it so.

It is impossible, my countrymen, to speak of peace without profound emotion. In thousands of homes in America, in millions of homes around the world, there are vacant chairs. It would be a shameful confession of our unworthiness if it should develop that we have abandoned the hope for which all these men died. Surely civilization is old enough, surely mankind is mature enough so that we ought in our own lifetime to find a way to permanent peace. Abroad, to west and east, are nations whose sons mingled their blood with the blood of our sons on the battlefields. Most of these nations have contributed to our race, to our culture, our knowledge, and our progress. From one of them we derive our very language and from many of them much of the genius of our institutions. Their desire for peace is as deep and sincere as our own.

Peace can be contributed to by respect for our ability in defense. Peace can be promoted by the limitation of arms and by the creation of the instrumentalities for peaceful settlement of controversies. But it will become a reality only through self-restraint and active effort in friendliness and helpfulness. I covet for this administration a record of having further contributed to advance the cause of peace.

Party Responsibilities

In our form of democracy the expression of the popular will can be effected only through the instrumentality of political parties. We maintain party government not to promote intolerant partisanship but because opportunity must be given for expression of the popular will, and organization provided for the execution of its mandates and for accountability of government to the people. It follows that the government both in the executive and the legislative branches must carry out in good faith the platforms upon which the party was entrusted with power. But the government is that of the whole people; the party is the instrument through which policies are determined and men chosen to bring them into being. The animosities of elections should have no place in our Government, for government must concern itself alone with the common weal.

Special Session of the Congress

Action upon some of the proposals upon which the Republican Party was returned to power, particularly further agricultural relief and limited changes in the tariff, cannot in justice to our farmers, our labor, and our manufacturers be postponed. I shall therefore request a special session of Congress for the consideration of these two questions. I shall deal with each of them upon the assembly of the Congress.

Other Mandates from the Election

It appears to me that the more important further mandates from the recent election were the maintenance of the integrity of the Constitution; the vigorous enforcement of the laws; the continuance of economy in public expenditure; the continued regulation of business to prevent domination in the community; the denial of ownership or operation of business by the Government in competition with its citizens; the avoidance of policies which would involve us in the controversies of foreign nations; the more effective reorganization of the departments of the Federal Government; the expansion of public works; and the promotion of welfare activities affecting education and the home.

These were the more tangible determinations of the election, but beyond them was the confidence and belief of the people that we would not neglect the support of the embedded ideals and aspirations of America. These ideals and aspirations are the touchstones upon which the day-to-day administration and legislative acts of government must be tested. More than this, the Government must, so far as lies within its proper powers, give leadership to the realization of these ideals and to the fruition of these aspirations. No one can adequately reduce these things of the spirit to phrases or to a catalogue of definitions. We do know what the attainments of these ideals should be: the preservation of self-government and its full foundations in local government; the perfection of justice whether in economic or in social fields; the maintenance of ordered liberty; the denial of domination by any group or class; the building up and preservation of equality of opportunity; the stimulation of initiative and individuality; absolute integrity in public affairs; the choice of officials for fitness to office; the direction of economic progress toward prosperity for the further lessening of poverty; the freedom of public opinion; the sustaining of education and of the advancement of knowledge; the growth of religious spirit and the tolerance of all faiths; the strengthening of the home; the advancement of peace.

There is no short road to the realization of these aspirations. Ours is a progressive people, but with a determination that progress must be based upon the foundation of experience. Ill-considered remedies for our faults bring only penalties after them. But if we hold the faith of the men in our mighty past who created these ideals, we shall leave them heightened and strengthened for our children.

Conclusion

This is not the time and place for extended discussion. The questions before our country are problems of progress to higher standards; they are not the problems of degeneration. They demand thought and they serve to quicken the conscience and enlist our sense of responsibility for their settlement. And that responsibility rests upon you, my countrymen, as much as upon those of us who have been selected for office.

Ours is a land rich in resources; stimulating in its glorious beauty; filled with millions of happy homes; blessed with comfort and opportunity. In no nation are the institutions of progress more advanced. In no nation are the fruits of accomplishment more secure. In no nation is the government more worthy of respect. No country is more loved by its people. I have an abiding faith in their capacity, integrity and high purpose. I have no fears for the future of our country. It is bright with hope.

In the presence of my countrymen, mindful of the solemnity of this occasion, knowing what the task means and the responsibility which it involves, I beg your tolerance, your aid, and your cooperation. I ask the help of Almighty God in this service to my country to which you have called me.

The Great Humanitarian

THE INAUGURAL ADDRESS OF HERBERT HOOVER

Kendrick A. Clements

IN HIS MEMOIRS, written nearly twenty years after he left the White House, Herbert Hoover admitted that the Inaugural Address he delivered on March 4, 1929, was not the speech he would have liked to have given. As secretary of commerce for eight years in the Harding and Coolidge administrations, Hoover had been an activist on the model of pre–World War I progressives like Theodore Roosevelt. But the postwar Republican party was dominated by small-government conservatives and isolationists like Warren Harding and Calvin Coolidge. Harding was willing to give the secretary considerable leeway to pursue his ideas, but Coolidge, who derided Hoover as "wonder boy," resisted or obstructed his efforts to expand the functions of the federal government to serve the growing population of an increasingly industrialized nation in an interconnected world.

Election to the presidency seemed to give Hoover an opportunity to press forward his ideas for expansion of the federal role, but when he sat down to write his Inaugural Address he was keenly aware that "certain differences" between his and Coolidge's "points of view" cast a chilling shadow over his ambitions. Given Coolidge's great popularity in the country and especially in the Republican Party, he risked splitting the party if he suggested taking the country in a dramatically different direction than his predecessor.

The question, then, was what he *could* propose to do. In the end, he decided that he had to confine himself mainly to uncontroversial generalities—to "American ideals and aspirations," as he put it in his memoirs. That was not a prescription for a stirring speech. Never a particularly good public speaker, and always better at dealing with the specific details of a problem than at enunciating broad principles or inspiring his listeners, Hoover began with some vague observations about a tricky issue, foreign policy. The country, he declared, had not only recovered from the war but had contributed to "the recovery and progress of the world," giving "renewed hope and courage to all who have faith in government by the people." Having thus staked a claim to world leadership without challenging his party's isolationism, with which he privately disagreed, he slipped away from that difficult topic with more platitudes about how the world had come to respect America's "influence and high purposes."

From foreign policy, Hoover moved on to the main theme of his 1928 campaign: the national prosperity for which Republicans had happily taken credit. The nation, he proclaimed, had achieved greater "comfort and security than ever existed before in the history of the world," a victory over "widespread poverty" that assured Americans "a higher degree of individual freedom than ever before." Although slightly less sweeping than his claim in his speech accepting the Republican nomination on August 11, 1928, that the United States was on the threshold of a "final triumph over poverty," the contrast between his assumption of permanent prosperity and the grinding poverty of the Great Depression would forever shape Americans' memories of the thirty-first president.

Hoover devoted the longest section of his speech to a discussion of lawlessness that had grown out of popular opposition to the Eighteenth Amendment to the Constitution, which had made the sale and consumption of alcoholic beverages illegal. Probably he would have preferred to avoid the topic. His friends remembered that when he lived in Europe before the war, he enjoyed a martini before dinner and sometimes drank a glass of wine, but he was neither strongly against nor for Prohibition. When the law passed, he declared that while secretary of commerce he would neither serve nor drink alcohol. He found personal abstention easy, but as a presidential candidate in the deeply divided America of 1928 the issue was inescapable. His opponent, Al Smith, was an outspoken advocate of repeal, which created a dilemma for Hoover. He doubted that complete enforcement of Prohibition was possible, but he was unwilling to simply concede to Smith the votes of the "wet" cities on the East and West coasts. Accordingly, he attempted to find a middle position that might pacify both sides. In the end, he issued a statement describing Prohibition as "a great social and economic experiment, noble in motive and far-reaching in purpose" and promising "the efficient enforcement" of the law.

His statement was widely ridiculed during the campaign as an attempt to straddle the problem, and Hoover apparently felt compelled to explain in his inaugural that he actually had a specific policy in mind. Ignoring the issue of repeal, he identified the central problem as "disregard and disobedience of law."

As long as Prohibition remained the law, he declared, individual Americans must respect and obey it, the states must make good faith efforts to enforce it, and even more important, "the entire Federal machinery of justice" must be overhauled to make enforcement swifter and more efficient. His only specific proposal, however, was the appointment of a "national commission" to study "the whole structure of our Federal system of jurisprudence" and to present recommendations for reform. To those listening to the speech, it appeared that the mountain had labored and brought forth a mouse.

Having thus attempted to divert the torrent of debate about repeal into the dry channels of legal reform, Hoover then turned for the remainder of his address to a laundry list of proposals he had been advancing throughout the previous decade. They included self-regulation of business (with strict government oversight), promotion of education, a strengthening and extension of public health programs, the assertion of American leadership in advancing "the reign of justice and reason toward the extinction of force" in the world, and the promotion of what has come to be called the "good neighbor policy" toward Latin America. Most of these ideas were vague enough to elicit broad but shallow support. A reiteration of President Harding's 1923 recommendation that the United States join the Permanent Court of International Justice, however, was sufficiently specific to awaken extreme isolationists and never won the approval of the Senate. A promise to call a Special Session of Congress to deal with the agricultural depression that had been haunting the country and to reform the tariff, though offered in the optimistic atmosphere of prosperity, would evoke very different responses in the post-Crash atmosphere of late 1929. As the Depression deepened, a forgettable speech would be buried by more pressing issues.

While Hoover spoke, the skies opened and cold rain poured down. Both the president and first lady were soaked and shivering by the time the event concluded. Hoover closed with an assurance that the country's future was "bright with hope," but the weather was a better omen for the fate of his administration than his optimistic words.

Franklin D. Roosevelt's First Inaugural Address

SATURDAY, MARCH 4, 1933

I AM CERTAIN that my fellow Americans expect that on my induction into the Presidency I will address them with a candor and a decision which the present situation of our Nation impels. This is preeminently the time to speak the truth, the whole truth, frankly and boldly. Nor need we shrink from honestly facing conditions in our country today. This great Nation will endure as it has endured, will revive and will prosper. So, first of all, let me assert my firm belief that the only thing we have to fear is fear itself—nameless, unreasoning, unjustified terror which paralyzes needed efforts to convert retreat into advance. In every dark hour of our national life a leadership of frankness and vigor has met with that understanding and support of the people themselves which is essential to victory. I am convinced that you will again give that support to leadership in these critical days.

In such a spirit on my part and on yours we face our common difficulties. They concern, thank God, only material things. Values have shrunken to fantastic levels; taxes have risen; our ability to pay has fallen; government of all kinds is faced by serious curtailment of income; the means of exchange are frozen in the currents of trade; the withered leaves of industrial enterprise lie on every side; farmers find no markets for their produce; the savings of many years in thousands of families are gone.

More important, a host of unemployed citizens face the grim problem of existence, and an equally great number toil with little return. Only a foolish optimist can deny the dark realities of the moment.

Yet our distress comes from no failure of substance. We are stricken by no plague of locusts. Compared with the perils which our forefathers conquered because they believed and were not afraid, we have still much to be thankful for.

Nature still offers her bounty and human efforts have multiplied it. Plenty is at our doorstep, but a generous use of it languishes in the very sight of the supply. Primarily this is because the rulers of the exchange of mankind's goods have failed through their own stubbornness and their own incompetence, have admitted their failure, and abdicated. Practices of the unscrupulous money changers stand indicted in the court of public opinion, rejected by the hearts and minds of men.

True they have tried, but their efforts have been cast in the pattern of an outworn tradition. Faced by failure of credit they have proposed only the lending of more money. Stripped of the lure of profit by which to induce our people to follow their false leadership, they have resorted to exhortations, pleading tearfully for restored confidence. They know only the rules of a generation of self-seekers. They have no vision, and when there is no vision the people perish.

The money changers have fled from their high seats in the temple of our civilization. We may now restore that temple to the ancient truths. The measure of the restoration lies in the extent to which we apply social values more noble than mere monetary profit.

Happiness lies not in the mere possession of money; it lies in the joy of achievement, in the thrill of creative effort. The joy and moral stimulation of work no longer must be forgotten in the mad chase of evanescent profits. These dark days will be worth all they cost us if they teach us that our true destiny is not to be ministered unto but to minister to ourselves and to our fellow men.

Recognition of the falsity of material wealth as the standard of success goes hand in hand with the abandonment of the false belief that public office and high political position are to be valued only by the standards of pride of place and personal profit; and there must be an end to a conduct in banking and in business which too often has given to a sacred trust the likeness of callous and selfish wrongdoing. Small wonder that confidence languishes, for it thrives only on honesty, on honor, on the sacredness of obligations, on faithful protection, on unselfish performance; without them it cannot live.

Restoration calls, however, not for changes in ethics alone. This Nation asks for action, and action now.

Our greatest primary task is to put people to work. This is no unsolvable problem if we face it wisely and courageously. It can be accomplished in part by direct recruiting by the Government itself, treating the task as we would treat the emergency of a war, but at the same time, through this employment, accomplishing greatly needed projects to stimulate and reorganize the use of our natural resources.

Hand in hand with this we must frankly recognize the overbalance of population in our industrial centers and, by engaging on a national scale in a redistribution, endeavor to provide a better use of the land for those best fitted for the land. The task can be helped by definite efforts to raise the values of agricultural products and with this the power to purchase the output of our cities. It can be helped by preventing realistically the tragedy of the growing loss through foreclosure of our small homes and our farms. It can be helped by insistence that the Federal, State, and local governments act forthwith on the demand that their cost be drastically reduced. It can be helped by the unifying of relief activities which today are often scattered, uneconomical, and unequal. It can be helped by national planning for and supervision of all forms of transportation and of communications and other utilities which have a definitely public character. There are many ways in which it can be helped, but it can never be helped merely by talking about it. We must act and act quickly.

Finally, in our progress toward a resumption of work we require two safeguards against a return of the evils of the old order: there must be a strict supervision of all banking and credits and investments, so that there will be an end to speculation with other people's money; and there must be provision for an adequate but sound currency.

There are the lines of attack. I shall presently urge upon a new Congress, in special session, detailed measures for their fulfillment, and I shall seek the immediate assistance of the several States.

Through this program of action we address ourselves to putting our own national house in order and making income balance outgo. Our international trade relations, though vastly important, are in point of time and necessity secondary to the establishment of a sound national economy. I favor as a practical policy the putting of first things first. I shall spare no effort to restore world trade by international economic readjustment, but the emergency at home cannot wait on that accomplishment.

The basic thought that guides these specific means of national recovery is not narrowly nationalistic. It is the insistence, as a first consideration, upon the interdependence of the various elements in all parts of the United States—a recognition of the old and permanently important manifestation of the American spirit of the pioneer. It is the way to recovery. It is the immediate way. It is the strongest assurance that the recovery will endure.

In the field of world policy I would dedicate this Nation to the policy of the good neighbor—the neighbor who resolutely respects himself and, because he does so, respects the rights of others—the neighbor who respects his obligations and respects the sanctity of his agreements in and with a world of neighbors.

If I read the temper of our people correctly, we now realize as we have never realized before our interdependence on each other; that we can not merely take but we must give as well; that if we are to go forward, we must move as a trained and loyal army willing to sacrifice for the good of a common discipline, because without such discipline no progress is made, no leadership becomes effective. We are, I know, ready and willing to submit our lives and property to such discipline, because it makes possible a leadership which aims at a larger good. This I propose to offer, pledging that the larger purposes will bind upon us all as a sacred obligation with a unity of duty hitherto evoked only in time of armed strife.

With this pledge taken, I assume unhesitatingly the leadership of this great army of our people dedicated to a disciplined attack upon our common problems.

Action in this image and to this end is feasible under the form of government which we have inherited from our ancestors. Our Constitution is so simple and practical that it is possible always to meet extraordinary needs by changes in emphasis and arrangement without loss of essential form. That is why our constitutional system has proved itself the most superbly enduring political mechanism the modern world has produced. It has met every stress of vast expansion of territory, of foreign wars, of bitter internal strife, of world relations.

It is to be hoped that the normal balance of Executive and legislative authority may be wholly adequate to meet the unprecedented task before us. But it may be that an unprecedented demand and need for undelayed action may call for temporary departure from that normal balance of public procedure.

I am prepared under my constitutional duty to recommend the measures that a stricken Nation in the midst of a stricken world may require. These measures, or such other measures as the Congress may build out of its experience and wisdom, I shall seek, within my constitutional authority, to bring to speedy adoption.

But in the event that the Congress shall fail to take one of these two courses, and in the event that the national emergency is still critical, I shall not evade the clear course of duty that will then confront me. I shall ask the Congress for the one remaining instrument to meet the crisis—broad Executive power to wage a war against the emergency, as great as the power that would be given to me if we were in fact invaded by a foreign foe.

For the trust reposed in me I will return the courage and the devotion that befit the time. I can do no less.

We face the arduous days that lie before us in the warm courage of the national unity; with the clear consciousness of seeking old and precious moral values; with the clean satisfaction that comes from the stern performance of duty by old and young alike. We aim at the assurance of a rounded and permanent national life.

We do not distrust the future of essential democracy. The people of the United States have not failed. In their need they have registered a mandate that they want direct, vigorous action. They have asked for discipline and direction under leadership. They have made me the present instrument of their wishes. In the spirit of the gift I take it.

In this dedication of a Nation we humbly ask the blessing of God. May He protect each and every one of us. May He guide me in the days to come.

Fear Itself

THE FIRST INAUGURAL ADDRESS OF FRANKLIN D. ROOSEVELT

Cynthia M. Koch

ON INAUGURATION DAY, March 4, 1933, Washington was cold and overcast. Homeless men wandered the streets. Flags hung at half-mast in memory of Senator Thomas J. Walsh, who had died while en route to Washington to serve as attorney general.

The president-elect and his family, Cabinet members, and close associates attended a precedent-setting prayer service at St. John's Episcopal Church directly across Lafayette Square from the White House. The Reverend Endicott Peabody, headmaster of Groton School (which Roosevelt had attended as a boy), officiated. When the service ended, Roosevelt remained on his knees in silent prayer.

At the Capitol, with his legs encased in steel braces, the president-elect steadied himself on the arm of his eldest son James as he made his way to the rostrum. He placed his hand on the ancient Roosevelt family Bible, printed in Amsterdam in 1686. It was open—as it always was when Roosevelt was sworn to office—to St. Paul's First Epistle to the Corinthians: "And now abideth faith, hope, charity, these three; but the greatest of these is charity." Breaking another tradition, he repeated word for word the solemn oath administered by Chief Justice Charles Evans Hughes. Then, as the crowd grew quiet, Franklin Roosevelt offered hope to a desperate people with bold words that still reverberate in public memory. "This great nation will endure as it has endured, will revive, and will prosper.... [T]he only thing we have to fear is fear itself."

The address was delivered in one of the nation's darkest hours, at a time when many objective observers felt Americans had plenty to fear. The country was in the third year of the worst economic depression in its history. By the end of 1932, fifteen million workers—one out of every three—had lost their jobs. U.S. Steel's payroll of full-time workers fell from 225,000 in 1929 to none in early 1933. In the steel town of Youngstown, Ohio, unemployment was 78 percent—more than three times the national average of 25 percent.

People were hungry. Ninety percent of the population of the coalfields of West Virginia and Kentucky suffered from malnutrition. In the cities, where there were some social services, only about one in four unemployed workers received any assistance from a patchwork of local government aid and charity. Long lines for bread and soup snaked through city streets.[1]

Farm income fell from $12 billion in 1929 to $5 billion in 1932. The price of a bushel of Iowa corn was worth less than a package of chewing gum. In the South, thousands of acres of cotton rotted in the fields, not worth the cost of harvest. Farmers could not meet their mortgage payments or taxes. Between 1929 and 1933, a third of all American farmers lost their farms.

By early 1933, nearly half of the $20 billion in home mortgages was in default. More than a thousand homeowners were foreclosed daily. Renters were evicted. People thrown out of their homes gathered in shantytowns derisively called Hoovervilles. Schools were closed as state and local governments ran out of money to pay their teachers.

Violence was in the air. In Iowa and Nebraska, a group known as the Farm Holiday movement announced a farmers' strike. They blocked highways leading to the agricultural markets in Omaha, Sioux City, and Des Moines. They dumped milk into ditches. They turned back cattle. When forty-nine picketers were arrested in Council Bluffs, Iowa, a thousand farmers assembled to break them out of jail.

A group of 43,000 desperate World War I veterans and their families arrived in Washington from all over the country in the summer of 1932. Known as the Bonus Army, they demanded early payment of bonuses due them for military service. Their camp was forcibly dispersed under orders from President Hoover, resulting in the death of two veterans.

* * *

Roosevelt was elected on November 8, 1932, but the Twentieth Amendment—which changed Inauguration Day from March 4 to January 20—would not be in effect until 1937. In the sixteen long weeks before March 4, 1933, conditions grew even more desperate as a new banking crisis gripped the nation. On inauguration morning, the New York Stock Exchange suspended trading, as did the Chicago Board of Trade. Thirty-eight states, including New York and Illinois, had already closed their banks.

It was an age of dictators, and democracy was in peril. For many, Mussolini's Italy and Stalin's Soviet Union seemed preferable to the dysfunction in the United States. Hitler's rise to power on January 31 only confirmed belief in the efficiency of the totalitarian state. Former New York Governor Al Smith, once a political mentor to Roosevelt and now a critic, compared America's plight to the crisis of war. "What does a democracy do in war," he asked. "It becomes a tyrant, a despot, a real monarch." In World War I, he declared with exaggeration, "[W]e took our Constitution, wrapped it up and laid it on the shelf and left it there until it was over." Alf Landon, the Republican governor of Kansas who would be Roosevelt's opponent in 1936, declared, "[E]ven the iron hand of a national dictator is in preference to a paralytic stroke." Visiting Roosevelt in Warm Springs, Georgia, in January, the respected columnist Walter Lippmann told Roosevelt, "The situation is critical, Franklin. You may have no alternative but to assume dictatorial powers."[2]

In February the country almost lost the president-elect to an assassin's bullet. After Roosevelt spoke from an open car to a crowd in Miami on February 15, gunshots rang out. An out-of-work anarchist named Guiseppe Zangara fired five bullets at Roosevelt from close range. A bystander deflected his hand, but Zangara wounded four people and fatally shot Chicago Mayor Anton Cermak. Roosevelt's calm and courage in the face of the attack gave confidence to a badly shaken nation.

* * *

Roosevelt began working on his Inaugural Address as the banking crisis deepened. On February 27, his advisor Raymond Moley arrived with a draft at the Roosevelt home in Hyde Park, New York. Roosevelt began to rework it (ultimately there were four drafts) and completed it the next day—except for the reference to fear, which was added after an introduction from Louis Howe arrived on February 28 containing the phrase, "We have nothing to fear but fear itself." Roosevelt added it to his speech and elaborated on it. The origins of the phrase are murky, and Sam Rosenman, Roosevelt's advisor and speechwriter, linked it to Henry David Thoreau's "[N]othing is so much to be feared as fear," but Moley—who was with the president-elect at the time—discounts the connection. Scholars have noted that the concept has a long history; Francis Bacon said essentially the same thing in the early seventeenth century.[3]

Roosevelt made one last change before delivering the nineteen-minute speech: the opening line "[T]his is a day of consecration," which he added by hand while waiting in the Senate Committee Room of the Capitol before the inauguration. In delivering the speech, he added one more crucial word: "This is a day of *national* consecration." This change encapsulates the intermingling of religious faith and patriotism that gives the speech its power.

In the famous opening paragraph, Roosevelt embellished the "fear" phrasing with a reassuring reminder of the nation's history. "This great Nation will endure as it has endured, will revive and will prosper." The memorable statement, "So, first of all, let me assert my firm belief that the only thing we have to fear is fear itself—nameless, unreasoning, unjustified terror which paralyzes needed efforts to convert retreat into advance," introduces the speech's war theme. "In every dark hour of our national life a leadership of frankness and vigor has met with that understanding and support of the people themselves which is essential to victory."

Roosevelt was summoning people to a holy war against "false leadership." The present crisis, he assured them, "comes from no failure of substance. We are stricken by no plague of locusts." At fault are the "unscrupulous money changers," who have now been driven from "their high seats in the temple of our civilization. We may now restore that temple to the ancient truths." And those ancient truths are "social values more noble than mere monetary profit."

The body of the speech describes his proposals for "action, and action now": jobs for the unemployed, "treating the task as we would treat the emergency of a war" with the workers "accomplishing greatly needed projects to stimulate and reorganize the use of our natural resources"; national planning to address the "overbalance of population in our industrial centers and ... to provide a better use of the land for those best fitted for the land"; and "two safeguards against a return of the evils of the old order": "strict supervision of all banking and credits and investments" and "provision for an adequate but sound currency."

Again, he returned to the martial theme. "These are the lines of attack," he assured his listeners, while pledging that he will use the instruments of democracy. "I shall presently urge upon a new Congress, in special session, detailed measures for their fulfillment, and I shall seek the immediate assistance of the several States."

He dismissed Hoover's focus on international trade as secondary to "first things first," that is, "putting our own national house in order and making income balance outgo." In terms of international relations, Roosevelt spoke of dedicating the nation to "the policy of the good neighbor—the neighbor who resolutely respects himself and, because he does so, respects the rights of others."

Approaching his conclusion, Roosevelt introduced "interdependence," an idea that would be repeated throughout his presidency. "[I]f we are to go forward, we must move as a trained and loyal army willing to sacrifice for the good of a common discipline." He called upon Americans to embrace "the larger purposes [that] will bind upon us all as a sacred obligation with a unity of duty hitherto evoked only in time of armed strife."

He then moved to his peroration, a declaration that Eleanor Roosevelt said "was very solemn and a little terrifying."

> I am prepared under my constitutional duty to recommend the measures that a stricken Nation in the midst of a stricken world may require. These measures, or such other measures as the Congress may build out of its experience and wisdom, I shall seek, within my constitutional authority, to bring to speedy adoption. But in the event that the Congress shall fail ... I shall ask the Congress for the one remaining instrument to meet the crisis—broad Executive power to wage a war against the emergency, as great as the power that would be given to me if we were in fact invaded by a foreign foe.

The speech electrified the nation and was soon followed by the remarkable legislative accomplishments of the First Hundred Days. The economic success of Roosevelt's declaration of war against the Great Depression is debated by historians, but one thing is clear from this speech and the leadership that followed: Roosevelt rallied the people and restored confidence in democracy at a time when its very survival was at stake.

Notes

1. I am indebted to Jean Edward Smith, *FDR* (New York: Random House, 2007), 289–303, *passim*, for the description of the background and circumstances of the inauguration.
2. Quoted from David M. Kennedy, *Freedom from Fear: The American People in Depression and War, 1929–1945* (New York: Oxford University Press, 1999), 111.
3. Smith, *FDR*, 299 fn.

Franklin D. Roosevelt's Second Inaugural Address

WEDNESDAY, JANUARY 20, 1937

WHEN FOUR YEARS ago we met to inaugurate a President, the Republic, single-minded in anxiety, stood in spirit here. We dedicated ourselves to the fulfillment of a vision—to speed the time when there would be for all the people that security and peace essential to the pursuit of happiness. We of the Republic pledged ourselves to drive from the temple of our ancient faith those who had profaned it; to end by action, tireless and unafraid, the stagnation and despair of that day. We did those first things first.

Our covenant with ourselves did not stop there. Instinctively we recognized a deeper need—the need to find through government the instrument of our united purpose to solve for the individual the ever-rising problems of a complex civilization. Repeated attempts at their solution without the aid of government had left us baffled and bewildered. For, without that aid, we had been unable to create those moral controls over the services of science which are necessary to make science a useful servant instead of a ruthless master of mankind. To do this we knew that we must find practical controls over blind economic forces and blindly selfish men.

We of the Republic sensed the truth that democratic government has innate capacity to protect its people against disasters once considered inevitable, to solve problems once considered unsolvable. We would not admit that we could not find a way to master economic epidemics just as, after centuries of fatalistic suffering, we had found a way to master epidemics of disease. We refused to leave the problems of our common welfare to be solved by the winds of chance and the hurricanes of disaster.

In this we Americans were discovering no wholly new truth; we were writing a new chapter in our book of self-government.

This year marks the one hundred and fiftieth anniversary of the Constitutional Convention which made us a nation. At that Convention our forefathers found the way out of the chaos which followed the Revolutionary War; they created a strong government with powers of united action sufficient then and now to solve problems utterly beyond individual or local solution. A century and a half ago they established the Federal Government in order to promote the general welfare and secure the blessings of liberty to the American people.

Today we invoke those same powers of government to achieve the same objectives.

Four years of new experience have not belied our historic instinct. They hold out the clear hope that government within communities, government within the separate States, and government of the United States can do the things the times require, without yielding its democracy. Our tasks in the last four years did not force democracy to take a holiday.

Nearly all of us recognize that as intricacies of human relationships increase, so power to govern them also must increase—power to stop evil; power to do good. The essential democracy of our Nation and the safety of our people depend not upon the absence of power, but upon lodging it with those whom the people can change or continue at stated intervals through an honest and free system of elections. The Constitution of 1787 did not make our democracy impotent.

In fact, in these last four years, we have made the exercise of all power more democratic; for we have begun to bring private autocratic powers into their proper subordination to the public's government. The legend that they were invincible—above and beyond the processes of a democracy—has been shattered. They have been challenged and beaten.

Our progress out of the depression is obvious. But that is not all that you and I mean by the new order of things. Our pledge was not merely to do a patchwork job with second-hand materials. By using the new materials of social justice we have undertaken to erect on the old foundations a more enduring structure for the better use of future generations.

In that purpose we have been helped by achievements of mind and spirit. Old truths have been relearned; untruths have been unlearned. We have always known that heedless self-interest was bad morals; we know now that it is bad economics. Out of the collapse of a prosperity whose builders boasted their practicality has come the conviction that in the long run economic morality pays. We are beginning to wipe out the line that divides the practical from the ideal; and in so doing we are fashioning an instrument of unimagined power for the establishment of a morally better world.

This new understanding undermines the old admiration of worldly success as such. We are beginning to abandon our tolerance of the abuse of power by those who betray for profit the elementary decencies of life.

In this process evil things formerly accepted will not be so easily condoned. Hard-headedness will not so easily excuse hardheartedness. We are moving toward an era of good feeling. But we realize that there can be no era of good feeling save among men of good will.

For these reasons I am justified in believing that the greatest change we have witnessed has been the change in the moral climate of America.

Among men of good will, science and democracy together offer an ever-richer life and ever-larger satisfaction to the individual. With this change in our moral climate and our rediscovered ability to improve our economic order, we have set our feet upon the road of enduring progress.

Shall we pause now and turn our back upon the road that lies ahead? Shall we call this the promised land? Or, shall we continue on our way? For "each age is a dream that is dying, or one that is coming to birth."

Many voices are heard as we face a great decision. Comfort says, "Tarry a while." Opportunism says, "This is a good spot." Timidity asks, "How difficult is the road ahead?"

True, we have come far from the days of stagnation and despair. Vitality has been preserved. Courage and confidence have been restored. Mental and moral horizons have been extended.

But our present gains were won under the pressure of more than ordinary circumstances. Advance became imperative under the goad of fear and suffering. The times were on the side of progress.

To hold to progress today, however, is more difficult. Dulled conscience, irresponsibility, and ruthless self-interest already reappear. Such symptoms of prosperity may become portents of disaster! Prosperity already tests the persistence of our progressive purpose.

Let us ask again: Have we reached the goal of our vision of that fourth day of March 1933? Have we found our happy valley?

I see a great nation, upon a great continent, blessed with a great wealth of natural resources. Its hundred and thirty million people are at peace among themselves; they are making their country a good neighbor among the nations. I see a United States which can demonstrate that, under democratic methods of government, national wealth can be translated into a spreading volume of human comforts hitherto unknown, and the lowest standard of living can be raised far above the level of mere subsistence.

But here is the challenge to our democracy: In this nation I see tens of millions of its citizens—a substantial part of its whole population—who at this very moment are denied the greater part of what the very lowest standards of today call the necessities of life.

I see millions of families trying to live on incomes so meager that the pall of family disaster hangs over them day by day.

I see millions whose daily lives in city and on farm continue under conditions labeled indecent by a so-called polite society half a century ago.

I see millions denied education, recreation, and the opportunity to better their lot and the lot of their children.

I see millions lacking the means to buy the products of farm and factory and by their poverty denying work and productiveness to many other millions.

I see one-third of a nation ill-housed, ill-clad, ill-nourished.

It is not in despair that I paint you that picture. I paint it for you in hope—because the Nation, seeing and understanding the injustice in it, proposes to paint it out. We are determined to make every American citizen the subject of his country's interest and concern; and we will never regard any faithful law-abiding group within our borders as superfluous. The test of our progress is not whether we add more to the abundance of those who have much; it is whether we provide enough for those who have too little.

If I know aught of the spirit and purpose of our Nation, we will not listen to Comfort, Opportunism, and Timidity. We will carry on.

Overwhelmingly, we of the Republic are men and women of good will; men and women who have more than warm hearts of dedication; men and women who have cool heads and willing hands of practical purpose as well. They will insist that every agency of popular government use effective instruments to carry out their will.

Government is competent when all who compose it work as trustees for the whole people. It can make constant progress when it keeps abreast of all the facts. It can obtain justified support and legitimate criticism when the people receive true information of all that government does.

If I know aught of the will of our people, they will demand that these conditions of effective government shall be created and maintained. They will demand a nation uncorrupted by cancers of injustice and, therefore, strong among the nations in its example of the will to peace.

Today we reconsecrate our country to long-cherished ideals in a suddenly changed civilization. In every land there are always at work forces that drive men apart and forces that draw men together. In our personal ambitions we are individualists. But in our seeking for economic and political progress as a nation, we all go up, or else we all go down, as one people.

To maintain a democracy of effort requires a vast amount of patience in dealing with differing methods, a vast amount of humility. But out of the confusion of many voices rises an understanding of dominant public need. Then political leadership can voice common ideals, and aid in their realization.

In taking again the oath of office as President of the United States, I assume the solemn obligation of leading the American people forward along the road over which they have chosen to advance.

While this duty rests upon me I shall do my utmost to speak their purpose and to do their will, seeking Divine guidance to help us each and every one to give light to them that sit in darkness and to guide our feet into the way of peace.

"One-Third of a Nation..."

THE SECOND INAUGURAL ADDRESS OF FRANKLIN D. ROOSEVELT

David M. Kennedy

FRANKLIN D. ROOSEVELT's Second Inaugural Address, the first to be delivered in the newly established inaugural month of January, is one of the most richly instructive of all such addresses. Its anaphoric litany of national failings, culminating in the famous declaration about "one-third of a nation ill-housed, ill-clad, ill-nourished," has echoed down the decades. But though frequently misunderstood, not least because of that resonant passage, the address, if read carefully, amounts to one of the American republic's great state papers and bears comparison with Abraham Lincoln's storied Second Inaugural.

Like Lincoln's in 1865, Roosevelt's address in 1937 was a model of concision and the compelling eloquence of simple, unadorned language. Like Lincoln, Roosevelt framed his remarks around moral as well as political precepts. Most importantly, both speeches open windows into the respective presidents' souls and their most deeply held philosophical values, even while brilliantly illuminating the transformative historical episodes of the Civil War and the Great Depression.

Like many second-termers, Roosevelt began by comparing the (improved) state of the nation on the instant occasion with the (parlous) moment when he had taken office four years earlier. Then, thirteen million workers were jobless, some 25 percent of the labor force; national income had plummeted to half its 1929 level; virtually all banks had shuttered their doors. On Inaugural Day in March 1933, Roosevelt had memorably begun the work of bracing up a despairing people when he intoned that "the only thing we have to fear is fear itself."

There followed the out-pouring of reforms that history knows as the New Deal. The Depression still weighed heavily on the land in 1937, but Roosevelt justifiably boasted that even as he spoke the economy was measurably recovering, while the national mood had markedly improved.

But Roosevelt devoted fewer than 100 of the address's 1,812 words to that familiar kind of self-congratulatory, political boilerplate.

Instead, he invoked a different historical reference point altogether, not the Depression's abysmal depth in 1933, but "the one hundred and fiftieth anniversary of the Constitutional Convention which made us a nation." He then launched into an exemplary presidential civics lesson, mounting a vigorous defense not simply of his own record, but of the whole concept of the positive, activist state as a legitimate, even necessary, feature of democratic governance.

Though many listeners at the time may not have fully appreciated it, Roosevelt proceeded to offer a commendably succinct summary of the critique of legacy political institutions and practices as well as laissez-faire economic nostrums that the Progressive generation of Roosevelt's youth had struggled to articulate. Government was not simply a necessary evil, as Thomas Paine had preached in the Revolutionary era and generations of Americans had ritually repeated (as some still do). Democratic government, said Roosevelt, also had the "power to do good." Like his predecessors, distant-cousin Theodore Roosevelt and scholar-in-politics Woodrow Wilson (in whose administration he had served as assistant secretary of the Navy), Roosevelt championed the positive role of the state as the instrument of society's collective will and citizens' shared purposes—and as counterpoise to the enormous accretions of power that had taken root in the modern industrial economy. That aspirational notion had galvanized an earlier generation, but it was Roosevelt's New Deal that finally brought to fruition many of the older Progressives' ambitions for reforms like capital market regulation, secure old-age pensions, unemployment relief, protections for labor-union organization, facilitation of home ownership, electrification of the countryside, conservation of landscapes and natural resources, and huge nation-building infrastructure investments like the dams and hydroelectric installations that jump-started the economic and social modernization of the South and sparked a second westward movement into the arid regions of the United States. "The Constitution of 1787," Roosevelt summed up, "did not make our democracy impotent."

It's worth noting that Roosevelt cast this robust assertion of government's proper scope in language appropriate to the substance of his argument. He used the word "we" no fewer than 70 times, "our" another 30 times, and the perpendicular pronoun "I" no more than a dozen times, five of them in the widely quoted passage about "I see one-third of a nation. . . ."

In due course Roosevelt returned to the ambient circumstances of 1937. "Our progress out of the depression is obvious," he said. "[W]e have come far from the days of stagnation and despair."

But then there followed one of the most remarkable statements in the annals of presidential addresses, inaugural addresses included, to which Roosevelt singularly attached an exclamation point: "Such symptoms of prosperity may become portents of disaster!"

One will look long and in vain for a comparable remark by any politician, anytime, anywhere. Here was a president in the very act of celebrating his electoral triumph, justifiably crowing about the progress made in his first administration. Why in the same breath would he appear to undercut that upbeat message with the highly unorthodox—even heretical—assertion that prosperity amounted to disaster?

The answer to that riddle lies in the passage immediately following Roosevelt's extraordinary lamentation about the dangers attendant on prosperity. It was here that Roosevelt turned to the plight of the "one-third of a nation," the "tens of millions" of Americans who were denied "what the very lowest standards of today call the necessities of life."

Casual students of the Roosevelt era might be forgiven for assuming that when the president rehearsed the fate of that suffering one-third, he was referring to the victims of the Great Depression. But a closer reading compels a different conclusion altogether. By early 1937, the president and others believed—mistakenly, as it turned out—that the worst was behind them, that the New Deal had broken the back of the Depression and put the nation on the road to recovery. But Roosevelt knew that "our present gains were won under the pressure of more than ordinary circumstances." The return to "normalcy," to business as usual, might well mean returning to politics as usual, to the kind of stasis that was purpose-built into the American constitutional architecture of checks and balances. The window of opportunity might slam shut well before Roosevelt's larger vision was fully realized.

That vision was capacious indeed. "We are going to make a country," Roosevelt once said to Labor Secretary Frances Perkins, "in which no one is left out."[1] The long-excluded one-third of American citizens who were his concern in 1937 conspicuously comprised rural Americans, Black and white alike, as well as the enormous immigrant communities that had arrived around the turn of the century.

Rexford Tugwell, a Roosevelt confidant and policy adviser, once described Roosevelt's vision as "a better life for all Americans, and a better America to live it in. I think it was that general. There were items in it, but only a few he saw as fixed. One of these was security; if Europeans could have that, so could Americans. Another was a new framework for industrialism, and still another was a physically improved country."[2] Later, on the occasion of his 1944 State of the Union Address, Roosevelt elevated his vision to the level of a sweeping philosophical principle: "necessitous men are not free men," he said, adding that "people who are hungry and out of a job are the stuff of which dictatorships are made."

It's important to emphasize the character and reach of Roosevelt's vision, because he is often wrongly accused of having none. Far too many accounts of Roosevelt's presidency mistakenly argue that his program had no internal coherence, that it amounted to little more than an opportunistic hodge-podge of ill-conceived policies with no overall pattern. But as his Second Inaugural Address makes clear, his deep commitment to the positive state, and to bringing that excluded one-third of his fellow citizens into the full richness of American life, gives the lie to such gross misunderstandings.

Notes

1. Frances Perkins, *The Roosevelt I Knew* (New York: The Viking Press, 1946), 113.
2. Rexford G. Tugwell, *The Brains Trust* (New York: Viking, 1968), 157–158.

Franklin D. Roosevelt's Third Inaugural Address

MONDAY, JANUARY 20, 1941

ON EACH NATIONAL day of inauguration since 1789, the people have renewed their sense of dedication to the United States.

In Washington's day the task of the people was to create and weld together a nation.

In Lincoln's day the task of the people was to preserve that Nation from disruption from within.

In this day the task of the people is to save that Nation and its institutions from disruption from without.

To us there has come a time, in the midst of swift happenings, to pause for a moment and take stock—to recall what our place in history has been, and to rediscover what we are and what we may be. If we do not, we risk the real peril of isolation, the real peril of inaction.

Lives of Nations are determined not by the count of years, but by the lifetime of the human spirit. The life of a man is three-score years and ten: a little more, a little less. The life of a Nation is the fullness of the measure of its will to live.

There are men who doubt this. There are men who believe that democracy, as a form of Government and a frame of life, is limited or measured by a kind of mystical and artificial fate—that, for some unexplained reason, tyranny and slavery have become the surging wave of the future—and that freedom is an ebbing tide.

But we Americans know that this is not true.

Eight years ago, when the life of this Republic seemed frozen by a fatalistic terror, we proved that this is not true. We were in the midst of shock—but we acted. We acted quickly, boldly, decisively.

These later years have been living years—fruitful years for the people of this democracy. For they have brought to us greater security and, I hope, a better understanding that life's ideals are to be measured in other than material things.

Most vital to our present and our future is this experience of a democracy which successfully survived crisis at home; put away many evil things; built new structures on enduring lines; and, through it all, maintained the fact of its democracy.

For action has been taken within the three-way framework of the Constitution of the United States. The coordinate branches of the Government continue freely to function. The Bill of Rights remains inviolate. The freedom of elections is wholly maintained. Prophets of the downfall of American democracy have seen their dire predictions come to naught.

No, democracy is not dying.

We know it because we have seen it revive—and grow.

We know it cannot die—because it is built on the unhampered initiative of individual men and women joined together in a common enterprise—an enterprise undertaken and carried through by the free expression of a free majority.

We know it because democracy alone, of all forms of government, enlists the full force of men's enlightened will.

We know it because democracy alone has constructed an unlimited civilization capable of infinite progress in the improvement of human life.

We know it because, if we look below the surface, we sense it still spreading on every continent—for it is the most humane, the most advanced, and in the end the most unconquerable of all forms of human society.

A Nation, like a person, has a body—a body that must be fed and clothed and housed, invigorated and rested, in a manner that measures up to the objectives of our time.

A Nation, like a person, has a mind—a mind that must be kept informed and alert, that must know itself, that understands the hopes and the needs of its neighbors—all the other Nations that live within the narrowing circle of the world.

A Nation, like a person, has something deeper, something more permanent, something larger than the sum of all its parts. It is that something which matters most to its future—which calls forth the most sacred guarding of its present.

It is a thing for which we find it difficult—even impossible—to hit upon a single, simple word.

And yet we all understand what it is—the spirit—the faith of America. It is the product of centuries. It was born in the multitudes of those who came from many lands—some of high degree, but mostly plain people—who sought here, early and late, to find freedom more freely.

The democratic aspiration is no mere recent phase in human history. It is human history. It permeated the ancient life of early peoples. It blazed anew in the Middle Ages. It was written in Magna Charta.

In the Americas its impact has been irresistible. America has been the New World in all tongues, and to all peoples, not because this continent was a new-found land, but because all those who came here believed they could create upon this continent a new life—a life that should be new in freedom.

Its vitality was written into our own Mayflower Compact, into the Declaration of Independence, into the Constitution of the United States, into the Gettysburg Address.

Those who first came here to carry out the longings of their spirit, and the millions who followed, and the stock that sprang from them—all have moved forward constantly and consistently toward an ideal which in itself has gained stature and clarity with each generation.

The hopes of the Republic cannot forever tolerate either undeserved poverty or self-serving wealth.

We know that we still have far to go; that we must more greatly build the security and the opportunity and the knowledge of every citizen, in the measure justified by the resources and the capacity of the land.

But it is not enough to achieve these purposes alone. It is not enough to clothe and feed the body of this Nation, to instruct, and inform its mind. For there is also the spirit. And of the three, the greatest is the spirit.

Without the body and the mind, as all men know, the Nation could not live.

But if the spirit of America were killed, even though the Nation's body and mind, constricted in an alien world, lived on, the America we know would have perished.

That spirit—that faith—speaks to us in our daily lives in ways often unnoticed, because they seem so obvious. It speaks to us here in the Capital of the Nation. It speaks to us through the processes of governing in the sovereignties of 48 States. It speaks to us in our counties, in our cities, in our towns, and in our villages. It speaks to us from the other Nations of the hemisphere, and from those across the seas—the enslaved, as well as the free. Sometimes we fail to hear or heed these voices of freedom because to us the privilege of our freedom is such an old, old story.

The destiny of America was proclaimed in words of prophecy spoken by our first President in his first Inaugural in 1789—words almost directed, it would seem, to this year of 1941: "The preservation of the sacred fire of liberty and the destiny of the republican model of government are justly considered ... deeply, ... finally, staked on the experiment intrusted to the hands of the American people."

If we lose that sacred fire—if we let it be smothered with doubt and fear—then we shall reject the destiny which Washington strove so valiantly and so triumphantly to establish. The preservation of the spirit and faith of the Nation does, and will, furnish the highest justification for every sacrifice that we may make in the cause of national defense.

In the face of great perils never before encountered, our strong purpose is to protect and to perpetuate the integrity of democracy.

For this we muster the spirit of America, and the faith of America.

We do not retreat. We are not content to stand still. As Americans, we go forward, in the service of our country, by the will of God.

Pathbreaker

THE THIRD INAUGURAL ADDRESS OF FRANKLIN D. ROOSEVELT

Michael Kazin

THE HEADLINES REMINDED everyone that no other president had ever been inaugurated three times. But browsed quickly or heard on the air, Franklin D. Roosevelt's address of just 1,380 words may have seemed to strike only familiar, if rather abstract, chords of congratulatory patriotism. He invoked the examples of Washington and Lincoln and lauded the democratic "spirit" instilled in iconic documents from the Mayflower Compact to the Declaration of Independence and the Constitution to the Gettysburg Address. That same spirit, Roosevelt claimed in a nod to the immigrants and their children who had again helped elect him, was "born in the multitudes of those who came from many lands." He concluded with a pledge: "We do not retreat. We are not content to stand still. As Americans, we go forward, in the service of our country, by the will of God."

The address was delivered with his usual flair. Roosevelt's moral urgency and his knack for dramatic pacing helped make him one of the greatest presidential orators. Yet, the throng that day of close to half a million appeared largely unmoved by his rhetoric, and Roosevelt later confessed his disappointment at the lukewarm reception. Arthur Krock, the influential Washington Bureau Chief of the *New York Times*, commented that "the spiritual tone" of the address, given before a bevy of "silk-hatted politicians" and an audience shivering in 24-degree weather, was "not calculated to bring forth great displays of popular enthusiasm."[1]

However, if read closely, the speech was more a call to defend the ideals of a system faced with "great perils never before encountered" than an anodyne hymn to the nation's past achievements. There was loose in the world that winter an evil and mighty force which the president was urging Americans to resist, even if he never named it in his speech. As he spoke, the armies of Nazi Germany and their Italian Fascist ally were occupying most of Europe. Only Great Britain, under the leadership of Prime Minister Winston Churchill, held off the totalitarian enemy, thanks to the Royal Air Force's defeat of the German Luftwaffe the previous fall. But Adolf Hitler's desire to conquer the island nation and its far-flung empire burned as brightly as ever.

A month earlier, in the wake of his third victory, Roosevelt had announced that the United States should be an "Arsenal of Democracy"—producing and selling the weapons of war to Britain and Canada. He knew a majority of Americans opposed throwing troops into the cauldron of war but also did not want Hitler and Mussolini to triumph. The impressive display of tanks and troops marching in close formation that dominated the Inaugural Parade served as a fitting response to anyone who doubted the administration's determination to prepare the public for the sacrifices that might be required of them in the near future.

Near the beginning of his speech, Roosevelt made clear that ideological combat was vital to defeating the (unnamed) menace abroad. Some men "believe that democracy, as a form of Government and a frame of life, is limited or measured by a kind of mystical and artificial fate" and that "tyranny and slavery have become the surging wave of the future." He quickly asserted, "But we Americans know that this is not true." Roosevelt's boundless confidence in the "spirit" of democracy which he elaborated in the rest of the short address was bounded with a warning: if citizens do not believe in their right and ability to govern themselves, they will never vanquish their sworn enemies.

As with all paeans to American exceptionalism, Roosevelt's speech was not free of hyperbole. The democratic system that he claimed "enlists the full force of men's enlightened will" did not allow most Black Americans who lived in the South, then run almost exclusively by politicians from Roosevelt's own party, to enjoy the "equal protection of the laws" or to vote—both of which the Constitution guaranteed. And he made no effort to explain how democracy could be in such danger if it were, at the same time, "still spreading on every continent—for it is . . . in the end the most unconquerable of all forms of human society." It is a bit odd that none of the speechwriters or the president who labored on an address that went through some six drafts noticed the contradiction.

Just two weeks before, Roosevelt had delivered a speech to a joint session of Congress whose significance has always overshadowed that of the Third Inaugural. In that State of the Union Address, he warned, similarly, that "the democratic way of life is at this moment being directly assailed in every part of the world . . . either by arms or by secret spreading of poisonous propaganda" and called for "a swift and driving increase in our armament production." But what made that speech so memorable was Roosevelt's bold statement that the world could be made "secure" only if it were "founded upon four essential human freedoms"—of speech, of worship, from want, and from fear. The Four Freedoms swiftly became the equivalent of war aims for a nation that had not yet been attacked (but would be eleven months later); it rendered the Inaugural Address something of an anticlimax. As desires both specific and universal, they infused the "democratic spirit" with a weightier, more appealing import. Perhaps that's one reason why the vast audience did not give Roosevelt's speech on the 20th of January the emotional ovation he expected. They had so recently heard or read a better one dedicated to the very same end.

Note

1. Arthur Krock, "In the Nation: Reflections on the Third Inaugural," *New York Times*, January 21, 1941, A20.

Franklin D. Roosevelt's Fourth Inaugural Address

SATURDAY, JANUARY 20, 1945

MR. CHIEF JUSTICE, *Mr. Vice President, my friends:*
You will understand and, I believe, agree with my wish that the form of this inauguration be simple and its words brief.

We Americans of today, together with our allies, are passing through a period of supreme test. It is a test of our courage—of our resolve—of our wisdom—our essential democracy.

If we meet that test—successfully and honorably—we shall perform a service of historic importance which men and women and children will honor throughout all time.

As I stand here today, having taken the solemn oath of office in the presence of my fellow countrymen—in the presence of our God—I know that it is America's purpose that we shall not fail.

In the days and in the years that are to come we shall work for a just and honorable peace, a durable peace, as today we work and fight for total victory in war.

We can and we will achieve such a peace.

We shall strive for perfection. We shall not achieve it immediately—but we still shall strive. We may make mistakes—but they must never be mistakes which result from faintness of heart or abandonment of moral principle.

I remember that my old schoolmaster, Dr. Peabody, said—in days that seemed to us then to be secure and untroubled: "Things in life will not always run smoothly. Sometimes we will be rising toward the heights—then all will seem to reverse itself and start downward. The great fact to remember is that the trend of civilization itself is forever upward; that a line drawn through the middle of the peaks and the valleys of the centuries always has an upward trend."

Our Constitution of 1787 was not a perfect instrument; it is not perfect yet. But it provided a firm base upon which all manner of men, of all races and colors and creeds, could build our solid structure of democracy.

And so today, in this year of war, 1945, we have learned lessons—at a fearful cost—and we shall profit by them.

We have learned that we cannot live alone, at peace; that our own well-being is dependent on the well-being of other Nations, far away. We have learned that we must live as men and not as ostriches, nor as dogs in the manger.

We have learned to be citizens of the world, members of the human community.

We have learned the simple truth, as Emerson said, that "The only way to have a friend is to be one."

We can gain no lasting peace if we approach it with suspicion and mistrust—or with fear. We can gain it only if we proceed with the understanding and the confidence and the courage which flow from conviction.

The Almighty God has blessed our land in many ways. He has given our people stout hearts and strong arms with which to strike mighty blows for freedom and truth. He has given to our country a faith which has become the hope of all peoples in an anguished world.

So we pray to Him now for the vision to see our way clearly—to see the way that leads to a better life for ourselves and for all our fellow men—to the achievement of His will to peace on earth.

Unprecedented

THE FOURTH INAUGURAL ADDRESS OF FRANKLIN D. ROOSEVELT

David B. Woolner

AT APPROXIMATELY 11:50 a.m. on Saturday, January 20, 1945, U.S. President Franklin D. Roosevelt took the arm of his son James, and with his steel braces locked in place, made his way carefully through a small crowd that had gathered on the south portico of the White House to a chair that had been placed there for him as the inaugural ceremony that would see Roosevelt take the oath of office for the fourth and final time got underway. With the nation at war, he had insisted that his unprecedented fourth swearing-in should be a brief, straightforward affair. There would be no inauguration day parade and no elaborate event on the steps of the Capitol. He also planned to keep his inaugural remarks short and to the point. Like the rest of the nation, Roosevelt was tired. Tired of the war, tired of the great sacrifices the war demanded, and—as he only admitted to his most intimate confidants—tired of being president.

Given the situation that the United States and its Allies faced at the beginning of 1945, Roosevelt had good reason to feel fatigued. It had taken many weeks of hard fighting for the Western Allies to recover from the massive counteroffensive that Hitler launched in the Ardennes on December 16, 1944. Even though the Allies had managed to halt the German advance, it was now clear that, in spite of the stunning success of the Allied drive across France in the wake of the Normandy invasion, the war was by no means over. Indeed, U.S. battle casualties for the month of December alone were the highest of the war. Worst still, these figures arrived at the very moment when the country faced a severe shortage in manpower, not only to fill the ranks of the Armed Forces, but also to maintain the critical levels of industrial production that were required to keep the offensive operations in Europe and Asia moving forward.

Equally important, Roosevelt had to worry about a growing sense of dissension among the three major Allied powers as the war entered its final phase, and the concomitant disillusionment among the American public that accompanied it. To many observers it was becoming more and more apparent, for example, that the Soviet Union was intent on exerting direct control over Poland, and just as obvious that Churchill's government was intent on establishing a conservative pro-British regime in Greece—even at the cost of armed conflict with Britain's former allies, the anti-monarchist and largely communist Greek resistance. Given these developments, some members of Congress argued that the much-heralded principles that had been articulated in the 1941 Atlantic Charter were being crucified in the current Polish and Greek crises. But the most serious issue confronting the president concerned the impact that internal Allied tensions might have on the main reason Roosevelt had decided to run for a fourth term: the fate of the United Nations.

All of these questions weighed heavily on Roosevelt's mind as he prepared to take on the responsibility of another four years in office. To meet these challenges, Roosevelt had already agreed to make the long journey to the Soviet resort town of Yalta, on the Crimean Peninsula, to converse with his British and Soviet counterparts. Here, the three leaders hoped to solidify their strategy for the final assault on Germany and Japan and come to an understanding over such outstanding issues as the future status of Poland and the structure of the United Nations.

Of course, the need for security meant that Roosevelt could not divulge the fact that he would be leaving for the Yalta conference a mere two days after he was sworn in as president. But in light of the growing uncertainty in the public's mind about the direction of the war, he planned to use the occasion of his fourth inaugural as a means to stress the need for Allied unity, and not let the differences that had begun to emerge as the specter of victory appeared on the horizon blind the American people to what he previously termed the "important common and continuing interests in winning the war and building the peace."

January 20 was a cold day, with a fresh dusting of snow glistening on the leaves of the nearby magnolia trees. On the steps below the portico, looking up in admiration and wonder, stood all thirteen of the president's grandchildren, and below them, the hundreds of official guests who filled a special section marked by a canvas spread on the ground to cover the snow. The president had also insisted—in a fitting reminder that the nation was still at war—that, amid the crowd of diplomats, governors, members of Congress, and other representatives of Washington officialdom, a space be reserved for a group of fifty wounded servicemen, many of whom, like their commander in chief, were confined to wheelchairs.

The first to take the oath of office was Vice President Truman. Then it was Roosevelt's turn. After making his way to the podium with the help of James and a Secret Service agent, Roosevelt placed his right hand on his family Bible and, discreetly gripping the reading podium with his left, turned to face U.S. Chief Justice Harlan Stone. He then swore to faithfully execute the office of president of the United States and to preserve protect and defend the nation's Constitution, "so help me God."

With the sight of the Jefferson Memorial glimmering in the distance, Roosevelt began his Fourth Inaugural Address by reminding the American people of the many trials they had yet to face as they struggled to bring the war to an end. The United States and its Allies were passing through "a period of supreme test," he said, "a test of our courage—of our resolve—of our wisdom—of our essential democracy. If we meet this test—successfully and honorably," he continued, "we shall perform a service of historic importance which men and women and children will honor throughout all time."

In short, winning the war was not going to be easy. Nor would the transition from war to peace be achieved without a great deal of effort and the occasional setback. Although we may "strive for perfection," he said, "we may make mistakes" along the way. Still, as his "old schoolmaster, Dr. Peabody, said in days that seemed to us then to be secure and untroubled," we should remember that "[t]hings in life will not always run smoothly. Sometimes we will be rising toward the heights—then all will seem to reverse itself and start downward." But the "great fact to remember is that the trend of civilization is forever upward; that a line drawn through the middle of the peaks and valleys of the centuries always has an upward trend."

And then, no doubt thinking about the structure of the peace to come, Roosevelt reflected on the character of the American Constitution. It "was not a perfect instrument," he said, Indeed, "it is not perfect yet. But it provided a firm base upon which all manner of men, of all races and colors and creeds, could build our solid structure of democracy." Having learned through the experience of war that we "cannot live alone, at peace" and that we must be "citizens of the world . . . community," he urged his fellow countrymen to recognize that a lasting peace could not be founded on suspicion or mistrust or fear. Instead, what was needed was the confidence and the courage that flow from conviction—the conviction that "the only way to have a friend is to be one."

Roosevelt then closed his address with the observation that the Almighty had blessed the United States in many ways: "He has given our people stout hearts and strong arms with which to strike mighty blows for freedom and truth," as well as "a faith which has become the hope of all peoples in an anguished world."

In many respects, Roosevelt's Fourth Inaugural Address represents a brief reiteration of the much longer remarks he delivered on the State of the Union, on January 6, 1945. On that occasion, he not only spoke forcefully about the specific requirements needed to bring the war to a successful conclusion, but also about the critical need for the American people not to lose faith in the process involved in laying the foundations for the future peace of the world, including the creation of the United Nations. His greatest fear was that the American people might turn away from their international responsibilities and revert to the destructive pattern that had followed the last war. Here, his warning about the importance of not expecting "perfection" in his Fourth Inaugural is of special interest, for as he explained in his State of the Union Address, "Perfectionism, no less than isolationism or imperialism or power politics," might obstruct the paths to international peace. "Let us not forget that the retreat to isolationism a quarter of a century ago was started not by a direct attack against international cooperation but against the alleged imperfections of the peace. In our disillusionment after the last war," he said, "we preferred international anarchy to international cooperation with Nations which did not see and think exactly as we did. We gave up the hope of gradually achieving a better peace because we had not the courage to fulfill our responsibilities in an admittedly imperfect world. We must not let that happen again," he continued, "or we shall follow the same tragic road again—the road to a third world war."

Roosevelt would not live long enough to see the Allied victory and the successful establishment of the United Nations that followed. And he was certainly correct when he warned about the numerous imperfections that might well accompany the transition of the world from war to peace. But the postwar international structure he helped establish has not only led to a period of unprecedented economic expansion, but has also helped the world avoid the onset of a new and even more destructive world war. Viewed from this perspective, Roosevelt was surely correct when he argued that the American people should never forget that they "cannot live alone, at peace" and will forever remain "citizens of the world, members of the human community."

Harry S. Truman's Inaugural Address

THURSDAY, JANUARY 20, 1949

MR. VICE PRESIDENT, *Mr. Chief Justice, fellow citizens:*

I accept with humility the honor which the American people have conferred upon me. I accept it with a deep resolve to do all that I can for the welfare of this Nation and for the peace of the world.

In performing the duties of my office, I need the help and prayers of every one of you. I ask for your encouragement and your support. The tasks we face are difficult, and we can accomplish them only if we work together.

Each period of our national history has had its special challenges. Those that confront us now are as momentous as any in the past. Today marks the beginning not only of a new administration, but of a period that will be eventful, perhaps decisive, for us and for the world.

It may be our lot to experience, and in large measure to bring about, a major turning point in the long history of the human race. The first half of this century has been marked by unprecedented and brutal attacks on the rights of man, and by the two most frightful wars in history. The supreme need of our time is for men to learn to live together in peace and harmony.

The peoples of the earth face the future with grave uncertainty, composed almost equally of great hopes and great fears. In this time of doubt, they look to the United States as never before for good will, strength, and wise leadership.

It is fitting, therefore, that we take this occasion to proclaim to the world the essential principles of the faith by which we live, and to declare our aims to all peoples.

The American people stand firm in the faith which has inspired this Nation from the beginning. We believe that all men have a right to equal justice under law and equal opportunity to share in the common good. We believe that all men have the right to freedom of thought and expression. We believe that all men are created equal because they are created in the image of God.

From this faith we will not be moved.

The American people desire, and are determined to work for, a world in which all nations and all peoples are free to govern themselves as they see fit, and to achieve a decent and satisfying life. Above all else, our people desire, and are determined to work for, peace on earth—a just and lasting peace—based on genuine agreement freely arrived at by equals.

In the pursuit of these aims, the United States and other like-minded nations find themselves directly opposed by a regime with contrary aims and a totally different concept of life.

That regime adheres to a false philosophy which purports to offer freedom, security, and greater opportunity to mankind. Misled by that philosophy, many peoples have sacrificed their liberties only to learn to their sorrow that deceit and mockery, poverty and tyranny, are their reward.

That false philosophy is communism.

Communism is based on the belief that man is so weak and inadequate that he is unable to govern himself, and therefore requires the rule of strong masters.

Democracy is based on the conviction that man has the moral and intellectual capacity, as well as the inalienable right, to govern himself with reason and justice.

Communism subjects the individual to arrest without lawful cause, punishment without trial, and forced labor as the chattel of the state. It decrees what information he shall receive, what art he shall produce, what leaders he shall follow, and what thoughts he shall think.

Democracy maintains that government is established for the benefit of the individual, and is charged with the responsibility of protecting the rights of the individual and his freedom in the exercise of those abilities of his.

Communism maintains that social wrongs can be corrected only by violence.

Democracy has proved that social justice can be achieved through peaceful change.

Communism holds that the world is so deeply divided into opposing classes that war is inevitable.

Democracy holds that free nations can settle differences justly and maintain lasting peace.

These differences between communism and democracy do not concern the United States alone. People everywhere are coming to realize that what is involved is material well-being, human dignity, and the right to believe in and worship God.

I state these differences, not to draw issues of belief as such, but because the actions resulting from the Communist philosophy are a threat to the efforts of free nations to bring about world recovery and lasting peace.

Since the end of hostilities, the United States has invested its substance and its energy in a great constructive effort to restore peace, stability, and freedom to the world.

We have sought no territory. We have imposed our will on none. We have asked for no privileges we would not extend to others.

We have constantly and vigorously supported the United Nations and related agencies as a means of applying democratic principles to international relations. We have consistently advocated and relied upon peaceful settlement of disputes among nations.

We have made every effort to secure agreement on effective international control of our most powerful weapon, and we have worked steadily for the limitation and control of all armaments.

We have encouraged, by precept and example, the expansion of world trade on a sound and fair basis.

Almost a year ago, in company with 16 free nations of Europe, we launched the greatest cooperative economic program in history. The purpose of that unprecedented effort is to invigorate and strengthen democracy in Europe, so that the free people of that continent can resume their rightful place in the forefront of civilization and can contribute once more to the security and welfare of the world.

Our efforts have brought new hope to all mankind. We have beaten back despair and defeatism. We have saved a number of countries from losing their liberty. Hundreds of millions of people all over the world now agree with us, that we need not have war—that we can have peace.

The initiative is ours.

We are moving on with other nations to build an even stronger structure of international order and justice. We shall have as our partners countries which, no longer solely concerned with the problem of national survival, are now working to improve the standards of living of all their people. We are ready to undertake new projects to strengthen the free world.

In the coming years, our program for peace and freedom will emphasize four major courses of action.

First, we will continue to give unfaltering support to the United Nations and related agencies, and we will continue to search for ways to strengthen their authority and increase their effectiveness. We believe that the United Nations will be strengthened by the new nations which are being formed in lands now advancing toward self-government under democratic principles.

Second, we will continue our programs for world economic recovery.

This means, first of all, that we must keep our full weight behind the European recovery program. We are confident of the success of this major venture in world recovery. We believe that our partners in this effort will achieve the status of self-supporting nations once again.

In addition, we must carry out our plans for reducing the barriers to world trade and increasing its volume. Economic recovery and peace itself depend on increased world trade.

Third, we will strengthen freedom-loving nations against the dangers of aggression.

We are now working out with a number of countries a joint agreement designed to strengthen the security of the North Atlantic area. Such an agreement would take the form of a collective defense arrangement within the terms of the United Nations Charter.

We have already established such a defense pact for the Western Hemisphere by the treaty of Rio de Janeiro.

The primary purpose of these agreements is to provide unmistakable proof of the joint determination of the free countries to resist armed attack from any quarter. Every country participating in these arrangements must contribute all it can to the common defense.

If we can make it sufficiently clear, in advance, that any armed attack affecting our national security would be met with overwhelming force, the armed attack might never occur.

I hope soon to send to the Senate a treaty respecting the North Atlantic security plan.

In addition, we will provide military advice and equipment to free nations which will cooperate with us in the maintenance of peace and security.

Fourth, we must embark on a bold new program for making the benefits of our scientific advances and industrial progress available for the improvement and growth of underdeveloped areas.

More than half the people of the world are living in conditions approaching misery. Their food is inadequate. They are victims of disease. Their economic life is primitive and stagnant. Their poverty is a handicap and a threat both to them and to more prosperous areas.

For the first time in history, humanity possesses the knowledge and the skill to relieve the suffering of these people.

The United States is pre-eminent among nations in the development of industrial and scientific techniques. The material resources which we can afford to use for the assistance of other peoples are limited. But our imponderable resources in technical knowledge are constantly growing and are inexhaustible.

I believe that we should make available to peace-loving peoples the benefits of our store of technical knowledge in order to help them realize their aspirations for a better life. And, in cooperation with other nations, we should foster capital investment in areas needing development.

Our aim should be to help the free peoples of the world, through their own efforts, to produce more food, more clothing, more materials for housing, and more mechanical power to lighten their burdens.

We invite other countries to pool their technological resources in this undertaking. Their contributions will be warmly welcomed. This should be a cooperative enterprise in which all nations work together through the United Nations and its specialized agencies wherever practicable. It must be a worldwide effort for the achievement of peace, plenty, and freedom.

With the cooperation of business, private capital, agriculture, and labor in this country, this program can greatly increase the industrial activity in other nations and can raise substantially their standards of living.

Such new economic developments must be devised and controlled to benefit the peoples of the areas in which they are established. Guarantees to the investor must be balanced by guarantees in the interest of the people whose resources and whose labor go into these developments.

The old imperialism—exploitation for foreign profit—has no place in our plans. What we envisage is a program of development based on the concepts of democratic fair-dealing.

All countries, including our own, will greatly benefit from a constructive program for the better use of the world's human and natural resources. Experience shows that our commerce with other countries expands as they progress industrially and economically.

Greater production is the key to prosperity and peace. And the key to greater production is a wider and more vigorous application of modern scientific and technical knowledge.

Only by helping the least fortunate of its members to help themselves can the human family achieve the decent, satisfying life that is the right of all people.

Democracy alone can supply the vitalizing force to stir the peoples of the world into triumphant action, not only against their human oppressors, but also against their ancient enemies—hunger, misery, and despair.

On the basis of these four major courses of action we hope to help create the conditions that will lead eventually to personal freedom and happiness for all mankind.

If we are to be successful in carrying out these policies, it is clear that we must have continued prosperity in this country and we must keep ourselves strong.

Slowly but surely we are weaving a world fabric of international security and growing prosperity.

We are aided by all who wish to live in freedom from fear—even by those who live today in fear under their own governments.

We are aided by all who want relief from the lies of propaganda—who desire truth and sincerity.

We are aided by all who desire self-government and a voice in deciding their own affairs.

We are aided by all who long for economic security—for the security and abundance that men in free societies can enjoy.

We are aided by all who desire freedom of speech, freedom of religion, and freedom to live their own lives for useful ends.

Our allies are the millions who hunger and thirst after righteousness.

In due time, as our stability becomes manifest, as more and more nations come to know the benefits of democracy and to participate in growing abundance, I believe that those countries which now oppose us will abandon their delusions and join with the free nations of the world in a just settlement of international differences.

Events have brought our American democracy to new influence and new responsibilities. They will test our courage, our devotion to duty, and our concept of liberty.

But I say to all men, what we have achieved in liberty, we will surpass in greater liberty.

Steadfast in our faith in the Almighty, we will advance toward a world where man's freedom is secure.

To that end we will devote our strength, our resources, and our firmness of resolve. With God's help, the future of mankind will be assured in a world of justice, harmony, and peace.

Cold Warrior

THE INAUGURAL ADDRESS OF HARRY S. TRUMAN

Andrew E. Busch

HARRY S. TRUMAN took the oath of office on January 20, 1949, after having been elected in one of the most dramatic political upsets in American history. He had served nearly all of what would have been Franklin Roosevelt's fourth term after Roosevelt's death in April 1945. He had big shoes to fill, and the consensus by political prognosticators—and more than a few ordinary citizens—was that he was falling short. Labor unrest, inflation, shortages, and remaining wartime restrictions added up to a challenging environment for the incumbent.

In the 1946 midterm elections, Republicans made big gains, winning majorities in the House and Senate for the first time since 1930. Even Democrats were so convinced of Truman's impending doom that Arkansas Senator William Fulbright suggested that Truman appoint a Republican secretary of state and then resign, a maneuver that would have given Republicans the presidency under the order of presidential succession in place at the time. In domestic policy, Truman and the new Congress clashed repeatedly, with Congress passing a large tax cut and the Taft-Hartley Act, hated by organized labor, over Truman's veto. His proposed civil rights program and other reforms designed to complete the New Deal languished. At the same time, Truman worked closely with Republicans to obtain passage of the Marshall Plan to rebuild Western Europe, aid to Greece and Turkey, and the National Security Act of 1947 creating the Defense Department, the Joint Chiefs of Staff, the Central Intelligence Agency, and the National Security Council.

In 1948, Truman was nominated by Democrats to serve another term as president, but the party was split. On one side, Strom Thurmond ran as a "States

Rights Democrat"—or Dixiecrat—hoping to punish Truman for his civil rights stand by winning enough Southern electors to throw the election into the House of Representatives. On the other side, former Vice President Henry Wallace ran as the candidate of the Progressive Party, a coalition of far-left Democrats and communists. Wallace sought to punish Truman for his policy of anti-communist containment by siphoning off Democratic votes in Northern and Western states.

Polling, which was in its infancy, showed Truman far behind Republican challenger Thomas Dewey, the governor of New York. Dewey played it safe, relying on vague platitudes and a leisurely speaking schedule. Truman was fiery and energetic (some said demagogic). He called Congress into special session and dared it to pass a number of liberal measures endorsed by Dewey, exploiting the long-standing rift between the Republicans' presidential wing and their more conservative congressional wing. When Congress failed to act, he slapped the label of the "Do-Nothing 80th Congress" on it and campaigned for a change on Capitol Hill.

In the end, Truman won, despite the unanimous prediction of the "experts." It was not a huge win, but it was solid. Truman won 49.6 percent of the nationally aggregated popular vote to Dewey's 45.1 percent; Thurmond and Wallace each won 2.4 percent. More importantly, Truman held a 303 to 183 advantage in Electoral College votes. Thurmond's 39 in Southern states was not enough to derail the president. When he returned to Washington after voting in Missouri, Truman gleefully held aloft the blazing, premature headline of the *Chicago Tribune*: DEWEY DEFEATS TRUMAN. His fight against the GOP Congress was also successful, as Democrats regained their majorities in both House and Senate.

Harry Truman's Inaugural Address contained some historically typical features. One was an appeal to unity after a contentious campaign. "The tasks we face are difficult," Truman said, "and we can accomplish them only if we work together." Another was frequent appeal to God, an important element of American political culture found in almost every presidential inaugural address since 1789.

What made Truman's address unique to that point—though less unique after—was the fact that it focused almost entirely on the world. It is easy to understand why he adopted that focus. The Cold War with the Soviet Union was underway in earnest. Since 1945, the Soviets had incorporated into their empire the countries of Eastern Europe, most recently through a communist coup d'état engineered in Czechoslovakia in early 1948. Even as Truman spoke, Berlin was under siege, its land corridors to the West cut off by the Soviets. The free part of the city was completely dependent on a massive airlift. Some in Washington had counseled preventive war while the United States still had a nuclear monopoly, but Truman had resisted.

Looking out at the world, Truman perceived that "[i]t may be our lot to experience, and in large measure to bring about, a major turning point in the long history of the human race." The first half of the century, Truman noted, had seen unprecedented assaults on human rights and destructive warfare never before seen. Thus, "[t]he supreme need of our time is for men to learn to live together in peace and harmony." Of course, Truman himself had witnessed firsthand the destruction of the First World War, in which he served as an artillery officer, and he had borne the heavy responsibility for the decision regarding the use of atomic bombs to end the Second.

The president held that the foundation for America's efforts abroad would be its religious and civic faith, "that all men have a right to equal justice... and equal opportunity to share in the common good... that all men have the right to freedom of thought and expression. We believe that all men are created equal because they are created in the image of God." To this summation of the Declaration of Independence, Truman contrasted the regime and the ideology that opposed not just the United States, but people around the world who wanted to be free. Communism, Truman observed, opposed self-government, crushed the individual, and embraced violence as the only route to justice, and war as the inevitable solution to international disputes. The actions resulting from the communist ideology "are a threat to the efforts of free nations to bring about world recovery and lasting peace."

Truman touted the Marshall Plan as an example of what the United States was already doing in cooperation with others to advance the cause of recovery and peace. "We are ready," he added, "to undertake new projects to strengthen the free world," falling under four "major courses for action":

1. "continue to give unfaltering support to the United Nations and related agencies";
2. "continue our programs for world economic recovery";
3. "strengthen freedom-loving nations against the dangers of aggression"; and
4. "embark on a bold new program for making the benefits of our scientific advances and industrial progress available for the improvement and growth of underdeveloped areas."

Truman briefly elaborated each point. The most potentially controversial was point number 3, which Truman explained by reference to a new North Atlantic security arrangement he would soon be proposing to Congress. That arrangement was the North Atlantic Treaty Organization (NATO), based on the principle that an attack upon one is an attack upon all. NATO would become a key piece of the American strategy of collective security up to the present day. As Truman put it, "If we can make it sufficiently clear, in advance, that any armed attack affecting our national security would be met with overwhelming force, the armed attack might never occur."

After laying out his goals, Truman expanded upon the superiority of democracy, which alone could provide the dynamism and growth necessary for progress among nations. In his one brief nod to domestic affairs, he acknowledged that "[i]f we are to be successful in carrying out these policies, it is clear that we must have continued prosperity in this country and we must keep ourselves strong."

The president wrapped up his address by returning to the theme with which he began:

> Events have brought our American democracy to new influence and new responsibilities. They will test our courage, our devotion to duty, and our concept of liberty.
>
> But I say to all men, what we have achieved in liberty, we will surpass in greater liberty.
>
> Steadfast in our faith in the Almighty, we will advance toward a world where man's freedom is secure.
>
> To that end, we will devote our strength, our resources, and our firmness of resolve.

Truman's Inaugural Address wound up being a serviceable blueprint for the next four years. Except for an important amendment to the Social Security Act, not much happened in domestic affairs; the administration was as focused on the world in practice as Truman had been rhetorically. In 1950, Truman committed the United States to the defense of South Korea after it was invaded by its communist neighbor to the North—a devotion of national strength, resources, and resolve that ultimately saved South Korea and established the seriousness of the containment policy but also consumed the remainder of the Truman presidency.

More broadly, Truman's address marked the triumph of liberal, anti-communist internationalism as something resembling the consensus foreign policy of the United States for the next two decades. America First isolationism was out, as was the Henry Wallace Popular Front with Stalin. Not until Vietnam was the consensus shattered in the Democratic party, and even then most of the pieces were picked up and revivified by Ronald Reagan. While little came of Truman's domestic Fair Deal, the foreign policy themes that dominated his 1949 Inaugural Address were not forgotten.

Dwight D. Eisenhower's First Inaugural Address

TUESDAY, JANUARY 20, 1953

MY FRIENDS, BEFORE I begin the expression of those thoughts that I deem appropriate to this moment, would you permit me the privilege of uttering a little private prayer of my own. And I ask that you bow your heads:

Almighty God, as we stand here at this moment my future associates in the Executive branch of Government join me in beseeching that Thou will make full and complete our dedication to the service of the people in this throng, and their fellow citizens everywhere.

Give us, we pray, the power to discern clearly right from wrong, and allow all our words and actions to be governed thereby, and by the laws of this land. Especially we pray that our concern shall be for all the people regardless of station, race, or calling.

May cooperation be permitted and be the mutual aim of those who, under the concepts of our Constitution, hold to differing political faiths; so that all may work for the good of our beloved country and Thy glory. Amen.

MY FELLOW CITIZENS:

The world and we have passed the midway point of a century of continuing challenge. We sense with all our faculties that forces of good and evil are massed and armed and opposed as rarely before in history.

This fact defines the meaning of this day. We are summoned by this honored and historic ceremony to witness more than the act of one citizen swearing his oath of service, in the presence of God. We are called as a people to give testimony in the sight of the world to our faith that the future shall belong to the free.

Since this century's beginning, a time of tempest has seemed to come upon the continents of the earth. Masses of Asia have awakened to strike off shackles of the past. Great nations of Europe have fought their bloodiest wars. Thrones have toppled and their vast empires have disappeared. New nations have been born.

For our own country, it has been a time of recurring trial. We have grown in power and in responsibility. We have passed through the anxieties of depression and of war to a summit unmatched in man's history. Seeking to secure peace in the world, we have had to fight through the forests of the Argonne, to the shores of Iwo Jima, and to the cold mountains of Korea.

In the swift rush of great events, we find ourselves groping to know the full sense and meaning of these times in which we live. In our quest of understanding, we beseech God's guidance. We summon all our knowledge of the past and we scan all signs of the future. We bring all our wit and all our will to meet the question:

How far have we come in man's long pilgrimage from darkness toward light? Are we nearing the light—a day of freedom and of peace for all mankind? Or are the shadows of another night closing in upon us?

Great as are the preoccupations absorbing us at home, concerned as we are with matters that deeply affect our livelihood today and our vision of the future, each of these domestic problems is dwarfed by, and often even created by, this question that involves all humankind.

This trial comes at a moment when man's power to achieve good or to inflict evil surpasses the brightest hopes and the sharpest fears of all ages. We can turn rivers in their courses, level mountains to the plains. Oceans and land and sky are avenues for our colossal commerce. Disease diminishes and life lengthens.

Yet the promise of this life is imperiled by the very genius that has made it possible. Nations amass wealth. Labor sweats to create—and turns out devices to level not only mountains but also cities. Science seems ready to confer upon us, as its final gift, the power to erase human life from this planet.

At such a time in history, we who are free must proclaim anew our faith. This faith is the abiding creed of our fathers. It is our faith in the deathless dignity of man, governed by eternal moral and natural laws.

This faith defines our full view of life. It establishes, beyond debate, those gifts of the Creator that are man's inalienable rights, and that make all men equal in His sight.

In the light of this equality, we know that the virtues most cherished by free people—love of truth, pride of work, devotion to country—all are treasures equally precious in the lives of the most humble and of the most exalted. The men who mine coal and fire furnaces, and balance ledgers, and turn lathes, and pick cotton, and heal the sick and plant corn—all serve as proudly and as profitably for America as the statesmen who draft treaties and the legislators who enact laws.

This faith rules our whole way of life. It decrees that we, the people, elect leaders not to rule but to serve. It asserts that we have the right to choice of our own work and to the reward of our own toil. It inspires the initiative that makes our productivity the wonder of the world. And it warns that any man who seeks to deny equality among all his brothers betrays the spirit of the free and invites the mockery of the tyrant.

It is because we, all of us, hold to these principles that the political changes accomplished this day do not imply turbulence, upheaval or disorder. Rather this change expresses a purpose of strengthening our dedication and devotion to the precepts of our founding documents, a conscious renewal of faith in our country and in the watchfulness of a Divine Providence.

The enemies of this faith know no god but force, no devotion but its use. They tutor men in treason. They feed upon the hunger of others. Whatever defies them, they torture, especially the truth.

Here, then, is joined no argument between slightly differing philosophies. This conflict strikes directly at the faith of our fathers and the lives of our sons. No principle or treasure that we hold, from the spiritual knowledge of our free schools and churches to the creative magic of free labor and capital, nothing lies safely beyond the reach of this struggle.

Freedom is pitted against slavery; lightness against the dark.

The faith we hold belongs not to us alone but to the free of all the world. This common bond binds the grower of rice in Burma and the planter of wheat in Iowa, the shepherd in southern Italy and the mountaineer in the Andes. It confers a common dignity upon the French soldier who dies in Indo-China, the British soldier killed in Malaya, the American life given in Korea.

We know, beyond this, that we are linked to all free peoples not merely by a noble idea but by a simple need. No free people can for long cling to any privilege or enjoy any safety in economic solitude. For all our own material might, even we need markets in the world for the surpluses of our farms and our factories. Equally, we need for these same farms and factories vital materials and products of distant lands. This basic law of interdependence, so manifest in the commerce of peace, applies with thousand-fold intensity in the event of war.

So we are persuaded by necessity and by belief that the strength of all free peoples lies in unity; their danger, in discord.

To produce this unity, to meet the challenge of our time, destiny has laid upon our country the responsibility of the free world's leadership.

So it is proper that we assure our friends once again that, in the discharge of this responsibility, we Americans know and we observe the difference between world leadership and imperialism; between firmness and truculence; between a thoughtfully calculated goal and spasmodic reaction to the stimulus of emergencies.

We wish our friends the world over to know this above all: we face the threat—not with dread and confusion—but with confidence and conviction.

We feel this moral strength because we know that we are not helpless prisoners of history. We are free men. We shall remain free, never to be proven guilty of the one capital offense against freedom, a lack of stanch faith.

In pleading our just cause before the bar of history and in pressing our labor for world peace, we shall be guided by certain fixed principles. These principles are:

- Abhorring war as a chosen way to balk the purposes of those who threaten us, we hold it to be the first task of statesmanship to develop the strength that will deter the forces of aggression and promote the conditions of peace. For, as it must be the supreme purpose of all free men, so it must be the dedication of their leaders, to save humanity from preying upon itself.
- In the light of this principle, we stand ready to engage with any and all others in joint effort to remove the causes of mutual fear and distrust among nations, so as to make possible drastic reduction of armaments. The sole requisites for undertaking such effort are that—in their purpose—they be aimed logically and honestly toward secure peace for all; and that—in their result—they provide methods by which every participating nation will prove good faith in carrying out its pledge.
- Realizing that common sense and common decency alike dictate the futility of appeasement, we shall never try to placate an aggressor by the false and wicked bargain of trading honor for security. Americans, indeed all free men, remember that in the final choice a soldier's pack is not so heavy a burden as a prisoner's chains.
- Knowing that only a United States that is strong and immensely productive can help defend freedom in our world, we view our Nation's strength and security as a trust upon which rests the hope of free men everywhere. It is the firm duty of each of our free citizens and of every free citizen everywhere to place the cause of his country before the comfort, the convenience of himself.
- Honoring the identity and the special heritage of each nation in the world, we shall never use our strength to try to impress upon another people our own cherished political and economic institutions.
- Assessing realistically the needs and capacities of proven friends of freedom, we shall strive to help them to achieve their own security and well-being.

Likewise, we shall count upon them to assume, within the limits of their resources, their full and just burdens in the common defense of freedom.
- Recognizing economic health as an indispensable basis of military strength and the free world's peace, we shall strive to foster everywhere, and to practice ourselves, policies that encourage productivity and profitable trade. For the impoverishment of any single people in the world means danger to the well-being of all other peoples.
- Appreciating that economic need, military security and political wisdom combine to suggest regional groupings of free peoples, we hope, within the framework of the United Nations, to help strengthen such special bonds the world over. The nature of these ties must vary with the different problems of different areas.
- In the Western Hemisphere, we enthusiastically join with all our neighbors in the work of perfecting a community of fraternal trust and common purpose.
- In Europe, we ask that enlightened and inspired leaders of the Western nations strive with renewed vigor to make the unity of their peoples a reality. Only as free Europe unitedly marshals its strength can it effectively safeguard, even with our help, its spiritual and cultural heritage.
- Conceiving the defense of freedom, like freedom itself, to be one and indivisible, we hold all continents and peoples in equal regard and honor. We reject any insinuation that one race or another, one people or another, is in any sense inferior or expendable.
- Respecting the United Nations as the living sign of all people's hope for peace, we shall strive to make it not merely an eloquent symbol but an effective force. And in our quest for an honorable peace, we shall neither compromise, nor tire, nor ever cease.

By these rules of conduct, we hope to be known to all peoples.

By their observance, an earth of peace may become not a vision but a fact.

This hope—this supreme aspiration—must rule the way we live.

We must be ready to dare all for our country. For history does not long entrust the care of freedom to the weak or the timid. We must acquire proficiency in defense and display stamina in purpose.

We must be willing, individually and as a Nation, to accept whatever sacrifices may be required of us. A people that values its privileges above its principles soon loses both.

These basic precepts are not lofty abstractions, far removed from matters of daily living. They are laws of spiritual strength that generate and define our material strength. Patriotism means equipped forces and a prepared citizenry. Moral stamina means more energy and more productivity, on the farm and in the factory. Love of liberty means the guarding of every resource that makes freedom possible—from the sanctity of our families and the wealth of our soil to the genius of our scientists.

And so each citizen plays an indispensable role. The productivity of our heads, our hands, and our hearts is the source of all the strength we can command, for both the enrichment of our lives and the winning of the peace.

No person, no home, no community can be beyond the reach of this call. We are summoned to act in wisdom and in conscience, to work with industry, to teach with persuasion, to preach with conviction, to weigh our every deed with care and with compassion. For this truth must be clear before us: whatever America hopes to bring to pass in the world must first come to pass in the heart of America.

The peace we seek, then, is nothing less than the practice and fulfillment of our whole faith among ourselves and in our dealings with others. This signifies more than the stilling of guns, easing the sorrow of war. More than escape from death, it is a way of life. More than a haven for the weary, it is a hope for the brave.

This is the hope that beckons us onward in this century of trial. This is the work that awaits us all, to be done with bravery, with charity, and with prayer to Almighty God.

My citizens—I thank you.

Ike

THE FIRST INAUGURAL ADDRESS OF DWIGHT D. EISENHOWER

Michael J. Birkner

ALWAYS A DISTINCTIVE moment in the life of a nation, the inauguration of a new chief executive takes on special significance when a transition from one party to another is involved. The inauguration of Dwight D. Eisenhower as the nation's thirty-fourth president, moreover, was conducted in the midst of a stalemated war in Korea, a war that was one of the factors contributing to Eisenhower's decisive victory over Democrat Adlai Stevenson in November 1952.

Eisenhower's election was predicated on his reputation as the man who orchestrated the defeat of Adolf Hitler's armies and voters' conviction in 1952 that it was time for a change. The American public was increasingly impatient with a drumbeat of petty corruption cases involving Truman administration officials, with rising inflation, and with a seemingly endless war in Asia. Throughout his exhausting whistle-stop campaign in the fall of 1952, Eisenhower hammered home three key themes—communism, corruption, and Korea—as central to his crusade. The slogan "C2, K1" became a Republican anthem. Democrats' response that Americans never had it so good did not resonate as well with voters. Eisenhower took 55 percent of the popular vote and earned a decisive 442–89 victory in the Electoral College.

Because he had promised in a late campaign speech in Detroit to "go to Korea" and determine the best course of action there, Eisenhower followed through in December. He quickly concluded, based on an on-the-ground assessment, that there was no easy path to victory. Eisenhower needed to find a way to achieve peace with honor—ending the war without sacrificing a foot of South Korea territory to the communists.

En route home, he spent a week on board the cruiser USS *Helena* bound for Hawaii, accompanied by Charles Wilson and Herbert Brownell, his designees for secretary of defense and attorney general, respectively. At Wake Island, they were joined by Eisenhower's choices for secretary of state, treasury, and budget director, along with his longtime confidant, General Lucius Clay. The purpose was to enable his key advisers to get to know one another and chart a course for the new administration.

Once home in Morningside Heights on the Columbia University campus in New York City, after a Christmas holiday break, Eisenhower began writing his Inaugural Address, working first with C. D. Jackson and later with Emmet John Hughes, both of whom were on loan to him from *Time/Life*. He shared a draft of the address at a pre-inauguration meeting with his Cabinet at New York's Commodore Hotel on January 12, 1953, eliciting vigorous applause. As one of his biographers has noted, "he wanted neither to lecture nor to preach as he tried to articulate the grounding principles of his administration."[1] Despite the positive response from his top aides, Eisenhower was not satisfied that he had struck the right notes. As recounted by Hughes, on January 17 he began working on an entirely new version of his address. According to Hughes, Eisenhower "felt a restless anxiety never displayed, before or later, about any speech." But the new draft did not jell. The president-elect then decided, with Hughes's help, to rework the version he had delivered to the Cabinet. He continued to do so right up to the 20th, removing references to Moscow after UN Ambassador-designate Henry Cabot Lodge commented about problems with the phrasing.

Inauguration day in Washington dawned cool and overcast, though the sun peeked through the clouds during the ceremony. Ike and Mamie attended a special service in the morning at the National Presbyterian Church. He was not yet a member, but would join the church within months of taking up residency in the White House. After changing into his inauguration dress, which included striped trousers and dark gray formal jacket as well as a precedent-breaking homburg in place of the traditional silk top hat, Eisenhower was driven to the White House. There he engaged in a brief, frosty interaction with President Harry Truman, declining Truman's offer of hospitality before they took a limousine ride, as per tradition, to the Capitol. The harsh campaign rhetoric each had directed at the other still stung and contributed to the atmosphere. Their conversation during the short ride was mundane, focused on the crowd, the weather, and the importance of an orderly transition. Eisenhower asked Truman who had ordered his son John home from Korea for the inaugural ceremonies. "I did," Truman replied. Eisenhower offered a brief thank you, and that was the extent of their exchange.

He reiterated his thanks in a letter to Truman three days later, expressing appreciation for "your thoughtfulness in ordering my son home from Korea... and even more especially for not allowing either him or me to know that you had done so."

At noon, before an impressive crowd eager to celebrate the Republicans' return to power in Washington, Eisenhower was sworn in by Chief Justice Fred Vinson, as was his young vice president, Richard M. Nixon. Eisenhower used two Bibles: a George Washington Bible and one his mother gave him when he graduated from West Point.

Breaking another precedent, Eisenhower offered a brief prayer before commencing with his formal address: "May cooperation be permitted and be the mutual aim of those who, under the concepts of our Constitution, hold to differing political faiths; so that all may work for the good of our beloved country and Thy glory. Amen."

The inaugural speech Eisenhower delivered was neither the longest nor the shortest of its kind, nor was it filled with florid expressions. But one biographer's dismissal of the speech as "tedious and instantly forgettable" is grossly unfair.

Eisenhower's major focus in the twenty-minute address was the future of mankind. Would it be slave or free? Would Americans respond effectively to the challenges of their times? Are we moving toward the light, he asked, "or are the shadows of another night closing in upon us?"

Eisenhower highlighted the importance of the nation's founding documents and the watchfulness of Divine Providence. The struggle against atheistic communism, he observed, was central to America's future. "Freedom is pitted against slavery; lightness against the dark." The leaders of the free world, in this telling, needed to work together; danger lay in "discord."

Eisenhower said his administration would be guided by certain fixed principles. He listed nine of them by number and briefly elaborated. Key examples included abhorring war and standing firm against aggression; placing love of country above comfort and convenience; recognizing that economic health was "the indispensable basis of military strength and the free world's peace"; support for the United Nations as a means of strengthening "special bonds the world over"; and a profound conviction that all peoples and nations were equal. No race, Eisenhower observed, is inferior or expendable. Underscoring his commitment to this last premise, Eisenhower said he wanted America's friends to know that he would "observe the difference between world leadership and imperialism; between firmness and truculence; between a thoughtfully calculated goal and a spasmodic reaction to the stimulus of emergencies." Above all, he insisted, his administration would defend the "deathless dignity of man."

As president, Eisenhower lived up to his commitments to prudent stewardship of American resources and an open hand of friendship offered even to the nation's major adversary, the Soviet Union. That his approach to waging the Cold War sometimes fell short of this high standard seems indisputable. That he kept the peace and oversaw eight years of increased material prosperity is equally indisputable.

Following delivery of his address, Eisenhower's day in the spotlight was not over. After a brief lunch, he and Mamie reviewed a parade of floats along Pennsylvania Avenue, including ten floats from his native state of Texas relating the various stages of his life, West Point cadets marching past the review stand, and even some saddled-up Kansas and California cowboys. Remarkably, Eisenhower permitted one of the cowboys to lasso him, surely the first and last time for such an occurrence at a presidential inauguration. The parade went on for what he later recalled was too many hours—five, in fact, rather than the scheduled three. "Not until nearly seven o'clock did the last two elephants go by,"[2] he recalled in his memoir, *Mandate for Change*. Then it was off to the White House to change clothes and attend two inaugural balls, where he offered brief comments. Around one in the morning on January 21, 1953, Dwight Eisenhower went to bed as president of the United States.

Notes

1. Jim Newton, *Eisenhower: The White House Years* (New York: Anchor Books, A Division of Random House, Inc., 2012), 91.
2. Dwight D. Eisenhower, *Mandate for Change, 1953–1956* (New York: Doubleday & Company, Inc., 1963), 102.

Dwight D. Eisenhower's Second Inaugural Address

MONDAY, JANUARY 21, 1957

MR. CHAIRMAN, MR. Vice President, Mr. Chief Justice, Mr. Speaker, members of my family and friends, my countrymen, and the friends of my country, wherever they may be:

We meet again, as upon a like moment four years ago, and again you have witnessed my solemn oath of service to you.

I, too, am a witness, today testifying in your name to the principles and purposes to which we, as a people, are pledged.

Before all else, we seek, upon our common labor as a nation, the blessings of Almighty God. And the hopes in our hearts fashion the deepest prayers of our whole people.

May we pursue the right—without self-righteousness.

May we know unity—without conformity.

May we grow in strength—without pride in self.

May we, in our dealings with all peoples of the earth, ever speak truth and serve justice.

And so shall America—in the sight of all men of good will—prove true to the honorable purposes that bind and rule us as a people in all this time of trial through which we pass.

We live in a land of plenty, but rarely has this earth known such peril as today.

In our nation work and wealth abound. Our population grows. Commerce crowds our rivers and rails, our skies, harbors, and highways. Our soil is fertile, our agriculture productive. The air rings with the song of our industry—rolling mills and blast furnaces, dynamos, dams, and assembly lines—the chorus of America the bountiful.

Now this is our home—yet this is not the whole of our world. For our world is where our full destiny lies—with men, of all people, and all nations, who are or would be free. And for them—and so for us—this is no time of ease or of rest.

In too much of the earth there is want, discord, danger. New forces and new nations stir and strive across the earth, with power to bring, by their fate, great good or great evil to the free world's future. From the deserts of North Africa to the islands of the South Pacific one third of all mankind has entered upon an historic struggle for a new freedom; freedom from grinding poverty. Across all continents, nearly a billion people seek, sometimes almost in desperation, for the skills and knowledge and assistance by which they may satisfy from their own resources, the material wants common to all mankind.

No nation, however old or great, escapes this tempest of change and turmoil. Some, impoverished by the recent World War, seek to restore their means of livelihood. In the heart of Europe, Germany still stands tragically divided. So is the whole continent divided. And so, too, is all the world.

The divisive force is International Communism and the power that it controls.

The designs of that power, dark in purpose, are clear in practice. It strives to seal forever the fate of those it has enslaved. It strives to break the ties that unite the free. And it strives to capture—to exploit for its own greater power—all forces of change in the world, especially the needs of the hungry and the hopes of the oppressed.

Yet the world of International Communism has itself been shaken by a fierce and mighty force: the readiness of men who love freedom to pledge their lives to that love. Through the night of their bondage, the unconquerable will of heroes has struck with the swift, sharp thrust of lightning. Budapest is no longer merely the name of a city; henceforth it is a new and shining symbol of man's yearning to be free.

Thus across all the globe there harshly blow the winds of change. And, we—though fortunate be our lot—know that we can never turn our backs to them.

We look upon this shaken earth, and we declare our firm and fixed purpose—the building of a peace with justice in a world where moral law prevails.

The building of such a peace is a bold and solemn purpose. To proclaim it is easy. To serve it will be hard. And to attain it, we must be aware of its full meaning—and ready to pay its full price.

We know clearly what we seek, and why.

We seek peace, knowing that peace is the climate of freedom. And now, as in no other age, we seek it because we have been warned, by the power of modern weapons, that peace may be the only climate possible for human life itself.

Yet this peace we seek cannot be born of fear alone: it must be rooted in the lives of nations. There must be justice, sensed and shared by all peoples, for, without justice the world can know only a tense and unstable truce. There must be law, steadily invoked and respected by all nations, for without law, the world promises only such meager justice as the pity of the strong upon the weak. But the law of which we speak, comprehending the values of freedom, affirms the equality of all nations, great and small.

Splendid as can be the blessings of such a peace, high will be its cost: in toil patiently sustained, in help honorably given, in sacrifice calmly borne.

We are called to meet the price of this peace.

To counter the threat of those who seek to rule by force, we must pay the costs of our own needed military strength, and help to build the security of others.

We must use our skills and knowledge and, at times, our substance, to help others rise from misery, however far the scene of suffering may be from our shores. For wherever in the world a people knows desperate want, there must appear at least the spark of hope, the hope of progress—or there will surely rise at last the flames of conflict.

We recognize and accept our own deep involvement in the destiny of men everywhere. We are accordingly pledged to honor, and to strive to fortify, the authority of the United Nations. For in that body rests the best hope of our age for the assertion of that law by which all nations may live in dignity.

And, beyond this general resolve, we are called to act a responsible role in the world's great concerns or conflicts—whether they touch upon the affairs of a vast region, the fate of an island in the Pacific, or the use of a canal in the Middle East. Only in respecting the hopes and cultures of others will we practice the equality of all nations. Only as we show willingness and wisdom in giving counsel—in receiving counsel—and in sharing burdens, will we wisely perform the work of peace.

For one truth must rule all we think and all we do. No people can live to itself alone. The unity of all who dwell in freedom is their only sure defense. The economic need of all nations—in mutual dependence—makes isolation an impossibility: not even America's prosperity could long survive if other nations did not also prosper. No nation can longer be a fortress, lone and strong and safe. And any people, seeking such shelter for themselves, can now build only their own prison.

Our pledge to these principles is constant, because we believe in their rightness.

We do not fear this world of change. America is no stranger to much of its spirit. Everywhere we see the seeds of the same growth that America itself has known. The American experiment has, for generations, fired the passion and the courage of millions elsewhere seeking freedom, equality, and opportunity. And the American story of material progress has helped excite the longing of all needy peoples for some satisfaction of their human wants. These hopes that we have helped to inspire, we can help to fulfill.

In this confidence, we speak plainly to all peoples.

We cherish our friendship with all nations that are or would be free. We respect, no less, their independence. And when, in time of want or peril, they ask our help, they may honorably receive it; for we no more seek to buy their sovereignty than we would sell our own. Sovereignty is never bartered among freemen.

We honor the aspirations of those nations which, now captive, long for freedom. We seek neither their military alliance nor any artificial imitation of our society. And they can know the warmth of the welcome that awaits them when, as must be, they join again the ranks of freedom.

We honor, no less in this divided world than in a less tormented time, the people of Russia. We do not dread, rather do we welcome, their progress in education and industry. We wish them success in their demands for more intellectual freedom, greater security before their own laws, fuller enjoyment of the rewards of their own toil. For as such things come to pass, the more certain will be the coming of that day when our peoples may freely meet in friendship.

So we voice our hope and our belief that we can help to heal this divided world. Thus may the nations cease to live in trembling before the menace of force. Thus may the weight of fear and the weight of arms be taken from the burdened shoulders of mankind.

This, nothing less, is the labor to which we are called and our strength dedicated.

And so the prayer of our people carries far beyond our own frontiers, to the wide world of our duty and our destiny.

May the light of freedom, coming to all darkened lands, flame brightly—until at last the darkness is no more.

May the turbulence of our age yield to a true time of peace, when men and nations shall share a life that honors the dignity of each, the brotherhood of all.

Thank you very much.

The Price of Peace

THE SECOND INAUGURAL ADDRESS OF DWIGHT D. EISENHOWER

Louis Paul Galambos

ON NOVEMBER 6, 1956, American voters gave Republican Dwight David (Ike) Eisenhower an impressive (57.4 percent) majority of their votes for a second term as president of the United States. This former Supreme Commander of Allied Forces in World War II, military commander of the North Atlantic Treaty Organization, and thirty-fourth U.S. president swept the Electoral College vote, 457 to 73, against his Democratic rival, Governor Adlai Stevenson. The breadth of this victory should have made the Second Inaugural Address a mere victory lap for his party and its acclaimed leader. There were, however, too many dark clouds around Washington and the nation to allow the inauguration to descend into pride and puffery.

 The president and the American voters still had reason to wonder if their elected leader would remain healthy through the next four years. Eisenhower had long experienced a number of stress-related problems, beginning with his years at West Point prior to American entry into World War I. He smoked throughout his military career and was chain-smoking as many as four packs of cigarettes a day when he commanded the successful D-Day landing in France. This habit and the pressures of his career caught up with him repeatedly, and in September 1955, he suffered a major heart attack. He had barely recovered before a massive attack of ileitis in June 1956 sent him back to the hospital and into surgery. Again, he recovered and won the 1956 election, but he, First Lady Mamie Eisenhower, and the nation could not be certain he would be able to provide the firm hand that he had displayed in the previous four years.

The president's vigorous participation in the inaugural ceremonies on January 21, 1957, gave reassurance that he had fully recovered from his heart attack and subsequent surgery. On a cold, gray day with occasional light flurries of snow, the president stood during the entire three hours of the parade. A similarly positive conclusion had been projected by Eisenhower's State of the Union Address on January 10, and his Annual Budget Message on January 17. In the Budget Message, he reported on a growing economy, a balanced budget, and a successful effort to control inflation. The State of the Union Address was a less optimistic call to hard duty in a dangerous world, but there, too, the president could see foreshadowed "a world transformed by the spirit of freedom."

His Second Inaugural Address offered a similar vision of America's "time of trial." While we enjoyed prosperity, he said, much of the world experienced "want, discord, danger. New forces and new nations stir and strive across the earth, with power to bring, by their fate, great good or great evil to the free world's future." The breakup of the old empires and the socialist- and communist-leaning new governments of Africa and Asia were at the forefront of the president's mind. Indeed, much of the world was swinging to the Left, toward the Soviet Union and away from the American model of democratic capitalism. Eisenhower frequently found that broad transition difficult to understand and confront, but in his Inaugural Address, he stamped the struggle in stark, moral terms.

In Europe, there was abundant evidence of international communism's "bondage." Soviet tanks had just recently crushed the Hungarian Revolution. "Budapest," Eisenhower said, "is no longer merely the name of a city; henceforth it is a new and shining symbol of man's yearning to be free." But of course, those men and women who had pledged "their lives to that love" had been defeated. Nor had the German problem been solved: "In the heart of Europe, Germany still stands tragically divided. So is the whole continent divided. And so, too, is all the world." He called for Americans to stay the course, to commit themselves to "our firm and fixed purpose—the building of a peace with justice in a world where moral law prevails."

The moral order and the American alliance system had both become shaky in 1956, when Israel, Britain, and France launched an invasion of Egypt over control of the Suez Canal. Egypt's President Nasser had provoked the attack by nationalizing the canal, but Eisenhower recognized that the Suez Canal Company, as well as the invasion, was a relic of a fast-fading colonial era of gunboat diplomacy. Incensed because he had not been informed of the attack, the president looked to "the authority of the United Nations. For in that body rests the best hope of our age for the assertion of that law by which all nations may live in dignity." Leaning hard against America's three allies, Eisenhower would shortly succeed in ending the invasion and performing "the work of peace" that he called for in his Inaugural Address.

The president left no doubt that the nation still needed its Cold War allies to continue their opposition to the "divisive force" of "International Communism and the power that it controls. The designs of that power, dark in purpose, are clear in practice. It strives to seal forever the fate of those it has enslaved. It strives to break the ties that unite the free. It strives to capture—to exploit for its own greater power—all forces of change in the world, especially the needs of the hungry and the hopes of the oppressed." Eisenhower was seeking support for the foreign aid that would satisfy some of those "needs" and fulfill some of those "hopes." He acknowledged that the international struggle would be expensive. "To counter the threat of those who seek to rule by force, we must pay the costs of our own needed military strength, and help to build the security of others. We must use our skills and knowledge and, at times, our substance, to help others rise from misery, however far the scene of suffering may be from our shores. For wherever in the world a people knows desperate want, there must appear at least the spark of hope, the hope of progress—or there will surely rise at last the flames of conflict."

As the address made clear, the Eisenhower strategy had not changed. He would, above all, avoid "the flames of conflict." "We seek peace," he said, "knowing that peace is the climate of freedom. And now, as in no other age, we seek it because we have been warned, by the power of modern weapons, that peace may be the only climate possible for human life itself." To that end, he would also seek continued prosperity for Americans and for the millions elsewhere "seeking freedom, equality, and opportunity." Other goals, foreign and domestic, were embodied in the dual themes of peace and prosperity. Left unexplored in the address was the great struggle of African Americans for their full civil rights, a struggle that President Eisenhower would soon be forced to push higher in the goals of his second administration. On January 21, 1957, however, President Eisenhower folded that and other formidable issues into his concluding prayer that Americans would someday see "the turbulence of our age yield to a true time of peace, when men and nations shall share a life that honors the dignity of each, the brotherhood of all."

John F. Kennedy's Inaugural Address

FRIDAY, JANUARY 20, 1961

VICE PRESIDENT JOHNSON, *Mr. Speaker, Mr. Chief Justice, President Eisenhower, Vice President Nixon, President Truman, reverend clergy, fellow citizens:*

We observe today not a victory of party, but a celebration of freedom—symbolizing an end, as well as a beginning—signifying renewal, as well as change. For I have sworn before you and Almighty God the same solemn oath our forebears prescribed nearly a century and three quarters ago.

The world is very different now. For man holds in his mortal hands the power to abolish all forms of human poverty and all forms of human life. And yet the same revolutionary beliefs for which our forebears fought are still at issue around the globe—the belief that the rights of man come not from the generosity of the state, but from the hand of God.

We dare not forget today that we are the heirs of that first revolution. Let the word go forth from this time and place, to friend and foe alike, that the torch has been passed to a new generation of Americans—born in this century, tempered by war, disciplined by a hard and bitter peace, proud of our ancient heritage—and unwilling to witness or permit the slow undoing of those human rights to which this nation has always been committed, and to which we are committed today at home and around the world.

Let every nation know, whether it wishes us well or ill, that we shall pay any price, bear any burden, meet any hardship, support any friend, oppose any foe to assure the survival and the success of liberty.

This much we pledge—and more.

To those old allies whose cultural and spiritual origins we share, we pledge the loyalty of faithful friends. United, there is little we cannot do in a host of cooperative ventures. Divided, there is little we can do—for we dare not meet a powerful challenge at odds and split asunder.

To those new states whom we welcome to the ranks of the free, we pledge our word that one form of colonial control shall not have passed away merely to be replaced by a far more iron tyranny. We shall not always expect to find them supporting our view. But we shall always hope to find them strongly supporting their own freedom—and to remember that, in the past, those who foolishly sought power by riding the back of the tiger ended up inside.

To those peoples in the huts and villages of half the globe struggling to break the bonds of mass misery, we pledge our best efforts to help them help themselves, for whatever period is required—not because the communists may be doing it, not because we seek their votes, but because it is right. If a free society cannot help the many who are poor, it cannot save the few who are rich.

To our sister republics south of our border, we offer a special pledge—to convert our good words into good deeds—in a new alliance for progress—to assist free men and free governments in casting off the chains of poverty. But this peaceful revolution of hope cannot become the prey of hostile powers. Let all our neighbors know that we shall join with them to oppose aggression or subversion anywhere in the Americas. And let every other power know that this Hemisphere intends to remain the master of its own house.

To that world assembly of sovereign states, the United Nations, our last best hope in an age where the instruments of war have far outpaced the instruments of peace, we renew our pledge of support—to prevent it from becoming merely a forum for invective—to strengthen its shield of the new and the weak—and to enlarge the area in which its writ may run.

Finally, to those nations who would make themselves our adversary, we offer not a pledge but a request: that both sides begin anew the quest for peace, before the dark powers of destruction unleashed by science engulf all humanity in planned or accidental self-destruction.

We dare not tempt them with weakness. For only when our arms are sufficient beyond doubt can we be certain beyond doubt that they will never be employed.

But neither can two great and powerful groups of nations take comfort from our present course—both sides overburdened by the cost of modern weapons, both rightly alarmed by the steady spread of the deadly atom, yet both racing to alter that uncertain balance of terror that stays the hand of mankind's final war.

So let us begin anew—remembering on both sides that civility is not a sign of weakness, and sincerity is always subject to proof. Let us never negotiate out of fear. But let us never fear to negotiate.

Let both sides explore what problems unite us instead of belaboring those problems which divide us.

Let both sides, for the first time, formulate serious and precise proposals for the inspection and control of arms—and bring the absolute power to destroy other nations under the absolute control of all nations.

Let both sides seek to invoke the wonders of science instead of its terrors. Together let us explore the stars, conquer the deserts, eradicate disease, tap the ocean depths, and encourage the arts and commerce.

Let both sides unite to heed in all corners of the earth the command of Isaiah—to "undo the heavy burdens . . . (and) let the oppressed go free."

And if a beach-head of cooperation may push back the jungle of suspicion, let both sides join in creating a new endeavor, not a new balance of power, but a new world of law, where the strong are just and the weak secure and the peace preserved.

All this will not be finished in the first one hundred days. Nor will it be finished in the first one thousand days, nor in the life of this Administration, nor even perhaps in our lifetime on this planet. But let us begin.

In your hands, my fellow citizens, more than mine, will rest the final success or failure of our course. Since this country was founded, each generation of Americans has been summoned to give testimony to its national loyalty. The graves of young Americans who answered the call to service surround the globe.

Now the trumpet summons us again—not as a call to bear arms, though arms we need—not as a call to battle, though embattled we are—but a call to bear the burden of a long twilight struggle, year in and year out, "rejoicing in hope, patient in tribulation"—a struggle against the common enemies of man: tyranny, poverty, disease, and war itself.

Can we forge against these enemies a grand and global alliance, North and South, East and West, that can assure a more fruitful life for all mankind? Will you join in that historic effort?

In the long history of the world, only a few generations have been granted the role of defending freedom in its hour of maximum danger. I do not shrink from this responsibility—I welcome it. I do not believe that any of us would exchange places with any other people or any other generation. The energy, the faith, the devotion which we bring to this endeavor will light our country and all who serve it—and the glow from that fire can truly light the world.

And so, my fellow Americans: ask not what your country can do for you—ask what you can do for your country.

My fellow citizens of the world: ask not what America will do for you, but what together we can do for the freedom of man.

Finally, whether you are citizens of America or citizens of the world, ask of us here the same high standards of strength and sacrifice which we ask of you. With a good conscience our only sure reward, with history the final judge of our deeds, let us go forth to lead the land we love, asking His blessing and His help, but knowing that here on earth God's work must truly be our own.

Camelot

THE INAUGURAL ADDRESS OF JOHN F. KENNEDY

Barbara Ann Perry

JANUARY 20, 1961, John F. Kennedy's Inauguration Day, dawned clear but frigid, after the eight-inch snowfall on the nation's capital overnight. Kennedy and his wife, Jacqueline, had already thrilled Washington on Inauguration Eve, looking like a couple just stepping out of a fairy tale about a handsome prince and beautiful princess, as they attended a star-studded gala, produced by their friend Frank Sinatra. After eight years of the elderly President Dwight Eisenhower, the New Frontier, as Kennedy's administration would be called, burst on the scene with panache and vigor, a favorite Kennedy description (pronounced with his Boston accent as "vigah") for the activism he envisioned to get "the country moving again."

Kennedy's election marked two unprecedented milestones: at age forty-three, he was the youngest candidate ever elected to the nation's highest office and the first Roman Catholic. As he stood to take the oath of office, placing his hand on his Church's version of the Bible, he represented the faith of a quarter of the U.S. population and an immigrant heritage of all but Native Americans. Kennedy was just three generations removed from his four great-grandparents who had emigrated as dirt-poor refugees from the mid-nineteenth century's devastating Irish potato famine.

The outgoing president who, at seventy, was the same age as Kennedy's mother, and had suffered serious illnesses during his two terms in the White House, sat bundled against the icy temperatures, a scarf swaddling his neck, and his wispy white strands of hair blowing in the breeze. What a contrast when his successor stood at the podium, sans topcoat, scarf, gloves, or hat, his thick shock of auburn hair not in the least out of place. He had spent the weeks leading up to this historic day at his parents' Florida beachfront compound, naming his Cabinet and sunning around the pool. Thus, despite his own medical issues, most of which remained hidden from the public, he looked the picture of health and vitality, even on the era's black and white TV screens.

In his acceptance speech at the 1960 Democratic Convention, Kennedy had introduced the metaphor that would identify his presidency: "We stand today on the edge of a New Frontier," he declared in Los Angeles, "—the frontier of the 1960s, the frontier of unknown opportunities and perils, the frontier of unfilled hopes and unfilled threats. . . . Beyond that frontier are uncharted areas of science and space, unsolved problems of peace and war, unconquered problems of ignorance and prejudice, unanswered questions of poverty and surplus." He then focused the frontier imagery primarily on domestic issues.

In his Inaugural Address, however, he chose to emphasize Cold War challenges that he would face in foreign and defense policy. Like all of Kennedy's most important and memorable speeches, this historic Inaugural Address featured pithy syntax, soaring rhetoric, and compelling symbolism. He and his wordsmith, Theodore Sorensen, perfected the use of political symbols, defined by scholar Barbara Hinckley as those that "convey a larger range of meaning beyond themselves, with emotional, moral, or psychological impact. This larger meaning need not be independently true but will tap ideas people want to believe in as true."[1]

Kennedy began his first address to the American people and the world as president with a paean to freedom, represented by his election and the peaceful transition of power, a not-so-veiled contrast to authoritarian regimes in the communist bloc. With a nod to the nation's Founders, he praised their "revolutionary beliefs" that "are still at issue around the globe—the belief that the rights of man come not from the generosity of the state but from the hand of God." Having fought anti-Catholicism to become president, vowing to maintain the constitutional separation of church and state, Kennedy did not hesitate to call on the deistic natural rights theory embraced by drafters of the Declaration of Independence and the Constitution.

Yet in the second paragraph of this speech, Kennedy cited how drastically the world had changed in the nuclear age: "For man holds in his mortal hands the power to abolish all forms of human poverty and all forms of human life." He could not have known that in October 1962, during the Cuban Missile Crisis, he would hold in *his* hands the fate of the world, as it faced the possibility of nuclear annihilation if the United States and the Soviet Union went to war over the latter's placement of atomic warheads just ninety miles off the Florida coast and aimed at all major U.S. cities.

Illustrating Kennedy's youth, in contrast to his predecessor, he fashioned one of the most memorable symbols of the entire speech. As the first president born in the twentieth century, he proclaimed, "Let the word go forth from this time and place, to friend and foe alike, that the torch has been passed to a new generation of Americans." He was leading the junior members of the World War II generation, many of whom, like him, were the young officers who served in Europe, where his brother Joseph, Jr., had lost his life as a Navy aviator, and in the Pacific, where he himself, a Navy PT boat skipper, nearly met his end when a Japanese destroyer rammed and sank his vessel. "The graves of young Americans who answered the call to service surround the globe," Kennedy declared. "Now the trumpet summons us again."

Whether fighting for "human rights" against fascism in the Second World War, or against communism in the Cold War, Kennedy signaled in the following passage—an exemplar of his and Sorensen's crisp phrasing that brought to mind the Gettysburg Address—that "we shall pay any price, bear any burden, meet any hardship, support any friend, oppose any foe to assure the survival and success of liberty."

A one-sentence paragraph introduced his promises to the world: "This much we pledge—and more." He spoke directly to our "old allies whose cultural and spiritual origins we share," to "those new states whom we welcome to the ranks of the free," to "those peoples in the huts and villages of half the globe struggling to break the bonds of mass misery," to "our sister republics south of the border," and to the United Nations. From his days as a teenager devouring Winston Churchill's history of the English people, magazines, and newspapers, and, as a college student, serving his father, Ambassador Joseph P. Kennedy, Sr., in the United Kingdom, and then writing his Harvard honors thesis on Britain's unpreparedness for World War II, Kennedy had been a staunch internationalist. He believed in the idealism of alliances and the practical contributions they made to America's geopolitical interests. President Kennedy's establishment of the Peace Corps, just two months after the inauguration, would embody both his ideals and pragmatism.

Now, as a Cold Warrior, he aimed his rhetoric at "those nations who would make themselves our adversary." He called for peace to avoid "accidental self-destruction," but swore to maintain parity in the arms race in order to avoid tempting the communists "with weakness." "So let us begin anew—remembering on both sides that civility is not a sign of weakness. . . . Let us never negotiate out of fear. But let us never fear to negotiate," JFK asserted. He offered an olive branch, along with a quiver of arrows, just as the American eagle possesses in the presidential seal.

Recognizing the potentially peaceful uses of science, Kennedy begged "both sides" in this bipolar world (free vs. communist) to invoke technology's "wonders . . . instead of its terrors. Together let us explore the stars." The latter goal would go unheeded as both the United States and the Soviet Union raced to be the first to land a man on the moon and return him safely to earth, with Americans, inspired by Kennedy, achieving that technological wonder in 1969, six years after his tragic assassination.

In the most quoted line from the address, Kennedy importuned his fellow Americans to "ask not what your country can do for you—ask what you can do for your country," a sentiment borrowed and paraphrased from his prep school headmaster. Yet it is Kennedy's concluding oration that remains the heart and soul of his applauded Inaugural Address: "Finally, whether you are citizens of America or citizens of the world, ask of us here the same high standards of strength and sacrifice which we ask of you. With a good conscience our only sure reward, with history the final judge of our deeds, let us go forth to lead the land we love, asking His blessing and His help, but knowing that here on earth God's work must truly be our own."

Note

1. Barbara Hinckley, *The Symbolic Presidency: How Presidents Portray Themselves* (New York: Routledge, 1990), 7.

Lyndon B. Johnson's Inaugural Address

WEDNESDAY, JANUARY 20, 1965

MY FELLOW COUNTRYMEN:

On this occasion, the oath I have taken before you and before God is not mine alone, but ours together. We are one nation and one people. Our fate as a nation and our future as a people rest not upon one citizen, but upon all citizens.

This is the majesty and the meaning of this moment.

For every generation, there is a destiny. For some, history decides. For this generation, the choice must be our own.

Even now, a rocket moves toward Mars. It reminds us that the world will not be the same for our children, or even for ourselves in a short span of years. The next man to stand here will look out on a scene different from our own, because ours is a time of change—rapid and fantastic change—bearing the secrets of nature, multiplying the nations, placing in uncertain hands new weapons for mastery and destruction, shaking old values, and uprooting old ways.

Our destiny in the midst of change will rest on the unchanged character of our people, and on their faith.

The American Covenant

They came here—the exile and the stranger, brave but frightened—to find a place where a man could be his own man. They made a covenant with this land. Conceived in justice, written in liberty, bound in union, it was meant one day to inspire the hopes of all mankind; and it binds us still. If we keep its terms, we shall flourish.

Justice and Change

First, justice was the promise that all who made the journey would share in the fruits of the land.

In a land of great wealth, families must not live in hopeless poverty. In a land rich in harvest, children just must not go hungry. In a land of healing miracles, neighbors must not suffer and die unattended. In a great land of learning and scholars, young people must be taught to read and write.

For the more than 30 years that I have served this Nation I have believed that this injustice to our people, this waste of our resources, was our real enemy. For 30 years or more, with the resources I have had, I have vigilantly fought against it. I have learned, and I know, that it will not surrender easily.

But change has given us new weapons. Before this generation of Americans is finished, this enemy will not only retreat, it will be conquered.

Justice requires us to remember: when any citizen denies his fellow, saying: "His color is not mine or his beliefs are strange and different," in that moment he betrays America, though his forebears created this Nation.

Liberty and Change

Liberty was the second article of our covenant. It was self-government. It was our Bill of Rights. But it was more. America would be a place where each man could be proud to be himself: stretching his talents, rejoicing in his work, important in the life of his neighbors and his nation.

This has become more difficult in a world where change and growth seem to tower beyond the control and even the judgment of men. We must work to provide the knowledge and the surroundings which can enlarge the possibilities of every citizen.

The World and Change

The American covenant called on us to help show the way for the liberation of man. And that is today our goal. Thus, if as a nation there is much outside our control, as a people no stranger is outside our hope.

Change has brought new meaning to that old mission. We can never again stand aside, prideful in isolation. Terrific dangers and troubles that we once called "foreign" now constantly live among us. If American lives must end, and American treasure be spilled, in countries we barely know, that is the price that change has demanded of conviction and of our enduring covenant.

Think of our world as it looks from the rocket that is heading toward Mars. It is like a child's globe, hanging in space, the continents stuck to its side like colored maps. We are all fellow passengers on a dot of earth. And each of us, in the span of time, has really only a moment among our companions.

How incredible it is that in this fragile existence we should hate and destroy one another. There are possibilities enough for all who will abandon mastery over others to pursue mastery over nature. There is world enough for all to seek their happiness in their own way.

Our Nation's course is abundantly clear. We aspire to nothing that belongs to others. We seek no dominion over our fellow man, but man's dominion over tyranny and misery.

But more is required. Men want to be a part of a common enterprise, a cause greater than themselves. Each of us must find a way to advance the purpose of the Nation, thus finding new purpose for ourselves. Without this, we shall become a nation of strangers.

Union and Change

The third article was union. To those who were small and few against the wilderness, the success of liberty demanded the strength of union. Two centuries of change have made this true again.

No longer need capitalist and worker, farmer and clerk, city and countryside, struggle to divide our bounty. By working shoulder to shoulder, together we can increase the bounty of all. We have discovered that every child who learns, and every man who finds work, and every sick body that is made whole—like a candle added to an altar—brightens the hope of all the faithful.

So let us reject any among us who seek to reopen old wounds and to rekindle old hatreds. They stand in the way of a seeking nation.

Let us now join reason to faith and action to experience, to transform our unity of interest into a unity of purpose. For the hour and the day and the time are here to achieve progress without strife, to achieve change without hatred; not without difference of opinion, but without the deep and abiding divisions which scar the union for generations.

The American Belief

Under this covenant of justice, liberty, and union we have become a nation—prosperous, great, and mighty. And we have kept our freedom. But we have no promise from God that our greatness will endure. We have been allowed by Him to seek greatness with the sweat of our hands and the strength of our spirit.

I do not believe that the Great Society is the ordered, changeless, and sterile battalion of the ants. It is the excitement of becoming—always becoming, trying, probing, falling, resting, and trying again—but always trying and always gaining.

In each generation, with toil and tears, we have had to earn our heritage again. If we fail now, we shall have forgotten in abundance what we learned in hardship: that democracy rests on faith, that freedom asks more than it gives, and that the judgment of God is harshest on those who are most favored.

If we succeed it will not be because of what we have, but it will be because of what we are; not because of what we own, but rather because of what we believe.

For we are a nation of believers. Underneath the clamor of building and the rush of our day's pursuits, we are believers in justice and liberty and union, and in our own Union. We believe that every man must some day be free. And we believe in ourselves.

And that is the mistake that our enemies have always made. In my lifetime, in depression and in war they have awaited our defeat. Each time, from the secret places of the American heart, came forth the faith they could not see or that they could not even imagine. It brought us victory. And it will again.

For this is what America is all about. It is the uncrossed desert and the unclimbed ridge. It is the star that is not reached and the harvest that is sleeping in the unplowed ground. Is our world gone? We say farewell. Is a new world coming? We welcome it, and we will bend it to the hopes of man.

And to these trusted public servants and to my family, and those close friends of mine who have followed me down a long winding road, and to all the people of this Union and the world, I will repeat today what I said on that sorrowful day in November last year: I will lead and I will do the best I can.

But you must look within your own hearts to the old promises and to the old dreams. They will lead you best of all.

For myself, I ask only in the words of an ancient leader: "Give me now wisdom and knowledge, that I may go out and come in before this people: for who can judge this thy people, that is so great?"

The Dawn of the Great Society

THE INAUGURAL ADDRESS OF LYNDON B. JOHNSON

Mark K. Updegrove

ON THE EVENING of November 3, 1964, Lyndon Baines Johnson sat in the Presidential Suite of the Driskill Hotel in Austin, Texas, monitoring the results of the election that would relieve him of the stigma of being an "accidental president." In fact, the election would deliver a decisive mandate. Nearly a year after assuming the presidency upon the assassination of John F. Kennedy, Johnson would find not only that he had won the office, but that he had done so by yielding the biggest electoral margin in American history to that point, garnering 61 percent of the popular vote against his Republican opponent, Arizona senator and conservative stalwart Barry Goldwater. The titanic Johnson, who had devoted nearly his entire adult life to the acquisition and exercise of power, climbing the political ladder in Congress to become the most powerful Senate majority leader of the century, then moving on to become Kennedy's vice president, had not only reached power's highest rung, he had done so with a landslide. "Our victory was a mandate for action," he wrote later in his memoir, *The Vantage Point*, "and I meant it to be used that way."[1]

Johnson had spent his first year in the presidency successfully achieving the legislative goals that had eluded Kennedy—a tax cut to stimulate a sluggish economy and the passage of the landmark Civil Rights Act, breaking the back of Jim Crow and its false promise of "separate but equal" segregated facilities. "Rightly or wrongly," he said, "I felt from the very first day in office that I had to carry on for President Kennedy. I considered myself the caretaker of both his people and policy." But he had begun to lay the groundwork for his own domestic agenda by picking up one unfinished by another president, Franklin D. Roosevelt, whom he would emulate more than any other. "This is Kennedy's program," he told aides soon after taking over the Oval Office, "and we're going to get it through. But if we're going to compete with Roosevelt's revolution... it's got to be bigger than anything that has been envisioned so far."[2]

Bigger it was. Johnson had come to Washington during depths of the Great Depression in the mid-1930s as Roosevelt's New Deal, unprecedented government programs to lift Americans from economic ravage, was in full swing, bringing hope and possibility. He saw his administration as not so much competing with the New Deal but completing it. Four months before the election, in a commencement address at the University of Michigan, he had planted the seeds of his own outsize domestic vision, unveiling the Great Society, an ambitious legislative agenda around civil rights, federal aid to education, immigration reform, poverty eradication, environmental preservation, and expanded healthcare. Now, with the presidency in hand for the next four years, he would use his inauguration early in the New Year to promulgate the Great Society as the hallmark of his term in office.

January 20, 1965, as Lady Bird Johnson wrote, "dawned bright and beautiful," with a temperature of 38 degrees and sunshine, blue skies, and scattered clouds over the U.S. Capitol. An estimated 1.2 million crowded into Washington for the thirty-sixth president's inauguration, besting the record set by Kennedy four years earlier by 200,000, further approbation for the brash but often insecure Johnson. Eschewing the top hat, cutaway coat, and striped trousers worn by his twentieth-century predecessors, he opted for decidedly less formal garb, donning a plain Oxford gray business suit. Marking an Inauguration Day first, Lady Bird Johnson held the Bible on which her husband rested his left hand as he took the oath of office, establishing a tradition upheld by future first ladies. After reciting the oath that thirty-four men had taken before him, Johnson stood behind the lectern and, for twenty-three minutes, sounded the overture of his administration.

In a slow, deliberate voice laden with his Texas Hill Country accent, he laid out a covenant for the American people comprising "justice, liberty, and union" that allowed us to become a nation "prosperous, great, and mighty."

> Let us now join reason to faith and action to experience, to transform our unity of interest into a unity of purpose. For the hour and the day and the time are here to achieve progress without strife, to achieve change without hatred; not without difference of opinion but without the deep and abiding divisions which scar the union for generations.

Portending his commitment to civil rights well beyond signing the Civil Rights Act into law the previous year, he made it clear that his vision of justice included all Americans. "Justice requires us to remember," he declared, "when any citizen denies his fellow, saying: 'His color is not mine or his beliefs are strange and different' ... he betrays America."

Eight hundred miles away—portending the challenges ahead and underscoring the need for racial justice—as many as two hundred Blacks were being arrested in Selma, Alabama, for attempting to register to vote as the president spoke.

In perhaps the speech's most memorable lines, Johnson elaborated on his view of the Great Society.

> I do not believe that the Great Society is the ordered, changeless, and sterile battalion of ants. It is the excitement of becoming—always becoming, trying, proving, falling, resting, and trying again—but always trying and always gaining.

While not on par with the century's most iconic Inauguration Day oratory, it reflected Johnson's prodigious commitment to deliver social change. It was also in keeping with the view of domestic policy as a fluid, experimental exercise held by Roosevelt, who said, "It is common sense to take a method and try it. If it fails, admit it freely and try another. But above all else, try something."[3]

Echoing a chorus of positive reviews for the speech, the *New York Times*' James "Scottie" Reston, the dean of White House correspondents, wrote, "President Johnson's Inauguration was a dramatization of the American Dream. It was 'bigger and better' than ever before.... In the poignant moment of commitment, he went back to the eternal things: justice, liberty, and unity."[4]

After formally being reinstated as president and watching the inaugural parade that followed, Johnson danced the night away at a series of five inaugural balls. As he left the last of them, a gathering at the Sheraton-Hilton where he danced only with women from Texas, he beseeched his fellow revelers, "Don't stay up too late. We're on our way to the Great Society."

In the days ahead, he would work tirelessly to make good on his promise. The Great Society was foremost on Johnson's mind as he began his new term in office, setting his sights on a flurry of laws that would indeed rival those that Roosevelt ushered in through the New Deal. Johnson had a good head start. In addition to decisively delivering him the presidency, the election tide of 1964 had also brought more Democrats into Congress than since the days of the New Deal, with many newly elected lawmakers riding into office on Johnson's back. Just as auspicious was a Gallup Poll later in the year that showed faith in government among the American people to be at an all-time high of 77 percent.

Still, Johnson took nothing for granted. Acutely aware of the ephemeral nature of political capital—"When a man is first elected President, he's a giraffe; six months later he's a worm," he said—he spent much of the capital he had accrued in the same year, standing at the peak of his presidency. In 1965 alone, he set in motion a breathtaking domestic agenda that included the fruition of the Voting Rights Act, the Immigration Act, the Elementary and Secondary Education Act, the Higher Education Act, the Highway Beautification Act, and the Clean Air Act; the creation of Medicare, Medicaid, the Department of Housing and Urban Development, the National Endowment for the Arts, and the National Endowment for Humanities; and the implementation of Head Start. In many ways, the progressive advances would create the foundation for modern America.

Conspicuously absent from Johnson's Inauguration speech was any reference to the war in Vietnam, which, along with his prodigious legislative accomplishments, would define his presidency. Nor was there any allusion to the Cold War or the threat of the spread of communism, which had been the centerpiece of Kennedy's celebrated "pay any price, bear any burden" rhetoric four years earlier. Unlike Kennedy, it was domestic policy that fired Johnson's imagination, not foreign policy.

Vietnam, which had landed on his desk the day he inherited the presidency from Kennedy, was an unwanted intrusion, threatening to encroach on the Great Society. While unity was central to Johnson's Inauguration Day message, it was his escalation of the war in Vietnam that would divide the country. "That bitch of a war," as Johnson would call it, would create fissures and tumult, contributing to his decision not to seek re-election in 1968, as he sought an honorable peace that ultimately eluded him.

But as Lyndon Johnson took the presidency in his own right in 1965, there was little indication that the distant war in Vietnam would crowd out his presidency. In his Inaugural Address, he called America "a nation of believers." At the dawn of his administration, as he played its opening notes, there was reason for him to believe in the promise that lay ahead.

Notes

1. Lyndon Baines Johnson, *The Vantage Point: Perspectives of the Presidency, 1963–1969* (New York: Holt, Rinehart and Winston, 1971), 110.
2. Mark K. Updegrove, *Indomitable Will* (New York: Crown, 2012), 91.
3. Franklin D. Roosevelt, "Address at Oglethorpe University in Atlanta, Georgia | The American Presidency Project," www.presidency.ucsb.edu, retrieved from https://www.presidency.ucsb.edu/documents/address-oglethorpe-university-atlanta-georgia.
4. James Reston, "Paradox and Reason; President Blends Religion and Politics in a Strong Appeal for Faith and Unity Paradox and Reason," *New York Times*, January 21, 1965, https://timesmachine.nytimes.com/timesmachine/1965/01/21/101523292.html?pageNumber=1.

Richard M. Nixon's First Inaugural Address

MONDAY, JANUARY 20, 1969

SENATOR DIRKSEN, MR. *Chief Justice, Mr. Vice President, President Johnson, Vice President Humphrey, my fellow Americans—and my fellow citizens of the world community:*

I ask you to share with me today the majesty of this moment. In the orderly transfer of power, we celebrate the unity that keeps us free.

Each moment in history is a fleeting time, precious and unique. But some stand out as moments of beginning, in which courses are set that shape decades or centuries.

This can be such a moment.

Forces now are converging that make possible, for the first time, the hope that many of man's deepest aspirations can at last be realized. The spiraling pace of change allows us to contemplate, within our own lifetime, advances that once would have taken centuries.

In throwing wide the horizons of space, we have discovered new horizons on earth.

For the first time, because the people of the world want peace, and the leaders of the world are afraid of war, the times are on the side of peace.

Eight years from now America will celebrate its 200th anniversary as a nation. Within the lifetime of most people now living, mankind will celebrate that great new year which comes only once in a thousand years—the beginning of the third millennium.

What kind of nation we will be, what kind of world we will live in, whether we shape the future in the image of our hopes, is ours to determine by our actions and our choices.

The greatest honor history can bestow is the title of peacemaker. This honor now beckons America—the chance to help lead the world at last out of the valley of turmoil and onto that high ground of peace that man has dreamed of since the dawn of civilization.

If we succeed, generations to come will say of us now living that we mastered our moment, that we helped make the world safe for mankind.

This is our summons to greatness.

I believe the American people are ready to answer this call.

The second third of this century has been a time of proud achievement. We have made enormous strides in science and industry and agriculture. We have shared our wealth more broadly than ever. We have learned at last to manage a modern economy to assure its continued growth.

We have given freedom new reach. We have begun to make its promise real for black as well as for white.

We see the hope of tomorrow in the youth of today. I know America's youth. I believe in them. We can be proud that they are better educated, more committed, more passionately driven by conscience than any generation in our history.

No people has ever been so close to the achievement of a just and abundant society, or so possessed of the will to achieve it. Because our strengths are so great, we can afford to appraise our weaknesses with candor and to approach them with hope.

Standing in this same place a third of a century ago, Franklin Delano Roosevelt addressed a Nation ravaged by depression and gripped in fear. He could say in surveying the Nation's troubles: "They concern, thank God, only material things."

Our crisis today is the reverse.

We have found ourselves rich in goods, but ragged in spirit; reaching with magnificent precision for the moon, but falling into raucous discord on earth.

We are caught in war, wanting peace. We are torn by division, wanting unity. We see around us empty lives, wanting fulfillment. We see tasks that need doing, waiting for hands to do them.

To a crisis of the spirit, we need an answer of the spirit.

To find that answer, we need only look within ourselves.

When we listen to "the better angels of our nature," we find that they celebrate the simple things, the basic things—such as goodness, decency, love, kindness.

Greatness comes in simple trappings.

The simple things are the ones most needed today if we are to surmount what divides us, and cement what unites us.

To lower our voices would be a simple thing.

In these difficult years, America has suffered from a fever of words; from inflated rhetoric that promises more than it can deliver; from angry rhetoric that fans discontents into hatreds; from bombastic rhetoric that postures instead of persuading.

We cannot learn from one another until we stop shouting at one another—until we speak quietly enough so that our words can be heard as well as our voices.

For its part, government will listen. We will strive to listen in new ways—to the voices of quiet anguish, the voices that speak without words, the voices of the heart—to the injured voices, the anxious voices, the voices that have despaired of being heard.

Those who have been left out, we will try to bring in.

Those left behind, we will help to catch up.

For all of our people, we will set as our goal the decent order that makes progress possible and our lives secure.

As we reach toward our hopes, our task is to build on what has gone before—not turning away from the old, but turning toward the new.

In this past third of a century, government has passed more laws, spent more money, initiated more programs, than in all our previous history.

In pursuing our goals of full employment, better housing, excellence in education; in rebuilding our cities and improving our rural areas; in protecting our environment and enhancing the quality of life—in all these and more, we will and must press urgently forward.

We shall plan now for the day when our wealth can be transferred from the destruction of war abroad to the urgent needs of our people at home.

The American dream does not come to those who fall asleep.

But we are approaching the limits of what government alone can do.

Our greatest need now is to reach beyond government, and to enlist the legions of the concerned and the committed.

What has to be done, has to be done by government and people together or it will not be done at all. The lesson of past agony is that without the people we can do nothing—with the people we can do everything.

To match the magnitude of our tasks, we need the energies of our people—enlisted not only in grand enterprises, but more importantly in those small, splendid efforts that make headlines in the neighborhood newspaper instead of the national journal.

With these, we can build a great cathedral of the spirit—each of us raising it one stone at a time, as he reaches out to his neighbor, helping, caring, doing.

I do not offer a life of uninspiring ease. I do not call for a life of grim sacrifice. I ask you to join in a high adventure—one as rich as humanity itself, and as exciting as the times we live in.

The essence of freedom is that each of us shares in the shaping of his own destiny.

Until he has been part of a cause larger than himself, no man is truly whole.

The way to fulfillment is in the use of our talents; we achieve nobility in the spirit that inspires that use.

As we measure what can be done, we shall promise only what we know we can produce; but as we chart our goals we shall be lifted by our dreams.

No man can be fully free while his neighbor is not. To go forward at all is to go forward together.

This means black and white together, as one nation, not two. The laws have caught up with our conscience. What remains is to give life to what is in the law: to ensure at last that as all are born equal in dignity before God, all are born equal in dignity before man.

As we learn to go forward together at home, let us also seek to go forward together with all mankind.

Let us take as our goal: Where peace is unknown, make it welcome; where peace is fragile, make it strong; where peace is temporary, make it permanent.

After a period of confrontation, we are entering an era of negotiation.

Let all nations know that during this administration our lines of communication will be open.

We seek an open world—open to ideas, open to the exchange of goods and people—a world in which no people, great or small, will live in angry isolation.

We cannot expect to make everyone our friend, but we can try to make no one our enemy.

Those who would be our adversaries, we invite to a peaceful competition—not in conquering territory or extending dominion, but in enriching the life of man.

As we explore the reaches of space, let us go to the new worlds together—not as new worlds to be conquered, but as a new adventure to be shared.

With those who are willing to join, let us cooperate to reduce the burden of arms, to strengthen the structure of peace, to lift up the poor and the hungry.

But to all those who would be tempted by weakness, let us leave no doubt that we will be as strong as we need to be for as long as we need to be.

Over the past twenty years, since I first came to this Capital as a freshman Congressman, I have visited most of the nations of the world. I have come to know the leaders of the world, and the great forces, the hatreds, the fears that divide the world.

I know that peace does not come through wishing for it—that there is no substitute for days and even years of patient and prolonged diplomacy.

I also know the people of the world.

I have seen the hunger of a homeless child, the pain of a man wounded in battle, the grief of a mother who has lost her son. I know these have no ideology, no race.

I know America. I know the heart of America is good.

I speak from my own heart, and the heart of my country, the deep concern we have for those who suffer, and those who sorrow.

I have taken an oath today in the presence of God and my countrymen to uphold and defend the Constitution of the United States. To that oath I now add this sacred commitment: I shall consecrate my office, my energies, and all the wisdom I can summon to the cause of peace among nations.

Let this message be heard by strong and weak alike:

The peace we seek—the peace we seek to win—is not victory over any other people, but the peace that comes "with healing in its wings"; with compassion for those who have suffered; with understanding for those who have opposed us; with the opportunity for all the peoples of this earth to choose their own destiny.

Only a few short weeks ago we shared the glory of man's first sight of the world as God sees it, as a single sphere reflecting light in the darkness.

As the Apollo astronauts flew over the moon's gray surface on Christmas Eve, they spoke to us of the beauty of earth—and in that voice so clear across the lunar distance, we heard them invoke God's blessing on its goodness.

In that moment, their view from the moon moved poet Archibald MacLeish to write: "To see the earth as it truly is, small and blue and beautiful in that eternal silence where it floats, is to see ourselves as riders on the earth together, brothers on that bright loveliness in the eternal cold—brothers who know now they are truly brothers."

In that moment of surpassing technological triumph, men turned their thoughts toward home and humanity—seeing in that far perspective that man's destiny on earth is not divisible; telling us that however far we reach into the cosmos, our destiny lies not in the stars but on earth itself, in our own hands, in our own hearts.

We have endured a long night of the American spirit. But as our eyes catch the dimness of the first rays of dawn, let us not curse the remaining dark. Let us gather the light.

Our destiny offers, not the cup of despair, but the chalice of opportunity. So let us seize it, not in fear, but in gladness—and, "riders on the earth together," let us go forward, firm in our faith, steadfast in our purpose, cautious of the dangers; but sustained by our confidence in the will of God and the promise of man.

"The Title of Peacemaker"

THE FIRST INAUGURAL ADDRESS OF RICHARD M. NIXON

Ken Hughes

IN HIS FIRST Inaugural Address, Richard Milhous Nixon wrote his own epitaph: "The greatest honor history can bestow is the title of peacemaker." Twenty-five years later he would have these words carved on his tombstone.

When he uttered them on Inauguration Day in 1969, the words were a political promise and a personal aspiration. Nixon won and assumed office during the bloodiest years of America's Vietnam War. A majority of Americans by then had concluded that the war was a mistake. As a motorcade took him from the White House to the U.S. Capitol, President-elect Nixon saw something his Cold War predecessors had not: protestors lining the streets. In the 1968 campaign, Nixon had promised to "end the war and win the peace," a goal short of victory, but one that seemed more realistic. It would be, he promised, "peace with honor," not "peace with surrender." All of America would be watching and judging whether he kept this promise.

When Nixon aspired to the honor of "peacemaker," however, he was talking about more than Vietnam. He hoped to change the terms of the entire Cold War, to see out the era of confrontation and usher in an era of negotiation.

In part this was a matter of necessity. When he left office as vice president on January 20, 1961, America's numerical advantage in nuclear weapons over the Soviet Union was at least 20-to-1. Eight years later, the two nations' doomsday arsenals were roughly equal. President Nixon would not approach the Cold War as his predecessors had, because he no longer could.

Practical necessity was not Nixon's only motive for changing course. He also possessed a particularly Nixonian vision of peace. Like his unexpected Democratic hero, President Woodrow Wilson, Nixon hoped to create an international framework to work out international differences without war. Wilson sought to create this framework idealistically, through open agreements openly negotiated. Nixon would try to get similar results through secret negotiations and backchannel deals. He thought he could play the Communist powers off one another, exploit the growing rift between the Soviet Union and the People's Republic of China, use the prospect of improved relations with China against Russia, with Russia against China, and with both against North Vietnam. In three years he would look like a smashing success, in twenty-five years like an elder statesman, and in fifty years like an exposed fraud.

On Inauguration Day in 1969, he looked like he was copying the most popular inaugural address of the Cold War, the one delivered by John F. Kennedy eight years earlier. Garry Wills identified numerous Nixonian echoes of the New Frontier.[1] "Let this message be heard by strong and weak alike." (Kennedy: "Let the word go forth to friend and foe alike.") "Those who would be our adversaries, we invite to a peaceful competition—not in conquering territory or extending dominion, but in enriching the life of man." (Kennedy: "To those nations who would make themselves our adversary, we offer not a pledge but a request: that both sides begin anew the quest for peace.") "To all those who would be tempted by weakness, let us leave no doubt that we will be as strong as we need to be for as long as we need to be." (Kennedy: "We dare not tempt them with weakness. For only when our arms are sufficient beyond doubt can we be certain beyond doubt that they will never be employed.") Comparison of the imitation to the original recalls Mark Twain's observation that the difference between the right word and the almost-right word is the difference between lightning and lightning bug.

Not that it mattered much in the long run. By 1972, Nixon appeared to have delivered on his promises and more. He had inaugurated an era of rapprochement with Communist China and détente with the Soviet Union. In that year he became the first president to visit the capitals of either of these Communist powers. He had negotiated a nuclear arms control agreement with the Soviets. And, by playing Moscow and Beijing off one another, he got both to pressure Hanoi to accept his Vietnam settlement terms. The agreement, he declared, was "peace with honor." In 1972, Nixon at least appeared to have some legitimate claim to history's greatest honor.

Until the end of his life, he fought successfully to keep the public from hearing most of his secretly recorded White House tapes and reading most of the records of his negotiations with Communist leaders. This secrecy proved to be essential to preserving his image as a peacemaker. When his struggle to conceal his record ended with his death in 1994, the government began the long, slow process of declassifying the tapes and documents. In the following decades, these records revealed that Nixon had forged a "decent interval" deal with the Communists. He had secretly assured Moscow and Beijing that North Vietnam could take over the South without fear of American intervention, just as long as the North waited a year or two after Nixon withdrew the last American troops. The deal he called "peace with honor" was no peace at all. It was designed to postpone, not prevent, the collapse of South Vietnam.

That was not the worst of it. Declassified tapes and documents reveal that Nixon realized early on that South Vietnam could not survive without American troops. This meant that "peace with honor" was never achievable. America could either leave and lose the war, or stay and fight it indefinitely. Neither alternative was peace.

But Nixon never admitted in public that he couldn't deliver what he had promised. To conceal this failure, he kept the war going through all four years of his first term. That was the only way to keep South Vietnam from falling before Election Day 1972, a defeat that would have destroyed his chances at a second term. The price of his re-election was the death of 20,000 Americans and many thousands more Vietnamese, North and South.

In his First Inaugural, Nixon laid out the terms by which history would judge his presidency. The test of his presidency would be whether he earned the title of peacemaker. In some ways, he did. Détente and rapprochement eased international tensions and improved relations with China and Russia. Those achievements were real, although we now see that they were tainted by Nixon's secret assurances to both Communist powers that he would accept defeat in Vietnam, as long as they delayed it long enough for him to duck responsibility. History has yet to devise a title to bestow on leaders who prolong wars to avoid losing elections, who fraudulently package delayed defeat as peace, who sacrifice human lives for political gain.

Note

1. Garry Wills, *Nixon Agonistes: The Crisis of the Self-Made Man* (Boston: Houghton Mifflin Company, 1970), 403.

Richard M. Nixon's Second Inaugural Address

SATURDAY, JANUARY 20, 1973

MR. VICE PRESIDENT, Mr. Speaker, Mr. Chief Justice, Senator Cook, Mrs. Eisenhower, and my fellow citizens of this great and good country we share together: Mr. Vice President, Mr. Speaker, Mr. Chief Justice, Senator Cook, Mrs. Eisenhower, and my fellow citizens of this great and good country we share together:

When we met here four years ago, America was bleak in spirit, depressed by the prospect of seemingly endless war abroad and of destructive conflict at home.

As we meet here today, we stand on the threshold of a new era of peace in the world.

The central question before us is: How shall we use that peace?

Let us resolve that this era we are about to enter will not be what other postwar periods have so often been: a time of retreat and isolation that leads to stagnation at home and invites new danger abroad.

Let us resolve that this will be what it can become: a time of great responsibilities greatly borne, in which we renew the spirit and the promise of America as we enter our third century as a nation.

This past year saw far-reaching results from our new policies for peace. By continuing to revitalize our traditional friendships, and by our missions to Peking and to Moscow, we were able to establish the base for a new and more durable pattern of relationships among the nations of the world. Because of America's bold initiatives, 1972 will be long remembered as the year of the greatest progress since the end of World War II toward a lasting peace in the world.

The peace we seek in the world is not the flimsy peace which is merely an interlude between wars, but a peace which can endure for generations to come.

It is important that we understand both the necessity and the limitations of America's role in maintaining that peace.

Unless we in America work to preserve the peace, there will be no peace.

Unless we in America work to preserve freedom, there will be no freedom.

But let us clearly understand the new nature of America's role, as a result of the new policies we have adopted over these past 4 years.

We shall respect our treaty commitments.

We shall support vigorously the principle that no country has the right to impose its will or rule on another by force.

We shall continue, in this era of negotiation, to work for the limitation of nuclear arms, and to reduce the danger of confrontation between the great powers.

We shall do our share in defending peace and freedom in the world. But we shall expect others to do their share.

The time has passed when America will make every other nation's conflict our own, or make every other nation's future our responsibility, or presume to tell the people of other nations how to manage their own affairs.

Just as we respect the right of each nation to determine its own future, we also recognize the responsibility of each nation to secure its own future.

Just as America's role is indispensable in preserving the world's peace, so is each nation's role indispensable in preserving its own peace.

Together with the rest of the world, let us resolve to move forward from the beginnings we have made. Let us continue to bring down the walls of hostility which have divided the world for too long, and to build in their place bridges of understanding—so that despite profound differences between systems of government, the people of the world can be friends.

Let us build a structure of peace in the world in which the weak are as safe as the strong, in which each respects the right of the other to live by a different system, in which those who would influence others will do so by the strength of their ideas, and not by the force of their arms.

Let us accept that high responsibility not as a burden, but gladly—gladly because the chance to build such a peace is the noblest endeavor in which a nation can engage; gladly also because only if we act greatly in meeting our responsibilities abroad will we remain a great nation, and only if we remain a great nation will we act greatly in meeting our challenges at home.

We have the chance today to do more than ever before in our history to make life better in America—to ensure better education, better health, better housing, better transportation, a cleaner environment—to restore respect for law, to make our communities more livable—and to insure the God-given right of every American to full and equal opportunity.

Because the range of our needs is so great, because the reach of our opportunities is so great, let us be bold in our determination to meet those needs in new ways.

Just as building a structure of peace abroad has required turning away from old policies that have failed, so building a new era of progress at home requires turning away from old policies that have failed.

Abroad, the shift from old policies to new has not been a retreat from our responsibilities, but a better way to peace.

And at home, the shift from old policies to new will not be a retreat from our responsibilities, but a better way to progress.

Abroad and at home, the key to those new responsibilities lies in the placing and the division of responsibility. We have lived too long with the consequences of attempting to gather all power and responsibility in Washington.

Abroad and at home, the time has come to turn away from the condescending policies of paternalism—of "Washington knows best."

A person can be expected to act responsibly only if he has responsibility. This is human nature. So let us encourage individuals at home and nations abroad to do more for themselves, to decide more for themselves. Let us locate responsibility in more places. Let us measure what we will do for others by what they will do for themselves.

That is why today I offer no promise of a purely governmental solution for every problem. We have lived too long with that false promise. In trusting too much in government, we have asked of it more than it can deliver. This leads only to inflated expectations, to reduced individual effort, and to a disappointment and frustration that erode confidence both in what government can do and in what people can do.

Government must learn to take less from people so that people can do more for themselves.

Let us remember that America was built not by government, but by people; not by welfare, but by work; not by shirking responsibility, but by seeking responsibility.

In our own lives, let each of us ask—not just what will government do for me, but what can I do for myself?

In the challenges we face together, let each of us ask—not just how can government help, but how can I help?

Your National Government has a great and vital role to play. And I pledge to you that where this Government should act, we will act boldly and we will lead boldly. But just as important is the role that each and every one of us must play, as an individual and as a member of his own community.

From this day forward, let each of us make a solemn commitment in his own heart: to bear his responsibility, to do his part, to live his ideals—so that together we can see the dawn of a new age of progress for America, and together, as we celebrate our 200th anniversary as a nation, we can do so proud in the fulfillment of our promise to ourselves and to the world.

As America's longest and most difficult war comes to an end, let us again learn to debate our differences with civility and decency. And let each of us reach out for that one precious quality government cannot provide—a new level of respect for the rights and feelings of one another, a new level of respect for the individual human dignity which is the cherished birthright of every American.

Above all else, the time has come for us to renew our faith in ourselves and in America.

In recent years, that faith has been challenged.

Our children have been taught to be ashamed of their country, ashamed of their parents, ashamed of America's record at home and of its role in the world.

At every turn, we have been beset by those who find everything wrong with America and little that is right. But I am confident that this will not be the judgment of history on these remarkable times in which we are privileged to live.

America's record in this century has been unparalleled in the world's history for its responsibility, for its generosity, for its creativity and for its progress.

Let us be proud that our system has produced and provided more freedom and more abundance, more widely shared, than any other system in the history of the world.

Let us be proud that in each of the four wars in which we have been engaged in this century, including the one we are now bringing to an end, we have fought not for our selfish advantage, but to help others resist aggression.

Let us be proud that by our bold, new initiatives, by our steadfastness for peace with honor, we have made a break-through toward creating in the world what the world has not known before—a structure of peace that can last, not merely for our time, but for generations to come.

We are embarking here today on an era that presents challenges great as those any nation, or any generation, has ever faced.

We shall answer to God, to history, and to our conscience for the way in which we use these years.

As I stand in this place, so hallowed by history, I think of others who have stood here before me. I think of the dreams they had for America, and I think of how each recognized that he needed help far beyond himself in order to make those dreams come true.

Today, I ask your prayers that in the years ahead I may have God's help in making decisions that are right for America, and I pray for your help so that together we may be worthy of our challenge.

Let us pledge together to make these next 4 years the best 4 years in America's history, so that on its 200th birthday America will be as young and as vital as when it began, and as bright a beacon of hope for all the world.

Let us go forward from here confident in hope, strong in our faith in one another, sustained by our faith in God who created us, and striving always to serve His purpose.

A Moment of Triumph before Disaster

THE SECOND INAUGURAL ADDRESS OF RICHARD M. NIXON

Thomas Alan Schwartz

SATURDAY, JANUARY 20, 1973, was a relatively mild day in Washington, cloudy but with no rain in the forecast. Richard Nixon's Second Inaugural Address took place in a very different atmosphere, both literally and figuratively, from his first one. That event, on a bitterly cold and overcast day, had brought to Washington thousands of antiwar demonstrators, who hurled objects at the presidential limousine and disrupted the inaugural parade. There were a few demonstrators present in 1973, but their cause no longer seemed as relevant or urgent. A settlement in Vietnam was only days away, and Richard Nixon used his short speech to proclaim that America now stood "on the threshold of a new era of peace in the world." Fresh off his impressive electoral triumph, carrying forty-nine states with a popular vote of 60 percent of the electorate, Nixon was at the peak of his political popularity and power. What is truly amazing is how quickly all of it would disappear. Nixon would resign in disgrace less than twenty months later.

With the help of his National Security Adviser, Henry Kissinger, Nixon had engineered a "trifecta" of foreign policy successes in 1972 that helped lead to his overwhelming electoral victory. His trip to China, the first of an American president, captured the imagination of Americans, and although it lacked any substantive agreements, it gave rise to the view of Nixon as a brilliant and shrewd foreign policy leader. His subsequent summit meeting in Moscow and the signing of the first Strategic Arms Limitation Treaty seemed to signal the end of the Cold War hostility that had shaped a generation of Americans. Finally, the imminent prospect of a Vietnam peace settlement, although delayed and seemingly threatened by the renewed Christmas bombing of North Vietnam, gave Americans hope that their prisoners of war would be returned and America's long nightmare in Indochina was finally over. To most Americans, Nixon's claim in his inaugural, that "1972 will be long remembered as the year of the greatest progress since the end of World War II toward a lasting peace in the world," did not seem like a classic Nixon exaggeration.

Having won his campaign against Senator George McGovern, a Democratic challenger whose slogan was "Come Home, America," Nixon made it clear that the peace he sought would not bring with it a return to pre–World War II isolationism. Nixon vowed to build a "structure of peace," in which America's role would remain "indispensable." However, he also made it clear that a post-Vietnam America would be cautious about using military force, and that "the time has passed when America will make every other nation's conflict our own." Nixon also encouraged the belief, widely shared among the public, that America would enjoy a "peace dividend" and could now redirect its energies toward its domestic challenges, "to make life better in America—to ensure better education, better health, better housing, better transportation, [and] a cleaner environment." Although the actual resources proved more limited than many Americans hoped, the federal government did begin spending far more on domestic programs in the 1970s.

Yet Nixon also sounded a more traditional Republican theme when he made the case for a more decentralized approach to decision-making and a more limited governmental role in American life. His choice of words foreshadows the Reagan Revolution of the 1980s when he argued, "The time has come to turn away from the condescending policies of paternalism — of 'Washington knows best.'" Although he was not specific in terms of amounts or dollar figures, he seemed to be calling for tax cuts by saying, "Government must learn to take less from people so that people can do more for themselves." And in what was clearly designed to be a play on the very famous closing line from John Kennedy's inauguration—"Ask not what your country can do for you, but what you can do for your country"—Nixon said, "In the challenges we face together, let each of us ask—not just how can government help, but how can I help?"

Lower taxes, limited government, less federal regulation, more individual responsibility—all of these arguments serve to connect Nixon's advocacy to ongoing themes in American conservatism and to issues that the Republican party has long embraced. There was also a specific reference to the tumultuous Vietnam period through which the country was emerging—"as America's longest and most difficult war comes to an end"—and that still seems quite relevant to the politically polarized America of 2022. Nixon called for greater "civility and decency" in public debate, urging "each of us" to show "a new level of respect for the rights and feelings of one another, a new level of respect for individual human dignity which is the cherished birthright of every American." In his First Inaugural Address, Nixon had called on Americans to "lower their voices," but the continuation of the Vietnam War did not lead to that. Instead, Nixon had faced in his first term massive protests and political division, including the Vietnam moratoriums, the huge protests after the Cambodia invasion, and the attempt to shut down Washington in the spring of 1971.

In one of the more curious passages in the speech, Nixon's rhetoric foreshadows a theme of President Donald Trump, who established a President's Advisory 1776 Commission to further "patriotic education." Nixon contended that in recent years American children "have been taught to be ashamed of their country, ashamed of their parents, ashamed of America's record at home and its role in the world." In what was likely a reaction to the first wave of revisionist historical instruction in some schools, Nixon contended, "We have been beset by those who find everything wrong with America and little that is right." Although Nixon did not use the now common expression "American exceptionalism," he did proclaim that America's "record in this century has been unparalleled in the world's history for its responsibility, for its generosity, for its creativity and for its progress." Closing the speech, he returned to the theme of a "structure of peace" that would last for "generations to come," and connected this to the forthcoming bicentennial celebrations of America's founding in 1976, over which he fully expected to preside. "Let us pledge together to make these next four years the best four years in America's history, so that on its 200th birthday America will be as young and as vital as when it began, and as bright a beacon of hope for all the world."

Richard Nixon is not a person with whom it is easy to sympathize. Listening to his voluminous tape recordings, which captured the man behind the public image he projected, it is not hard to be repelled by his cynical manipulation of issues and his crude prejudices and hatreds. Yet there is still an element of tragedy in his presidency that is reflected in this speech. Nixon had extricated America from an unwinnable war and reconciled the country with its two giant Cold War enemies, and he clearly hoped that this would allow the country the opportunity to heal and address its numerous domestic problems. But the Watergate scandal, a reflection of some of his worst political instincts and insecurities, would soon overshadow the vision presented in this speech and lead to his downfall. The tragedy may not be fully Shakespearean, but it is still epic.

Gerald Ford's Remarks upon Taking the Oath of Office as President

FRIDAY, AUGUST 9, 1974

MR. CHIEF JUSTICE, *my dear friends, my fellow Americans:*

The oath that I have taken is the same oath that was taken by George Washington and by every President under the Constitution. But I assume the Presidency under extraordinary circumstances never before experienced by Americans. This is an hour of history that troubles our minds and hurts our hearts.

Therefore, I feel it is my first duty to make an unprecedented compact with my countrymen. Not an inaugural address, not a fireside chat, not a campaign speech—just a little straight talk among friends. And I intend it to be the first of many.

I am acutely aware that you have not elected me as your President by your ballots, and so I ask you to confirm me as your President with your prayers. And I hope that such prayers will also be the first of many.

If you have not chosen me by secret ballot, neither have I gained office by any secret promises. I have not campaigned either for the Presidency or the Vice Presidency. I have not subscribed to any partisan platform. I am indebted to no man, and only to one woman—my dear wife—as I begin this very difficult job.

I have not sought this enormous responsibility, but I will not shirk it. Those who nominated and confirmed me as Vice President were my friends and are my friends. They were of both parties, elected by all the people and acting under the Constitution in their name. It is only fitting then that I should pledge to them and to you that I will be the President of all the people.

Thomas Jefferson said the people are the only sure reliance for the preservation of our liberty. And down the years, Abraham Lincoln renewed this American article of faith asking, "Is there any better way or equal hope in the world?"

I intend, on Monday next, to request of the Speaker of the House of Representatives and the President pro tempore of the Senate the privilege of appearing before the Congress to share with my former colleagues and with you, the American people, my views on the priority business of the Nation and to solicit your views and their views. And may I say to the Speaker and the others, if I could meet with you right after these remarks, I would appreciate it.

Even though this is late in an election year, there is no way we can go forward except together and no way anybody can win except by serving the people's urgent needs. We cannot stand still or slip backwards. We must go forward now together.

To the peoples and the governments of all friendly nations, and I hope that could encompass the whole world, I pledge an uninterrupted and sincere search for peace. America will remain strong and united, but its strength will remain dedicated to the safety and sanity of the entire family of man, as well as to our own precious freedom.

I believe that truth is the glue that holds government together, not only our Government but civilization itself. That bond, though strained, is unbroken at home and abroad.

In all my public and private acts as your President, I expect to follow my instincts of openness and candor with full confidence that honesty is always the best policy in the end.

My fellow Americans, our long national nightmare is over.

Our Constitution works; our great Republic is a government of laws and not of men. Here the people rule. But there is a higher Power, by whatever name we honor Him, who ordains not only righteousness but love, not only justice but mercy.

As we bind up the internal wounds of Watergate, more painful and more poisonous than those of foreign wars, let us restore the golden rule to our political process, and let brotherly love purge our hearts of suspicion and of hate.

In the beginning, I asked you to pray for me. Before closing, I ask again your prayers, for Richard Nixon and for his family. May our former President, who brought peace to millions, find it for himself. May God bless and comfort his wonderful wife and daughters, whose love and loyalty will forever be a shining legacy to all who bear the lonely burdens of the White House.

I can only guess at those burdens, although I have witnessed at close hand the tragedies that befell three Presidents and the lesser trials of others.

With all the strength and all the good sense I have gained from life, with all the confidence my family, my friends, and my dedicated staff impart to me, and with the good will of countless Americans I have encountered in recent visits to 40 States, I now solemnly reaffirm my promise I made to you last December 6: to uphold the Constitution, to do what is right as God gives me to see the right, and to do the very best I can for America.

God helping me, I will not let you down.

Thank you.

"Just a Little Straight Talk"

GERALD FORD'S REMARKS UPON TAKING THE OATH OF OFFICE AS PRESIDENT

John Robert Greene

THE INAUGURAL ADDRESS of Gerald R. Ford as the thirty-eighth president of the United States, delivered from the White House East Room at 12:05 p.m. on Friday, August 9, 1974, was unique in the annals of American history. Ford was the first vice president to accede to the presidency under the terms of the Twenty-fifth Amendment, following the resignation that morning of Richard M. Nixon. Moreover, while he was the eighth vice president to inherit his office from a sitting president, he was the first to deliver an address to the American people upon the occasion of his taking power.

Vice-presidential speechwriter Robert Hartmann, soon to serve as a counselor to President Ford, remembered that Ford gave him only one day's notice to craft comments that would follow his swearing-in. In light of the implosion of the Nixon presidency, Hartmann remembered that, as he began thinking, he jotted down three key themes—"Take Charge," "Legitimacy," and "Truth is the Glue."

Hartmann then worked to set the tone for the speech. A large part of this was deciding what to call it. It would be delivered in the shadow of a presidential resignation, and the air of sheer exhaustion and relief that permeated the nation that August negated the use of any of the pomp and circumstance that would normally accompany a presidential inauguration. Moreover, one of Ford's immediate goals was to distance himself from his predecessor, a man known for his formal, often stilted speech delivery. With these thoughts in mind, Hartmann settled upon Ford's opening line—that what he was about to deliver was "not an inaugural address, not a fireside chat . . . just a little straight talk among friends."

The speech continued along a path designed to exorcise the ghost of Nixon Past. Hartmann's dismissal of Watergate—"My fellow Americans, our long national nightmare is over"—was the most quoted passage of the speech, and it became one of the most memorable lines in modern inaugural history. However, when Hartmann had Ford claim that "[o]ur constitution works; our great republic is a government of laws and not men," he was on less solid ground. Many Americans, upset that Nixon had yet to be indicted for crimes that included at minimum an obstruction of justice that had been recorded on the White House taping system, were about to deflate Ford's honeymoon with charges of a deal between himself and Nixon—charges that would only be intensified exactly one month after Ford took office, when he pardoned Nixon. Still, the line exuded an optimism that Americans desperately wanted to experience, and few observers challenged this assessment at the time.

When Ford strode into the White House East Room, holding the hand of his wife Betty and surrounded by White House staffers, Cabinet members, and congressional leaders who had just witnessed Nixon's rather maudlin farewell (indeed, the Fords were the last to say goodbye to Nixon and his wife, Pat, as they boarded Marine One on the South Lawn of the White House) he was understandably tense. Immediately following his swearing-in by Chief Justice Warren Burger, Ford began his speech in a tight, stilted delivery. This was unlike Ford, who loved the speechmaking and gladhanding of a political campaign and had a professional politician's grace and ease in front of both crowds and camera. But as he moved through his address, Ford loosened up. He delivered Hartmann's "long national nightmare" line with both conviction and forcefulness, as the new president looked square into eyes of his audience and proclaimed the start of his own administration.

But even this line was not enough for Ford to feel comfortable that he had separated himself from his predecessor: "If you have not chosen me by secret ballot, neither have I gained office by any secret promises. I have not campaigned either for the Presidency or the Vice Presidency. I have not subscribed to any partisan platform. I am indebted to no man, and only to one woman—my dear wife—as I begin this very difficult job." The latter portion of that phrase was a break with tradition, as Ford became the first president to reference his wife in his Inaugural Address, a line that, when he delivered it, nearly caused his voice to break. The rest of the talk emphasized Ford's Midwestern roots and his deeply held Episcopalian faith, as when he asked the nation for "your prayers, for Richard Nixon and his family. May our former President, who brought peace to millions, find it for himself." When he was finished, instead of attending parades and inaugural balls in his honor, Ford walked down the hall to the Oval Office and immediately began a series of meetings with those in his new administration.

It all took less than fifteen minutes. At 850 words, it was the fourth shortest inaugural address in history (only Washington's First Inaugural, Lincoln's Second, and Franklin Roosevelt's Fourth were shorter). It was so brief that many in the press did not know what to make of it—*CBS News*, for example, called Ford's speech "Inaugural Remarks." But whatever it was called, the speech was a resounding success. Ford's reassuring presence, equally as much as Hartmann's words, helped the country start to breathe again. Articulating the feelings of many Americans, when Ford's speech was over, Warren Burger turned to Senate Minority Leader Hugh Scott and said, "Hugh, it worked. Thank God it worked."

Jimmy Carter's Inaugural Address

THURSDAY, JANUARY 20, 1977

FOR MYSELF AND for our Nation, I want to thank my predecessor for all he has done to heal our land.

In this outward and physical ceremony we attest once again to the inner and spiritual strength of our Nation. As my high school teacher, Miss Julia Coleman, used to say, "We must adjust to changing times and still hold to unchanging principles."

Here before me is the Bible used in the inauguration of our first President, in 1789, and I have just taken the oath of office on the Bible my mother gave me just a few years ago, opened to a timeless admonition from the ancient prophet Micah: "He hath showed thee, O man, what is good; and what doth the Lord require of thee, but to do justly, and to love mercy, and to walk humbly with thy God." (Micah 6:8)

This inauguration ceremony marks a new beginning, a new dedication within our Government, and a new spirit among us all. A President may sense and proclaim that new spirit, but only a people can provide it.

Two centuries ago our Nation's birth was a milestone in the long quest for freedom. But the bold and brilliant dream which excited the founders of this Nation still awaits its consummation. I have no new dream to set forth today, but rather urge a fresh faith in the old dream.

Ours was the first society openly to define itself in terms of both spirituality and of human liberty. It is that unique self-definition which has given us an exceptional appeal, but it also imposes on us a special obligation, to take on those moral duties which, when assumed, seem invariably to be in our own best interests.

You have given me a great responsibility—to stay close to you, to be worthy of you, and to exemplify what you are. Let us create together a new national spirit of unity and trust. Your strength can compensate for my weakness, and your wisdom can help to minimize my mistakes.

Let us learn together and laugh together and work together and pray together, confident that in the end we will triumph together in the right.

The American dream endures. We must once again have full faith in our country—and in one another. I believe America can be better. We can be even stronger than before.

Let our recent mistakes bring a resurgent commitment to the basic principles of our Nation, for we know that if we despise our own government we have no future. We recall in special times when we have stood briefly, but magnificently, united. In those times no prize was beyond our grasp.

But we cannot dwell upon remembered glory. We cannot afford to drift. We reject the prospect of failure or mediocrity or an inferior quality of life for any person. Our Government must at the same time be both competent and compassionate.

We have already found a high degree of personal liberty, and we are now struggling to enhance equality of opportunity. Our commitment to human rights must be absolute, our laws fair, our natural beauty preserved; the powerful must not persecute the weak, and human dignity must be enhanced.

We have learned that *more* is not necessarily *better*, that even our great Nation has its recognized limits, and that we can neither answer all questions nor solve all problems. We cannot afford to do everything, nor can we afford to lack boldness as we meet the future. So, together, in a spirit of individual sacrifice for the common good, we must simply do our best.

Our Nation can be strong abroad only if it is strong at home. And we know that the best way to enhance freedom in other lands is to demonstrate here that our democratic system is worthy of emulation.

To be true to ourselves, we must be true to others. We will not behave in foreign places so as to violate our rules and standards here at home, for we know that the trust which our Nation earns is essential to our strength.

The world itself is now dominated by a new spirit. Peoples more numerous and more politically aware are craving, and now demanding, their place in the sun—not just for the benefit of their own physical condition, but for basic human rights.

The passion for freedom is on the rise. Tapping this new spirit, there can be no nobler nor more ambitious task for America to undertake on this day of a new beginning than to help shape a just and peaceful world that is truly humane.

We are a strong nation, and we will maintain strength so sufficient that it need not be proven in combat—a quiet strength based not merely on the size of an arsenal, but on the nobility of ideas.

We will be ever vigilant and never vulnerable, and we will fight our wars against poverty, ignorance, and injustice—for those are the enemies against which our forces can be honorably marshaled.

We are a purely idealistic nation, but let no one confuse our idealism with weakness.

Because we are free we can never be indifferent to the fate of freedom elsewhere. Our moral sense dictates a clearcut preference for these societies which share with us an abiding respect for individual human rights. We do not seek to intimidate, but it is clear that a world which others can dominate with impunity would be inhospitable to decency and a threat to the well-being of all people.

The world is still engaged in a massive armaments race designed to ensure continuing equivalent strength among potential adversaries. We pledge perseverance and wisdom in our efforts to limit the world's armaments to those necessary for each nation's own domestic safety. And we will move this year a step toward ultimate goal—the elimination of all nuclear weapons from this Earth. We urge all other people to join us, for success can mean life instead of death.

Within us, the people of the United States, there is evident a serious and purposeful rekindling of confidence. And I join in the hope that when my time as your President has ended, people might say this about our Nation:

- that we had remembered the words of Micah and renewed our search for humility, mercy, and justice;
- that we had torn down the barriers that separated those of different race and region and religion, and where there had been mistrust, built unity, with a respect for diversity;
- that we had found productive work for those able to perform it;
- that we had strengthened the American family, which is the basis of our society;
- that we had ensured respect for the law, and equal treatment under the law, for the weak and the powerful, for the rich and the poor; and
- and that we had enabled our people to be proud of their own Government once again.

I would hope that the nations of the world might say that we had built a lasting peace, built not on weapons of war but on international policies which reflect our own most precious values.

These are not just my goals—and they will not be my accomplishments—but the affirmation of our Nation's continuing moral strength and our belief in an undiminished, ever-expanding American dream.

Thank you very much.

The Peanut Farmer

THE INAUGURAL ADDRESS OF JIMMY CARTER

Mark Atwood Lawrence

REFLECTING ON THE day he became the thirty-ninth president of the United States, Jimmy Carter recorded a revealing shard of memory in his diary. Even though he had pursued the nation's highest office with uncommon energy over many months, Carter wrote, he was "genuinely surprised" when the Bishop of Minnesota, in delivering the benediction at the inauguration ceremonies, bestowed "blessings on President Carter." The words "President Carter" were "startling to me," he recalls.

The whole day, January 20, 1977, was like that for Carter. Rarely had a newly elected president been less invested in the pomp and fanfare that usually went with the nation's highest office. The former governor of Georgia—a peanut farmer quick to extol his small-town roots—wore a store-bought suit and a borrowed overcoat. He passed up the traditional inaugural service at the stately St. John's Episcopal Church near the White House, joining instead his co-religionists at the humbler First Baptist Church several blocks away. He declined to hold the usual inaugural luncheon.

Following his swearing-in, Carter made his most striking gesture of the day. Moments after boarding a limousine for the mile-and-a-half ride to the White House, he ordered the driver to stop, got out, and began strolling down Pennsylvania Avenue hand in hand with First Lady Rosalynn, while their nine-year-old daughter Amy ambled—and sometimes skipped—alongside. Carter hoped his walk would offer a "tangible indication of some reduction in the imperial status of the president and his family." It worked. The crowds along the parade route warmly cheered the Carters, who won broad acclaim for the egalitarianism they projected.

Less celebrated was Carter's Inaugural Address, hardly a masterpiece of the genre. To be sure, the speech earned dutiful applause and respectful coverage at the time. But it has seldom garnered favorable comment from historians and biographers. It was, writes historian Randall Balmer, a "workmanlike" mélange of well-worn themes from the campaign. Biographer Jonathan Alter calls the speech "disjointed" and "loosely structured," gentle ways of critiquing the lack of intellectual coherence, poetic flow, or emotional punch.[1]

Better speechwriting might have helped knit Carter's ideas together into something more powerful, and a more polished delivery—almost always an elusive goal for Carter—might have left a better impression. But there was a more fundamental reason why Carter fell well short of the grandest inaugural orations. The speech's tepidness owed much to the very modesty that had enabled Carter to win the White House and underlay his most memorable gestures on Inauguration Day. To have asked Carter for something grander would have meant asking him to be a different sort of leader and to have understood the national mood in a different way.

The address oozed humility. Indeed, perhaps the most extraordinary moment came when Carter thanked his predecessor and political rival, Gerald R. Ford, an unprecedented gesture of selflessness in an inaugural speech. Otherwise, the address stands out for its brevity (1,228 words, taking a mere fourteen and a half minutes to deliver) and studied lack of pretension. Carter opened by quoting not the founding fathers or other luminaries of American history but his high school teacher, Miss Julia Coleman, whose admonition to her students in a humble Georgia schoolhouse—"We must adjust to changing times and still hold to unchanging principles"—set the tone for everything that followed.

Aides talked Carter out of going so far as to quote a biblical passage (2 Chronicles 7:14) condemning "wicked ways" and calling for national healing through forgiveness of "sin." Such fervid self-criticism seemed too strong for Americans who did not share Carter's particular brand of Christianity. But the verse Carter selected instead—Micah 6:8—sent a broadly similar message by stressing his dedication to justice, mercy, walking "humbly" with God. And Carter retained other notes of self-effacement in his text. "Your strength can compensate for my weakness," he told the American people, "and your wisdom can help to minimize my mistakes."

Carter hit much the same theme when he turned from his personal shortcomings to the nation's. "We have learned that *more* is not necessarily *better*, that even our great Nation has its recognized limits, and that we can neither answer all questions nor solve all problems," Carter averred in perhaps the most arresting lines of the speech. He appealed for a "spirit of individual sacrifice for the common good," urging that Americans "must simply do our best" rather than striving to do everything.

These words unquestionably suited the political moment. Although America's bicentennial in 1976 had triggered a wave of patriotic fanfare, Carter's rise to the presidency took place against a backdrop of national setbacks and demoralization. The Watergate scandal, culminating in Richard Nixon's resignation in 1974, caused many Americans to distrust the integrity, even the decency, of their leaders. America's final defeat in Vietnam the following year stirred profound doubts about the nation's entitlement to global leadership and the efficacy of the vast material power it wielded. Soaring inflation and other economic difficulties suggested, meanwhile, that the postwar economic boom was over. Cities crumbled, and environmental woes multiplied. All in all, as California Governor Jerry Brown put it in 1976, an "era of limits" appeared to be at hand.

Carter's victory in the 1976 presidential race owed much to his image as a political outsider, innocent of the corruption and error that had led the nation astray. From the moment he declared his candidacy, he gained traction largely because of who he was—a morally upright man who promised never to lie to the American people—and the promises of contrition and renewal that he offered. By the time of his inaugural, his professions of humility had become routine. If Americans looked past the speech and remembered other moments in a long day of political pageantry, it's not difficult to understand why.

The cost of Carter's approach—apparently one he was willing to pay—was a missed opportunity to highlight some intriguing big ideas that ran, if only vaguely, through the speech. These ideas were not entirely new, and Carter would articulate all of them more fully on other occasions. But if Carter had invoked them more eloquently at the outset of his administration, they might have resonated more powerfully with the public, helping to cast Carter in a glow of not just moral conviction, but also ingenuity and vision. Three such insights in particular stand out, all of which deserve to be recalled now at another moment of national doubt.

First, Carter called attention to his commitment to the advancement of human rights as a core concern of U.S. foreign policy. "Our moral sense dictates a clearcut preference," he insisted, "for these societies which share with us an abiding respect for individual human rights." What made the point especially notable was Carter's suggestion that dedication to principle would not undercut American power, as the Republican administrations of the earlier 1970s had tended to believe. Rather, Carter insisted "the trust which our Nation earns" through adherence to its core values "is essential to our strength." More abstractly, he declared that the pursuit of "moral duties" seemed "invariably to be in our own best interests."

Second, Carter proposed a military policy that would balance the pursuit of arms control with the preservation of national strength. The president's dedication to arms reduction was plain to see, as it had been throughout the campaign. "We pledge perseverance and wisdom in our efforts to limit the world's armaments to those necessary for each nation's own domestic safety," intoned Carter, suggesting a desire for deterrence at minimum levels of weaponry. He even held out "the elimination of all nuclear weapons from this Earth" as his ultimate goal. But, as usual with Carter, peacemaking ambitions coexisted with a concern for national defense befitting a former Naval officer. While the United States would never seek to "intimidate" its foes, he declared, "it is clear that a world which others can dominate with impunity would be inhospitable to decency and a threat to the well-being of all people."

Third, Carter declared his dedication to making the government not only more "compassionate" but also—a word easy to miss among the jumble of more high-minded adjectives—"competent." He declared that his inauguration marked a "new beginning" for the nation and encapsulated a "new spirit" among Americans. In a slight contradiction, he even suggested that a "serious and purposeful rekindling of confidence" had already taken hold across American society. But his more intriguing assertion was to herald a "new dedication within our Government"—the start, he hoped, of a new era in which Americans could be "proud" of what occurred in Washington.

Carter went no further with this theme or, for that matter, any other elements of domestic or foreign policy. In sticking to broad generalities, he was, of course, hardly alone; few presidents have used their inaugurals to engage the intricacies of policy matters. Moreover, Carter had good reason to believe that his primary task at the outset of his administration was to establish a new tone as the country grappled with pervasive doubt and distrust. Low national morale was a real problem.

Yet the speech fell short of Carter at his best. A master of detail who was often criticized for micromanagement of complicated policy issues, Carter showed few hints of the intellectual command that had made him an effective leader back in Georgia. His repeated expressions of humility, meanwhile, highlighted traits that many Americans would come to see as naïveté and excessive meekness as the United States faced mounting economic woes as well as foreign policy crises in the later years of his term. The political mood that brought Carter to office proved fleeting. By 1980, many Americans had lost interest in the genuine innovations that Carter espoused and rallied around a very different notion of renewal associated with Ronald Reagan and a revitalized nationalist wing of the Republican party.

Note

1. Jonathan Alter, *His Very Best: Jimmy Carter, a Life* (New York: Simon and Schuster, 2020).

Ronald Reagan's First Inaugural Address

TUESDAY, JANUARY 20, 1981

SENATOR HATFIELD, MR. *Chief Justice, Mr. President, Vice President Bush, Vice President Mondale, Senator Baker, Speaker O'Neill, Reverend Moomaw, and my fellow citizens:*

To a few of us here today, this is a solemn and most momentous occasion, and yet in the history of our Nation it is a commonplace occurrence. The orderly transfer of authority as called for in the Constitution routinely takes place, as it has for almost two centuries, and few of us stop to think how unique we really are. In the eyes of many in the world, this every-4-year ceremony we accept as normal is nothing less than a miracle.

Mr. President, I want our fellow citizens to know how much you did to carry on this tradition. By your gracious cooperation in the transition process, you have shown a watching world that we are a united people pledged to maintaining a political system which guarantees individual liberty to a greater degree than any other, and I thank you and your people for all your help in maintaining the continuity which is the bulwark of our Republic.

The business of our nation goes forward. These United States are confronted with an economic affliction of great proportions. We suffer from the longest and one of the worst sustained inflations in our national history. It distorts our economic decisions, penalizes thrift, and crushes the struggling young and the fixed-income elderly alike. It threatens to shatter the lives of millions of our people.

Idle industries have cast workers into unemployment, human misery and personal indignity. Those who do work are denied a fair return for their labor by a tax system which penalizes successful achievement and keeps us from maintaining full productivity.

But great as our tax burden is, it has not kept pace with public spending. For decades, we have piled deficit upon deficit, mortgaging our future and our children's future for the temporary convenience of the present. To continue this long trend is to guarantee tremendous social, cultural, political, and economic upheavals.

You and I, as individuals, can, by borrowing, live beyond our means, but for only a limited period of time. Why, then, should we think that collectively, as a nation, we are not bound by that same limitation? We must act today in order to preserve tomorrow. And let there be no misunderstanding: We are going to begin to act, beginning today.

The economic ills we suffer have come upon us over several decades. They will not go away in days, weeks, or months, but they will go away. They will go away because we, as Americans, have the capacity now, as we have had in the past, to do whatever needs to be done to preserve this last and greatest bastion of freedom.

In this present crisis, government is not the solution to our problem; government is the problem. From time to time, we have been tempted to believe that society has become too complex to be managed by self-rule, that government by an elite group is superior to government for, by, and of the people. But if no one among us is capable of governing himself, then who among us has the capacity to govern someone else? All of us together, in and out of government, must bear the burden. The solutions we seek must be equitable, with no one group singled out to pay a higher price.

We hear much of special interest groups. Well, our concern must be for a special interest group that has been too long neglected. It knows no sectional boundaries or ethnic and racial divisions, and it crosses political party lines. It is made up of men and women who raise our food, patrol our streets, man our mines and our factories, teach our children, keep our homes, and heal us when we are sick—professionals, industrialists, shopkeepers, clerks, cabbies, and truckdrivers. They are, in short, "We the people," this breed called Americans.

Well, this administration's objective will be a healthy, vigorous, growing economy that provides equal opportunity for all Americans, with no barriers born of bigotry or discrimination. Putting America back to work means putting all Americans back to work. Ending inflation means freeing all Americans from the terror of runaway living costs. All must share in the productive work of this "new beginning" and all must share in the bounty of a revived economy. With the idealism and fair play which are the core of our system and our strength, we can have a strong and prosperous America, at peace with itself and the world.

So, as we begin, let us take inventory. We are a nation that has a government—not the other way around. And this makes us special among the nations of the Earth. Our Government has no power except that granted it by the people. It is time to check and reverse the growth of government which shows signs of having grown beyond the consent of the governed.

It is my intention to curb the size and influence of the Federal establishment and to demand recognition of the distinction between the powers granted to the Federal Government and those reserved to the States or to the people. All of us need to be reminded that the Federal Government did not create the States; the States created the Federal Government.

Now, so there will be no misunderstanding, it is not my intention to do away with government. It is, rather, to make it work—work with us, not over us; to stand by our side, not ride on our back. Government can and must provide opportunity, not smother it; foster productivity, not stifle it.

If we look to the answer as to why for so many years, we achieved so much, prospered as no other people on Earth, it was because here in this land we unleashed the energy and individual genius of man to a greater extent than has ever been done before. Freedom and the dignity of the individual have been more available and assured here than in any other place on Earth. The price for this freedom at times has been high, but we have never been unwilling to pay that price.

It is no coincidence that our present troubles parallel and are proportionate to the intervention and intrusion in our lives that result from unnecessary and excessive growth of government. It is time for us to realize that we are too great a nation to limit ourselves to small dreams. We're not, as some would have us believe, doomed to an inevitable decline. I do not believe in a fate that will fall on us no matter what we do. I do believe in a fate that will fall on us if we do nothing. So, with all the creative energy at our command, let us begin an era of national renewal. Let us renew our determination, our courage, and our strength. And let us renew our faith and our hope.

We have every right to dream heroic dreams. Those who say that we're in a time when there are no heroes, they just don't know where to look. You can see heroes every day going in and out of factory gates. Others, a handful in number, produce enough food to feed all of us and then the world beyond. You meet heroes across a counter, and they are on both sides of that counter. There are entrepreneurs with faith in themselves and faith in an idea who create new jobs, new wealth and opportunity. They're individuals and families whose taxes support the Government and whose voluntary gifts support church, charity, culture, art, and education. Their patriotism is quiet, but deep. Their values sustain our national life.

I have used the words "they" and "their" in speaking of these heroes. I could say "you" and "your," because I'm addressing the heroes of whom I speak—you, the citizens of this blessed land. Your dreams, your hopes, your goals are going to be the dreams, the hopes, and the goals of this administration, so help me God.

We shall reflect the compassion that is so much a part of your makeup. How can we love our country and not love our countrymen; and loving them, reach out a hand when they fall, heal them when they're sick, and provide opportunities to make them self-sufficient so they will be equal in fact and not just in theory?

Can we solve the problems confronting us? Well, the answer is an unequivocal and emphatic "yes." To paraphrase Winston Churchill, I did not take the oath I have just taken with the intention of presiding over the dissolution of the world's strongest economy.

In the days ahead I will propose removing the roadblocks that have slowed our economy and reduced productivity. Steps will be taken aimed at restoring the balance between the various levels of government. Progress may be slow, measured in inches and feet, not miles, but we will progress. Is it time to reawaken this industrial giant, to get government back within its means, and to lighten our punitive tax burden. And these will be our first priorities, and on these principles there will be no compromise.

On the eve of our struggle for independence a man who might have been one of the greatest among the Founding Fathers, Dr. Joseph Warren, president of the Massachusetts Congress, said to his fellow Americans, "Our country is in danger, but not to be despaired of.... On you depend the fortunes of America. You are to decide the important questions upon which rests the happiness and the liberty of millions yet unborn. Act worthy of yourselves."

Well, I believe we, the Americans of today, are ready to act worthy of ourselves, ready to do what must be done to ensure happiness and liberty for ourselves, our children, and our children's children. And as we renew ourselves here in our own land, we will be seen as having greater strength throughout the world. We will again be the exemplar of freedom and a beacon of hope for those who do not now have freedom.

To those neighbors and allies who share our freedom, we will strengthen our historic ties and assure them of our support and firm commitment. We will match loyalty with loyalty. We will strive for mutually beneficial relations. We will not use our friendship to impose on their sovereignty, for our own sovereignty is not for sale.

As for the enemies of freedom, those who are potential adversaries, they will be reminded that peace is the highest aspiration of the American people. We will negotiate for it, sacrifice for it; we will not surrender for it, now or ever.

Our forbearance should never be misunderstood. Our reluctance for conflict should not be misjudged as a failure of will. When action is required to preserve our national security, we will act. We will maintain sufficient strength to prevail if need be, knowing that if we do so we have the best chance of never having to use that strength.

Above all, we must realize that no arsenal or no weapon in the arsenals of the world is so formidable as the will and moral courage of free men and women. It is a weapon our adversaries in today's world do not have. It is a weapon that we as Americans do have. Let that be understood by those who practice terrorism and prey upon their neighbors.

I am told that tens of thousands of prayer meetings are being held on this day, and for that I am deeply grateful. We are a nation under God, and I believe God intended for us to be free. It would be fitting and good, I think, if on each Inaugural Day in future years it should be declared a day of prayer.

This is the first time in history that this ceremony has been held, as you have been told, on this West Front of the Capitol. Standing here, one faces a magnificent vista, opening up on this city's special beauty and history. At the end of this open mall are those shrines to the giants on whose shoulders we stand.

Directly in front of me, the monument to a monumental man: George Washington, father of our country. A man of humility who came to greatness reluctantly. He led America out of revolutionary victory into infant nationhood. Off to one side, the stately memorial to Thomas Jefferson. The Declaration of Independence flames with his eloquence. And then beyond the Reflecting Pool the dignified columns of the Lincoln Memorial. Whoever would understand in his heart the meaning of America will find it in the life of Abraham Lincoln.

Beyond those monuments to heroism is the Potomac River, and on the far shore the sloping hills of Arlington National Cemetery, with its row on row of simple white markers bearing crosses or Stars of David. They add up to only a tiny fraction of the price that has been paid for our freedom.

Each one of those markers is a monument to the kinds of hero I spoke of earlier. Their lives ended in places called Belleau Wood, The Argonne, Omaha Beach, Salerno and halfway around the world on Guadalcanal, Tarawa, Pork Chop Hill, the Chosin Reservoir, and in a hundred rice paddies and jungles of a place called Vietnam.

Under one such marker lies a young man, Martin Treptow, who left his job in a small town barber shop in 1917 to go to France with the famed Rainbow Division. There, on the western front, he was killed trying to carry a message between battalions under heavy artillery fire.

We are told that on his body was found a diary. On the flyleaf under the heading, "My Pledge," he had written these words: "America must win this war. Therefore I will work, I will save, I will sacrifice, I will endure, I will fight cheerfully and do my utmost, as if the issue of the whole struggle depended on me alone."

The crisis we are facing today does not require of us the kind of sacrifice that Martin Treptow and so many thousands of others were called upon to make. It does require, however, our best effort and our willingness to believe in ourselves and to believe in our capacity to perform great deeds, to believe that together with God's help we can and will resolve the problems which now confront us.

And after all, why shouldn't we believe that? We are Americans.

God bless you, and thank you.

The Great Communicator

THE FIRST INAUGURAL ADDRESS OF RONALD REAGAN

Gil Troy

IN THE FIRST 105 words of his 1981 inauguration speech, Ronald Reagan painted the horizons—and defined the limits—of what would be known as the Reagan Revolution. In celebrating this "solemn and most momentous occasion" as "an orderly transfer of authority," he rejoiced: what "we accept as normal is nothing less than a miracle." Reagan was suggesting that the answer to America's malaise could be found in a patriotic renewal, by returning to core principles and the irrepressible confidence that had propelled Americans forward since the American Revolution. That faith in the past as a solution to present problems and the key to a proud, prosperous, and peaceful future is why Reagan never claimed to be launching a revolution. It was, he would say eight years later in his Farewell Address, the "Great Rediscovery: a rediscovery of our values and our common sense."

The new president had much riding on his twenty-minute address that bright, balmy January day. Americans were, he noted, "confronted with an economic affliction of great proportions," stagflation—a debilitating combination of high inflation and surging unemployment. Those problems were exacerbated by an unwieldy, unproductive, and ever-growing federal government, bankrolled by "a tax system which penalizes successful achievement and keeps us from maintaining full productivity." Beyond that, reeling from the revolutions and disillusionments of the 1960s and 1970s, Americans had lost faith in themselves and their government. Too many feared "that society has become too complex to be managed by self-rule." Reagan's predecessor Jimmy Carter unintentionally fed that crisis of confidence, with his constant emphasis on America's new limits and his listless handling of the humiliating Iranian hostage crisis, as Iranian radicals held fifty-two American diplomats and Marines captives for 444 days. Further adding tension and sowing doubt were "the enemies of freedom," especially the menace Reagan chose not to name explicitly: Soviet Communism.

Finally, Reagan knew that many Americans doubted him. He had won only 50.7 percent of the vote, despite his advisers' claim of a "Reagan mandate." Ignoring his two terms as California governor and nearly twenty years of political speechifying, Democrats mocked Ronald Reagan as a Hollywood B-movie actor and failed Las Vegas pitchman, who lacked a presidential CV, aura, or smarts.

Nevertheless, Reagan was inviting Americans to trust him, their country, and themselves, as one, integrated, red-white-and-blue package. Splashy consumption became one colorful way to take back the night. The president's thousand-dollar morning suit, the first lady's ten-thousand-dollar gown, the 16 million-dollar inaugural price tag, the private planes landing at National (later renamed Reagan) Airport, the limousines deployed on the ground, all signified Reagan's new direction. Although even some Republicans found the consumption too conspicuous, the festivities revealed a characteristically open American approach to wealth, not as something to be resented because aristocrats monopolized it, but as something accessible to be enjoyed, or at least revered. Ultimately, the celebration of wealth reflected the Reagan paradox: his odes to traditional values coexisted with his role as an avatar of American consumption, a maestro of materialism.

Ronald Reagan used his inauguration and his "first hundred days" to establish a new national tone. Proof of a collective desire for a new mood bubbled up in 1980. The national euphoria—and sense of vindication—which greeted the "Miracle on Ice," the American Olympic team's surprise hockey triumph over the Soviet Union in February 1980, demonstrated what the *Washington Post* called "hero-starved" Americans' yearning for a return to patriotism and national "self-esteem." Two months after the inauguration, Walter Cronkite would retire as the *CBS News* anchor. Reagan would replace "Uncle Walter" as the kindly paterfamilias of America's ever-changing family. All this required, he told his fellow Americans, "our willingness to believe in ourselves and to believe in our capacity to perform great deeds."

Reagan sought to restore faith in American individualism by targeting big government. This debate had been intensifying since Franklin D. Roosevelt's New Deal. Democrats became the party of government expansion, as Republicans tried putting on the brakes. Anxious to preserve "this last and greatest bastion of freedom," Reagan proclaimed: "In this present crisis, government is not the solution to our problem; government is the problem."

Subtly needling the Democrats, whom Republicans caricatured as the party of special interests, Reagan appealed to one "special interest group that has been too long neglected. . . . 'We the people,' this breed called Americans."

Seeing to restore the balance, Reagan insisted: "We are a nation that has a government—not the other way around."

Ronald Reagan had been singing this song of limiting government and empowering Americans since the mid-1950s, when he became a pitchman for General Electric as his Hollywood career faded. It surged with "The Speech," his ringing endorsement of Barry Goldwater in 1964. And it echoed in many of his riffs as California governor and on the speakers' circuit as he built toward his 1976, then 1980, presidential runs. He had no "intention to do away with government," he insisted. He just wanted "to make it work—work with us, not over us; to stand by our side, not ride on our back."

Reaffirming his faith in "freedom" and "the dignity of the individual," he insisted that "our present troubles parallel and are proportionate to the intervention and intrusion in our lives that result from unnecessary and excessive growth of government." Then, one of Reagan's defining lines: "It is time for us to realize that we are too great a nation to limit ourselves to small dreams."

Leaping from the political realm to the existential, he rhapsodized: "let us begin an era of national renewal." Seeing heroes as walking bundles of hope, Reagan saluted "individuals and families whose taxes support the Government and whose voluntary gifts support church, charity, culture, art, and education." And after honoring the American Revolution, warning "those who practice terrorism and prey upon their neighbors," and toasting Inauguration Day as a "day of prayer," he turned toward his home, to the West.

Noting that the ceremony had never been held on the West front of the Capitol, he saluted the men behind the monuments he now faced: George Washington, Thomas Jefferson, Abraham Lincoln. Looking toward "the sloping hills of Arlington National Cemetery" across from the Potomac, he honored America's soldiers who had sacrificed everything so we could enjoy our freedom. "Under one such marker lies a young man—Martin Treptow," he said. Treptow died in World War I. In his diary he wrote: "I will fight cheerfully and do my utmost, as if the issue of the whole struggle depended on me alone."

Reagan ended by summoning "our best effort, and our willingness to believe in ourselves and to believe in our capacity to perform great deeds; to believe that together, with God's help, we can and will resolve the problems which now confront us." Dismissing the cynics, he declared: "And, after all, why shouldn't we believe that? We are Americans. God bless you, and thank you."

Naysayers would note that Treptow wasn't buried in Arlington National Cemetery—although the phrase "one such marker" could apply to any military gravesite anywhere in the world. But believers—and the newly converted—delighted in the next triumphal few minutes. Striding into the President's Room of the Senate, Reagan signed an Executive Order freezing federal civilian hiring.

"This begins the process of restoring our economic strength and returning the Nation to prosperity," he said.

As the inaugural luncheon in Statuary Hall ended, Reagan announced the perfect coda to his red, white, and blue inaugural: "With thanks to Almighty God, I have been given a tag line, the get-off line everyone wants at the end of a toast or speech," the shameless showman admitted. The hostages "now are free of Iran." Ayatollah Khomeini had given the old performer a great gift to help "begin an era of national renewal."

After a shrewd courtesy visit to the Speaker of the House, Tip O'Neill—who felt snubbed by his fellow Democrat Jimmy Carter at the 1977 inauguration—Reagan rode down Pennsylvania Avenue to his new home. The inaugural parade celebrated the themes of the inaugural—and the three pillars on which Ronald Reagan's historical reputation still stands: peace, prosperity, and patriotism.

He promised all three in his twenty-minute talk. Eight rocky years later, he was able to make the case that he delivered all three—at least partially. With the Soviet Union imploding, the Cold War was ending. The stock market was booming, and inflation had faded. Meanwhile, the celebration of traditional American values that Reagan launched in the inaugural continued.

True, various problems persisted. Debates about Reagan's legacy continue to rage among historians. But there's a clear line between the vision he articulated in 1981 and the case he made emphasizing his successes eight years later. And, as he would say in his Farewell Address in his folksy, aw shucks way, looking back on his administration, and his first inauguration: "All in all, not bad. Not bad at all."

Ronald Reagan's Second Inaugural Address

MONDAY, JANUARY 21, 1985

SENATOR MATHIAS, CHIEF *Justice Burger, Vice President Bush, Speaker O'Neill, Senator Dole, reverend clergy, members of my family and friends, and my fellow citizens:*

This day has been made brighter with the presence here of one who, for a time, has been absent. Senator John Stennis, God bless you and welcome back.

There is, however, one who is not with us today. Representative Gillis Long of Louisiana left us last night. I wonder if we could all join in a moment of silent prayer.

(The President resumed speaking after a moment of silence.)

Amen.

There are no words adequate to express my thanks for the great honor that you have bestowed on me. I will do my utmost to be deserving of your trust.

This is, as Senator Mathias told us, the 50th time that we, the people, have celebrated this historic occasion. When the first President, George Washington, placed his hand upon the Bible, he stood less than a single day's journey by horseback from raw, untamed wilderness. There were 4 million Americans in a union of 13 States. Today, we are 60 times as many in a union of 50 States. We've lighted the world with our inventions, gone to the aid of mankind wherever in the world there was a cry for help, journeyed to the Moon and safely returned. So much has changed, and yet we stand together as we did two centuries ago.

When I took this oath 4 years ago, I did so in a time of economic stress. Voices were raised saying we had to look to our past for the greatness and glory. But we, the present-day Americans, are not given to looking backward. In this blessed land, there is always a better tomorrow.

Four years ago, I spoke to you of a New Beginning, and we have accomplished that. But in another sense, our New Beginning is a continuation of that beginning created two centuries ago when, for the first time in history, government, the people said, was not our master, it is our servant; its only power that which we the people allow it to have.

That system has never failed us, but for a time we failed the system. We asked things of government that government was not equipped to give. We yielded authority to the National Government that properly belonged to States or to local governments or to the people themselves. We allowed taxes and inflation to rob us of our earnings and savings and watched the great industrial machine that had made us the most productive people on Earth slow down and the number of unemployed increase.

By 1980, we knew it was time to renew our faith, to strive with all our strength toward the ultimate in individual freedom, consistent with an orderly society.

We believed then and now: There are no limits to growth and human progress when men and women are free to follow their dreams. And we were right to believe that. Tax rates have been reduced, inflation cut dramatically, and more people are employed than ever before in our history.

We are creating a nation once again vibrant, robust, and alive. But there are many mountains yet to climb. We will not rest until every American enjoys the fullness of freedom, dignity, and opportunity as our birthright. It is our birthright as citizens of this great Republic.

And if we meet this challenge, these will be years when Americans have restored their confidence and tradition of progress; when our values of faith, family, work, and neighborhood were restated for a modern age; when our economy was finally freed from government's grip; when we made sincere efforts at meaningful arms reduction and by rebuilding our defenses, our economy, and developing new technologies, helped preserve peace in a troubled world; when Americans courageously supported the struggle for liberty, self-government, and free enterprise throughout the world, and turned the tide of history away from totalitarian darkness and into the warm sunlight of human freedom.

My fellow citizens, our nation is poised for greatness. We must do what we know is right, and do it with all our might. Let history say of us: "These were golden years—when the American Revolution was reborn, when freedom gained new life, when America reached for her best."

Our two-party system has solved us—served us, I should say, well over the years, but never better than in those times of great challenge when we came together not as Democrats or Republicans, but as Americans united in a common cause.

Two of our Founding Fathers, a Boston lawyer named Adams and a Virginia planter named Jefferson, members of that remarkable group who met in Independence Hall and dared to think they could start the world over again, left us an important lesson. They had become, in the years then in government, bitter political rivals in the Presidential election of 1800. Then, years later, when both were retired and age had softened their anger, they began to speak to each other again through letters. A bond was reestablished between those two who had helped create this government of ours.

In 1826, the 50th anniversary of the Declaration of Independence, they both died. They died on the same day, within a few hours of each other, and that day was the Fourth of July.

In one of those letters exchanged in the sunset of their lives, Jefferson wrote: "It carries me back to the times when, beset with difficulties and dangers, we were fellow laborers in the same cause, struggling for what is most valuable to man, his right to self-government. Laboring always at the same oar, with some wave ever ahead threatening to overwhelm us, and yet passing harmless ... we rode through the storm with heart and hand."

Well, with heart and hand let us stand as one today—one people under God, determined that our future shall be worthy of our past. As we do, we must not repeat the well-intentioned errors of our past. We must never again abuse the trust of working men and women by sending their earnings on a futile chase after the spiraling demands of a bloated Federal Establishment. You elected us in 1980 to end this prescription for disaster, and I don't believe you reelected us in 1984 to reverse course.

At the heart of our efforts is one idea vindicated by 25 straight months of economic growth: Freedom and incentives unleash the drive and entrepreneurial genius that are the core of human progress. We have begun to increase the rewards for work, savings, and investment; reduce the increase in the cost and size of government and its interference in people's lives.

We must simplify our tax system, make it more fair and bring the rates down for all who work and earn. We must think anew and move with a new boldness, so every American who seeks work can find work, so the least among us shall have an equal chance to achieve the greatest things—to be heroes who heal our sick, feed the hungry, protect peace among nations, and leave this world a better place.

The time has come for a new American emancipation—a great national drive to tear down economic barriers and liberate the spirit of enterprise in the most distressed areas of our country. My friends, together we can do this, and do it we must, so help me God.

From new freedom will spring new opportunities for growth, a more productive, fulfilled, and united people, and a stronger America—an America that will lead the technological revolution and also open its mind and heart and soul to the treasures of literature, music, and poetry, and the values of faith, courage, and love.

A dynamic economy, with more citizens working and paying taxes, will be our strongest tool to bring down budget deficits. But an almost unbroken 50 years of deficit spending has finally brought us to a time of reckoning. We've come to a turning point, a moment for hard decisions. I have asked the Cabinet and my staff a question and now I put the same question to all of you. If not us, who? And if not now, when? It must be done by all of us going forward with a program aimed at reaching a balanced budget. We can then begin reducing the national debt.

I will shortly submit a budget to the Congress aimed at freezing government program spending for the next year. Beyond that, we must take further steps to permanently control government's power to tax and spend. We must act now to protect future generations from government's desire to spend its citizens' money and tax them into servitude when the bills come due. Let us make it unconstitutional for the Federal Government to spend more than the Federal Government takes in.

We have already started returning to the people and to State and local governments responsibilities better handled by them. Now, there is a place for the Federal Government in matters of social compassion. But our fundamental goals must be to reduce dependency and upgrade the dignity of those who are infirm or disadvantaged. And here, a growing economy and support from family and community offer our best chance for a society where compassion is a way of life, where the old and infirm are cared for, the young and, yes, the unborn protected, and the unfortunate looked after and made self-sufficient.

Now, there is another area where the Federal Government can play a part. As an older American, I remember a time when people of different race, creed, or ethnic origin in our land found hatred and prejudice installed in social custom and, yes, in law. There is no story more heartening in our history than the progress that we have made toward the brotherhood of man that God intended for us. Let us resolve there will be no turning back or hesitation on the road to an America rich in dignity and abundant with opportunity for all our citizens.

Let us resolve that we, the people, will build an American opportunity society in which all of us—white and black, rich and poor, young and old—will go forward together, arm in arm. Again, let us remember that though our heritage is one of blood lines from every corner of the Earth, we are all Americans, pledged to carry on this last, best hope of man on Earth.

I have spoken of our domestic goals and the limitations which we should put on our National Government. Now let me turn to a task which is the primary responsibility of National Government—the safety and security of our people.

Today, we utter no prayer more fervently than the ancient prayer for peace on Earth. Yet history has shown that peace will not come, nor will our freedom be preserved, by good will alone. There are those in the world who scorn our vision of human dignity and freedom. One nation, the Soviet Union, has conducted the greatest military buildup in the history of man, building arsenals of awesome offensive weapons.

We have made progress in restoring our defense capability. But much remains to be done. There must be no wavering by us, nor any doubts by others, that America will meet her responsibilities to remain free, secure, and at peace.

There is only one way safely and legitimately to reduce the cost of national security, and that is to reduce the need for it. And this we're trying to do in negotiations with the Soviet Union. We're not just discussing limits on a further increase of nuclear weapons; we seek, instead, to reduce their number. We seek the total elimination one day of nuclear weapons from the face of the Earth.

Now, for decades, we and the Soviets have lived under the threat of mutual assured destruction—if either resorted to the use of nuclear weapons, the other could retaliate and destroy the one who had started it. Is there either logic or morality in believing that if one side threatens to kill tens of millions of our people our only recourse is to threaten killing tens of millions of theirs?

I have approved a research program to find, if we can, a security shield that would destroy nuclear missiles before they reach their target. It wouldn't kill people; it would destroy weapons. It wouldn't militarize space; it would help demilitarize the arsenals of Earth. It would render nuclear weapons obsolete. We will meet with the Soviets, hoping that we can agree on a way to rid the world of the threat of nuclear destruction.

We strive for peace and security, heartened by the changes all around us. Since the turn of the century, the number of democracies in the world has grown fourfold. Human freedom is on the march, and nowhere more so than our own hemisphere. Freedom is one of the deepest and noblest aspirations of the human spirit. People, worldwide, hunger for the right of self-determination, for those inalienable rights that make for human dignity and progress.

America must remain freedom's staunchest friend, for freedom is our best ally and it is the world's only hope to conquer poverty and preserve peace. Every blow we inflict against poverty will be a blow against its dark allies of oppression and war. Every victory for human freedom will be a victory for world peace.

So, we go forward today, a nation still mighty in its youth and powerful in its purpose. With our alliances strengthened, with our economy leading the world to a new age of economic expansion, we look forward to a future rich in possibilities. And all this because we have worked and acted together, not as members of political parties, but as Americans.

My friends, we live in a world that is lit by lightning. So much is changing and will change, but so much endures, and transcends time.

History is a ribbon, always unfurling. History is a journey. And as we continue our journey, we think of those who traveled before us. We stand again at the steps of this symbol of our democracy—well, we would have been standing at the steps if it hadn't gotten so cold. (*Laughter*) Now we're standing inside this symbol of our democracy, and we see and hear again the echoes of our past: a general falls to his knees in the hard snow of Valley Forge; a lonely President paces the darkened halls and ponders his struggle to preserve the Union; the men of the Alamo call out encouragement to each other; a settler pushes west and sings a song, and the song echoes out forever and fills the unknowing air.

It is the American sound. It is hopeful, big-hearted, idealistic, daring, decent, and fair. That's our heritage, that's our song. We sing it still. For all our problems, our differences, we are together as of old. We raise our voices to the God who is the Author of this most tender music. And may He continue to hold us close as we fill the world with our sound—in unity, affection, and love—one people under God, dedicated to the dream of freedom that He has placed in the human heart, called upon now to pass that dream on to a waiting and hopeful world.

God bless you, and God bless America.

The Teflon President

THE SECOND INAUGURAL ADDRESS OF RONALD REAGAN

Iwan Morgan

RONALD REAGAN'S INAUGURATION to a second term as president marked the fiftieth inaugural ceremony in American history and the only one ever to be held indoors in the Capitol Rotunda, as bitterly cold weather had ruled out the traditional open-air ceremony. At 2,561 words, Reagan's Second Inaugural Address was the longest for a second-term president since James Monroe's tally of 4,472 in 1821. Reagan had delivered his First Inaugural Address in 1981 amid the worst economic conditions since the Great Depression of the 1930s and at a dangerous time in the Cold War when the Soviet Union appeared to have gained ascendancy over the United States. In 1985, however, the country was once more prosperous, secure, and optimistic about the future. In recognition of this, voters had re-elected Reagan to a second term in 1984 by a landslide over Democrat Walter Mondale—he received 58.8 percent of the popular vote and carried every state except Minnesota (plus the District of Columbia). His Second Inaugural Address spoke to America's restored confidence in expressing pride at the progress made in the last four years and looking ahead to what needed to be done in the next four to consolidate national renewal. In many ways, it followed on in spirit from the iconic political commercial of his re-election campaign, "It's morning again in America."

In his First Inaugural Address, Reagan insisted that restoration of prosperity depended on reducing the size of the federal government and cutting federal taxes in order to incentivize wealth creation by individual Americans. This conservative anti-statist message was also at the heart of his 1985 address, which identified the two key domestic goals of his second administration as being tax reform and deficit elimination. With regard to the former, he avowed, "We must simplify our tax system, make it more fair and bring the rates down for all who work and earn." These words heralded the enactment of the Tax Reform Act of 1986, the most significant tax reform measure of the second half of the twentieth century. This simplified the tax code into two brackets (instead of fourteen), removed the working poor from the tax rolls, and eliminated or reduced numerous tax breaks enjoyed by business and investors to pay for this largesse.

In contrast, Reagan fell far short in his pursuit of a balanced budget because he wanted to achieve one entirely through domestic program retrenchment, whereas Democrats and Republican fiscal hawks in Congress called for military cutbacks and tax increases. This failure to find political agreement also doomed Reagan's advocacy in the 1985 Inaugural Address of a constitutional amendment to stop the federal government from spending more than it took in annually in taxes. Instead of restoring fiscal discipline, he would preside over an era of unprecedented deficit expansion and public debt growth. In 1981 he had told Americans that gross federal debt was equivalent to a stack of $1,000 bills 67 miles high, but when he left office the pile was some 200 miles high.

Reagan's 1985 Inaugural Address also referenced America's recent progress in advancing African-American civil rights, but acknowledged that more needed to be done to build a country "rich in dignity and abundant with opportunity for all our citizens." These good intentions fell on largely deaf Black ears. African Americans were the one group who remained resistant to his optimistic vision of America's future because they resented his first-term retrenchment of public assistance programs and his continuing toleration of lily-white private Christian schools in the South. In his last year in office, Reagan would veto the Civil Rights Restoration Act of 1988 to strengthen educational desegregation on grounds that this represented an unjustified expansion of federal authority over the decisions of private organizations. This made him the first president since Andrew Johnson in 1866 to veto a civil rights bill, but he was quickly overridden by Congress.

If Reagan's upbeat inaugural vision of America's future did not endear him to African Americans, it was also out of step with the constrained economic prospects of millions of ordinary Americans, regardless of their race. Notwithstanding the Great Depression, the U.S. economy performed remarkably well in the first seventy-five years of the twentieth century in keeping average income mostly rising and economic inequality mainly falling. In the years from the late 1970s to the present, the former has stagnated and the latter has soared. Broader structural changes in the economy pertaining to the growing significance of finance and technology and the loss of manufacturing jobs made it harder for many in the lower half of the income distribution to secure decently paid employment.

Nevertheless, Reagan's economic policies contributed to rising income inequality because they disproportionately benefited the wealthy in reducing government and cutting taxes.

Reagan's 1985 Inaugural Address focused mainly on domestic issues but gave much more attention to foreign and defense issues than its 1981 predecessor. In his first term he had launched America's greatest defense expansion since the Korean War to overtake the perceived lead that the Soviets had gained in defense capabilities in the 1970s. This had intensified the Cold War, causing many Americans to grow concerned that the world was heading for nuclear confrontation. Seeking to reassure them that his goal was "peace through strength," Reagan put increasing emphasis on his desire to negotiate nuclear arms reduction in his re-election campaign. Continuing this theme, his 1985 Inaugural Address looked forward to "the total elimination one day of nuclear weapons from the face of the Earth." In it, he also spoke of his plans for research into the development of the Strategic Defense Initiative (SDI), popularly dubbed "Star Wars," to construct a space-based security shield that could prevent incoming missiles from reaching America in the event of a nuclear attack.

In his second term, Reagan's determination to follow through on nuclear arms reduction made greater progress than almost everyone but him expected. He was fortunate to deal with a new Kremlin leader, Mikhail Gorbachev, who realized that the Soviet economy could not sustain the arms race. In four summit meetings at Geneva, Reykjavik, Washington, and Moscow, their negotiations produced the Intermediate Nuclear Force Treaty of 1987, which eliminated an entire class of nuclear weapons for the first time in history and laid the foundations for the peaceful termination of the Cold War in the early 1990s. Paradoxically, SDI was a stumbling block in their early talks because Reagan would not agree to its elimination. Gorbachev decided, however, that he should not throw away the chance of lasting peace for a weapon still only in the research phase of development.

Reagan's second term would end on a great foreign policy triumph, but international affairs nearly undid him prior to this success. In contrast to his 1981 address that portrayed the rising threat of communism, his 1985 inaugural spoke of freedom, "one of the deepest and noblest aspirations of the human spirit," being on the march in the world, nowhere more so than in America's own hemisphere, and promised support for its advance. This was a veiled reference to the secret financial assistance to buy arms that the Reagan administration was providing, in violation of congressional prohibitions, for the Contra rebels in their campaign to overthrow the Marxist Sandinista government of Nicaragua. This illegal initiative soon intersected with another to sell arms to Iran, in violation of American and international law, in return for its help in freeing U.S. hostages held by Islamist groups in Lebanon. In late 1986, shortly after funds from these sales began to be diverted to the Contras, both operations came to light. Reagan found himself under scrutiny for his role in the so-called Iran-Contra affair that might have become his Watergate, but investigators accepted his disavowals of detailed knowledge of the transactions.

Reagan had no thought of what lay ahead with Iran-Contra when delivering his 1985 Inaugural Address, one of the most optimistic of all time. The fortieth president's confidence in his country shines through it. The address contained several historical references to how Americans had endured difficult times in the past while remaining united in their common cause of advancing freedom. An extended passage spoke of how two of the founders, John Adams and Thomas Jefferson, had renewed their friendship in old age after falling out over the election of 1800. Far from being nostalgic for bygone times, Reagan's historical parables were intended to guide America's future, which he believed would be even greater than its past. Essential for this, in his mind, was that his fellow citizens should focus on what united rather than divided them. Today's Americans might profitably read (or listen to) the 1985 Inaugural Address to heed its stress on national unity. Ronald Reagan, one suspects, would have been uncomfortable with the political polarization of the early twenty-first century.

George H. W. Bush's Inaugural Address

FRIDAY, JANUARY 20, 1989

MR. CHIEF JUSTICE, *Mr. President, Vice President Quayle, Senator Mitchell, Speaker Wright, Senator Dole, Congressman Michel, and fellow citizens, neighbors, and friends:*

There is a man here who has earned a lasting place in our hearts and in our history. President Reagan, on behalf of our nation, I thank you for the wonderful things that you have done for America.

I have just repeated word for word the oath taken by George Washington 200 years ago, and the Bible on which I placed my hand is the Bible on which he placed his. It is right that the memory of Washington be with us today not only because this is our bicentennial inauguration but because Washington remains the Father of our Country. And he would, I think, be gladdened by this day; for today is the concrete expression of a stunning fact: our continuity these 200 years, since our government began.

We meet on democracy's front porch. A good place to talk as neighbors and as friends. For this is a day when our nation is made whole, when our differences, for a moment, are suspended. And my first act as President is a prayer. I ask you to bow your heads.

Heavenly Father, we bow our heads and thank You for Your love. Accept our thanks for the peace that yields this day and the shared faith that makes its continuance likely. Make us strong to do Your work, willing to heed and hear Your will, and write on our hearts these words: "Use power to help people." For we are given power not to advance our own purposes, nor to make a great show in the world, nor a name. There is but one just use of power, and it is to serve people. Help us to remember it, Lord. Amen.

I come before you and assume the Presidency at a moment rich with promise. We live in a peaceful, prosperous time, but we can make it better. For a new breeze is blowing, and a world refreshed by freedom seems reborn. For in man's heart, if not in fact, the day of the dictator is over. The totalitarian era is passing, its old ideas blown away like leaves from an ancient, lifeless tree. A new breeze is blowing, and a nation refreshed by freedom stands ready to push on. There is new ground to be broken and new action to be taken. There are times when the future seems thick as a fog; you sit and wait, hoping the mists will lift and reveal the right path. But this is a time when the future seems a door you can walk right through into a room called tomorrow.

Great nations of the world are moving toward democracy through the door to freedom. Men and women of the world move toward free markets through the door to prosperity. The people of the world agitate for free expression and free thought through the door to the moral and intellectual satisfactions that only liberty allows.

We know what works: Freedom works. We know what's right: Freedom is right. We know how to secure a more just and prosperous life for man on Earth: through free markets, free speech, free elections, and the exercise of free will unhampered by the state.

For the first time in this century, for the first time in perhaps all history, man does not have to invent a system by which to live. We don't have to talk late into the night about which form of government is better. We don't have to wrest justice from the kings. We only have to summon it from within ourselves. We must act on what we know. I take as my guide the hope of a saint: In crucial things, unity; in important things, diversity; in all things, generosity.

America today is a proud, free nation, decent and civil, a place we cannot help but love. We know in our hearts, not loudly and proudly but as a simple fact, that this country has meaning beyond what we see, and that our strength is a force for good. But have we changed as a nation even in our time? Are we enthralled with material things, less appreciative of the nobility of work and sacrifice?

My friends, we are not the sum of our possessions. They are not the measure of our lives. In our hearts we know what matters. We cannot hope only to leave our children a bigger car, a bigger bank account. We must hope to give them a sense of what it means to be a loyal friend; a loving parent; a citizen who leaves his home, his neighborhood, and town better than he found it. What do we want the men and women who work with us to say when we're no longer there? That we were more driven to succeed than anyone around us? Or that we stopped to ask if a sick child had gotten better and stayed a moment there to trade a word of friendship?

No President, no government, can teach us to remember what is best in what we are. But if the man you have chosen to lead this government can help make a difference; if he can celebrate the quieter, deeper successes that are made not of gold and silk but of better hearts and finer souls; if he can do these things, then he must.

America is never wholly herself unless she is engaged in high moral principle. We as a people have such a purpose today. It is to make kinder the face of the Nation and gentler the face of the world. My friends, we have work to do. There are the homeless, lost and roaming. There are the children who have nothing, no love and no normalcy. There are those who cannot free themselves of enslavement to whatever addiction—drugs, welfare, the demoralization that rules the slums. There is crime to be conquered, the rough crime of the streets. There are young women to be helped who are about to become mothers of children they can't care for and might not love. They need our care, our guidance, and our education, though we bless them for choosing life.

The old solution, the old way, was to think that public money alone could end these problems. But we have learned that that is not so. And in any case, our funds are low. We have a deficit to bring down. We have more will than wallet, but will is what we need. We will make the hard choices, looking at what we have and perhaps allocating it differently, making our decisions based on honest need and prudent safety. And then we will do the wisest thing of all. We will turn to the only resource we have that in times of need always grows: the goodness and the courage of the American people.

I am speaking of a new engagement in the lives of others, a new activism, hands-on and involved, that gets the job done. We must bring in the generations, harnessing the unused talent of the elderly and the unfocused energy of the young. For not only leadership is passed from generation to generation but so is stewardship. And the generation born after the Second World War has come of age.

I have spoken of a Thousand Points of Light, of all the community organizations that are spread like stars throughout the Nation, doing good. We will work hand in hand, encouraging, sometimes leading, sometimes being led, rewarding. We will work on this in the White House, in the Cabinet agencies. I will go to the people and the programs that are the brighter points of light, and I will ask every member of my government to become involved. The old ideas are new again because they are not old, they are timeless: duty, sacrifice, commitment, and a patriotism that finds its expression in taking part and pitching in.

We need a new engagement, too, between the Executive and the Congress. The challenges before us will be thrashed out with the House and the Senate. And we must bring the Federal budget into balance. And we must ensure that America stands before the world united, strong, at peace, and fiscally sound. But of course things may be difficult. We need compromise; we've had dissension. We need harmony; we've had a chorus of discordant voices.

For Congress, too, has changed in our time. There has grown a certain divisiveness. We have seen the hard looks and heard the statements in which not each other's ideas are challenged but each other's motives. And our great parties have too often been far apart and untrusting of each other. It has been this way since Vietnam. That war cleaves us still. But, friends, that war began in earnest a quarter of a century ago, and surely the statute of limitations has been reached. This is a fact: The final lesson of Vietnam is that no great nation can long afford to be sundered by a memory. A new breeze is blowing, and the old bipartisanship must be made new again.

To my friends, and, yes, I do mean friends—in the loyal opposition and, yes, I mean loyal—I put out my hand. I am putting out my hand to you, Mr. Speaker. I am putting out my hand to you, Mr. Majority Leader. For this is the thing: This is the age of the offered hand. And we can't turn back clocks, and I don't want to. But when our fathers were young, Mr. Speaker, our differences ended at the water's edge. And we don't wish to turn back time, but when our mothers were young, Mr. Majority Leader, the Congress and the Executive were capable of working together to produce a budget on which this nation could live. Let us negotiate soon and hard. But in the end, let us produce. The American people await action. They didn't send us here to bicker. They ask us to rise above the merely partisan. "In crucial things, unity"—and this, my friends, is crucial.

To the world, too, we offer new engagement and a renewed vow: We will stay strong to protect the peace. The offered hand is a reluctant fist; but once made—strong, and can be used with great effect. There are today Americans who are held against their will in foreign lands and Americans who are unaccounted for. Assistance can be shown here and will be long remembered. Good will begets good will. Good faith can be a spiral that endlessly moves on.

Great nations like great men must keep their word. When America says something, America means it, whether a treaty or an agreement or a vow made on marble steps. We will always try to speak clearly, for candor is a compliment; but subtlety, too, is good and has its place. While keeping our alliances and friendships around the world strong, ever strong, we will continue the new closeness with the Soviet Union, consistent both with our security and with progress. One might say that our new relationship in part reflects the triumph of hope and strength over experience. But hope is good, and so is strength and vigilance.

Here today are tens of thousands of our citizens who feel the understandable satisfaction of those who have taken part in democracy and seen their hopes fulfilled. But my thoughts have been turning the past few days to those who would be watching at home, to an older fellow who will throw a salute by himself when the flag goes by and the women who will tell her sons the words of the battle hymns. I don't mean this to be sentimental. I mean that on days like this we remember that we are all part of a continuum, inescapably connected by the ties that bind.

Our children are watching in schools throughout our great land. And to them I say, Thank you for watching democracy's big day. For democracy belongs to us all, and freedom is like a beautiful kite that can go higher and higher with the breeze. And to all I say, No matter what your circumstances or where you are, you are part of this day, you are part of the life of our great nation.

A President is neither prince nor pope, and I don't seek a window on men's souls. In fact, I yearn for a greater tolerance, and easygoingness about each other's attitudes and way of life.

There are few clear areas in which we as a society must rise up united and express our intolerance. The most obvious now is drugs. And when that first cocaine was smuggled in on a ship, it may as well have been a deadly bacteria, so much has it hurt the body, the soul of our country. And there is much to be done and to be said, but take my word for it: This scourge will stop!

And so, there is much to do. And tomorrow the work begins. And I do not mistrust the future. I do not fear what is ahead. For our problems are large, but our heart is larger. Our challenges are great, but our will is greater. And if our flaws are endless, God's love is truly boundless.

Some see leadership as high drama and the sound of trumpets calling, and sometimes it is that. But I see history as a book with many pages, and each day we fill a page with acts of hopefulness and meaning. The new breeze blows, a page turns, the story unfolds. And so, today a chapter begins, a small and stately story of unity, diversity, and generosity—shared, and written, together.

Thank you. God bless you. And God bless the United States of America.

"*A Thousand Points of Light*"

THE INAUGURAL ADDRESS OF GEORGE H. W. BUSH

Mary Kate Cary

PRESIDENT GEORGE H. W. Bush gave his Inaugural Address on the 200th anniversary of George Washington's Inauguration. To mark the occasion, he chose to be sworn in on two Bibles: the one that George Washington used and a family Bible opened to the Beatitudes. As historian and author Jon Meacham pointed out to him, George Bush was one of only three presidents—along with Washington and Eisenhower—to open his address with a prayer. Meacham quoted that prayer years later at Bush's funeral in his famous eulogy for the late president.

President Bush once reminisced about his Inaugural Address in a compilation of his favorite speeches entitled *Speaking of Freedom*. In it, he remembered the details of the day:

> Inauguration Day at dawn was beautiful and sunny, with just a little chill in the air nothing like the bitter cold of some past inaugurations in Washington. We were all up early, and the day began with a family prayer service at St. John's Church on Lafayette Square. Afterward, Barbara and I met the Reagans for coffee at the White House, which was very relaxing.[1]

Once they arrived at the ceremonies, the president-elect enjoyed being surrounded on the podium by his wife, children, grandchildren, and his eighty-seven-year-old mother, as Justice Sandra Day O'Connor swore in Vice President Quayle, and Chief Justice William Rehnquist "did the honors" for President

Bush. Then the president remembered this about the address itself, which was written with the help of former Reagan speechwriter Peggy Noonan:

> When we began working on the speech earlier in January, I knew I wanted to begin with a prayer. A few other presidents have done that, but not too many. Then the speech went on to describe what I called "the age of the offered hand." We were seeking a new engagement with others—whether domestically, through those Americans already known as "the thousand points of light," as we sought to solve our nation's toughest challenges; through our relations with Congress, to work together without partisan rancor; or through our efforts to work with other nations to promote freedom for all people and end oppression. All over the world, the day of the dictator was over, and a "new breeze was blowing."[2]

The theme of the speech was built upon a powerful but unattributed quote: "I take as my guide the hope of a saint: In crucial things, unity; in important things, diversity; in all things, generosity."

For example, in the speech, the president made a reference to President Kennedy's Inaugural Address. Kennedy had said in 1960: "Now the trumpet summons us again—not as a call to bear arms, though arms we need—not as a call to battle, though embattled we are."

President Bush added to Kennedy's allegory: "Some see leadership as high drama and the sound of trumpets calling, and sometimes it is that. But I see history as a book with many pages, and each day we fill a page with acts of hopefulness and meaning. The new breeze blows, a page turns, the story unfolds. And so, today a chapter begins, a small and stately story of unity, diversity, and generosity — shared and written, together."

He referred to this theme of unity, diversity, and generosity again when he turned dramatically to face the assembled House and Senate leadership next to him on the steps of the U.S. Capitol: "To my friends, and yes, I do mean friends— in the loyal opposition, and yes, I mean loyal—I put out my hand. I am putting out my hand to you, Mr. Speaker. I am putting out my hand to you, Mr. Majority Leader. For this is the thing: This is the age of the offered hand.... The American people await action. They didn't send us here to bicker. They ask us to rise above the merely partisan. 'In crucial things, unity'—and this, my friends, is crucial." To critics, the "age of the offered hand" sounded naive, given that both houses of Congress were under Democratic control—in fact, Democrats were then nearing forty years of majority rule in the House—and increasing partisanship roiled Washington. However, President Bush went on to win bipartisan support for landmark legislation such as the 1990 Civil Rights Act, the Clean Air Act of 1990, and the Americans with Disabilities Act—as well as congressional approval for the successful first Persian Gulf War.

But perhaps the biggest legacy of the speech was its foreshadowing of the end of the Cold War and the fall of the Soviet empire. President Bush rightly sensed that the great nations dominated by the Soviets were moving toward democracy, and that their citizens knew how to secure a more just and prosperous life for themselves. We wouldn't need to invent a new system for them, he said, because, "We know what works: Freedom works. We know what's right: Freedom is right." Within a year of his inaugural, the Berlin Wall would come crashing down and millions of East Europeans would be freed from totalitarianism—without a shot being fired. He later spoke often of "Europe, whole and free."

"Re-reading the speech now," President Bush wrote years later, "I am struck by the feeling we all had that tremendous change was about to take place, and the sense of momentum that was with us all that day."[3]

How right he was. The world events that took place soon after his inaugural address changed the lives of millions of people all over the globe. George Bush will best be remembered for standing for unity, diversity, and generosity during a crucial moment in world history.

Notes

1. George H. W. Bush, *Speaking of Freedom* (New York: Simon and Schuster, 2009), 17.
2. Bush, *Speaking of Freedom*, 17–18.
3. Bush, *Speaking of Freedom*, 18.

Bill Clinton's First Inaugural Address

WEDNESDAY, JANUARY 20, 1993

MY FELLOW CITIZENS:
 Today we celebrate the mystery of American renewal. This ceremony is held in the depth of winter, but by the words we speak and the faces we show the world, we force the spring, a spring reborn in the world's oldest democracy that brings forth the vision and courage to reinvent America. When our Founders boldly declared America's independence to the world and our purposes to the Almighty, they knew that America, to endure, would have to change; not change for change sake but change to preserve America's ideals: life, liberty, the pursuit of happiness. Though we march to the music of our time, our mission is timeless. Each generation of Americans must define what it means to be an American.
 On behalf of our Nation, I salute my predecessor, President Bush, for his half-century of service to America. And I thank the millions of men and women whose steadfastness and sacrifice triumphed over depression, fascism and communism.
 Today, a generation raised in the shadows of the Cold War assumes new responsibilities in a world warmed by the sunshine of freedom but threatened still by ancient hatreds and new plagues. Raised in unrivalled prosperity, we inherit an economy that is still the world's strongest but is weakened by business failures, stagnant wages, increasing inequality, and deep divisions among our own people.
 When George Washington first took the oath I have just sworn to uphold, news travelled slowly across the land by horseback, and across the ocean by boat. Now, the sights and sounds of this ceremony are broadcast instantaneously to billions around the world. Communications and commerce are global. Investment is mobile. Technology is almost magical. And ambition for a better life is now universal.
 We earn our livelihood in America today in peaceful competition with people all across the Earth. Profound and powerful forces are shaking and remaking our

world. And the urgent question of our time is whether we can make change our friend and not our enemy. This new world has already enriched the lives of millions of Americans who are able to compete and win in it. But when most people are working harder for less; when others cannot work at all; when the cost of health care devastates families and threatens to bankrupt our enterprises, great and small; when the fear of crime robs law-abiding citizens of their freedom; and when millions of poor children cannot even imagine the lives we are calling them to lead, we have not made change our friend.

We know we have to face hard truths and take strong steps, but we have not done so; instead, we have drifted. And that drifting has eroded our resources, fractured our economy, and shaken our confidence. Though our challenges are fearsome, so are our strengths. Americans have ever been a restless, questing, hopeful people. And we must bring to our task today the vision and will of those who came before us. From our Revolution to the Civil War, to the Great Depression, to the civil rights movement, our people have always mustered the determination to construct from these crises the pillars of our history. Thomas Jefferson believed that to preserve the very foundations of our Nation, we would need dramatic change from time to time. Well, my fellow Americans, this is our time. Let us embrace it.

Our democracy must be not only the envy of the world but the engine of our own renewal. There is nothing wrong with America that cannot be cured by what is right with America. And so today we pledge an end to the era of deadlock and drift, and a new season of American renewal has begun.

To renew America we must be bold. We must do what no generation has had to do before. We must invest more in our own people, in their jobs, and in their future, and at the same time cut our massive debt. And we must do so in a world in which we must compete for every opportunity. It will not be easy. It will require sacrifice, but it can be done, and done fairly, not choosing sacrifice for its own sake but for our own sake. We must provide for our Nation the way a family provides for its children.

Our Founders saw themselves in the light of posterity. We can do no less. Anyone who has ever watched a child's eyes wander into sleep knows what posterity is. Posterity is the world to come: the world for whom we hold our ideals, from whom we have borrowed our planet, and to whom we bear sacred responsibility. We must do what America does best: offer more opportunity to all and demand more responsibility from all. It is time to break the bad habit of expecting something for nothing from our Government or from each other. Let us all take more responsibility, not only for ourselves and our families but for our communities and our country.

To renew America, we must revitalize our democracy. This beautiful Capital, like every capital since the dawn of civilization, is often a place of intrigue and calculation. Powerful people maneuver for position and worry endlessly about who is in and who is out, who is up and who is down, forgetting those people whose toil and sweat sends us here and pays our way. Americans deserve better. And in this city today there are people who want to do better. And so I say to all of you here: Let us resolve to reform our politics so that power and privilege no longer shout down the voice of the people. Let us put aside personal advantage so that we can feel the pain and see the promise of America. Let us resolve to make our Government a place for what Franklin Roosevelt called "bold, persistent experimentation, a government for our tomorrows, not our yesterdays." Let us give this Capital back to the people to whom it belongs.

To renew America, we must meet challenges abroad as well as at home. There is no longer a clear division between what is foreign and what is domestic. The world economy, the world environment, the world AIDS crisis, the world arms race: they affect us all. Today as an old order passes, the new world is more free but less stable. Communism's collapse has called forth old animosities, and new dangers. Clearly, America must continue to lead the world we did so much to make.

While America rebuilds at home, we will not shrink from the challenges nor fail to seize the opportunities of this new world. Together with our friends and allies, we will work to shape change, lest it engulf us. When our vital interests are challenged or the will and conscience of the international community is defied, we will act, with peaceful diplomacy whenever possible, with force when necessary. The brave Americans serving our Nation today in the Persian Gulf, in Somalia, and wherever else they stand, are testament to our resolve. But our greatest strength is the power of our ideas, which are still new in many lands. Across the world we see them embraced and we rejoice. Our hopes, our hearts, our hands are with those on every continent who are building democracy and freedom. Their cause is America's cause.

The American people have summoned the change we celebrate today. You have raised your voices in an unmistakable chorus. You have cast your votes in historic numbers. And you have changed the face of Congress, the Presidency, and the political process itself. Yes, you, my fellow Americans, have forced the spring. Now we must do the work the season demands. To that work I now turn with all the authority of my office. I ask the Congress to join with me; but no President, no Congress, no Government can undertake this mission alone.

My fellow Americans, you, too, must play your part in our renewal. I challenge a new generation of young Americans to a season of service: to act on your idealism, by helping troubled children, keeping company with those in need, reconnecting our torn communities. There is so much to be done; enough, indeed, for millions of others who are still young in spirit to give of themselves in service, too. In serving, we recognize a simple but powerful truth: We need each other, and we must care for one another.

Today we do more than celebrate America. We rededicate ourselves to the very idea of America, an idea born in revolution and renewed through two centuries of challenge; an idea tempered by the knowledge that, but for fate, we, the fortunate, and the unfortunate might have been each other; an idea ennobled by the faith that our Nation can summon from its myriad diversity the deepest measure of unity; an idea infused with the conviction that America's journey long, heroic journey must go forever upward.

And so, my fellow Americans, as we stand at the edge of the 21st century, let us begin anew with energy and hope, with faith and discipline. And let us work until our work is done. The Scripture says: "And let us not be weary in well doing: for in due season we shall reap, if we faint not." From this joyful mountaintop of celebration we hear a call to service in the valley. We have heard the trumpets. We have changed the guard. And now, each in our own way and with God's help, we must answer the call.

Thank you, and God bless you all.

The Comeback Kid

THE FIRST INAUGURAL ADDRESS OF BILL CLINTON

Steven M. Gillon

AS HE STOOD before the flag-draped façade of the Capitol, with a sea of people stretching to the Washington Monument, Arkansas governor William Jefferson Clinton witnessed a deeply divided and demoralized nation. His party had been out of power for twelve years, during which a revitalized conservative movement led by Ronald Reagan scaled back cherished Democratic social programs. While Reagan's successor, George H. W. Bush, had skillfully led the nation's response to the end of the Cold War, he had neglected problems on the home front. After seven booming years, the economy sputtered. The GNP increased at an anemic 2.2 percent, a reflection of rising unemployment, falling housing starts, and low consumer confidence.

Despite Bush's economic failures, the Democratic party in 1993 was still trying to recover from old political wounds. During the 1960s, the once powerful New Deal coalition had shattered in the face of hot button social issues involving race, crime, and taxes. These deep divisions reached a boiling point in 1992 after the acquittal of four white police officers accused of savagely beating an African-American motorist, Rodney King. Shortly after the verdicts were announced, African Americans in South Central Los Angeles erupted in the deadliest urban riot in over a century. By the time the violence ended three days later, 58 people lay dead, over 800 buildings were destroyed, and thousands more were damaged or looted. During his campaign, Clinton had attributed the riots to "12 years of denial and neglect" of festering racial issues under Reagan and Bush. But an opposing explanation—first touted by Nixon in the late 1960s—argued that such unrest revealed the necessity for "law and order." Once elected, Clinton would also embrace this alternate narrative, striking a balance between activist social policy and more punitive measures.

By straddling political divides in this way, the Clinton presidency seemed for many observers to promise a turning point, a shift away from the stale partisan debates that had divided the nation since the 1960s. After all, Clinton had won the presidency by blending liberal and conservative positions. He had campaigned for office as a "New Democrat," someone who understood the economic concerns of the struggling middle class, while also adopting traditionally conservative positions on crime and welfare. In the weeks before the address, Clinton made clear to speechwriters that he wanted to use this moment to emphasize the concept of an "American renewal" that fused elements of both tradition and innovation.

His inaugural address, just fourteen minutes long, was the third shortest in history, but it did not lack substance. After thanking his predecessor and others of his generation for their service and sacrifice, Clinton proclaimed that a new generation had come to power—"a generation raised in the shadows of the Cold War." He challenged this subset of "young Americans" to embark on what he called "a season of service" and pledged that his administration, as the standard-bearer for this generation, would do its part to revitalize the country.

It was not difficult for Clinton to make the case that his election represented a thorough changing of the guard. Only forty-six years old, Clinton was the third youngest president in history, after John F. Kennedy and Theodore Roosevelt. As America's first "baby boomer" president, Clinton possessed no memory of World War II. Instead, his political views were shaped by the tumultuous events of the 1960s—the Civil Rights Movement, antiwar protests, and a youth-led rebellion against authority. With an identity born from this revolutionary era, Clinton appeared to intimately understand the nature of radical change.

But Clinton's novelty did not mean an ignorance of the past, and his speechwriters made sure to sprinkle his address with subtle references to previous presidents. In addition to invoking George Washington and Thomas Jefferson, Clinton paid homage to Abraham Lincoln's Gettysburg Address by calling for a celebration of "the mystery of American renewal." The inauguration, he continued, was "held in the depth of winter, but by the words we speak and the faces we show the world, we force the spring." This season signaled a renaissance, when "the world's oldest democracy" would manifest "the vision and courage to reinvent" itself. Hinting at what would guide this reinvention, Clinton invoked Franklin Roosevelt's call during the Great Depression for "bold, persistent experimentation." Most significantly, America's rebirth would embrace the spirit of John F. Kennedy, someone Clinton had idolized since the age of sixteen. Echoing Kennedy's Inaugural Address, Clinton emphasized the necessity of sacrifice and service. "My fellow Americans," he stated in his casual, conversational tone, "you, too, must play your part in our renewal." In summoning these themes—rebirth, experimentation, sacrifice—Clinton positioned himself within a specific political genealogy, one that stood for liberalism's deepest values.

Yet, his words were also tinged with more conservative overtones regarding responsibility and limited government. In an obvious reference to his campaign promise to "end welfare as we know it," Clinton asserted that the time had come to "break the bad habit of expecting something for nothing from our Government or from each other." He then offset this statement with an appeal for togetherness: "Let us all take more responsibility, not only for ourselves and our families but for our communities and our country." By yoking individual responsibility to social awareness, Clinton was starting to present the contours of a new kind of centrism.

Clarifying this centrism also meant criticizing the Bush presidency, an approach that Clinton had honed during his campaign for president. People, he declared, were "working harder for less," while healthcare costs devastated families and "the fear of crime" sowed distrust among many Americans. "We know we have to face hard truths and take strong steps, but we have not done so," he said in an obvious jab at his predecessor. "Instead, we have drifted, and that drifting has eroded our resources, fractured our economy, and shaken our confidence." The Bush administration, Clinton implied, had left the nation lost and unmoored without a robust social safety net.

Significantly, though, Clinton's approach to these problems blended aspects previously seen as incompatible. His campaign booklet, "Putting People First," had outlined how his administration planned to expand social programs that had been starved during the previous twelve years. Indeed, before the election, he rarely even mentioned the deficit. But by the time of his inauguration, Clinton switched gears and decided to make deficit reduction, not new spending, his top priority. "To renew America we must be bold," he said. "We must do what no generation has had to do before. We must invest more in our own people, in their jobs and in their future, and at the same time cut our massive debt." That seeming contradiction—practicing financial discipline while also investing in the future—would prove to be one of the greatest challenges faced by the Clinton administration.

But embracing those challenges, Clinton claimed, was necessary to adapt to the new world order. For the previous half-century, the threat of Soviet aggression abroad and communist subversion at home had forged a fragile consensus in favor of an interventionist foreign policy. With the Cold War over, Clinton stressed how advances in technology and global trade bound the world together, presenting both unprecedented opportunities and challenges. This globalized "new world" was "more free but less stable," because "profound and powerful forces" exerted constant, unpredictable change. Thus, America's most urgent task would be to discover how to "make change our friend and not our enemy." One way to do that, he suggested, was to adopt new frameworks for thinking about and doing politics.

However, the high-minded tone of this speech disguised a troubling political reality. Clinton fully realized that he had secured only 43 percent of the popular vote. To assemble a governing coalition, he needed to win over the 19 percent of the electorate who had cast a ballot for eccentric Texas billionaire Ross Perot, whose campaign had focused on deriding the corruption and waste in Washington. In a direct appeal to these voters, Clinton acknowledged that, while the capital "is often a place of intrigue and calculation," under his administration, politics would be reformed so that "power and privilege no longer shout down the voice of the people."

After this mildly populist promise, the new president concluded with a rhetorical flourish, invoking God's help in achieving his agenda. "From this joyful mountaintop of celebration, we hear a call to service in the valley," Clinton concluded. "We have heard the trumpets. We have changed the guard. And now, each in our own way and with God's help, we must answer the call."

But no appeal to the Almighty could erase an indisputable fact: not everyone embraced Clinton's call for change. Soon enough, the intensity of that opposition would become boldly apparent, as controversy and scandal engulfed his administration.

Bill Clinton's Second Inaugural Address

MONDAY, JANUARY 20, 1997

MY FELLOW CITIZENS:

At this last Presidential Inauguration of the 20th century, let us lift our eyes toward the challenges that await us in the next century. It is our great good fortune that time and chance have put us not only at the edge of a new century, in a new millennium, but on the edge of a bright new prospect in human affairs, a moment that will define our course and our character for decades to come. We must keep our old democracy forever young. Guided by the ancient vision of a promised land, let us set our sights upon a land of new promise.

The promise of America was born in the 18th century out of the bold conviction that we are all created equal. It was extended and preserved in the 19th century, when our Nation spread across the continent, saved the Union, and abolished the awful scourge of slavery.

Then, in turmoil and triumph, that promise exploded onto the world stage to make this the American Century. And what a century it has been. America became the world's mightiest industrial power, saved the world from tyranny in two World Wars and a long cold war, and time and again reached out across the globe to millions who, like us, longed for the blessings of liberty.

Along the way, Americans produced a great middle class and security in old age, built unrivaled centers of learning and opened public schools to all, split the atom and explored the heavens, invented the computer and the microchip, and deepened the wellspring of justice by making a revolution in civil rights for African Americans and all minorities and extending the circle of citizenship, opportunity and dignity to women.

Now, for the third time, a new century is upon us and another time to choose. We began the 19th century with a choice: to spread our Nation from coast to coast. We began the 20th century with a choice: to harness the industrial revolution to our values of free enterprise, conservation, and human decency. Those choices made all the difference. At the dawn of the 21st century, a free people must now choose to shape the forces of the information age and the global society, to unleash the limitless potential of all our people, and yes, to form a more perfect Union.

When last we gathered, our march to this new future seemed less certain than it does today. We vowed then to set a clear course to renew our Nation. In these 4 years, we have been touched by tragedy, exhilarated by challenge, strengthened by achievement. America stands alone as the world's indispensable nation. Once again, our economy is the strongest on Earth. Once again, we are building stronger families, thriving communities, better educational opportunities, a cleaner environment. Problems that once seemed destined to deepen, now bend to our efforts. Our streets are safer, and record numbers of our fellow citizens have moved from welfare to work. And once again, we have resolved for our time a great debate over the role of Government. Today we can declare: Government is not the problem, and Government is not the solution. We—the American people—we are the solution. Our Founders understood that well and gave us a democracy strong enough to endure for centuries, flexible enough to face our common challenges and advance our common dreams in each new day.

As times change, so Government must change. We need a new Government for a new century, humble enough not to try to solve all our problems for us but strong enough to give us the tools to solve our problems for ourselves, a Government that is smaller, lives within its means, and does more with less. Yet where it can stand up for our values and interests in the world, and where it can give Americans the power to make a real difference in their everyday lives, Government should do more, not less. The preeminent mission of our new Government is to give all Americans an opportunity, not a guarantee but a real opportunity, to build better lives.

Beyond that, my fellow citizens, the future is up to us. Our Founders taught us that the preservation of our liberty and our Union depends upon responsible citizenship. And we need a new sense of responsibility for a new century. There is work to do, work that Government alone cannot do: teaching children to read, hiring people off welfare rolls, coming out from behind locked doors and shuttered windows to help reclaim our streets from drugs and gangs and crime, taking time out of our own lives to serve others.

Each and every one of us, in our own way, must assume personal responsibility not only for ourselves and our families but for our neighbors and our nation. Our greatest responsibility is to embrace a new spirit of community for a new century. For any one of us to succeed, we must succeed as one America. The challenge of our past remains the challenge of our future: will we be one Nation, one people, with one common destiny, or not? Will we all come together, or come apart?

The divide of race has been America's constant curse. And each new wave of immigrants gives new targets to old prejudices. Prejudice and contempt cloaked in the pretense of religious or political conviction are no different. These forces have nearly destroyed our nation in the past. They plague us still. They fuel the fanaticism of terror. And they torment the lives of millions in fractured nations all around the world.

These obsessions cripple both those who hate and of course those who are hated, robbing both of what they might become. We cannot, we will not, succumb to the dark impulses that lurk in the far regions of the soul everywhere. We shall overcome them. And we shall replace them with the generous spirit of a people who feel at home with one another. Our rich texture of racial, religious and political diversity will be a Godsend in the 21st century. Great rewards will come to those who can live together, learn together, work together, forge new ties that bind together.

As this new era approaches, we can already see its broad outlines. Ten years ago, the Internet was the mystical province of physicists; today, it is a commonplace encyclopedia for millions of schoolchildren. Scientists now are decoding the blueprint of human life. Cures for our most feared illnesses seem close at hand. The world is no longer divided into two hostile camps. Instead, now we are building bonds with nations that once were our adversaries. Growing connections of commerce and culture give us a chance to lift the fortunes and spirits of people the world over. And for the very first time in all of history, more people on this planet live under democracy than dictatorship.

My fellow Americans, as we look back at this remarkable century, we may ask, can we hope not just to follow, but even to surpass the achievements of the 20th century in America and to avoid the awful bloodshed that stained its legacy? To that question, every American here and every American in our land today must answer a resounding, "Yes!" This is the heart of our task. With a new vision of Government, a new sense of responsibility, a new spirit of community, we will sustain America's journey.

The promise we sought in a new land, we will find again in a land of new promise. In this new land, education will be every citizen's most prized possession. Our schools will have the highest standards in the world, igniting the spark of possibility in the eyes of every girl and every boy. And the doors of higher education will be open to all. The knowledge and power of the information age will be within reach not just of the few, but of every classroom, every library, every child. Parents and children will have time not only to work, but to read and play together. And the plans they make at their kitchen table will be those of a better home, a better job, the certain chance to go to college.

Our streets will echo again with the laughter of our children, because no one will try to shoot them or sell them drugs anymore. Everyone who can work, will work, with today's permanent under class part of tomorrow's growing middle class. New miracles of medicine at last will reach not only those who can claim care now but the children and hard-working families too long denied.

We will stand mighty for peace and freedom and maintain a strong defense against terror and destruction. Our children will sleep free from the threat of nuclear, chemical, or biological weapons. Ports and airports, farms and factories will thrive with trade and innovation and ideas. And the world's greatest democracy will lead a whole world of democracies.

Our land of new promise will be a nation that meets its obligations, a nation that balances its budget, but never loses the balance of its values, a nation where our grandparents have secure retirement and health care and their grandchildren know we have made the reforms necessary to sustain those benefits for their time, a nation that fortifies the world's most productive economy even as it protects the great natural bounty of our water, air, and majestic land. And in this land of new promise, we will have reformed our politics so that the voice of the people will always speak louder than the din of narrow interests, regaining the participation and deserving the trust of all Americans.

Fellow citizens, let us build that America, a nation ever moving forward toward realizing the full potential of all its citizens. Prosperity and power, yes, they are important, and we must maintain them. But let us never forget, the greatest progress we have made and the greatest progress we have yet to make is in the human heart. In the end, all the world's wealth and a thousand armies are no match for the strength and decency of the human spirit.

Thirty-four years ago, the man whose life we celebrate today spoke to us down there, at the other end of this Mall, in words that moved the conscience of a nation. Like a prophet of old, he told of his dream that one day America would rise up and treat all its citizens as equals before the law and in the heart. Martin Luther King's dream was the American Dream. His quest is our quest: the ceaseless striving to live out our true creed. Our history has been built on such dreams and labors. And by our dreams and labors, we will redeem the promise of America in the 21st century.

To that effort I pledge all my strength and every power of my office. I ask the Members of Congress here to join in that pledge. The American people returned to office a President of one party and a Congress of another. Surely, they did not do this to advance the politics of petty bickering and extreme partisanship they plainly deplore. No, they call on us instead to be repairers of the breach and to move on with America's mission. America demands and deserves big things from us, and nothing big ever came from being small. Let us remember the timeless wisdom of Cardinal Bernardin, when facing the end of his own life. He said: "It is wrong to waste the precious gift of time, on acrimony and division."

Fellow citizens, we must not waste the precious gift of this time. For all of us are on that same journey of our lives, and our journey, too, will come to an end. But the journey of our America must go on.

And so, my fellow Americans, we must be strong, for there is much to dare. The demands of our time are great, and they are different. Let us meet them with faith and courage, with patience and a grateful, happy heart. Let us shape the hope of this day into the noblest chapter in our history. Yes, let us build our bridge, a bridge wide enough and strong enough for every American to cross over to a blessed land of new promise.

May those generations whose faces we cannot yet see, whose names we may never know, say of us here that we led our beloved land into a new century with the American dream alive for all her children, with the American promise of a more perfect Union a reality for all her people, with America's bright flame of freedom spreading throughout all the world.

From the height of this place and the summit of this century, let us go forth. May God strengthen our hands for the good work ahead, and always, always bless our America.

The Politician

THE SECOND INAUGURAL ADDRESS OF BILL CLINTON

Russell L. Riley

THE HISTORICAL IMAGE of Bill Clinton as president is dominated by Bill Clinton the politician. Both favorable and unfavorable accounts of Clinton's incumbency tend to focus on his political pliancy. The upside, for those who find merit in Clinton's ways, was a rare level of success for a Democratic president in an epoch typically unfriendly to his party at the presidential level. In the three elections before Clinton succeeded in 1992, his party had secured only 173 electoral votes in *total*, nearly one hundred short of the level needed for victory in a single cycle. Moreover, two years into his presidency, the so-called permanent Democratic majority in the House of Representatives fell victim to Newt Gingrich's Republican Revolution, joining a newly Republican Senate, too. Presidential achievement in this environment, using any standard metric, is difficult. Thus Clinton's successes, including a rare Democratic re-election and a balanced federal budget, built on an innovator's flexibility in setting objectives and a mariner's skill in tacking toward them. He was, by the favorable portraiture of journalist Joe Klein, "the Natural."

However, for his opponents, this adaptability was a sign that Clinton had no principles, either in matters of public business or in his private affairs. He was "Slick Willie," spineless, unmoored to anything other than his own success. Ironically, then, Bill Clinton's shape-shifting was, by this common characterization, at the center of both his extraordinary successes and his extreme failures as president.

Clinton's Second Inaugural Address, however, demonstrates a flaw in this interpretation. It reveals a consistent and durable core to Bill Clinton's approach to politics. Three familiar keywords stand out: opportunity, responsibility, and community. History shows that these are not casual references tossed into the speech as polite applause lines. They are instead cornerstones to a persistent philosophy of government.

They appear together most prominently in Clinton's May 1991 keynote address to the Democratic Leadership Council (DLC), the centrist party organization he helped to develop in the lean decade of the 1980s. Bruce Reed, who would become Clinton's White House domestic policy advisor, later observed that this "was the speech of [Clinton's] life . . . and still one of the best political speeches I've ever seen anyone give. . . . [It was] pitch perfect." Its core message? A call "to give the people a new choice . . . that offers *opportunity*, demands *responsibility*, gives citizens more say . . . — all because we recognize that we are a *community*, we are all in this together, and we are going up or down together"[1] (emphasis added). The remainder of the speech was devoted to elaborating on each element of that triad. Then, as DLC founder Al From was to observe, these concepts were at the heart of Clinton's presidency, buttressing his efforts to reform the national welfare system, his sense of fiscal responsibility, his embrace of free trade, and his focus on national service.

These themes were demonstrably not the ephemeral product of a focus group or a tactical response to the dynamics of a single campaign season. They were, instead, the product of long and hard thought by Clinton about how his chosen party could succeed in a nation that had in five of six elections voted overwhelmingly against it.

Clinton was a Southerner and a Democrat. But he was not in any conventional sense a Southern Democrat. On cultural issues, especially race and gender, he was decidedly a product of the 1960s, his inclusive sensibilities whetted at Oxford and Yale. And he retained a faith in activist government that did not much survive the Civil Rights Movement in the white South. Yet because he chose to pursue a political career in his native Arkansas, Southern Democrats dominated his world. Their reactions determined whether he would succeed or fail. Thus he learned how to lead among people who were often skeptical of his intentions. He knew they had to be brought along. *Opportunity, responsibility, and community* was an incantation, intended to help Americans accept a role for government that might not occur naturally to them.

Still, it is tempting to dismiss these as mere catchwords, meaningless because they are so common in our political discourse—standards, as it were, in the Great American Songbook. But a review of all the inaugural speeches since World War II indicates otherwise. In only one address before Clinton's time, Reagan's second (in 1985), were all three words included—and even that instance is not a direct parallel, because Reagan spoke solely of "the responsibility *of the*

National Government," not personal responsibility in the Clintonian sense. So Clinton's invocation was practically unique. Given that history, a second discovery is equally striking: George W. Bush included all three in his 2001 Inaugural, echoing (without acknowledging the fact) Clinton on all points. For example, "America, at its best," Bush noted, "is a place where personal responsibility is valued and expected. Encouraging responsibility is... a call to conscience." This suggests that Clinton's influence on his times—notwithstanding his own personal irresponsibilities—was more substantial than has been previously acknowledged, and might have persisted had the events of September 11, 2001, not completely upturned the nation's political terrain.

These notes of remarkable consistency, however, are embedded in a speech otherwise infused with great uncertainty. Clinton's Second Inaugural exposes a president laboring to fathom the obscure currents of history engulfing his times and how best to respond to them. There are two components of the speech where these uncertainties are especially notable.

The first is in the state of America's foreign relations. For the previous fifty years, presidents could always fall back on Cold War rhetoric, and the unifying mission of defeating global communism, as a consistent element of the job description. But Clinton was elected immediately after the Cold War had ended. His foreign policy team had tried fruitlessly throughout his first term to identify what would come next—a simple organizing principle that would communicate the nation's approach to an indeterminate new era. Absent that new consensus, the 1997 Inaugural Address was far less concerned with foreign affairs than most since the Second World War. The term "terror" does get two quick mentions, foreshadowing a world to come. Otherwise, foreign policy gets comparatively meager attention.

Second, this speech reveals a leader trying to find his own way in these uncharted waters. Clinton had always wanted to be not just a good president, but a great one. His fine grasp of American history, however, told him that the greats were mainly the product of war or some other major emergency. And he knew that he was serving in an almost uniquely peaceful era for the United States. That reality sent him on an intellectual quest—to identify a powerful example unconnected to those common kinds of crises, who in turn might be a model for the heroic presidency he wanted his to be. This search led him to Theodore Roosevelt.

By Clinton's (idiosyncratic) reading, Roosevelt drew his strength from his ability to navigate the United States successfully through the dramatic economic upheavals at the beginning of the twentieth century. His use of the national government to rein in the excesses of industrial America and to moderate the disruptive forces caused by mass relocations "from farm to factory... [and] from country to city" were what, by Clinton's reading, put Roosevelt on Mount Rushmore. But they also gave Clinton reason to see parallels in his own time.

Theodore Roosevelt is nowhere mentioned in Clinton's Second Inaugural Address. But much of the speech is given over to describing a political and economic environment much like Roosevelt's. The country was "at the edge of a new century," an era of sweeping change.

> We began the 20th century with a choice: to harness the industrial revolution to our values of free enterprise, conservation, and human decency. Those choices made all the difference. At the dawn of the 21st century, a free people must now choose to shape the forces of the information age and the global society, to unleash the limitless potential of all our people.... We need a new Government for a new century.

That historical predicate provided Roosevelt the foundations for presidential greatness. Perhaps it would do the same for him.

It did not. Although Clinton's second term difficulties had little to do with anything related to this address, his attempt to define the times was too abstract for most to grasp, and his claim to Roosevelt's mantle met with a disdainful reaction as trial balloons circulated in the press. Theodore Roosevelt biographer Edmund Morris, for example, penned a dismissive op-ed for the *New York Times* pungently headed "The Rough Rider and the Easy One." So on these grounds, the speech didn't work. But it isn't alone.

Second Inaugural Addresses are notoriously difficult. Indeed some presidential speechwriters have suggested that they should be graded on a generous curve, perhaps tossing out Lincoln's entirely to make things fair. The huge benefit inherent in most—meaning first—inaugural addresses is that they have all the advantages of newness, of turning the page, just months after the electorate has announced that change is exactly what it wanted. Every second inaugural address, conversely, is freighted with the weight of continuity. The excitement of a new beginning can seldom be replicated. Thus, second inaugurals are always written on unwashed blackboards. The words may be meaningful and well-constructed, but the chalk is never as vibrant as when the slate was clean.

Note

1. "DLC: Keynote Address of Gov. Bill Clinton to the DLC's Cleveland Conv ...," 1991, retrieved June 20, 2024, from https://archive.ph/20050904033847/http://www.dlc.org/ndol_ci.cfm?contentid=3166&kaid=86&subid=194.

George W. Bush's First Inaugural Address

SATURDAY, JANUARY 20, 2001

PRESIDENT CLINTON, DISTINGUISHED guests and my fellow citizens, the peaceful transfer of authority is rare in history, yet common in our country. With a simple oath, we affirm old traditions and make new beginnings.

As I begin, I thank President Clinton for his service to our nation.

And I thank Vice President Gore for a contest conducted with spirit and ended with grace.

I am honored and humbled to stand here, where so many of America's leaders have come before me, and so many will follow.

We have a place, all of us, in a long story—a story we continue, but whose end we will not see. It is the story of a new world that became a friend and liberator of the old, a story of a slave-holding society that became a servant of freedom, the story of a power that went into the world to protect but not possess, to defend but not to conquer.

It is the American story—a story of flawed and fallible people, united across the generations by grand and enduring ideals.

The grandest of these ideals is an unfolding American promise that everyone belongs, that everyone deserves a chance, that no insignificant person was ever born.

Americans are called to enact this promise in our lives and in our laws. And though our nation has sometimes halted, and sometimes delayed, we must follow no other course.

Through much of the last century, America's faith in freedom and democracy was a rock in a raging sea. Now it is a seed upon the wind, taking root in many nations.

Our democratic faith is more than the creed of our country, it is the inborn hope of our humanity, an ideal we carry but do not own, a trust we bear and pass along. And even after nearly 225 years, we have a long way yet to travel.

While many of our citizens prosper, others doubt the promise, even the justice, of our own country. The ambitions of some Americans are limited by failing schools and hidden prejudice and the circumstances of their birth. And sometimes our differences run so deep, it seems we share a continent, but not a country.

We do not accept this, and we will not allow it. Our unity, our union, is the serious work of leaders and citizens in every generation. And this is my solemn pledge: I will work to build a single nation of justice and opportunity.

I know this is in our reach because we are guided by a power larger than ourselves who creates us equal in His image.

And we are confident in principles that unite and lead us onward.

America has never been united by blood or birth or soil. We are bound by ideals that move us beyond our backgrounds, lift us above our interests and teach us what it means to be citizens. Every child must be taught these principles. Every citizen must uphold them. And every immigrant, by embracing these ideals, makes our country more, not less, American.

Today, we affirm a new commitment to live out our nation's promise through civility, courage, compassion and character.

America, at its best, matches a commitment to principle with a concern for civility. A civil society demands from each of us good will and respect, fair dealing and forgiveness.

Some seem to believe that our politics can afford to be petty because, in a time of peace, the stakes of our debates appear small.

But the stakes for America are never small. If our country does not lead the cause of freedom, it will not be led. If we do not turn the hearts of children toward knowledge and character, we will lose their gifts and undermine their idealism. If we permit our economy to drift and decline, the vulnerable will suffer most.

We must live up to the calling we share. Civility is not a tactic or a sentiment. It is the determined choice of trust over cynicism, of community over chaos. And this commitment, if we keep it, is a way to shared accomplishment.

America, at its best, is also courageous.

Our national courage has been clear in times of depression and war, when defending common dangers defined our common good. Now we must choose if the example of our fathers and mothers will inspire us or condemn us. We must show courage in a time of blessing by confronting problems instead of passing them on to future generations.

Together, we will reclaim America's schools, before ignorance and apathy claim more young lives.

We will reform Social Security and Medicare, sparing our children from struggles we have the power to prevent. And we will reduce taxes, to recover the momentum of our economy and reward the effort and enterprise of working Americans.

We will build our defenses beyond challenge, lest weakness invite challenge.

We will confront weapons of mass destruction, so that a new century is spared new horrors.

The enemies of liberty and our country should make no mistake: America remains engaged in the world by history and by choice, shaping a balance of power that favors freedom. We will defend our allies and our interests. We will show purpose without arrogance. We will meet aggression and bad faith with resolve and strength. And to all nations, we will speak for the values that gave our nation birth.

America, at its best, is compassionate. In the quiet of American conscience, we know that deep, persistent poverty is unworthy of our nation's promise.

And whatever our views of its cause, we can agree that children at risk are not at fault. Abandonment and abuse are not acts of God, they are failures of love.

And the proliferation of prisons, however necessary, is no substitute for hope and order in our souls.

Where there is suffering, there is duty. Americans in need are not strangers, they are citizens, not problems, but priorities. And all of us are diminished when any are hopeless.

Government has great responsibilities for public safety and public health, for civil rights and common schools. Yet compassion is the work of a nation, not just a government.

And some needs and hurts are so deep they will only respond to a mentor's touch or a pastor's prayer. Church and charity, synagogue and mosque lend our communities their humanity, and they will have an honored place in our plans and in our laws.

Many in our country do not know the pain of poverty, but we can listen to those who do.

And I can pledge our nation to a goal: When we see that wounded traveler on the road to Jericho, we will not pass to the other side.

America, at its best, is a place where personal responsibility is valued and expected.

Encouraging responsibility is not a search for scapegoats, it is a call to conscience. And though it requires sacrifice, it brings a deeper fulfillment. We find the fullness of life not only in options, but in commitments. And we find that children and community are the commitments that set us free.

Our public interest depends on private character, on civic duty and family bonds and basic fairness, on uncounted, unhonored acts of decency which give direction to our freedom.

Sometimes in life we are called to do great things. But as a saint of our times has said, every day we are called to do small things with great love. The most important tasks of a democracy are done by everyone.

I will live and lead by these principles: to advance my convictions with civility, to pursue the public interest with courage, to speak for greater justice and compassion, to call for responsibility and try to live it as well.

In all these ways, I will bring the values of our history to the care of our times.

What you do is as important as anything government does. I ask you to seek a common good beyond your comfort; to defend needed reforms against easy attacks; to serve your nation, beginning with your neighbor. I ask you to be citizens: citizens, not spectators; citizens, not subjects; responsible citizens, building communities of service and a nation of character.

Americans are generous and strong and decent, not because we believe in ourselves, but because we hold beliefs beyond ourselves. When this spirit of citizenship is missing, no government program can replace it. When this spirit is present, no wrong can stand against it.

After the Declaration of Independence was signed, Virginia statesman John Page wrote to Thomas Jefferson: "We know the race is not to the swift nor the battle to the strong. Do you not think an angel rides in the whirlwind and directs this storm?"

Much time has passed since Jefferson arrived for his inauguration. The years and changes accumulate. But the themes of this day he would know: our nation's grand story of courage and its simple dream of dignity.

We are not this story's author, who fills time and eternity with his purpose. Yet his purpose is achieved in our duty, and our duty is fulfilled in service to one another.

Never tiring, never yielding, never finishing, we renew that purpose today, to make our country more just and generous, to affirm the dignity of our lives and every life.

This work continues. This story goes on. And an angel still rides in the whirlwind and directs this storm.

God bless you all, and God bless America.

Common Ground

THE FIRST INAUGURAL ADDRESS OF GEORGE W. BUSH

James Mann

GEORGE W. BUSH was the first president in more than a century to lose the popular vote but win the Electoral College; one had to go back to Benjamin Harrison in 1888 to find a comparable election. Bush had, moreover, won in the Electoral College only after the Supreme Court had ruled, by the close vote of 5 to 4, that Florida's electoral votes should be awarded to him and not to his Democratic opponent, Al Gore. Under those circumstances, Bush chose the theme for his Inaugural Address to be one of civility, delivering a speech that offered only a few glimpses of the initiatives and ideas that would follow in his presidency. Yet they were in the speech, if one looked closely.

The dispute in Florida had been bitter and prolonged, arousing passions and partisanship that were still raw on Inauguration Day. Despite the damp, foggy weather, roughly 300,000 people turned out on the streets of Washington. Protesters carried signs that said, "Hail to the Thief." Bush supporters, in turn, countered with placards that said, "W Stands for Winner."

Gathered around the stage for the swearing-in was an array of leaders who had dominated public life in America in previous years or would do so in the years to come. The leaders of the past started with Bush's proud, teary father, George H. W. Bush; the Bushes were that day about to become the first father-son team of presidents since the Adams family. The outgoing president Bill Clinton sat on the stage, too, along with Gore, the outgoing vice president. Hillary Clinton, who had two weeks earlier been elected to the U.S. Senate, sat alongside her husband. The master of ceremonies for the day's events was Mitch McConnell, who was then the Senate majority whip. Looking on from a choice seat just off the stage was the mayor of New York, Rudy Giuliani, just entering into what many assumed would be a relatively uneventful final year in office.

What George W. Bush gave them, and those who watched on television that day, was a fourteen-minute paean to civic virtues, repeatedly emphasizing the importance of showing respect to political opponents. He first thanked Clinton for his service and then thanked Gore for "a contest conducted with spirit and ended with grace." Bush alluded to the partisan divisions of the election in soothing terms. "Sometimes our differences run so deep, it seems we share a continent, but not a country. We do not accept this, and we will not allow it," Bush said. Not just once but three times he returned specifically to the theme of civility in political discourse. "Civility is not a tactic or a sentiment. It is the determined choice of trust over cynicism, of community over chaos," he asserted.

After all the tensions of the disputed election, the reaction to these passages would be overwhelmingly positive. "A Step Toward Common Ground," a headline on the front page of the *Washington Post* said the following day. The *New York Times* news analysis said Bush had "started to dispel the challenges to his legitimacy." Liberal columnist E. J. Dionne called the speech "excellent" and "Bush at his best."[1]

The address, written by Bush's speechwriter Michael Gerson, was cast mostly in terms of abstractions and ideals. Yet within the speech, there were also just a few words and phrases that served brief notice of the political battles that would later come to dominate George W. Bush's presidency. In fact, the speech contained offerings to each of the three conservative constituencies that had helped Bush win the Republican nomination.

Some history is in order here. Ronald Reagan had assembled a Republican coalition that had brought together tax-cutting libertarians, foreign policy hawks, and evangelicals. All three of these constituencies had then, in different ways, become disaffected with President George H. W. Bush. Throughout the 1990s, in the wake of his father's failure to win re-election, George W. Bush forged strong links to all three of these conservative factions within the party. He had, for example, promised substantial tax cuts during his presidential campaign.

In his inaugural address, George W. Bush gave a nod to each constituency. For economic conservatives, Bush promised, "We will reform Social Security and Medicare.... And we will reduce taxes to recover the momentum of our economy." As it turned out, Bush would not press hard to privatize Social Security until his second term, and even then he failed. But he would move for significant tax cuts in the first six months of his presidency, and in that he succeeded.

For evangelicals, the speech contained religious references, indeed ten of them in the short address. "When we see that wounded traveler on the road to Jericho, we will not pass to the other side," said Bush, referring to the parable of the Good Samaritan. This and the other references were offered as part of Bush's campaign theme of compassionate conservatism. It included, among other things, the idea of faith-based initiatives that would take social programs out of the control of the government and into the hands of churches and charities. That idea, too, could be found in the Inaugural, though couched in abstract wording: "Compassion is the work of a nation, not just a government," Bush asserted. "And some needs and some hurts are so deep they will only respond to a mentor's touch or a pastor's prayer."

So then what about foreign policy? Where in this Inaugural Address are any precursors to the future war in Iraq, the single aspect of Bush's presidency for which he would most be remembered? Where, in other words, are the references in the speech aimed at hawks or neoconservatives?

One answer might be that the September 11 attacks, which set in motion the chain of events leading up to the Iraq War, hadn't happened yet. On Inauguration Day, there were already a few within the administration who were pressing for more aggressive action against Saddam Hussein, but at that point, it was a secondary issue. At the time of the Inaugural, the neoconservatives had other priorities. At the top of their wish list was the desire for the United States to withdraw from the ABM Treaty of 1972, which stood in the way of the United States constructing missile-defense systems. In the careful phrasing of Bush's Inaugural, they could find a passage alluding to missile defense: "We will confront weapons of mass destruction, so that a new century is spared new horrors." Eleven months later, Bush would announce that the United States was formally withdrawing from the ABM treaty.

The word *Iraq* isn't in the speech. But look carefully and one finds a seemingly cryptic seven-word phrase that hints at some of the broader ideas and the intellectual debates that led up to the Iraq War. Bush declared at one point that America sought to shape "a balance of power that favors freedom."

That phrase almost certainly came from Condoleezza Rice, who had served as the principal foreign policy advisor during Bush's campaign and was that day taking over as his national security advisor. The phrase was an allusion to the longstanding debates over realism versus idealism in foreign policy. Rice had written an article for *Foreign Affairs* the previous year that discussed the idea and limits of a balance-of-power approach to the world, and in the fall of 2002, as the United States was moving determinedly toward war with Iraq, she gave a speech entitled "A Balance of Power That Favors Freedom."

What did that mean? Again, some background is relevant here. The neoconservative movement first became galvanized in foreign policy during the Nixon administration, in opposition to Henry Kissinger's balance-of-power diplomacy in general and to détente with the Soviet Union in particular. Careful balance-of-power considerations then once again dominated the thinking of the George H. W. Bush administration, during which the president and his national security advisor Brent Scowcroft had labored to avoid a break in relations with China and had sought to slow down the breakup of the Soviet Union. Indeed, one of the several reasons the George H. W. Bush administration had decided not to go on to Baghdad at the end of the Persian Gulf War in 1991 had been a balance-of-power consideration: the desire to leave Iraq in a position to serve as a counterweight to Iran.

Rice herself had been a protégé of Scowcroft. She and others in the administration were not prepared, at the very start of the new administration, to throw out completely the concept of balance-of-power diplomacy. But they also wanted to acknowledge the neoconservative argument that a reliance on balance-of-power considerations fails to take into account the ideals of freedom and democracy. Hence, "a balance of power that favors freedom" amounted to a declaration that the new administration would not be governed by realist, balance-of-power concerns to the extent that Bush's father's administration had been.

Finally, the wording of Bush's Inaugural suggested an activist, interventionist role for the United States overseas. A decade after the end of the Cold War, more than a few Americans were arguing that there were not many causes America needed to become involved in overseas. Bush rejected that notion. "The stakes for America are never small," he said. "If our country does not lead the cause of freedom, it will not be led."

There was very little commentary concerning these phrases in the speech on Inauguration Day or the days afterward. They were mostly lost amid Bush's repeated appeals for civility and unity. Indeed, at the time of the Inauguration, there was considerable speculation that the new president, having come to the White House without a majority of the popular vote, would of necessity have to move to the center of the political spectrum and to win Democratic support in order to govern.

It didn't turn out that way. Bush pressed hard for tax cuts in the earliest months of his presidency and got them passed in the face of substantial Democratic opposition. The following year he began driving toward a war with Iraq that produced even more intense divisions within the country than had the 2000 election.

Throughout it all, Bush remained generally civil to his political opponents, in striking contrast with the next Republican president, Donald Trump. But for Bush, civility in style definitely did not mean centrism in substance.

Note

1. E. J. Dionne Jr., "The Best of Bush . . .," *Washington Post,* January 23, 2001, https://www.washingtonpost.com/archive/opinions/2001/01/23/the-best-of-bush/78c5f41b-b401-4688-aefc-2cc226e35122/.

George W. Bush's Second Inaugural Address

THURSDAY, JANUARY 20, 2005

VICE PRESIDENT CHENEY, *Mr. Chief Justice, President Carter, President Bush, President Clinton, members of the United States Congress, reverend clergy, distinguished guests, fellow citizens:*

On this day, prescribed by law and marked by ceremony, we celebrate the durable wisdom of our Constitution, and recall the deep commitments that unite our country. I am grateful for the honor of this hour, mindful of the consequential times in which we live, and determined to fulfill the oath that I have sworn and you have witnessed.

At this second gathering, our duties are defined not by the words I use, but by the history we have seen together. For half a century, America defended our own freedom by standing watch on distant borders. After the shipwreck of communism came years of relative quiet, years of repose, years of sabbatical—and then there came a day of fire.

We have seen our vulnerability—and we have seen its deepest source. For as long as whole regions of the world simmer in resentment and tyranny, prone to ideologies that feed hatred and excuse murder, violence will gather, and multiply in destructive power, and cross the most defended borders, and raise a mortal threat. There is only one force of history that can break the reign of hatred and resentment, and expose the pretensions of tyrants, and reward the hopes of the decent and tolerant, and that is the force of human freedom.

We are led, by events and common sense, to one conclusion: The survival of liberty in our land increasingly depends on the success of liberty in other lands. The best hope for peace in our world is the expansion of freedom in all the world.

America's vital interests and our deepest beliefs are now one. From the day of our founding, we have proclaimed that every man and woman on this Earth has rights and dignity and matchless value, because they bear the image of the Maker of heaven and Earth. Across the generations we have proclaimed the imperative of self-government, because no one is fit to be a master, and no one deserves to be a slave. Advancing these ideals is the mission that created our nation. It is the honorable achievement of our fathers. Now it is the urgent requirement of our nation's security, and the calling of our time.

So it is the policy of the United States to seek and support the growth of democratic movements and institutions in every nation and culture, with the ultimate goal of ending tyranny in our world.

This is not primarily the task of arms, though we will defend ourselves and our friends by force of arms when necessary. Freedom, by its nature, must be chosen, and defended by citizens, and sustained by the rule of law and the protection of minorities. And when the soul of a nation finally speaks, the institutions that arise may reflect customs and traditions very different from our own. America will not impose our own style of government on the unwilling. Our goal instead is to help others find their own voice, attain their own freedom, and make their own way.

The great objective of ending tyranny is the concentrated work of generations. The difficulty of the task is no excuse for avoiding it. America's influence is not unlimited, but, fortunately for the oppressed, America's influence is considerable, and we will use it confidently in freedom's cause.

My most solemn duty is to protect this nation and its people from further attacks and emerging threats. Some have unwisely chosen to test America's resolve, and have found it firm. We will persistently clarify the choice before every ruler and every nation: the moral choice between oppression, which is always wrong, and freedom, which is eternally right. America will not pretend that jailed dissidents prefer their chains, or that women welcome humiliation and servitude, or that any human being aspires to live at the mercy of bullies.

We will encourage reform in other governments by making clear that success in our relations will require the decent treatment of their own people. America's belief in human dignity will guide our policies. Yet rights must be more than the grudging concessions of dictators; they are secured by free dissent and the participation of the governed. In the long run, there is no justice without freedom, and there can be no human rights without human liberty.

Some, I know, have questioned the global appeal of liberty—though this time in history, four decades defined by the swiftest advance of freedom ever seen, is an odd time for doubt. Americans, of all people, should never be surprised by the power of our ideals. Eventually, the call of freedom comes to every mind and every soul. We do not accept the existence of permanent tyranny because we do not accept the possibility of permanent slavery. Liberty will come to those who love it.

Today, America speaks anew to the peoples of the world:

All who live in tyranny and hopelessness can know: The United States will not ignore your oppression, or excuse your oppressors. When you stand for your liberty, we will stand with you.

Democratic reformers facing repression, prison, or exile can know: America sees you for who you are, the future leaders of your free country.

The rulers of outlaw regimes can know that we still believe as Abraham Lincoln did: "Those who deny freedom to others deserve it not for themselves, and, under the rule of a just God, cannot long retain it."

The leaders of governments with long habits of control need to know: To serve your people you must learn to trust them. Start on this journey of progress and justice, and America will walk at your side.

And all the allies of the United States can know: We honor your friendship, we rely on your counsel, and we depend on your help. Division among free nations is a primary goal of freedom's enemies. The concerted effort of free nations to promote democracy is a prelude to our enemies' defeat.

Today, I also speak anew to my fellow citizens:

From all of you I have asked patience in the hard task of securing America, which you have granted in good measure. Our country has accepted obligations that are difficult to fulfill, and would be dishonorable to abandon. Yet, because we have acted in the great liberating tradition of this nation, tens of millions have achieved their freedom. And as hope kindles hope, millions more will find it. By our efforts, we have lit a fire, as well—a fire in the minds of men. It warms those who feel its power; it burns those who fight its progress; and one day this untamed fire of freedom will reach the darkest corners of our world.

Few Americans accepted the hardest duties in this cause—in the quiet work of intelligence and diplomacy, the idealistic work of helping raise up free governments, the dangerous and necessary work of fighting our enemies. Some have shown their devotion to our country in deaths that honored their whole lives—and we will always honor their names and their sacrifice.

All Americans have witnessed this idealism, and some for the first time. I ask our youngest citizens to believe the evidence of your eyes. You have seen duty and allegiance in the determined faces of our soldiers. You have seen that life is fragile, and evil is real, and courage triumphs. Make the choice to serve in a cause larger than your wants, larger than yourself—and in your days you will add not just to the wealth of our country, but to its character.

America has need of idealism and courage, because we have essential work at home—the unfinished work of American freedom. In a world moving toward liberty, we are determined to show the meaning and promise of liberty.

In America's ideal of freedom, citizens find the dignity and security of economic independence, instead of laboring on the edge of subsistence. This is the broader definition of liberty that motivated the Homestead Act, the Social Security Act, and the G. I. Bill of Rights. And now we will extend this vision by reforming great institutions to serve the needs of our time. To give every American a stake in the promise and future of our country, we will bring the highest standards to our schools, and build an ownership society. We will widen the ownership of homes and businesses, retirement savings and health insurance—preparing our people for the challenges of life in a free society. By making every citizen an agent of his or her own destiny, we will give our fellow Americans greater freedom from want and fear, and make our society more prosperous and just and equal.

In America's ideal of freedom, the public interest depends on private character—on integrity, and tolerance toward others, and the rule of conscience in our own lives. Self-government relies, in the end, on the governing of the self. That edifice of character is built in families, supported by communities with standards, and sustained in our national life by the truths of Sinai, the Sermon on the Mount, the words of the Koran, and the varied faiths of our people. Americans move forward in every generation by reaffirming all that is good and true that came before—ideals of justice and conduct that are the same yesterday, today, and forever.

In America's ideal of freedom, the exercise of rights is ennobled by service and mercy, and a heart for the weak. Liberty for all does not mean independence from one another. Our nation relies on men and women who look after a neighbor and surround the lost with love. Americans, at our best, value the life we see in one another, and must always remember that even the unwanted have worth. And our country must abandon all the habits of racism, because we cannot carry the message of freedom and the baggage of bigotry at the same time.

From the perspective of a single day, including this day of dedication, the issues and questions before our country are many. From the viewpoint of centuries, the questions that come to us are narrowed and few: Did our generation advance the cause of freedom? And did our character bring credit to that cause?

These questions that judge us also unite us, because Americans of every party and background, Americans by choice and by birth, are bound to one another in the cause of freedom. We have known divisions, which must be healed to move forward in great purposes—and I will strive in good faith to heal them. Yet those divisions do not define America. We felt the unity and fellowship of our nation when freedom came under attack, and our response came like a single hand over a single heart. And we can feel that same unity and pride whenever America acts for good, and the victims of disaster are given hope, and the unjust encounter justice, and the captives are set free.

We go forward with complete confidence in the eventual triumph of freedom. Not because history runs on the wheels of inevitability; it is human choices that move events. Not because we consider ourselves a chosen nation; God moves and chooses as He wills. We have confidence because freedom is the permanent hope of mankind, the hunger in dark places, the longing of the soul. When our Founders declared a new order of the ages; when soldiers died in wave upon wave for a union based on liberty; when citizens marched in peaceful outrage under the banner "Freedom Now"—they were acting on an ancient hope that is meant to be fulfilled. History has an ebb and flow of justice, but history also has a visible direction, set by liberty and the Author of Liberty.

When the Declaration of Independence was first read in public and the Liberty Bell was sounded in celebration, a witness said, "It rang as if it meant something." In our time it means something still. America, in this young century, proclaims liberty throughout all the world, and to all the inhabitants thereof. Renewed in our strength—tested, but not weary—we are ready for the greatest achievements in the history of freedom.

May God bless you, and may He watch over the United States of America.

A Vision of America

THE SECOND INAUGURAL ADDRESS OF
GEORGE W. BUSH

Mark J. Rozell

PRESIDENT GEORGE W. Bush delivered his Second Inaugural Address on January 20, 2005, after having won re-election with a majority of the national popular vote and a clear Electoral College majority. Bush's first term initially stood under the cloud of his having lost the popular vote to Democrat Al Gore and emerging barely victorious after a disputed election settled by the U.S. Supreme Court by a one-vote margin thirty-six days after Election Day.

The terrorist attacks on the United States on September 11, 2001, transformed Bush's presidency and established the context for a Second Inaugural Address that differed greatly from his First. Bush began his first term committed to a robust domestic policy agenda, having pledged that the United States should not embark on regime change abroad, but rather should focus on challenges at home.

After the terrorist attacks, the president pivoted from a domestic policy focus to protecting the homeland and combating forces of terrorism abroad. The United States thus initiated military actions and eventual occupations in Afghanistan and Iraq, with strong bipartisan support in Congress and the nation generally. As the Middle East wars dragged on long beyond public expectations and American casualties grew, support for the president's actions abroad declined, and thus he entered the 2004 election cycle in a difficult political position.

Bush's victory in 2004 over Democratic Senator John Kerry gave the president the opportunity to define his legacy—a task he would begin to take up in his Second Inaugural Address and second-term policy agenda. The president's address projected a bold vision of the United States' worldwide leadership in promoting human freedom and liberty. It was a speech that harkened back to the ideals of Woodrow Wilson and John F. Kennedy.

Bush opened by establishing the historic context of the times—that the United States had fought a long Cold War for freedom and, once victorious, "came years of relative quiet, years of repose, years of sabbatical—and then there came a day of fire," referring to 9/11. The president then noted that this country that stood tall and victorious after the collapse of communism had now "seen our vulnerability." He attributed that vulnerability to an ideology of hate that posed "a mortal threat." He proclaimed that only "the force of human freedom" around the world could break this threat. Here the president made his call for the United States to lead the worldwide quest for human freedom and liberty, as a necessary means to protect this country: "The survival of liberty in our land increasingly depends on the success of liberty in other lands. The best hope for peace in our world is the expansion of freedom in all the world." Whereas John F. Kennedy had called upon the nation to defend freedom around the world wherever it was under threat, Bush called for the United States to both protect and expand freedom throughout the world.

In making this call for the expansion of freedom around the globe, the president was at once providing a defense of his administration's military actions in the Middle East and calling on the United States to embark on an even larger role of international leadership in defense of freedom. Bush then tied this bold internationalist vision to the foundational beliefs of our Republic, that all people have inalienable rights best protected by a system of self-government. Advancing the ideals of our Founding Fathers, the president extolled, "is the urgent requirement of our nation's security, and the calling of our time."

The president then issued his boldest proclamation: "The survival of liberty in our land increasingly depends on the success of liberty in other lands. The best hope for peace in our world is the expansion of freedom in all the world."

The president's soaring rhetoric of the United States' obligation to protect its homeland by promoting liberty abroad recalled his oft-stated controversial claim during his first term that preventing terrorism at home required fighting the terrorists abroad. It was clear at the time of the second inauguration that the United States' efforts to advance liberty and democratic institutions abroad through military interventions in Afghanistan and Iraq had been a failure, and the costs of the Middle East wars were piling up with no apparent end in sight. What had begun from a conviction that military interventions would topple oppressive regimes and democratic institutions would then emerge throughout the region had instead turned into a long-term military engagement seen by many of the peoples of the Middle East as a hostile occupation.

The Second Inaugural Address thus can be seen in part as Bush's legacy having largely hinged on his administration's policies of military intervention abroad, and these needed a rationale. Bush drew on American ideals of its founding and also its past role in fighting tyranny abroad to preserve those ideals and bring freedoms to others. Critics of the president at the time noted that the threat of terrorism was not analogous to the great twentieth-century threats to the United States and required a very different twenty-first-century strategy. No one questioned the president's assertions of the rightness of the cause of freedom from oppression, so well expressed in his Second Inaugural Address, but whether the foreign policies of the United States during his administration were conducive to advancing freedoms abroad.

Bush's Second Inaugural Address had little to say of the domestic policy challenges of his second term. With such a grand vision for the nation's role in the world framing the first and most substantial portion of the address, his modest goals for America at home stand out in striking contrast. Briefly the president mentioned several issues that later he would put forth in his annual State of the Union Address—home ownership, retirement savings, and health insurance reforms. These stand in this speech as mere foreshadowing of a second-term domestic agenda.

Finally, the president spoke of advancing freedom depending on the "private character" of the people—"on integrity, and tolerance toward others, and the rule of conscience in our own lives." He noted that the foundations of character are families, community, and faith. These values are at the core of a highly decentralized governing system that relies on citizen virtue and strong communities. He acknowledged that the country had its divisions, by "party and background," but we were united by "the cause of freedom."

The common thread of the speech was the president's call to the nation to advance freedom in the world as the aspiration of all humanity, at a time when many did not live free. He did not present in his Inaugural Address any specific policies to advance freedom internationally. Like many inaugural addresses, this one was large on articulating a broad vision, but very short on specifics.

As of 2024, President Bush's vision of a nation united in purpose significantly stands in contrast to the contemporary image of the United States as an intensely polarized nation unable to agree on much at all. At a time when many of the nation's leaders have advanced politically by stoking divisions in the nation, Bush's call to a common national purpose may seem a hopeless aspiration now. It was a noble quest, presented at a time when the country already was in the throes of partisan division that would only intensify during the presidencies of Barack Obama, Donald J. Trump, and Joe Biden. President Bush could not then heal the nation of its divisions, but he set forth the words that addressed a fundamental challenge of our times.

Barack Obama's First Inaugural Address

TUESDAY, JANUARY 20, 2009

MY FELLOW CITIZENS:

I stand here today humbled by the task before us, grateful for the trust you've bestowed, mindful of the sacrifices borne by our ancestors.

I thank President Bush for his service to our nation as well as the generosity and cooperation he has shown throughout this transition.

Forty-four Americans have now taken the presidential oath. The words have been spoken during rising tides of prosperity and the still waters of peace. Yet, every so often, the oath is taken amidst gathering clouds and raging storms. At these moments, America has carried on not simply because of the skill or vision of those in high office, but because we, the people, have remained faithful to the ideals of our forebears and true to our founding documents.

So it has been; so it must be with this generation of Americans.

That we are in the midst of crisis is now well understood. Our nation is at war against a far-reaching network of violence and hatred. Our economy is badly weakened, a consequence of greed and irresponsibility on the part of some, but also our collective failure to make hard choices and prepare the nation for a new age. Homes have been lost, jobs shed, businesses shuttered. Our health care is too costly, our schools fail too many—and each day brings further evidence that the ways we use energy strengthen our adversaries and threaten our planet.

These are the indicators of crisis, subject to data and statistics. Less measurable, but no less profound, is a sapping of confidence across our land; a nagging fear that America's decline is inevitable, that the next generation must lower its sights.

Today I say to you that the challenges we face are real. They are serious and they are many. They will not be met easily or in a short span of time. But know this America: They will be met.

On this day, we gather because we have chosen hope over fear, unity of purpose over conflict and discord. On this day, we come to proclaim an end to the petty grievances and false promises, the recriminations and worn-out dogmas that for far too long have strangled our politics. We remain a young nation. But in the words of Scripture, the time has come to set aside childish things. The time has come to reaffirm our enduring spirit; to choose our better history; to carry forward that precious gift, that noble idea passed on from generation to generation: the God-given promise that all are equal, all are free, and all deserve a chance to pursue their full measure of happiness.

In reaffirming the greatness of our nation we understand that greatness is never a given. It must be earned. Our journey has never been one of short-cuts or settling for less. It has not been the path for the faint-hearted, for those that prefer leisure over work, or seek only the pleasures of riches and fame. Rather, it has been the risk-takers, the doers, the makers of things—some celebrated, but more often men and women obscure in their labor—who have carried us up the long rugged path towards prosperity and freedom.

For us, they packed up their few worldly possessions and traveled across oceans in search of a new life. For us, they toiled in sweatshops, and settled the West, endured the lash of the whip, and plowed the hard earth. For us, they fought and died in places like Concord and Gettysburg, Normandy and Khe Sahn.

Time and again these men and women struggled and sacrificed and worked till their hands were raw so that we might live a better life. They saw America as bigger than the sum of our individual ambitions, greater than all the differences of birth or wealth or faction.

This is the journey we continue today. We remain the most prosperous, powerful nation on Earth. Our workers are no less productive than when this crisis began. Our minds are no less inventive, our goods and services no less needed than they were last week, or last month, or last year. Our capacity remains undiminished. But our time of standing pat, of protecting narrow interests and putting off unpleasant decisions—that time has surely passed. Starting today, we must pick ourselves up, dust ourselves off, and begin again the work of remaking America.

For everywhere we look, there is work to be done. The state of our economy calls for action, bold and swift. And we will act, not only to create new jobs, but to lay a new foundation for growth. We will build the roads and bridges, the electric grids and digital lines that feed our commerce and bind us together. We'll restore science to its rightful place, and wield technology's wonders to raise health care's quality and lower its cost. We will harness the sun and the winds and the soil to fuel our cars and run our factories. And we will transform our schools and colleges and universities to meet the demands of a new age. All this we can do. All this we will do.

Now, there are some who question the scale of our ambitions, who suggest that our system cannot tolerate too many big plans. Their memories are short, for they have forgotten what this country has already done, what free men and women can achieve when imagination is joined to common purpose, and necessity to courage. What the cynics fail to understand is that the ground has shifted beneath them, that the stale political arguments that have consumed us for so long no longer apply.

The question we ask today is not whether our government is too big or too small, but whether it works—whether it helps families find jobs at a decent wage, care they can afford, a retirement that is dignified. Where the answer is yes, we intend to move forward. Where the answer is no, programs will end. And those of us who manage the public's dollars will be held to account, to spend wisely, reform bad habits, and do our business in the light of day, because only then can we restore the vital trust between a people and their government.

Nor is the question before us whether the market is a force for good or ill. Its power to generate wealth and expand freedom is unmatched. But this crisis has reminded us that without a watchful eye, the market can spin out of control. The nation cannot prosper long when it favors only the prosperous. The success of our economy has always depended not just on the size of our gross domestic product, but on the reach of our prosperity, on the ability to extend opportunity to every willing heart—not out of charity, but because it is the surest route to our common good.

As for our common defense, we reject as false the choice between our safety and our ideals. Our Founding Fathers our Founding Fathers, faced with perils that we can scarcely imagine, drafted a charter to assure the rule of law and the rights of man—a charter expanded by the blood of generations. Those ideals still light the world, and we will not give them up for expedience sake.

And so, to all the other peoples and governments who are watching today, from the grandest capitals to the small village where my father was born, know that America is a friend of each nation, and every man, woman and child who seeks a future of peace and dignity. And we are ready to lead once more.

Recall that earlier generations faced down fascism and communism not just with missiles and tanks, but with the sturdy alliances and enduring convictions. They understood that our power alone cannot protect us, nor does it entitle us to do as we please. Instead they knew that our power grows through its prudent use;

our security emanates from the justness of our cause, the force of our example, the tempering qualities of humility and restraint.

We are the keepers of this legacy. Guided by these principles once more we can meet those new threats that demand even greater effort, even greater cooperation and understanding between nations. We will begin to responsibly leave Iraq to its people and forge a hard-earned peace in Afghanistan. With old friends and former foes, we'll work tirelessly to lessen the nuclear threat, and roll back the specter of a warming planet.

We will not apologize for our way of life, nor will we waver in its defense. And for those who seek to advance their aims by inducing terror and slaughtering innocents, we say to you now that our spirit is stronger and cannot be broken—you cannot outlast us, and we will defeat you.

For we know that our patchwork heritage is a strength, not a weakness. We are a nation of Christians and Muslims, Jews and Hindus, and non-believers. We are shaped by every language and culture, drawn from every end of this Earth; and because we have tasted the bitter swill of civil war and segregation, and emerged from that dark chapter stronger and more united, we cannot help but believe that the old hatreds shall someday pass; that the lines of tribe shall soon dissolve; that as the world grows smaller, our common humanity shall reveal itself; and that America must play its role in ushering in a new era of peace.

To the Muslim world, we seek a new way forward, based on mutual interest and mutual respect. To those leaders around the globe who seek to sow conflict, or blame their society's ills on the West, know that your people will judge you on what you can build, not what you destroy.

To those who cling to power through corruption and deceit and the silencing of dissent, know that you are on the wrong side of history, but that we will extend a hand if you are willing to unclench your fist.

To the people of poor nations, we pledge to work alongside you to make your farms flourish and let clean waters flow; to nourish starved bodies and feed hungry minds. And to those nations like ours that enjoy relative plenty, we say we can no longer afford indifference to the suffering outside our borders, nor can we consume the world's resources without regard to effect. For the world has changed, and we must change with it.

As we consider the role that unfolds before us, we remember with humble gratitude those brave Americans who at this very hour patrol far-off deserts and distant mountains. They have something to tell us, just as the fallen heroes who lie in Arlington whisper through the ages.

We honor them not only because they are the guardians of our liberty, but because they embody the spirit of service—a willingness to find meaning in something greater than themselves.

And yet at this moment, a moment that will define a generation, it is precisely this spirit that must inhabit us all. For as much as government can do, and must do, it is ultimately the faith and determination of the American people upon which this nation relies. It is the kindness to take in a stranger when the levees break, the selflessness of workers who would rather cut their hours than see a friend lose their job which sees us through our darkest hours. It is the firefighter's courage to storm a stairway filled with smoke, but also a parent's willingness to nurture a child that finally decides our fate.

Our challenges may be new. The instruments with which we meet them may be new. But those values upon which our success depends—honesty and hard work, courage and fair play, tolerance and curiosity, loyalty and patriotism—these things are old. These things are true. They have been the quiet force of progress throughout our history.

What is demanded, then, is a return to these truths. What is required of us now is a new era of responsibility—a recognition on the part of every American that we have duties to ourselves, our nation and the world; duties that we do not grudgingly accept, but rather seize gladly, firm in the knowledge that there is nothing so satisfying to the spirit, so defining of our character than giving our all to a difficult task.

This is the price and the promise of citizenship. This is the source of our confidence—the knowledge that God calls on us to shape an uncertain destiny. This is the meaning of our liberty and our creed, why men and women and children of every race and every faith can join in celebration across this magnificent mall; and why a man whose father less than 60 years ago might not have been served in a local restaurant can now stand before you to take a most sacred oath.

So let us mark this day with remembrance of who we are and how far we have traveled. In the year of America's birth, in the coldest of months, a small band of patriots huddled by dying campfires on the shores of an icy river. The capital was abandoned. The enemy was advancing. The snow was stained with blood. At the moment when the outcome of our revolution was most in doubt, the father of our nation ordered these words to be read to the people:

> "Let it be told to the future world . . . that in the depth of winter, when nothing but hope and virtue could survive . . . that the city and the country, alarmed at one common danger, came forth to meet [it]."

America: In the face of our common dangers, in this winter of our hardship, let us remember these timeless words. With hope and virtue, let us brave once more the icy currents, and endure what storms may come. Let it be said by our children's children that when we were tested we refused to let this journey end, that we did not turn back nor did we falter; and with eyes fixed on the horizon and God's grace upon us, we carried forth that great gift of freedom and delivered it safely to future generations.

Thank you. God bless you. And God bless the United States of America.

A New Birth of Freedom

THE FIRST INAUGURAL ADDRESS OF BARACK OBAMA

Tracy Denean Sharpley-Whiting

BARACK OBAMA'S SPEECHES in the run-up to his inauguration in January 2009 were a brew of soaring oration, Aristotelian rhetoric, and elements of the Black Jeremiad. Authors such as Frederick Douglass, with his "What to the Slave Is the Fourth of July?" (1852), Martin Luther King, Jr.'s speech "The Other America" (1967), James Baldwin's epistolary *The Fire Next Time*, and Jeremiah Wright's social gospel-infused sermons were parts of a canon of literature and performance that gave intellectual form and substance to Obama's oratorical stylings and rhetorical grace. His campaign had used variations of a hope and change motto, while the candidate himself embodied a multiracial America, brimming with expectancy and possibility. And yet, his First Inaugural Address was decidedly understated. Barack Obama appeared to have taken clearer-eyed stock of the moment.

On Tuesday, January 20, besides his inauguration, the nation was also celebrating the 200th-year anniversary of the birth of America's sixteenth president, Abraham Lincoln. Lincoln, the Great Emancipator and uniter in post–Civil War America, had always figured centrally as a point of political comparison and emulation for the Democratic president-elect. Springfield, Illinois, was where both Lincoln and then Senator Obama served as state lawmakers and where the late Republican president delivered his 1858 "A House Divided" speech. And Springfield, rather than his adopted hometown of Chicago, was where Barack Obama announced his candidacy for the presidency. As Lincoln's 1858 speech, as well as his two subsequent Inaugural Addresses of 1861 and 1865 had, Obama's First Inaugural Address broached the themes of unity, war, healing, reconciliation, and rebirth. Despite his having garnered over 65 million votes, the most in a presidential election at that time, an Electoral College rout of 365 votes, and an approval rating of 67 percent that January, America's house at the start of 2009 was ablaze and surreptitious partisan chicanery was afoot. Obama would need to rally the nation after a hard-fought and hard-won election, remind them of the guiding principle of *E pluribus unum*.

Before taking the podium, Obama took a commemorative train ride from Philadelphia, Pennsylvania, to Washington, D.C., in honor of Lincoln. Philadelphia, "The City of Brotherly Love," had also played host to Obama's campaign-saving speech on race: "A More Perfect Union." In many respects, his First Inaugural Address picked up where "A More Perfect Union" left off. America's forty-fourth president, a mixed-race man who identifies as African American, understood his journey as improbable when he offered that his "father less than sixty years ago might not have been served in the local restaurant." But there he was now "stand[ing] before you to take a most sacred oath" on "this magnificent mall" with "men and women and children of every race and every faith . . . every language and culture, drawn from every end of this Earth. . . . Christians and Muslims, Jews and Hindus, and non-believers." That what was improbable became possible is, for Obama, a uniquely American story, "the meaning of our liberty and our creed." The American experiment of democracy is necessarily bound up with this braided history. In his recounting of the diversity of the American experience, of those who "traveled across oceans in search of a new life . . . toiled in sweatshops, and settled the West, endured the lash of the whip, and plowed the hard earth," one hears echoes of Langston Hughes's "I Too Sing America" and Walt Whitman's "I Hear America Singing." And in a few subtle rhetorical moves, he makes short work of the oversimplified idea of America as a Christian nation of voluntary immigrants. Barack Obama is only the second president in an inaugural address to concede the "peculiar and powerful interest," as Lincoln so eloquently remarked in his Second Inaugural Address, of enslaved Blacks as involuntary arrivals on America's shores at its founding. He is also the only president to recognize atheists and agnostics alike in an inaugural address.

Obama had inherited a nation at a bleak crossroads, "amidst gathering clouds and raging storms." His lesson on our "patchwork heritage" as a signal call to unity, as a benchmark of "our strength," was the address's prelude to realism, his ticking off of the dire predicament in which the country found itself. America was enmeshed in two seemingly never-ending wars in Afghanistan and Iraq, the latter of which he had given a full-throated denunciation of as a "dumb war" in 2002 as an Illinois state senator. Rejecting as "false the choice between our safety and our ideals . . . the rule of law and rights of man," Obama argued that "our security" emanates from "the justness of our cause." Unapologetic with respect to America's "way of life" and unwavering in "its defense," he was nonetheless unsparing in his criticism of the previous administration's squandering of America's resources and use of "power" as unaligned with "the justness of our cause" and "the tempering qualities of humility and restraint." If wars abroad proved fiscally imprudent and morally dubious, "greed and irresponsibility" ravaged the domestic economy whose automotive, banking, and other financial institutions were on the brink of collapse. Failing schools and "[t]oo costly" healthcare rounded out the new president's litany of indicators of crises. The indices pointed to a "nagging fear that America's decline is inevitable."

Obama demanded that Americans marshal their collective strength. In looking backward, he cast the war over slavery and secession and its deleterious aftermath of segregation as one of America's greatest challenges. For having "tasted the bitter swill of civil war and segregation," a rebirthed nation "emerged from that dark chapter stronger and more united," he assured his audience. Obama walks his listeners even further back in America's history to its birth, where "patriots huddled ... on the shores of an icy river," while "the enemy advance[ed]" as evidence of Americans' strength and solidarity. Here he turned to progressive pamphleteer Thomas Paine, whose inspirational words General George Washington would have read to his soldiers: "Let it be told to the future world ... that in the depth of winter, when nothing but hope and virtue could survive ... that the city and the country, alarmed at one common danger, came forth to meet [it]."

Given the hardships overcome during these watershed moments in American history, Obama understood that Americans could once again rise to these new challenges by leaning into the values of "honesty and hard work, courage and fair play, tolerance and curiosity, loyalty and patriotism .... [which] have been the quiet force of progress throughout our history." American exceptionalism, first articulated by Thomas Jefferson, is the sinewy thread throughout the address. And it is this exceptionalism that will compel Americans to "set aside childish things" that "strangled our politics" and sowed division. If American exceptionalism is the thread, then an indivisible America, not a red or a blue America, a theme that resonated throughout his campaign for the presidency, is the needle. Threading the needle, Obama forecasts to the global community that America will be "ready to lead once more."

"This election," he argued, represented a pivot in the American mind, the choosing of "hope over fear, unity of purpose over conflict and discord." But Barack Obama's election also ushered in a new and premature way of thinking about America as post-racial. Celebrated as the realization of a dream deferred, the actualization of our democratic ideals in practice, post-racial America was but a fever dream, ripe for the breaking. Reveling in America's promise and progress, "gathering clouds" were already on the horizon and swollen to bursting with the emergence of the Tea Party and an era of white grievances and tribalism.

Barack Obama's Second Inaugural Address

MONDAY, JANUARY 21, 2013

VICE PRESIDENT BIDEN, Mr. Chief Justice members of the United States Congress, distinguished guests, and fellow citizens:
Each time we gather to inaugurate a President we bear witness to the enduring strength of our Constitution. We affirm the promise of our democracy. We recall that what binds this nation together is not the colors of our skin or the tenets of our faith or the origins of our names. What makes us exceptional—what makes us American—is our allegiance to an idea articulated in a declaration made more than two centuries ago:

> We hold these truths to be self-evident, that all men are created equal; that they are endowed by their Creator with certain unalienable rights; that among these are life, liberty, and the pursuit of happiness.

Today we continue a never-ending journey to bridge the meaning of those words with the realities of our time. For history tells us that while these truths may be self-evident, they've never been self-executing; that while freedom is a gift from God, it must be secured by His people here on Earth. The patriots of 1776 did not fight to replace the tyranny of a king with the privileges of a few or the rule of a mob. They gave to us a republic, a government of, and by, and for the people, entrusting each generation to keep safe our founding creed.

And for more than two hundred years, we have.

Through blood drawn by lash and blood drawn by sword, we learned that no union founded on the principles of liberty and equality could survive half-slave and half-free. We made ourselves anew, and vowed to move forward together.

Together, we determined that a modern economy requires railroads and highways to speed travel and commerce, schools and colleges to train our workers.

Together, we discovered that a free market only thrives when there are rules to ensure competition and fair play.

Together, we resolved that a great nation must care for the vulnerable, and protect its people from life's worst hazards and misfortune.

Through it all, we have never relinquished our skepticism of central authority, nor have we succumbed to the fiction that all society's ills can be cured through government alone. Our celebration of initiative and enterprise, our insistence on hard work and personal responsibility, these are constants in our character.

But we have always understood that when times change, so must we; that fidelity to our founding principles requires new responses to new challenges; that preserving our individual freedoms ultimately requires collective action. For the American people can no more meet the demands of today's world by acting alone than American soldiers could have met the forces of fascism or communism with muskets and militias. No single person can train all the math and science teachers we'll need to equip our children for the future, or build the roads and networks and research labs that will bring new jobs and businesses to our shores. Now, more than ever, we must do these things together, as one nation and one people.

This generation of Americans has been tested by crises that steeled our resolve and proved our resilience. A decade of war is now ending. An economic recovery has begun. America's possibilities are limitless, for we possess all the qualities that this world without boundaries demands: youth and drive; diversity and openness; an endless capacity for risk and a gift for reinvention. My fellow Americans, we are made for this moment, and we will seize it—so long as we seize it together.

For we, the people, understand that our country cannot succeed when a shrinking few do very well and a growing many barely make it. We believe that America's prosperity must rest upon the broad shoulders of a rising middle class. We know that America thrives when every person can find independence and pride in their work; when the wages of honest labor liberate families from the brink of hardship. We are true to our creed when a little girl born into the bleakest poverty knows that she has the same chance to succeed as anybody else, because she is an American; she is free, and she is equal, not just in the eyes of God but also in our own.

We understand that outworn programs are inadequate to the needs of our time. So we must harness new ideas and technology to remake our government, revamp our tax code, reform our schools, and empower our citizens with the skills they need to work harder, learn more, reach higher. But while the means will change, our purpose endures: a nation that rewards the effort and determination of every single American. That is what this moment requires. That is what will give real meaning to our creed.

We, the people, still believe that every citizen deserves a basic measure of security and dignity. We must make the hard choices to reduce the cost of health care and the size of our deficit. But we reject the belief that America must choose between caring for the generation that built this country and investing in the generation that will build its future. For we remember the lessons of our past, when twilight years were spent in poverty and parents of a child with a disability had nowhere to turn.

We do not believe that in this country freedom is reserved for the lucky, or happiness for the few. We recognize that no matter how responsibly we live our lives, any one of us at any time may face a job loss, or a sudden illness, or a home swept away in a terrible storm. The commitments we make to each other through Medicare and Medicaid and Social Security, these things do not sap our initiative, they strengthen us. They do not make us a nation of takers; they free us to take the risks that make this country great.

We, the people, still believe that our obligations as Americans are not just to ourselves, but to all posterity. We will respond to the threat of climate change, knowing that the failure to do so would betray our children and future generations. Some may still deny the overwhelming judgment of science, but none can avoid the devastating impact of raging fires and crippling drought and more powerful storms.

The path towards sustainable energy sources will be long and sometimes difficult. But America cannot resist this transition, we must lead it. We cannot cede to other nations the technology that will power new jobs and new industries, we must claim its promise. That's how we will maintain our economic vitality and our national treasure—our forests and waterways, our crop lands and snow-capped peaks. That is how we will preserve our planet, commanded to our care by God. That's what will lend meaning to the creed our fathers once declared.

We, the people, still believe that enduring security and lasting peace do not require perpetual war. Our brave men and women in uniform, tempered by the flames of battle, are unmatched in skill and courage. Our citizens, seared by the memory of those we have lost, know too well the price that is paid for liberty. The knowledge of their sacrifice will keep us forever vigilant against those who would do us harm. But we are also heirs to those who won the peace and not just the war; who turned sworn enemies into the surest of friends—and we must carry those lessons into this time as well.

We will defend our people and uphold our values through strength of arms and rule of law. We will show the courage to try and resolve our differences with other nations peacefully—not because we are naïve about the dangers we face, but because engagement can more durably lift suspicion and fear.

America will remain the anchor of strong alliances in every corner of the globe. And we will renew those institutions that extend our capacity to manage crisis abroad, for no one has a greater stake in a peaceful world than its most powerful nation. We will support democracy from Asia to Africa, from the Americas to the Middle East, because our interests and our conscience compel us to act on behalf of those who long for freedom. And we must be a source of hope to the poor, the sick, the marginalized, the victims of prejudice—not out of mere charity, but because peace in our time requires the constant advance of those principles that our common creed describes: tolerance and opportunity, human dignity and justice.

We, the people, declare today that the most evident of truths—that all of us are created equal—is the star that guides us still; just as it guided our forebears through Seneca Falls, and Selma, and Stonewall; just as it guided all those men and women, sung and unsung, who left footprints along this great Mall, to hear a preacher say that we cannot walk alone; to hear a King proclaim that our individual freedom is inextricably bound to the freedom of every soul on Earth.

It is now our generation's task to carry on what those pioneers began. For our journey is not complete until our wives, our mothers and daughters can earn a living equal to their efforts. Our journey is not complete until our gay brothers and sisters are treated like anyone else under the law for if we are truly created equal, then surely the love we commit to one another must be equal as well. Our journey is not complete until no citizen is forced to wait for hours to exercise the right to vote. Our journey is not complete until we find a better way to welcome the striving, hopeful immigrants who still see America as a land of opportunity until bright young students and engineers are enlisted in our workforce rather than expelled from our country. Our journey is not complete until all our children, from the streets of Detroit to the hills of Appalachia, to the quiet lanes of Newtown, know that they are cared for and cherished and always safe from harm.

That is our generation's task—to make these words, these rights, these values of life and liberty and the pursuit of happiness real for every American. Being true to our founding documents does not require us to agree on every contour of life. It does not mean we all define liberty in exactly the same way or follow the same precise path to happiness. Progress does not compel us to settle centuries-long debates about the role of government for all time, but it does require us to act in our time.

For now decisions are upon us and we cannot afford delay. We cannot mistake absolutism for principle, or substitute spectacle for politics, or treat name-calling as reasoned debate. We must act, knowing that our work will be imperfect. We must act, knowing that today's victories will be only partial and that it will be up to those who stand here in four years and 40 years and 400 years hence to advance the timeless spirit once conferred to us in a spare Philadelphia hall.

My fellow Americans, the oath I have sworn before you today, like the one recited by others who serve in this Capitol, was an oath to God and country, not party or faction. And we must faithfully execute that pledge during the duration of our service. But the words I spoke today are not so different from the oath that is taken each time a soldier signs up for duty or an immigrant realizes her dream. My oath is not so different from the pledge we all make to the flag that waves above and that fills our hearts with pride.

They are the words of citizens and they represent our greatest hope. You and I, as citizens, have the power to set this country's course. You and I, as citizens, have the obligation to shape the debates of our time—not only with the votes we cast, but with the voices we lift in defense of our most ancient values and enduring ideals.

Let us, each of us, now embrace with solemn duty and awesome joy what is our lasting birthright. With common effort and common purpose, with passion and dedication, let us answer the call of history and carry into an uncertain future that precious light of freedom.

Thank you. God bless you, and may He forever bless these United States of America.

Faith in America's Future

THE SECOND INAUGURAL ADDRESS OF BARACK OBAMA

James T. Kloppenberg

BARACK OBAMA'S SECOND Inaugural Address invokes Thomas Jefferson's Declaration of Independence and Abraham Lincoln's Second Inaugural in support of principles and policies that Obama championed from his first political campaigns. Obama entered public life as a community organizer in the impoverished Far South Side of Chicago, where he worked with a network of progressive religious activists to address glaring inequalities. His first electoral victory put him in the Illinois State Senate, where he struggled to forge compromises and address partisan gerrymandering. His 2004 speech at the Democratic National Convention, which stressed Americans' unity at a time of increasingly stark divisions, launched his rapid, unlikely ascent from obscurity to the U.S. Senate in 2004 and the presidency just four years later. In 2012, re-elected by a smaller margin than in 2008 and confronting an increasingly hostile Republican majority in Congress, he delivered an inaugural address that showed his debts to the American democratic tradition and highlighted the distinctiveness of his sensibility.

For Obama, liberty always meant more than freedom from constraint. The libertarian idea of freedom, doing whatever an individual wants to do, has dominated Republican party ideology ever since Ronald Reagan declared government the "problem" in his First Inaugural. Instead, Obama contends that freedom, consistent with the tradition of "ordered liberty" central to American political thought since the seventeenth century, is always bounded by law. Individuals exercise their liberty when they act according to ethical maxims and within legal guidelines, not when they follow their preferences, or their impulses, regardless of the consequences for others. For Obama, freedom is but an empty promise when individuals lack the means to develop their capacities. In his book *The Audacity of Hope*, Obama embraced the principles that Franklin D. Roosevelt articulated in his final campaign for the presidency in 1944, a "second bill of rights" that includes the right to a job, food, clothing, housing, healthcare, education, and insurance against the hazards of unemployment and old age. When Obama proclaims that "preserving our individual freedoms ultimately requires collective action," he has in mind securing individuals' freedom to fulfill their potential, not freedom from government. He calls for the nation to shoulder its responsibilities to "care for the vulnerable," to guard everyone from "life's worst hazards and misfortune," and to secure for all citizens "a basic measure of security and dignity."

Equality, as Obama understands it, requires more than equal protection before the law, crucial as that principle is. Like Benjamin Franklin, John Adams, Thomas Jefferson, and James Madison, Obama insists that "our country cannot succeed when a shrinking few do very well and a growing many barely make it." The nation's eighteenth-century founders believed that the rough equality of condition enjoyed by American men—with the glaring exceptions of dispossessed Indigenous people and enslaved Black people—not only distinguished the democratic United States from European monarchies, with their traditions of inherited aristocratic privilege, but it also made possible self-government. Like those earlier champions of democracy, Obama argues for a system of taxation in which the amount owed to the community increases along with the wealth derived from the conditions secured, and the laws enacted, by that community. Working from the premise that "all of us are created equal," Obama locates more recent campaigns for equality, regardless of gender, race, or sexual preference, in the tradition of earlier struggles against white male supremacy waged by abolitionists and advocates of woman suffrage.

Much as Americans celebrate "initiative and enterprise," and productive as America's market economy has been, Obama argues that the economy "thrives" for all only when it "rewards the effort and determination of every single American." He rejects the neoliberal idea that increasing innovation and productivity require lavish compensation for some, while others cannot escape "the brink of hardship," let alone "find independence and pride in their work." Although Obama denies that "all society's ills can be cured through government alone," he rejects the shibboleth that all economic regulation is an illegitimate intrusion. Government has set the rules for the marketplace since the eighteenth century, and the nation's greatest economic growth came through establishing "rules to ensure competition and fair play." When conditions are as unequal as they are in twenty-first-century America, the idea of equal opportunity, like the abstract idea of purely negative freedom from constraints, rings hollow.

Obama also departs from some aspects of earlier American political thought. He denies the existence of uniquely privileged perspectives and universal, unchanging truths. Shaped by late twentieth-century ideas of anti-foundationalism, cultural anthropology, historicism, and philosophical pragmatism, Obama insists that we must not "mistake absolutism for principle." From his point of view, all ideas should be seen as cultural creations that reflect particular historical circumstances. The meaning of abstract principles such as liberty, equality, and democracy changes over time. Every generation must interpret the Constitution, the living law that "We the People" authorized and possess the power to amend. We must make persuasive arguments based on our values, rather than venerating the document as sacred writ. Earlier Americans of European descent took for granted their right to possess lands occupied by Indigenous people and their superiority to women and non-white people, assumptions about white male supremacy that most Americans now question. For centuries, many Americans failed to recognize the need to preserve and protect rather than simply exploit the natural resources of the continent. Now, Obama observes, the hard fact of climate change requires us to develop "sustainable energy sources" to "preserve our planet."

Finally, Obama accepts not only the inevitability of different points of view, but also the potentially productive quality of disagreement. We must not "substitute spectacle for politics" or allow "name-calling" to take the place of "reasoned debate," because deliberation is the lifeblood of democracy. Americans need not understand liberty, equality, and the role of government in exactly the same way in order to respect, debate with, and learn from each other. Self-rule does not require consensus. It demands only reverence for the rule of law, a commitment to marshaling evidence in support of arguments, reliance on persuasion rather than violence, and a willingness to acknowledge our own limitations. Obama concedes that he does not have all the answers; he admits "that our work will be imperfect." That epistemic humility, which has inspired his admirers and frustrated his critics on the left as well as the right, has from the start been integral to Obama's understanding of American democracy.

Donald Trump's Inaugural Address

FRIDAY, JANUARY 20, 2017

CHIEF JUSTICE ROBERTS, *President Carter, President Clinton, President Bush, President Obama, fellow Americans, and people of the world:* thank you.

We, the citizens of America, are now joined in a great national effort to rebuild our country and to restore its promise for all of our people.

Together, we will determine the course of America and the world for years to come.

We will face challenges. We will confront hardships. But we will get the job done.

Every four years, we gather on these steps to carry out the orderly and peaceful transfer of power, and we are grateful to President Obama and First Lady Michelle Obama for their gracious aid throughout this transition. They have been magnificent.

Today's ceremony, however, has very special meaning. Because today we are not merely transferring power from one Administration to another, or from one party to another—but we are transferring power from Washington, DC and giving it back to you, the American People.

For too long, a small group in our nation's Capital has reaped the rewards of government while the people have borne the cost.

Washington flourished—but the people did not share in its wealth.

Politicians prospered—but the jobs left, and the factories closed.

The establishment protected itself, but not the citizens of our country.

Their victories have not been your victories; their triumphs have not been your triumphs; and while they celebrated in our nation's Capital, there was little to celebrate for struggling families all across our land.

That all changes—starting right here, and right now, because this moment is your moment: it belongs to you.

It belongs to everyone gathered here today and everyone watching all across America.

This is your day. This is your celebration.

And this, the United States of America, is your country.

What truly matters is not which party controls our government, but whether our government is controlled by the people.

January 20th 2017, will be remembered as the day the people became the rulers of this nation again.

The forgotten men and women of our country will be forgotten no longer.

Everyone is listening to you now.

You came by the tens of millions to become part of a historic movement the likes of which the world has never seen before.

At the center of this movement is a crucial conviction: that a nation exists to serve its citizens.

Americans want great schools for their children, safe neighborhoods for their families, and good jobs for themselves.

These are the just and reasonable demands of a righteous public.

But for too many of our citizens, a different reality exists: Mothers and children trapped in poverty in our inner cities; rusted-out factories scattered like tombstones across the landscape of our nation; an education system, flush with cash, but which leaves our young and beautiful students deprived of knowledge; and the crime and gangs and drugs that have stolen too many lives and robbed our country of so much unrealized potential.

This American carnage stops right here and stops right now.

We are one nation—and their pain is our pain. Their dreams are our dreams; and their success will be our success. We share one heart, one home, and one glorious destiny.

The oath of office I take today is an oath of allegiance to all Americans.

For many decades, we've enriched foreign industry at the expense of American industry;

Subsidized the armies of other countries while allowing for the very sad depletion of our military;

We've defended other nation's borders while refusing to defend our own;

And spent trillions of dollars overseas while America's infrastructure has fallen into disrepair and decay.

We've made other countries rich while the wealth, strength, and confidence of our country has disappeared over the horizon.

One by one, the factories shuttered and left our shores, with not even a thought about the millions upon millions of American workers left behind.

The wealth of our middle class has been ripped from their homes and then redistributed across the entire world.

But that is the past. And now we are looking only to the future.

We assembled here today are issuing a new decree to be heard in every city, in every foreign capital, and in every hall of power.

From this day forward, a new vision will govern our land.

From this moment on, it's going to be America First.

Every decision on trade, on taxes, on immigration, on foreign affairs, will be made to benefit American workers and American families.

We must protect our borders from the ravages of other countries making our products, stealing our companies, and destroying our jobs. Protection will lead to great prosperity and strength.

I will fight for you with every breath in my body—and I will never, ever let you down.

America will start winning again, winning like never before.

We will bring back our jobs. We will bring back our borders. We will bring back our wealth. And we will bring back our dreams.

We will build new roads, and highways, and bridges, and airports, and tunnels, and railways all across our wonderful nation.

We will get our people off of welfare and back to work—rebuilding our country with American hands and American labor.

We will follow two simple rules: Buy American and Hire American.

We will seek friendship and goodwill with the nations of the world—but we do so with the understanding that it is the right of all nations to put their own interests first.

We do not seek to impose our way of life on anyone, but rather to let it shine as an example for everyone to follow.

We will reinforce old alliances and form new ones—and unite the civilized world against radical Islamic terrorism, which we will eradicate completely from the face of the Earth.

At the bedrock of our politics will be a total allegiance to the United States of America, and through our loyalty to our country, we will rediscover our loyalty to each other.

When you open your heart to patriotism, there is no room for prejudice.

The Bible tells us, "how good and pleasant it is when God's people live together in unity."

We must speak our minds openly, debate our disagreements honestly, but always pursue solidarity.

When America is united, America is totally unstoppable.

There should be no fear—we are protected, and we will always be protected.

We will be protected by the great men and women of our military and law enforcement and, most importantly, we are protected by God.

Finally, we must think big and dream even bigger.

In America, we understand that a nation is only living as long as it is striving.

We will no longer accept politicians who are all talk and no action—constantly complaining but never doing anything about it.

The time for empty talk is over.

Now arrives the hour of action.

Do not let anyone tell you it cannot be done. No challenge can match the heart and fight and spirit of America.

We will not fail. Our country will thrive and prosper again.

We stand at the birth of a new millennium, ready to unlock the mysteries of space, to free the Earth from the miseries of disease, and to harness the energies, industries and technologies of tomorrow.

A new national pride will stir our souls, lift our sights, and heal our divisions.

It is time to remember that old wisdom our soldiers will never forget: that whether we are black or brown or white, we all bleed the same red blood of patriots, we all enjoy the same glorious freedoms, and we all salute the same great American flag.

And whether a child is born in the urban sprawl of Detroit or the windswept plains of Nebraska, they look up at the same night sky, they fill their heart with the same dreams, and they are infused with the breath of life by the same almighty Creator.

So to all Americans, in every city near and far, small and large, from mountain to mountain, and from ocean to ocean, hear these words:

You will never be ignored again.

Your voice, your hopes, and your dreams, will define our American destiny. And your courage and goodness and love will forever guide us along the way.

Together, we *will* Make America Strong Again.

We *will* Make America Wealthy Again.

We *will* Make America Proud Again.

We *will* Make America Safe Again.

And, yes, together, we *will* Make America Great Again. Thank you, God bless you, and God bless America.

Uniquely American

THE INAUGURAL ADDRESS OF DONALD TRUMP

Nicholas F. Jacobs

THE MORNING OF Friday, January 20, 2017, began as one might expect. The peaceful and orderly transition of presidential power to the forty-fifth president, Donald John Trump, contained all the pomp and circumstance of the traditional Washingtonian affair: morning church services at St. John's Episcopal Church across from the White House, followed by tea with the Obamas; the incoming and outgoing presidents shared a motorcade down Pennsylvania Avenue to the Capitol. In the aftermath of one of the most bitterly contested elections in American history, featuring two of the most historically disliked candidates for office, Trump's Inauguration Day festivities seemed to clamor for a return to normalcy. Welcoming the crowds that had gathered on the Mall to hear the new president speak, Senator Roy Blunt echoed all the trappings of the day's symbolic importance, quoting Jefferson, Lincoln, Franklin Roosevelt, Kennedy, and Reagan in a quick three-minute speech. After all, he argued, presidential inaugurals were "not a celebration of victory, but a celebration of democracy," that every American could, and should, honor.

But as he had done so many times before, Trump shattered those expectations. For the newly sworn in president, Inauguration Day—politics in general—was only ever about winning. Trump had built a personal brand around the idea that in life, as in business, there are only winners or losers. As president, he was to be no loser.

Trump won the Electoral College, although he lost the popular vote by 2.8 million ballots. No matter, this was a day when "the people" would "start winning again, winning like never before." Standing before former presidents, congressional leaders, and other long-serving political dignitaries, Trump spoke about "their victories," but echoed his campaign's central refrain that "their triumphs have not been your triumphs."

Contemporaneous accounts of Trump's speech use a variety of adjectives to describe his message: unprecedented, dismal, nationalist, authoritarian, populist. But more than anything else, the simplistic and unadorned notion of "winning" defines the address, as it defines so much of Trump's public philosophy: the purpose of government is to help those that win, and to help them keep winning; winners get to rule and losers must accept their fate; especially in the global arena, Americans must win first. Despite his speech's relative simplicity and brevity, this single idea captures much about the state of American politics on the eve of Trump's inaugural, and what the next four years under a Trump administration would bring. There were winners and losers in politics—no middle ground.

Steve Bannon, one of the architects of Trump's campaign and likely coauthor of the speech, often commented that its anti-establishment rhetoric and disdain for convention were in homage to Andrew Jackson's grassroots assault on America's governing institutions in the 1830s. In this view, Trump was tapping into a deep history of populist protest, led by strong presidents. Trump's speech, however, was decidedly modern. Even Jackson's inaugural referenced the Constitution, and the limits it contained on executive power; even Jackson gave "reverence" for "the examples of public virtue left by my illustrious predecessors." For Trump, compromise, moderation, and restraint were not ancient virtues, but rather outdated excuses made by "a small group in our nation's Capital," the real victors, who perpetually "reaped the rewards of government while the people have borne the cost."

Trump styled himself as a leader of a new movement—a movement, ironically, of losers. In the days leading up to the inaugural, Trump supporters celebrated at "DeploraBalls"—galas named in homage to Hillary Clinton's off-the-cuff remark that most of her electoral opponents' supporters could be placed in what she liked to call "the basket of deplorables." On the campaign trail, as in his inaugural, Trump described the communities in which his movement thrived as one in a state of permanent decline: "trapped in poverty," "deprived of knowledge," "robbed . . . of unrealized potential," the victims of "American carnage." Unlike other catastrophes that elevated presidents to office and motivated their calls to unity, Trump portrayed this crisis as one purposely and deliberately constructed by a ruling class, and which disproportionately affected his followers, the "righteous public."

For most of those listening to Donald Trump's address, this was, perhaps, an unrecognizable image of their country. But, to those who voted for Trump, there was enough truth in his message to catapult him into office. As Hillary Clinton would pointedly recognize two years after losing, "I won the places that represent two-thirds of America's gross domestic product. So I won the places that are optimistic, diverse, dynamic, moving forward, and his whole campaign, 'make America great again.' was looking backwards."[1] Trump won, in other words, the losers in the new global economy. Trump won because he blamed the recognizable, if simplistic, problems of open borders, immigrants, racial antagonisms, China's unfair business practices, and a ruling elite who profited from the arrangement, including, and perhaps most importantly, members of his own Republican party. Of course, poor Americans also voted for Clinton as did the wealthy vote for Trump, but Clinton's comments are a testament to the bipartisan legitimacy bestowed on Trump's self-serving idea of a deeply fractured America. Whether it was objectively true is largely beside the point. Perceptions are what counts in politics, and Trump seemed to understand that more than most of his opponents were willing to concede.

The administration's obsession with the image of winning defined its governing approach from the start. Trump became the first president to formally declare his re-election campaign on Inauguration Day. Barely twenty-four hours had passed before the White House called its first press conference to accuse the media of intentionally portraying the new president as a loser, because the crowds at his inauguration were visibly smaller than those of the Women's March on Washington—a rally drawing hundreds of thousands held the day after Inauguration Day, largely in protest of the new president's perceived hostility to reproductive rights and gender equality. The president's chief political advisor and former campaign manager, Kellyanne Conway, gave an unvarnished view of the White House's decision to challenge the reporting. Conway's claim that the administration simply gave "alternative facts" to the media's narrative captured the political double-speak or absurdity of the false numbers the White House produced about TV ratings and attendance. Even more, it was demonstrable proof of Trump's demand that he be seen as a winner. And winners do not have fewer attendees at their inaugural than the president he supposedly repudiated.

Throughout his term, the former reality TV star's actions fit the pattern he established on Inauguration Day. He bragged about large crowds and maintained an exhausting schedule of rallies that crisscrossed the nation—a "thank you tour" that he continued even after he took the oath of office. He intentionally refused to play to presidential expectations—from shrugging off questions about whether he would use his powers to go after political opponents, to refusing to condemn white supremacists in the aftermath of neo-Nazi demonstrations in Charlottesville, Virginia. No matter his personal sympathies, any other course of action would have suggested that somebody had power over what the president could or should say. That is how losers talk.

Accepting the party's nomination at the Republican National Convention in 2016, he declared that he "alone" could fix America's ailments. Whereas other presidents had downplayed the degree to which they relied on executive authority, Trump staged carefully choreographed media ops for almost every executive order he signed, always lifting them up for the cameras to capture his bold signature at the bottom of the page. He signed his first, a largely symbolic order to undermine the implementation of the Affordable Care Act, known popularly as Obamacare, just after his inaugural parade ended. Throughout his campaign, Trump promised to "Make America Great Again"—not wealthier, more equal, or run with smaller government. Understanding that "greatness" is always in the eye of the beholder, Trump's approach to the presidency reflected the orientation of an image-obsessed brand-builder. On June 1, 2020, Trump returned to St. John's Church in the midst of nationwide protests against systemic racism and police violence—an extraordinary moment of public reckoning that the promise of American greatness demands that we address these enduring challenges. In contrast, and after ordering the National Guard to disperse peaceful protestors with tear gas, Trump invited the press to photograph him holding up a Bible in front of the damaged church—the image of a president in control, and winning.

Almost four years to the day of Donald Trump's Inaugural Address, on January 6, 2021, the president returned to the National Mall, this time in front of the White House as the Congress convened to certify the electoral victory of Joe Biden. For weeks, the president and his allies had concocted every conceivable tale of fraud and twisted every possibility of voting irregularity to prop up the myth that he was the true winner. "We won in a landslide," he repeated, "This was a landslide. They said it's not American to challenge the election. This [is] the most corrupt election in the history, maybe of the world. With your help over the last four years, we built the greatest political movement in the history of our country and nobody even challenges that. We fight like hell. And if you don't fight like hell, you're not going to have a country anymore."[2]

As the president spoke to his followers, rioters—convinced that they could not have rightfully lost—broke through barriers and stormed the Capitol building. They climbed the scaffolding erected for Biden's inaugural address and raced through the halls to track down members of Congress. Perhaps more than any of his predecessors, Trump revealed the power of the president's words. And he made history with those words—the first president to actively use his powers to sow distrust and overturn the constitutional process for ensuring a peaceful transition of power, the first president to actively court a movement to "fight like hell" to win at all costs, even if it meant violence against the government.

When President Biden delivered his Inaugural Address, he did so in an occupied Capitol city, behind rows of soldiers, barbed wire, metal fences, and unprecedented levels of security. Donald Trump envisioned a nation at war with itself—between winners and losers. Despite losing himself, his imprint on the next administration remains clearly visible. His brand of politics—an unvarnished and unequivocal tribalism—may come to define this era of American governance. It will be up to future presidents, through their actions and their words, to recognize the great task the Constitution demands of its political leaders. It remains as true today as it was when George Washington first took the oath of office that the "preservation of the sacred fire of liberty and the destiny of the republican model of government are justly considered, perhaps, as deeply, as finally staked on the experiment entrusted to the hands of the American people."

Notes

1. "Hillary's New Stat: I Won Districts Representing 2/3 of U.S. GDP," Axios, March 13, 2018, retrieved from https://www.axios.com/2018/03/13/hillary-clinton-india-two-thirds-gdp-trump.
2. "Transcript of Trump's Speech at Rally before US Capitol Riot," AP NEWS, January 13, 2021, retrieved from https://apnews.com/article/election-2020-joe-biden-donald-trump-capitol-siege-media-e79eb5164613d6718e9f4502eb471f27.

Joe Biden's Inaugural Address

WEDNESDAY, JANUARY 20, 2021

CHIEF JUSTICE ROBERTS, *Vice President Harris, Speaker Pelosi, Leader Schumer, Leader McConnell, Vice President Pence, distinguished guests, and my fellow Americans.*

This is America's day.

This is democracy's day.

A day of history and hope.

Of renewal and resolve.

Through a crucible for the ages America has been tested anew and America has risen to the challenge.

Today, we celebrate the triumph not of a candidate, but of a cause, the cause of democracy.

The will of the people has been heard and the will of the people has been heeded.

We have learned again that democracy is precious.

Democracy is fragile.

And at this hour, my friends, democracy has prevailed.

So now, on this hallowed ground where just days ago violence sought to shake this Capitol's very foundation, we come together as one nation, under God, indivisible, to carry out the peaceful transfer of power as we have for more than two centuries.

We look ahead in our uniquely American way—restless, bold, optimistic—and set our sights on the nation we know we can be and we must be.

I thank my predecessors of both parties for their presence here.

I thank them from the bottom of my heart.

You know the resilience of our Constitution and the strength of our nation.

As does President Carter, who I spoke to last night but who cannot be with us today, but whom we salute for his lifetime of service.

I have just taken the sacred oath each of these patriots took—an oath first sworn by George Washington.

But the American story depends not on any one of us, not on some of us, but on all of us.

On "We the People" who seek a more perfect Union.

This is a great nation and we are a good people.

Over the centuries through storm and strife, in peace and in war, we have come so far. But we still have far to go.

We will press forward with speed and urgency, for we have much to do in this winter of peril and possibility.

Much to repair.

Much to restore.

Much to heal.

Much to build.

And much to gain.

Few periods in our nation's history have been more challenging or difficult than the one we're in now.

A once-in-a-century virus silently stalks the country.

It's taken as many lives in one year as America lost in all of World War II.

Millions of jobs have been lost.

Hundreds of thousands of businesses closed.

A cry for racial justice some 400 years in the making moves us. The dream of justice for all will be deferred no longer.

A cry for survival comes from the planet itself. A cry that can't be any more desperate or any more clear.

And now, a rise in political extremism, white supremacy, domestic terrorism that we must confront and we will defeat.

To overcome these challenges—to restore the soul and to secure the future of America—requires more than words.

It requires that most elusive of things in a democracy:

Unity.

Unity.

In another January in Washington, on New Year's Day 1863, Abraham Lincoln signed the Emancipation Proclamation.

When he put pen to paper, the President said, "If my name ever goes down into history it will be for this act and my whole soul is in it."

My whole soul is in it.

Today, on this January day, my whole soul is in this:
Bringing America together.
Uniting our people.
And uniting our nation.
I ask every American to join me in this cause.
Uniting to fight the common foes we face:
Anger, resentment, hatred.
Extremism, lawlessness, violence.
Disease, joblessness, hopelessness.
With unity we can do great things. Important things.
We can right wrongs.
We can put people to work in good jobs.
We can teach our children in safe schools.
We can overcome this deadly virus.

We can reward work, rebuild the middle class, and make health care secure for all.

We can deliver racial justice.

We can make America, once again, the leading force for good in the world.

I know speaking of unity can sound to some like a foolish fantasy.

I know the forces that divide us are deep and they are real.

But I also know they are not new.

Our history has been a constant struggle between the American ideal that we are all created equal and the harsh, ugly reality that racism, nativism, fear, and demonization have long torn us apart.

The battle is perennial.

Victory is never assured.

Through the Civil War, the Great Depression, World War, 9/11, through struggle, sacrifice, and setbacks, our "better angels" have always prevailed.

In each of these moments, enough of us came together to carry all of us forward.

And, we can do so now.

History, faith, and reason show the way, the way of unity.

We can see each other not as adversaries but as neighbors.

We can treat each other with dignity and respect.

We can join forces, stop the shouting, and lower the temperature.

For without unity, there is no peace, only bitterness and fury.

No progress, only exhausting outrage.

No nation, only a state of chaos.

This is our historic moment of crisis and challenge, and unity is the path forward.

And, we must meet this moment as the United States of America.

If we do that, I guarantee you, we will not fail.

We have never, ever, ever failed in America when we have acted together.

And so today, at this time and in this place, let us start afresh.

All of us.

Let us listen to one another.

Hear one another.

See one another.

Show respect to one another.

Politics need not be a raging fire destroying everything in its path.

Every disagreement doesn't have to be a cause for total war.

And, we must reject a culture in which facts themselves are manipulated and even manufactured.

My fellow Americans, we have to be different than this.

America has to be better than this.

And, I believe America is better than this.

Just look around.

Here we stand, in the shadow of a Capitol dome that was completed amid the Civil War, when the Union itself hung in the balance.

Yet we endured and we prevailed.

Here we stand looking out to the great Mall where Dr. King spoke of his dream.

Here we stand, where 108 years ago at another inaugural, thousands of protestors tried to block brave women from marching for the right to vote.

Today, we mark the swearing-in of the first woman in American history elected to national office—Vice President Kamala Harris.

Don't tell me things can't change.

Here we stand across the Potomac from Arlington National Cemetery, where heroes who gave the last full measure of devotion rest in eternal peace.

And here we stand, just days after a riotous mob thought they could use violence to silence the will of the people, to stop the work of our democracy, and to drive us from this sacred ground.

That did not happen.

It will never happen.

Not today.

Not tomorrow.

Not ever.

To all those who supported our campaign I am humbled by the faith you have placed in us.

To all those who did not support us, let me say this: Hear me out as we move forward. Take a measure of me and my heart.

And if you still disagree, so be it.

That's democracy. That's America. The right to dissent peaceably, within the guardrails of our Republic, is perhaps our nation's greatest strength.

Yet hear me clearly: Disagreement must not lead to disunion.

And I pledge this to you: I will be a President for all Americans.

I will fight as hard for those who did not support me as for those who did.

Many centuries ago, Saint Augustine, a saint of my church, wrote that a people was a multitude defined by the common objects of their love.

What are the common objects we love that define us as Americans?

I think I know.

Opportunity.

Security.

Liberty.

Dignity.

Respect.

Honor.

And, yes, the truth.

Recent weeks and months have taught us a painful lesson.

There is truth and there are lies.

Lies told for power and for profit.

And each of us has a duty and responsibility, as citizens, as Americans, and especially as leaders—leaders who have pledged to honor our Constitution and protect our nation—to defend the truth and to defeat the lies.

I understand that many Americans view the future with some fear and trepidation.

I understand they worry about their jobs, about taking care of their families, about what comes next.

I get it.

But the answer is not to turn inward, to retreat into competing factions, distrusting those who don't look like you do, or worship the way you do, or don't get their news from the same sources you do.

We must end this uncivil war that pits red against blue, rural versus urban, conservative versus liberal.

We can do this if we open our souls instead of hardening our hearts.

If we show a little tolerance and humility.

If we're willing to stand in the other person's shoes just for a moment.

Because here is the thing about life: There is no accounting for what fate will deal you.

There are some days when we need a hand.

There are other days when we're called on to lend one.

That is how we must be with one another.

And, if we are this way, our country will be stronger, more prosperous, more ready for the future.

My fellow Americans, in the work ahead of us, we will need each other.

We will need all our strength to persevere through this dark winter.

We are entering what may well be the toughest and deadliest period of the virus.

We must set aside the politics and finally face this pandemic as one nation.

I promise you this: as the Bible says weeping may endure for a night but joy cometh in the morning.

We will get through this, together.

The world is watching today.

So here is my message to those beyond our borders: America has been tested and we have come out stronger for it.

We will repair our alliances and engage with the world once again.

Not to meet yesterday's challenges, but today's and tomorrow's.

We will lead not merely by the example of our power but by the power of our example.

We will be a strong and trusted partner for peace, progress, and security.

We have been through so much in this nation.

And, in my first act as President, I would like to ask you to join me in a moment of silent prayer to remember all those we lost this past year to the pandemic.

To those 400,000 fellow Americans—mothers and fathers, husbands and wives, sons and daughters, friends, neighbors, and co-workers.

We will honor them by becoming the people and nation we know we can and should be.

Let us say a silent prayer for those who lost their lives, for those they left behind, and for our country.

Amen.

This is a time of testing.

We face an attack on democracy and on truth.

A raging virus.

Growing inequity.

The sting of systemic racism.

A climate in crisis.

America's role in the world.

Any one of these would be enough to challenge us in profound ways.

But the fact is we face them all at once, presenting this nation with the gravest of responsibilities.

Now we must step up.

All of us.
It is a time for boldness, for there is so much to do.
And, this is certain.
We will be judged, you and I, for how we resolve the cascading crises of our era.
Will we rise to the occasion?
Will we master this rare and difficult hour?
Will we meet our obligations and pass along a new and better world for our children?
I believe we must and I believe we will.
And when we do, we will write the next chapter in the American story.
It's a story that might sound something like a song that means a lot to me.
It's called "American Anthem" and there is one verse stands out for me:

> "The work and prayers
> of centuries have brought us to this day
> What shall be our legacy?
> What will our children say? . . .
> Let me know in my heart
> When my days are through
> America
> America
> I gave my best to you."

Let us add our own work and prayers to the unfolding story of our nation.
If we do this then when our days are through our children and our children's children will say of us they gave their best.
They did their duty.
They healed a broken land.
My fellow Americans, I close today where I began, with a sacred oath.
Before God and all of you I give you my word.
I will always level with you.
I will defend the Constitution.
I will defend our democracy.
I will defend America.
I will give my all in your service thinking not of power, but of possibilities.
Not of personal interest, but of the public good.
And together, we shall write an American story of hope, not fear.
Of unity, not division.
Of light, not darkness.
An American story of decency and dignity.

Of love and of healing.
Of greatness and of goodness.
May this be the story that guides us.
The story that inspires us.
The story that tells ages yet to come that we answered the call of history.
We met the moment.

That democracy and hope, truth and justice, did not die on our watch but thrived.

That our America secured liberty at home and stood once again as a beacon to the world.

That is what we owe our forebearers, one another, and generations to follow.
So, with purpose and resolve we turn to the tasks of our time.
Sustained by faith.
Driven by conviction.
And, devoted to one another and to this country we love with all our hearts.
May God bless America and may God protect our troops.
Thank you, America.

"Democracy Is Precious, Democracy Is Fragile"

THE INAUGURAL ADDRESS OF JOE BIDEN

Kate Masur

JOE BIDEN DELIVERED his Inaugural Address of January 20, 2021, to a jittery nation rocked by the lethal coronavirus pandemic and a horrific assault on American democracy just two weeks earlier. He met the moment by stressing unity and empathy and by invoking American history to convey that the people of this imperfect nation should have reason for optimism.

Fourteen days before the inauguration, on January 6, the U.S. Capitol building was attacked and overrun by Americans hoping to overturn the results of the 2020 presidential election and stop Joe Biden from taking office. Whipped up by the false claims of President Donald Trump and his allies, rioters had attempted to stop Congress from formally counting and then announcing the votes of the Electoral College in accordance with the Constitution and federal law. Members of the mob had turned temporary risers and platforms constructed for the inauguration into ladders as they scaled the Capitol and tried to force their way inside.

Members of the House and Senate evacuated during the worst of the onslaught, returning that evening and working into the next morning to conduct the count and affirm that Biden was the next president. As least seven deaths were associated with the day's violence, and about 150 law enforcement officers were injured.[1]

Over the next two weeks, Washington, D.C., came to resemble a fortress. The Capitol itself had sustained extensive damage. In the words of J. Brett Blanton, Architect of the Capitol, "The [inauguration] platform was wrecked. There was broken glass and other debris. Sound systems and photography equipment was damaged beyond repair or stolen. Two historic Olmsted lanterns were ripped from the ground, and the wet blue paint was tracked all over the historic stone balustrades and Capitol building hallways."[2]

A sense of danger persisted as the inauguration drew closer. Many people feared that Trump's supporters were not finished trying to violently disrupt the transfer of power. Lawmakers were briefed on continuing threats. The Secret Service was on high alert; its inauguration planning involved the FBI and the Defense Department, as well as representatives from railroads and the area's gas company.[3] Authorities were coming to understand that organizers had used encrypted digital communications to plan the January 6 insurrection.[4] On the eve of Biden's inauguration, Washington's bridges[5] were closed to inbound traffic and a record-setting 25,000 National Guard[6] troops were in the area.

As they speculated on Biden's inauguration, many commentators invoked Abraham Lincoln, who took office as civil war threatened the nation and who had quietly sneaked into Washington before his inauguration amid threats on his life. Calling for a calming message from Biden, opinion writers frequently invoked the concluding passages of Lincoln's First Inaugural, particularly the lines in which he urged his "dissatisfied fellow-countrymen": "We are not enemies, but friends."[7]

Conjuring up Lincoln as a peacemaking president who brought Americans together required quite a bit of forgetting. In the months immediately before and after taking office, Lincoln had refused to compromise with secessionists on the question of slavery in the territories, even if it might have helped avert a war. "We have just carried an election on principles fairly stated to the people," he wrote to an ally in Illinois.[8] "If we surrender, it is the end of us, and of the government." Over the next four years, Lincoln prosecuted the Civil War with notable relentlessness, stretching the powers of the presidency as no previous president had done, provoking opposition verging on hatred not only from white Southerners but also from white Northern Democrats as well.

As Joe Biden spoke that day, it was clear that he and his speechwriter, likely Vinay Reddy, had Lincoln on their minds too. The overall theme of the speech was unity, but Biden started by talking about the insurrection. He affirmed at the outset that the inauguration represented "the triumph not of a candidate, but of a cause, the cause of democracy." Noting that this was a transition of power provided for in the Constitution (and even calling the transition "peaceful"), Biden lamented that "just days ago violence sought to shake this Capitol's very foundation." Outlining the challenges the nation would face, he emphasized that there was much to "repair," "restore," "heal," "build," and "gain." The threats to

American democracy, he said, included not solely the January 6 insurrectionists, but "white supremacy" and "domestic terrorism."

Lincoln was the only past president featured in a vignette during the speech, and Biden prefaced his remarks on Lincoln with a forthright call for "Unity." Yet Biden did not, as some commentators might have predicted, characterize Lincoln as a unifier. Instead, he quoted the reminiscences of artist Francis B. Carpenter, who recalled in an 1866 book that, just before signing the Emancipation Proclamation on January 1, 1863, Lincoln had turned to William Seward, his secretary of state, and said, "If my name ever goes into history it will be for this act, and my whole soul is in it."[9]

In selecting this quotation from Carpenter, Biden made Lincoln sound human and humble and steered by moral principles. By invoking the signing of the Emancipation Proclamation, Biden also brought forth an acclaimed example of presidential leadership and courage, even as he also alluded to the shame of slavery itself and the continuing importance of its aftermath to American politics today.

Biden proceeded to align himself with Lincoln's sentiments. He repeated: "My whole soul is in it" and added, "on this January day, my whole soul is in this." From there he elaborated on the speech's theme of unity in troubled times. It was a straightforward message that echoed past inaugural addresses that had sought to heal the divisions created by electoral competition and call forth a nation that could come together to accomplish shared goals; among those Biden named were creating jobs, educating children, and defeating COVID-19.

Much of Biden's inaugural address was concerned with offering reasons for optimism amid a myriad of crises. It was helpful that he took office alongside Vice President Kamala Harris, the first woman and first person of color to hold the office. Harris and Biden had previously competed for the 2020 Democratic nomination. In the first Democratic debate, Harris, of Black and Indian descent, had criticized Biden for having opposed busing for school desegregation when he was a U.S. senator in the 1970s and for recently recalling that he had worked smoothly with segregationist senators. Harris called those comments "hurtful" and invoked her own experiences as "a little girl in California who was part of the second class to integrate her public schools, and she was bused to school every day."[10] Harris's words highlighted the generational difference between the two former senators (he was already a politician when she was a schoolchild). In drawing attention to her own Blackness, Harris also illuminated Biden's whiteness, a political identity that often remains unspoken or invisible. Biden stumbled in response, and many observers wondered what the exchange portended for the future of the primary campaign.

As Biden campaigned for the presidency, he repeatedly showed his understanding that Black Americans, and Black women in particular, were a key constituency. In August, he announced that Kamala Harris had agreed to be his running mate.[11] He introduced her midway through his Inaugural Address with a lead-in that referenced, in quick succession, several key trials of American democracy: "the Civil War, when the Union itself hung in the balance," "the great [National] Mall where Dr. King spoke of his dream," and "another inaugural" (that of President Woodrow Wilson) when "thousands of protesters tried to block brave women from marching for the right to vote." Then he called out Kamala Harris by name, identifying her as "the first woman in American history elected to national office." Ending this portion of the speech, Biden concluded: "Don't tell me things can't change."

Before the inauguration, commentators had wondered how the Biden team would balance the celebratory and ritualistic aspects of an inauguration—aspects whose importance was heightened by the January 6 insurrection—with the somberness of a nation in mourning and the fact that the outgoing administration had steadfastly refused to acknowledge the severity of the pandemic and the grief so many were experiencing. The night before the inauguration, Biden took part in a poignant ceremony at the Lincoln Memorial that recognized the lives lost to COVID-19. In the speech itself, he said his first act as president, performed then and there, was to ask Americans to "join me in a moment of silent prayer to remember all those we lost this past year to the pandemic. To those 400,000 fellow Americans—mothers and fathers, husbands and wives, sons and daughters, friends, neighbors, and co-workers." With these words, Biden signaled that he would approach the pandemic in a wholly different way than his predecessor.

Indeed, Biden had campaigned in part on being a man of great empathy whose life had been shaped by the death of his wife and daughter in a car accident in 1972 and, more recently, the passing of his eldest son, Beau, of cancer.[12] He seemed to acknowledge his own history when he asked Americans to "stand in the other person's shoes just for a moment. Because here is the thing about life: There is no accounting for what fate will deal you." Perhaps those who had lost loved ones and livelihoods during the pandemic believed those difficult experiences gave Biden some sense of what they were going through. Directly evoking the nation's grief and fear he affirmed: "We will get through this, together."

Biden was frank about where the nation stood at this juncture, his vision of the past likewise a significant change from that of his predecessor. Donald Trump had made history itself a battleground during the summer of 2020, amid a swelling movement for racial justice and calls to remove monuments that honored advocates of slavery and genocide. Trump had chosen Mt. Rushmore, in South Dakota, for a July 4 speech in which he claimed that "a new far-left fascism" was overtaking the nation's schools and boardrooms and that "our children are taught in school to hate their own country, and to believe that the men and women who built it were not heroes, but that [they] were villains."[13] What they were learning was "a web of lies."

What was the proper subject of American history? Trump advanced the idea that the story of the nation was "miraculous" and that the goal was to "raise the next generation of American patriots." That fall, Trump established the "1776 Commission" to advance his agenda for turning history into patriotic education and to beat back the threats, among them the *New York Times*' 1619 Project, published a year earlier, which emphasized the centrality of slavery to U.S. history. Two days before Biden's inauguration, the 1776 Commission released its report, framed as a "rebuttal of reckless 're-education' attempts that seek to reframe American history around the idea that the United States is not an exceptional country but an evil one."[14]

The vision of American history Biden offered in his Inaugural Address was far more truthful and far more consistent with what historians have come to understand about the past, if pared down to is most basic premises. As he put it in the speech: "Our history has been a constant struggle between the American ideal that we are all created equal and the harsh, ugly reality that racism, nativism, fear, and demonization have long torn us apart," he said. If there was something we should take away from this history, he emphasized (optimistically), it was that at critical moments, Americans had "acted together" to overcome their most significant challenges.

Upon taking office, the Biden administration quickly archived the 1776 Commission's report and disbanded the commission. Yet in the year that followed, many Republican leaders enthusiastically echoed Trump's attacks on how American history is taught and pressed for state legislation that would monitor teachers and public schools' curricula and stop discussion of what they considered "divisive concepts."

Biden's Inaugural Address was not a particularly profound speech or very distinguished as an inaugural address. He hit plenty of conventional notes by repeatedly invoking American exceptionalism, promising to be the president for all the people, and calling on Americans to have courage as they faced a difficult future. In the version published on the White House website, almost every sentence is on its own line, making it look more like a poem than a conventional speech and perhaps reflecting the influence of social media and our sound-byte driven culture. But Biden's speech met a moment of crisis relatively unstintingly. It established a new tone for the presidency and tried to place the nation on the road to a better place, a road everybody knew would be bumpy at best.

Three and a half years later, in the summer of 2024, the nation was on the cusp of another presidential election. Most people thought it would be a reprise of 2020, with former president Donald Trump challenging Biden, now the incumbent. All that changed on July 21, when Biden announced his decision not to run for re-election just weeks before his party's convention. A terrible performance in the first of two projected debates against Trump had prompted panic among prominent Democrats and pundits, many of whom were already concerned about whether Biden, age eighty-one, was physically and mentally strong enough to defeat Trump, who was himself seventy-eight.

Biden arrived at the decision reluctantly, after failing to persuade his erstwhile allies that he was ready. And in stepping aside, he endorsed Kamala Harris, his vice president and former rival for the presidency. In an address explaining his decision, Biden invoked George Washington, Abraham Lincoln, and Franklin D. Roosevelt as admirable examples and portrayed a nation at an "inflection point." He recalled the "peril and possibilities" that had defined the moment of his inauguration day and described what he considered the greatest successes of his presidency. He invoked the nation's founding ideals of equality and individual rights and declared that it was time "for new voices, fresh voices, yes, younger voices." Then, without referencing Trump by name, he emphasized that in the United States "kings and dictators do not rule—the people do" and called on Americans to "act together" to "preserve our democracy."

Notes

1. Chris Cameron, "These Are the People Who Died in Connection with the Capitol Riot," *New York Times*, January 5, 2022, https://www.nytimes.com/2022/01/05/us/politics/jan-6-capitol-deaths.html.
2. Bill Chappell, "Architect of the Capitol Outlines $30 Million in Damages from Pro-Trump Riot," *NPR*, February 24, 2021.
3. Carol D. Leonnig, Karoun Demirjian, Justin Jouvenal, and Nick Miroff, "Secret Service Launches Massive Security Operation to Protect Biden Inauguration," *Washington Post*, January 13, 2021, https://www.washingtonpost.com/national/biden-inauguration-security-dc/2021/01/12/b1a9781a-54e9-11eb-89bc-7f51ceb6bd57_story.html.
4. Ibid.
5. *NBC4 Washington*, "'Not Taking Any Chances': 25K National Guard in DC on Eve of Inauguration Day," *NBC4 Washington*, January 19, 2021.
6. Leonnig, Demirjian, Jouvenal, and Miroff, "Secret Service Launches Massive Security Operation to Protect Biden Inauguration."

7. *Inaugural Addresses of the Presidents of the United States: From George Washington 1789 to George Bush 1989*. Avalon Project—Documents in Law, History and Diplomacy (n.d.).
8. Abraham Lincoln, *Collected Works of Abraham Lincoln*, Vol. 4 (New Brunswick, NJ: Rutgers University Press, 1953), 172.
9. F. B. Carpenter, *Six Months at the White House with Abraham Lincoln: The Story of a Picture* (New York: Hurd and Houghton, 1866).
10. Isabella Grullón Paz, "Kamala Harris and Joe Biden Clash on Race and Busing," *New York Times*, June 27, 2019, https://www.nytimes.com/2019/06/27/us/politics/kamala-harris-joe-biden-busing.html.
11. Alexander Burns and Katie Glueck, "Kamala Harris Is Biden's Choice for Vice President," *New York Times*, August 11, 2020, https://www.nytimes.com/2020/08/11/us/politics/kamala-harris-vp-biden.html.
12. "Biden Commemorates 49th Anniversary of Crash That Killed His First Wife," *Guardian*, December 18, 2021, https://www.theguardian.com/us-news/2021/dec/18/joe-biden-anniversary-car-crash-first-wife-daughter.
13. Donald J. Trump, "Remarks by President Trump at South Dakota's 2020 Mount Rushmore Fireworks Celebration, Keystone, South Dakota," National Archives and Records Administration, July 4, 2020.
14. "1776 Commission Takes Historic and Scholarly Step to Restore Understanding of the Greatness of the American Founding," National Archives and Records Administration, January 18, 2021.

Contributors

This book would have been impossible without the kindness, generosity, and grace of others. I will remain indebted to each scholar and historian who devoted the time necessary to contribute an essay. They are listed, along with a little more information, in the most reasonable manner I could think of—by order of appearance.

Ted Widmer is Distinguished Lecturer at Macaulay Honors College, City University of New York. He is the author and editor of numerous books on the presidency, including *Lincoln on the Verge: Thirteen Days to Washington*; *Campaigns: A Century of Presidential Races*; and *American Speeches: Political Oratory from Abraham Lincoln to Bill Clinton*. He served as a speechwriter and senior adviser in the Clinton White House.

Stephen H. Browne is a rhetorical critic and Professor in the Department of Communication Arts and Sciences at Pennsylvania State University. Among his many books are *The First Inauguration: George Washington and the Invention of the Republic*; *The Ides of War: George Washington and the Newburgh Crisis*; and *Jefferson's Call for Nationhood: The First Inaugural Address*.

Kevin Butterfield is the Director of the John W. Kluge Center at the Library of Congress. Previously, he was the Executive Director of what is now the George Washington Presidential Library at Mount Vernon, the historic home of George Washington. He is the author of *The Making of Tocqueville's America: Law and Association in the Early United States*.

R. M. Barlow is Assistant Editor for The Adams Papers at the Massachusetts Historical Society. A specialist in early American diplomatic and military history, she earned a PhD in History from the University of Virginia.

Peter S. Onuf is Thomas Jefferson Memorial Foundation Professor Emeritus at the University of Virginia. A noted Thomas Jefferson scholar, Onuf is the author of several books about the third president, including *"Most Blessed of the Patriarchs": Thomas Jefferson and the Empire of the Imagination* (coauthored with Annette Gordon-Reed); *The Mind of Thomas Jefferson*; *Jefferson's Empire: The Language of American Nationhood*; and *Jeffersonian America* (coauthored with Leonard Sadosky).

Annette Gordon-Reed is the Carl M. Loeb University Professor of History at Harvard Law School. Among her books are *Thomas Jefferson and Sally Hemings: An American Controversy*; *The Hemingses of Monticello*, which won the National Book Prize and the Pulitzer Prize in History; and *Andrew Johnson* for Times Books' The American Presidents Series.

Stuart Leibiger is Professor and Chair of the History Department at La Salle University. He is the author of *Founding Friendship: George Washington, James Madison and the Creation of the American Republic*. He has worked on the editorial staffs of the Papers of George Washington and the Papers of Thomas Jefferson. In 2015, he won the George Washington Memorial Award, a lifetime achievement award given annually by the George Washington Masonic Memorial Association in Alexandria, Virginia.

J. C. A. Stagg is a Professor at the University of Virginia and the Editor of The Papers of James Madison. He has published *The War of 1812: Conflict for a Continent*; *Borderlines in Borderlands: James Madison and the Spanish-American Frontier, 1776–1821*; and *Mr. Madison's War: Politics, Diplomacy, and Warfare in the Early American Republic, 1783–1830*.

Daniel F. Preston is the recently retired Editor of The Papers of James Monroe at the University of Mary Washington. He is the author of *James Monroe: An Illustrated History*.

Sandra Moats is Associate Professor of History at the University of Wisconsin–Parkside. She is the author of *Celebrating the Republic: Presidential Ceremony and Popular Sovereignty, from Washington to Monroe* and *Navigating Neutrality: George Washington and the American Government in the Turbulent Atlantic*.

C. James Taylor edits the John Quincy Adams Digital Diary. He is the former Editor-in-Chief of the Adams Papers at the Massachusetts Historical Society and previously served as the Editor and Project Director for The Papers of Henry Laurens.

Harry L. Watson is the Atlanta Distinguished Professor of Southern Culture at the University of North Carolina at Chapel Hill. He was a founding editor of *Southern Cultures*, a peer-reviewed quarterly journal on the history, culture, society, and experience of the American South. His books include *Building the American Republic, Volume 1: A Narrative History to 1877*; *Liberty and Power: The*

Politics of Jacksonian America; and *Andrew Jackson vs. Henry Clay: Democracy and Development in Antebellum America.*

Thomas Coens is an editor with the Papers of Andrew Jackson and Research Associate Professor of History at the University of Tennessee, Knoxville. He earned his BA in history from Yale and his PhD from Harvard with a dissertation titled "The Formation of the Jackson Party, 1822–1825." To date, Dr. Coens has co-edited six volumes of Jackson's presidential papers, covering the years 1829 to 1834. He is currently writing a monograph on nuclear fear in the 1980s.

Michael J. Gerhardt is the Burton Craige Distinguished Professor of Jurisprudence at the University of North Carolina at Chapel Hill School of Law. His books include *The Forgotten Presidents: Their Untold Constitutional Legacy*; *The Federal Impeachment Process: A Constitutional and Historical Analysis*; *The Power of Precedent*; and *Lincoln's Mentors: The Education of a Leader.*

Daniel Walker Howe is Rhodes Professor of American History Emeritus at Oxford University in England and Professor of History Emeritus at the University of California, Los Angeles. His book *What Hath God Wrought: The Transformation of America, 1815–1848*, the fifth volume in the Oxford History of the United States series, won the Pulitzer Prize in History. Other books include *Making the American Self: Jonathan Edwards to Abraham Lincoln* and *The Political Culture of the American Whigs.*

Christopher J. Leahy is a Professor of History at Keuka College. He is the author of *President without a Party: The Life of John Tyler.*

Walter R. Borneman is an American historian and lawyer. He is the author of several books, including *Polk: The Man Who Transformed the Presidency and America*; *1812: The War That Forged a Nation*; *The French and Indian War: Deciding the Fate of North America*; and *Brothers Down: Pearl Harbor and the Fate of the Many Brothers Aboard the USS Arizona.*

Michael F. Holt is Langbourne M. Williams Professor of American History Emeritus at the University of Virginia. He is the author of several books, including *Franklin Pierce* for the Times Books' American Presidents Series; *The Fate of Their Country: Politicians, Slavery Extension, and the Coming of the Civil War*; and *The Rise and Fall of the American Whig Party: Jacksonian Politics and the Onset of the Civil War.*

Claude Welch is a SUNY Distinguished Service Professor and Professor of Political Science Emeritus at the University at Buffalo. He earned his BA at Harvard University and his PhD at Oxford University. His books include *Protecting Human Rights in Africa*; *Human Rights in Asia*; and *Anatomy of Rebellion.*

Peter A. Wallner is Professor of History Emeritus at Franklin Pierce College. He is the author of *Franklin Pierce: New Hampshire's Favorite Son* and *Franklin Pierce: Martyr for the Union*.

Jean H. Baker is Professor Emerita of History at Goucher College. Her books include *Mary Todd Lincoln: A Biography*; *James Buchanan* for the American Presidents Series; *Sisters: The Lives of America's Suffragists*; *Margaret Sanger: A Life of Passion*; and *Building America: The Life of Benjamin Henry Latrobe*.

David S. Reynolds is a Distinguished Professor of English at The Graduate Center at the City University of New York. He is the author of several books, including *Abe: Abraham Lincoln in His Times*; *Mightier than the Sword: Uncle Tom's Cabin and the Battle for America*; *Waking Giant: America in the Age of Jackson*; *John Brown, Abolitionist: The Man Who Killed Slavery, Sparked the Civil War, and Seeded Civil Rights*; and *Walt Whitman's America: A Cultural Biography*, which won the Bancroft Prize.

Richard John Carwardine is Rhodes Professor of American History Emeritus at Oxford University and former President of Corpus Christi College, Oxford. He is the author of *Lincoln: A Life of Purpose and Power*, which won the Lincoln Prize, co-editor of *The Global Lincoln*, and *Evangelicals and Politics in Antebellum America*.

Michael Les Benedict is Professor of History Emeritus at Ohio State University. His books include *The Impeachment and Trial of Andrew Johnson* and *The Blessings of Liberty*.

Joan Waugh is Professor of History Emerita of the University of California, Los Angeles. Her publications include *The American War: A History of the Civil War Era* and *U. S. Grant: American Hero, American Myth*.

John F. Marszalek is the Executive Director of the Ulysses S. Grant Association's Grant Presidential Library at Mississippi State University, where he was a Giles Distinguished Professor. He is the author of *Sherman: A Soldier's Passion for Order* and *Assault at West Point, the Court Martial of Johnson Whittaker*, among other books. He serves on the board of advisors of the Lincoln Forum, the Lincoln Prize, the national Lincoln Bicentennial Commission, and the Monitor Museum.

Dustin McLochlin is the Curator at the Rutherford B. Hayes Presidential Library and Museum and Instructor at Bowling Green State University.

Charles W. Calhoun is Professor Emeritus of History at East Carolina University. His books include *The Presidency of Ulysses S. Grant*; *Benjamin Harrison* for the American Presidents Series; and *From Bloody Shirt to Full Dinner Pail: The Transformation of Politics and Governance in the Gilded Age*.

Walter Nugent (1935–2021) was the Andrew V. Tackes Professor of History Emeritus at the University of Notre Dame. Among his books are *The Tolerant Populists: Kansas Populism and Nativism*; *Money and American Society, 1865–1880*; *Crossings: The Great Transatlantic Migrations, 1870–1914*; *Into the West: The Story of Its People*; *Habits of Empire: A History of American Expansion*; and *Color Coded: Party Politics in the American West, 1950–2016*.

Mark W. Summers is the Thomas D. Clark Professor of History at the University of Kentucky. His books include *A Dangerous Stir: Fear, Paranoia, and the Making of Reconstruction*; *Rum, Romanism, and Rebellion: The Making of a President, 1884*; and *The Press Gang: Newspapers and Politics, 1865–1878*.

Allan B. Spetter is Professor Emeritus of History at Wright State University. He is the coauthor of *The Presidency of Benjamin Harrison* with Homer E. Socolofsky.

Matthew Algeo is an award-winning journalist and author. He holds a degree in Folklore from the University of Pennsylvania. His books include *The President Is a Sick Man*; *Harry Truman's Excellent Adventure*; *All This Marvelous Potential*; and *Abe & Fido*.

Christopher Capozzola is a Professor of History at the Massachusetts Institute of Technology. He is the author of *Bound by War: How the United States and the Philippines Built America's First Pacific Century* and *Uncle Sam Wants You: World War I and the Making of the Modern American Citizen*.

Christopher McKnight Nichols is a Professor of History and the Wayne Woodrow Hayes Chair of National Security Studies at The Ohio State University. He is the author of *Promise and Peril: America at the Dawn of a Global Age* and the co-editor of *Prophesies of Godlessness*; *The Oxford Encyclopedia of American Military and Diplomatic History*; *The Wiley Blackwell Companion to the Gilded Age and Progressive Era*; *Rethinking American Grand Strategy*; and *Ideology in U.S. Foreign Relations: New Histories*.

Jean M. Yarbrough is the Gary M. Pendy, Sr., Professor of Social Sciences at Bowdoin College. She is the author or editor of *Theodore Roosevelt and the American Political Tradition*; *The Essential Jefferson*; and *American Virtues: Thomas Jefferson on the Character of a Free People*.

Jonathan Lurie is Professor Emeritus of History at Rutgers University. He is the author of *William Howard Taft: The Travails of a Progressive Conservative* and *The Chief Justiceship of William Howard Taft*.

Contributors

Robert A. Enholm is the former Executive Director of the Woodrow Wilson House and Global Fellow at the Wilson Center.

John Milton Cooper, Jr., is Professor Emeritus of History at the University of Wisconsin, Madison. His books include *Woodrow Wilson: A Biography*, a finalist for the Pulitzer Prize in Biography; *Breaking the Heart of the World: Woodrow Wilson and the Fight for the League of Nations*; and *Pivotal Decades: The United States, 1900–1920*.

James D. Robenalt is a lawyer and author. His books include *Ballots and Bullets: Black Power Politics and Urban Guerrilla Warfare in 1968 Cleveland*; *The Harding Affair: Love and Espionage during the Great War*; and *January 1973: Watergate, Roe v. Wade, Vietnam, and the Month That Changed America Forever*.

Amity Shlaes is an author and columnist who currently serves as the Chair of the Board of Trustees at the Calvin Coolidge Presidential Foundation. She is the author of several books, including *Coolidge*; *The Forgotten Man: A New History of the Great Depression*; *The Greedy Hand: How Taxes Drive Americans Crazy and What to Do about It*; and *Great Society: A New History*.

Kendrick A. Clements is Professor Emeritus of History at the University of South Carolina. He has published books that include *Hoover, Conservation, and Consumerism: Engineering the Good Life*; *The Life of Herbert Hoover: Imperfect Visionary, 1918–1928*; and *The Presidency of Woodrow Wilson*.

Cynthia M. Koch is Historian in Residence and Director of History Programming for the Franklin Delano Roosevelt Foundation. She was Director of the Franklin D. Roosevelt Presidential Library and Museum and Senior Advisor to the Office of Presidential Libraries at the National Archives.

David M. Kennedy is the Donald J. McLachlan Professor of History Emeritus at Stanford University. He is also the current editor of *The Oxford History of the United States*. His books include *Freedom from Fear: The American People in Depression and War, 1929–1945*, a volume in the *Oxford History of the United States* that won the Pulitzer Prize in History and the Francis Parkman Prize; *Over Here: The First World War and American Society*, a Pulitzer Prize finalist; and *Birth Control in America*, which won the Bancroft Prize.

Michael Kazin is a Professor of History at Georgetown University and the editor emeritus of *Dissent* magazine. He is the author of several books, including *A Godly Hero: The Life of William Jennings Bryan*; *The Populist Persuasion: An American History*; *War against War: The American Fight for Peace, 1914–1918*;

American Dreamers: How the Left Changed a Nation; and *What It Took to Win: A History of the Democratic Party*.

David B. Woolner is Senior Fellow and Resident Historian of the Roosevelt Institute and Professor of History at Marist College. He has authored or co-edited numerous works, including *The Last 100 Days: FDR at War and at Peace*; *Progressivism in America: Past, Present, and Future*; *FDR's World: War, Peace, and Legacies*; and *FDR and the Environment*.

Andrew E. Busch is the Crown Professor of Government and George R. Roberts Fellow at Claremont McKenna College. He is the author or coauthor of *The Rules and Politics of American Primaries*; *Defying the Odds: The 2016 Elections and American Politics*; *Reagan's Victory: The Presidential Election of 1980 and the Rise of the Right*; and *Truman's Triumphs: The 1948 Election and the Making of Postwar America*, among others.

Michael J. Birkner is Professor of History at Gettysburg College. He is the author of editor of several books, including *The Governors of New Jersey: Biographical Essays*; *Encounters with Eisenhower*; and *The Worlds of James Buchanan and Thaddeus Stevens: Place, Personality, and Politics in the Civil War Era*.

Louis Paul Galambos is a Research Professor at Johns Hopkins University, where he is also the Editor of the Papers of Dwight D. Eisenhower. In addition to the volumes of the *Papers*, Dr. Galambos is the author of *Eisenhower: Becoming the Leader of the Free World* and *The Creative Society—and the Price Americans Paid for It*.

Barbara Ann Perry is the Gerald L. Baliles Professor and Director of Presidential Studies at the University of Virginia's Miller Center, where she co-chairs the Presidential Oral History program. She is the author of several books, including *Jacqueline Kennedy: First Lady of the New Frontier*; *Rose Kennedy: The Life and Times of a Political Matriarch*; and co-editor of *41: Inside the Presidency of George H. W. Bush*; *42: Inside the Presidency of Bill Clinton*; and *Edward M. Kennedy: An Oral History*.

Mark K. Updegrove is the President and CEO of the LBJ Foundation and serves as Presidential Historian for ABC News. He was Director of the LBJ Presidential Library. His books on the presidency include *The Last Republicans: Inside the Extraordinary Relationship Between George H. W. Bush and George W. Bush*; *Indomitable Will: LBJ in the Presidency*; and *Incomparable Grace: JFK in the Presidency*. He has conducted exclusive interviews with six U.S. presidents.

Ken Hughes is an American historian and expert on secret presidential recordings. He is the author of *Chasing Shadows: The Nixon Tapes, the Chennault Affair,* *and the Origins of Watergate* and *Fatal Politics: The Nixon Tapes, the Vietnam War, and the Casualties of Reelection*.

Thomas Alan Schwartz is Distinguished Professor of History at Vanderbilt University. He is the author of several books, including *Henry Kissinger and American Power: A Political Biography*; *America's Germany: John J. McCloy and the Federal Republic of Germany*; and *Lyndon Johnson and Europe: In the Shadow of Vietnam*.

John Robert Greene is Paul J. Schupf Professor of History at Cazenovia College. His works include *I Like Ike: The Presidential Election of 1952*; *The Presidency of George H. W. Bush*; *Betty Ford: Candor and Courage in the White House*; and *The Presidency of Gerald R. Ford*.

Mark Atwood Lawrence is the Director of the LBJ Presidential Library and Professor of History at the University of Texas at Austin. He has published several books, including *The Vietnam War: A Concise International History*; *The Vietnam War: An International History in Documents*; and *Assuming the Burden: Europe and the American Commitment to War in Vietnam*.

Gil Troy is Professor of History at McGill University. He is the author of several books, including *The Age of Clinton: America in the 1990s*; *The Reagan Revolution: A Very Short Introduction*; *Morning in America*; and *Leading from the Center*.

Iwan Morgan is Emeritus Professor of U.S. Studies at the Institute of the Americas, University College London. His books include *The Age of Deficits: Presidents and Unbalanced Budgets from Jimmy Carter to George W. Bush*; *Reagan: American Icon*; *Nixon*; and *FDR: Transforming the Presidency and Renewing America*.

Mary Kate Cary is a former speechwriter for President George H. W. Bush and an executive producer for *41 on 41*, a documentary about the president. She also teaches political speechwriting as an Adjunct Professor of Politics and is a Senior Fellow at the Miller Center at the University of Virginia.

Steven M. Gillon is Scholar-in-Residence at The History Channel and a professor of history at the University of Oklahoma. He has authored or edited several books, including *The Pact: Bill Clinton, Newt Gingrich, and the Rivalry That Defined a Generation*; *Separate and Unequal: The Kerner Commission and the Unraveling of American Liberalism*; and *America's Reluctant Prince: The Life of John F. Kennedy Jr.*

Russell L. Riley is Co-chair of the Miller Center's Presidential Oral History Program and is the White Burkett Miller Center Professor of Ethics and

Institutions at the University of Virginia. He is the author of *Inside the Clinton White House*; *Bridging the Constitutional Divide: Inside the White House Office of Legislative Affairs*; and co-editor of *The President's Words: Speeches and Speechwriting in the Modern White House*.

James Mann is an American journalist and author and a Scholar-in-Residence at Johns Hopkins University. He wrote for the *Los Angeles Times*, the *Washington Post*, and the *Baltimore Sun*. He is the author of several books, including *Rise of the Vulcans: The History of Bush's War Cabinet*; *George W. Bush* for the American Presidents Series; *The Obamians: The Struggle Inside the White House to Redefine American Power*; *About Face: A History of America's Curious Relationship with China*; and *The Great Rift: Dick Cheney, Colin Powell, and the Broken Friendship That Defined an Era*.

Mark J. Rozell is the Founding Dean of the Schar School of Policy and Government at George Mason University, where he also holds the Ruth D. & John T. Hazel Chair in Public Policy. He is the author or coauthor of books including *Federalism: A Very Short Introduction*; *The South and the Transformation of U.S. Politics*; and *Executive Privilege: Presidential Power, Secrecy, and Accountability*.

Tracy Denean Sharpley-Whiting is the Gertrude Conaway Vanderbilt Distinguished Professor of French at Vanderbilt University, as well as the Chair of African American and Diaspora Studies. She has authored several books, including *Bricktop's Paris: African American Women in Paris between the Two World Wars*; *Black France/France Noire: The History and Politics of Blackness*; and *The Speech: Race and Barack Obama's "A More Perfect Union."*

James T. Kloppenberg is the Charles Warren Research Professor of American History Emeritus at Harvard University. He is the author of books including *Reading Obama: Dreams, Hope, and the American Political Tradition*; *The Virtues of Liberalism*; and *Toward Democracy: The Struggle for Self-Rule in European and American Thought*.

Nicholas F. Jacobs is an Assistant Professor of Government at Colby College. His work appears in numerous journals, including *Perspectives on Politics*; *Political Science Quarterly*; and *Presidential Studies Quarterly*.

Kate Masur is a Professor of History at Northwestern University. She is the author of several books, including *Until Justice Be Done: America's First Civil Rights Movement, from the Revolution to Reconstruction* and *An Example for All the Land: Emancipation and the Struggle over Equality in Washington, D.C.*, as well as co-editor of *The World the Civil War Made*.